ANGUS WILSON

ANGUS WILSON

A Biography

Margaret Drabble

St. Martin's Press ♨ New York

To Tony Garrett

ANGUS WILSON: A BIOGRAPHY. Copyright © 1995
by Margaret Drabble.
All rights reserved. Printed in the United States of America.
No part of this book may be used or reproduced in any
manner whatsoever without written permission except in the
case of brief quotations embodied in critical articles or
reviews. For information, address St. Martin's Press,
175 Fifth Avenue, New York, N.Y. 10010.

Library of Congress Cataloging-in-Publication Data

Drabble, Margaret
Angus Wilson : a biography / by Margaret Drabble.
p.   cm.
Includes bibliographical references (p. 673) and index.
ISBN 0-312-14276-5
1. Wilson, Angus—Biography.   2. Novelists, English—
20th century—Biography.   I. Title.
PR6045.I577Z63   1996
823'.914—dc20   [B]   96-1479   CIP

First published in Great Britain by Martin Secker
& Warburg Limited

First U.S. Edition: May 1996
10   9   8   7   6   5   4   3   2   1

CONTENTS

LIST OF ILLUSTRATIONS

(First eight-page section)

1 View of West Street, Durban, 1855
2 Angus Wilson's mother, Maud Johnstone-Wilson, Durban 1898
3 Willie Johnstone-Wilson with the young Angus (c. 1914)
4 Angus Wilson with his mother, at Bexhill, 1914
5 Angus Wilson with his brother Winn, Bexhill, 1915
6 Angus Wilson, aged nine, in a rickshaw in Durban, 1923
7 Angus Wilson in HMS *Pinafore* at Ashampstead
8 Angus Wilson with John Pattisson in a Westminster school production, 1931
9 Angus Wilson with his parents, 1929.
10 The Myrmidons at Merton College, Oxford, 1935
11 Angus Wilson with RN and WRNS at Bletchley Park
12 Angus Wilson with Geoffrey Wright at Little Hadham
13 Angus Wilson with Ian Calder
14 Angus Wilson with Bentley Bridgewater
15 Angus Wilson at Providence House
16 Angus Wilson with George Painter
17 Viva King
18 Forrest Fulton
19 Tony Garret in uniform, 1948
20 Ian Calder
21 Chris Arnold as an undergraduate
22 Perkin Walker
23 Angus Wilson on the steps of the British Museum, 1954

(Second eight-page section)

24 A holograph page from Angus Wilson's first short story

(Third eight-page section)

ACKNOWLEDGEMENTS

I would like to thank all those people and institutions (and people in those institutions) who have helped me with my research. My principal thanks, however, must go to Tony Garrett, without whose generosity, time and encouragement this book could never have been written. This book is dedicated to him and he must stand at the head of the list. My warmest thanks are also due to Angus Wilson's nieces Jeanne Davies and Sybil Scott, and their families, who have given me every assistance.

I would also like to thank the Anti-Apartheid Movement, the BBC Written Archives Centre at Caversham Park, the Bletchley Park Trust, Bristol Special Collections, the British Library, the British Library Sound Archive, the Campbell Collections of the University of Natal, Churchill College, Cambridge, Archives Centre (Cecil Roberts Papers), Girton College, Cambridge, the Provost and Scholars of King's College, Cambridge (for permission to quote from unpublished E.M. Forster material), the University Library of Delaware, Durham University Library (Plomer Collection), the University of East Anglia, the Gay and Lesbian Humanist Association, the Hall-Carpenter Archives, GCHQ, the Home Office, the Imperial War Museum, the Lancing College Archives, the Brotherton Library at University of Leeds, Alderman Newton's School in Leicester, Merton College, Oxford, New College, Oxford, PEN, the Peace Pledge Union, University of Reading (Secker & Warburg Archives), St Katherine's School, St Andrews, the National Library of Scotland in Edinburgh (Muriel Spark Papers), Sussex University Library (Gorer Papers, Sonia Orwell Papers, Woolf Papers), St Paul's School, Harry Ransom Humanities Research Center, University of Texas at Austin, the Theatre Museum, Tonbridge School, University of Tulsa (McFarlin Library, Department of Special Collections), UCLA Special Collections, the National Library of Wales at Aberystwyth, Westminster School.

Particular mention should be made of the magnificent Angus Wilson MSS Collection at the University of Iowa. I was granted generous access to this by Robert A. McCown, Head of Special Collections and Manuscripts Librarian, and I would like to thank him and all the library staff for their help, and for making my visit so pleasant. The British Library, with which Angus Wilson himself was so closely connected, has also given me every assistance and I am most grateful.

The following have all helped me in various ways and I thank them all:

Peter Ackroyd, Bernard Adams, Maria Aitken, John Alston, Martin Amis, Anastasia Anrep, Murray Arbeid, R.C.G. Ashby, Sandra Atkinson, Edward St Aubyn, L.W. Bailey, E.H. Ball, Michael Barrett, Professor E.C. Baughan, Lord Beaumont, Robin E. Berry, Kathleen Betterton, David Binns, Victor Bonham-Carter, Michael Bott, John Bowen, Douglas Boyce, Susan Boyd, Richard Brain, George Broadhead, Sally Brown, Steve Brown, Frederick Busch, Margot Butt, James Callaghan, The Reverend A.H. Christian, Adrienne Clarkson, Charles S. Clayton, Philip Collins, Jon Cook, Peter Copley, Kathleen B. Cory, Mrs Basil Creighton, John Croft, Anthony Curtis, Masolino D'Amico, Mark Davies, Hugh and Sarah Davies-Jones, Ann Longford Dent, the Duchess of Devonshire, Ghislain de Diesbach, Kirkpatrick Dobie, Alan Drop, Nell Dunn, A.E. Dyson, Lord Eden, Michael Erben, John Field, Norman Field, Michael Fordham, Professor Roy Foster, Christina Foyle, Antonia Fraser, David Freeman, Caroline Garland, Dr Kenneth Garlick, Jonathan Gili, Sir William Golding, William Gooddy, Ranjan Goonetilleke, Nadine Gordimer, Richard Gordon, Elizabeth Gordon, Graham C. Greene, Harry Guest, Emily Hahn, Christopher Hall, Ian Hamilton, Dr Teresa Hankey, Dr Jacob Harskamp, Frank Hauser, Denis Healey, F.W.J. Hemmings, Bill Hetherington, Sir Harry Hinsley, Reverend Jim Hobbs, Gwen Hollington, Gerald Holmes, Michael Holroyd, Penelope Holt, Professor Ted Honderich, Frank Hooper, Michael Horniman, Paula Hostrup-Jessen, Mrs Pat Kelly, Elizabeth Jane Howard, David Hughes, Mrs David Huxley, Dr Alec Hyatt King, Ikeshiro, Elizabeth Inglis, Stephen Jacobi, Jaidev, Sarah Johnson, Adil Jussawalla, David Michael Kaplan, Sue Keable, Pat Keen, Donald Keene, Mrs Patricia Kelly, Rachel Kempson, Miss M.J.O. Kennedy, Prince Shararyar M. Khan, Francis King, James Kirkup, T.E.D. Klein, Professor H.W. Kosterlitz, Mary Lago, Richard Lamb, Robert Lambert, Judith Landry, Esther Langdon, Claire Larrière, Melvin Lasky, Edward Legg, Jack Leggett, Jeremy Lewis, Sir Hugh Lloyd-Jones, Tim Manderson, C. Masterman, Neville Masterman, Masaie Matsumura, Guy McDonald, Professor Roy MacGregor-Hastie, James McPherson, Kerry McSweeney, Dina Mehta, George Melly, Peter Milward SJ, Julian Mitchell, Jessica Mitford, Lady Moser, Charlotte Mosley, Frank Muir,

Alan Munton, Michael Ondaatje, Charles Palliser, Pauline Paucker, Gertrude Perkins, Dr Ludo Pieters, Drury Pifer, Joseph Prescott, F.T. Prince, Sir Victor Pritchett, Josephine Pullein-Thompson, S. Gorley Putt, Jonathan Raban, Antoine and Pamela Rachet, John Ralphs, Michael Ramsbotham, Donald Richie, Dorothy Robinson, William Rose, Michael Rook, Richard Rowson, John Russell, Mrs Kit Russell, Lord St John of Fawsley, Daniel B. Saferstein, John Ralston Saul, Mike Shaw, Valerie Shaw, Moira Shearer, John Shearman, Arnold Simmel, Professor J. Simmons, David Simpson, Clive Sinclair, Helen Sinclair-Wilson, Dr Sinha, Marjorie Smith, Dame Muriel Spark, Dr Hilda Spear, Colin Spencer, M. Spiering, John and Hilary Spurling, John Standing, Anthony Storr, the Hon Guy Strutt, Anthony Symondson SJ, Gerald Taylor, Nemone Thornes, Ann and Anthony Thwaite, Miriam Tlali, Tokunaga Shozo, Polly Toynbee, Sally Toynbee, Rose Tremain, Raleigh Trevelyan, Cliff Tucker, Alan Tuckett, Robyn Turner, Sir Brian Urquhart, Randolphe Vigne, David Walker, George Weidenfeld, Arnold Wesker, Simon Westcott, Professor Marcus Wheeler, Rajiva Wijesinha, Patrick Wilkinson, Mary Day Woolheim, Victoria Wood, Michael Woolley, Major R.V.J. Young.

I am also much indebted to the many individuals interviewed, who are listed separately under "sources" on p. 674.

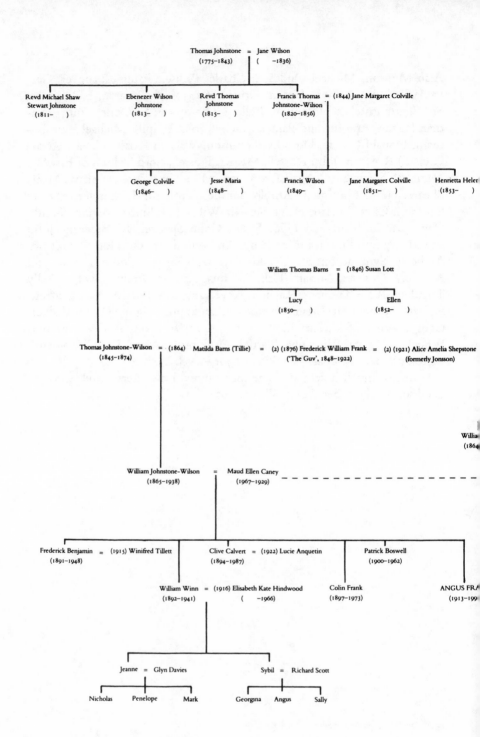

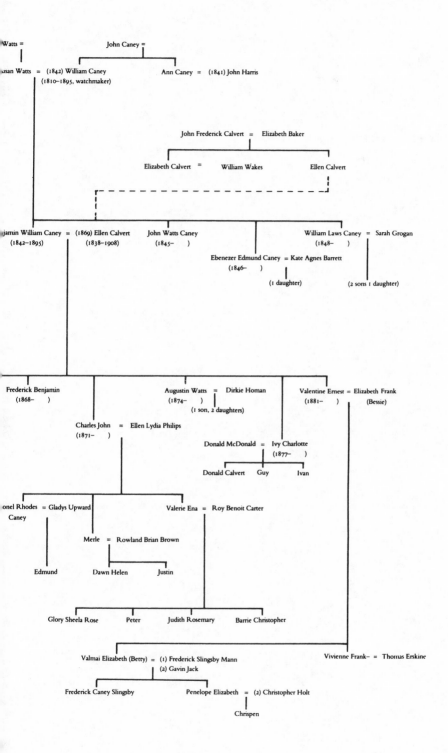

Watts =

John Caney =

usan Watts = (1842) William Caney
(1810–1895, watchmaker)

Ann Caney = (1841) John Harris

John Frederick Calvert = Elizabeth Baker

Elizabeth Calvert = William Wakes

Ellen Calvert

jamin William Caney = (1869) Ellen Calvert
(1842–1895)   (1838–1908)

John Watts Caney
(1845–)

William Laws Caney = Sarah Grogan
(1848–)

Ebenezer Edmund Caney = Kate Agnes Barrett
(1846–)

(1 daughter)

(2 sons 1 daughter)

Frederick Benjamin
(1868–)

Augustin Watts = Dirkie Homan
(1874–)

(1 son, 2 daughters)

Valentine Ernest = Elizabeth Frank
(1881–)   (Bessie)

Charles John = Ellen Lydia Philips
(1871–)

Donald McDonald = Ivy Charlotte
(1877–)

Donald Calvert   Guy   Ivan

onel Rhodes = Gladys Upward
Caney

Valerie Ena = Roy Benoit Carter

Merle = Rowland Brian Brown

Edmund

Dawn Helen   Justin

Glory Sheela Rose   Peter   Judith Rosemary   Barrie Christopher

Valmai Elizabeth (Betty) = (1) Frederick Slingsby Mann
(2) Gavin Jack

Vivienne Frank– = Thomas Erskine

Frederick Caney Slingsby

Penelope Elizabeth = (2) Christopher Holt

Chrispen

PREFACE

Angus Wilson often said that if he were to write his own autobiography, half of what he wrote would be family legend. He came
from a family of story-tellers and he excelled in what he liked to call
"the disreputable art of fiction". He was a brilliant raconteur, a fine
mimic, and an overflowing source of anecdote. Talking of himself, his
family, his friends, his misadventures, he was, or so it seemed, effort-
lessly entertaining. He was fantastic and hyperbolic, and his stories
improved with the years. He himself was building on the stories of his
father and his brothers. How to disentangle fact from fantasy, how to
unpick the embroidery without destroying the fabric?

He intended to write his own life, but the ill-health of his last years
prevented him. The most directly autobiographical work he wrote, *The
Wild Garden*, was published in 1963, when he was fifty. It is frank and
revealing – too revealing for some of its critics – but it was by no means
intended as his final statement upon himself. He was constantly revising
his own reading of the past. And as he grew older, he became less and
less interested in discretion and self-protection. Had he lived, we may
believe, he would have wanted to speak out.

This conviction makes a biographer's task easier. As Wilson did not
protect his own privacy too closely, the biographer may feel less
intrusive. He himself approved of biographical speculation, and exercised it himself when he wrote on Zola, Dickens and Kipling. It never
occurred to him that a writer's life was not the mainspring of his work
– and in his own case, as with Dickens, he saw childhood as the
primary source. He presents his biographer with some problems, but
not with a sense of trespass.

The story of how I came to be appointed his biographer is told in
this volume, but perhaps I should here explain why I wanted to write

about him. There is no point in my concealing the fact that I came to this task as a committed admirer of Wilson's works. I have long considered him one of the major novelists of the post-war world, indeed of the century, and this was my starting point. I knew the research for this book would give me a chance to explore the connections between life and work in a writer whose novels I knew well, and which had greatly influenced me. I hoped that perhaps, as I traced his progress, I would uncover the mystery of the source of creativity itself. I am not sure if I did, but at times I felt near to glimpsing it. His was a brave life, which transformed pain, despair and disorder into art. He himself subscribed to a belief in the creative wound, in the grains of sand which become pearls. Trying to find the grains of sand, trying to understand the process of their transformation was an enterprise he would have approved.

I first discovered his fiction when I was still an undergraduate, at Cambridge, in the late 1950s, when his early works began to appear in paperback. I remember the excitement with which I fell upon them, an excitement echoed by many of the witnesses in this book. Here was something entirely adult, and entirely new. He was the first contemporary writer I had discovered for myself, and he opened a window onto a world which seemed infinitely rich and wonderfully problematic. His worldliness had a powerful appeal to a generation of semi-sheltered young readers. Here was a writer who spoke with wit and authority about high life and low life, about society hostesses and rent boys, about civil servants and television personalities, about nightclub pianists and blackmailers and leftwing progressives and women on the edge of a nervous breakdown. He broke down the categories and confines of sex and gender, and wrote as a liberator and a pioneer. (I read Wilson at the same time as I first read Simone de Beauvoir: together this improbable couple redefined the post-war post-Freudian map.) Some called his work unpleasant, but those who admired him knew they also heard in him the voice of compassion and understanding. Here was a writer to trust. He swallowed no party doctrines, no received wisdom. He told no lies.

He demonstrated that it was still possible to write a great novel. This ought to have seemed obvious, but it did not. The universities in the 1940s and 50s were intent on bringing literature to a halt at the end of the nineteenth century: Cambridge was progressive in that it allowed and obliged students of English Literature to read D.H. Lawrence. But Lawrence's world was already remote from the world we inhabited. Wilson wrote about here and now. The excitement of realising that great fiction was still on the agenda was almost overwhelming. It was as exciting as learning to read for the first time as a child.

Much was expected of Wilson. In no time he found himself exalted as the only writer capable of carrying on the Great Tradition of serious moral fiction established by Dr Leavis. This was, we may now see, a considerable burden to him, a burden that might have crushed a lesser talent and a less courageous man. He was subjected to praise and blame, to critical analysis, to expressions of faith. He was the repository of hope. One of the joys of first discovering him had been the pleasure of finding a writer as yet unplaced by academe, a writer not on any syllabus, but academe was hard at his heels. I well remember the curious sensation of reading an article on his work by A.O.J. Cockshutt called "Favoured Sons: The Moral World of Angus Wilson" in *Essays in Criticism* in 1959: I sat in Newnham College Library poring over this text, disagreeing with much of it, and torn between dismay and delight at finding that here was a critical text with which I could disagree. I found I was not alone in my Wilson addiction – yet part of me wanted to be alone. (By odd coincidence, it was this same article that inspired one of Wilson's warmest admirers in the United States, Jay L. Halio, to write about Wilson's work: he too disagreed with Cockshutt's position, and wrote to say so.)

This biography is not a work of literary criticism, though it does use the fiction to illumine the life, and vice versa. It does not quote extensively from or attempt to give an account of the considerable mass of critical opinion on Wilson's work. I have not tackled the question of Wilson's distinctive style, though I am haunted by a remark of his friend and one-time colleague, George Painter, who said that the stamp of Wilson's style was evident in every sentence he wrote. This is to a certain extent true, yet it is hard to say why. Wilson, unlike some of his own dandy writer heroes and heroines, did not produce a carefully polished prose (though Martin Amis was to accuse it of "mandarin brio"): he was reckless with punctuation and spelling and seemed to write best (as he spoke) in rapid and spontaneous (and more or less illegible) bursts of speed. Yet his sense of structure was solid, far more solid than was always appreciated, and he put in a great deal of preliminary work, in the form of many pages of notes. Each book was preceded by months of planning, and the passages of high-speed and quickfire wit were the result of much thinking and rethinking.

He was, in much of his work, a satirist, which meant that he spoke (often wickedly) in many voices: *No Laughing Matter*, which many consider his masterpiece, is triumphantly polyphonic. He enjoyed his own gift as a ventriloquist, his own versatility, and like Dickens he enjoyed reading from his own work – at one point he had seriously considered becoming an actor. Yet this gift posed a hazard for his biographer. One could hear Angus Wilson's own voice ring out, as he delivered an anecdote or read a passage or imitated a friend: it was difficult, at times impossible, not to try to appropriate his voices and his manner.

Easier to define than the Wilson style, perhaps, is the Wilson matter. A decade or two ago anyone would have known what was meant by the phrase "a very Angus Wilson moment" or "a very Angus Wilson scene". He specialised in the domestic macabre, in family manipulations, in social embarrassments, in acute analysis of fading fashions and progressive ideologies. The Kensington of his youth provided a rich source of material, and it was interesting to discover how many of his close friends had been reared on the same terrain. But he did not rest there: his work would have been easier to categorise if he had. He moved into other, very different areas, both in Britain, and eventually in the world. As he moved, he lost some of his readers, and acquired others. An overview of his career as a whole shows his sense of his own destiny as a writer, his sense of the seriousness of the novel as a form. He remained true to his own vision, to what he saw as his own high calling. He ignored fashion, and it could be argued that he ignored it at some cost. The story of his last years is not a happy one. But it is not a story of compromise or failure.

★

The writing of this book would not have been possible without the full co-operation of Angus Wilson's friend and companion of nearly fifty years, Tony Garrett. Wilson made no secret of the fact that he was a homosexual, and this volume is in part a history of what we now call gay liberation, and the decreasing need for discretion. When I was first approached to write it, it had not occurred to me that the fact that Wilson was a male homosexual and I a woman might present me with problems. I now realise that others would have written this book very differently, and that some would have pressed more questions and written more fully about certain aspects of Wilson's life.

Tony Garrett and Angus Wilson were very much a couple for many years, and although they were loyal and faithful to one another they both at times had independent sexual encounters, as this biography indicates. But there are few details about sexual activity here. Tony Garrett said at the outset that although he was prepared to talk about his relationship with Wilson and about aspects of their homosexuality, he was not prepared to talk about "actual sexual activity for the following reasons:

"Firstly because I cannot ask Angus for his permission, and I must rely upon my judgement of his wishes, and they would have been, I believe, that sexual activity should be left out. Since so much has been revealed about his life by me and by others, it may seem odd (or infuriating to those who delight in intimate exposure) to stop short at this point. I have tried to explain my further reason for this reticence in what follows ... I find it impossible to recall the precise emotional content, the exact ethos of non-physical love, in any given sexual intercourse. To record the physical love only, therefore, would be to leave out the greater part of love, and to risk debasing the purely physical."

I find nothing odd or infuriating in this reticence, and I have respected it. On the other hand, Angus Wilson's homosexuality is one of the major themes in the book, which is also, I believe, as he would have wished it. One can only regret that more of his own voice cannot be heard on these matters. He was still seeking understanding of his own experiences and sexual nature in the very last interviews of his life. Yet he was probably right to say, as he wrote to Kenneth Tynan, that the truth about his sexual adventures and fantasies was to be found in his fiction. There, in his novels, he could and did speak out.

For he was, first and foremost, a writer of fiction, and the facts of his life, along with his friends and the members of his family, were swept into the mainstream of his great fictional enterprise. As one of his editors, John Blackwell, commented, he tended to treat "all fiction, the authors *and* the characters, as though they were part of some gigantic extended family", and he tended to treat his family as though they were characters from fiction. His own father emerges from his reminiscences as from the pages of Dickens and Dostoevsky. The "crazy family" theme was one that recurred again and again in his own work, and for good reason: as he claimed, his own family had a gift for creating legends. Angus Wilson himself was a fiction. For the first fact about him that confronts us is that he did not begin life as Angus Wilson. He was registered after his birth on 11 August 1913 in Bexhill-on-Sea as Angus Frank Johnstone Wilson, and a Johnstone-Wilson, more often hyphenated than not, he was for many years to remain. Our story begins in Scotland with the Johnstone-Wilsons of Stroquhan.

THE FAMILY ROMANCE

Within the bounds of Annandale
The Gentle Johnstones ride.
They have been there a thousand years,
And a thousand years they'll bide.

The family romance begins in Scotland. The Johnstone-Wilsons were a
Scottish family from Dumfriesshire, the second largest county in southern
Scotland. Angus's father, William Johnstone-Wilson, liked to talk of the
family estate at Dunscore, some ten miles to the northwest of Dumfries.
He finally took his youngest son Angus to the borders in 1929 as a boy of
fifteen to see the Lowland country of small lochs and downland and salmon
rivers that had been the background of his own youth.

The parish is bounded by the rivers Nith and Urr, and the river Cairn
flows through it. This is Burns country, and Robert Burns, who had
farmed in the parish unsuccessfully at Ellisland, had also been one of the
founders of Dunscore circulating library, though this, too, was not a
particularly successful venture. The higher Dumfriesshire terrain did not
yield easily. The library, of which Burns had been treasurer, librarian and
censor, struggled on until the Second World War, when some of its books,
with Burns's writing in them, were sent for salvage.[1]

Although they were only fifteen miles away, Angus and his father did
not go to see the old family home, the source of many boyhood tales of
stoats, badgers, ravens and ratting.[2] Was this because of his father's regret at
what might have been his life, Angus later wondered? We do not know
whether on this occasion they went to see Dunscore church, a brave plain
building built on an eminence above the village, which commands the
neighbourhood for miles around. (When Emerson visited Carlyle at

nearby Craigenputtock a century earlier in the summer of 1833, the two metaphysicians were moved by the sight of the lonely church amidst the heathery hills to discuss the immortality of the soul, and Carlyle memorably declared to his new American friend "Christ died on the tree: that built Dunscore kirk yonder; that brought you and me together."[3] Their conclusion was that "time has only a relative existence".)

It was many years before Angus returned to seek the fictitious wild Scottish garden of his imagination and to see for himself the big solid ancestral house of Stroquhan and the family tombstones in Dunscore churchyard. By this time, none of the estate was left. But the Johnstone-Wilsons had once had land and money. The story of their disappearance is an important part of Angus Wilson's own story.

The Johnstone-Wilson dynasty was founded at the beginning of the nineteenth century, in February 1810, when a Miss Jane Wilson (b. 1776) married a Reverend Thomas Johnstone in Edinburgh. Both are well known border names. Family tradition has it that Jane Wilson was an heiress, sister of Francis Wilson of Croglin, an eminent Scottish solicitor and Writer to the Signet, and that the Wilsons insisted on the linking of the names as a condition of the union. Jane's father, Ebenezer Wilson, was a bookseller of Dumfriesshire, who had at least four other children – though there is no record of the birth of a son Francis. The Wilsons had long been important landowners in the parish of Tynron just north of Dunscore. A Wilson of Croglin is mentioned in Robert Simpson's *Traditions of the Covenanters* (1843) and Wilsons had owned the properties of Croglin, Appin, Marqueston, Birkhill, Kirkonnel and Lann. One tradition has it that the Wilsons sold Croglin at the end of the eighteenth century and went to Ireland. William Wilson of Tynron, local poet and antiquarian, identified the family seat of the Wilsons of Croglin in a converted sheep fold, where a weather-worn tombstone dated 1700 bears a heart-shaped shield and what seems to be a sprig of juniper, the Wilson badge.[4] The Wilsons of Croglin were proud of their heritage, and claim President Wilson as a kinsman.

A certain tenderness breathes from Tynron. The parishioners, wrote the Reverend J.M. McWilliam, in *The Third Statistical Account of Scotland* (1951, 1958), gave an important place in their domestic life to cats and dogs, and erected a sign on the road near the village with the word "Caution" and the figure of a cat, to commemorate the sad place where one had met its untimely end.

The Johnstones, ironically known as the gentle Johnstones, were a more bloodthirsty lot. They feature prominently in many border stories, particularly of violent sixteenth-century feuds with the Maxwells. The name of Johnstone is said by some to date from the grant of lands in Dumfriesshire to a Norman knight Jean, Jehan, or John in the twelfth century, and by others to date from a native settler who held land from c. 1174 from the Bruces of Annandale. It still survives in the landscape – in the parish of Johnstone, and in Johnstonebridge – and wild tales of Johnstone exploits were woven into Johnstone-Wilson family legend (and occasionally exhumed to entertain American lecture audiences in later years when Angus Wilson found himself called upon to follow the haggis).

The Johnstones were a powerful, prolific and belligerent clan. One of the most famous or infamous incidents of their history is that of the "Lockerby Lick". In 1593, the lord Maxwell, "having conveened two thousand men or thereby, in arms . . . with intention to have besieged the laird of Johnston's house of Lochwood, and razed out the memory of him and his name in these bounds", was ambushed by the laird of Johnstone and forty men: as the laird of Maxwell stood unarmed, the laird of Johnston "approached to him, and gave him the first stroke on the head, by which he fell from his horse, and was there cruelly murdered, with sundry others of his kindred and his friends. A great number were hurt in the face, which was called *A Lockerby Lick*."[5]

Angus's father, who greatly liked blood sports, relished such a heritage. Luckily there were other ancestral role models for other members of the family, including Secretary of State James Johnstone, who backed William of Orange, was chief instigator of the inquiry into the Massacre of Glencoe, and in later years devoted himself to gardening and planting at his home, Orleans House in Twickenham. He achieved a reputation for possessing one of the best collections of fruits and vines in the country. (Swift, however, thought him "one of the greatest knaves, even in Scotland".)

And then there was the engaging Miss Sophie Johnstone, permanent house guest at Balcarres Castle, the childhood home of the poet and South African pioneer Lady Anne Barnard. Sophie was subjected to a Rousseau-esque education by her "odd dog" of a father; she was as an experiment taught nothing at all and was never contradicted from the hour of her birth, with the result that "nature seems to have entered into the jest, and hesitated to the last whether to make her a boy or a girl. Her taste led her to hunt with her brothers, to wrestle with the stable boys, and to saw wood with the carpenter . . . She . . . played well on the fiddle, sung a man's song in a bass voice, and was by many people suspected of being one. She learnt to write of the butler at her own request, and had a taste for reading which she greatly improved. She was a droll, ingenious fellow; her talent for mimicry made her enemies, and the violence of her attachments to those she called her favourites secured her a few warm friends."[6]

Over the whole of the Johnstone family, warriors and eccentrics alike, shone the distant reflected glory of the extinct Earldom of Annandale, and the dormant Marquessate. This was an ancestry of vanished splendour to inspire dreams of romance, and the Johnstone-Wilsons were not indifferent to it. The crest badge of the Johnstones of Annandale was a winged spur, its plant badge was the red hawthorn, and its motto was *Nunquam Non Paratus*. The Flying Spur, memory of desperate searches for provender, re-entered the family history as the emblem of Angus's brother's preparatory school at Seaford, and as the title of the school magazine in which the earliest examples of Wilson juvenilia appear. Angus's niece, Sybil Scott, says that she was told as a child that when the Johnstone clan of old sat down to eat the womenfolk would serve up a covered dish, which, when opened, would be found to contain nothing but spurs – a hint to the menfolk to take to their horses and ride over the border to steal some Cumberland sheep. For, despite their motto (Never Unprepared), the Johnstones were not always provident.

We leave the world of legend and enter that of fact with Thomas Johnstone (1775–1843), Angus's great-great-grandfather. He was no swashbuckler. He was educated at the University of Edinburgh and was tutor in the families of Sir Michael Shaw Stewart of Blackhall and of Robert Baird of Newbyth: he was ordained as a Presbyterian minister in the Low Meeting of Berwick-on-Tweed on 15 September 1809. Jane (or Janet) Wilson, the presumed heiress of Croglin, was his first wife (he remarried, without issue, after her death in 1836) and by her he had four sons, two of whom, Michael Shaw Stewart and Thomas, also became ministers. Ebenezer died in 1839 aged 26 in Canada. The youngest son, Francis Alexander Wilson Johnstone, born on 18 November 1820, is the son who transformed himself into a Johnstone-Wilson and rebuilt the family home of Stroquhan. Under him, the estate of 300 acres prospered.

Stroquhan, the house which Angus's father signally failed to revisit, still stands prominently on the slopes of a hillside just beyond Dunscore, in a pleasant rolling border landscape. It is a country of drystone dykes where narrow bridges arch over clear and rapidly flowing burns. It is not rich agricultural land, but it provided grazing for sheep and cattle, and shooting and fishing for gentlemen. Lunchie holes, through which sheep but not cows could pass, can still be found in the dykes, indicating the former extent of the property, which until the 1920s included the neighbouring estates of Glenesslin and Dunesslin. The estate was well known to neighbour Carlyle, who mentions it in his letters, and it was sold in the

1830s when its owners, the Andersons, fell into debt. Family lawsuits accompanied the sale, and Carlyle records his wife Jane's visit in 1840 to "Miss Anderson of Stroquhan, poor woman, who seems to live now about Islington (tutoring some yellow or black children of her brother's, as we understand); a most melancholy wreck of baffled pride, – sullen, bare, ceremonious narrow, like an old Whinstone Border-tower!"[7]

The loss of the Andersons was the gain of the Johnstone-Wilsons, and Francis lived in the house from 1841. The 1851 census return shows him well established as head of a considerable household. He had married Jane Margaret Colville on 10 December 1844: she was a minister's daughter, born in 1827 in Kilwinnning Manse, County Ayr. By 1851 she had four children between the ages of one and five, and Stroquhan also housed a sister-in-law, a couple of cousins, and four servants. The estate employed nine labourers.

The house itself, of which the foundations date back to the early 1600s, is now approached by a long drive sweeping up past a gatehouse. There may once have been a moat: the house's site could easily have been fortified and defended. Francis Johnstone-Wilson added to the original structure a tall square wing, and an imposing front door with a porch and pediment over which can be seen the family coat-of-arms. It is a handsome house, a house of consequence, finely positioned.

This was the family seat, source of a dwindling *rentier* income and of much myth-making and not wholly reverent speculation amongst younger generations of Johnstone-Wilsons. Francis himself was a prominent local figure, a Justice of the Peace, and he prospered, perhaps too merrily, until his early death aged thirty-five in 1856 of "organic disease of liver and stomach". Almost immediately, it seems, the family fortunes became entangled. Francis's wife, Jane Margaret, is said to have fallen under the undue influence of her half-brother Francis Colville. Her brother George Colville was Minister of nearby Canonbie, and reported the death of his brother-in-law, but of Francis we know nothing but rumour. Jane was left a young widow with five children born in rapid succession, the heir Thomas Johnstone (b.1845), George Colville (b.1846), Jessie Maria (b.1848), Francis Wilson (b.1849) and Jane Margaret Colville (b.1851). (Baby Henrietta Helen, born in 1853, had died the following year.) The estate was mismanaged, and money was alleged to have been misappropriated by the Colvilles. It was said that Thomas contemplated legal action for embezzlement against his uncle Francis, but was dissuaded when he realised the proceedings would compromise his own mother.

Whatever the truth of these persisting suspicions, rumour becomes more interesting but, alas, as difficult to resolve as we come to the history of Angus's grandfather, Thomas Johnstone-Wilson. He was under ten years old when his father died, and details of his education are obscure. Angus in later years claimed Thomas had been sent to an English public school, but nobody seemed to know which one: he did not attend any of those at which his son and grandsons were educated. He almost certainly did not go to university. It was believed in the family that he became a captain with either a Scottish or an English border regiment and that he served in Canada, where he was injured by a kick from a horse. (The injury was to prove fatal, for the family believed it caused or precipitated his early death.) He was then invalided out of his regiment.

It was also said that he had married Angus's grandmother, Matilda, in St James, Piccadilly, without the blessing of that regiment, and that his marriage for this reason was "off the strength" – that is, her name was not included in the roll of officers' wives.

Marry he certainly did, on 10 May 1864, and family tradition identified the church correctly. On his marriage certificate he gives his profession or rank as Esquire, and his bride, West Susan Matilda Barns, claims at this stage to be the daughter of William Thomas Barns, Gentleman. Both bride and groom are described as minors, marrying with consent. Who gave the consent to Thomas's marriage is not clear: the witnesses at the wedding were both from the Barns side. What we do know is that Matilda, or Tillie, as she was known, came from a public house in the Haymarket called The Grapes. This cannot have been quite what was desired or expected of the Laird and Heir of Stroquhan, nephew and descendant of several Scottish ministers.

The Grapes, 52 Haymarket, was the Barns family residence. Angus, writing of Matilda in *The Wild Garden*, describes her as "a beautiful woman who ended her days as an exceedingly snobbish, rather vulgar Edwardian Kensington hostess. She always spoke of her father as a diamond merchant; whatever his profession, he lived in the eighteen-sixties in the Haymarket (where my father was born), which, remembering Dostoevsky's lurid accounts of that street in that decade, has always struck me as very odd for a diamond merchant's dwelling. My brothers placed my grandmother as a publican's daughter who caught the Scottish captain on his way through London to Canada where his regiment was sent to put down rebellion."

The brothers seem to have been right, at least about the placing of her as a "publican's daughter". (They would have known and remembered Matilda well, whereas Angus, the youngest of the family, was only two years old when she died.) Angus's father, William Thomas Frank Johnstone Wilson, was indeed born at 52 Haymarket, on 6 December

1865, a date which disposes of a simple theory of shotgun marriage. Thomas's occupation, on the birth certificate, is given as "Gentleman" – again, no mention of any regiment. And the Haymarket was at that period, as Angus recorded with relish, a street with very mixed associations – it had some elegant shops and two well known theatres, but it also had many famous and infamous public houses and hostelries, and its western side leaked out into many little dark alleyways where thieves swarmed and fights were frequent.

The family background of the Barns was modest: Matilda's father William had been a picture dealer, son of a picture dealer, before he became a licensed victualler, and her mother's father was a park keeper. Matilda herself was born in Hatton Garden. Business at The Grapes seems to have prospered, despite competition from The Waterloo, The White Horse, The Black Horse, The Cock, The Unicorn, The Blue Posts, and many other historic landmarks in the neighbourhood. The 1871 Census shows Angus's father Willie as a little boy of five in a bustling establishment in the heart of London, in one of its most notorious streets, together with his Barns grandparents, his mother, a couple of aunts, five barmaids, a cook and a parlour maid. No sign of any diamonds, though the address of Hatton Garden, famous in the diamond trade, may have given rise to the family legend. No sign, either, of Willie's father, Thomas, and no more pretence that grandfather Barns was an unemployed Gentleman.

It must have been a strange upbringing for the grandson of Presbyterian Scottish gentry, and we have no means of knowing how much the Johnstone-Wilsons at Dunscore knew of what was happening in London. We do not know when Willie first visited his inheritance and his Scottish aunts at Dunscore and Stroquhan. Nor do we know what happened to his paternal grandmother, for she, unlike most of the rest of the family, is not buried in Dunscore churchyard. One story has it that she and the embezzling brother ran off together to Canada. The Scottish aunts, Jessie and Cissie, certainly disapproved of Matilda.

And where was his father, Thomas, on Census day, 10 April 1871? Where, indeed, had he been and what had he been doing ever since his marriage? Family tradition held that he was in Canada serving with the King's Own Scottish Borderers. This regiment, the Twenty-Fifth, had been in Canada from June 1864 until August 1867, and had he been with them, Thomas could well have received out there the fatal kick. The next sighting we have of him, after his early marriage, is on his early deathbed, aged twenty-nine, in 1874, in Worcester Park, Cuddington, when he died of dropsy. The certificate describes him as "Formerly Captain 25th Regiment", and the death was reported by an illiterate servant.

The only problem here is that the Twenty-Fifth Regiment denies all knowledge of any Captain Johnstone-Wilson. Indeed, had Thomas ever joined the Kings's Own Scottish Borderers, he would, on his marriage to a publican's daughter, have been obliged, says the regiment's archivist, to resign. So not only does it seem that he never joined: he has also been both contemporaneously and posthumously dismissed, in double ignominy. Extensive searches of army lists and muster lists have so far failed to reveal any records of Thomas. Was he, like his son Willie and several of his grandsons, a fantasist?

It may well be that he joined some other regiment, and that the records will one day be discovered. The only clue we have is in a letter from Angus's brother Colin, the self-appointed family historian, to one of his cousins, in which he says that Thomas "was an officer in a quite reputable regiment – but not as my pretentious grandmother liked to allege – the Black Watch – but quite a good regiment . . . disbanded some years ago." This may indeed prove to have been the case, and the inscription of the Twenty-Fifth on the death certificate a simple error rather than a deliberate falsification. But as yet mystery surrounds Thomas's life and death. We do not even know when son Willie and wife Matilda left The Grapes and settled in the new and pleasant South West London suburb of Worcester Park. This branch of the Johnstone-Wilsons was, and continued to be, elusive. It seemed to enjoy giving the Census and the Street Directory the slip.

Up in Scotland, the family estate, which by now had swelled to 1700 acres, all firmly entailed, stood firm, and the house was let, first by the curators of Thomas, then by the curators of his son William, to a succession of tenants. Matilda's father was made a trustee.

Matilda of The Grapes, left a young, handsome and ambitious widow, did not stand firm. In March 1876, sixteen months after her husband's death, she remarried.

★

Matilda's second husband, a wholesale poulterer named Frederick William Frank, was an important intruder into the Johnstone-Wilson fortunes, and he was heartily disliked by some of his step-grandchildren. Known as "The Guv", he was described by Colin as one of the ugliest men ever seen. Why on earth had Matilda married him? She was, for all her social disadvantages, generally acknowledged to be a beauty, and could surely have done better the second time round: her first effort, despite the irritating entail, had been pretty successful, and she clearly had no intention of staying in purdah in quiet Cuddington. A family photograph (now lost?) showed her as a young widow, with Willie pressed uncomfortably against her knee, flounced in massive crape, but wearing no cap, which showed that "vanity scored over convention" (Colin). She told grandson Colin that after Thomas's death she had received an offer from a colonel in the Indian army, which she had refused as she did not want to leave her little boy. Why, then, did she accept the hideous Mr Frank, risking their being announced together in Edwardian drawing-rooms, as Colin conjectured, as Beauty and the Beast?

Her style of beauty can be guessed from Colin's letters and stories, from family legend as it was to reappear reworked in Angus Wilson's novels, and from an opulent portrait in oils painted in 1906 when she was in her fifties. She was, says Colin (who did not much like her), radiant and full of charm, much in demand as a guest: she had natural gold hair with just a tint of copper, small and rather plump hands, a "marvellous skin . . . very very fine brilliantly sparkling blue eyes – and fine cut features." She reminded him of the clear snowy peak of Mont Blanc on an azure night, hard and brilliant and slightly repellent like a diamond. In the portrait, painted for Mr Frank by Alfred Priest R.P.* as a birthday present (or perhaps as a thirtieth wedding anniversay present?), she appears fashionable and triumphant in a black evening dress, with an aigrette in her hair. It is said that she asked the artist to paint out her sequins, as they detracted from her beauty. It is also said that Mr Frank was delighted with his gift until Matilda presented him with the bill.

Matilda was not a character to be hidden under a bushel in Cuddington. Mr Frank had a solid long-established business in Leadenhall Market, where the Frank family had been dealing in poultry and game since the 1850s. He could provide a handsome dress allowance and pay for bridge parties and theatres. On 29 March 1876, Matilda and he were married in Malden, and Willie Johnstone-Wilson acquired a stepfather. (Curiously, on the marriage certificate Matilda inexplicably changed her name to Maude, but she continued to be known in the family as Tillie.)

Willie's mind was said by Colin to have been poisoned against the Franks by his snobbish Scottish aunts, who could not accept a dealer in chickens as a substitute for an officer and a gentleman. But Colin's testimony on this is not wholly reliable. He did not like his father either – indeed, he did not like most people. Angus himself said that while his father was less "socially boastful" than his mother, and less inclined to talk about lineage, he did exude an air of Scottish country gentry – and this

---

* Priest (1874–1929) was at the beginning of a career which combined paintings of society and public figures with popular and sentimental pieces with such titles as "Mother, Mother", "Got 'im" and "The Old Maid".

cannot have been wholly compatible with the urban Frank ethos. The
Guv, with his whisky-drinking grey Amazon parrot, in the Cromwell
Road flat, appeared to young Angus as "the very embodiment of bald-
headed, monocled Forsyteism", and Matilda, leaning against a side-table
of expensive ornaments and looking boldly back over her shoulder,
embodies something equally fleshly, comfortable and quietly ostentatious.
The riches of generations of prosperous middle-class trade handsomely
adorned the fine shoulders of the daughter of The Grapes.

Mr Frank's stepson Willie Johnstone-Wilson, however, was not
destined for a career in fish, poultry, game or any other commodity. He
was not destined for a career at all. According to his sons, he never did a
stroke of work in his life, and never seriously contemplated any profession,
apart from a brief flirtation with the law. As heir to what he believed to be a
considerable Scottish estate, he cherished delusions that money would
flow forever. It was enough to be a Gentleman of No Occupation. If The
Guv was an embodiment of the Forsytes, Willie was to become an
archetypal *rentier*, and in that he was also a child of his time. Not for nothing
was *rentier* to be one of Angus's favourite words. Its italics spatter his prose
like grapeshot.

Willie received a gentleman's public-school education, at Lancing
College in Sussex, which he attended from January 1881 to 1884, as a
boarder in the Head Master's House (which happened to be the most
expensive). We do not know why this school was selected: we do know
that while no London address is given for the young scholar, he is proudly
entered as son of Thomas Johnstone Wilson Esq of Stoguhar (*sic*) Croglin.

This was a flourishing period in the school's life. With the Reverend
Edward Sanderson as Head, the famous landmark of the new chapel was
built: the school was also renowned for its soccer.[8] But Willie Johnstone-
Wilson made little mark there. He did not contribute to the School
Magazine, and is not known to have taken part in any dramatic or literary
events. Nor is there any record of his having won any prizes, although he
was to tell Angus that he had. He does appear as "Heads, Cricket XI 1883"
in the Lancing Register but that seems to have been his only achievement.

After leaving Lancing, he had a brief stab at the law, applying on 5
January 1885 to be admitted to the Inner Temple. The Frank family was
still based in South West London, and his address was given as Udney Park,
Teddington. He was admitted on 26 February 1885 "as a gentleman of
respectability and proper person", on the recommendation of a couple of
barristers, and may well have attended a few lectures and eaten some
dinners, but no more is heard of his legal ambitions. Like many other
young men, he seems to have joined because it was the thing to do.

He was by now nineteen, and without any known occupation. How did he pass his time? Not, it seems, very productively. He was a man-about-town, a stage-door Johnny, a chain-smoker, a diner at Simpson's and Scott's and the Cri. He boasted of having "attended cockfights on islands in the Seine and illegal, non-Queensberry-rule boxing bouts". He credited The Guv with having taught him "to fight – not to box, mind you . . . That's what you've got to learn, laddie, to fight, not to box." He spoke of bloody wagers with Cockney porters in Covent Garden. The violence of Regency life lingered on in the undercurrents and by-ways of London, and resurfaced in the nightlife of the 1880s and 1890s. This was the London of Queensberry's son Alfred Douglas and his friend Oscar Wilde, who frequented the Café Royal, another of Willie's favourite haunts. Here, in a newly risqué café society, the upper and middle classes feasted with poets and pugilists and panthers from the jungle of the streets. Willie went in for "gambling obsessively, whoring rather mildly".[9] This was the great age of music hall, and Willie was to be seen at Gatti's and the Gaiety, those fun-palaces of the people, where social distinctions dissolved in the seedy glamour of the footlights. The laird's son could merge here with the publican's grandson, in the presence of the great entertainers – Vesta Tilley, Marie Lloyd, Florrie Forde, Hetty King. (At Gatti's, he might well have met Kipling, for it was also Kipling's favourite haunt.) Some fascinating tail-ends of gossip linger on in family correspondence – why did Willie Johnstone-Wilson claim to be responsible for launching upon her musical career the celebrated Gertie Millar, the humble girl from Bradford who became Countess Dudley? What fantastic improvisation made him think he had saved Jenny Lee's mother from the cobblestones of Aberdeen?

A young man-about-town with a penchant for actresses and gambling is a dangerous liability. Willie kept a notebook of his flirtations, like all young men of his day, and Tillie found it. Or so the story goes. As a punishment, he was sent off to seek prosperity in South Africa. Willie joined all the other remittance men and fortune-seekers of the Empire, and sailed boldly off to Port Natal. Off he went, "an attractive young heir of a foolish young widow", spoiled and indulged, with a taste for both high life and low life. On board that ship he met a young red-headed South African beauty with a green feather in her hair, Maud Ellen Caney.

THE CONVERGENCE OF THE TWAIN

The Caney family came from Lincolnshire. By the time Willie met Maud on the high seas, the Caneys were well established in Durban society. Their pioneering days were over, and they had entered a period of rising social respectability. A young Scottish landowning gentleman aged twenty-four with a double-barrelled name might well have seemed an attractive match for Maud, the second child and oldest daughter of a family of six. She is said to have ditched in his favour a Durban beau, a doctor, who was waiting faithfully for her return from England. (She is also said to have lived to regret her choice.)

If Willie Johnstone-Wilson liked to romance to his sons about his forebears, Maud Caney felt obliged by social pressures to be more seriously misleading about her own. She tried to dissociate herself from her trade background in South Africa and her family roots in England, and became, as the Caneys agreed, a fearful snob. Her desperate pretences pained, distressed and amused her children. Why could she not have been openly proud of the remarkable success story of the Caneys, instead of trying to hide it in circumlocution and misleading hints through which her horribly perceptive offspring (and, they feared, their friends and neighbours) could all too easily see?

The Caneys, like many other families of the period, had travelled far from their roots. The first Caney had gone out to Natal to make his fortune as a young man in 1860. Christened William Benjamin Caney, but later always known as B.W., he was born at Market Rasen, a small market town in Lincolnshire, on 2 December 1842. His father William, a labourer's son, was a watchmaker, born in the village of Barton Bendish, near Swaffham, in Norfolk: his mother Susan (née Watts) was a mariner's daughter, born far inland in the tiny agricultural parish of Dry Doddington, Lincolnshire, near Newark. The couple had married in Kent, where William Caney had worked as a clockmaker in Tunbridge Wells, then moved to Market Rasen, where William set himself up as "watchmaker and cutler" in the early 1840s in Queen Street. Market Rasen was, in effect, one long street on the Gainsborough to Louth road, with a market place in the centre, and King Street to the west, Queen Street to the east. It was a prosperous and expanding town (1600 inhabitants in 1842) known for its Tuesday markets, its fairs and racing – and for its high proportion of "teetotallers and Rechabites": one of its most splendid buildings is the Centenary Wesleyan Chapel (1863), complete with Ionic portico and pediment. Methodism flourished in the neighbourhood, and there was a Caney preaching on the Methodist circuit in 1844 who may well have been Great-Grandfather William Caney.

William played an active part in parish affairs, sitting on committees, assessing parish property, speaking at meetings: in 1878 he was the subject of a lampoon in the *Market Rasen Mail*, "The Lay of the Intelligent One", which took him to task for a flowery letter he had written to the *Mail* against secret nominations for local elections. Caney's prose had been impassioned: "The region of secrecy is full of danger. From thence came Guy Fawkes of old, and Hodel the Berlin would-be regicide of today, and it would not be far wrong to say from the same dark abode proceeded that black-visioned monster, dagger or pistol in hand, in all ages by whose evil machinations some of the fairest and choicest of mankind have been cut off . . ."[1]

William's son B.W. Caney was the oldest of four, two of whom (William Laws and Ebenezer) were eventually to follow their brother to South Africa: the other boy, John Watts, said to be "not right in the head", stayed on after his mother's death in 1856 with his father in Queen Street, working as shop assistant. The reason for the departure of the three boys was rumoured to have been a quarrel with a stepmother, but the story of William Caney's having once had a French wife and a daughter Charlotte by her seems to be apocryphal.[2] It is more probable that the decline of local trade following the arrival of the railway in 1848 influenced their departure. William Laws Caney is said to have worked for a while as a photographer in London in Bond Street, then to have travelled to India, where he painted miniatures of maharajahs: he was the last arrival in South Africa.

Whatever his reasons, B.W. Caney, Angus's maternal grandfather, left Market Rasen and sailed for Port Natal and the new town of Durban in South Africa. During the 1850s and 60s a flood of emigrants poured from Britain to the new colonies, some on government-assisted passages, and by the 1860s Natal had become a popular destination. Early years of settlement were harsh: an advance party setting out from Cape Town on the *Julia* in 1824 to the largely unexplored East Coast of Africa was greeted by hyenas and warring Zulus, and most of them died a violent death or succumbed to fever. Ivory was not as plentiful as had been expected, and many settlers turned back, but a few adventurers persisted and by 1835 the settlement of Durban had thirty inhabitants. In 1843, Natal was annexed as a colony by Britain, and gradually the town developed, with a school, a mission station, and grandiose dreams of promenades and civic buildings.

By 1850, there were two double-storey warehouse-shops and several brick structures – an inn, a billiards room, a print shop. But many houses were still built in African-hut style, of wattle and daub, with mat-lined roofs of thatched grasses. Corrugated iron was popular and considered more desirable than slate and tile. When Queen Victoria's son Prince Alfred visited in 1860 "the streets remained rutted, unhardened and unlit; there were open drains, and piles of miasmic rubbish littered the vacant lots of the town . . ."[3]

B.W. Caney was greeted by the same sights and smells that greeted the Prince. He probably arrived on 14 March 1861, on the *Leila*, a ship which left London on 25 November 1860 with 133 passengers: one of these was listed as William B. Carney, aged 17. The young man lost no time in setting up shop. He started up a jewellery, watchmaking and photography business and soon acquired permanent premises in West Street. This street, named after Lieutenant-Governor Martin West in 1845, became one of the principal shopping thoroughfares of Durban, but in 1860 the *Natal Mercury* was complaining about the town's "cesspools of stagnant filth" and condemning West Street in particular for its "pig sties, manure heaps and open privies". At high tide children fished in a salt stream that ran across the road, and contemporary photographs show smartly-dressed women dragging their crinolines through the mud. Early West Street landmarks were W.H. Savory's grocery store, Mrs Moffat's thatched boarding-house, the Wesleyan church and the town gaol: Acutt's famous auction rooms stood round the corner on Gardiner Street. Yoked oxen provided transport, and stores displayed an exotic mixture of ivory, pumpkins, almonds, dates, aromatic spices, hides and ammunition.

Caney's Building, erected in 1864, was proudly described as the first three-storeyed building in town, and one of the first jewellery stores in South Africa. It was also to be for years the family home and birthplace of several of the young Caneys. Its situation was exposed, as it stood lonely, aspiring, unprotected by neighbours. High winds blew in from the Bay, making the rickety top storey sway.

By the time B.W. Caney married in 1864 he was advertising watches, clocks, wedding rings, concertinas and photographic cases, and carrying out repairs for patrons at his "New Store, West End, West Street". The colony was growing fast, and ships were pouring into port with European settlers, indentured Indian labourers and imported goods. There was great demand for all civilising commodities: "Blue and White Damask, Black and Colored Goffered Braids, Hemmed Lace Handkerchiefs, Children's Kid Top Goloshed Patent Boots". B.W.'s store stocked gold watch-chains and sovereign cases for men, muff chains and mizpah brooches for the women, and, after the gold rush of 1886, hundreds of pick-and-shovel brooches to celebrate South Africa's growing prosperity.

B.W.'s bride, Ellen Calvert, had also emigrated in 1861. We have more details of her voyage than of his. She had travelled with her older sister Elizabeth, who was newly married to a joiner, William Wakes. They too were of Lincolnshire Noncomformist tradesman stock: the Calvert girls had been born in Horncastle, daughters of a grocer, and Elizabeth had married William Wakes in the Independent Chapel, just off the South High Street in Lincoln. This was a few minutes' walk from the Queen Inn, a commercial and family hotel where Ellen had worked as a barmaid. (It is now a Pizza Parlour.) Above the Inn loomed the great cathedral, high on its hill, but the Calverts belonged firmly to the lower town.*

Ellen, her sister and brother-in-law sailed out on a full-rigged sailing ship, the *Catherine*. Neither journey nor arrival were easy. The *Catherine* took ten days to reach Plymouth from Victoria Docks, and had to be recaulked; she took another four months to reach Durban. A small cabin was shared by eight married couples and fourteen children, and the passage was stormy; nearly everybody, Elizabeth Wakes remembered, was violently ill. A pirate ship was sighted, and a food shortage threatened when fresh meat hanging overboard was eaten by sharks. Arrival on 9 March 1862 offered new terrors. Durban had as yet no harbour, and ships often had great difficulty crossing the bar. (The advertising boast of *The Silvery Wave*, on which Caney tradition held that B.W. had gone out, was that it was "Guaranteed to Cross the Bar".) Passengers had to be lifted off the boat in baskets or carried ashore by Zulus. Elizabeth was so terrified of the black faces that at first she refused to disembark, and had to be assisted by a white sailor.

---

* It is worth mentioning that Colin claimed that Ellen was the seventh child of a seventh child, and that she was thus endowed with second sight: he also believed that Ellen's mother was a Blake of Kildare, and that the older Calverts had been born in Ireland of a father who had unwisely emigrated to Ireland instead of going, like the Kennedys, to America. All this is in a letter to his cousin Vivienne, 1 September 1973, and repeated in other letters. There is no evidence for any of it and some against it. Ellen's mother was not a Blake but a Baker. Calvert is a common Lincolnshire name. Colin, as we shall see, was very pro-Irish.

But Elizabeth settled in, and spent the rest of her life in South Africa. It was said that she and William Wakes eventually tired of dragging around an unmarried sister, and persuaded her to accept the precocious B.W. Caney on his third proposal. The wedding took place on 16 February 1864, at Bay Terrace, Durban. The bride was four years older than the groom. The weather was hot and oppressive, "about as hot as we ever have it in Durban", and the temperature (85–92 in the shade, 125 in the sun) was the favourite topic of conversation, as it might have been back in the old country. But almost everything else in this brave new colonial world was to be very different.

The couple established themselves as leading figures in their new country, embarking on a way of life far removed from that of their modest relatives back home. Ellen had seven children (one of whom died as a boy) and became matriarch to a prolific tribe of Caneys, several of whom achieved distinction in the arts, in law, in politics. In early days the family passion was for sport. Val Caney, the fifth son, born in 1877, kept a diary which records bicycle rides, swimming, and fishing expeditions in the Bay catching smelts, soles, tigers and grunters – a relief after long hot hours working in the store. There was often "great fun on the Bluff".[4] There were meetings at the Royal Natal Yacht Club, and sails in a succession of Caney-owned sailing and rowing boats – the *Flirt*, the *Alley Sloper*, the *Sprat*, the *Masher*, the *Ivy*. (Their very names are redolent of the music hall so dear to Willie Johnstone-Wilson.) The shooting was rather different from the shooting at Stroquhan, for Val pursued not only snipe and plover but also kingfishers, bushbirds, divers and green swallows. The Durban races were another attraction, and the Caneys owned racehorses, though unlike their approaching Scottish son-in-law they did not have a reputation as gamblers.

The family expanded in all directions. B.W.'s brothers, attracted by news of the good life, followed him out from England; both married and produced large families. There was an unhappy ending for the unfortunate Ebenezer, clearly not an outdoor man, for he was drowned when he fell off the pier while photographing a sailing ship. But the others fared better. South Africa was booming in the wake of discoveries of rich deposits of gold and diamonds: who better placed than a jeweller to prosper? Ellen grew stout and respectable, B.W.'s solid downward-drooping moustache was set with a determination to succeed. The jewellery business flourished, and there was money to spare for luxuries. Maud went on her first voyage to England in style to visit her grandfather, the watchmaker, still in Queen Street in Market Rasen. (He died in 1898, aged eighty-nine.) It was on the return journey that she met Willie Johnstone-Wilson, and embarked on a shipboard romance.

Maud, like Matilda, was renowned as a beauty. What marriageable young lady is not? She had abundant masses of long red-gold hair and she captivated Willie (who, according to Colin, could never resist red hair) by the green feather in her grey squirrel toque. Was Willie Johnstone-Wilson handsome as well as debonair? It is hard to reconstruct his youthful appearance, so heavily is it overlaid with images of his later self – walrus-moustached, nicotine-stained, bowler-hatted, a handkerchief dangling from his tweed coat pocket. But acceptable at twenty-four he certainly was. He employed his celebrated charm and won Maud over as they sailed towards her home.

The outdoor life of the Caneys in South Africa appealed to Willie, for he too was passionate about all forms of sport, and tales of Zulu wars, slaughters, and heroic rides through the bush matched his recital of fights in Covent Garden and the bloody exploits of the Johnstones. The Battle of Blood River (1838) and the massacre at Rorke's Drift (1879) had already passed into folklore, and rivalled tales of the Lockerbie Lick. This was bracing frontier stuff, at least in the telling. The reality was more relaxing. Willie did not have to rely for his pleasures on the beach, the Turf Club and the Yacht Club: Durban had acquired a magnificent Theatre Royal in 1882, and offered concerts, music hall, dancing, opera. Durban had splendid hotels, with turbanned waiters and palm courts and verandahs; it had promenades and esplanades where a gentleman could stroll with a cigarette or be conveyed by a fine feathered Zulu in a rickshaw. (Brother-in-law Val, who was a bit of a dandy, waistcoated, straw-hatted, white-suited, was famous for taking a rickshaw to work long after the advent of the motorcar.) Servants, both European and Kaffir, were plentiful and cheap.

The Caneys lived well. Willie Johnstone-Wilson knew when he was on to a good thing. (The elder Caneys, for their part, were not so sure about Willie.)

He and Maud were married privately at B.W.'s double-fronted residence, Beacon House, Bayside, on 17 April 1890, in the presence of many Caneys. Brother Charlie was best man, and sister Ivy and cousin Edie were bridesmaids. The wedding rated a paragraph in the *Natal Mercury* – not as long a paragraph as that devoted to the orange-flower-bedecked, lace-and-tulle wedding of one of the Acutts, but a whole paragraph nevertheless. It was a changeable autumn day, with a refreshing shower of rain: Boucicault's *London Assurance* was playing at the Theatre Royal, and it was off to the uncertainties of London that they sailed, after a short honeymoon by the famous waterfall at Howick. They left on 27 April on the *Norham Castle* (first class, of course), accompanied by the good wishes "of a large circle of friends" to start a new life together in Richmond.

Had the Caney parents approved more whole-heartedly of the match, the wedding might have been less private. Maud would have liked posterity to know more of her bridal attire.

*

On their return from South Africa, the newly-wed Johnstone-Wilsons settled in Richmond in a pleasant new development of undistinguished semi-detached three-storey yellowish brick houses near – perhaps even a little too near? – the railway station. Almost at once they began to produce a family of six surprising sons. The first of these, Frederick Benjamin, was born at 21 Larkfield Road, on 12 March 1891. His father Willie is described as "living on his own means", which may at that stage have been true. He was soon to live on his wife's. A second son, Winn William, was born at the same address on 20 September 1892. He was not expected to live, and was peremptorily christened on the kitchen table, but despite being cast off at birth into the care of the family treasure, Nurse Sopp, he managed to struggle on, to the great advantage of the rest of his family. He was a born fighter. A third son, Clive Calvert, was born on 2 September 1894, and a fourth, Colin Frank, on 12 September 1897. By this time the family had started a series of migrations, and had crossed the river to settle for a while at 33 Perham Road, Fulham. A fifth, and, they must have assumed an ultimate son, Patrick Boswell, was born on 16 October 1900.

This was a large family for a gentleman of independent but diminishing means who had expensive tastes and did not seem to be in any way employable. His wife, although she came from hard-working stock, had not been trained to look after herself or anyone else; unlike her mother, she had been brought up to be a lady. She had been educated at the Durban Young Ladies' Collegiate Institution, and for the rest of her life she remained incapable of cooking or attending to any household chores. Like most women of her class and time, she had servants and expected to be waited on. Some of the names of these attendants, like that of Nurse Sopp and a governess-nurse, Mrs Tatham, have come down to us (along with Nurse Sopp's recipes for fairy cakes and scones) but many of them, ill-selected and themselves ill-trained, have vanished beyond recall. Small children at that period were not expected to see much of their parents. They lived a nursery life, a life of rice and batter puddings, of prickly and much-loathed Jaeger combinations, of secret games. Mother would control the nursery from afar, with occasional bodily incursions, but Father hardly knew it existed. He spent his afternoons and evenings at the club or at the Long Bar of the newly opened Trocadero, and his mornings preventing the maids from doing Mother's bedroom.

Nurse Sopp was a powerful presence. She intruded on Cook's territory with her famous shortbreads, and nourished a violent prejudice against Catholics – she had once been jilted by a Catholic fishmonger. She also had a fearsome code of manners in which she drilled her subjects. The family legend went thus: Winn was Nurse's favourite, Clive was his mother's favourite, Pat was his father's favourite, Colin was nobody's favourite.

Winn had auburn hair like his mother, but the others were dark like their father. Winn was serious, Clive was talkative. Colin, olive-complexioned, was physically the odd one out – hardly a Johnstone-Wilson at all, some thought. Pat as a baby was famed for his angelic curls: ladies would stop his perambulator in the street to coo at them in admiration. He was a pretty child and won drawing-room acclaim during the Sino-Japanese war when Britain was backing Japan: English women dressed themselves up in kimonos (Maud was sent a much-envied silk kimono from Grandma Caney in Durban) and little Pat would sing

> Only a little Jappy soldier
> Only a mother's son
> Prone on the field of battle
> Only his duty done

to the applause and sniggers of his audience.

The Johnstone-Wilsons were a play-acting family, and Maud in particular liked to be the star. They could create dramas out of very little. The serious side of life did not much appeal to them. All these boys had to be sent to proper schools, of course, though neither Willie nor Maud had much real respect for education or erudition – indeed, they thought them rather provincial. But society set standards which had to be obeyed. Fred, Winn and Colin went along the road to Colet Court and St Paul's (though Colin's stay there was suspiciously brief), and Pat went to Tonbridge. None of them except Pat had particularly distinguished school careers: perhaps a certain anxiety as well as insouciance in the home hindered concentration. Where, after all, were the fees to come from? And to go *on* coming from?

Clive proved less expensive. He was let off the rigours of education after an attack of meningitis at the age of five: he was thought to be too delicate. He was nursed through the illness at home by Maud, Tillie, and various cousins called up from the depths of Lincolnshire: the door knocker was swathed in washleather to preserve silence, which, according to Colin, was broken by the sound of angelic voices singing to Maud and Tillie to annouce that the child was about to take a turn for the better. The family doctor, Dr Armstrong, also claimed credit for the recovery, and thereafter is said to have treated the family free of charge.

Despite these savings, life was costly. The family liked to put on a good show. In this pre-war world, the boys would be taken on rounds of afternoon calls by Maud or the finely-corseted Tillie, and they were expected to dress accordingly. The slightest social occasion called for a morning suit, and a young man had to perch on a small drawing-room chair with top hat, stick and gloves (only a "bounder" left his hat in the hall) while balancing a cup and saucer in one hand and a cake from a silver basket in the other. Five morning suits, five sticks, five hats, five pairs of gloves would be a tall order.

The Drury Lane Christmas pantomime was the occasion for a full-dress family parade, with satin-ribboned boxes of Turkish delight or marrons glacés and corsages of Parma violets. The regal Tillie would inspect the scene through her lorgnettes, the Guv through his monocle, and on one occasion Mother was obliged by request to remove her enormous rose-covered picture hat and hand it to little Colin, who never forgot the responsibility of clutching it and its murderous assegais of hat pins upon his lap.

Luckily for the family fortunes, the despised "Guv" with his heavy humour and enormous bald head stepped in and took over the upbringing of the eldest, Fred. Fred moved into the childless Frank household and grew up somewhat apart from his parents and brothers. The frequently shifting Johnstone-Wilson ménage, despite its pretensions, was very different from this solid and disciplined world of eight-course dinners, servants in their proper places, airless basements. Fred was displaced, rejected. Despite this early separation, Fred took after his father in tastes, in lack of application, and in a somewhat dubious charm. He was the only one of the sons who did not give in to his mother's passionate desire for admiration and surrender. He rejected her, and eventually went into the Frank poultry business, where he did not shine.

Clive's career was more successful though hardly more illustrious. At the age of sixteen he was packed off to Ceylon, on some vague recommendation of the possibility of a job with a tea planter. Luckily, he made friends with a couple on the boat, who managed to get him shipped home when it turned out that the tea planter was a hopeless drunk. Clive too was then rescued by the Franks, who eventually set him up in a poultry shop called J.W. Clive in Chandos Street, Charing Cross. He, the least educated of a sadly under-educated family, was the only one to show any financial shrewdness or sense of self-preservation. (Angus thought he had more of the South African business sense in him.)

Of Colin and Pat, that strange and devoted pair, there are many strange stories to tell, as the saga unfolds. Winn was the brother who most closely approached middle-class normality, and he found it uphill work trying to stand by the rest of his family, to whom he was loyally devoted.

In those deceitfully calm pre-war years the Johnstone-Wilson parents were struggling to stay afloat upon the social tide. Would they, like the unsinkable *Titanic*, founder? Some marital crisis in 1909 was survived, but long remembered by the boys. Willie continued to gamble and get into debt and dine at the Trocadero: bankruptcy was a word that floated in the nursery air. Maud, like so many of her generation, took refuge in Christian Science, and refused to believe that anything could go seriously wrong. Willie was unfaithful, and there were unseemly domestic quarrels. He was forever packing up his tennis bags and declaring that he was about to leave home forever. Maud was forever telling the maid to lay a place for Mr Johnstone-Wilson just the same, as he would be sure to be home for his dinner. (Or was it the maid who comforted an hysterical Mrs Johnstone-Wilson? The scenario varied.) And home he always came.

Maud herself had admirers rather than lovers. She needed above all to be admired, and as Willie's attentions were somewhat diffused, she allowed the attentions of "pseudo-uncles" who brought her chocolates, courted her from afar, and fetched and carried for her, reminding her of her days as a Durban belle. Mother-in-law Tillie disapproved. The children watched with sharp eyes.

Home was not really much of a home. Pursued by debts, the family decamped from one private hotel to another, sometimes hastily, pursued by bailiffs. There were rows, reconciliations, humiliations. Winn got a job working in a school in Eastbourne, and perhaps drawn by this small beacon of security the family moved in 1912 to Bexhill-on-Sea on the South Coast, to a suburban house in Dorset Road which they nostalgically renamed Dunscore. There, as a result of one of Willie Johnstone-Wilson's renewed pledges of good behaviour, on Monday, 11 August 1913, baby Angus was born.

He was something of a surprise to his mother, to his father and to the congregation of the First Church of Christ Scientist, Bexhill. Maud was, after all, forty-five years old, and the youngest of her sons, Pat, was already thirteen. Inevitably, it was said that she had really wanted a little girl. Had she had one, she would have called her Violet Sybil. Angus did his best to oblige her by turning out to be a very pretty baby with masses of striking blond curls. (His brother Clive dubbed him Blond and thus addressed him for most of his life.) Angus appeared very charmingly in little white dresses with double frills of broderie anglaise. He played on the beach with his bucket and spade, in a little sunhat, surrounded by bathing belles in cloches and picture hats and bathing hats. He was taken for rides along the promenade in little donkey carts and goat carts. And Willie loved his unexpected Benjamin child.

Baby Angus was spoiled. He had to put up with being described as a little mistake and a little afterthought, but he was also indulged by all. His parents made much of him, and his older brothers, particularly Pat and Colin, petted him and let him into their somewhat surprising secrets. He was precocious: "Baby wants to go to Monte Carlo" was one of his earliest *bons mots*. He was a child amongst adults, an eavesdropper on an incomprehensible world of double meanings and jokes and half-guessed allusions. On one mysterious occasion Daddy disappeared to Jersey, and came back with a beard: he was kept out of sight indoors, taking an occasional airing on the balcony, until "things blew over". What was a child to make of this?

Angus was indulged, but he was also often ignored. Kept up late, alternately cossetted and forgotten, his baby face occasionally looks truculent and perplexed in the old seaside snapshots, and it soon took on an expression that was old before its time. He belonged to no generation. He was a spy, a go-between, an unseen witness, as well as the darling baby of the house.

3

ARMAGEDDON AND AFTER

Angus was only a baby when the First World War broke out, but he was just old enough to have a remembered sense of the world that it so violently disrupted. Of the progress of the war itself, just across the English Channel, he was certainly aware. It was said that on a still day the shelling could be heard in Bexhill, and those who did not hear it imagined it. Angus's mother was on the alert. She had three sons of fighting age, two approaching maturity, and it seemed hardly likely, as the war dragged on and took its devastatingly high toll, that they would all be spared.

The family had moved from Dorset Road to Marina Court, a large block of flats on the sea front with enormous corridors where Angus and his brothers played at air raids: the Christian Science Reading Room was housed in the same building, at 5 Marina Arcade, and Maud went there for comfort, as a regular attender – though there is no record of her having been, now or later, a member. Bexhill tried to keep calm in the face of the threat of war, urging its population of preparatory school children that it was "business as usual": local dignitary Earl De La Warr issued a patriotic message from Cooden Beach Golf Club promising that, "In a small way Bexhill can and will help."[1] Xenophobia raged, and there was a cry to purge Bexhill and Britain of all orchestras and bands with German- or Austrian-sounding names, and to change the name of the Bexhill Kursaal, famous for its musical entertainments, to something less Teutonic: but Madame Ceres continued to sell her hats, Giller's Library continued to prosper, the Cinema-de-Luxe with its full orchestral accompaniments did a fine trade, and the hotels persisted in publishing their lists of summer visitors.

Recruiting fever seized the little town, and there were many rallies. Sussex men disappeared, to be replaced, over the years, by an influx of Canadian forces. Angus's war effort consisted of dressing up in blue satin and piping up musically at recruiting concerts with "We don't want to lose you, but we think you ought to go . . ." He looked very charming with his Buster Brown haircut – as charming as the shopgirls from Plummer Roddis's department store who, according to his brothers, used to parade up and down outside the shop at Eastbourne singing

> Your arms are our defence
> Our arms your recompense.

His older brothers were amongst those who had to go, and off they went.

Winn went first. He volunteered and was commissioned on 1 December 1914, as temporary second Lieutenant of the Tenth Battalion of the Royal Sussex Regiment. He had embarked that spring on a courtship of Elizabeth Hindwood, a Froebel-trained teacher living in nearby Wallington, and the war interrupted but perhaps intensified their romance. The courtship continued in a touching correspondence, as Betty was slowly translated from Miss Hindwood to Betty, Dearest, Darling, Kiddy, Girlie, Mon Enfant: shyly she confessed that she was a little older than he, gallantly he reassured her that this was of no consequence. They exchanged views as well as endearments, Winn writing to Betty in September 1914 "I hope you never joined that hysterical and perfectly disgusting White Feather brigade . . . It is a sacrilege to suggest that you would. I apologise." He also sent her a snapshot of baby Angus. He left the peaceful South Coast world of tennis and amateur theatricals for barracks in Dover and Colchester and proposed to her, diffidently, by letter from Dover, on 23 May 1915, adding that the rumour was that he was about to go off to the Dardanelles. She accepted him, and off he went, not to the Dardanelles but to France, with the Ninth Battalion, transferred from the Tenth.

The other brothers were not quite so quick off the mark. Clive joined the Inns of Court OTC on 11 October 1915, and was commissioned into the Royal Army Service Corps the following year. He was to serve in France, Flanders and Italy, and was promoted to lieutenant on 19 December 1917. He survived the war unwounded.*

Fred, the idle well-dressed charmer, was still living with his stepfather Frank in the flat at 225 Cromwell Road. His grandmother Tillie, she of the glacé kid gloves and millinery extravaganzas, had died on 8 June 1914, aged sixty-seven, her death marking the end of the era in which she had risen so far above her original station. Winn, not Fred, was in attendance at her

---

* Clive stayed on with the RASC after the war, working as Instructor and Inspector of Mechanical Transport until 1922 or 23, towards the end of the period on half-pay.

deathbed. Fred, who like his father had a reputation as a roué, married an actress, Winifred Tillett, on 23 September 1915. She was two years older than he, and the daughter of a ship broker. On his marriage certificate, inexplicably, he gives his profession as Able Seaman. Winn, who adored his brother Fred, was sad not to have been asked to the wedding. (Much about Fred's career was inexplicable and better left unexamined, the family thought: he may already have had some kind of brush with the law.) He was commissioned as a temporary Second-Lieutenant in the Royal Garrison Artillery in April 1918. He too survived the war and was not wounded.

Winn was not as lucky as his brothers. His parents received the dreaded telegram on 22 November 1915 with the news that Winn had received a gunshot wound in the chest and was at the 10th Casualty Clearing Station. More telegrams followed, bringing little comfort. REGRET SLIGHT IMPROVEMENT NOT MAINTAINED, STILL CRITICAL, NO WORSE, came the various bulletins. He was not better, he was much the same. Winn was not expected to live. The chaplain wrote a long handwritten letter of explanation to his fiancée, and Betty's heart must have sunk when she read the words "He was a great favourite with his men and was hit while insisting on his men taking cover."

But the chaplain had given up too easily. Winn struggled and began to improve. The chaplain encouraged his faltering letters to Miss Hindwood. His strength seemed to return. Winn survived, and on 17 June 1916 he and Elizabeth Kate Hind-Wood were married at St Andrews, Westminster. He returned to active service, was promoted as Acting Lieutenant in October, was wounded again ("a small shrapnel wound") in March 1917 and again recovered. This time Willie and Betty went down to Folkestone and Willie crossed the channel to see his son. Betty was not allowed across, and sight of the hotel in Folkestone where she waited for news filled her with lasting horror. Willie's glimpse of the Field Station improved in the telling – "that nightmare place, there with the screams you could hardly hear for the guns and the stench of vomit . . . unrecognisable forms, more like landed fish than men – you know, white and gaping . . ."[2] After this second injury Winn came home to convalesce for a while at the Countess of Pembroke Hospital at Wilton; October 1918 found him sailing from Liverpool to America, on a mission which involved travelling from New York to Washington, Chicago, Atlanta and other cities, lecturing on the war in Red Cross halls, schools and churches, trying to rally support for a cause to which many Americans seemed indifferent, even hostile. He was in Detroit in November and noted in his diary "November 11. Wake to Armistice celebrations at 5 am. Amazed at Americans who can enthuse in cold blood at such an hour." Then back to England, on 27 December, and a new life. His had been an honourable war, and one that Winn was to fight again for the benefit of admiring boys with the cutlery and salt cellars on his prep-school dining table. He was lucky. The 24th Division, with which the 9th Battalion of the Royal Sussex Regiment served, lost 35,362 men.

And what of the mysterious Colin whom nobody loved, and Pat who was loved by all? Pat was still a schoolboy at Tonbridge during the war, safely out of harm's way. He had grown up from an angelic baby into a beautiful adolescent whose physical attractions may be judged by the chronologically impossible but long-believed family legend that he was the model for Gilbert's statue of Eros in Piccadilly.

Colin had left school before the war began. He had entered St Paul's from Colet Court in the spring of 1912 and left in April 1913 at the age of sixteen; he was described in reports as being "very poor" at most of his lessons, apart from English History. He then lived with the family at Bexhill, indulging the family talent for doing nothing much. At one point he decided to call himself Ronnie. At another he fancied himself as a William. He had already embarked on a rich fantasy life. These were the first of several transformations and conversions.

Towards the end of the war, Colin joined the Black and Tans and went to Ireland where he was seduced by a sergeant, who gave him a make-up box and encouraged him to paint his face. He became a practising homosexual, and developed a dislike of the Protestant church that culminated in his becoming a Roman Catholic convert. Or so the family said.

A Firbankian character was in the making. But what here is fact and what is fiction? Was Colin really a member of the Black and Tans? Was it truly the English atrocities in Ireland that drove him into the arms of Rome? Was there ever a dashing sergeant with rouge and *poudre-de-riz* in a secret box? Certain it is that Colin was obsessed by the subject of cosmetics, and wore red nail varnish in public, thus shocking his South African Caney relatives; he seems also to have taken to wearing ladies' underwear. (He was and remained very interested in corsets, a fixation derived from those amazing garments of his mother's Edwardian days: poring through the advertisments in *The Gentlewoman*, who might not turn transvestite or fetishist at the sight of those ravishingly curved Specialité models from Dickins and Jones, in superfine French coutille, prettily trimmed with lace-ribbon, with fancy rubber suspenders in front?)

The dates for his Irish expedition could be made to fit with family legend. The Black and Tans were an irregular force recruited in England to reinforce the Royal Irish Constabulary in 1920: the first British recruit joined in January 1920, and the numbers rose over the following months. These were the years of severe post-war unemployment, and a motley assortment of waiters, barmen, cinema operators, motor mechanics, swimming instructors, footmen, clerks, ex-soldiers and ex-officers were glad – at least initially – to find paid employment. Was Colin among them? His name does not appear in Home Office listings of the RIC or the Auxiliary Division Register, but he may have been serving with a regular regiment rather than with the Black and Tans themselves – there were over 37,000 troops in Ireland in November 1919. (It is worth noting that at least one recruit gave as his reasons for resigning not the more common "intimidation" or "threats to family" or "dislike of militarism of job" but "sympathy with the Irish people" – a sympathy Colin and his brother Pat were to feel all their lives.)

Whatever the nature of Colin's adventures in Ireland, we can have little doubt of some of his activities during the 1920s in England. From an early age Angus was aware that both Colin and Pat were homosexual, and when he was a small child his brothers would admit him to their dressing-up games. His accounts of what happened in these games varied, but they seemed to have revolved principally round tableaux of executed royalty. In one version, little Angus, dressed as Marie Antoinette or Mary Queen of Scots, would be led to the block, there to die bravely, admired by his older brothers. In view of the differences in their ages, there was clearly some sexual undercurrent in these rituals, though one need not endorse the suggestion of one friend who speculated that Angus, like Frederick Ashton, had probably been seduced by his brothers. (Ashton was also the youngest child of a large family of boys.) But some erotic frisson in these games there must have been.*

Colin and Pat were fascinated by tragic royal ladies. Had they not a beautiful mother who cast herself in the role of tragedy queen? Pat had been born on 16 October, the anniversary of the execution of Marie Antoinette, a date which seemed to both brothers to be highly significant. They were also intrigued by the strange story of the Empress Eugénie, wife of Napoleon the Third, who after her husband's expulsion from France had lived in exile in Chislehurst. There she would beautify herself, like Pauline Borghese, by bathing in milk. (Unlike Marie Antoinette, she had

---

* Compare Nancy Mitford's revelation: "I used to masturbate whenever I thought about Lady Jane Grey, so of course I thought about her continually & even executed a fine water colour of her on the scaffold . . . This sublimation of sex might be recommended to Harriet . . ." Letter to Evelyn Waugh, 21 May 1948. *Letters*, ed. Charlotte Mosley (Hodder & Stoughton 1993).

some thought for the needs of others: the milk was then recycled and given to the poor.) She even, satisfyingly, had a South African connection, for her son, the impetuous Prince Imperial, was killed in the Zulu war of 1879. His body was returned to the family mausoleum in Chislehurst, but she travelled out to Natal the following year to see the spot where he had fallen. She spent fifty days under canvas up-country on this pilgrimage. Not quite a pioneering Caney, but a sort of spiritual relation nevertheless.

Mata Hari was another favourite, a femme fatale and Queen of Spies who appeared in innumerable post-war movies. She became a central figure in Angus's imaginative games: he spent much time in a transparent spotted blouse playing Chopin on the piano while the firing squad waited. Did Pat and Colin embody the firing squad?

In notes on these games made late in life (in 1985) Angus jotted down "Pat – much closer to me – still schoolboy – yet nothing except with both of them continuous charades – . . . Lipstick, powder etc. Colin with dyed hair. Scotch tea rooms lady about 'the brothers' (me as well) when I was 16."

Well did Angus, years later in an *Observer* review, describe his brothers as queenly. And the brothers went further than charades. They indulged their regal daydreams with their baby brother, but at night they earned their meagre living trolling the Dilly in ladies' underwear. Or so the family believed. They operated as prostitutes, though no one could say for how long, or from what base. And at some point in his teens Angus seems to have overheard an interchange through a wall in a room in Villiers Street – a notoriously louche area near Charing Cross – "Regent Palace Hotel, no room for two men in Charing X. Room next to ours. Villiers St. Purposeful fantasy or just fantasy or real? My complaints to Clive. Could I have heard so much?" (Faulkner's Hotel, Villiers St featured as a location jotted down in notes for an autobiography: brother Clive lived nearby respectably in the Adelphi at some point: what was schoolboy Angus doing there? The young Kipling also had strong associations with this street, one might note.)

Whatever the time sequence of these events, Colin and Pat introduced Angus young to the underworld. But they did not remain long as Painted Ladies soliciting in the City of Dreadful Night. Some time in the 1920s both of them were rescued by Our Lady of the Sorrows, and they were received into the Roman Catholic Church. Colin was baptised on 9 June 1926, in St Mary's on the Fulham Road. Pat was received at much the same time, and thenceforth both of them presented themselves as devout converts. Colin, briefly, thought of becoming a Servite monk, but found the monastery kitchens too disgusting – thus consciously or unconsciously concurring with Frederick Rolfe, alias the Rev. Frederick William Rolfe, alias Fr. Rolfe, alias Baron Corvo, alias George Arthur Rose, alias Hadrian the Seventh, alias the poor student Jameson at "St Andrew's College" (alias Scots College) who told Hadrian the Seventh that he lived on bread, boiled eggs and water because "I have been into the kitchen; and I have seen – things."[3] And Colin was to develop more characteristics in common with Rolfe than a fastidiousness about food.

Both Colin and Pat remained, despite and through their conversion, camp to a degree. They were eccentric Twenties figures who might have starred at the Oxford of Evelyn Waugh and Harold Acton if anyone had thought of purchasing them an education. Had they had the money of a Stephen Tennant (whom Pat somewhat resembled), or the ambition and discipline of a Cecil Beaton, they could have joined the gilded youth of their time. As it was, Pat wore white gloves and a black sombrero, Colin painted his nails carmine, and they both affected knitting, anklets and earrings.

They were Corvine or Firbankian figures – had not Firbank also adored the Empress Eugénie, his close neighbour in Chislehurst, his very own Artifical Princess? Had not Firbank rouged and powdered? Angus, writing of the Twenties and Firbank, comments: "maquillage for courageous tapettes of all classes was in those years a convention"[4], and his own brothers were no exceptions. These were the days when Stephen Tennant sprinkled his finger-waved hair with gold dust and wrote to his friend Cecil Beaton from Fallodon in the wilds of Northumberland: "My dear! please hurry to Selfridges for the elixir as I am becoming a mournful sight, daily navy blue hair sprouts from my head – do be an angel and send it quick!"[5] Beaton himself had been thrown in the river at a grand ball at Wilton House in that summer of 1927 for wearing an excess of rouge, face powder and mascara. (But poor E.M. Forster did not dare even to powder his nose.*)

Pat and Colin could not expect to live the High Life except in fantasy. Pat is said to have worked for a while as personal secretary to Sir Timothy Eden, but this may be mere family gossip, and the Eden family cannot confirm it – though the present Lord Eden says that it is possible that "he may have helped my father in connection with his own writing."[6] The possibility does not seem too far-fetched, for there was much in Sir Timothy that would have appealed both to Pat and to Angus – Sir Timothy published a gentle, whimsical little work about his pet dogs,

---

* Jan 2, 1925. "Famous, wealthy, miserable, physically ugly – red nose enormous . . . Take no bother over nails or teeth but would powder my nose if I wasn't found out." P.N. Furbank, *E.M. Forster: A Life* Vol. 2, Ch. 6 (1978).

dedicated to one of them by his "unworthy MASTER",[7] and a life of his own fox-hunting aesthete father Sir William.[8] This recounts Sir William's famous quarrel with Whistler over the price of a portrait, and quotes Sir William's very strong views on gardening – he waged war on flower pots, begonias and calceolarias, roundly declared that "it is flowers that ruin a garden" and urged his readers "never mix reds or pinks or yellows – put blues and mauves and greys together . . ."

Pat would have felt more at home with such preoccupations, but this temporary post, if it existed at all, did not last long, and Pat and Colin moved on to various semi-respectable but hopeless jobs – selling Electrolux vacuum cleaners, working as supers at Elstree – but public schoolboys were a drug on the market, and eventually they went to live off brother Winn in sober Seaford. In this setting they were highly conspicuous and long remembered.

Angus deeply loved Pat, whom he described as "a youth of exceptional histrionic powers, strangely combining sharpness of wit and tenderness of heart, extremely effeminate, with deep powers of creation . . ."[9] His relationship with the difficult Colin was more complex, but Pat he loved, and so did everyone. Kindness itself, such a gentleman, so gentle, so sweet-natured – these are the tributes of the family who remember him, of pupils whom he taught. A great-niece still cherishes the fairy that he gave her for the top of her Christmas tree.

The third brother, Clive, had also become a Catholic, but for different reasons. In June 1922 he married a shrewd bourgeoise Frenchwoman, Lucie Anquetin, whose family came from La Ciotat, near Marseilles. The Anquetins claimed kinship with the French Impressionist Louis Anquetin (1861–1932), friend and patron of Toulouse-Lautrec; he had exhibited in the 1890s with Gauguin at the Café Volpini, and his racetrack scenes and sketches of Parisian café society would have appealed to Willie Johnstone-Wilson. But Lucie's branch of the family had closer connections with the catering business than with art; Lucie's father was a hotel manager. This may have been a marriage of convenience: it was to be as unconventional as it was durable. And it began badly, from the family point of view, for the Anquetins were deeply offended by the fact that almost immediately before the wedding, indeed offensively close to the wedding, Maud and William Johnstone-Wilson, and young Master Angus Johnstone-Wilson, set sail for Durban on the *Dunluce Castle*.

Maud and Willie had had enough of post-war Bexhill and Eastbourne, of financial anxiety and pursuing creditors. F.W. Frank, The Guv, that despised but reliable standby, had married again in November 1921; his new wife Alice Jonsson Shepstone (or Alys, as she sometimes spelled it) was a South African divorcée with two spinster daughters whom she bullied unmercifully. This new step-step-grandmother (whose exact relationship to the Johnstone-Wilsons caused lasting confusion) could not be good news. The Guv stuck by Fred and helped to set up Clive and Lucie in business, but the rest of the Johnstone-Wilsons got the message that they had to fend for themselves. There must, Willie thought, be better pickings elsewhere. Stroquhan, with its ten bedrooms, its gardens and greenhouses, its grouse moor and trout fishing, was now let to a family called Cobden Ramsay ("Mrs Frank's Trustees" still had the shooting at neighbouring Glenesslin) but there was not enough money coming in. In Dunscore, the Johnstone-Wilsons were quite forgotten – only a distant memory of a lady with pearls, of a chauffeur-driven car still lingered, and they had probably belonged to a previous tenant called General Johnston.[10] The *rentiers* were at bay. So off they went, in the spring of 1922, first class, to revisit the Caneys, and to see what life was like in the sun.

Angus too was ready to depart, though his memories of his pampered life on the South Coast were on the whole happy. He claimed that he got out of attending his first Bexhill kindergarten by having tantrums when he got a black mark for complaining that another boy had been sick over his India rubber. He attended several other kindergartens, but none for very long, as the family was always on the move. When they moved briefly along the coast to Gildredge Road in Eastbourne he went to a school called Knockmaroon: here he blotted his copybook by spreading the rumour that one of the mistresses had a sweetheart.[11] He said that it was in the Eastbourne lodgings that he precociously began to read grown-up books like *Emma* and the novels of E. Phillips Oppenheim, though he also had juvenile favourites, like *The Swiss Family Robinson*, Julia Horatia Ewing's *Miscellanea*, and a fascinatingly terrifying picture book by Bertha and Florence Upton called *Golliwogg's Polar Adventures*. In Eastbourne he had also followed more childish pursuits, catching cabbage whites in a green butterfly net while his parents watched tennis at Devonshire Park, and enjoying maple sundaes at Bobby's. (He always had a sweet tooth.) He strolled along the promenade with his mother, listening to gossip about the aristocratic Devonshires who owned, as far as he could gather, most of Eastbourne, and owned it, moreover, in some way that shed credit on the Johnstone-Wilsons. Credit with the bank they might lack, but reflected social glory they enjoyed. He was particularly enraptured by the wonderful Camera Obscura, which allowed you to see all the same people that you'd just seen walking along the front contained, as it were, in a vast bowl of cream. And then there was the sea itself, the source of many delightful solitary games and imaginings.*

At this point of the South Coast experience, Angus was threatened with boarding school. He threw another tantrum, and won. South Africa was a way out of difficulties for all of of them.

                                             *

The *Dunluce Castle* set off on 11 May 1922 on its thirty-three day voyage, carrying Willie and Maud, aged fifty-six and fifty-two, and Angus, aged seven. Sea voyages had changed out of all recognition since the days of the early Caney pioneers. The ships of the Union Castle line had a long and romantic history. The maiden voyage of the *Pembroke Castle* in 1893 was graced by Tennyson, Gladstone, and a banquet in Copenhagen for twenty-nine royal personages, including the King and Queen of Denmark, the Emperor and Empress of Russia, the King and Queen of Greece and the Royal Family of Hanover. It was a ship of the Union Castle line that escorted Empress Eugénie to Port Natal on her pilgrimage to the site of her son's last stand. Sir Redvers Buller sailed for Cape Town on 14 October 1899 on the *Dunottar Castle* to fight the Boer War, accompanied by cries of "Remember Majuba!" and "Bring back a piece of Kruger's whiskers!" Kipling loved the Castle ships, and so did Laurens van der Post, who once found a silvery flying fish upon the pillow in his cabin.

The *Dunluce Castle*, built in 1904, kept its first-class passengers happy with fancy-dress balls, classical concerts, gaming tables. It was a *tableau vivant* of Empire. Great stars like Dame Clara Butt and Nellie Wallace had sung their way over the seas with the Union Castle line, and every voyage offered first-class entertainment. Willie felt quite at home in this spectacular floating hotel. Maud too was in her element. An ocean bride, she loved to talk of great sea disasters like the sinking of the *Titanic* and the *Lusitania*. The *Waratah* was a particular favourite, for she had gone down without trace after leaving Durban for Cape Town in 1909, and nothing of her was ever seen again, except the floating body of a little girl wearing a red dressing-gown – or was it perhaps a little pink dress? As Maud gossiped in the lounge, young Master Johnstone-Wilson (who never learned to

---

* A letter from Angus dated 3 February 1987 to local historian Gerald Newson says "Before leaving [for South Africa] we had given up the decision to live at Hampden Park (although I adored the Park and everything connected with it) and had become lodgers in a house in, could it be, Gildredge Terrace, from which we only left in order to go to SA . . . I acquired a real affection for Eastbourne, particularly walking on the front with my Mother, who was, although a middle aged woman, very chic."

swim) was kept well away from the rails by the steward, who taught the children in his care to sing a jolly ditty which began

> There were three Jews of Amsterdam –
> Damn, Damn, Damn.

Smartly dressed in his little sailor suit, Angus saluted the future as he sailed on towards Tenerife.

Maud was returning to a country that had changed much during her thirty-two-year absence. The Boer War had been fought and won, years of constitutional negotiation had followed, and in 1910 Natal had joined the Cape Colony, the Transvaal and the Orange Free State to form the new Union of South Africa. In Natal, Africans outnumbered whites by ten to one, and the region was threatened by Zulu rebellion: in 1906 Bambatha, a former Zulu chief, had been defeated, and three thousand Zulu and thirty whites had been killed. Many voters in Natal felt political union, even with their late enemies, offered the best chance of security.

The Caney family, too, had changed. The patriarch, B.W. himself, would not be there to greet Maud amidst the flutter of flags and handkerchiefs, for he was buried back in Kingston, beneath a magnificent headstone and some carved ivy, in the family mausoleum. He had died there on a return visit to England with his wife in 1895, the year of the Jameson Raid. This trip had been intended as a reconciliation, for there had been friction between the families, but the effort had killed B.W., who died of pneumonia and was buried on 23 September. He was fifty-two years old. Ellen Caney and her younger daughter Ivy had sailed back two months later without him. Ellen herself had died in 1908.

But these were among the few losses. The next generation prospered. Charlie, Gus and Val Caney had all gone into the family business, married and reproduced. The sisters had also married. Angus found himself greeted by a vast new array of cousins, much nearer in age than his own brothers, and by a country which struck him as thrilling and exotic. The year and a half he spent with the Caneys expanded in his memory to occupy great tracts of his childhood.

Back in Bexhill he had heard many stories about the pioneering life, and he was not disappointed. Visiting Great-Uncle Wakes on his pineapple farm in Bellair (now a suburb of Durban) was a journey into the remote jungle, and Great-Uncle, blind, with a huge white beard, looked his part to perfection. There was a rawness, a hint of violence in the manners of the elder Wakes and Caneys that both attracted and appalled. Great-Uncle Wakes was said to have beaten his daughters as well as his servants with the sjambok, and it was in his pineapple fields that Angus saw, to his great delight, his first black mamba: like the heroes of *The Swiss Family Robinson*, he responded to this highly dangerous creature with interest rather than terror. (All his life he was to be fascinated by strange creatures and exotic flora, and would disconcertingly rush towards beasts in the wild rather than take cover from them. He had an instinctive trust in all animals.) He also, to the disgust of his cousins, spent much time talking to the native servants in their huts. Maud had not managed to instil in him the correct attitude towards Kaffirs.

He was not allowed to run free: for some time he attended the Berea Road Infants School with cousin Ivan McDonald and a brother of Roy Campbell, and may have met there the girl whom he was to remember as his only heterosexual passion. Alas, we know nothing of her, but he insisted until his final years that she had been "very important" to him. He also remembered vividly Miss Grace Tutton, the headmistress, who was (like Mother and Aunt Ivy) a Christian Scientist, and the classes out of doors under the jacaranda tree where he imbibed "a mixture of outworn genteel English teaching and watered down Nationalist history."[12]

According to Ivan's brother Guy, Angus's schooldays did not last long. The Johnstone-Wilsons were as restless and unsettled in Durban as they had been in Bexhill, and lived mainly in hotels – the Orisdale, the Esplanade – or in rented lodgings near the racecourse – a way of life that was many years later held responsible for Angus's unsound left-wing political views. Guy, son of Maud's sister Ivy, had heard much about Aunt Maud and tennis-playing Scottish Uncle Bill, for Ivy had kept in close touch with her sister. He was disappointed in his new aunt, who appeared to him as "a stoutish elderly woman of a somewhat stern countenance and manner". Angus, however, impressed him. Strikingly fair-skinned, pink-cheeked, and nattily clothed in grey flannel jacket and short trousers with white collar and tie, Angus seemed confident, precocious, a child accustomed to shining in adult company.[13] The memories of cousin Merle are similar – of a small boy with huge blue eyes and yellow curly hair who talked all the time with great excitement at the top of his voice. (Merle did not like her godmother Maud, who was, she thought, a fearful snob: when Merle got engaged Maud responded with "Oh well, if you must marry into trade . . .") Angus spent much time playing with his McDonald cousins at their home, Blinkbonnie: Aunt Ivy there pressed on him a copy of Mrs Mary Baker Eddy's writings, which he kept all his life.

Angus wrote only two pieces of fiction set in South Africa. The first of these, "Union Reunion",[14] is set in the 1920s at the time of his first visit,*

* The second, "No Future for Our Young", relates to his second visit in 1961, and is unpublished.

and draws on childhood memories. It has a satiric ferocity and a coarseness of caricature that he was later somewhat to regret. It is written largely from the point of view of Laura, returning to her childhood home in Durban with her English husband Harry, and finding herself shocked by the changes that have taken place in the family. Judged by the standards of bridge parties in Kensington and Worthing (what *would* Lady Ampleforth have said?) her sisters-in-law are gross, over-rouged, over-brightly-dressed; for their part, they find her "still very much the Duchess". Harry, with his other women and his gambling and his extravagance, is clearly modelled on Willie Johnstone-Wilson. The discovery of mutual hostility, the sense that Laura is an alien and Harry a patronising braggart, is dissolved only in whisky and soda, memories of South African heroism on the Somme in 1916 at that "damned fine fight at Delville Wood", racing tips, talk of native servants and the threat of Kaffir revolt. Animosity slumps under the weight of a vast meal of goose, turkey, duck, pumpkin, rice, sweet potato, mealie cobs and peas, all covered in a thick brown gravy. It is Aunt Liz's eighty-eighth birthday, but Aunt Liz, like Elizabeth Wakes, is wandering in her wits as she looks back to the Good Old Days of the sjambok and the frontier. The older generation eats and drinks itself into a stupor of crude jokes: Lincolnshire lewdness breaks through both Durban and Kensington gentility in an orgy of farting and flirting around the piano. And from the midst of this grotesque tableau arises the ghost of Laura's poor little eight-year-old boy who had died in Durban during the war while visiting his aunts. Dead of meningitis, drowned on the *Waratah* – it is the little children who suffer. (A Master Wilson had attended the funeral of grandmother Ellen Caney in 1908, along with all the Caneys and Wakes and McDonalds – could this have been one of the older brothers, on a solitary visit?)

The story gives an unflattering portrait of the Caney tribe. It is a set piece, a scene of coarse Jan Steen revelry. But it was not the whole truth about the family, nor about Maud's feelings about her roots. The Durban of the Caneys was by no means as barbarous as "Union Reunion" paints it, and the family, despite its predilection for the Turf Club and the Yacht Club, had its cultured members. Charlie's wife, Nellie, was known as one of the first ladies in Durban. (This in itself would have annoyed Maud.) Famed as the first woman in Durban to drive a car (number plate ND 153), she played the piano well, made sure her daughters Merle and Val studied the violin and the cello, and held musical soirées that bore no resemblance to the jumbled, drunken sing-song of Aunt Liz's birthday party. Charlie was proud of her talents, and one of the Caney boats was named *Trio*, in double tribute – to Nellie's musical evenings, and to the trio of brothers

and business partners, Charlie, Val and Gus. Grogan Caney, the son of
B.W.'s youngest brother, was a fine singer with the Durban Choir and
became one of the best-known music teachers in Natal.*

Angus, like his Uncle Charlie, was not musical, and therefore was not
best placed to appreciate the particular Caney talent. But he discovered a
secret garden of his own in Durban. Rudyard Kipling, a Child of Empire,
had played with Indian children and been mothered by his ayah: Frederick
Ashton, a diplomat's son in Lima, played with the little Peruvian boys of
the neighbourhood more happily than with his own brothers. And the boy
Angus could escape from the constraints of grey flannel jackets into the
magic world of Kim and Mowgli. He played with the natives, and
remembered with lasting affection the old Zulu servant George: writing of
Kipling's early boyhood in Bombay, he says "where parents . . . knew that
their own love was needed as well as that of the servants, a little Sahib's life
could be very idyllic, however little we may condone the racial or class
basis on which it rested. (I know this from my own experience as a little
baas in Durban from the age of seven to eleven years: I have never felt such
warm love as I did then from my beloved 'Kaffir', George.)"[15] (Note how a
period of time that was in fact less than two years has expanded in his
memory to a vague five years or so: he was far more accurate about
Kipling's dates than about his own.)

The intimacy of this relationship could not last. The Caneys at this stage
held the normal South African attitudes to the native population –
condescension, mistrust, fear. Black faces remained as foreign and as
dangerous as they had appeared to the terrified girl stepping ashore from
Lincolnshire in 1861. Memories of Zulu revolt and the murders of white
farmers were fresh in everyone's memory. It is clear that Angus, in his
Kipling biography, is thinking of the climate of his own Durban childhood
when he says "Ayahs, native servants of all kinds were 'wonderful with
children', but they spoiled them, indulged them too much, especially,
given their ideas about women, spoiled the boys too much. Then the
standards of all natives were not ours – in matters of truth-telling, of hard
work, of hygiene, and (only to be mentioned in intimate club or memsahib
gatherings) in sexual life. . . ."[16]

A more socially embarrassing form of racism was aroused by Gus
Caney's blonde, tennis-playing wife Dirkie, who was an Afrikaner. The
family patronised and looked down on her from the solidity of their
British-born credentials. And the whole lot of them, British and South
African, Caney and Johnstone-Wilson alike, were anti-Semitic. Most of

---

* Val's grandson, Peter Carter, is lead violinist with the Allegri String Quartet: Merle's
daughter Dawn trained in Europe and became an opera singer.

their anti-Semitism was merely the unthinking and idle talk of the period (even gentleman Winn had referred to a fellow officer as "a member of the tribe of Judah") but some of it was more deeply felt. This was a family tradition against which Angus and other younger members of the family were to react strongly.*

Maud and Willie thought of settling in Durban. They had been joined by twenty-six-year-old Colin, who shocked the Caneys with his extravagant dress and curious name-changes. ("I think I'll be David today.") But both Colin and Maud were asthmatic, and the climate did not really suit them. Colin sailed home on 9 February 1924, third class, on the P and O boat the *Balranald*, and ten days later the first-class Willie, Maud and Master Angus followed on the *Nestor*, an Australian liner of the Blue Funnel line. They were accompanied by Maud's sister-in-law Bessie (Elizabeth Frank Caney) and her two daughters, Betty (Valmai Elizabeth) and Vivienne.† Betty (whom Angus was to remember for many years at a party on the Island surrounded by 124 young men with straw boaters and ukeleles – "the most attractive flapper that you ever knew . . . so fast and smart and yet so kind to a small boy . . ."[17]) was sent to Seaford to acquire some English polish, which she seems to have resisted with spirit.

Bessie's marriage to Valentine Caney was, oddly enough, an indirect result of Tillie's marriage to Guv Frank: Suffolk-born Bessie, described by her daughter Vivienne as "a real blushing English rose", was one of several Franks who had gone out to Durban, where they were naturally enough looked after by the family of the Guv's stepson's wife.

The South African experiment was over, though there were to be many comings and goings of Caneys and Franks and Carters and Johnstones and Wilsons in the years to come. Charlie's daughter Merle, sailing to London in May 1924, was one of the first of many visitors, and she remembers Angus in the return role of host, showing her around London on the top of a double-decker bus, talking loudly and very fast and enjoying the attention of other passengers. What a clever little boy, how well-informed, how amusing!

The Johnstone-Wilsons settled back into their vagrant life, abandoning the South Coast for a succession of Kensington hotels. But one of the first things that Maud did on her return, before leaving Eastbourne, was to

* One descendant believes that some of the Caney anti-Semitism may have sprung from a fear that the Caneys, emigrants running a successful jewellery business, might be mistaken for Jews: perhaps they were not Caneys after all, but Cohens? They were very anxious not to sell the business to a Jew.
† Vivienne was to marry and settle in England, as Mrs Thomas Erskine: Betty's first husband was Frederick Slingsby Mann, and her second Gavin Jack.

make her will. It was a wise move. She left all her possessions (jewels, trinkets, furniture, plate, articles of vertu) to her husband, made small bequests to her executor Winn and his daughters, and put everything else in trust for Angus.

4

THE FLYING SPUR

While Maud and Willie and Master Angus were abroad in the sun, Winn and his wife Betty were working hard to establish their family and its fortunes. They had two daughters, Jeanne, born in 1917, and Sybil, born in 1920. After leaving the army Winn had returned as senior assistant master to Ashampstead in Eastbourne. The headmaster was about to retire, and Winn was looking around for a building in which to open a school of his own. The house that he found was to play an important part in the lives of the Johnstone-Wilson clan. It replaced the legendary Stroquhan as the family seat.

It was not unworthy of its role. Like Stroquhan, Sutton Place in Seaford was built upon old foundations. These date back to a Norman priory, connected with St Nicholas Church, one of the five churches of Sutton-cum-Seaford. Both priory and church vanished with the Reformation, and the land and dwellings passed through the hands of various fabled families, both Regicide and Royalist, until the main building was substantially rebuilt round about 1760. Traces of its ancient origins can still be seen, in an old flint wall at the end of the rose garden, in an aged mulberry tree, in old brick arches in the extensive cellars, and in suggestions of an underground passage leading towards the ha-ha. The eighteenth-century house was improved and enlarged at the end of the nineteenth century by its owner, Viscount Selby, Speaker of the House of Commons, and a Bill of Sale described the property as "a charming country residence", standing in well-timbered pleasure grounds, with a lodge entrance, kitchen gardens, and ranges of farm buildings. It was conveniently close to the golf links.

Seaford was refined: it prided itself on its lack of pierrots. It was also well known for its preparatory schools. The King's surgeon had personally recommended its sea air and new buildings sprang up all over the town, taking advantage of the rates, which were lower than in Eastbourne. The education industry boomed. Jeremy Lewis, himself in later years a Seaford schoolboy, recalled a glorious past: "Edwardian prep schools, like golf clubs, embody English institutional architecture at its best, and Seaford in its heyday was chock-a-block with white mullioned windows, overhung balconies with curious fire escapes attached, dormer windows with sheets hung out to dry, belfries, clock towers and crunching gravel drives."[1] But Lewis's is a post-Betjeman enthusiasm, and at the time the ancient priory felt much superior to its younger neighbours. Winn and Betty Wilson were proud of the fact that they were the only school with a garden large enough to accommodate the famous travelling Ben Greet players with their annual Shakespeare open-air production. Pupils from other schools would be invited, and performances of *Twelfth Night* or *A Midsummer Night's Dream* would be interrupted at a dramatic moment by the arrival of the Royal Mail or the barking of Lion, the school bulldog, or Rollo, the Great Dane. (Rollo was well known in the neighbourhood, as were his Great Dane successors; they are still remembered in Seaford.)

Winn opened his new school in the spring of 1923, renaming the building "Ashampstead" after its Eastbourne predecessor. He also brought with him some of the pupils and staff from the old school, including Charlie, his former batman, who served as caretaker; Captain Chudleigh, who had been in the same regiment; and the burly, mannish matron, ex-nanny Miss Ellis, who crackled impressively with blue-and-white starch as she made her cascara-carrying rounds or inspected the boys in their baths. Captain Wilson was famed on the sportsfield as an ardent and sometimes over-excited referee, who occasionally had to gasp for breath as his old war wound inhibited his zeal. This wound was a source of wonder to the boys. It was clearly visible as two indented scars on chest and back, and some of them spread the rumour that the bullet had entered the Captain and passed right through his body to kill the man behind him.

Winn, like all the Johnstone-Wilsons, was a great story-teller. He loved to dramatise the campaigns of Julius Caesar and Napoleon, or the battles of Gilbert with Sullivan. High on the white cliffs amidst the scabious and rabbit warrens, to the cries of seagulls, he would describe the retreat from Mons. He recited Kipling and "Jabberwocky", and on a Sunday evening would read aloud, compellingly, from Dumas, Dickens, Rider Haggard and Henty. He had a great admiration for Galsworthy, and was a wizard with improvised history quizzes. With his thin, pale, almost cadaverous face, his habitual monocle, and a certain lean and hungry intensity of expression, he was a hero to many of the boys, and a figure of authority to all. Some found him uncertain of temper, but this, like his breathlessness, was attributed to the war wound. He was not a light-hearted man: when a South African cousin, Calvert McDonald, arrived and asked Uncle Winn to "do his conjuring tricks", his daughters were astonished. Whoever could have put an idea like that into young Calvert's head?

Opinions of Betty were unanimous. She was gentle, pretty and petite, and she always wore a black cloche hat. She was perhaps a little put-upon at times, but she never complained. Sick boys with fever she nursed tenderly, and she cut the toenails of the little ones. She taught painting and nature studies (her teaching qualifications were better than those of some of the masters) and she named the dormitories not after statesmen or soldiers but after Landseer, Whistler, Romney and Millais. Reproductions of works by these artists hung upon the walls. She made elaborate costumes for the Gilbert and Sullivan productions. She was a mother-substitute for many small boys whose families were abroad in the army, in business, or with the Indian civil service. Those who came into her care fared better than Rudyard Kipling and his sister Trix in their famously terrible sojourn with landlady Mrs Holloway in the House of Desolation at Southsea. The presence of the two daughters, Jeanne and Sybil, did much to soften the institutional atmosphere. Several of the boys fell madly in love with sportive Sybil and her long yellow plaits. The more bookish ones favoured the studious Jeanne.

Ashampstead was an unconventional school. The approach was conventional enough – the reserved railway carriage from Victoria to Seaford, the horse-drawn carriages from the station up to the school – but thereafter a certain eccentricity flourished. Much smaller than many of its neighbours, with an average intake of about thirty-five, it rejoiced in what one boy called "a relaxed discipline". Some of the masters, like the delightful maths master Mr Barry, who was always borrowing money for his gambling debts from pupils and parents alike, were a little strange. And Winn was impressively improvisatory. Not all headmasters taught their flock to play auction bridge, or marched them on impulse up the Wilmington Giant in the snow, or would suddenly announce that today everyone was to stay in bed on a diet of bread, marmalade and Bovril. Boys were encouraged to pot at rooks with a shotgun, and rook pie was often on the menu. They were also sent off to gather kindling in the woods for the school fires. When asked to translate the Johnstonian school motto, *Semper Paratus*, one baffled youngster piped up "Gathering sticks, Sir?" In early years Winn and Betty Wilson, who had shed the pomposity of the hyphenated Johnstone, would join in romps, and the end of term was marked by wild games of Sardines in the house and Dragons and Ogres in the garden.

Beatings occasionally took place, but the most feared punishment was to be "chosen". This involved being deprived of choice in the main meal of the day. A "chosen" boy was given a large helping of what he most disliked, and was made to finish it. The most dreaded item was stuffed ox heart. Did anyone ever choose stuffed heart unless himself "chosen"? There was economic method in this madness. School food – liver and bacon, tripe and onions, curry and mince, spotted dick, tapioca – was not a treat, though ginger pudding was popular. Boys looked forward eagerly to the socialised distribution of tuck. Poor little Raynor Sharp, of Sharp's toffees, a perhaps unwilling public benefactor, had to share his large tins with the whole school.

Why, offered such variety of choice in Seaford, did parents choose Ashampstead? Some parents were attracted to the building itself, which did not have to try very hard to look like a stately home. Grandmother Tillie's portrait in black tulle hung proudly over the stairwell, the mounted heads of Scottish beasts adorned the walls, and there were pseudo-Jacobean oak fireplaces. The Hardy-esque Mr Boniface tended a fine kitchen garden and greenhouses which supplied cabbages, caulifowers, brussel sprouts, even asparagus. Then there were the free extras: as well as bridge, there was rugger, soccer, cricket, swimming, rifle-shooting, riding, blackberrying on the downs, ping-pong, billiards, music and dancing with Mrs Wilson. Religious tolerance was the rule, and the school admitted Roman Catholics and Jewish boys, for whom special provision was made – though there was one awful row about beef with a small Hindu, over which Betty had to exercise all her tact. There was all the fun of the Sports Day, with mothers arriving in ostentatious rivalry in chauffeur-driven limousines. (In the Fathers' Race one year, a father carrying his son upon his shoulder fell, broke his leg, and subsequently died. Or so the Waugh-like legend persists.)

Some parents were swayed by the good heart of Betty Wilson, others by the discounts offered to large families. The fees were modest (less than half those of the Leys in Cambridge) and reductions were offered to younger brothers. Whole clutches of Reids, Thurstans, Culmers and Bartleys passed through Ashampstead and on to public school or Naval College. The Le Poer Trench brothers Power and Brinsley, offspring of the Earl of Clancarty, were able by aristocratic privilege to infiltrate one of the school's rare girls, the Honourable Alma.

All these attractions Ashampstead could boast. And it also offered, absolutely free of charge, the interesting spectacle of the rest of the family of the Johnstone-Wilsons. For, however hard Winn and Betty tried to pin their régime to something like normality, the bizarre Johnstone-Wilsons would keep breaking in.

Maud and Willie were frequent visitors. Maud in her silks and picture hat was quite the Duchess as she sat in a deck chair and watched the tennis or presented the school prizes. Willie did not think much of school grub but was occasionally obliged to fall back on it. He would arrive, bearing a little offering of raspberries or chocolate cake, and would later in his stay make do with spotted dick while he borrowed money off Winn. Fred, who was rapidly getting through shares left to him by the Guv (who had died in November 1922, not long after his remarriage) would also turn up, sometimes with a pheasant from Leadenhall Market, more often with Auntie Winnie, long remembered by small boys as "quite an eyeful". He presented the school with a bad-tempered goat which lived in the paddock. Winnie was at some point mysteriously and without explanation replaced by Auntie Phyllis. (Phyllis was a manicurist from *Chez Antoine* who had appeared with gilded nipples strumming the banjo before Edward VII.) But Winnie remained on very good terms with her brother-in-law Mr Colin, another frequent visitor to Ashampstead. He would stay for long periods, all extras free, doing nothing much, though he did entertain twelve-year-old William Rose as they walked together to Mass on a Sunday morning.

And then there was Mr Pat. He worked. Fresh from Tonbridge, with school prizes to his credit, he taught French and English literature. He was as tall and willowy as matron was stocky, a conspicuous figure with his tightly waved hair, dark blue suit, white gloves, spats, grey trilby, long cigarette-holder, perfume and penchant for peppermint creams. He was a born class-room teacher, full of anecdotes. His readings from Jane Austen were brilliant, and his teaching of French irregular verbs was accompanied by "choreographic motions with his long arms and legs: extended lunges dips and pirouettes . . . at his most ladylike, he somehow preserved dignity. There was no hint of persuasiveness for his conception of himself. He made no bid for imitation, he was simply him(her)self. And he conveyed affection for all of us, without constraint. Further, I never heard any of us taunt him behind his back."

This is the record of an American boy at Ashampstead, Tom Wood, who further recalled the fascination of the dazzling and fantastic conversations of Pat and Colin. He used to hang around listening and trying to join in. Winn discouraged this. "Don't bore Mr Pat and Mr Colin," he would say to this eager acolyte.

Angus entered this interesting establishment in May 1924, and stayed there for three years. The school magazine, *The Flying Spur*, offers a

revealing commentary on the school and Angus's progress there. A page of
light verse published in one of the undated volumes over the initials
"A.J.W." is possibly by Angus himself – it records Sybil's "mighty power"
and "Spartan limbs", and Lady Jane's love of reading:

> No, don't disturb her at her book,
> It is an honour but to look.

Brother Pat is affectionately evoked:

> There was a man named Mr. P –
> Who had a wondrous garden hat,
> The fame of it spread near and far,
> Reporters came from the Evening Star.
> They asked him for some garden hints
> And what went best with autumn tints . . .

Angus was introduced to the game of rugby ("Forward. Does not yet
know the game. Tries hard in the scrum and one of the few forwards with
any idea of hooking") and cricket ("unorthodox, a very safe catch at close
quarters"). This was not his field, though he eventually got his rugger
colours. He featured more prominently in the school dramas. He put
expression into his role as Leila, a gipsy, in Hamilton Clarke's musical *King
Pepin*, and although he had no singing voice, appeared with panache as Sir
Joseph Porter in *H.M.S. Pinafore*. He greatly enjoyed the "hammy but
rapturous" visits of Ben Greet and his strolling players, and gave his own
Shylock and Malvolio in scenes from Shakespeare. In the school holidays,
in collaboration with a small boy called Dragon Stevenson, he composed
dramas which would be performed by Jeanne, Sybil, and those homeless
children whose parents were everlastingly in India: these were usually
Agatha Christie-style dramas involving violent death. One Firbankian line
stands out in Jeanne's memory: "Oh, there's the inspector, I'm sure he's a
duck!"* He also organised Scarlet Pimpernel games in which he himself
played "Blakeney, Lady Blakeney, Chauvelin, Fouquier-Tinville with a
bell, Robespierre, Marie Antoinette, the Prince Regent, and Madame
Elizabeth, leaving only the boring parts of the King and the Dauphin for
two other boys; the rest shouted happily under my direction as 'the
mob'."[2]

Life was never dull. Angus was much nearer in age to Jeanne and Sybil
than to his brother-headmaster, and he spent a lot of time with them. But
he also spent time in London with his parents and his bridge-playing step-

---

* Compare Ronald Firbank's possibly mythical postcard to the Sitwells: "To-morrow I go
to Hayti. They say the President is a *Perfect Dear*." Osbert Sitwell, *Noble Essences*, 1950, pp.81–2.

grandmother Alys, acquiring under their influence adult tastes which he brought back to school: in his last term, as a prefect, he set a "sophisticated" tone, and preached the virtues of the two wonderful new long-running musicals, *Rose Marie: a Romance of the Canadian Rockies*, which opened in 1925 at Drury Lane with a huge chorus and *No, No, Nanette*, which opened later in the same year at the Palace. He imitated George Grossmith, Billy Merson and Leslie Henson, and persuaded the very young new dancing mistress to teach them all the Charleston and the Black Bottom.

It all seemed innocent fun, as they graduated from collecting lead soldiers and cigarette cards to more adult diversions. But Angus was already uncomfortably aware that the family home was under siege. He was not alone in noticing this. All surviving Ashampsteadians bear witness to the encroaching presence of hangers-on, to the difficulty that Winn and Betty had in fighting off their demands. The school was run on a shoestring, and long visits from non-paying relatives did not help the budget. Angus Wilson's short story, "Rex Imperator", looks back to a period covering both the 1920s and the 1930s, and paints a depressing picture of Rex and Brenda trying to struggle on while surrounded by gathering vultures – Rex's sister, waiting for her alimony, Brenda's father with his gambling debts, drunken and cynical brother Basil with his unemployed "alpha brain". It is a place of waiting. The rooks caw in the nearby copse. "Sometimes it seemed that there were too many windows, too much bleak light; at others the house seemed perpetually sombre and dark."[3]

It was just as well for Angus that his mother had made her will. Whatever had prompted her to this – the behaviour of Willie and Colin in Durban, or the death of Guv Frank and observations of Fred's increasing unreliability – she had been gifted with a glimmer of the second sight for which her mother was renowned. At least Angus's education was secure.

★

In 1927, Angus left for Westminster School. The choice was inspired. It was evident to all that he was unsuited for a sporting school, but of all possible options, Westminster, as he himself said, was the best.

He did not lose touch with Ashampstead, which provided a form of continuity. In the summer after his last Ashampstead term, the whole tribe went on a family holiday to the small town of Watchet, on the coast of West Somerset, overlooking the Bristol Channel – Winn, Betty, Jeanne, Sybil, Maud, Willie, and two boys called Tony Bloomfield and Victor Toeg. Victor was one of those boys whose parents lived abroad: his father was a stockbroker in Shanghai, and Victor had been sent back to Ashampstead, discovered on a "recce" by a governess who liked its homely atmosphere. In the first year his holidays had been spent in France with a married uncle who turned out to lead an unsuitably unmarried life: he did not speak French and his only friend had been another hotel orphan. Victor was much relieved when it was agreed that Betty should look after him all the year round.

So off they went to the West Country, in the old maroon "Winnie-the-Wolseley" which the Captain had bought from the Culmer parents. On their way they met, quite by chance, Fred driving back from Cornwall with one of his ladies, and stopped for a chat. (There were not many cars in those days: easy, perhaps *too* easy, to spot a friend on the road.)

They spent a fortnight of glorious weather staying in a rented house overlooking the sea. Photographs of the group taking picnics on Exmoor present a reassuring image of normality – there is Sybil, with her golden Rapunzel plaits, there is Jeanne, there is Betty in her cloche and Willie clutching a mug of tea. It is all very English. Angus's face, oddly mature and sharp, is highly distinctive. He has entered his thin, anxious phase. He is the oldest of the young ones, set slightly apart.

They would set off for the day, drive for ten miles or so to the Quantocks or up onto Exmoor, getting out to push the protesting old car up the notoriously steep Porlock hill, and then park, to carry the picnic hamper along a river bank until they found a pleasant spot. The children would explore and play in the river, jumping from boulder to boulder. Over sandwiches, Willie told stories of his cricketing triumphs – "I used to turn out for Middlesex occasionally, you know, old man." Victor Toeg, a keen sportsman, listened entranced. On one occasion Victor found himself walking all the way back to the car side-by-side with the formidable Mrs Johnstone-Wilson Senior: it was a good hour's walk, but she chatted pleasantly to him all the way. There was on this occasion no sign of the asthma that often troubled her.

For Victor Toeg, this was a happy summer. What was Angus thinking of, down by the river? In *The Wild Garden*, he mentions a holiday by the sea when he was fifteen when he deliberately burned the wings of moths in the flame of the candle in his bedroom. The episode had unpleasant sexual connotations. Did it take place at Watchet? Was this one of the reasons why he never liked the West Country? He also records that on this seaside visit he was reprimanded by his parents for playing imaginative games with the nieces – games that resurfaced later in his short stories – games that they considered unsuitable for his age. Something was troubling him.

There is a look of alert and cautious awakening on the adolescent face in those holiday snaps. And Porlock, for him, remained a bad place. When he mentioned it in his notebooks, the connotation was usually sinister.

"Mother and me, on the road to Porlock" was one of the notes he made when assembling his thoughts for his first novel.

THE BOY WITH THE HAIR

Angus was taken to Westminster on his first day by his father, somewhat to his distress. It was 3 May 1927. The first twenty minutes of his new school career were the worst. One of the school's well-intentioned rituals was to assign each new boy, known as a "shadow", to a "substance", in the form of a second- or-third term boy who would introduce the newcomer to the school regulations and customs. Here is his own description of his initiation. "It so happened that another new boy was Pierre Turquet, son of the head of the famous Scoone's diplomatic coaching school. He was late – as was my 'substance'. In the space of twenty minutes or so I suffered the worst experience of my whole days there. It seemed that again and again I was asked 'Are you Turkey?' I took it to be a reference to what I knew must be by now my scarlet face. If they could do this with my father standing by, what terrible bullying was in store?"[1]

This stylised account demonstrates his own survival technique at Westminster. He learned to clown, to make himself ridiculous before others had a chance to do so. Thus would he divert the imagined bullies. He decided to become a curiosity.

He had a need of defences. Although Westminster was a notably civilised school, where intellect was more prized than muscle, Angus Johnstone-Wilson stood out as an oddity. Physically, he was highly conspicuous. His shock of crinkly untidy yellow hair, his pale protruding blue-grey eyes, his high-pitched voice, his savagely bitten nails and knuckles, his dirty collars, his general untidiness and ink-stained appearance were vividly remembered by contemporaries half a century later. But so were his stories. Like David Copperfield, he saved himself by story-telling. He seemed always to be the centre of an attentive circle who listened, rapt, as he wove fantasies about his family so extreme that some friends were forbidden to go anywhere near the Johnstone-Wilson household – wherever it might be, if there *was* such a thing? Angus mimicked the masters, and produced endless instalments of "a sophisticated precursor of Mrs Dale's Diary, set in Ruislip."[2] He invented a character called Mulligawny engaged in an epic restoration of Tower Bridge. He became known as "the mad boy", or "the boy with the hair". He wore these labels with pride.

Westminster boys had to learn to withstand the public gaze. The uniform of the day was designed to attract attention. Small boys wore an Eton jacket, and the older ones graduated to an imposing assortment of black gowns, stiff white collars, white bow ties, top hats, striped trousers and coat tails. These looked all very well in Little Dean's Yard or in the cloisters, but they looked pretty odd on the underground on the way home to Putney or Streatham. Westminster pupils had to run the gauntlet of mocking "slum boys" and "Cockney barrow boys", and Angus was once loudly reprimanded by a woman in the Royal Academy for letting the school down by keeping his hands in his pockets.

As a day boy, a Homeboarder, Angus had the freedom of the streets, and soon became familiar with the surrounding square mile. Everything of interest was within walking distance, and there was much to explore. Richard Gorer, younger brother of the writer Geoffrey Gorer, was one of Angus's closest friends in the Lower School. They spent hours together over walnut cake at Fuller's in Victoria Street as Angus made up stories about their fellow customers. Angus recalled that they composed together "a never-to-be written novel, the plot of which was played out in the Army and Navy stores." (Richard Gorer's memory is slightly different: "I wrote a whole novel while at Westminster, which is more than Angus did.") It was from Richard that Angus learned how to avoid games on the compulsory sports afternoons: the thing to do was to sign up for fencing. Pierre Turquet, who had got Angus off to such a bad start, came in useful here, for he was a brilliant fencer, a future champion, and the instructor was so keen on coaching him that others could sit around unnoticed for hours. There, in the Gothic setting of the school armoury, approached through the dark cloister near the Chapel of the Pyx, the young Turquet would flash his shining foil while Gorer and Johnstone-Wilson held their juniors spellbound.

The very buildings and fabric of Westminster School had a haunting effect on its pupils. Angus may not have paid much attention to them at the time – his interest in architecture developed much later – but he unconsciously absorbed their influences. The School had been the Monastery of Westminster Abbey before the Reformation, and the adjoining institutions remained closely connected. "Westminster was a fabulous place, recalls Brian Urqhart. "The tomb-stones and tombs in the Abbey and Cloisters, through which, dimly gas-lit on winter evenings, we made our way to College Hall, were an encyclopedia of English history. Ghosts abounded, including a recumbent stone figure reading a book who had been seen to turn the pages. On foggy evenings we ran rather than walked to supper . . ."[3] The school's foundation dated back to the Middle Ages, and its status was redefined by Henry VIII in 1540 and again by in 1560 by Queen Elizabeth. An early master was Nicholas Udall (or Uvedale), author of the Elizabethan comedy *Ralph Roister Doister*: he had been dismissed from Eton for pederasty in 1541 and imprisoned for a while in the Marshalsea, but had emerged to become Schoolmaster of Westminster in 1555. Westminster's tolerance began early. The school's mighty dead included Ben Jonson, Dryden, Locke, George Herbert and Gibbon; Christopher Wren, another Old Boy, had built the Scholars' House. The dramatic candle-lit Abbey services, with their magnificent choral interludes, were rich and strange to one reared on a wholesome plain sunny diet of Christian Science.

The social composition of the school also offered a many-layered variety. There were six houses, two for day boys, and a new pupil found a promising range of acquaintance. (The whole school, in 1927, had 366 pupils, of whom 237 were day boys.) Sons of politicians and peers and professors mingled with the offspring of stockbrokers and soldiers and singers and solicitors. These were all upper, upper middle, or middle-middle class boys, nearly all from comfortable or even wealthy back-grounds – though some parents scraped hard to provide what they knew would be a good educational and social investment. The tone was both worldly and high-minded: the ragging and fagging of the typical geographically isolated neo-Arnoldian late-nineteenth-century public school did not prevail here. This was not an outdoor hearty world of rugger fields, cold baths, lonely goalposts, and enraged referees on a muddy touchline, but a cosmopolitan monastic island in the heart of London. "We were like little men: we were expected to be self-disciplined: we were old before our time." The OTC existed, but PT was an acceptable alternative, and several of the masters (including the Rev. H.K. "Hippo" Luce, Master of the Kings' Scholars) had pacifist leanings. To a boy like Angus, this was a propitious atmosphere, and he made friendships which lasted till death.

His closest friends were to be Forrest Fulton, son of a solicitor in Notting Hill, who was precisely two days younger than Angus, and who entered the school on the same day: and Daniel Pickering Walker (always known as Perkin), son of an artist, who was a year younger and entered the school a year later. But there were many other friendships and acquaintances which gave delight or amusement. There was Neville Masterman, son of the liberal politician and journalist C.F.G. Masterman, and Neville's close friend Alan Campbell-Johnson. There was the athletic Turquet, the flautist Pinder-Wilson, the musical Engleheart, the brilliant Bill Deakin, the Wicked Panting,* and Bunty Whitney-Smith, son of an entertaining sculptor. Anthony Beyts, who modestly thought of himself as a bit of a duffer, was oppressed by a cleverer younger brother (and remembers that Angus too was once bottom of the class). There was Norman Parkinson, and John Freeman, and Francis Bailey, and Francis Pagan, and Jack Simmons and John Shearman, and an array of future bishops, vice-chancellors, knights, captains of industry and spies. There was Frank Hooper and Peter Copley and Hilary Gardner and John Pattisson, all with histrionic talents. There was John Ridley, who was "shadow" to Angus's "substance", and who remembers his kindness and generosity with lasting gratitude. Then there were the talented Mangeot brothers, Sylvain and Fowke, sons of the distinguished bohemian Belgian violinist André Mangeot: young Sylvain had had the good fortune to be tutored by Christopher Isherwood, who had worked with the Mangeots in 1925 for about a year after coming down from Cambridge. (Isherwood has left a lively portrait of the Mangeots in his autobiographical *Lions and Shadows*, 1938, where they are disguised as the Cheurets: "the Cheuret veil was a pretty thin and transparent one, and to call that work fiction is to do an injustice to the disarmingly accurate portraits which certain members of my family have been trying to live down ever since," Sylvain's nephew Andrew was to write in 1982 in a preface to a book of verses and illustrations written in collaboration by twenty-one-year-old tutor and eleven-year-old pupil in 1925.)[4] And, a little older, watching the inky boy with the hair from an amused distance, was Bentley Bridgewater.

These were the pupils. The staff included Laurence (Laurie) Tanner, the civilised Augustan Senior History Master and Keeper of the Abbey Muniments, who read to them from the works of Max Beerbohm and Lord Chesterfield in the comfortable Asburnham Library, reputed to be designed by Inigo Jones (though Pevsner suggested John Webb as a more probable candidate). Tanner described himself as a "pre-Reform Bill Tory" and liked to tell anecdotes of long-dead Oxford and Cambridge academics. The housemaster of Homeboarders, D.J. Knight, was remembered with affection. Feelings about the Headmaster, the Reverend Dr Harold Costley-White (a Balliol First, and joint editor of *Periods of Old*

---

* Anthony Panting, so nicknamed because of his discovery of some loophole in the school rules.

Testament History), were more mixed. Angus described him as "a clergyman very like Doctor Grantly" (the worldly archdeacon of Trollope's Barchester novels): others remember him as histrionic, "a Stentorian prelate-figure" and "a sanctimonious old bore". (Peter Ustinov, a pupil from 1934–7, was famed for his imitations of him.) "In his mortar board, gown, and clerical bibs, he did *look* like a Headmaster – of the eighteenth century. He spoke in a sing-song voice aimlessly accenting particular syllables, apparently to give an impression of sincerity" and "was muddle-headed in the extreme."[5]

But the most sensational schoolmaster at Westminster was the notorious John Edward Bowle, who arrived in the spring of 1930 at precisely the right moment to make a dramatic impact upon young Johnstone-Wilson. Angus's school record up to this point had not been distinguished, and his home life had been disturbed. Bowle came in the nick of time. Full of a passionate and slightly displaced energy, he was one of those teachers who alter lives. His own trajectory was strange enough. Educated at Marlborough ("really the most awful barbarous place") with Anthony Blunt and John Betjeman, he struck out even in his schooldays as an aesthete, designing the cover for the school magazine, *The Heretick* (1924), with its motto *Upon Philistia Will I Triumph*; it portrayed " a scowling 'tough' with a hockey stick, seated on a mound in front of rugby posts, while fauns . . . played pipes and taunted him."[6] Bowle won a Brackenbury Scholarship to Balliol, whereupon his delighted father gave him a huge allowance. There young Bowle continued in the same vein, throwing himself into the alcoholic pleasure-loving mood of the 1920s with such success and commitment that he gained a reputation as a wit and was the cause of wit in other men. (Maurice Bowra famously dubbed him "the inverted Bowle of night".) He also gained, in his last year, a Third Class Degree. (Here he was following closely in the footsteps of another – ostentatiously heterosexual – playboy Brackenbury Scholar, Cyril Connolly, who had pulled off the same coup a couple of years earlier. The Balliol interviewers must have been growing puzzled by the performance of their selections.) Bowle, abruptly rejected by his father, adored by his mother, then worked briefly as secretary for the literary Irish statesman and agricultural reformer Sir Horace Plunkett, before turning up at Westminster for a decade of significant schoolmastering.

Here he scored a notable hit, though not with all his colleagues, some of whom regarded him as a dangerous subversive. To the boys, he was a wonder. He was young, intense, smartly-suited, omniscient. He had thick curly blond hair, a translucently pale skin, horn-rimmed glasses and a slight stoop. He never smiled. He brought with him an air of immense sophistication and great intellectual excitement. He took the boys out to the Café Royal, that old haunt of Ronald Firbank, Oscar Wilde and Willie Johnstone-Wilson, and treated them to gin and tonic. (They had to pretend it was water.) He invited them singly or in pairs to his aesthetic bachelor flat for more highly-coloured drinks. He knew everybody who was anybody, and he not only knew them, he brought them to school to meet his favoured pupils. Bertrand Russell, A.L.Rowse, John Sparrow, Aldous Huxley, H.G. Wells, Harold Nicolson, Arnold Toynbee and that polymath guru of the 1930s, Gerald Heard, all trooped along at the bidding of Bowle. He fed his students on an amazingly potent cocktail of the new ideas of a new decade.

Angus recorded "The keywords of his teaching were 'absolutely modern', 'civilized', and an 'alpha mind'. I nearly died of mental indigestion under the diet of Spengler, Croce, Roger Fry, Freud, Cole, Gerald Heard, Uncle Tom Cobley and all that he provided."[7] Under his influence Angus was to move to "the history side" and become a member of the small, distinguished History Seventh. Bowle was not only brilliantly entertaining, he got results. Costley-White might mumble, but the boys got into Oxford, where they did better than Bowle had himself.

The changing climate of the school was marked. In 1926, the year before Angus arrived, Costley-White had addressed a special assembly to announce "The General Strike is over. This is a great day for Westminster and the Empire." By 1930, the very concept of Empire was crumbling, and a new generation of schoolboys was being reared not to become automatic strike-breakers, but to challenge orthodoxy. The debating society discussed the motion that "socialism is the only remedy for the present evil" and lost only by the presidential vote. Church disestablishment, corporal and capital punishment, and confidence in the metropolitan police were all hotly discussed, and on Monday, 10 November 1930, a joint meeting with the Debating Society and the school branch of the League of Nations deplored by 13 to 9 the lack of friendly relations between the British Empire and Soviet Russia. A.F. Johnstone-Wilson from the floor suggested that individualism was not a virtue but only a phase in history and "then dealt with the press, Lord Beaverbrook, Empire Free Trade, books by Russians on Russia, and some other topic, about which he spoke too quickly for it to be caught."[8]

Ideas were tumbling around the school with exhilarating and alarming speed. Bliss was it in those days for those who were young, middle-class, and not yet in need of a job. Angus devoured the novels of Aldous Huxley (who had two half-brothers at the school) and heard him speak on World Peace. He read Virginia Woolf, Lytton Strachey, Evelyn Waugh, Dorothy

Richardson, and all the Russian novelists. Galsworthy was forgotten as he plunged into political theory, psychology, modernism. Even Hugh Walpole, to whom he maintained a greater loyalty, took a back seat. "Bogus" and "shame-making" became catchwords. He and his set were determined to be thoroughly modern. Heard had a powerful impact upon him – Angus visited him once or twice with Bowle at his huge apartment in Portman Square, and listened to him as he spoke "continuously with his eyes cast down as though reading from a crystal ball." He was "knocked over" like a convert on the Road to Damascus by *The Ascent of Humanity*, and years later was to declare that Heard's concepts of consciousness and supraconsciousnesss had poured a poetry into his view of the past that Marxist and utilitarian approaches had never quite supplanted.[9]

School was stimulating, but home life was as unsettled as ever. Angus was a Homeboarder in name, but a Hotelboarder in practice. His parents continued to wander around South Kensington, recording various addresses as they passed on – 34 Cambridge St, Hyde Park: 83 Queensgate: 85 Queensgate: Craven Hill Gardens: The Glendower Hotel; 52 Cranley Gardens . . . (His mother at one point suggested that Angus might keep his address quiet and hint – only a white lie, dear – that he lived somewhere a little more chic.) While Angus was precociously reading Tolstoy and Spengler at school, he was equally precociously overhearing hotel conversations about adultery, bailiffs, bridge losses and gambling debts. Gone were the days when, a darling little curly-headed infant, he would wait for a pause in the conversation and then lisp winningly as he offered an advertisement cut out from a newspaper "Oh look, I do think you should try these Kruschen's Salts, they'll do wonders for your rheumatism!" No longer did he mishear "strumpet" as "trumpet". No longer, accompanying his mother to the Church of Christ Scientist, could he leap up and bear witness, declaring "I'm only a little boy but I do wish to say that Christian Science has done me so much good and cured me of the error and false claim of adenoids!" He had tried some of these ploys once too often and even Mother could see through them now. But other roles had come his way. Women seemed eager to take him into their confidence, and told him their secrets. Divorce and bankruptcy were no longer mysteries to him. A brilliant talker, he was (and remained) an attentive listener. No longer a pretty little mascot, he had become a little man, an old head on young shoulders. In the summer of 1928 he crossed the Channel and travelled alone to the South of France to stay with his sister-in-law Lucie's family, who introduced him to the pleasures of red Rhône table wine – possibly the first of what became annual visits. He was growing up fast.

(One of his Westminster contemporaries remarked "I don't think he ever had any childhood.")

The atmosphere in those Kensington hotels was charged with uncertainty. There were flamboyant characters, like step-grandmother Alys, who lived in Bailey's Hotel with a little gold bag perpetually on her wrist and a parrot on her shoulder, running up bridge debts. But even she was perched on the edge of a void: indeed, she was largely a mythical character. Angus and the brothers loved to tell the story of how she died in a bath in Harrogate, and left her money to the parrot. In fact, she died in Harrow, and left the money to her daughters in Chelsea. This was an unconvincing existence. After her death. Angus dubbed her, for her life of evasions. "The Artful Dodger": "gilt and paste from Harrods" was another of her epitaphs.

Angus's satirical sketch, "Kensingtonian", published anonymously when he was sixteen in the school magazine[10] catches the mood of place and period with something of his future sharpness. "The larger proportions of Kensingtonians, young and old, belong to that vague class which calls itself 'the new poor,' or, sometimes more internationally, 'les nouveaux pauvres' . . . They are largely 'retired' and play bridge, but there are a great number of younger 'new poor' who vainly try to keep up an air of modernity and naughtiness." A whole class of dwindling *rentiers* was, like the Johnstone-Wilsons, trying to keep up appearances, to live Knightsbridge lives on Kensington purses. Even before the financial crisis of 1931, this group felt threatened by smaller stock-market crashes. Some of these hotel transients, like Willie, had never worked in their lives. How could they start now? They looked back, nostalgically, to the Forsyte days of Edwardian prosperity which would never come again.

Angus took it all in. He lay in his bed and stared at the stains on the wall, at the cracks in the ceiling, at the crumbling of the ornate but second-rate plaster moulding. He worried about his father's debts, his mother's plucky pretences.

Did he know that Maud had secured his educational future, or did he fear that at any moment, like his brothers, he might be snatched away from the privileges of Westminster and sent out to work for his living? Was brother Fred already trying to break the trust? Was Angus aware that Fred had run into some legal difficulty that had obliged him to provide proof of his legitimacy in a court of law? Thin ice, thin ice. One might fall through it so easily, like Golliwog on the way to the North Pole.

On 6 March 1929, Maud Johnstone-Wilson died, quite suddenly, at 52 Cranley Gardens, of a heart attack brought on by bronchitis and asthma. She was sixty. Angus got home from school just in time to see her before she died. Her death was quite unexpected. She was, it was true, a little overweight, but she had not seemed ill. Anyway, she did not believe in illness. Illness was Error. Doctors were unnecessary. It was all a mistake.

The event affected Angus strangely. He never wrote about it, nor, directly, did he write about her, though he was to record that his distress at the time was aggravated by the fact that his mother had died, as she feared she would, not in a home of her own but in a boarding-house. The manageress and the other boarders let it be known that Death was not socially acceptable. At school, her departure went largely unremarked. Costley-White informed Angus that he was "a nice, plucky boy" and seized the opportunity to tell him to get his hair cut. Richard Gorer was not even aware that Maud had died. But Gorer's own father had gone down on the *Lusitania* in 1915 and nobody had talked much about that. It was not the sort of thing to talk about. Many children in those days did not see much of their parents anyway. A parent more or less did not count for much.*

Maud had departed, after a life of stress and pluck. Things had not been easy for the bright colonial girl. She had had to endure the sneers of mother-in-law Tillie, as she tried to conform to London drawing-room ways. Her husband had been openly unfaithful. Some of her six sons had been a disaster. She had battled on (even, it is said, trying to make a little pin money by writing under the Japanese pen-name of Ful Nana for *The Gentlewoman*) but in the end it had all been too much for her. She had gone under, gasping for breath.

She was buried at Kingston, with her father B. W. Caney. There is no record of the funeral. Angus selected a Christian Science verse for her tombstone, by Mary Baker Eddy, which he later dismissed as "mawkish": it reads

> No snare, no fowler, pestilence or pain
> No night drops down upon the troubled breast
> When heaven's after smile earths tear drops gain
> And mother finds her home and heavenly rest.

The Flying Spur reported her death with reverence, in a special black box. "It is with the deepest regret and sorrow that we have to report the sudden death of Mrs Johnstone-Wilson, Senr., mother of Captain Wilson, who died on March 6th, 1929. The School has lost a benefactor and one who always took the greatest personal interest in everything concerning it."

* In 1965 Geoffrey Gorer, who was old enough to remember his father's death vividly, published a sociological survey entitled *Death, Grief and Mourning* (Doubleday, Cresset in UK) which dealt with this topic.

★

What on earth was to happen to Angus and Willie? They were an odd couple. Angus was fifteen, and Willie was in his early sixties, old enough to be Angus's grandfather. Both of them were shabby, and Willie grew shabbier with the years. But they stuck together. There was always the substitute home of Ashampstead, and they could take refuge with Clive and Lucie – Clive and Lucie, true to family tradition, moved around, at one point living in the Adelphi off the Strand, within walking distance of the shop in Chandos Street, and later moving to a mansion flat in Barons Court. (Angus did visit them for meals occasionally, as a schoolboy and later as an undergraduate: one friend, revealingly, mistook Lucie for Angus's stepmother, and recalled her thrifty disquisition on the relative weight and price of dried or cooked pasta.) But most of the time it was father and son against the world. Angus, who increasingly appreciated that, despite all, his parents had been curiously loyal to one another, was loyal to Daddy. Daddy, after Maud's death, made a gesture to the boy by taking him up to Dumfriesshire in the summer of 1929, but as we have seen he did not have the courage to revisit Stroquhan. There was no return to boyhood for either of them, but instead a succession of lodgings and depressing small apartments. Willie grew to depend on Angus. And Angus became protective towards Daddy – taking Mummy's place, playing the daughter of the house, as Colin (who despised his father) spitefully remarked.

Colin and Pat, at this vulnerable period, attempted to convert Angus to their own Catholic faith, and possibly came somewhere near succeeding. Angus claimed to have taken instruction from Father Martindale at Farm Street before rejecting belief or being rejected as "not yet ready" by the church. He was certainly interested in spiritual alternatives to Christian Science, and was reading Dostoevsky with an intensely personal passion. In Dostoevsky's blustering, boastful, sentimental and inadequate fathers, he found echoes of his own. Willie was a cross between Mr Micawber and old Karamazov. In Dostoevsky's descriptions of the cities of the night, Angus found the underworld of London that he was coming to know so well. He cast himself as the little saint, the little hero. It was a new role. He saw himself as Alyosha Karamazov, victimised, eccentric, unworldly-wise. His friends called him Alyosha. He even found a Dostoevskyean daughter in distress to befriend.

This was Rachel Gardner, sister of Westminster pupil Hilary Gardner, who found herself at the age of seventeen in a position even more unlikely than that of Angus. Rachel's father had been a Jesuit who fell in love with and married his ward, a woman twenty-five years younger than himself: he left the Jesuits and turned stockbroker. In 1929, the year of Maud's death, he lost his money in the stock-market crash. His wife left him, there was an acrimonious and mud-slinging divorce, and she remarried. In 1930–31 Rachel, who had been the belle of the Westminster boys, was living alone with her father in a gloomy flat in the Old Brompton Road in considerable poverty, earning six shillings a week in the rag trade. She was desperately unhappy. Her stage-struck brother Hilary had left Westminster in July 1930 and gone off to work at the Maddermarket Theatre in Norwich with Nugent Monck. Her father was courting another woman, this time thirty-five years younger than himself. This is where Angus came in.

Angus befriended Rachel Gardner, took her to the cinema and the theatre, walked her home and sat with her for the long hours until her delinquent father came home. Angus would read to Rachel, mainly from Dostoevsky. The Grand Inquisitor's Speech was a great favourite. She felt safe alone with him. She trusted him. He was, she says, her education. She was his first student.

He mothered Rachel and his own father. Luckily, there were others who in turn could take a maternal interest in him. One of these was Neville Masterman's mother, who had been through a few difficulties herself – her husband, a drinking and depressive melancholic, had died in November 1927 after a dramatically downward career spiral. She herself (a high-born Lyttelton) was something of a Mrs Jellyby, high-principled, hard-working, disorganised and hopeless with money – a Liberal type that continued to intrigue Angus. She liked Angus, and made him welcome at her somewhat chaotic home at 46, Gillingham Street, near Victoria Station. The house itself captured his imagination. He was also a welcome guest at the house of Forrest Fulton's mother, Mabel Fulton at 27 Ladbroke Grove.

There were two other older women, also mothers of Westminster boys, who became very important to him. One was Helen Pattisson, mother of John and Alister Pattisson: the other was Miriam Laura Walker, mother of Perkin and wife of Pickering Walker – she was always known as "Bump".

★

Helen Pattisson was, in Angus's terminology, a plucky widow. Her husband, a solicitor, died in 1931 at the age of fifty in unfortunate circumstances – a suicide, it was rumoured, and victim of some professional disaster. (He shot himself in the head with a shotgun.) Helen was left to bring up her boys on a much reduced income, moving from a comfortable home in Tedworth Square, Chelsea, to a flat over a builder's in Holland Street off Kensington High Street. There she contrived to live in some style, dressing in smart if eccentric fashion, and flirting with the friends of her sons, dazzling them with her sophistication. John and Alister were quite outshone. She took to Angus, as foil and admirer, and he was fascinated by her. She was to play an important role in his adult life.

Bump Walker ran a very different kind of household. Her maiden name was Crittall, and she came from a family which had embarked on prosperity in the mid-nineteenth century from a small ironmonger's business in Braintree: her father, Francis Henry Crittall (1860–1935), made a fortune from manufacturing mass-produced metal-frame doors and windows. He was well known as a parlour pink, a supporter of the Union movement, a member of the Labour Party from 1918, a Utopian and a hearty bon viveur who enjoyed good food, good wines, and large cars: he had built for his workforce a showpiece model village at Silver End, a few miles south-east of Braintree. (He died, in 1935, in characteristic style, on board ship, on his way back from a Caribbean cruise.) Bump inherited his largesse. Her husband, Pickering Walker, was an artist and architect, who designed the house at Maresfield Park which Angus visited so often.

This house, The Wilderness, was not built until after Angus's schooldays, but it played so large a part in the lives of the family and their friends that it seems to have subsumed all memories of other Walker homes, including the large North London house, 135 King Henry's Road in Primrose Hill, where the family lived in the 1920s and early 30s. Perkin Walker himself, writing of his Westminster friendship with Angus, insists that Angus visited him at Maresfield Park during his schooldays, and Angus himself seems to have had similar recollections. The spirit of the place swallowed the surrounding years. And it would be hard to find a greater contrast with the boarding-houses of South Kensington. The Wilderness was, and remained, a potent symbol, an immemorial place.

Maresfield, in Sussex, is on the southern fringe of Ashdown Forest, some thirty miles south of London, and twelve miles north of Lewes. The country estate on which Pickering Walker built his new, absolutely modern home had romantic associations: it had belonged to the Shelley family in the nineteenth century and in 1898 the property had been given by the Shelleys to their friend of a summer holiday, Count (later Prince) Munster von Deineberg, German Ambassador to Britain. The Anglophile Count was obliged to abandon Maresfield at the outbreak of the Great War, leaving behind him not only his estate but also a Swiss summerhouse which became the delight of visiting children. In 1924 the Public Trustee began to sell off the estate in lots.

The neighbourhood was colonised in the 1920s by the painter Edward Wadsworth and his wife Fanny, who bought the Dairy Farm of the old

Manor House in 1926 to use as a weekend cottage. They liked it so much that they settled there permanently, and their garden sprouted sculptures by Zadkine. The Wadsworths were followed by the buccaneering painter Richard Wyndham, who moved into nearby Tickerage Mill House. Musicians, painters and actors discovered the attractions of this deeply rural corner of Sussex, and visited one another for weekend house parties, Sunday drinks, games of charades and croquet, Guy Fawkes celebrations, dumb crambo, concerts and flirtations. Tristram Hillier, Max Ernst, Tom Driberg, A.J.A. Symons, Cyril Connolly, Peter Quennell, the Sitwells, Robert Byron, Constant Lambert and various refugees from the Gropius group visited Maresfield and Tickerage: Connolly in particular loved Tickerage.

Young Barbara Wadsworth, Edward Wadsworth's daughter, watched the building of the Wilderness beyond the primrose wood with intense interest, and was particularly delighted with the creation of a superb hard tennis court with a miracle surface of wonderful green squashed stones.

The Pickering Walkers were an asset to Maresfield. Artistic, musical, amusing, they spent their money, like the Wadsworths, on serious things like paintings and cars and pianos and violins. They were also extremely generous. They kept a fine table, in days when English food was still infamous. No boiled ox heart here, but good wines, pineapples, French cheeses, cocktails, home-made ice creams. Brilliant conversation flowed freely after dinner to the perfume of expensive cigars. The house was made for company. It had a high reception room with a Minstrels' Gallery and an open log fire, it had panelled doors and maple floors, well-planned kitchens, many bedrooms and (more remarkably) plenty of bathrooms. It had space, ease, and unpretentious luxury. Bump became a keen gardener, and the long brick house with its hipped tiled roof soon blossomed with clematis and vine, while the grounds spread from herbaceous borders and banks of azalea into wild woodland. It was a happy house, and it became a second home to Angus, and to Perkin's cousin Elizabeth Crittall – who, like Angus, had lost her mother, and been comforted by Bump. They were all welcomed in, along with the Mangeot brothers and their musical instruments. Perkin himself was a fine pianist.

Yet all was not wholly idyllic. The Garden of Eden had its dangers. Angus, who was fiercely loyal to Perkin Walker all his life, was viewed by his best friend with a curious detachment which sheds an odd light on the happy times at King Henry's Road and The Wilderness. Perkin's own distinguished career was overshadowed by a brooding melancholia, and one senses something very strange behind his account of their early friendship (written while Angus was very much alive, to celebrate his seventieth birthday). Walker describes himself, at the age of thirteen, as "an ordinary looking boy, rather large and strong for my age, withdrawn and taciturn owing to extreme timidity . . . In contrast Angus, then as now, was courageous and extremely talkative, an amusing and brilliant conversationalist; and his appearance, I thought, was very strange indeed, and I want to dwell on this fact, because it partly explains, though it does not excuse, the way that I and my family behaved to him. He was very thin, giving an appearance of weakness, with a babyish face, dominated by protruding blue eyes and topped by very fair crinkly hair . . . he gave the impression, in fact false, of being vulnerable, defenceless and easily intimidated. I had already decided, at my preparatory school, owing to some mysterious moral grace, perhaps deriving from my parents, that odd-looking, timid boys must not be bullied, though I had a natural inclination to do so, but strenuously protected. This decision meant that I had no inhibitions in trying to become friends with Angus – not that he was in any danger of being bullied, for he was a year older than I and already happily established at the school – but without that decision I might have despised bizarre and feeble-looking boys and sought my friends among robust and dominating types. But being myself cowardly, I preferred friends who were gentle and powerless to injure me . . ."

This seems a tortuous apologia for a friendship, the stranger when one knows that Perkin Walker was to become (perhaps at the age of thirteen already was?) a conventionally good-looking young man, tall, extremely attractive to both sexes, athletic, strong, physically courageous, and a first-class tennis player as well as a fine pianist. "Something of a hero," Barbara Wadsworth's son Alex Hollweg remembered.

Perkin Walker, in this same tribute, describes with a peculiar frankness the way in which his parents – who were, he insists, extremely fond of Angus – could not resist teasing him for the oddities of his personal appearance. He presented "so bizarre a figure as to seem hardly human" and the Walker parents, amazed by his bitten nails, his scruffiness, his odd and inexplicable self-confidence, treated him as "a kind of clown or court jester, an amusing but hardly human pet". On one occasion, Bump appeared holding "a filthy looking little brush that had been used for cleaning tennis shoes. She brought it into the living-room, almost speechless with laughter, exclaiming; 'Angus's toothbrush.'" On another occasion Angus let it be known that he thought he might be considered sexually attractive by some (had not his grateful shadow John Ridley found him a "near-Adonis"?[11]) and this too had reduced the Walkers to helpless laughter. In a later draft, Perkin modified some of these comments, but the gist remained the same. **Angus was a freak, and he was made to feel it.**[12]

There were snakes in the wilderness garden, and Angus occasionally retreated to the woodland in tears. There were terrible moments, like the time when Bump found him reddening his lips with the red stain from a book binding. There were also evenings when Bump herself, presaging a sad old age, had too much to drink. Pickering and Perkin Walker were both heavy steady drinkers with cast-iron heads who never showed the slightest sign of excess, and they poured for others as they poured for themselves. Some succumbed.

(It was said that Helen Pattisson and Bump Walker *hated* one another.)

*

Angus's schooldays, meanwhile, were drawing to a close of muted triumph. Under the influence of John Edward Bowle, he sparkled in several directions. Great expectations were held out for him. A sketch by Alan Campbell-Johnson, written as an exercise set by Bowle for the History Sixth at this period, gives a vivid picture of Angus towards the end of his Westminster career (and of the tone of the school): "Few of his friends in the early 30's could have forecast his fate correctly; It is probable that none of them seriously attempted the task; – they were all too concerned with analysing their own immaturity to bother about his. But some were interested, some envious, all amused. He was able to advertise his own personality, and, at the same time, conceal his aims:– 'Some prefer to be notorious; others to be thought merely more clever than they are; *I prefer to be a curiosity*.' It was only natural:– retreating forehead, retreating hair, the back of his head, in silhouette, a wavy question mark; little round watery eyes sparkling with cultured joviality; a rather small white nose which tried hard to apologise for its presence on his face; nor did his mouth dominate – discoloured teeth, and pale lips often hidden from the stranger through a habit he had of biting his fingers (which, with constant erosion had lost much of their former beauty) – a slightly receding chin, a high pitched consequential voice – *a curiosity, but a precious one*. 'I never used to leave his presence without the strong impression of his charm and vivacity' wrote a friend of his with surprising sincerity."

Angus had developed into a personality, and his last year was a triumph, which pointed him in several directions. In 1931 he performed with conspicuous success in a production of Oscar Wilde's *The Importance of Being Earnest*, a bold choice for a school more noted over the centuries for its Latin plays.

It was a lavish affair. There were three performances at the end of March, in the Napier Hall, Vincent Square: the show was dressed by the theatrical costumiers W.Clarkson of Wardour Street, furniture was hired from High Holborn, and coffee, milk, ices and ice spoons were supplied by Cadby Hall. John Pattisson gave a performance as Cicely Cardew which the school mgazine, *The Elizabethan*, considered "little short of consummate", Frank Hooper was a wonderfully dressed and spoken Lady Bracknell, and "A. Johnstone-Wilson's Miss Prism suggested that she had considerable knowledge of the variety stage." Young Peter Copley, later of the Old Vic, was a stage manager. It was all an enormous success.

But the production's climax was off-stage. Bowle had invited Lord Alfred Douglas himself to watch this production of his martyred lover's finest play. Lord Alfred turned up with his young friend John Betjeman, and after the show they adjourned with members of the cast to Bowle's flat in Middle Temple Lane. (Or was it somewhere in Belgravia? Memories of its location seem a little fuddled.) Here there were celebrations. A strangely potent black drink flowed, and Angus, emboldened, suggested to "Bosie" that Mr Wilde might have preferred Shakespeare's plays in the days when the women's parts were performed by boys – a question which he might well have thought doubly relevant, in view of Lord Alfred's passion for Shakespeare's sonnets. Had not Wilde himself suggested that Shakespeare's dedicatee, Mr W.H., was a boy actor called Will Hughes?* And was it true, the precocious Angus wanted to know, that Wilde had wanted all the parts in his *Salome* to be played by boys?

Douglas refused to rise to the Shakespearean bait. He seemed rather cross, Angus complained, and much more interested in who had won the 2.30 at Lingfield.

Bosie was by this time an ageing figure in whose features it was difficult to discern those of one once renowned as the most beautiful young man in England. He was living quietly with his mother in Hove, and his primary interest was gambling. He had owned horses, in better days, and now, like Angus's father, he put his money on them.† Slightly depressed and downtrodden, worn out by years of successful and unsuccessful litigation, this descendant of the Black Douglases bore a strange resemblance to that other Lowland Scot, William Johnstone-Wilson, descendant of the Gentle Johnstones. They had for decades inhabited intersecting worlds, and now those worlds, in old age, converged.

The post-performance show went from bad to worse, to the delight of all. Bowle, overcome by triumph and champagne, fell over or fell asleep, in the bath or under the table. (Some claim he was *thrown into* the bath.)

---

* In 1933 Martin Secker published Douglas's *True History of Shakespeare's Sonnets*, in which he "utterly rejected the notion that Shakespeare was a homosexualist".

† His dying words were said to have been instructions to his bookmaker – "Mixed bark doubles – Nicholson's mounts." See Rupert Croft-Cooke, *Bosie* (W.H.Allen), p.378.

Betjeman leaped onto the table and uttered a rallying cry. "Now, boys, your master is feeling a little unwell. We must all stand by him! We must not peach on John Edward Bowle!" How Bosie got back to Hove, legend does not record. It was a night to remember, however vaguely.

In July, another theatrical event was mounted, in the form of a ballet and musical divertissement, produced by H.S. Williamson (later Head of Chelsea College of Art). The music was by John Engleheart, Lully and others; costumes by Mrs Costley-White; choreography by Engleheart; with Pierre Turquet and Francis Pagan on the secretarial staff. Bentley Bridgewater played the piano. Angus appeared, masked, as both Athena and Aphrodite in *Tales of Troy* and in this double role was acclaimed by Harold Hobson himself. The production raised a few parental eyebrows.

Another, equally memorable, yet sharply contrasted event took place at the end of that year, when Mahatma Gandhi was invited by Bowle to speak to a group of boys in the Ashburnham Library. Gandhi, recently released from prison in the latest phase of his long march of civil disobedience, was attending a London Round Table Conference on Indian Constitutional Reform, and he arrived on a cold, foggy evening to attend one of the first meetings of the Westminster Political and Literary Society. Bowle (referring to a sketch by himself eventually published in *The Elizabethan*, February 1983) remembered that he arrived, scantily clad, "with two white clad attendants in little square caps. He had a jaw like a pike, and though his head was much smaller than it appears in the drawing I made at the time, such was the power of his discourse that it appeared much larger, as depicted. It is no exaggeration to say that he hypnotised his audience . . . he spoke of his vision of India, free and united, with primitive peasant industry as an example to a world over-shadowed by the abuse of economic and political power." Everyone remembered it as a strange and impressive occasion. An alert, wide-eyed, crinkle-haired Angus is captured by Bowle's pen, and Angus himself recalled asking a question about the danger of a Russian invasion of an independent India. (Not for nothing was he a student of Kipling's *Kim*.) Gandhi replied, emphatically, that there was no such danger.

The two sides of Angus Wilson illustrated in these Bowle-orchestrated encounters with two weirdly contrasted prisoners of conscience, Bosie and Gandhi, were to continue to play against one another throughout his life. Angus could never quite reject either.

6

AN UNCERTAIN OXFORD

The next step was Oxford. Westminster had a particularly cosy relationship with Christ Church, and Bowle groomed his boys carefully for the
closed Hinchcliffe Scholarship. It was said that Bowle had it all sewn up,
and that the Christ Church dons simply took his recommendation. Angus
must have thought he was in with a good chance. He was one of Bowle's
favoured protégés – indeed one friend remembers him as Bowle's "prize
pupil, so brilliant as to be almost an associate teacher".[1]

The examinations took place in November 1931. Three boys were put
in for the Hinchcliffe – Angus, Alan Campbell-Johnson and Paul Gedye
(later of London and Montreal Transport). The essay subject was "Never
maltreat an enemy by halves" – an invitation to discuss what were
increasingly perceived as the disastrous economic consequences of the
peace and the Versailles treaty. One of the interviewers was Patrick
Gordon Walker, later a prominent Labour politician, and Angus, with
hindsight, wondered if he had offended this young left-wing don by
would-be sophisticated jokes about his South African ancestry. His first
published story, "The Interview at Oxford", which appeared in his
Ashampstead school magazine *The Flying Spur*, is a comic sketch which
betrays some uneasiness about over-confident behaviour on the part of the
narrator, and its confident satiric tone foreshadows its author's later work.
"There were six of them. A tall man with a hooked nose; a short fat man
with a bushy red moustache; a thin one with an 'arty' tie; a dim one with
watery features; a huge fat one with a broken nose; and 'Weeping Willow'.
I called the last one 'Weeping Willow', because his hair, his hands, his
waistcoat, everything upon him, sagged and drooped. He looked at one
with a piteous expression that was a mixture between that of the
bloodhound in 'Dignity and Impudence' and those many men who
'haven't had a bite of food all day, guv'nor.'

"It was rather a shock when he spoke. 'Sit down!', he snapped . . ."

The narrator proceeds to make a mess of the interview by an ill-judged jest about his hobbies; he modestly confesses to acting a little and writing a little, but when asked if he also goes in for carpentry, he replies "No, nor meccano either." This raises a smile, but loses him his place at "Blackpool University".

This would seem to be a parody of what went on at Christ Church. For Angus Johnstone-Wilson did not get the Hinchcliffe. Alan Campbell-Johnson did, to his own surprise.

One may assume that whatever they said later (and both claimed to have predicted this outcome) Angus and Bowle were surprised too. Fortunately for Angus, the Caney money enabled him to accept a place at Merton as a commoner. The scholarship had not been an all-or-nothing bid, as it was for the characters from lower-middle-class backgrounds so vividly described in the works of C.P. Snow, who sat their Oxbridge and Bar examinations as though their lives depended upon it. There was still a future for him at Oxford. The trust gave him £300 a year on top of his tuition fees, college payments and vacation expenses. This was riches. He could live like a lord – particularly at Merton, where there were fewer wealthy undergraduates than at Christ Church.

Merton was a handsome, historic, intellectually respectable, predominantly middle-class college – "a prudish college", according to Richard Cobb. It was not socially intimidating, nor did it tempt its young men into debt. Yet Angus seems to have approached both Merton and Oxford with a surprising degree of timidity. As on his first day at Westminster, he feared the worst. He feared bullies who never materialised. Just as he had dwelt too much on the brutalities of Kipling's Stalky stories before entering Westminster, now he seemed to expect to find himself an immediate victim of the battles of Athletes and Aesthetes of an earlier decade. His father had helped him to choose rooms – III/3, in St Albans Quad, over the Junior Common Room – and they were excellent, save for what seemed to be bloodcurdling yells from drunken evenings below. Was he about to be thrown out of a window, plunged in a river, or otherwise assaulted for his "pansy" manner?

He hid in fear, never eating in hall, where he had in his first days seen undergraduates throwing bread at one another. An obscure practice called sconcing, involving beer and forfeits, did not much attract him either. He told himself that he was avoiding "the too appalling food and company", but later admitted that an ill-conceived terror of savage rituals was his real motive for dining out.[2]

He found comfort with a small group of old friends from Westminster.

Perkin Walker went up to Christ Church in the same term, Michaelmas 1932: Forrest Fulton was already at Pembroke, reading medicine. Francis Bailey was at New College. These three formed the nucleus of a slightly larger group which met regularly, eating out at the George or at a restaurant in the Cornmarket which served good asparagus omelettes, and spending their evenings reading plays or poetry over port or madeira. They were to strike some of Angus's theatrical chums as rather a dull, bookish, serious-minded lot, without many laughs, and Angus himself described them as "a civilised, old maidish group, whose genuine wit was incommunicable because it was so inturned . . . we had a lot of laughter and interesting talk, but I think we were inevitably rather smug."[3] (Others found them "bitchy, literary and quarrelsome, always picking at one another".)

There were other familar Westminster faces beyond this small circle – Richard Gorer and Neville Masterman had disappeared to Cambridge, but Bentley Bridgewater, Sylvain Mangeot, Bill Deakin, Alan Campbell-Johnson and the Wicked Panting clustered at Christ Church. Angus ought to have felt safe enough. But he took time to branch out.

As at Westminster, he raised high his defences. He took to smoking expensive, ostentatious Turkish cigarettes in a long holder, and sported canary-coloured brass-buttoned waistcoats and brightly-coloured ties. He bought shot-silk cushions for his room and collected hot jazz gramophone records. When his friends could not join him for a meal, he defiantly ate alone, imitating his father's expensive tastes, "elaborately consuming Sole Mornay and Meringue Chantilly with a book propped up against the vase of flowers that ornamented the table."[4]

He did not dare to stay in his room in the afternoons for fear of being identified as an aesthete or a swot, or of being invited to take part in some unwelcome sporting activity, so would set off for long and tedious walks in the countryside. He noticed other lonely young men in the college, but "in those first weeks, I could as easily have confessed my loneliness and alarms to them as a warthog can communicate his fears of a lion to a herd of zebras."[5]

He was at first disappointed in his studies, finding himself obliged to take elementary classes in Latin and Economics for Pass Mods. His first term, despite some efforts at bravado, was "hell", and after Christmas he came down with an attack of psychosomatic jaundice and pleaded with his father and brothers to be allowed to leave Oxford for good. "However, they nobly persuaded me against their financial interest, and I came back to what were to be uniformly happy (though not ecstatic) years."[6]

It was a slow, surprisingly uncertain start. But gradually he made new friends, some of them from worlds very different from any he had known before. Merton, unlike Christ Church, took in several clever young men from the North. Norman Morris, a "very small Jewish man from the Midlands", was a new and invigorating experience. He too was reading history at Merton, he too was born in August 1913, but there any obvious resemblance ended. Norman's family were Jewish, his mother from the Riga area of Latvia, his father's family from Poland, and they had settled in Bilston, Staffordshire, where his father (when lucky enough to be in employment) worked at a factory bench. The Morrises were the only Jewish family in Bilston, a small Black Country working-class conservative constituency. Norman's mother (although not as political as Angus believed) was friendly with the Labour Party people and ambitious for her children. She wanted them to go to University and become teachers, for that way lay security.

Norman went from Elementary School to Wolverhampton Grammar School, then to Merton, where he switched from classics to history. (The Morrises were a highly-motivated family: a brother went to St John's, Oxford, a sister to Birmingham University.) At Merton, Morris's circumstances were very different from Angus's. He had scholarships to the tune of £150.00 a year, out of which he had to pay £125.00 in fees, dues and hall dinners, leaving about ten shillings a week for all other living expenses. At the beginning of his third year the fees were remitted and he was put on free dinners, leaving him the whole £150.00 to live on – this was about the annual wage of a skilled worker at that period.

Norman Morris and Angus met in a tutorial, and got on well. They were both members of the Labour Club, but they were not seriously political – unlike Dick Crossman, a young don, and undergraduates Michael Foot and Anthony Greenwood, who were already in full voice at the Oxford Union. Angus and Norman attended the occasional meeting or demonstration together, but were given to fits of giggles. They took to sitting up late at night over a dying fire in Angus's rooms, talking the night away. The contrasts in their own lives were a source of mutual revelation. Norman Morris had never heard of homosexuality, and now began to understand some of the innuendoes of this mysterious town of Oxford. Angus was equally fascinated by Norman's accounts of "real life" up north, of factory work, unemployment and anti-Semitism.

Norman introduced Angus to tinned salmon. "What do you do with the bones?" asked Angus. "Eat them," said Norman. Angus was amazed.

Angus visited the Morris family in its Bilston council house, and marvelled at "a certain exoticism" in this lively household. He had never seen anything like it before. The Morrises were only semi-orthodox, but they ate kosher food and lit candles on Friday nights, and this struck Angus as strangely exciting. He also, with Norman, saw the Black Country at the height of the Depression, a sight more instructive than many an economics lesson, more telling than the visiting lecturers who addressed undergraduates of the day on "Unemployment and How to Cure It" and "Is Poverty a Crime?"

Norman Morris, in turn, has vivid memories of Angus's father. "Angus hated his father. It was a positive loathing. He despised his father and adored his mother. He painted his father as a third-rate imitation man-about-town who never earned a penny in his life and made off with his wife's money. He loathed intellectuals and aesthetes. Angus made out that his father boasted that the high point in his life was when he was in South Africa and helped to chase Gandhi out of town with a whip." But Norman Morris himself did not recognise Willie from this portrait. "He invited me and Angus to lunch in London at the Café Royal, a typical Edwardian restaurant. I went full of trepidation but he was very different from Angus's painting of him. He was kindness itself, he chatted away, he put me at my ease, and he was obviously as proud as he could be of his intellectual aesthete son."

Another northern friend at Merton was Denis Barnes from Manchester, who "always spoke as though he was a working class boy; but his father was, in fact, I believe, an Inspector of Education."* Denis Barnes was educated on scholarships at Hulme Grammar School and Merton, and struck Angus as an interesting new type of ambitious, career-minded left-wing public servant, a representative of the new hard-working meritocracy – a type that recurred in his fiction. Denis was quick, clever, amusing and ironic; he was to remain a close friend for life.

It was a little hard on Norman and Denis to be portrayed in "My Oxford" as representatives of the whole of Britain north of Hampstead, and of the mass of the English working classes. (Norman, although he was an atheist, also had to stand in for the whole of Judaism.) But thus does the irresponsible novelist's imagination work: one detail stands for a way of life, one clue leads to an undiscovered country. And there is a hint that these two friends also stood for something else. They stood for a predominantly heterosexual non-public-school world which cared nothing for Oxford figures such as Maurice Bowra, John Sparrow and John Edward Bowle. Had Angus been at Christ Church or Balliol instead of Merton, he might never have made such friendships.

Long before Angus arrived at Oxford, it was evident to anyone who noticed such things that he was homosexual. Westminster took a tolerant

---

* Denis Barnes was the fifth of sixth children: his father was a school welfare officer.

"boys will be boys, they'll grow out of it" attitude towards such matters, and some of them did. Angus's sexual experiences had so far been confined largely to what he called "Cockney boys" (he confessed to finding the very accent attractive) and to encounters on the other side of the Channel. Homosexual activity was illegal in England, and Angus, who had twitted his father about Oscar Wilde ("What did Oscar Wilde *do*, Daddy?" "Oh, he messed about – with – with little girls"), was well aware of this. But its illegality did not mean it was never mentioned. On the contrary, some talked about it all the time. Oxford in the 1920s had been famous for its all-male parties: references in the novels of Evelyn Waugh were quite unambiguous.

It does, however, seem clear that Angus had never had a serious sexual attachment. His group of Westminster friends provided a safe house and he was not romantically involved with any of them. In a deleted passage of "My Oxford" he says "I remember only twice when I made pick ups in Oxford's streets (both times what I think would now be called hustlers) and in each case I rapidly withdrew with the sense that that this was a London or French holiday activity not to be pursued in Oxford." It was many years before he began happily to connect working-class pick-ups with real life, "and certainly Oxford was for me something quite apart from active sexual life."

The Golden Age Oxford of Harold Acton and Waugh and Betjeman was over, and so was the bisexual Silver Age of W.H. Auden, Stephen Spender and Isaiah Berlin. The early 1930s were what Berlin calls the Leaden or Copper Age, when moral earnestness and financial insecurity were irresistibly rising in the face of the growing challenge of Hitler and Mussolini. Parents like Bowle Senior no longer showered their under-graduate sons with money to spend on wild drinking-parties. They were too worried about their own investments. Their sons would have to fend for themselves. A sobriety, an apprehension was in the air. Even the least committed sensed it. Only a brave few, like the beautiful Titian-haired Bunny Roger, continued to camp it up in Twenties style, and he got sent down.* Angus, at Merton, worked harder than Bowle and Connolly had done at Balliol. Heavyweight history texts purchased at Blackwells in October 1933 at the beginning of his second year survive as an earnest of good intentions: F.M. Stenton's *English Feudalism*, K. Feiling's *History of the Tory Party 1640–1714*, Burckhardt's *The Civilization of the Renaissance in Italy*. (Renaissance Italy became one of his special periods.) He was elected

---

* Bunny Roger = Neil Monroe Roger, son of wealthy stockbroking parents, a designer for Hardy Amies at Fortnum and Mason, famous for his maquillage, eccentric dress and spectacularly coloured entertainments.

in the autumn of 1934 to the Bodley Club, a Merton society which discussed papers on subjects such as "Clio and the Whigs" and "Byzantine Art". (He was an intermittent attender, less loyal than Norman Morris and Denis Barnes.) He read enormously, making his way through yards of English, French and German novels. He got on well with some of his tutors, but unfortunately never hit it off with Professor H.W. Garrod, who was the key to Merton's social life, a figure to be compared with the influential "Sligger" Urquhart at Balliol. Garrod, classical scholar and Professor of Poetry, had a keen eye for interesting young men, and entertained them generously, but the lunch at which he met Angus was not a success: "Angus made some very clever remarks to Garrod – too clever probably and over-sophisticated. Garrod just did not like him. He said afterwards to Idris Deane Jones [Angus's History Tutor] much to Deane Jones's annoyance that he disliked Angus's sissy voice."[7] It was the Christ Church interview story all over again.

Nor did anything come of an introduction to the other great man of letters of Merton, the much-marrying cricket-playing poet Edmund Blunden, who was tutor to Hugh Carleton Greene, Douglas LePan, Northrop Frye and Paul Engle from Iowa. Blunden chaired many gatherings of the Bodley Club, and gave a well-attended paper on "Uneducated Poets" followed by mulled claret – Angus was there, but there is no record that Blunden and Angus had any personal contact.

Two intermediaries tried to integrate Angus into college social life. One was a gilded youth from the rich set, Stuart Daniel, who struck Angus as "the very epitome of a Byronic public schoolboy. Tall, handsome, enormously charming, with a wide Oxford range, an easy culture, he seemed to me a figure out of a book." This benevolent Steerforth and another young man called Richard Lamb introduced Angus to a smart Merton dining club called The Myrmidons: despite the special violet evening coats with their shiny wide lapels; the prevailing club tone was sporting rather than aesthetic, and Angus in the group photograph looks, as he felt himself to be, a little out of place. He, Daniel and One Other display the most exquisitely neat waved and crimped hair – Angus had clearly got himself up very carefully for the occasion. (A fellow Myrmidon in this 1935 photograph is Airey Neave.)

Richard Lamb confirms Angus's account of his unhappy Oxford début. Sylvain Mangeot told him that Angus, having been very popular at Westminster, was disappointed in his reception in Oxford. "He tried to speak in his first term at the Union but was not successful. Nor did he get on well with the dons at Merton. His appearance was odd; his hair was indescribable and he had an extraordinary camp way of talking which put many people off." But the Myrmidons, Lamb says, liked him – he made them all laugh.

Another friendly Mertonian was Basil Royal-Dawson. He was one of the theatre crowd, and he and Daniel persuaded Angus to join the Merton Floats, the college dramatic society. Angus appeared as the maid Emmy in *The Doctor's Dilemma* in November 1933: Emmy, Shaw tells us, "has the complexion of a never-washed gypsy, incurable by any detergent; and she has, not a regular beard and moustaches, which could at least be trimmed and waxed into a masculine presentableness, but a whole crop of small beards and moustaches . . . She has only one manner, and that is the manner of an old family nurse to a child just after it has learnt to walk. She has used her ugliness to secure indulgences unattainable by Cleopatra or Fair Rosamund . . ." This piece was directed by Felix Felton, President of OUDS (the Oxford University Dramatic Society), with Royal-Dawson as Redpenny and Daniel as Sir Ralph Bloomfield-Bonnington. Diana Churchill played Jennifer Dubedat: she was at the beginning of her professional career, and was fresh from an autumn season at the Oxford Playhouse. From the Floats, Angus graduated to OUDS, where he appeared in February 1934 as a Hostess in a production of Marlowe's *Doctor Faustus*, produced by Gyles Isham, with Felix Felton as Faustus and Peter Glenville as Mephistophilis.

This was glittering Oxford: these were the names of the future. Angus McBean designed the sets, Stuart Daniel played the Emperor, and Helen of Troy was played by the daughter of Major General H.E.Salt, the endlessly interviewed and photographed Deb of the Year Miss Primrose Salt, who confided to Cherwell that Oxford sherry parties were more amusing than London ones, and that the OUDS were "awfully nice people". (Her theatrical career did not take off, but she kept her flair for publicity: when she married in November 1935 in New Delhi she had just broken her arm in a riding accident and her wedding photos appeared in the British press captioned as the "Arm-in-a-Sling Bride".)

Belonging to the OUDS was a way of life. There were long Sunday breakfasts in the club rooms, with good food and witty company. Peter Glenville was one of the stars. He was the son of a famous theatrical couple: his father was Shaun Glenville, of *Blue Train, Razzle Dazzle* and *Frivolity*, and his mother was Dorothy Ward, one of the idols of the twenties. One of her songs, as Angus fondly remembered two decades later was "Ain't We Got Fun?"[8] She was famous as principal boy in many a pantomime: during her son's Oxford years she played Jack in *Jack and the Beanstalk*. (Her husband played Dame Trot.)

Peter Glenville's tastes were necessarily more classical. He appeared as

Edward II, Richard III, and Mephistophilis: he was Puck in Max Reinhardt's spectacular borzoi-enhanced open-air production of *A Midsummer Night's Dream* (June 1933) and Hamlet in an OUDS Jubilee production in February 1935, directed by Nevill Coghill with décor by Richard Buckle. He was President of OUDS, reviewed regularly in *Isis*, spoke at the Union, and was frequently quoted in *Cherwell*'s "Sayings of the Week".*

Peter Glenville liked Angus. From his gilded Christ Church perspective, he remembers him at Oxford as "a scholar, not a rich boy – with a curious, darting, humming-bird authority". He would talk endlessly about Daddy in his light eccentric voice: "Daddy's ill in the hotel, I've got to go and look after Daddy." He was not at all decadent, not at all outrageous, not at all in the Brian Howard/Harold Acton mode, not at all embarrassed by his own lack of machismo: he was a "serious, hard working, *respectable little body*." He had everything under control. "In his own chihuahua way, he was always the overdog."

Angus collaborated with another rising star in the theatre world, Paul Dehn, to write for an OUDS smoker. To this event, Peter Glenville brought Ivor Novello, and, against the club's all-male rules, Gladys Cooper. Novello, once a choral scholar at Magdalen College School, was now the actor-writer-director king of musical comedy: Gladys Cooper, who had appeared with him ten years earlier in one of his few failures, *Enter Kiki*, was one of the most celebrated actresses of the day. And here the two of them were to watch Angus as he played in a novel interpretation of the Seven Deadly Sins. He represented Buggery, wearing flame-coloured pyjamas and carrying a madonna lily. (Terence Rattigan gave his Treachery in the same tableau.) Angus also did an imitation of Primrose Salt, and appeared as a comic charlady who sang "I've got a boy in India, so I won't be kissed on the lips." Or so remembers the Wicked Panting, who was himself to prove "an irresistible heroine" the following year. It was all a great success.

Angus put on one other performance which was handed down as legend. In "My Oxford", he reports that an Oxford don's wife once remarked to him "I hear you spent nearly all your time at Oxford dressed as a woman." This story originated in an occasion when he dressed up in

---

* Glenville was to swim up two decades later at the Mardi Gras ball of Marie-Laure de Noailles dressed as Byron fresh from the Hellespont, "with an effect of seaweed and brine still clinging to his close-fitting costume, which had been designed by Oliver Messel". (Harold Acton, *More Memoirs of an Aesthete*, Methuen, 1970, p.343) Other British revellers included Lady Diana Cooper as Lady Blessington, Violet Trefusis as Lady Hester Stanhope, Ann Fleming as Harriet Wilson, and Patrick Leigh-Fermor as Bulwer-Lytton.

tweeds borrowed from his friend Sally Graves.* Thus attired, he impersonated the famously smart mother of John Freeman for the benefit of the parents of one J.R. Morris at a tea party at Brasenose. His smoker clothes were lent to him by another undergraduate friend, Barbara (Ward) Jackson. He was a natural in drag.

Unlike some homosexuals, Angus liked women and had good friends at Somerville. Women liked him and connived with him: some were prepared to play "the girlfriend" when Daddy came to visit. Some of them got rather fond of Daddy. Alison Hope was Daddy's pet, but Sally Graves, Barbara Ward, and a decorative and silent young Argentinian called Hebe were also favoured. Daddy would come up to Oxford two or three times a term, and would take them all out to meals at The George, where he would enjoy advising the young ladies on what to order. Sally Graves remembers Angus's protective sweetness to his rather small, red-cheeked, elderly father.

And so the Oxford years sped by. What next, some of them began to wonder? Angus toyed with the idea of becoming an actor: many of his theatre friends were turning professional. Terence Rattigan's first play *First Episode* (written in collaboration with Philip "Whoopee" Heimann) was put on while he was still an undergraduate: it transferred from a small theatre in Kew to become a West End box-office success in the autumn of 1933, encouraging Rattigan to leave Oxford without bothering to take his degree. Other OUDS men, including George Devine and Giles Playfair, also moved on to the professional stage. After all, what else was there, where else could one go? The future was not bright.

The First World War had taken the Oxford of Harold Macmillan by surprise. Nobody was expecting it. The Second crept up more slowly, accompanied by all sorts of ominous creakings and groanings from the machinery of state, and by a crescendo of ugly noises from Europe and the Far East. Britain's departure from the gold standard in 1931, soaring unemployment (nearly three million by 1933), Hunger Marches, the rise of Hitler and Mussolini – these could not be avoided, even in Oxford. Pacifism and disarmament were the themes of the day. How could a second catastrophe be averted? Undergraduates learned of the horrors of Armageddon through newly published works by Sassoon, Graves, Remarque, Wilfred Owen. Never again, was the cry from Westminster schoolmasters, from Beverley Nichols and Aldous Huxley and Gerald Heard and Dick Sheppard. We must fight back, replied militant

---

* Sally Graves, Elizabeth Millicent Graves, later Sally Chilver, was a niece of Robert Graves and known as the Zuleika of Somerville. She was Principal of Lady Margaret Hall, Oxford, 1971–1979.

MacNeice. But the more the subject was debated, the more the situation deteriorated.

Oxford played a singular part in the pacifist debate. Many, including characters as diverse as the Wicked Panting and Norman Morris, favoured pacifism; many joined Sheppard's Peace Movement (later the Peace Pledge Union). They believed Germany had been unfairly treated at Versailles, and that the economic consequences of the peace were our own fault. Some were active Marxists. Union debates reflected these concerns: was Russia the only country in Europe with a future, did the House condemn the selfishness of French foreign policy, did it prefer Fascism to Socialism, should the League of Nations be abolished? But the most famous debate of all took place on 14 February 1933, when the House, swayed by the rhetoric of C.E.M. Joad and his quotations from Lytton Strachey, decided by 275 votes to 153 that "this House will in no circumstances fight for its King and its Country". The subsequent furore in the national press was tremendous, as boxes of white feathers arrived at the Union and Mosley's Fascists tore up the minutes of the meeting.

But all this was frivolity, compared with the economic and political realities behind the debate. The real world waited.

7

THE OLD MEN AT THE MUSEUM

Angus sat for his finals in May 1935. He got a respectable Second. Was this a disappointment? Would getting a Third, like Auden, Bowle and Connolly, have been more thrilling? Had he really got an "alpha mind", or was it only beta after all? He had hoped to get a First, and put his failure down to having spent too much time with OUDS.

Real life presented itself in unattractive colours. Too clever to be an actor, not clever enough to be a don: this was how, retrospectively, he summed up his plight. Many graduates newly exiled from the charmed university world are assailed by a sense of hopelessness, sometimes prolonged, occasionally terminal. Angus had the advantage that he had not invested his all in Oxford. He had not become a celebrity. But a disadvantage, shared with hundreds of other graduates, was that there was nowhere to go. Depression ruled, within and without.

The next year of his life is poorly recorded. He was unhappy. His father was now very dependent on him: he had turned into a shabby, frail old man. Job prospects were dismal. Angus went to the cinema, dreary afternoon after dreary afternoon, sometimes alone and sometimes with Daddy, and bit his nails and smoked and occasionally wept in the dark. A childhood taste for Great War tragedies about heroic nurses and Mary Pickford as Kiki in a transparent spotted blouse had matured into an enjoyment of the satiric comedy of American cinema: he took to Mary Boland, Kay Francis, Carole Lombard, Jean Harlow, Miriam Hopkins, Bette Davies, Rosalind Russell, Margaret Dumont.* He hated Westerns, and despite a brief undergraduate flirtation with the Oxford Film Club, never really liked serious films about peasants and slum dwellers: and neither he nor Daddy liked Shirley Temple or Charlie Chaplin. (But Daddy *particularly* admired Claudette Colbert.)

* *Vogue*, August 1956.

On those dark afternoons he could not avoid newsreel of Mussolini marching through Abyssinia, and he took Rachel Gardner to see Lothar Mendes's adaptation of Feuchtwanger's *Jew Süss*, a warning of worse to come.

He and Daddy also filled in time by visiting Ashampstead, but Angus was depressed by the atmosphere there. It was like a railway waiting-room, where people sat around hoping that something would turn up. Mr Pat had bravely tried to branch out on his own, and opened a tea-room with Mr Colin's assistance in nearby Pevensey, in a charming seventeenth-century beamed cottage: Angus visited Pat at Lyons Close with his Oxford friends Norman Morris, Denis Barnes, Perkin Walker and Forrest Fulton, and admired Pat's gallantry as he baked coconut fingers and Durban buns and ginger biscuits and shortbreads and eggless cakes from Nurse Sopp's handwritten recipes. A couple of lady lodgers lived upstairs and helped with the rent. But there wasn't much money in this, and Colin and Pat gave up and set off on their travels, to Yugoslavia, Alexandria and the beyond of beyond.

Angus claimed that he himself tried a spell as a waiter, and was imbued by the experience with democratic sympathies – was this with Pat at Pevensey, or at some other establishment? He contemplated other activities: perhaps he could become secretary to Sir Stafford Cripps, as Betjeman and Bowle had been secretaries to Plunkett, as Cyril Connolly had been secretary to Logan Pearsall Smith? Or he could follow in Christopher Isherwood's footsteps and find some nice boy to tutor? Could he ask Pierre Turquet's father to find him a place at Scoone's, where Ronald Firbank had been a pupil? Could he go off, like Forster or Joe Ackerley, on a Hindoo Holiday to instruct an Indian princeling? Such occupations were fairly undemanding, and left free time for a literary man to find his feet as novelist or poet.

But it had not really crossed Angus's mind to want to be a literary man. Writing as a profession had not seriously occurred to him.

Others were finding life difficult. Norman Morris, who wanted to be a journalist, worked for six months without pay on the *Wolverhampton Express*, then taught in an elementary school in Bilston. "Grammar Schools would not take a Jew." His brother was two to three years without a job. Both suspected anti-Semitism. Denis Barnes had got a First in Modern History and a degree in PPE, so his prospects were brighter: in 1937 he went straight from Oxford into the Ministry of Labour, a first step in a successful public career. Perkin Walker had a First and a private income: he now embarked on a life's work as a gentleman scholar of the Renaissance. Forrest Fulton at Pembroke had switched after two years

from law to animal physiology, and went on to clinical work at the London
Hospital as a prelude to a career in virology. Stuart Daniel launched himself
as a successful barrister: Francis Bailey, perhaps less happily, worked as an
archivist.

The possibility of anti-homosexual prejudice in a depressed employment market must have occurred to Angus, as the possibility of anti-
Semitism occurred to the Morrises. Many professions were not open to
someone who could not disguise a camp manner. Bunny Roger said it
would have been out of the question for him to have survived in the
stockbroking world to which his family belonged. "I wouldn't have done
well as a tycoon, would I?" Roger struck a defiant pose and got away with
it, becoming a familiar figure as he strolled down Piccadilly in Edwardian
costume. Of an evening he preferred ostrich feathers and sequins. The
press loved him.

Actors and stage designers were allowed, even expected to be camp.
Social proprieties bowed to the Gielguds and Rattigans and Cowards and
Novellos. But if you got caught in a public lavatory or with a guardsman, if
some scandal alienated your unsuspecting matineé audiences – that was
another matter. Concealment, even here, was necessary.

Angus looked around him, and wondered. Doors closed in his face even
when he did not particularly want to open them. He went off to a few
fashion shows with Bump Walker and some Somerville friends – maybe he
was toying with the idea of being a fashion journalist? Why not, after all?
He protected himself by pretending that he had obtained "the most
improbable positions of importance" – including Secretary to the Socialist
League – but the pretence gave him no satisfaction. He was ashamed of it.[1]
One job he did find, through an advertisment in the *Evening Standard*: he
became, for a while, the amanuensis of a Mrs MacLachlan.

Mrs MacLachlan, as Elizabeth Morris, had been a student at Girton from
1882 to 1885, where she read Greek and Sanskrit. She had appeared
imposingly as Clytemnestra in *Elektra* in the college play in 1883, a role for
which her domineering personality and handsome prow of a nose finely
suited her. She also had a passion for horoscopes and folk dancing and made
a study of schizophrenia. She married a journalist and pscychologist in
1885, and became a governor of Christ's Hospital. In the mid-thirties she
thought it was time she wrote her memoirs, and to this end hired a
succession of young people, including Angus and a Somerville graduate,
Kathleen Betterton. She did not seem able to give them very clear
instructions or indeed any biographical material, and a mixture of
boredom and mistrust drove her employees away. Mrs MacLachlan,

despite her invigorating curry lunches, her mystic leanings, her yoga and her antique clothing, was a dead-end job.

Angus believed she kept an adopted child in cruelly deprived conditions in her flat in Soho. He felt he ought to go to the police about this. According to Kathleen Betterton, Mrs MacLachlan had a large apartment in Bayswater and a single dusty room in Regent Street which she used as an office. It had a huge table piled high with ancient magazines and dusty balance sheets. Kathleen Betterton felt the atmopshere was sinister: she feared the visit of a malign stranger, and became convinced that a face was staring through the window at her back.[2] (Can there be any connection between these two stories and Girton College Register's comment that in 1919 Mrs MacLachlan "adopted eight war orphans"?)

Time dragged for Angus in this haunted void as it had dragged for Dickens in his blacking factory. Without purpose, with diminishing funds, he felt insecure. Wandering aimlessly around South Kensington, he bumped once or twice into the tall conspicuous figure of Bentley Bridgewater. They chatted, compared notes on progress and lack of progress, had a drink together. Bentley was living with his parents in Kensington, having spent some time after Oxford studying German in Austria: he was now at a London crammers, trying at his ambitious mother's insistence to enter the diplomatic service.

Bridgewater failed to get one of the five available Foreign Office places. His crammers suggested applying for a job at the British Museum, where he was lucky enough to get a post as Assistant Secretary in the Director's Office. At much the same time, Angus came to hear that there were jobs available at the Museum in the Department of Printed Books. His informant was Arthur Ellis, the diminutive Superintendent of the Reading Room, and by good chance a close friend of Pierre Turquet's mother, Professor Gladys Turquet. (Vacancies were never advertised.) Angus applied, in April 1936: his nomination was put forward by the Archbishop of Canterbury, who was one of the three principal Trustees responsible for appointments at the Museum. The Civil Service Commission interviewed Angus, and confirmed that he was qualified for the post.

Angus started work as a "temporary assistant cataloguer" in the Department of Printed Books in January 1937. Twenty new posts had recently been created to deal with arrears in cataloguing. He got one of them. In the midst of his bewilderment, "so near the family knuckle and the thirties knuckle", this job "came as heaven".*

---

* The Museum's own records show that Angus had in fact applied for a job there as early as November 1935, but nothing had materialised. Quotes taken from essay notes for "Seven Ages of Man".

The word "temporary" did not mean quite what it implied. The new recruits, all with good degrees and high linguistic qualifications, were given this title in order to avoid paying them a salary commensurate with the equivalent status of assistant keeper: they received £250.00 per annum and had no pension rights. (C.P Snow, the son of a petty bourgeois Leicester bankrupt, says that by 1930 he was in receipt of "750 a year plus perks" as a young Fellow of Christ's College, Cambridge.)[3] Some of these twenty were to spend their entire working lives in the Museum: others left and were replaced. Their task was to work on a new General Catalogue, begun in 1931 to replace the old General Catalogue. The work was expected to last about fifteen years. (By 1955, twenty years on, they had reached the letter D.) They also had to process new acquisitions. They were paid by the Treasury as temporary civil servants, but were in fact the "servants" of the Trustees, a group which included the Archbishop, the Lord Chancellor, the Speaker of the House of Commons, and members of wealthy families which had made bequests to the Library.

The Department of Printed Books had close links with its Victorian past. Great men of earlier days – Edmund Gosse, Richard Garnett and the Biblical scholars Russell Martineau and Sir Frederic Kenyon – were still vividly remembered. Ancient traditions flourished. The senior-grade staff were darkly suited (though the Keeper of Printed Books, Wilfred Alexander Marsden, sported a dapper spotted bow tie and spats). Two of them spent much of their time composing competitive Alcaic verses to the restaurant cat. One of the older Assistant Keepers, L.C. Wharton, "a gentle delightful bachelor with a long, thin nose and a mass of white hair and a drooping moustache, which gave him the appearance of Lewis Carroll's White Knight", was the last man to wear a top-hat on duty in the Reading Room.[4] Another keeper (F.G. Rendall) was to tell Angus that requests for Private Case Books (i.e. books withheld from the general public on moral or legal grounds) would come only from "anarchists, unfrocked clergymen or swine".[5] G.D.R. Tucker, the Incorporator of the catalogue, was an Alpinist, a croquet player, and a composer of verses upon the subject of croquet: he had a slight stammer. "Mac" (Alan Grant MacFarlane) had a severe stammer, attributed to his wartime experiences in Flanders. Henry Thomas, Hispanologist, bachelor and bibliographer, was Deputy Keeper: he was a devoted pilgrim on the road to Santiago de Compostela, and wrote about miracles, translated his own work into Spanish, and was suspected of being very pro-Franco. Thomas Kendrick, also war-wounded, and assistant keeper in the department of British and medieval antiquities, was a keen fly-fisherman and wrote about druids and earthquakes. Arthur Ellis, the Superintendent of the Reading Room, was a perfect little man, demure and sugary, and charming to all the readers, even when they tried to borrow money off him.

Such were the senior staff, the chiefs of the Department. Further down the hierarchy, the Attendants, "carefully chosen largely from the families of servants of the Trustees, or other well-to-do people", carried themselves, according to Alec Hyatt King, with "a dignity of fussy importance" which bore the marks of their class origins.[6] These poorly paid lower-grade staff eked out their income by acting as butlers and footmen at banquets of the Trustees. Some mornings they would arrive looking very somnolent, and would snooze quietly in the lower reaches of the ironwork below the Reading Room as they wore off the after-effects of a very late night and the gift of half a partridge or half a bottle of champagne.

"Dickensian", "mummified", "mulligatawny" and darkened by "a sad fog of Victorianism" – these were some of the phrases Angus later used to describe the Library of the 1930s. They offended more loyal colleagues, who preferred to insult their own institution in their own way. But change was on the way, and the new intake represented the first wave of it. After much grumbling, a few women had been given employment. These included Audrey Brodhurst and Wendy Charles from Somerville, and Anne O'Donovan from Girton. Laurence Wood, a French specialist, and Howard Nixon, later librarian of Westminster Abbey, were also part of the team. Transients included Peter du Sautoy, who went on to a career in publishing; George Clutton, who became an ambassador; and the Irish baritone, Frederick Fuller, who went off to sing with Villa-Lobos in Brazil. This group represented another generation. They even addressed one another by their first names.

The work itself was not inspiring. Cataloguing had moved on a little since the *fin-de-siècle* days of the first General Catalogue when the geographer John de Villiers complained that he often fell asleep after working for hours "upon some particularly dull job that an intelligent youngster of fourteen could have dealt with".[7] Nevertheless, it was still monotonous. Catalogue entries had to be written for every single published item that the library possessed, or that came in under the Copyright Act – a disparate and ever-swelling mass of material. Angus, who could already deal with entries in Greek, Latin, German, French and Italian, now set himself to learn Norwegian (partly in homage to Ibsen) but was taken aback when he found he was also expected to deal with books in Welsh, Dutch and Danish. They all learned on the job, after a short course on "incorporation" (i.e. the arrangement of the catalogue), and picked up the details of a system that had been laid down a century earlier – a fine

system, perhaps too fine for practicality. (Its suppression on the advent of
photolithography is still deplored in some quarters.)

Work offered some surprises – Angus was amazed by the quantities of
religious literature and romantic fiction that the nation poured forth.
Working conditions were not very romantic. The cataloguers worked in
one room under the eye of three minders, at long wooden tables, waiting
for manually-propelled barrowloads to arrive: they were expected to get
through a certain number of items each day. The chairs were uncomfortable. There was one telephone in the room, manned by a Mr Pennycad,
who would put incoming calls onto extensions. It was soon noticed that
the new young man with the double-barrelled name was receiving more
than his fair share of calls.

Cliques and factions formed in the cataloguing room, and a little salon
began to build up around Angus. This group never took its forty-five
minute lunch break in the Museum canteen, but ate at Oddi's restaurant in
nearby Coptic Street. The dining-room was unpromisingly narrow and
the tables were covered in nasty American cloth, but the fat Mrs Oddi
(variously remembered as French, Italian or Greek) doted upon Angus,
and sent out for French pastries for him. The food was cheap – stew or
sausage lyonnaise or liver and bacon for tenpence or a shilling, a three-
course meal with soup, exotic chicken risotto and fruit salad for three and
six. Perkin Walker and other Oxford friends (a Marxist botanist, a
journalist working with G.D.H. Cole, Kathleen Betterton, and fashion
journalist Peggy Reekie) dropped in to join them.

George Painter, large of heart and small of stature, was a brilliantly gifted
later arrival in the group. He started work in January 1938, and came from
a First Class degree in Birmingham to find the group already established,
with Angus holding court. It was a republican, even a revolutionary court.
Several of them, including Angus, were Labour Party members: some had
Communist sympathies. Audrey Brodhurst (some said the cleverest of
them all) brought with her from her Birmingham-Somerville background
strong left-wing principles. Wendy Charles was the *tricoteuse*: famed at
Somerville for going everywhere with her knitting, she was now a
member of the Chelsea Labour Party, and with the Mangeots supported
the Popular Front and distributed the *Daily Worker*. "We were all very
red," she remembers.

They would talk and talk. They read Firbank, John Cowper Powys,
Djuna Barnes, Dickens, Henry James, Proust, Ignazio Silone. They talked
books and politics, discussing the Spanish Civil War, pacifism, the PPU,
Oswald Mosley. (Angus himself seems to have shifted his support from the
Peace Pledge Union to Stafford Cripps's "United Front of the Working

Class to fight Fascism and War", a platform which threatened to split the Labour Party in its attempts to unite the Left.) And Angus entertained. He told tales about his brothers and South Africa, about Aunt Alys and her parrot: he imitated Queen Elizabeth at Tilbury, and did Keats in Cockney. And, of course, they all gossipped, though a halt would be called if things got too personal – *"pas de secrets de boudoir!"* Audrey Brodhurst would cry.

Some talked, some attended demonstrations. Wendy Charles and Peter du Sautoy were at the Tooley Street and Cable Street marches in the East End. Assistant Keeper Hugh Chaplin and his wife Ina were also very active on the left.* Political activity staved off fear. It was a worrying time, but they made themselves too busy to worry.

For Angus, home life was also troubled. Willie Johnstone-Wilson was in a bad way. He and Angus were living together in a service flat in Hogarth Road, just off Earls Court: Wendy Charles called in there and found the old man listening to the boxing results on a large brown radio sitting on a green chenille tablecloth. Gallantly he pulled himself together for this pretty little creature, and promised her that when he felt better he would take her to see the ponies jump over the sticks at Sandown. Sally Graves remembers him sitting on a bed in the corner, not very well, wrapped up in a woman's shawl. He was pleased to see her: he always took an interest in the gals. Angus and his circle used to organise evening play-readings at weekends, where Museum and Oxford and theatre friends would mingle: when the reading took place in Hogarth Road, the old man would listen in deeply polite boredom to Ibsen or adaptations of Evelyn Waugh declaimed by Perkin Walker, Forrest Fulton, Alison Hope, John Pattisson. "It's all very clever," he would say, and at the end would leap to attention to entertain the prettiest young woman in the room. He did not care for the new post-Shavian theatre. Popular historical biographies were more his line, Agnes Strickland one of his favourite authors. Richard the Third, Henry the Eighth and Charles the Second were his heroes. Royal mistresses he also approved. He depended greatly on the circulating library.

Willie was by now very frail. Angus tried to keep him going, but it was hard work. Angus shared so few of the old man's amusements – he would go along to Lord's or the Oval to keep him company and read Dostoevsky in the sun while his father watched the cricket or greeted friends in the Members' Bar, but he could not bring himself to go with him to rugby matches at Twickenham. One day when Angus was visiting Clive and

---

* Arthur Hugh Chaplin (b.1905), was Principal Keeper of Printed Books at the British Museum 1966–70; his wife Irene (Ina) Marcousé remained active in local politics for many years.

Lucie Johnstone-Wilson news came from Twickenham Police Station that Willie had collapsed. He seemed to have had a slight stroke. Angus rushed off in a taxi and rescued him. Father and son moved to a ground-floor flat across the street in one of the tall terraced houses of Hogarth Road but from now on it was downhill all the way. Willie stumbled when he walked, would set off in the wrong direction towards familiar haunts like the Trocadero.

By the spring of 1938 Willie needed nursing. He was taken in an ambulance to his faithful son Winn at Ashampstead, but Betty Johnstone-Wilson could not cope with him. Winn himself was not well: the old war wound was playing up. Willie was moved up the hill to a nursing home at Weir Cottage, Bramber Road, Seaford. He was suffering from memory loss while stubbornly insisting that he was not senile. He was not an easy patient. There he died, on 6 May 1938, at the age of 73. The causes of death were given as cardiac muscle failure, arteriosclerosis and chronic nephritis (i.e. kidney failure). He was buried at Seaford.

It was a sad ending, but one that Angus was able to face more openly than his mother's. He wrote a short story based on it, "A Story of Historical Interest", in which he tells the story from a daughter's viewpoint, and hints at the possibility of another cause of death.

"Dr Filby laughed. 'No meat or eggs,' he repeated. 'The kidneys are affected. There's definite albumen in the water. I suppose your father was a bit wild when he was younger. You'll excuse my asking but do you know of any V.D. story?' 'I've never heard of anything,' said Lois. 'I'm just a bit puzzled by those marks on his legs,' said the doctor. 'There's a possibility of a tertiary syphilis, but don't worrry about it, even if it is so, it can only be of historical interest.' "[8]

And so goodbye to the stage-door Johnny. The sins of his youth had revisited him. The fact that Angus at the time mentioned a possibility of syphilis to George Painter, who had come to know Angus's family well, indicates that this was not a piece of fictitious embroidery. Willie, in his days of wild oats, had contracted some form of venereal disease. Syphilis or not, as Dr Filby knew, the end had come.

★

With his father gone, Angus left Earls Court and moved to Bloomsbury to be nearer work. He was free to grow up at last. The decade since Maud's death had brought him unnaturally close to his father – at one point in their wanderings they shared a double bed. The more his brothers criticised Willie, the more Angus stood up for him. He had even done the cooking – a shopping list, scribbled inside his Norwegian dictionary, itemises ham, butter, caster sugar, a one-pound loaf, a half-pound pack of Indian tea, a dozen eggs, greengages. Prematurely responsible in some ways, he had been mildly (and willingly) retarded in others, like many a dutiful spinster – an analogy his story recognises. How could one have an affair or even a casual sexual encounter while sharing a flat, let alone a bed, with one's father? War was on the way, but so, perhaps, was liberation.

His one-bedroom Bloomsbury apartment (3/11) was on the eighth floor in Endsleigh Court, a large block of featureless flats on the north side of Tavistock Square. Niece Jeanne, the bookish one, now working for a publisher and living in a girls' hostel, visited him there, got to know his Museum colleagues, and took part in play readings. (She shared Angus's histrionic talents.) Angus made a new sort of home life for himself, giving Sunday lunches with elaborate puddings: he always had a sweet tooth and particularly enjoyed pears covered in a rich chocolate sauce – a dish to which he remained faithful, and which provoked years later the cry from an American guest, the critic Ellen Moers, "How cruel can you get to a pear?"

Angus had by now established a closer friendship with Bentley Bridgewater. Bridgewater had at first seemed rather a distant figure, tennis-playing, piano-playing, double-bass-playing – but his background, Angus discovered, had striking similarities to that of the Johnstone-Wilsons. The Bridgewaters were Kensingtonians who had come down in the world: Bentley's mother Violet was Canadian-born, and his father had read for the bar. In early days the family had private means and lived it up with a nanny and a French maid. In 1912 when Bentley was a baby they went off to British Columbia and "bought up some of Vancouver Harbour Front". They came back across the Atlantic in 1917 and proceeded to ruin not only themselves but also Violet's Canadian pioneer father with hideously ill-advised investments. Mr Bridgewater became lame, was converted to Christian Science by the second wife of Maharajah Duleep Singh, and resorted to faith healers. His final illness, a succession of small strokes, devoured the last remnants of the family fortunes, and although he did not die until 1963 (having obtained an OBE for his work with the National Federation of Housing Services in 1957) Violet was prematurely forced into the role of Plucky Wife – a role in which Angus got to know her well.

She had more resources than Maud Johnstone-Wilson. She had studied music in Paris, and when her husband fell ill she played for her living. She had composed patriotic little songs in the First War: "Fight, Canada, for Empire!", "A Maori's Dream of Home". She taught singing and piano, played for the chorus rehearsals of Ivor Novello's musicals, accompanied at auditions, taught at the Webber-Douglas School. She coached soprano Audrey Mildmay who in 1931 married John Christie, founder of Glyndebourne: Mrs Christie always took a kindly interest in young Bentley Bridgewater. Noticing Bentley's lack of interest in young ladies, she told him to "Fight against it!" and offered to pay for his piano lessons. Bentley was not best pleased.

One of the hazards of being a single and apparently eligible young man, as both Bentley and Angus discovered, was the unwanted attention of the mothers of eligible daughters. This was still the age of the arranged marriage. Angus was relentlessly pursued by the untiring barracuda Phyllis Tucker, the wife of Raffles Tucker, one of his seniors at the Museum: she had two marriageable daughters, and Angus was frequently solicited to play tennis with them – this despite the fact that Raffles Tucker and Angus seem to have heartily disliked one another. Angus evaded as best he could, as he claimed to have evaded his own mother's attempts to introduce him to suitable girls at hotel tea-dances. Angus's mother was no longer there to pursue his matrimonial prospects, but Violet Bridgewater was very much there – it was said that she even consulted Angus about how to find a female friend for Bentley. But she was quite clear about one thing – until Bentley married, he was not to be allowed to leave home. He had to stay in Clareville Grove with Mother and her tortoise. His rebellions consisted of refusing to play on demand at her soirées, and of walking out into the night.

Bentley was ever a wanderer, a cat who walked by himself. Walking the streets late was one way to get away from Mother. And who knows what might turn up in the great outdoors of London? Bentley had an extraordinary mixture of recklessness and docility; he was a great risk-taker who continued conscientiously to worry about feeding his mother's cat.

Bentley Bridgewater introduced Angus to his musical friends, including Geoffrey Wright, ex-organ scholar, late of the Cambridge Footlights, now successfully composing music for film and stage shows.* Wright's Bloomsbury flat in Great Ormond Street was a popular meeting place – it was here that Angus first met Bunny Roger, journalist Nancy Spain and theatre director Frith Banbury.

Musicals offered a respite from the tedium of work and politics, and Angus, George Painter and other somewhat incongruous Museum scholars took themselves off to see Noël Coward, Nellie Wallace, Lupino Lane, Beatrice Lillie and Douglas Byng, the high priest of camp. Walter

---

* Wright had written for various revues, including *Charlot's Char-a-Bang* at the Vaudeville, *Let's Go Gay* at the Shaftesbury, and the immensely successful *Gate Revue* (March, 1939) at the Ambassadors, in which Hermione Gingold made her name.

Crisham, who had danced with Dorothy Dickson in Ivor Novello's spectacular oriental fantasy *Careless Rapture* (1936–7) at Drury Lane, and with Hermione Gingold in the *Gate Revue*, was a particular favourite. As war approached, the need for escapism grew.

Angus was beginning to feel the futility of political protest. Like many of his generation, he was never to forget the shadow of "the ghastly hysterical days of Godesberg and Munich". He had managed for years to keep himself distracted with "that most satisfactorily escapist of all activities – busy political work to prevent the coming of war – a world in which the menace did not seem quite real, because it was the current change of all our talk, a world where the terrible wood was never seen for the party political trees."[9] Despairing, he reacted against this useless agitation, and now set out to enjoy himself – going to parties, taking a holiday in Corsica, trying to have fun before the end came.

Crisis lurched into crisis. Spain fell to Franco. Mussolini took Abyssinia. Hitler had invaded the Rhineland, and despite Neville Chamberlain's desperate slogan of "peace for our time" (1 October 1938) Hitler continued to invade neighbouring territories, and London's ARP (Air Raid Precautions) continued to call for volunteers. Gas masks were issued, recalled, reissued. Trenches were dug in Hyde Park itself.

Trenches, gas masks, barrage balloons and sandbags confirmed the expectation of invasion. We would suffer this time as France and Flanders had suffered. And this war would add a new dimension of horror. Londoners were gripped with fear of aerial bombardment. There had been a successful rehearsal in the Spanish Civil War, and at the time of Munich bombs were still dropping on Barcelona and Alicante. Documentaries, leaflets and works of fiction had been prophesying this cataclysm for years, some with considerable relish – a whole new genre of The Gas Bomb Novel had evolved.[10] Taking off from H.G. Wells and his *The Shape of Things to Come* (1933), George Orwell, T.H. White, Henry Green, Graham Greene, John Lehmann, Stephen Spender, W.H. Auden, F.L. Lucas and Virginia Woolf looked up at the skies and shuddered.

Gerald Heard, that fast-talking polymath who had entertained the Westminster boys so pleasantly to tea, who had sat on so many platforms and written so many pamphlets and attended so many peace conferences, had come to believe his own propaganda: when war broke out, a modern city could be wiped out by modern technology in a day.[11] Resistance would be ineffectual. Europe was doomed. Heard, his friend Christopher Wood, and Aldous and Maria Huxley and their son had set sail for the United States on 7 April 1937. They left Britain to its fate. For years they had worked for peace, they had issued warnings in every possible form, but nobody important had listened.

They were the fortunate, prescient refugees, and they knew it. Others were propelled by more urgent circumstances. On 13 December 1938, a twelve-year-old Jewish refugee called Arnold Simmel arrived at Captain Wilson's school in Seaford. Ashampstead was to young Simmel a cold foreign world of barbaric ritual. Nobody spoke any German, and he spoke little English. He was mildly bullied as "a little Nazi boy", he got chilblains, and he was frightened of the fierce jokes of Captain Wilson. He did not like the "all boys" atmosphere, so alien to a Jewish child. He cheered himself up by developing a crush on Miss Sybil, and he liked working with the old gardener Boniface in the vacations. He studied the puzzling English class system in the form of Trixie who served in the dining-room: she had embarrassingly red painted lips, a troubling sensuousness, and spoke with a local accent. The other boys called her "ordinary". The unthinking contempt for what they called "ordinary people" intrigued him.[12]

Angus met Arnold Simmel at Ashampstead, and recognised him as a portent. It was no longer possible to be unaware of the future. Angus was with the Walkers at Maresfield for Easter 1939 when news came that Mussolini had invaded Albania. This new crisis seemed all the more dreadful because it reached him in surroundings that were associated with the good life. As in *Heartbreak House*, war was about to break into the idyll of country-house England. None of these erstwhile disciples of Gerald Heard thought they had much hope of surviving it.

THE SLOUGH OF DESPOND

Angus Johnstone-Wilson, temporary civil servant, was given a personal forewarning of the outbreak of war. On 23 August 1939, a directive came from the Home Office ordering the transport of valuables from the British Museum to hidden locations in the countryside. Packing was to start at 7 a.m. the next morning. Staff were urgently summoned to help by telephone or telegram. This was the moment, Angus was to recall, when "I knew, my God, I knew that it was coming."[1]

Contingency plans for evacuating art treasures from the metropolis had been discussed as early as 1933, and practical preparations made. Kenneth Clark, the patrician young director of the National Gallery, organised the removal of paintings from his and other public collections to various safe houses. Many went to Penrhyn Castle, near Bangor, in North Wales, a gloomy spot selected because it was remote, strong, dry, and had a door large enough to allow the passage of King Charles I on horseback, as painted by Van Dyck. Smaller works went to the National Library of Wales in Aberystwyth, where a bomb-proof and air-conditioned tunnel was being dug into the rock beneath the hill on which the library stood. And thither, too, went manuscripts and drawings from the Museum, along with the most valuable books from the King's Library. Larger items were to be hidden in the Aldwych Tube tunnel: yet others went to country houses in Northamptonshire. The newly-excavated riches of Sutton Hoo which had lain quietly beneath the earth for centuries had barely arrived at the Museum before they were whisked off again into a new hiding-place. This whole operation was superintended by Sir John Forsdyke, Director and Principal Librarian.

Angus was one of those in charge of overseeing the packing of container-vans. He also escorted the sealed vans to their destination in Aberystwyth and handed them over to a reception committee trained in fire-fighting. These were uncomfortable, worrying journeys on the Great Western Railway, shrouded in a secrecy which never came naturally to Angus, and delayed by Welsh stationmasters who refused to let trains run on Sundays. Hours were spent waiting in sidings or stuck in the Severn tunnel, cheered only by a bit of across-the-ranks camaraderie, and by the unintended comedy of a railway inspector who talked so much and so proudly of his brilliant daughter, bound to do well because she was "so unenterprising, so very unenterprising". Flashes of macabre humour lit a nervous dreariness of expectation that made one almost long for the worst to happen.

Aberystwyth was the end of the line, and it looked safe enough as it glittered in the August sun: the magnificent temple of a library, commanding the heights with a fine view over the bay, was to prove a landmark for German bombers, but they always flew safely over it to drop their cargo on Liverpool. The library kept its treasures safely, and even maintained scholarly access to the hidden books throughout the war. The British Museum was not the only instititution to entrust its possessions to the caves in the cliff: in the ensuing panic others followed. Some forgot where they had sent their archives. At the end of the war, some remained unclaimed. Some are there still. The townspeople whispered that the Crown Jewels were down there somewhere beneath the gorse, the ivy and the brambles.

The unreality of this lull before the storm was heightened for Angus by a strange interlude. War was declared on Sunday, 3 September 1939, and it caught much of the nation at the seaside, enjoying its summer break. The Morrises from Bilston had taken for a month a little wooden beach bungalow at Borth, a few miles along the single-track railway north of Aberystwyth. Borth was a quiet unpretentious family resort with a sandy beach set in rolling unspoiled countryside – bucket-and-spade and donkey-ride terrain. It was a glorious summer. Norman Morris and his brother Ronnie now had teaching jobs and could afford a self-catering holiday: they took with them mother and father, sister Sheila, and Cousin Doris to do the cooking. And there, for a week, Angus joined them, arriving by train to be met at the tiny station.

Where exactly did he arrive *from*? Did he turn up before or after his secret journeys to and from London – which, of course, he did not mention to his hosts? Norman Morris cannot remember. It seems likely that Angus's visit was not, geographically, a coincidence. Angus thoroughly enjoyed it, according to Sheila, helping Doris with the meals, and chattering away to all of them at tremendous speed. Did they discuss the political crisis? Not much, Norman thinks, or at least not *en famille*.

(Norman suspected that Angus thought Borth a bit ordinary – not quite Le Touquet or Eastbourne. Sheila disputed this. Both think Angus stayed for a whole week.)

Angus returned to London and the Museum, and the Morrises cut short their holiday when war was announced and drove back without headlights to Bilston and the black-out. Somewhat further east, brothers Pat and Colin, who had been teaching for the British Council and/or spying in Yugoslavia, in the company of many handsome sailors, had a more dramatic escape: they got out of Yugoslavia and into Egypt, and from Egypt made their way to India.

The Home Front was quiet. For a whole year nothing much happened to London or the major cities. Official evacuation of schoolchildren and private evacuation of the wealthy and the nervous took place, but most stayed put. Some hastened to volunteer, others waited to see what happened next. Old Westminster friend Francis Bailey was one of the first to disappear: he enlisted in the Royal Air Force in January 1940 and was killed in October of the same year. Work at the Museum continued as usual. It was all a bit of an anti-climax. The worst casualties were from people walking into things or falling downstairs in the black-out. In the bitter winter of 1939, deep snow lay in Russell Square. The doomed city waited. George Painter and Angus went to see Douglas Byng as Widow Twankey at Golders Green, and comforted themselves with a block of chocolate made of unsweetened cocoa. They went to visit Winn and Betty and the nieces at Seaford at Christmas, and found the school deserted, semi-derelict, also waiting. The South Coast readied itself for invasion with barbed wire and anti-tank traps: most of the schoolboys fled. Some stayed on, because they had nowhere to go. (Arnold Simmel was reunited with his family from Germany: his father had escaped from Dachau, and in March 1940 they all sailed to New York.)

Events in Europe – in Norway, Finland, then Belgium and France – were more dramatic. France fell, and the British scrambled away from Dunkirk. In August 1940, the Battle of Britain followed, as the Luftwaffe tried to wipe out the aerodromes and coastal radar stations of the RAF. Then, on 7 September, bombs at last began to fall on London. The first to hit the British Museum fell on 18 September 1940. It went through several floors but failed to explode. Others followed, and on 29 September the King's Library had a direct hit which destroyed 150 volumes. The Reading Room and the Students' Room of the Manuscripts Department were closed, and all remaining manuscripts were sent away. But the worst came on 10 May 1941, when, beneath a bomber's moon, many small incendiaries fell, causing uncontrollable destruction. It was what they had all feared. Forsdyke strode around bravely in a tin hat labelled Director. The Museum staff were trained in fire-fighting, but this was beyond them.

"The first roof to catch fire was that of the Roman Britain Room, and we had time enough to try all means of getting hoses down through the copper or up through the plaster before our attention was called to similar fires elsewhere. It was then evident that the task was beyond the strength of our night staff, and for the only time during the war we called in the London Fire Brigade. The Brigade sent eight pumps, but they could not all be brought into use on the available supply of water, and indeed no concentration of pumps and men could have prevented the roofs from burning out. It was rather a matter of putting them out when they fell on the floors, and none of the accessible floors were in fact damaged."[2] But by this time the books in the South-West Quadrant bookstack were ablaze, burning like a blast-furnace. Girders twisted like sticks of rhubarb. 250,000 volumes were lost by fire and water. The Reading Room, fortunately, escaped.

10 May was a night of many disasters. Not only books were lost. It was the worst night of the London Blitz. 1,436 people were killed, and 1,792 seriously injured. There were 2,200 fires, from Hammersmith in the west to near Romford in the east. "Next morning, a drifting cloud of brown smoke blotted out the sun. Charred paper danced in the woods thirty miles from the City. Churchill wept over the ruins of the House of Commons. A third of the streets of Greater London were impassable; 150,000 families were without gas, water or electricity. Every main railway station but one was blocked for weeks. Not for eleven days were the last pumps withdrawn from the fires, while exhausted civil defenders and a badly shaken population waited for the blow which must surely finish off the capital: the blow which never came."[3]

Angus, on the eighth floor of Endsleigh Court, overlooking the rooftops of Bloomsbury, was too near too many targets, including three main railway stations. For a while, he and a group of Museum colleagues moved north to Hampstead, where one of their friends, Peggy Reekie, had a flat. She was a Manchester-born graduate from St Hugh's, who had met Angus through fellow Mancunian Denis Barnes: she was also a close friend of Audrey Brodhurst, and had joined the lunch club at Oddi's. Before the war she had worked for Illustrated Newspapers, writing on fashion and telling young ladies what to wear to the hunt ball: Angus had loved her gossip from the Deb of the Year world. She had now moved on to more serious business at the Ministry of Information and the Board of Trade.

It was a little quieter at 21 Frognal, though still the sirens wailed. They could hear the rumbling of the trains on the little North London line, which they renamed "the strategic railway": it shook the very foundations of the house as it made its way from Richmond in the west to Hackney and Dalston in the east. From the Hampstead heights they could see the city burning below them. The house was a large late-Victorian barracks of a building, and it had eight or nine rooms each with its own little kitchenette or gas ring. There they gathered – Peggy Reekie, Angus Johnstone-Wilson, George Painter, Audrey Brodhurst, John Pattisson, Laurence Wood. An Italian woman called Pierina would sometimes cook for them, but George was said to prefer his own pickled herring. A previous resident had abandoned a piano and a mass of 1920s sheet music. Audrey played and Angus sang – he knew the lot, from his mis-spent youth. "Mercenary Mary", "Paper Doll", "Ain't We Got Fun", "Miss Otis Regrets", "I Want to be Happy", "Tea for Two", "Sophisticated Lady", "Bye Bye Blackbird" . . . Angus kept everyone's spirits up: he was the life and soul of the party. Angus, Peggy and John also played bridge through the night, relentlessly. This was not quite so popular with some of the others. Nerves were taut.

(George Painter, who had been bombed out of Mecklenburgh Square, remembers that Angus was very brave. Angus conversely remembered that he and George, "the two most openly frightened, retreated (quite absurdly) to the deepest cellars with the thickest earplugs.")[4]

Work at the Museum changed its nature completely. With the library closed to the public, it was brown overalls and gloves for everyone – even the women were seen climbing up and down ladders, clearing shelves, continuing the evacuation of books, working on salvage of damaged volumes.* A smell of charred paper, cloth and leather filled the Reading Room and spread to other parts of the building. They all got very dirty. The books were brought up from the basement of the South West Quadrant and spread out on the Reading Room floor, and everyone mucked in, including the Deputy Head Saleswoman Miss Knight (much imitated by Angus) and the keeper of the ladies' lavatory, Mrs Mainwaring. Mrs Mainwaring was a character, with her little fox fur, her little eye-veil, her unrealistically red hair and her outrageous stories from her previous incarnation as a theatrical dresser. Her conversation would swoop from the heights of refinement to the depths of obscenity, hardly registering the transition. She took a shine to George Painter and would cry out anxiously

---

* Alec Hyatt King's official diary for the period records that he started on salvage work on Monday, 12 May, working from 9 to 4: he was still working intermittently on salvage in December.

"Where's the boy today? Isn't he in yet?" Social barriers fell around them as the bombs fell.

Bentley Bridgewater took advantage of the war to run away from home. His mother had patriotically volunteered her house in Clareville Grove as an Air Raid Wardens' Outpost, and this was the last straw. Bentley decided he had had enough. He got on his bike and went. He cycled off and found himself some comfortable digs with landlady Mrs Elizabeth Baker in a village called Little Hadham, near Bishops Stortford, some thirty miles north of London. He commuted to the Museum daily by train. He was one of many who were moving out into what were jauntily known as "funk-holes" – when the house in Frognal was finally bombed and the water supply cut off, some of its inmates moved to Amersham, and George Painter went to King's Langley, while Angus joined Bentley in Little Hadham. The indulgent Mrs Baker took to Angus at once, and gave him the best bedroom on the ground floor.

Providence House was a welcome refuge from the air-raid shelters and battered buildings of London, from the surreal landscapes of the blanched and ruined city. An attractive, timbered, white-washed, seventeenth-century village dwelling, at one time the village school, it stood just a little way up from the bridge over the river. Beyond it stretched the rolling open country. A peaceful rural spot, almost eerily quiet after Frognal. Angus and Bentley visited the pub of an evening, where Bentley would play the piano. They were petted by Mrs Baker, a rosy-cheeked Mrs Tiggywinkle of a woman whose second husband ran a pub in Bishops Stortford; she cooked a good plain English meal, kept a coal fire burning, and entertained the boys with tales about her days as a bedmaker in Cambridge. She was easy-going, and she enjoyed a drink. Her large knickers flapped merrily unashamed upon the clothesline. There was only an outside lavatory, but the boys were comfortable enough.

Angus and Bentley were thrown much into one another's company, on the journeys in the blackout, on the long evenings in the village. Occasionally they were stranded overnight in London, when they would sometimes sleep at Geoffrey Wright's flat at 28 Great Ormond Street – from his windows they could see the talisman of St Paul's, still bravely standing. (One night in the war the pipes froze and burst and the staircase and the street became a waterfall of ice, remembers Ronald Crichton, a Christ Church friend of Bentley's.) And one night at Geoffrey's, Angus and Bentley found themselves in bed together.

This affair brought, at first, comfort and reassurance. *Pas de secrets de boudoir*, of course, but the news got about, and Oddi's lunch club accepted them as a couple. Audrey Brodhurst went out once or twice to see them at

Little Hadham, and George Painter, writing poetry and himself surviving an unhappy love affair, cycled over on his new bike. One weekend early in 1940 he and Angus walked for miles in the wintry twilight over the wet fields and low ridges of the undulating Hertfordshire countryside. Angus walked at amazing speed. It was by walking that he numbed anxiety and fear. George Painter took to the bicycle.

Painter's volume of verse, *The Road to Sinodun: A Winter and Summer Monodrama*,[5] evokes the emotional stress of those days. Overhead flew the bombers.

> Women hate me, but above,
> Wicked planes express their love.
> Over my bed the bombers drone
> And I never feel alone.
>
> Hark, the bomber beats above,
> Raven of eclectic fate,
> Bearing death to those I love,
> Passing over those I hate.

George Painter, like Angus and Bentley, had escaped to the country from the "couloir of burning and stone" after the break-up of the household in Frognal, and the poems were written in London, King's Langley and the Thames Valley: "Misted is the grey escarpment, dim with mist the aerodromes . . ." The very landscape of Britain was changed by the war, and those aerodromes spreading through the countryside were an ambiguous symbol: they simultaneously offered protection and invited wrath, they represented discipline and patriotism yet suggested the extended horrors of a new totalitarian era should Britain fall. Rex Warner's *The Aerodrome*, an interesting variant of the Gas Bomb Novel, published in 1941, is a disturbing Kafkaesque allegory contrasting the ruthless Fascist glamour of the Air Force — not, Warner hastens to assure the reader, *our* Air Force — and the muddled sensuousness of the Village — not, of course, any of *our* villages. Angus greatly admired this novel, which seemed to him to catch the mood of the pre-war years when the young had felt nothing but "disgust and scorn" for the muddles made by Baldwin, MacDonald and Neville Chamberlain, and some on the right had been tempted by the "siren song of a clean aesthetic society".[6]

Painter became a true friend and confidant to Angus in those dark uncertain days. Angus told him his family worries, and Painter, who had watched the slow decline of Daddy, consoled Angus when he learned that Winn Johnstone Wilson was also dying, a war late, of the old wound. (Winn was a "brilliant talker", recalls Painter, with his long stories of the

Fifth Army in 1918 – but "his dear sweet wife said hardly a word".) Winn died on 20 April 1941 (a month after Virginia Woolf's suicide, news of which had deeply depressed Angus) and was buried at Seaford with his father – "Captain Winn Johnstone Wilson of Ashampstead School. Died on April 20 1941 of wounds received 1915–17. Aged 48." The mainstay of the clan had gone, and Angus, the baby of them all, found the burden of responsibility fell upon him: he seemed to have become, somewhat prematurely, the head of the family. Betty Wilson faced a quarter of a century as a plucky widow.

George Painter cycled over to Little Hadham again on 21 June, 1941 – he remembers the date, for it was the day that Hitler invaded Russia. The war was not going well. It called for more and more manpower and womanpower. On 24 May HMS *Hood* had been sunk by the *Bismarck*, and down with it went Dragon Stevenson from Ashampstead. The British pulled out of Crete with heavy losses, the Japanese marched into Vietnam. More and more of Angus's friends joined the armed services.

Geoffrey Wright joined the navy, composing songs on the train to and from Chatham, was released for a while to write a film score for *Ships with Wings* and the music for a Cochran revue, *Big Top*, and then ended up in London in Naval Intelligence. John Pattisson served in the desert with the XII Royal Lancers, and Alan Campbell-Johnson joined the RAF and became a Wing-Commander. Anthony Beyts was already a veteran of the Rajputana Rifles. Others whose health or principles made them unable to fight became fire-watchers. Sandy Parnis, a friend of Bentley Bridgewater's from the Treasury, was treasurer for the Friends' Ambulance Unit during the war, and spent much time on the roof of the Middlesex Hospital watching out for flying bombs and V-2s. Stephen Spender, William Sansom and Henry Green also joined the Fire Service.

The Museum staff were being called up, their occupations no longer reserved. In the First War, nearly all the staff fit for military service had eventually been summoned. The same was happening now. Bentley Bridgewater was seconded to the Dominions Office. Laurence Wood had disappeared to an unknown destination early in 1941, amidst rumours that there was work available for linguists and scholars in some kind of Intelligence.

The unknown destination was Bletchley Park. Geoffrey Wright had also spent some time there and there both Angus and Bentley went, in the autumn of 1942.

Bletchley Park was one of the best-kept secrets of the Second World War. It is a secret no longer, and since Group-Captain F.W. Winterbotham broke the silence by publishing *The Ultra Secret* in 1974 many volumes have been devoted to its activities. Nevertheless, much of what happened there remains unrecorded, and not all accounts are reliable. And many of the official documents relating to it have not yet reached the Public Record Office. It is difficult to trace even one man's progress through this carefully constructed maze.

It is now widely known that Bletchley Park, a nineteenth-century country house in Buckinghamshire, was the wartime operational headquarters of the Government Code and Cypher School (GCCS).* The house and grounds, which stand roughly half way between Oxford and Cambridge in the dull brick railway-crossed midlands of England, had been purchased by the government in 1937 from its owner Sir George Leon, to house the School. GCCS had grown out of the Naval Intelligence Division, formed in 1886, which in 1917 had taken in civilian experts in decyphering. A group of cryptographers, enigmatically known as "Room 40" after their original workplace attached to the Old Admiralty Building, managed to remain intact in the inter-war period, although control was transferred from the Admiralty to the Foreign Office. The operation was moved from its shared accommodation with the Special Intelligence Services† at 54 Broadway Buildings, by St James's underground station, to Bletchley Park. Some new recruits were interviewed for work at Bletchley Park in 1938 before the Munich crisis, and then, after the Chamberlain agreement, told to go away again and wait. They did not wait for long. Some reported for duty promptly on 3 September 1939. Others had to make their way back from the seaside.

Here, behind the rapid sprouting of iron railings and barbed wire, unknown to any but insiders, an extraordinary team began to assemble. Their fields of expertise were curiously diverse. Here were crossword-puzzle addicts and chess players and bridge players and linguists and mathematicians and historians and statisticians and economists and archaeologists. Here were scholars of Greek, Latin, Anglo-Saxon and Chinese. Here were versifiers and actors. Dillwyn ("Dilly") Knox and Frank Adcock and Frank Birch, all three from Room 40 and King's College, Cambridge, were here. So were Alan Turing, a young mathematics Fellow from King's, and Patrick Wilkinson, Lay Dean of the same college: these two had attended their first 1938 briefing in London together.

---

* It was built by Sir Herbert Leon (1850–1926), stockbroker, Liberal MP, local philanthropist and cricket fanatic, descendant of a wealthy Jewish family which had come to England from Spain in the eighteenth century. The heir to the baronetcy is his grandson, the actor John Standing.

† SIS: also known to GCCS as "The Other Side".

It was a strange bunch, and Frank Birch was one of the more colourful figures of an eccentric collection. A conspicuous career as a theatrical undergraduate had attracted the attention of John Masefield, who had seen him in 1914 wandering around King's with a bottle of wine in each hand celebrating his famous performance as Face in the Marlowe Society's production of *The Alchemist*. Goldsworthy Lowes Dickinson had prophesied that he was a young man who might do anything, and he had. He served in the Dardanelles before joining Room 40, married the flamboyant Vera, a sister of Viscount Gage, in 1919, directed for the Marlowe while teaching history as a fellow of King's in the 1920s, gave a famous Widow Twankey in *Aladdin* at the ADC and the Lyric Hammersmith in 1931, and spent ten years acting, directing and writing for the professional stage. He was to be head of the Naval Section at Bletchley Park throughout the war.

Here, also, came a great many young men and women, from all three armed services and from none, who had very little idea of what was going on. They served in their own section, did their day's work, and went back to their billets. The last thing that was encouraged was intelligent discussion. The right hand must on no account know what the left hand was doing. To this day, some of those who were there do not know what their close friends were up to. Some did not understand what they themselves were doing. Some, later, were anxious to forget. Some thought that the local gossip which held that the place was the Lunacy Commission was all too apt.

The notion of Bletchley Park as war effort was suggested to Angus by fellow-cataloguer Laurence Wood, who had been taken on early at Bletchley Park, exempted from military service because of noisy lungs. Wood was invited to recruit amongst his old colleagues on the Museum staff. The Museum, like the Oxbridge colleges, was a potentially rich source of the right kind of brainpower – were not Alcaic verses, catalogue slips, ancient papyri and the Rosetta stone all forms of code? Recruiting for Bletchley Park was done by word-of-mouth, by Old Boy or Old Girl networks – a clutch of clever young women was secured through a senior cryptographer whose sister had been a fellow of Newnham College, Cambridge. Angus, who was weary of trundling up and down from Bishops Stortford on cold slow trains, often delayed by time-bombs, was willing to try.

He left no record of his original interview, though others indicate that this tended to be an eccentric, even perfunctory procedure. "Do you speak Italian?" one young woman was asked. "Only opera Italian," she replied. "That's quite good enough," she was told. And off she went. Another candidate was asked if he enjoyed chess. Off he went too. S. Gorley Putt's account suggests the style of the times: ". . . from the very beginning of my appointment to Naval Intelligence, there had been a puzzling mixture of formality and fecklessness. Summoned in early September of 1941 for interview at the Admiralty, after convoy service in a 1917 V-and-W destroyer, I had been conducted by a small female child wearing a pale blue crochet dress into the presence of Captain Haines, RN, and packed off by him to Frank Birch at Bletchley, who having discovered that my German was non-existent and my Italian Dantesque but hardly naval, accepted me without demur."[7]

Angus could offer good Italian, and in October he found himself in Bedford on what he fully expected would be an induction course to prepare for the highly specialised work at Bletchley Park. Here, he had a most unpleasant surprise. Instead of being welcomed by a like-minded group of scholars, he found that he appeared to be in the army. To be specific, he seemed to be in the General Service Corps. He was bewildered. What had gone wrong? For three days he wondered, and just as he was about to don some kind of uniform and vanish into the ranks forever, he was summoned to a higher authority and told he had been "sent for". And off he went, as he had originally expected, to a training course.

He never worked out what had happened during this three-day gap, but it seems more than likely that his name had got muddled up with that of his brother Clive, who had served in the RASC during the First War, was an Aide-de-Camp under Command and Staff in 1941–2, and was then re-employed as Inspector of Mechanical Transport by the RASC from 21 October 1942. It was a case of mistaken identity. With six brothers to choose from, such things might well happen. (Clive became Acting Captain on 17 July 1943, and chose to remain a Captain for the rest of his life.)

The initiation into the ways of GCCS was gentle. Bedford, the gateway to BP, was a more interesting and attractive town than Bletchley. Pleasantly sited on the River Ouse, it boasted embankment walks, punts, a large park, a Town and Country Club. It had some fine domestic and industrial architecture, good second-hand bookshops and a large Granada cinema. Its two most famous sons were John Bunyan and prison reformer John Howard, both connected in their different ways with the County Gaol in Silver Street: Bunyan had been shut up in it, from 1660–1672, and almost exactly a hundred years later Howard had inspected it. Bedford was a high-minded self-respecting little town, but it did not strike the trainee cryptographers as puritanical or claustrophobic. The punts reminded them of their Oxbridge days, and even with rationing the handsome Swan Hotel overlooking the river offered decent meals.

Angus put up at a small boarding-house near the bridge, and embarked on a course of cryptography (possibly supplemented by a language course in German or Japanese). It was like being back at school, and those who liked school could enjoy themselves. The courses lasted for a few months, and the age of trainees ranged from 18 to 38; Angus's fellow-students included Edward Boyle from Christ Church; Roland Oliver, a young historian from Cambridge; John Croft, a Christ Church Hinchcliffe Scholar whose Old Westminster tie Angus immediately spotted; and a twenty-year-old Welshman, Hywel Jones, who had just rushed through his degree at Corpus, Oxford, and demanded to be called up. (Jones's Italian wasn't bad, he says: anyway it was quite good enough for them.)

Hywel Jones and Angus shared the same digs and Jones made sure that Angus, as the senior, got the best room. This was a diplomatic move. Angus appreciated it, and took a friendly interest in the young man. Hywel Jones, a minister's son from Cardiff, had been brought up a pacifist, and his family had supported the Popular Front. Angus and Jones whiled away their evenings at the boarding-house talking of politics and sex. Angus made no secret of his own life: he expressed sympathy with the lonely lives of the sad queer commercial travellers who were their fellow lodgers, and reprimanded Jones for teasing them. He also informed the younger man of the dangers of public lavatories and of blackmail. Jones listened, enthralled, to this worldly discourse.

John Croft was an older and more sophisticated observer. He found Angus "fey rather than camp", with his tripping walk, his raffish and slightly down-at-heel appearance, his prematurely white hair – a chip off the old Fitzrovian block. Angus affected large, brightly coloured bow ties – orange, viridian, old rose, turquoise.[8] Clearly a camp – or fey – manner was not considered a security risk. Was not Frank Birch himself one of the campest figures of his day?*

The course over, off they went to Bletchley Park. Angus went into the Naval Section, in Block B of "Hut 8", to work on Italian naval codes, translating signals picked up by interceptors. Professor E.R.P. Vincent (Vinca) from Magdalen, Cambridge, was in charge. (Angus did not care for Vinca.) When Bentley Bridgewater arrived, shortly after Angus, he

---

* Nor were communist sympathies or membership of the Communist Party at this stage of the war a barrier, it should be noted: some felt they were rejected by Intelligence on political grounds, but there were many communist sympathisers at BP, and scientists like J.D. Bernal, whose views on the Soviet Union were well known, were in the inner ring of the British war effort.

went into the German naval section: Roland Oliver found himself working at the same table as Bentley at a frequently-changed German naval hand cipher used by tugs and ice-breakers. Boring work, thought Bentley. Mechanical, repetitive, and moreover somewhat undervalued, compared with work on the more glamorous German Enigma machine: the morale of cryptographers working on hand signals was not high.[9]

The phrase "Hut 8" was more a way of life and a description of a function than an address, as all the original huts had multiplied as Bletchley Park grew and the sections spread. Hut 4, with Frank Birch in charge, was also in the naval section, Hut 3 was in the Air and Military Section. (In Hut 3 worked a very young WAAF officer called Christine Brooke-Rose.) Hut 6 was where the cryptographers decoded, and other huts dealt with intelligence from these decodings. Huts 1 and 2 seem to have been either so dull or so secret that nobody mentions them. Joanne Woodward, who worked from 1941 to 1945 in "Room Seven", cannot even remember what Hut this was in, nor what she really did there: "I could draw a map of where we all sat, but am now not nearly so certain about what we all did. Even at the time the pattern was mystifyingly vague. There has been much praise of B.P.'s security . . . but I've always suspected its true basis lay in this very vagueness. Very few of us had any real grasp of what was going on, or of where our own contributions would be slotted in, let alone of what was involved in the work of the other Huts. Foreign interrogators would have had a thin time trying to extract information from us, the dogsbodies."

Working conditions were miserable, and the one-storey huts were gloomy and ugly. The original wooden ones were replaced by brick buildings, less draughty but no more attractive. There they worked, night and day, on round-the-clock eight- or twelve-hour shifts. The birthplace of the first computer started off from a very low technological base. It was a world of paperclips and sealing-wax and string, and Carpenter "Titch" was often sent down a hole to retrieve telegrams that had fallen by the wayside. Hut 6 and Hut 3 communicated by "the top high-sided box of a butler's tray, two kitchen hatches, and a broomstick. Hut 6 put the just decoded signs in the tray, shoved it through their hatch, and then banged on the inside of Hut 3's hatch with the broomhandle. A final later improvement was made when a piece of string was installed by Hut 3 so that the empty tray could be dragged back to Hut 6's side."

Work was intermittent: sometimes a flood of documents would arrive, causing frenzied activity, followed by a tedious lull. Clever young women who had volunteered fresh from university thinking they could help win the war found themselves bored out of their minds as they sat on Z watch sorting out decoded messages for the index of the library store. The atmosphere was claustrophobic, the food in the canteen was unimaginably horrible. Who wanted reheated yellow cabbage and dried-egg omelettes filled with spaghetti or bright yellow slabs of NAAFI cake with seeds in it at three in the morning? The Joe Lyons Individual Fruit Pies were known as "targets for tonight" but they were hard enough to find, for it was not easy to locate the canteen itself as you stumbled across the Park grounds in the pitch dark.

The big house was used only by the very top brass. A few ducks hung on from the previous régime, floating aimlessly around on the little ornamental lake. And Bletchley itself, unlike Bedford, was not an attractive town. Pevsner comments bleakly, "There is no perambulation needed of Bletchley." Patrick Wilkinson complained that if you wanted to go for a country walk, it was always the same walk – to Shenley Church End and back. Kingsman Christopher Morris, with a keen eye for topography sharpened by study of Celia Fiennes, considered it "no kind of a place, no kind of a place at all." (He shook his head sadly as he reiterated this.)

A few lived on site in "a horrid little hostel built for single girls", where the talk was of unwanted pregnancies and clothes–swops. Most were billeted in the neighbouring villages in pubs or private homes. Some were in caravans, some were in Woburn Abbey, where a batch of Wrens slept in bunks in the Duchess's bedroom, with the bell-pushes marked MAID, EMERGENCY, HIS GRACE. The chess-players C.H.O'D. Alexander and Stuart Milner-Barry, heroes of the Enigma story, were at The Shoulder of Mutton in Old Bletchley. Gorley Putt was invited to join Patrick Wilkinson at The Duncombe Arms, on Bunyan's Hill of Difficulty at Great Brickhill: it was run by a Mr and Mrs Frank Stabb who kept two large pigs called Roosevelt and Churchill, and one Christmas they had Churchill's liver for breakfast. Many of the billets had no running water and no indoor lavatories: Alan Pryce-Jones recalls that his little brick cottage at Fenny Stratford on Simpson Road was "icily cold" in winter, and of "a workday ugliness which evoked high praise from John Betjeman."[10] It was all very makeshift, and finding a good billet tested survival skills. John Plumb, the gifted and ambitious son of a Leicester clicker, was yet another Cambridge historian who became a power at Bletchley Park: he stayed for a while in a billet with Donald Lucas but soon found it more convenient to move ten miles out to the Rothschilds at Ascott, near Wing, where he dined on unrationed lobster and game instead of on whalemeat stew. Plumb had a talent for finding himself in the right company, and he was at home with the Rothschilds, who were big in

Buckinghamshire: Ascott was only one of their several stately homes in the county.

Angus was billeted a couple of miles outside Bletchley, in the village of Simpson. Simpson lay beyond Fenny Stratford, over the level crossing and under the railway bridge, down by the hump-bridged canal. He was placed with a gardener's widow, Mrs Emily Hill, who lived with her schoolmistress daughter Nellie in an old cottage in the middle of the village. He slept in the bed vacated by her son Arthur, unfortunately taken prisoner-of-war by the Japanese: Arthur, a regular soldier, had been about to come home when war broke out and caught him in Singapore. Angus felt he was the cuckoo in the nest. (Cuckoos always interested Angus.) When Bentley arrived at Bletchley Park he was first placed in a pub, but then managed to find a room in Simpson in a council house with the milkman and his wife.

Others who found their way to Simpson to puzzle and amuse its old inhabitants included Professor Hinsley himself, later Bletchley Park's historian. He was remembered as very polite and generous with his sherry. A young couple, Tony and Trudie Perkins (he from Hut 6), were at the Mount in Simpson: it was good to be in with the Perkins, as they had a bath with hot running water, and would let you use it if you were nice to them. They also had a telephone and a baby: Angus would borrow the former, and entertain the latter with animal noises.

This was Angus's second stretch of village life, and he found that Mrs Hill was a very different character from the easy-going Mrs Baker. Mrs Hill was devout and attended the thriving local Methodist Chapel. She deplored alcohol and wished the young men would not go to the pub. She protested at a vocal rendering of the Indian Love Lyrics with Bentley at the piano: "Less than the dust beneath thy chariot wheels" was pagan stuff. She read local author Bunyan's *Holy War* regularly, and also, rather guiltily, the more sensational works of Mrs Henry Wood, relishing what she called "the superstitious bits". She could not stop Angus's incessant smoking, although she tried, making "dry little chapel coughs" every time he lit up. She noticed that he had a tendency to get very overwrought. She also discovered that although the queer little chap was obviously very brainy, he was not really very practical. He hadn't a clue about everyday things. He couldn't ride a bike, for instance: Mr Bridgewater's was far too big for him, and when a kind young lady called Pamela Griffiths tried to teach him to ride hers on Gypsy Lane on the way out to Wolverton, he just couldn't really seem to get the hang of it. He had to stick to those camouflaged buses. Sometimes he would absent-mindedly set off for work in his pyjamas. Mrs Hill tried to cheer him up with her treacle puddings. He had some terrible tantrums. Sometimes she could hear him screaming in his bedroom.

Treats, these days, were few and far between. Once there was a duck, collected by Angus from the Bates at Orchard Cottage, where Nellie Hill's young man, an electrician called Albert Baden Powell, was lodging.* "I've come for the duck," piped Angus, in his unforgettable squeak. Pamela Griffiths remembers Angus arriving one day with a knob of garlic, the first she had ever seen. He had been presented with it by a woman friend in London.

Pamela Griffiths was a quick young Italian graduate working in naval technical intelligence. She was a wizard at crosswords and picked up Japanese in no time: Angus encouraged her to learn to cook, commenting helpfully one day upon her potatoes: "I think they're nicer with the eyes taken out, don't you?" She garnered the hedgerows for salads and discovered supplies of rabbit. She and Angus became good friends, and she would often walk him home. They would visit The Rising Sun or The Leather Bottle for a gin and orange, or treat themselves in The Railway Inn at Bletchley. (Here Bentley Bridgewater celebrated his thirtieth birthday, and Christine Brooke-Rose her twenty-first.) The cheese omelettes in the café next to the Odeon weren't bad. And they would talk of books: he educated her, chattering away with what seemed superficial brilliance of Anglo-Saxon history or George Eliot, Jane Austen or Virginia Woolf. She realised as she listened to him that it was the superficiality that was superficial.

Yes, there were diversions. Some really enjoyed life at Bletchley Park – the games of rounders on the lawn, the tennis on courts provided at Churchill's own command, the record concerts, the madrigals on the banks of the Grand Union Canal. Lack of transport was a problem, but you could make your own amusements, just as though you were in a prisoner-of-war camp, and occasionally visiting artistes came who were amazed by the discrimination of their audience – Maggie Teyte, Dorothy Dickson's daughter Dorothy Hyson, Cecil Day-Lewis all did their turns. The amateur theatricals were particularly lively: Bill Marchant (later Sir Herbert) put on the annual revue, and Pamela Gibson, a professional actress who had turned down a part in repertory in Lillian Hellman's new anti-Nazi play *Watch on the Rhine* to work at Bletchley Park, found herself directing a production of *Pygmalion*. Social events were organised by a spirited young Irishwoman called Caroline Linehan.

* Nellie Hill (Ellen Hill) married Baden Powell in 1946, had two children, and then returned to her career as a teacher: she taught in Simpson until retirement.

Even the Home Guard provided entertainment. The sheer incompetence of some of these clever chaps when confronted with a simple exercise was impressive. It was amazing that none of them killed themselves as they blundered about the grounds at night hooting and pretending to be owls. It was a miracle that Bletchley Park suffered only one casualty – a self-inflicted bayonet wound in the upper thigh. Security too provided some mirth: there was said to be a notice saying "In case of fire, ring for the Fire Brigade, but on no account tell them where the fire is." Baden Powell recalls that all summons for electricians to go to BP were treated as high priority, but you could never say where you were going, or why – "Nobody breathed a word."

There were love affairs and emotional dramas. Marriages were made and broken. Here Neville Masterman met his wife, Brenda Tongue, a BP sergeant and Anglo-Saxon linguist. Here Christine Brooke-Rose met and married her first husband. Caroline Linehan was to marry historian Roland Oliver. Here the poet Henry Reed, who wrote some of the best poems to come out of the Second World War, met Michael Ramsbotham. The poet F.T. Prince and his wife Elizabeth Bush were both at Bletchley Park. Some of these unions lasted: some did not. As Gorley Putt writes: "In the hot-house secret confinement of Bletchley Park, personal relations were as grotesquely falsified as in an Iris Murdoch novel. Sexual infatuations and personality clashes alike became obsessional. One after another, in one way or another, we would all go off our rockers. Some would be sent to absent themselves from felicity awhile in discreet rest-centres where they could babble o' green fields without betraying secrets. (Absences of any kind, whether caused by mental or ordinary physical ailments, meant extra mind-stretching hours for the survivors – for one can hardly replace overnight a cryptographer when messages start to flow or a top secret intelligence officer when enemy forces advance or set sail.) We shot up and down from elation to despair and back again. Nerves tautened to breaking-point by round-the-clock speedy exactitude would fumble, in off-hours, for emotional nourishment."[11]

This was the darker side of a kind of determined good humour. There were many emotional casualties. Some confessed to dreadful nightmares. Although themselves safe from attack (only a few bombs fell accidentally in the neighbourhood during the entire war) they knew what was happening to London. They knew more of what was happening abroad than those who relied on censored newspapers and deliberate disinformation. Ships were sinking, men were dying in the desert. Angus dreamed of drowning in polar seas. Only a handful of them could feel that their own contribution was individually worthwhile. Bletchley Park was claustrophobic, dead-ended: once you were in, it was rumoured, you could never get out. It was not every day that Churchill turned up in his boiler suit to thank you for helping to sink the *Bismarck*.

Camaraderie and co-operation were not universal. There was a great deal of naked careerism, of quarrelling over status and rank, of petty malice and jealousy. Christopher Morris was to note chronic tensions between cryptography and intelligence: "To the intelligence officer, cryptographers were apt to appear as unworldly, absent-minded, eccentric, ill-dressed academics. To the cryptographer, the intelligence officer could appear to be too political by half and often as a shameless empire builder."[12] Angus reacted to this atmosphere with distress: he found his new career a rat race. This was a larger, fiercer world than the Museum, and he felt intellectually outclassed by the pure mathematicians, by the trained and keenly competitive minds of the Cambridge dons.

★

It is now impossible to reconstruct the details of Angus's working life at Bletchley Park. Accounts vary. Some said he sat conspicuously on a raised platform overlooking a posse of Wrens – *hundreds*, one claims, but more probably thirty or forty, as Angus himself would say. They were working away on an enormous index of naval codes. (Some, in contrast, remember him hiding away in a small side office, no bigger than a filing cupboard.) The posse included debutantes, bright young graduates, and "call-up" girls – a potentially explosive social mix. Occasionally Angus seems to have been let out to go to teach on an induction course at Bedford – this is the impression he later gave to Ian McEwan.

How important was his work? Some say it was routine, "somewhere way down the line": others claim it was high-powered. One enthusiast believes that Angus Johnstone-Wilson and Bentley Bridgewater between them won the war: according to this source, Angus was a "complete memory bank", an expert on Japanese call-signs who could identify from meaningless groups of alphabetical jumble an air station 300 miles north of Australia or a supply base in the Phillipines. He had a computer in his head: it was not surprising that he had to disappear to BP's special rest home in Devon for a while.

Did his Wrens love him or hate him, pet him or tease him? They called him Johnnie-Willie to his face, but what did they call him behind his back? Had he overheard the word *Nanny*? These girls were not all sweetness. They nicknamed Henry Reed "Millicent". Angus always had sharp ears for hearing the worst about himself, could pluck insults from the air. One of the Wrens, on her first interview with him, thought his falsetto voice was affected as a joke, and replied in kind: she was embarrassed when she discovered her mistake. Ann Dent, niece by marriage of Raffles Tucker at the British Museum, and in charge of her own small group of Wrens and a map with coloured drawing-pins, assumed from telephone conversations that "John Willie" was a girl, and was taken aback when she confronted him in person. Unlike many of the young women, she never fell under the spell of his charm – she felt that he played the spoilt child, that he flattered his flock and tried to gain their sympathy by gazing up at them winningly from his large blue eyes. (Her attitude to him may have been coloured by the fact that she once overheard him holding court in the next hut as he made devastating fun of Uncle Raffles, Aunt Phyllis and her cousins.)

Angus had always been subject to tantrums, and now mad fits of rebellion boiled up in him. On one occasion he insisted on smoking in a non-smoking compartment of a train, and invited a court case rather than put out his cigarette. He knew this was crazy, but he did it. He refused to accept authority. He hated the rules and the shift system. He was furious because Bentley was on nights, he on days. How dare Bletchley Park mess up his private life in this way? Did it do this to married couples? The endless files of pointlessly circulating paper enraged him. There was no sense in any of it. All these not-very-secret Top Secret messages with labels like Ultra/Zip/Zg/303, all these call-signs from halfway round the world – it was so important and so dull. He had never cared for crosswords, for intellectual puzzles. They gave him no satisfaction.

Stories began to circulate about Angus's outbursts. He had thrown a bottle of Quink at a Wren.* He had thrown a large book at a Wren. He had beaten one lady on her flat little chest like a tom-tom when she had asked him why he was in such a hurry. He had torn out handfuls of Bentley's hair. He had hit Bentley on the head with a copy of *Middlemarch*. He had quarrelled with Bentley about his sweetie rations. He had ripped a tablecloth from a restaurant table. He had torn up official papers and scattered them round the room like rose petals. He had assaulted a young female officer on Bletchley station, hitting her on the knees with his suitcase. He had been seen weeping as he sat on the steps of the cinema. He had run round the lake. He had jumped into the lake. He had jumped naked into the lake.

These were the stories, and there was some truth in them – save, perhaps, for the last, which almost every personal memoir of Bletchley Park repeats in one form or another. Run round the lake he may have done ("Johnstone-Wilson's running round the lake again" became a euphem-

---

* Ink-spilling incidents occur twice in his fiction – in the unfinished fragment *Goat and Compasses* and in *As If By Magic* – which seems to support this story.

ism for his losing his temper) but his nakedness has surely been invented, as no eye-witnesses have come forward: all versions are second-hand. But his state of tension was noticed by all who dealt with him. You couldn't miss it. It even had permanent signs. His lip was scarred from an accident caused by — well, the official version was that he had walked off the end of a station platform or fallen into a hedge during the blackout, but insiders knew it was the result of beating against Bentley's windows late at night while drunk. He had broken the glass and fallen through. Or something like that.

His Wrens tried to look after him, and gave him nice cups of tea made with that awful dried milk. They got him double rations of tea buns — one for Wren Johnstone, please, and one for Wren Wilson. They did their best. They did not like to see him sitting on a bench staring at the river like a crazed man, with great dark rings round his eyes, when they knew he could be so amusing, so delightful, so understanding of their own problems. Mrs Hill also endured his weeping and wailing and shouting with equanimity. He used to fly into a rage when Nellie Hill called Bentley "Bent". That was *his* nickname. Bentley belonged to him.

★

The great storm was, it seems, precipitated by a row that Angus engineered between Jack Plumb and Jack's friend and ex-teacher, Bert Howard. Both Plumb and Howard were from Leicester: Howard had been accepted at Bletchley Park on the recommendation of C.P. Snow, who was now in charge of the allocation of scientists and other civilian personnel. Herbert Edmund Howard, Like Bowle (though in very different style), had been one of those teachers who changes lives. He was the intellectual talent-spotter of Leicester, and Plumb was one of his star pupils at Alderman Newton's School, where Snow himself had just missed being taught by him. Snow had, however, become a close friend of Bert Howard, and they had spent much time together drinking in the pubs of Leicester.

Born in Norfolk in 1900, the son of a postmaster, Howard had been at the King Edward VI Grammar School in King's Lynn, then had got a First Class degree at King's College, London. In the 1930s he published a history text book and several pseudonymous thrillers (as R. Philmore) for Gollancz, and took part in many extra-curricular activities — he also edited the school magazine (in which Plumb published short stories), ran the chess club and the debating society, and, more dangerously, took groups of selected boys sailing on the Norfolk broads with the Green Wyvern Club. He appears in the Snow novel sequence "Strangers and Brothers" as the unorthodox and charismatic lawyer and WEA lecturer George Passant. Snow's prophetic portrait is of a "big fish in a small pond", an unworldly sensualist whose notions of freedom court and eventually precipitate disaster.

Passant is an oversexed heterosexual, who spends his time with prostitutes in Nottingham and with a crowd of young people from his home town at a nearby country retreat. In real life, Howard was, according to Snow, polysexual, with a growing and eventually uncontrollable interest in young boys. Years later, in the 1960s, Snow was to help Howard to leave the country for Holland when he was threatened with prosecution for seducing the son of a prison warder — but even at this stage (and after Howard's death in exile at Hilversum in 1963) Snow remained inexplicably loyal to Howard's memory, extravagantly insisting that Howard "was one of our great men of genius, one of our real men of genius. When still quite a young man, at age 55, he was still infinitely more useful to us in the war than any General. He had this taste, and killed himself with it. Don't think that he wasn't surrounded by people who'd have made themselves blue in the face to get him anywhere in the world."[13]

At Bletchley Park, the story goes, Howard and Plumb were very close. Plumb, who built himself a successful power base at Bletchley Park, was one of Frank Birch's deputies, and Angus's superior, and Angus had a tendency to resent superiors. Plumb thought Bentley and Angus were lazy. "Angus was like a fifteen-year-old child." Angus, Plumb said, sowed dissension. Who can tell, at this distance, what went on? The situation was inbred, claustrophobic, hysterical. It got out of hand. Angus was on the verge of a serious breakdown.

Something had to be done. Angus was offered leave in a convalescence or mental home — some say he went to a naval rest home at Holne in Devon, or to St Andrew's Hospital in Northampton, where the poet John Clare had once been treated. Angus's own version is that he rejected hospital internment: he says he was taken to see "a private mental home in Oxford — a stately hall, I remember, filled with the war's nervous casualties, all very genteel and middle class they looked to me, playing progressive ping-pong. And wouldn't I feel happer to join them? No, I wouldn't and I refused the suggestion again and again. I should stay on and pluckily do the job."[14] But he agreed to see a doctor in Bedford, who arranged for him to make a twice-weekly visit to a psychotherapist, a Dr Rolf Kosterlitz, in Oxford.

Angus was fortunate to receive such a civilised recommendation. Many fared worse. Wartime had produced a range of psychiatric troubles and neuroses in the civilian population as well as in the armed forces, and a recognised treatment consisted of pumping patients full of drugs in the hope of producing a therapeutic "abreaction". Sometimes it worked, sometimes it didn't. It was all a bit hit-and-miss. Angus, already heavily dependent on sleeping pills, was perhaps lucky to escape more dramatic medication.

Psychotherapy was also hit-and-miss. Churchill, predictably, did not think much of "trick cyclists", as psychiatrists were known in military slang. And psychotherapy could be as dangerous as the wrong medication. In 1939 Angus's old acquaintance from OUDS, Terence Rattigan, depressed by the short run of his new play *After the Dance* (only 60 performances!) elected to see a Dr Keith Newman of the Oxford City and County Hospital, with bizarre results. Newman (originally Odo Neuman, from Austria) advised Rattigan to give up his pacifism and join the RAF, which Rattigan, mesmerised by this strange figure, did: Newman then in turn became mesmerised by Rattigan, and claimed to have superintended and attended every single performance of the indirect result of Rattigan's RAF experiences, *Flare Path*, a play which had a long run in 1942–3 at the Apollo.*

Angus's therapeutic encounters were less dramatic. Bentley would accompany him on the train to Oxford, and sit in the waiting-room of 110B Banbury Road while Angus talked to Kosterlitz. Sometimes a young woman from the Italian Section, Elizabeth Wyndham, would travel with them; she went on a different healing mission to play the piano in Oxford with Ernst Gombrich's sister. Elizabeth was one of those young debutantes whose social standing intimidated the mainly middle-class intake: a member of the Egremont family from Petworth, her uncle was First Lord of the Admiralty. She got on well with Angus and Bentley, and sympathised with Angus's hysteria. She knew he knew he needed help. "He was always so frightened," she remembered.

Angus gives an account of this period of breakdown in *The Wild Garden*, written nearly twenty years later. He describes his self-communing in the long dark Methodist evenings at Mrs Hill's, when even books would not serve as an opiate. "And the communings were painful, for in the organization in which I worked by day I was one of some thousands, and I

---

* Newman wrote up this obsession in *250 times I saw a play*, Pelago Press, Oxford, 1944: a sequel to his *Mind, Sex and War*, 1941. He claims to have given *Flare Path* its title.

soon learned that the weapons by which I had gained my way in the past were inapplicable to so large a community. I put up a good fight – indeed it still astonishes me that so many adult people responded to my childish methods before I had to give in; but in the end my will was defeated, and this was the more galling because my will was by no means an ill will, on the contrary it was often very sensible, very hard-working, and friendly towards others to the point of sentimentality. Such a defeat would have been bad enough, but I also fell really in love for the first time – perhaps my father's death three years before had liberated me – and I painfully learned that I had far too little capacity for anything except demanding in such a relationship . . . Although I suffered from an acute and hysteric anxiety state I continued to try to win approval and to gain my wishes by carrying on at work – an example of an ambiguously desirable 'pluck' learned from my mother . . . But what matters at this point is that this defeat finally forced me to rearrange my experience of life in imaginative terms, to try to make sense by making fictional patterns." He goes on to say that he also discovered for the first time "that I could hate intensely, if not for long periods, and that I was capable of cruelty, indeed addicted to it, particularly towards those who attracted me most strongly."[15] The lid came off the panic that had been packed down since his childhood, and it broke loose. The ice cracked.

This account condenses a struggle stretched over months, indeed years, into a few paragraphs. It is impossible now to reconstruct the chronology of breakdown and recovery: he probably could not have done it himself, had he wished to. He did not like to talk about Bletchley Park, although he never tried to conceal his breakdown. Years of official secrecy inhibited analysis, and much is irrecoverable.* But we can make some kind of a guess as to what went on between Angus and Dr Kosterlitz.

★

Rolf-Werner Kosterlitz (1906–1989) was one of many intellectual refugees who made their way to Oxford. He was the son of a doctor, Bernhard Kosterlitz, and he was educated at the Kiel-Gymnasium in Berlin: he had passed examinations to graduate at both Berlin and Freiburg, but was unable to take his degree "for political reasons" – i.e. because he was Jewish. He left Germany in 1937, and came to Oxford with his mother. (His older brother was to become a Professor in the University of Aberdeen.) In 1941 was admitted as an advanced B. Litt student at New

---

* GCHQ were unable to help with information about Angus's medical history: they acknowledged he had been at Bletchley Park, but their records had his birth date wrong by ten years.

College, giving his nationality as Czech. Somewhere on the route to Oxford he had lost an eye: his remaining eye stared piercingly through a monocle.

He began to practise as a psychotherapist while working on his D.Phil. on "The Problem of the Ego". He described himself as a Jungian, and encouraged his patients to keep dream diaries. He made a valuable collection of paintings and tribal artefacts, but seems to have been a lonely and eccentric figure in his long exile, credited with a "difficult" personality: he attached himself to odd philosophical and religious societies. One of these, the Psychological Study Group, was run by Doris and John Layard, a psychoanalytical couple influenced by Jung and deeply interested in the psychosomatic nature of illness.*

Layard, in 1940, had undertaken a Jungian analysis of a fifty-four-year-old countrywoman and had encouraged her to record and to sketch her dreams.† His subject, "Mrs Wright", dreamed interestingly and obligingly; the crucial symbol was a sacrificial hare, but her dreams also include fears of air raids and an encounter with a friendly German pilot. "She was a little puzzled about the 'friendly' German until I pointed out to her that almost everyone was now having dreams about friendly Germans, this representing the esoteric complement to our overt defence against their attack. The spirit called forth by their attack and our defence against it was regenerating an England that sorely neeeded it, and in this sense Germans, by attacking us, were indeed proving our best friends." (p.72) In similar optimistic vein, Layard interprets a dream of an air raid on an open courtyard as "indicating the powerful spirit of God descending out of the clear heavens upon man".

Kosterlitz seems to have employed a similar technique with Angus, encouraging him to record his dreams. Angus kept his dream diaries with some relish, and, characteristically, made a public joke of them. "These are my dreams," he would tell his friends, showing them a lined exercise book full of pencilled notes. Everybody got to know about his dreams. One of these notebooks survives, in twelve fading, stained, partly illegible pages of handwriting.

The notes refer to several identifiable characters – his brother Fred, Daddy/Father (both terms are used, and he appears many times), Dr K.,

* Layard (1891–1974), a social anthropologist, had a bizarre early career: he was an early friend and very briefly a lover of W.H. Auden, whom he had met in Berlin in 1928. He was himself a wounded healer, and had been through a complete breakdown followed by a period of paralysis. Auden was fascinated by him.

† Layard wrote up this successful analysis in *The Lady of the Hare* (Faber 1944). A promised sequel never appeared.

Mrs Baker, Mrs Hill, Geoffrey, Winn, Bentley, Bentley's landlady Mrs Matthews, Jack Plumb, Perkin, Forrest, John Pattisson, Nelly Hill, niece Jane and one of his more supportive Wrens, Rona. There are some one cannot identify: Ruth, Mrs Feather, Jill Dent, Hugh, Lisa, and several others. (Jill Dent may be intended for Ann Dent, and Mrs Feather is more than likely to refer to a feather-brained, dithering middle-class comic character created by South African-born radio actress, Jeanne de Casalis.) Who is Mr Mayne, whose name appears several times in a somewhat threatening context? Angus also refers to known places from various periods of his life: Earls Court; Hadham; Thurloe Square, where his friends Viva and Willie King lived; Dolphin Square, where his friends the Wormalds had taken a flat; the Adelphi, where brother Clive had lived. The dream plots revolve round several theatrical events – a meeting in a mental institution, a hotel room, a meeting on the steps of South Kensington Underground, an air raid and fog in Thurloe Square, an air raid at the Methodist Chapel, a children's party, a scene with a woman murderer from Dundee wearing a red blouse, a cinema visit which turns into a trial, a musical reception. Churchill and Stalin both surface, and references to war, communism, Trotskyites, bombs, fires, the ARP, sirens are frequent. There are some not very explicit sexual references – to sodomy, to two nancy boys, to two arty-tarty boys.

One confusing sequence about "a german run" and "transport bounds" gives rise to a query about confidentiality: was Angus allowed to discuss his work with Kosterlitz? How much did Kosterlitz know about where Angus was working?

Some lines are not within the dream sequences, but are notes from the conscientious dreamer to himself:

> Tell Dr K about Friday's two temptations to rage. 1. Jack's notice. 2. B's getting up later.
> To tell Dr K. B. says I am acutely concerned with poss social inferiority.

There are also some sections that make sense within themselves:

"I am with Arthur, he is my employer instead of Jack. I suggest I may have to take off work for some hrs in next days he asks what on earth is wrong. I say I may be temperamentally unstable. He says not good enough, he himself could be temperamentally unstable any day he liked. Would I like to take a few days off to meet my beloved (A. sarcasm type) if such could be managed – I say A. there *is* no beloved away from here, it is B. I tell A. I regard his integrity as as great as his lack of sympathy and rely on him to say nothing."

Others have a different interest:

"I am making a necklace from string fox terrier and two rats – rat & rat's mother – rat's mother no use but cannot offend her by saying so – will use all rats for rest of necklace as cheaper – fox terrier in control (as me) as strain oneself when pulled out by thread, this strain allows me to reject mother rat without offence – ie I am sufferer too – I am pulling necklace thread straight have to brush my cheek by dog, fear next by rats – weaker struggling to get my head away."*

Angus was a rich and abundant dreamer all his life. He provided Kosterlitz with a wealth of material. Kosterlitz's record as a healer is obscure and he has left few traces in Oxford or elsewhere. But in the kingdom of the blind, the one-eyed man is king. Faced with this interesting, white-haired, baby-faced, desperate, fluent, plucky, weeping, amusing young-old man, he made a suggestion. Your dreams are interesting, Mr Johnstone-Wilson, he said. Why don't you try to write some short stories? Why don't you join a Writer's Circle?

Angus's version of events is that he did indeed join a Writers' Circle in Bletchley, but when he read the contributions by his fellow members and was asked to write one of his own, he was so depressed that he decided not to bother. Well, he did have a go at it, perhaps, he admitted, but when he showed them to Perkin Walker, Perkin told him he was writing pastiche Dickens, so he gave up. And then Kosterlitz said, who not try painting instead? Or collect wild flowers?

★

In the flat below Kosterlitz, in the large brick double-fronted house in North Oxford, lived a more orthodox young scientist and lecturer, Peter Medawar, with his wife Jean and their three children. Jean Medawar wrote: "No 110 Banbury Road was divided into three flats: the top flat above us was soon occupied by the Kosterlitz family . . . Dr Kosterlitz was a psychoanalyst and until he was rounded up as an enemy alien, Peter

---

* On the last page of the notebook is a highly eclectic reading list, which includes Wordsworth, Berlioz's Autobiography, Arthur Symons and J.A. Symonds, Hardy, Yeats, Eliot, Trollope, Meredith and Shenstone: Angus read voraciously during these years. On the Bishops Stortford train he claims to have read Keats's letters, *Aurora Leigh*, Diderot's *La Religieuse*, and *To the Finland Station*. The only contemporary item in his list is William Plomer's *Autobiography* (i.e. *Double Lives*: Cape, 1943) – a work which he would have found of particular interest, as Plomer, ten years older than himself, was the son of a remittance man who was sent off in mild debt from Yorkshire to South Africa in 1895, took part in the Jameson raid, and then turned sheepfarmer. Young William, born in Pietersburg, spent his childhood between "the rush of sensuous experience" and the touch of warm brown skins that meant Africa, and prep schools back in the English countryside: like Angus, he paid tribute to the Zulu houseboys, "warm-hearted, warm-blooded beings, handsomely made, and perfect in their goodness to this child."

sometimes played chess with him. This entertainment was mixed with frustration by Dr Kosterlitz's habit of asking if he could take a move back 'because I have made a mistake'. A fairly steady stream of patients made their way up the stairs for treatment. Peter was already sceptical about the therapeutic value of psychoanalysis and saw and heard nothing from the top flat to change his views."[16]

Her daughter Caroline's memories are slightly different. She recalls no difficulties over the chess board, and used to enjoy going upstairs to see the Kosterlitzes. Caroline Medawar, now Caroline Garland, is herself a psychoanalyst.

Was Kosterlitz ever rounded up as an enemy alien? Possibly, but if so it must have been for a brief period during the panic of June 1940, when thousands of German Jews and others of alien origin were interned in camps – most famously on the Isle of Man – or deported to Canada and Australia. Many were released after a matter of months, following strong protests in the press and Parliament – although in October 1941 there were still 6,928 "Category C" (i.e. "No Security Risk") aliens interned in the U.K. Kosterlitz, if he had been behind barbed wire, had not stayed there for long.

Many years later, Angus discovered Kosterlitz's last bill. It was for five guineas, or some such small sum: it turned up inside a jacket pocket or folded inside a book. It was unpaid.*

---

* Dr Kosterlitz, still living at 110B Banbury Road, died intestate on 18 September 1989: the *Oxford Times* (8 December 1989) reported that a "treasure trove" of paintings, tribal artifacts and furniture had been found in his flat, and the *Oxford Magazine*, Fourth week, Trinity Term, 1992, in an article on refugees called "Exile in Oxford" by J.M.Ritchie, mentioned that "Three hundred paintings . . . were auctioned raising £122,335."

9

THERAPIES AND CONVALESCENCES

Dr Kosterlitz provided official therapy: others provided a more informal variety. BP was not a prison or a high-security asylum: it was possible to get out for a night in town or a week on leave. Wrens got on their bikes, hitched lifts on military transport, and braved the gropings of licentious soldiery on darkened trains. Angus and Bentley managed to get to London from time to time to enjoy the reviving hospitality of Viva King, or to call on Honoria Wormald.

Before the war, Angus and Bentley had been frequently entertained by these two women, both of whom were wives of Museum colleagues: Viva, wife of Willie King and Honoria, wife of Francis Wormald. Honoria and Viva's social circles overlapped. They did not much care for one another.

The Wormalds lived before the war at 14 Mecklenburgh Square, Bloomsbury, where they were already famed for their somewhat eccentric hospitality: both had a habit of falling asleep after dinner, and Honoria would wake suddenly, observe her guests struggling to maintain a conversation, and cry out "Oh, what a refreshing snooze!" or alternatively, to Francis, "Don't *snore*, Crocky!" Francis was sometimes a little slow with his prized cocktail-shaker, and Honoria, born to money and married to money, was on the careful side, but despite this they were persistent entertainers. Honoria wore the same evening dress and rode the same bicycle for decades, and once was discovered trying to serve a bargain offer of non-alcoholic communion wine. But secretly they were immensely generous. They had no children of their own and gathered around them a group of talented people in whom they took a parental and occasionally overbearing interest – artists, aesthetes, scholars, priests. Charles Ginner, Edward Le Bas, Hermione Hammond, Ivor Jones and young doctor Patrick Woodcock were of their entourage. They lent money to these protégés, bought their books and their paintings, advised them on their curtains, told them when they needed to use deodorants.

Francis came from a wealthy woollen family from Yorkshire, and was one of two sets of twins – the older were boys, John and Francis, and the younger were girls, Anne and Ellen. Their mother died when they were children, and the boy twins were informed of this at Eton: Francis was to remember going home for the holidays that term, to find for the first time nobody on the station. (They were all a little frightened of their father, Thomas Marmaduke Wormald. It had not occurred to him to meet his motherless sons.) Francis, widely known as Puff or Puffy, became a distinguished palaeographer and liturgist, first at the Museum and then at King's College, London. Others confess to calling him Wormie: "Wormie – we always called him Wormie – was *very very* clever, but he never made you feel stupid. He was always full of jokes, such a *jolly* man" – or so said Mrs Basil Creighton.[1] Honoria, his cousin on her mother's side, was born Honoria Mary Rosamund Yeo, the daughter of a barrister: strong-willed and outspoken, handsomely white-haired in her twenties, she defied her mother's disapproval and studied medicine, taking her second MB in 1935 – the year in which it was discovered that Francis had Bright's disease and might have only months to live. This was also the year of their marriage. Both were devout churchgoers, combining the highest of principles in great things with the broadest tolerance of what they considered peccadilloes. A threat of a death sentence concentrated the mind. They were progressive, egalitarian intellectuals, with strong but personal moral views combined with a deep respect for artistic creation. To discourage artistic ambition was, for them, the sin against the Holy Ghost.

Francis, a neat, precise, dapper, pink, bouncy, sexless little man, was thought by some to have a doppelgänger who was a nun, occasionally to be seen of an evening in the twilit square. As a boy, he had liked to play a game in which he was Mother Superior and his twin sisters were naughty nuns.

In 1941, bombed out of Bloomsbury, the Wormalds moved to a flat in Beatty House, Dolphin Square. Honoria, who lost a brother in the bombing, joined the Red Cross, and Francis moved from the Museum to the Ministry of Home Security to make Civil Defence films. He also became a member of St Paul's Watch, dedicated to the preservation of the cathedral – a building which miraculously survived the war unscathed. With such distractions, they entertained somewhat less, spending alternate weeks with friends in Essex and Hertfordshire, but they did not forget their large brood of lame ducklings. Honoria sent Angus postcards at Bletchley, and she it was who presented him with the treasured knob of garlic.

Testimony to their goodness comes from the painter, Hermione Hammond, who was at the Frances Holland school with Ann and Ellen Wormald. Hermione's mother had taken a kindly interest in the old-fashioned, motherless girls, and Francis and Honoria Wormald in turn took care of Hermione Hammond when she suffered a severe mental breakdown during the war. She had been rushing manically around the country inspecting billets for the Ministry of Health when her own health gave way, and she found herself in hospital – for a spell in St Andrew's, Northampton, then in Wembley. "I was absolutely cuckoo," she claims. Puff and Honoria (Puff bullied by Honoria) were her most faithful visitors, and sustained her during these grim patches. They invited her to Dolphin Square, when she was out and about, and it was there that she met Angus. He at once recognised a fellow sufferer, and did much to restore her battered self-esteem: inviting her out to dinner, listening patiently to her woes. (According to Vincent Brome, for many decades an habitué of the Reading Room, it was Francis Wormald who paid for Angus's visits to Kosterlitz. This would certainly have been in character.)

Honoria Wormald's salon was a meeting place for invalids. She liked people she could help. She preferred them to the independent. Her Christmas parties were notorious for their bizarre combination of screaming queens and lame ducks.

Viva King was a more flamboyant figure, and her entertainments, though perhaps equally therapeutic, were less decorous. (Viva thought Honoria was a bit of a frump.) Viva was an opulent beauty, with a clear pink-and-white complexion: such perfect skin, her many admirers never fail to note. It was perhaps the more remarkable in contrast with the pickled complexion of her husband Willie, whose nose beneath his marmalade hair resembled a whiskered raspberry. Her Sunday salon at 15 Thurloe Square attracted a crowd of devoted if occasionally waspish acolytes. Like the Windmill, it never closed – well, hardly ever – and like the Windmill, its attractions were sometimes on the louche side.

Viva King was the Queen of queens. She was dubbed by Osbert Sitwell "The Scarlet Woman", or "The Queen of Bohemia". Her family background was somewhat irregular. The Booths were landed gentry from Yorkshire, whose money had mysteriously disappeared over recent decades. She had a non-practising barrister grandfather, uncles who were remittance men, a divorced aunt, and lord knows what other skeletons in the family cupboard. Her mother, like Angus a child of the menopause, was a granddaughter of the writer Captain Marryat. She herself was born in Mendoza, Argentina, and christened Dorothy Elizabeth Leonora Ursula Booth, although she was always known as Viva.

Her parents separated when she was a girl, and Viva was given a Convent education in Bruges, interspersed with extremely secular visits to her father in Paris. Her account of him, to one acquainted with Willie Johnstone-Wilson, sounds oddly familiar: "His Savile Row clothes became old, but they never looked it . . . we would sometimes find in the *Tatler*, on the 'Priscilla in Paris' page, a photograph of him at the races. And once, 'Captain (sic) Booth takes a stroll in the Bois . . .' For a time he wrote sporting articles for the *Westminster Gazette* and covered the Carpentier-Wells contest. He also found the racecourse profitable . . ." His friends were trainers and jockeys, and for a while Father himself became a horse-coper at Compiègne. "Practical jokes and tall stories were, in his period, the height of wit . . . He would tell long stories in the first person, 'I once knew a Hottentot girl who . . .' It is strange now to think that anyone had the time or patience to listen, but I noticed that his yarns went down with much laughter and merriment and made him very popular. I had sometimes read 'his' story that same morning in his copy of the *Pink' Un* (the *Sporting Times*)."[2]

Did his friends eventually tire of this "shady and deceptive" sponger? She suspected so. She also recognised that he was "too fond" of her and attributed her own diverted sexual development to the experience of being chased around the furniture by him and other elderly gentlemen with moustached lips smelling of bear's grease and whisky. (She implies that her father went further than the chase.)

Back in London, her mother opened a private hotel in Kensington – one of those hotels so familiar to Angus from his own youth. After a disastrous spell as a governess, Viva joined her mother in this enterprise, branching out as a maker of costumes for ballet and opera. She got to know everybody, was invited out everywhere, was painted by Augustus John, spent her time at parties, began to give parties. She met Ronald Firbank and Djuna Barnes. She was an adventuress in Chelsea. (She was not very pleased when, years later, reviewing her memoirs, Angus Wilson referred to her, admiringly, as a Becky Sharp.) After various brief amours (one with the composer Peter Warlock who later committed suicide) she became engaged to Willie King, and married him in August 1926 at a point when he found himself in transit between the Victoria and Albert Museum and the Ceramic Department of the British Museum. ("We moved, without violence to our senses, into an affectionate intimacy.")[3] His parents had money, and she hoped they would die soon. They did not approve of her – despite or because of the fact that Willie's father Colonel King showed a dangerous tendency towards being "too fond" of her. Together, she and Willie embarked on a brave partnership.

Viva loved the outrageous. She was generous and cruel, malicious and tender-hearted, motherly and fiendish. She liked the famous (the Sitwells, Somerset Maugham, Augustus John) but she liked the infamous too. She collected people – the rich, the ambitious, the artistic, the suicidal, the slightly crazy. The unashamed raincoated pederast Norman Douglas was one of the stars of her salon. (Willie became his literary executor.) Ivy Compton-Burnett and her friend Margaret Jourdaine were often to be seen. Beverley Nichols, Ernest Thesiger, Simon Harcourt-Smith, Isobel Strachey and Madge Garland joined the throng. Mrs Frances Watson, whose withered brown Egyptian visage betrayed decades of cat-worship, would come to seek homes for stray moggies: if Viva's network failed, she would advertise in the Personal Column of *The Times*. Nina Hamnett would arrive at four, a good half hour before the other guests, in order to start drinking on time. And Angus and Bentley were among the regulars.

Angus was first taken to Viva King's in pre-war days, or so he recalled, by Una Pope-Hennessy, author of a biography of one of his father's favourite authors, Agnes Strickland.* It was a successful overture. Angus and Viva had a great deal in common. Her house in the square signalled to him like a beacon during the blackout. He escaped when he could from the Slough of Despond and the Bletchley of Boredom to Vanity Fair. Stumbling there one wartime night in a thick fog, Angus was accosted by an elderly gentleman of military bearing. "Madam," he said. "I see you are lost. May I escort you?" And he took Angus's arm, saw him safely to Viva's door, bowed, and departed without another word. On another occasion, after leaving Viva's he found himself standing with a weeping Norman Douglas at a bus stop outside South Kensington station: Douglas was attracting the sympathy of motherly old ladies in the queue with his heart-rending sobs, when all of a sudden he looked around him, brightened up, and declared "I think this is where I had my first suck-off!"

This is a characteristic Thurloe Square story. Viva's entourage was the source of scandal and gossip and everything connected with her was heightened in the telling. Her name was legend. It became a password in the homosexual underworld: "Oh," people would say, "I didn't know *he* was a friend of Mrs King's." Two stories are told of her and Angus: one, that she proposed to him that she should have a child by him: the other, that one evening when alone with him upon the brown velvet sofa she suddenly threw herself upon the hearthrug, passionately solicited his advances, and, to render her offer irresistible, extracted from her person a

* Dame Una Pope-Hennessy, d.1949, mother of James and John Pope-Hennessy, and author of works on Dickens, Scott, Poe, and the French Revolution.

bloody tampon which she flung upon the fire with the cry "I'm not too old, you see! There's life in the old dog yet!"

Willie King's advances were also unorthodox. One young man from Bletchley Park recounts that he was propositioned over the dinner table by Willie King in the immortally seductive words of Catullus: "*Pedicabo et irrumabo!*" (Catullus, 16). And Viva, on an evening at the opera, cried out to this same young man "Oh, look at those curtains closing! Just like a little anus!" Viva and Willie King were both outrageous. That was their attraction. Viva was seriously interested in underwear, in gussets and suspenders and fastenings; she possessed a pair of Queen Victoria's drawers, and introduced Angus to a fascinating fetishistic semi-pornographic weekly magazine called *London Life* which took off where the *Gentlewoman* ended. It advertised Gentlemen's Corsets and "rare books", ran articles on "The Appeal of Macs", and stories with titles like "What Sadie Knew". What on earth would Mrs Hill and Bunyan have made of all this? No wonder Angus felt that Mrs Hill looked at him as though he were a member of a different species.

Willie King, like Francis Wormald, was a true scholar. He may not have looked up to much, with his red nose, his scrubby orange hair, his mottled hands, his skinny dried frame and jerky walk – like a monkey on a stick, one friend remarked. But he was the Real Thing. He was a true eccentric, famed for walking briskly to work every day like clockwork across Hyde Park to the Museum from Thurloe Square reading the newspaper through rain or shine, the pages sometimes disintegrating into papier mâché in his hands. He was a very heavy drinker, though opinion divides on whether he favoured sherry, gin, rum or whisky. (Perhaps he drank the lot.) Was he the right man to have in a Ceramics Department? It seems so. Famously, he never dropped a piece. (Or so one legend has it. Another records that he would sometimes cry out "I'm sick of all this fucking rubbish!" and sweep a pile of priceless pots from his desk to the floor.)

He had romantic family connections (the Byrons, the Lovelaces) and an upper-class insouciance. When war broke out, he completely ignored the blitz, refusing to acknowledge the existence of air raids. He nobly drank himself into a stupor every night and passed out. Viva joined the WVS, and then the Red Cross, where she found herself, to her indignation, being bossed about by Honoria Wormald. Willie applied for MI5 but was sent with the Royal Artillery to a gun site in Liverpool: Hermione Baddeley, who was there entertaining the troops, was amazed at the manner in which he took to the spartan life, sleeping on a camp-bed with blankets. He was transferred to Carlisle as Education Officer, and thence made his way to Bletchley Park, where he was reunited with Angus and Bentley

Bridgewater and other friends: he spent one day and night a week in London with Viva. He was famed for the military precision with which he planned ahead for his drinks while changing trains at Bletchley station: the instructions were that three (or four, or five) double gins (or rums, or whiskies, or sherries) were to be lined up for him on the bar counter. He would toss them back, one after the other, and then stride stiffly upon his way to catch the train to Wolverton.

*

Viva King and Honoria Wormald were both well aware of Angus's precarious mental state at this period. And so were others. At one point he was invalided home to Seaford, where Winn's widow, Betty Wilson, was now struggling to run a small pre-prep school. Ashampstead itself had been taken over by the pistol-happy Canadian forces, who made free of the place, indulged in domestic target practice, and kept themselves warm by lighting fires with a lot of old papers up in the attics – Johnstone-Wilson diaries, letters, scrap books, mementoes. When the house was bought up at the end of the war, it was in a terrible state.

Angus had visited Seaford several times earlier in the war – once or twice with Museum friends, to camp out at Ashampstead with a bottle of Empire Sherry and a partridge provided by Fred. (On one of these occasions, they all had terrible colds – physical as well as mental health was at low ebb.) Nobody can remember whether Angus attended brother Winn's funeral in 1941: Seaford, along with much of the east and south coast, was designated as a "Defence Area", not to be visited for "holidays, recreation or pleasure" – even for a funeral you needed a special permit and there were military police on the station, waiting to arrest you, or so it was believed. An eerie sense of semi-desertion prevailed: Elizabeth Bowen's short story, "Ivy Gripped the Steps", which Angus much admired, evokes a similar resort: "The houses at the sea end of the avenue had, like those on the Promenade, been requisitioned; but some of those at the theatre end stayed empty. Here and there, portions of porches or balustrades had fallen into front gardens, crushing their overgrowth; but there were no complete ruins ... effects of blast, though common to all of Southstone, were less evident than desuetude and decay ... in the shuttered shopping streets along the Promenade, in the intersecting avenues, squares and crescents, vacuum mounted up."[4]

In June 1943, despite her mother's premonitions ("She'll never get married, living with that lot," Betty Wilson had told schoolboy Michael Pitt) Jeanne Wilson married Glyn Davies in Seaford, wearing an old evening dress decorously refurbished for church with sleeves made from some yards of white material provided by Peggy Board-of-Trade Reekie – a useful friend in the days of clothes coupons. Angus attended the wedding and gave her away – this was a true war wedding, for Glyn Davies immediately disappeared into the army and did not see Jeanne again until the war was over. (When they were reunited in Canterbury, so much time had passed that they were not sure if they would recognise one another.)

Angus's later appearances in Seaford were less festive. They were during his treatment by Kosterlitz, for he went armed with his dream notebook. Jean Rickwood, an old schoolfriend of Jeanne and Sybil, had returned to Seaford to help Betty while her husband was stationed in North Africa: she had a daughter, Anne, born in January 1942, with whom Angus was very friendly – they used to go for walks together, jumping in all the puddles, and would come back soaking wet. Angus, who loved to give people nicknames, called her "Piedie". Angus seemed quite normal to Anne and the other schoolchildren. (Michael Pitt remembers his kindness and generosity – Angus treated him to his first Pimm's, he recalls, though this must be a post-war memory.) But Jean Rickwood knew all about Angus's breakdown – she could hardly avoid knowing about it, for from time to time he would bang on her bedroom door, wake her up, and insist on telling her his dreams.

He would also go for long, long walks alone, over the Downs, past the dew ponds. Once he walked over to Glyndebourne. And he would tie his belt around his raincoat and drag it behind him like a dog.

Were these periods of official convalescence? Pamela Griffiths at Bletchley received a postcard from Angus in Seaford, dated October 1943, with the message "Feeling so very much better and hope to be with you soon." This is one clear date in a period of misery that extended over years.

★

Angus made at least one other long recuperative holiday away from Bletchley Park. He was invited to Scotland by his early surrogate mother from Westminster days, Helen Pattisson.

Helen was one of the three celebrated Gillespie sisters of St Andrews. Daisy married well and disappeared to live in Weybridge: Helen married a solicitor, Edmond Langshaw Pattisson, who, as we have seen, left her a young widow with two tall sons: Madge, an old Girtonian, made her home in St Andrews, where for many years she most effectively taught mathematics to the girls of St Katharine's School. Her teaching methods are still remembered there, as is her nickname "Gollie".

Madge Gillespie lived at 15 College Street, a couple of minutes' walk from the University, in a small and pretty house that fronted directly onto the street, and there Helen joined her for long periods during the war: John was off with the Desert Rats, and Alister, who had just taken his degree at St Andrews, was working on a farm as a conscientious objector. (He was a gentle man: "*Please* do move over," he would implore the cows.)

The suggestion that Angus should convalesce in the bracing East Coast Scottish sea air must have come from Helen. But Madge's small house could not accommodate him, and two doors along the street at Number 19 (with the date 1622 engraved over the door) the Wardale family turned their only child Carol out of her bedroom into the boxroom in order to take Angus in as a paying guest. (They needed the extra income: a university lecturer's pay was miserable.) Carol did not resent his intrusion: on the contrary, she enjoyed Angus's company and his breakneck conversation, and had many a game of ping-pong with him. Like Jean Rickwood she was treated to some of the secrets of his dream diary. She was still in her mid-teens, but her parents always talked about everything in front of her: she was aware both of homosexuality and the holocaust, and recognised at once that Angus was inescapably, in her view biologically, queer. (At times she too heard him weeping in the night.)

St Andrews is a finely situated town, where Angus met with much long-remembered kindness – as did many Norwegian and Polish refugees who also found their way there. "The Polish Boys", as they were affectionately called by the locals, were warmly welcomed, and 82 of them entered the university in 1942–3, with waived fees and crash courses in English: most of them were in uniform and on Army pay. (Some were called back to their Army units in 1944: others went on to graduate.) But despite these acts of wartime generosity, the academic community in St Andrews was small, conservative, ingrown and isolated. It was still customary to change into evening dress for dinner, and in College Chapel the congregation was divided by rank and sex. Horse-drawn omnibuses survived, and the old university porter, bent double above a barrowload of books as he battled his way against a stiff wind, offered a nineteenth-century spectacle. But it also housed some citizens with strong, even radical views.

Angus was lucky to find in Byoon and Kling Wardale (*sic*: what extraordinary names and sobriquets Angus's friends possessed!) a couple with advanced opinions – Kling Wardale was a German scholar who had been a member of the PPU until a pre-war visit to Prague had opened his eyes to Hitler's real intentions. The Wardales were good friends of their neighbour Madge Gillespie, who was a formidable character and a personality in the town – austere, no-nonsense, independent, scrupulous, bridge-playing, plainly dressed, but of an evening bejewelled. "A bit of a dragon," some said. She was certainly not a churchgoer: she left her body, rather inconveniently for her nephew, to Science. (He was put out when, months after her death, the medical school rang and asked what he wanted done with "the bits left over".)

Her sister Helen was also a character. She was "of striking and original appearance, with nut-brown skin, dark hair, and large, expressive eyes. Uncommonly tall, she had her clothes made at Liberty's in a C19 style the Brontes might have worn, and wore them till they were beyond repair. Striding along in her dark blue broadcloth coat with its coachman's cape, her sable muff, her buckled hat and shoes, she had the air and character of 'Shirley'. She sang well, though rarely in public . . . her interest was in Scottish ballads and traditional Scottish and French songs."[5] Her two sons were also very tall.

Helen, like the heroine of Angus's story "Totentanz", brought London ways and London Library books back with her to College Street. She filled the window-ledges of No.15 with flowers, played the virginals, taught young Carol Wardale to sing, and introduced her to gin and lime. Later, Helen gave Carol a silk stole and the fur coat in which she was married. She was famously generous. She brightened up her sister Madge, and became a close friend of Carol's parents. But not even she could reform St Andrews single-handed.

Angus was to catch the distinctive character of its academic community in a not wholly flattering manner in the opening sequences of "Totentanz", which owes its setting to this war-time visit.

"In their sub-arctic isolation, cut off from the main stream of Anglo-Saxon preferments, sodden with continual mists, pinched by perpetual north-east gales, kept always a little at bay by the natives with their self-satisfied homeliness and their smugly traditional hospitality, the dons and their wives formed a phalanx against spontaneous gaiety that would have satisfied John Knox himself." But on a bright day, he concedes its beauties: "The Master's lawns, surfeited with rain and mist, lay in flaunting spring green beneath the deep even blue of the July sky. The neat squares of the eighteenth-century burghers' houses and the twisted shapes of the massive grey loch-side ruins recovered their designs from the blurring mists. The clumps of wallflowers, gold and copper, filling the crevices of the walls, seemed to mock the solemnity of the covenanting crows . . ." Perhaps wisely, he concealed his location by transforming the famous warm scarlet of the scholars' gowns into pale blue.[6]

Angus ate with the Gillespie-Pattissons, slept with the Wardales. The cuckoo was welcomed into a warm nest in St Andrews. But Bletchley Park beckoned him back.

★

His last year at Bletchley was enlivened and complicated by an extraordinary new arrival. Angus's relationship with Bentley Bridgewater was pursuing its occasionally troubled but never-ending never-to-be-ended course when in upon them both burst a terrible and disruptive new force, in the form of a brilliant young man called Ian Calder.

Ian's sister Rosemary Calder was one of Angus's more recently recruited Wrens. She had arrived at Bletchley Park from Nottingham and had fallen under Angus's spell. She was a lively, sociable, indeed irrepressibly energetic and talkative young woman. She had left school at sixteen, at her mother's insistence, and had made her way via a secretarial course, studies in Social Sciences at Nottingham University College, and various ladylike odds and ends to the freedom of the huts and public houses of Bletchley Park. Many a drink and many a laugh there was at The Rising Sun or The Leather Bottle: it was wonderful to be away from her mother, although she also found herself separated from her young man, Ian Merry, who was off in the navy. But Angus's company made up for a great deal. In October 1944 she wrote home in glowing terms of Angus, who "is the sweetest thing and spoils us all and we spoil him too." She was delighted to be with him permanently, which means "that I never do nights, only days and evenings." Her bit of the war was Bermuda: the Japanese war was drawing to its close, and she thought it an honour as well as a pleasure to be in Angus's room, where all the brains were. It was a power-house. It was a think tank. "Anything difficult, take it to Angus's room!" He got the cream.

Rosemary Calder had a hunch that Angus would hit it off with her older brother Ian, who was now in the RAF, waiting for the war to end to return to Cambridge.* She was keen to introduce them, and thinks they may have met first at Bletchley Park in February 1945 at her birthday party. (She was only fifteen months younger than Ian.) Or was it a little later in the year? Anyway, at some point in 1945, Angus and Ian came together, took to one another, and did not look back.

Ian Calder, like Angus, was famous for talking. He was also a remarkable-looking young man, small, strikingly blond, with hair that stood on end like a ziggurat. He has been described as a destroying angel, a boy with chocolate-box good looks, a Shelley, a genius, a doomed Faust, a spoiled teacher's pet, an arch procrastinator. He was generous, sweet-natured, erratic, gifted, idealistic, impractical. Nobody who met him forgot him, and those who liked him liked him very much. Ideas excited

* Ian Calder, born 23 October 1923. He had already spent a year (1941–2) as an exhibitioner in History at Caius.

Ian Calder intensely, and he would declaim from Blake or Marlowe with unstoppable zest. He was restlessly swept by new enthusiasms. He had no sense of self-preservation at all.

This bright young boy with the blazing hair exploded into Angus's life like a comet. Angus was instantly captivated by him, and so, it appears, was Bentley. As the war drew to an end, their three-way friendship intensified. If Angus had been emotional about Bentley Bridgewater, he was now passionate about Ian Calder. The scene was set for the dramas of the Little Hadham Experiment.

THE WRONG SET

One would have thought that Angus would have been eager to escape from Bletchley Park and all that it had meant to him. But he hung on for a few months after the war, somewhat to his own bewilderment. He did not know where to go. And at the moment of leaving "terror seized me completely. A friend was leaving the same day as I, so together we gave a party to all our colleagues who had been so friendly, and with me, so patient. In the security guard's hut we gave it, outside the wires, so that we could leaven the occasion with London friends and avoid shop talk. We drank rum and orange and beer – the wartime luxuries . . . There amid the bright chatter and the filthy drink and the spam rolls, I suddenly knew that what I longed for was that one of the security guards should take me by the arm and lead me back into the hated compound for a safe life sentence, never to leave again. But it was too late. I was free."[1]

The attractions of the General Catalogue were not overwhelming. Angus and Bentley – the Heavenly Twins, as their Wrens had called them – contemplated seeking a career elsewhere, but eventually both of them found themselves where they had been years earlier – living with Mrs Baker at Little Hadham, and commuting to the British Museum. Bentley was back in the Director's Office, but Angus found himself redeployed on a new task: that of replacing the quarter of a million books lost by bomb damage. It was more enjoyable than sitting all day at a table, and from October 1946 he had the company of an agreeable young man called O.W. "Tim" Neighbour, who helped him in his mission and listened to Angus's chatter about the contents rather than the bindings of books. Together they rummaged around post-war London of an afternoon, persuading antiquarians to dig deep in dirty basements, and occasionally finding an unexpected treasure or a cache of books outside London.[2] The twenty-three-year-old, himself in bad shape after being obliged to abandon a university education at Cambridge, knew all about Angus's reputation for excitability, but found he kept his outbursts for the evenings. Angus and Tim Neighbour encouraged one another, talking of Victorian and French literature, seeing one another through low patches. It was reconstruction work, on more levels than one.*

Although the war was over, Britain was rationed, dull, and full of unsorted rubble, broken relationships, broken ambitions. Some regretted the end of their wartime service: Angus had had a bad war – miserable to the point of despair, unhappy in his work, and apparently unpromoted within the Bletchley Park hierarchy – but others had done well. For Christine Brooke-Rose, Bletchley Park had been an education, and a spur to further achievement. (The form of her cryptographic novels surely owes something to decoding at Bletchley Park.) Gwenda David, one-time Lady Reader in the Reading Room, had been amazed to find herself recruited to the BBC and working there on equal terms with equal pay (£450.00 a year, no less) along with Geoffrey Grigson and William Empson. Old Mertonian poet and scholar Douglas LePan had had a glorious war, first as a gunner in Italy with the First Canadian Field Regiment, then in the diplomatic service in London: in civilian life he found himself missing the masculine camaraderie of battle.

The end of the war brought no irresponsible surge of high spirits. This was the age of austerity, the time of the snoek and the rook. The atrocities of Nazi Germany were revealed as worse than the worst of fears, and human nature stood condemned at Nuremberg. Faith had failed, liberalism had failed, humanism had failed. Christian Science, Maud's refuge, had failed even more dismally than other creeds, and Angus came to see its favour in the 1930s with Nancy Astor and the Cliveden Set as an ominous marker on the way to war: "the optimism with which Lady Astor's world approached the question of changing Germany's heart, however well-intentioned, was in the circumstances frivolous as well as disastrous. I was brought up as a Christian Scientist and I know well the unreal sweetness that hangs around that Church. It would be hard to choose a creed – and it was that of Lady Astor and Lord Lothian – better fitted to play into the hands of Hitler's gang. It is never, I suppose, very wise to deny the existence of evil, but it was peculiarly unwise from 1933 to 1939."[3] Evil may not have triumphed on the battlefield, but neither had it died in the bunker. It left a huge question-mark hanging over the very concept of progress. The self-delusions of self-styled progressive thinkers were to be one of Angus Wilson's favourite targets.

---

* O.W. Neighbour went on to a degree at Birkbeck and a distinguished career with the Museum as a musicologist.

★

Post-war life, however, had gained considerable colour through the
addition of Ian Calder. Angus and Bentley Bridgewater did not exactly
fight for possession of him, for that was not their way: instead, they entered
upon what Bentley called the Little Hadham Experiment – a *ménage à trois*
at Mrs Baker's, where Bentley, Angus and Ian attempted a three-way love
affair. Ian Calder was now back at Cambridge, but he spent weekends at
Providence House. The situation was disturbing, emotional, electric.

Angus and Bentley were not the only contenders for Ian Calder's favour. His mother was also determined not to relinquish him. Molly Calder (*née* Alice Maud Fyson, from East Anglia), large, strong-willed and
manipulative, dominated her headmaster husband and was unwilling to
lose her grip on any of her three children. Towards the end of the war
she had been with the WVS in Europe, but she now returned and bought
a house and farm in Suffolk, the White House at Mettingham, with five
acres and a kitchen garden where she kept ducks and cows and pigs. A
Canadian lover also seems to have been associated with this deal. (Mr
Calder, meanwhile, was thinking of becoming a vicar.) There were to be
endless dramas and struggles for possession of Ian, and Mrs Calder was
quite a fighter. She was desperate to hang on to Ian and Rosemary, creating tremendous scenes when either of them showed signs of independence, jealously accusing Rosemary's fiancé Ian Merry and his brother
Loudon of battening on her hospitality, jealously resenting Angus's influence over Ian. When she did not get her own way she would throw a fit,
in Marshall and Snelgrove or some other conveniently conspicuous spot:
she was said to have hurled herself down the stairs on the day of Rosemary's wedding. John Wain was to describe her as "a Clytemnestra of the
provinces". She was one of those Monster Mothers who simultaneously
delighted and horrified Angus. Angus and Bentley often went to the
White House on visits, where Bentley would soothe Molly by playing to
her upon the piano and Angus entertained her, Ian and Rosemary by making
up stories about their county neighbours, the Bogus-Smiths. (Angus enjoyed
inventing these appallingly memorable nicknames: the multi-coloured coif-
fure and vivacious ways of the mother of an Oxford friend earned her the
never-to-be-forgotten Firbankian sobriquet of "Mrs Hell".)

For young Ian Calder, things were looking good. Everybody was
squabbling over him delightfully, and the dons at Cambridge thought he
was brilliant: he had become quite a protégé of Shakespeare scholar Basil
Willey. A contemporary of his at Caius, Nicholas Brooke, who had rooms
near by, remembers him vividly – they wrote a pastiche Restoration play

together for the Caius Shadwell Society, inspired by Francis Bennett, who had in his youth been a protégé of E.M. Forster. These were the days when there was a curfew at ten in the evening, and Ian Calder and Nicholas Brooke would drop in on one another to chat. Brooke remembers that Angus read the pastiche play, and called in to college to see Ian to talk about it – he recalls Angus, very thin and sharp, leaning against the mantelpiece and talking away. Ian Calder, he says, was known as "the man with green hair" – he always created an impression. (His impression on Brooke was not wholly favourable.)

Some thought that Angus enjoyed the drama of the *ménage à trois*, and all its attendant tensions – "he always liked a threesome," Bentley Bridgewater said. And, curiously enough, Angus's brother Clive had meanwhile become involved in a threesome at least as odd as Angus's own, if not odder. The two trios were to meet on one explosive evening at Clive's red-brick mansion flat in Baron's Court. The occasion was a party given by Clive and Lucie Johnstone-Wilson, and one of the guests was Alan Rook, wine dealer and poet of the Second World War. Clive Johnstone-Wilson and Alan Rook were in the throes of a reciprocated and long-lasting passion.

They had met in Chelmsford in 1943 while Clive was serving with the RASC. Clive, ever a wheeler and dealer, had smoothed young Alan's army life, wheedling tit-bits for the general and thus preferment for Alan, according to Alan's younger brother, Robin Rook. The affair had been commemorated in verse: Alan Rook's second volume of mildly homo-erotic war poetry, *These are my Comrades,*[4] was dedicated to Clive Calvert Johnstone-Wilson, Lieutenant Royal Army Service Corps Aide-de-Camp. The affair survived the war and another publication, *Not as a Refuge,*[5] is a prose meditation on the nature of poetry addressed to an absent friend "from whom I have been divided by the necessary separations of war": it refers to a game he and his comrade used to play together in public places, which recalls the games Angus and his friend Richard Gorer had played at Westminster. "We tell each other stories about the people around us. We fill in their home background, outline their activities, detail the activities of their days. We are not always kind . . ."

Alan Rook already had a history. The oldest of four brothers, he had set his heart on becoming a poet, but his father, as fathers will, had decided he should be an accountant. Accountancy gave Alan a nervous breakdown, and he was invalided off to the South of France where he took up with a mysterious older figure called Cecil St John Le Grand, an ageless playboy in his mid-forties. Alan brought St John back to England with him, and moved (with St John) into a cottage lent to him by an aunt, in which he was expected to finish his accountancy examinations. He then prevailed upon his father to allow him to go up to Oxford (still in the company of St John) to read English Literature. There he became the pet of C.S. Lewis and Tolkien, who encouraged him, despite his Second-Class degree, to think of an academic career, and sent him off to Germany in 1938 to be a *Lektor* in Freiburg. This suited him no better than accountancy, and he returned, to be rescued by the war. St John was dumped, without a ration card, on the Rook family up in Nottinghamshire, and Alan, after a bit of fun with the Local Defence Volunteers in Sherwood Forest, joined the army, and met Clive Johnstone-Wilson.

Both St John and Clive had backed a winner in Alan Rook. He abandoned literature as a profession, and went into the family wine business, Skinner and Rook. Under his management it prospered, and for some years Clive and Lucie were to prosper with it.

What did Lucie make of this new attachment? It is not recorded. For some years the threesome co-existed in a complaisant manner. She was present on the night of the party in Baron's Court, although she stayed in her bedroom, entertaining visitors there: there were plenty of young men happy to go and chat to this dark beady-eyed exotic French woman, and she enjoyed their flattery. It was all quite sophisticated.

The other threesome of Ian Calder, Bentley Bridgewater and Angus attended the party, and at some point there was a tremendous row between Bentley and Angus: according to Robin Rook, Angus became hysterical, and pulled Bentley's forelock "*right off*". Angus then rushed into the street, followed by Bentley, and neither of them were seen again that night. Ian Calder remained behind, as did Robin Rook, and they all slept upon the floor. Robin was glad he had not taken his respectable Oxford girlfriend: he had somehow guessed it would not be that kind of party. It was high jinks with the wrong set.

★

At least it was a change from the BM, where the circle at Oddi's had reconvened. George and Joan Painter had married in 1942, and Laurence Wood, detached from Audrey Brodhurst, was now attached to Angus's ex-Wren Rona Ross, whom he met at Geoffrey Wright's in Great Ormond Street, and married in August 1947. Many jokes were exchanged in the museum corridors: Painter and Johnstone-Wilson had a routine of literary repartee as they hurried past one another in the course of duty. They were all good at word games and paper games: Audrey Brodhurst recalls Jeanne Davies's talents at the dramatic monologue, and Angus's skill at finishing quotations –

"Oh sirs, we have a noble father lost!"
"Just when we'd got the calling cards embossed."

But it was not always easy to keep one's wits sharp in the cosy atmosphere exuded by the new BM staff magazine, *Under the Dome*, with its columns on rose-growing and chicken-rearing and angling. And the world beyond the dome could be sinister, even threatening. On one occasion a young man of menacing demeanour arrived at the Museum demanding to see Mr Johnstone-Wilson, and was turned away by the warder, who said that if he came back, he would call the police. Wendy Charles recalls little scraps of paper pushed under the door of Angus's flat which, from Angus's anxious response to them, she took to be blackmail notes. Charlie, the butcher's boy, was up to his tricks again.

Angus did not much enjoy this high-risk life. He got little thrill out of breaking the law. But he was eternally inquisitive by nature, and temperamentally and ideologically unwilling to believe ill of anybody with a Cockney accent: when he paid for a meal in a Lyons' Corner House by cheque, he did not at once spot the eager eyes of his guest (presumably Charlie again) as they fixed on that promising cheque book, and was shocked when the young man announced his intention of "putting the muckers [*sic*] on him".* (This alarming phrase, "putting the muckers", probably misheard from the Cockney "putting the mockers", is one that fascinated Angus: he repeated it several times, in early and late fiction and in interviews, with a kind of unwilling admiration, which seems to suggest a biographical link with Charlie, probably the source of most of these incidents.)

Nor were casual pick-ups the only threats to Angus's cheque book. Brother Fred in Parsons Green had fallen on hard times. Winifred had left him and had remarried (rather well), and Phyllis had left him too. Fred would turn up at the Museum trying to cadge off Angus, spinning him tall stories about investments in surprising commodities like raisins. Fred also cadged off Clive. Fred, as both Clive and Angus could not fail to observe, was going downhill rapidly, and would soon be Under the Hill. Colin and Pat, meanwhile, were far, far away, beyond the reach of his begging bowl, in distant India.

Angus's life, unlike Fred's, was secure (though he still had not qualified for a pension). But it didn't at this stage seem to be going anywhere. There were friends, there were parties – he saw much of Viva King and the

---

* The Lily Pond at the Lyons' Corner House in Coventry Street was a Sunday afternoon homosexual meeting place: James Kirkup loved its "razzle-dazzle", and met there a scarf-bedecked Quentin Crisp. In the post-war gloom the Corner House represented the height of affordable splendour.

Wormalds, and of Rosemary Calder, now, despite her mother, married to
Ian Merry. He often popped in for breakfast with the hospitable Merrys in
St George's Square. And he also continued to see much of Denis Barnes,
who had in 1938 married Patricia Abercrombie, familiarly known as Patsy:
she was the cousin of Ralph Abercrombie, who worked for some years at
the High Hill Bookshop in Hampstead, and was herself to become known
as the novelist, P.B. Abercrombie. (She records that in the immediate pre-
war years she and Denis Barnes saw a good deal of Angus – they met at least
three times a week, going to films and the theatre together, or calling on
one another at home. Angus was often accompanied by Jeanne Davies.)
He occasionally dropped in on a club – at the Gargoyle he met Philip and
Ann Toynbee, Maurice Richardson and David Tennant, and he
occasionally visited the discreetly homosexual Rockingham, where
everyone wore ties and looked very respectable. But he was not really a
club person. He did not like drinking in public places, any more than he
enjoyed the illicit and dangerous world of the cottage, though he confessed
that he found the messages written upon lavatory walls quite interesting.
(So did Honoria Wormald, to whom her male friends would obligingly
recite them – one of the minor incidental pleasures of the war was the
exposure of the bombed lavatory wall to the enquiring female eye.)

Socially Angus was and remained a divided soul. Part of him longed for
the risky glamour and the glitter, part of him preferred the safe, loyal, quiet
family life of his old Westminster friends – Forrest Fulton and his mother in
Ladbroke Grove, Perkin Walker and his mother at Maresfield, were
comforting fixtures who would never let him down or reject him. He
introduced Ian Calder to Forrest and Perkin, and they all seemed to get on
well enough. But despite Ian, Angus still had a roving eye. Both Angus and
Bentley began to take a slightly more than friendly interest in a young man
at the British Museum, another golden-haired boy who at once sprang to
the attention as a rival candidate for the title of The Fairest Youth in the
World.

Angus maintains that he first set eyes upon Anthony Garrett on Garrett's
first day at the Museum on 31 December 1945: the new young attendant
was startled to be addressed in familiar fashion by a white-haired senior,
who strangely commented "It's very cold up your end of the Museum."
But, as Garrett was soon to learn, Angus Johnstone-Wilson was familiar
with everybody: several colleagues at the BM credit him with insisting on
first names across the ranks. Angus and Bentley noticed that young
Anthony often arrived at the Museum in the morning with a serious-
looking young man, from whom he would take his farewell at the
Museum gates as each went off to work. They drew their own correct

conclusions, and invited Anthony to join them from time to time for lunch or dinner at one of their regular spots – The Horseshoe Tavern, or Fava's in Greek Street. Anthony was happy to tag along. But this relationship, like Angus's career as a librarian, did not at this stage seem to hold out any particular promise.

On 14 July 1946, Angus became an Assistant Keeper, Second Class. Here was promotion. Was this not what he had always wanted? Well, perhaps not.

★

One Sunday morning, in November 1946,[6] or so Angus himself tells the tale, he sat down at Providence House in Little Hadham and wrote a short story. He sat down at ten and finished at six. This story was to be called "Raspberry Jam". Perhaps he had decided that he could at least do better than the other members of the Bletchley Writers' Circle. Or perhaps the kindly, obsessional affection of a village neighbour in Little Hadham, Valentia Graham Young, had put the idea into his head. He always, in later years, credited Val with playing a large part in his emergence as a writer.

Val Graham Young, daughter of a musician, had retired from dancing to run the Little Hadham Post Office and sell knick-knacks with her friend Connie Hackett. Val, who had grown too tall for classical ballet, was famed for having appeared at the Hippodrome in the chorus of that great show, *Hit the Deck*, with Stanley Holloway, in 1927: she was a good sort, a trouper, a friend to Angus and the boys, turning up at unexpected moments to polish Bentley Bridgewater's piano, confiscating Bentley's naughty copies of *London Life*, and bullying Angus out of his depressions into trying to enjoy the flowers of spring. The Little Hadham Experiment with all its oddities deterred her not at all. Once when Angus failed to appear for lunch, she drove over to Providence House and forced her way into his bedroom, where he sat weeping in his underwear. "Get dressed!" she insisted, herself always somewhat overdressed and lavish with cosmetics. And he did. She bundled him into her little car, and drove him off to lunch, haranguing him the while about the wickedness of despair. She told him to write down his thoughts, to make stories out of village life. Write about those wicked, wicked people at the end of the road, she said.

She loved him. She rushed in where angels feared to tread, and Angus was ever grateful to her for it: her impulsive holy folly appears in several of his works, her name surfaces again and again in his notebooks. She was Nurse turned Muse, and her visitations were sensationally effective.

★

Angus Wilson's first story is a macabre performance, about a little boy who is befriended by two eccentric village ladies and becomes witness to their cruel and bizarre killing of a bullfinch. He says he wrote it very fast, and he must have known that it was good. It is quite different in kind and quality from anything he had written so far – the schoolboy pieces, although clever enough, show no promise of this burst of sophisticated and sustained accomplishment.

Where did this shocking story come from? He himself said it was inspired by two old ladies he had met while in his twenties. These may be identified with two women who lived in Pevensey, where Pat and Colin Johnstone-Wilson ran their tea-room. Jeanne Davies remembers visiting these two women with her father Winn some time in the 1930s – possibly to take them something? "Anyway my father knocked on the door several times and finally it opened and a peculiar figure stood there brandishing a broom and screaming at us to go away . . . later, I went there on my own, or possibly with one of the Uncles. I remember the inside of the house which was very dark and fusty like some medieval cottage. On the stove was a large pot of soup, very watery, and with two peas floating in it! I remember this very well as it seemed such an extraordinary thing to be cooking. Angus also went there to help and I think these two women may be the basis for Raspberry Jam."[7]

It seems likely that these are also the two sisters referred to by Colin in a letter to Angus, dated 25 July 1965. "Do you remember the 2 Miss Fentons at Pevensey? With only the smallest encouragent they would jump to drape a shawl and play Boadicea, assault Pevensey castle . . ."

Two real old ladies, then, who impressed several members of Angus's family. Do they connect with an entry in the only extant dream notebook, which reads "B and I and Geoffrey (Jane at times)* were having holiday at Hadham (week's holiday) – it was last day – we called at some tea room (?) there were two hard made up 38ish women there – I talked to blonde woman. We were coming back in car – I was looking forward to raspberry jam and last evening with B." etc.

The presence of raspberry jam seems, at least, a strange coincidence. Has it a sexual connotation? And if so, is it intentional?

★

Here, from various tangled memories, from dreams and analyses of dreams, in the home of the Hadham Experiment, was born Angus Wilson

---

* Angus for some reason always called Jeanne Davies Jane.

the short-story writer. But the birth was not quite as sudden as he later claimed.

He had certainly written one or two earlier sketches before this story: two notebooks, one of them dated August 1941, show what seem to be drafts of earlier fragments of and ideas for stories, some of which were later developed as "Saturnalia", "Mother's Sense of Fun" (here entitled "Lonely without Mother") and "Christmas Day at the Workhouse", and some of which (including an intriguing title "Incubation Period", about VD) disappear forever: what may well be the very first of all the sketches, a four-page meditation on gloom and loneliness, seems to refer to the period of breakdown in Simpson. "It is just this house, these petty and shabby possessions, this shifting domesticity that have wrecked his hopes and narrowed down his dreams, sucking him deep into the Slough of Despond . . ." (Could this be one of his very first attempts to write for Dr Kosterlitz? Dr K's initials appear on one of the end papers.)

Other unfinished scraps indicate his later modes – a satiric country dialogue ("Old Man Brock is very active this season"), a somewhat fey picture of Henry in the Aviary and the Dell, a substantial piece of narrative about village boys "putting the muckers" (*sic*) on an elderly Jew, and an extended piece of self-mockery with Angus himself as the posturing Janet Ogilvie. But the dating of these scraps is difficult: they were certainly not all written during the war, for the Janet Ogilvie piece, entitled "The Audience was in a Critical Mood", has references to the post-war Labour government.[8]

A yellowing scrap of two pages of flimsy typed paper with the beginning of a story called "Whitney Smith" by J. Wilson is also preserved, separately, in the archives, labelled "Earliest Piece of AW's Writing". (It is most unlikely to have been typed by Angus himself for he never learned to type, and this is quite professionally done.) It too features a "Janet Ogilvy" – and a Miranda Harcourt, and a "Nutty" Smith, and an Odette Lavery – more of the Proustian dandy mode here than of Dickens, and we know that Angus read Proust obsessively during the war.

Despite this evidence of preliminary efforts, it is the memory of the suddenness of the creation of "Raspberry Jam" ("I sat down, as they say in faith-healing testimonies, and 'just wrote a story one Sunday' ") that stayed with him.[9] He turned it into a comic tale about his landlady ("'Allo! Fancy sitting indoors on a day like this! Lovely warm day like this! '"[10]) but the anxious sense of miraculous delivery remains. This surely reflects his own sense of the narrowness of his victory. So easily he might have stayed put, frozen, or gone under. The ice had cracked once, it might crack again. He still had dreams of drowning. But here he was, up on his skates, spinning. Would the ice hold, the gift be renewed?

It did, it was. He sat in his olive-green rocking chair and wrote, over eight weekends, eight stories, and all of them were good.

What was he to do with these unexpected emissions? Should he try to publish them? Had he written them for publication? He showed them to a few friends, some of whom made encouraging noises, some of whom did not. (A postcard from Angus to Henry Reed survives, demanding their return, as copies were expensive. Legend has it that Reed replied that he had no talent, and Reed's friend Michael Ramsbotham confirms that he did not think much of Angus's work when it was published.*) It was Robin Ironside who made the decisive act of support. He visited Little Hadham, read the stories, and took them away with him. "My friend Robin Ironside, the painter, saw enough talent in them to show them to the editor of *Horizon*, Cyril Connolly. Like many another author it is to him and his then secretary, Sonia Brownell, that I owe my first appearance in print."[11]

Robin Ironside, a friend of Mrs King, had already embarked on a precarious freelance life. Before the war he had worked as an Assistant Keeper at the Tate; during the war he had been sent off into the secret places where the Tate's treasures were stored. He was one of the earliest contributors to Connolly's *Horizon*.† In 1946 he resigned in order to paint and write full-time. Pale, thin and elegant, he was frequently invited at the last moment as a spare man to smart dinners by hostesses such as Emerald Cunard, Ann Fleming, Lady Clementine Beit: he would gratefully abandon his tiny flat in Kinnerton Yard, Knightsbridge, glad of the prospect of a square meal. (Left to himself, he hardly ate at all.) His evening attire consisted of an old grey flannel jacket of his brother's, dyed black, black jeans and black espadrilles.

Ironside's paintings, sometimes commissioned in exchange for weekend hospitality, were worked and reworked in obsessional detail: he found it almost impossible to finish anything. They were a strange, elaborate, ghostly mixture of the Chirico surreal and the Pre-Raphaelite romantic, with their own arcane iconography: titles include "Man Dying on a Flight

* Letter Michael Ramsbotham to M.D. 8 May 1993:
"As you know, there were other literary people there" [at Bletchley Park] "including my friend Henry Reed, Vernon Watkins (even funnier than Angus), F.T. Prince, F.L. Lucas. I didn't know about Angus's literary ambitions until towards the end of his time there when he asked Henry for his opinion about the drafts of some of his short stories. I remember only that Henry was not enthusiastic (I don't know what he said) and in later years he didn't rate Angus very highly."
† He contributed an article on Burne-Jones and Gustave Moreau to *Horizon* No.6 in 1940.

of Public Steps" and "Famous Statues visiting a Museum of People". His was not an easy life: he was always hard up. By the time he read Angus's stories, he had himself sampled the splendours and miseries of Bohemia, had sought psychotherapy, and become mildly addicted to Dr Collis Browne's Chlorodine, a well-known and delicious remedy for indigestion, which contained a helpful boost of laudanum.*

Angus professed surprise when Robin whisked his stories away, and more suprise when Sonia Brownell rang him out of the blue at the BM to tell him that Connolly was interested in them. And in November 1947 "Mother's Sense of Fun" appeared in *Horizon* No. 95 (in the company of Herbert Read, Franz Borkenau† and Eric Walter White) to be followed in April of the next year by "Crazy Crowd" (in the company of Robin Ironside on Balthus and Edith Sitwell). Angus Wilson was a published writer, published in good company, in the magazine that considered itself the literary showcase of the day.

Angus was quick to see the possibilities of supplementing his modest salary. His notebooks of this period show that he was seriously investigating the short-story market – the *Cornhill, Occident, The Windmill, Argosy, Orion, Life and Letters, The Wind and the Rain* are all listed. But he was saved from freelance soliciting when his old schoolfriend John Pattisson (nicknamed Pattipans), late of the Desert Rats and now at Secker & Warburg, expressed interest in a collection. Angus at once obligingly produced several more stories. Pattisson and Secker's reader Julia Strachey liked them, and a contract was drawn up, dated 1 March 1948, for an as yet untitled "First Collection", promising an advance of fifty pounds, half payable on signing, half on publication. In March, 1949, *The Wrong Set and Other Stories* appeared, to great acclaim. It was dedicated "To Bentley & Ian, in gratitude". Angus had ceased to be Angus Johnstone-Wilson, Assistant Keeper. He had become Angus Wilson, writer. It was no longer jam tomorrow. It was jam today.

*

Angus's fortunes were on the turn. Even the routine at the British Museum

* He had some public successes: he designed a *Rosenkavalier* for Covent Garden in 1948, and later worked with Frederick Ashton and Hugh Casson. His younger brother Christopher Ironside (1913–1992) collaborated with him in various theatre projects, and also designed the new decimal coinage. His niece Virginia Ironside is a well-known journalist: she was very fond of her uncle and commented, "He was a lot thinner and a lot poorer than John Richardson."

† Franz Borkenau, the distinguished political historian, had been deported as an enemy alien to Australia on the infamous *Dunera*: after the war he returned to Europe, where after a lonely and restless life he died in a hotel room in Zürich in 1957 at the age of fifty-six. He knew Angus through the British Museum, and appears as himself, briefly, in *No Laughing Matter*.

soon began to change for the better, when Angus found himself increasingly indispensable not in the dusty basements of booksellers but in the more congenial forum of the Reading Room. The Superintendent, Robert A. Wilson (another Wilson from Westminster, and a classical scholar, born in 1905), was a man of uncertain temper who terrified many of his subordinates, but Angus stood up to him and the two got on well together: in his report on the Reading Room for 1 April 1950 to 31 March 1951 Wilson senior noted that he had had "to a much greater extent than previously, the assistance of Mr Johnstone-Wilson. While in the Reading Room Mr Johnstone-Wilson has constantly pursued his work on the temporary Subject-Index. Despite this his presence has not only greatly lightened the burden of the Superintendent but has also been of signal advantage to his readers. In the view of the Superintendent, Mr Johnstone-Wilson might with advantage be officially recognised as Deputy Superintendent. At present his position in relation to other members of the staff is ambiguous, as it is not clear that in the absence of the Superintendent he is, under the Director, the controlling officer."

So Deputy Superintendent Angus Johnstone-Wilson became, and he enjoyed it very much – indeed, he often said that had he been appointed to his position before writing his stories he might have stayed on happily at the Museum all his working life. His elevation placed him conspicuously on a raised dais in the centre of the Reading Room beneath Panizzi's beautiful dome, a colourful bird in a vast circular cage, bow-tied, blue-rinsed, chattering loudly to readers and staff and friends on the telephone (was that really John Gielgud he was talking to, wondered one eavesdropper?) and confidently offering advice or even reading manuscripts or proofs for students, displaced Americans, Polish refugees, crazy scholars, and aspiring novelists. He dealt with "old ladies seeking nursery rhymes they had read in their youth – even one who sang a little unrecognisable tune in her high cracked voice – people who [had] been conducting hopeless law suits throughout their lives, sailors who [had] jumped ship and wanted to know what rights they [had] to claim wages."[12]

He was warmly remembered for his personal kindnesses – by Christine Brooke-Rose for helping her out over some misdemeanour over a library book, by her second husband Jerzy Pieterkiewicz with whom Angus talked at length about beavers, by American novelist Mary Lee Settle and Colin Wilson for his interest in their unpublished works, by South African short-story writer Eileen Barnard from Durban for helping her to get a Reader's Ticket – "The Reading Room was one of the few places you could keep warm in those days." He was the most unconventional of librarians – when he heard Emily Hahn and Elizabeth Harman (later Lady Longford) gossiping at adjacent desks, he rushed over, not to silence them, but to try to join in the conversation. He never ever said "Shh!"

He felt a tenderness for this strange assembly of readers, some of them survivals from the nineteenth-century Grub Street world of George Gissing for whom "in a manner, absurd but true, the British Museum Reading Room really is the sort of Republic of Letters that they imagine ancient Athens to have been",[13]* and some of them, like Pieterkiewicz himself, representatives of the new influx from Europe – those to whom MacNeice alluded in his poem of 1939:

> Between the enormous fluted Ionic columns
> There seeps from heavily jowled or hawk-like foreign
> faces
> The guttural sorrow of the refugees.[14]

The Reading Room was full of oddities at that time, remembers Pieterkiewicz, some newly demobbed, some exiled, some plain crazy, and Angus was kind to the cranky and the ridiculous: Angus was vain, but with a generous, colourful vanity.†

Angus watched and he was watched. From his new vantage-point he kept an eye not only on the poor and struggling but also on the great scholars and writers of the day as they consulted the catalogue or studied in the North Library – Rose Macaulay, Sir Lewis Namier, Veronica Wedgwood, Christopher Sykes, Fredson Bowers, Cecil Woodham Smith, Sir Charles Webster, Ephraim Lipson, Hester Chapman, Geoffrey Tillotson, Vincent Brome. Sacheverell Sitwell told him that his father had possessed one of the old green tickets given to him by his guardian Archbishop Tait in 1876.

It was a great meeting-place, and many not wholly intellectual assignations were made beneath the dome. One Lady Reader, misled by Angus's friendly and helpful manner, fell importunately in love with him, and had to have her ticket withdrawn. Christine Brook-Rose's first novel, *The Languages of Love* (Secker, 1957), could be subtitled "A Reading Room Romance", for many of its exchanges, philological and otherwise, take place in the Museum and its immediate neighbourhood.

In later years, Angus was to dine out on his Reading Room stories.

---

* Angus himself, writing under his new name of Angus Wilson, contributed a short article on "The British Museum in English Fiction" to *Under the Dome* in December 1949, in which he cited Gissing's *New Grub Street*, E. Nesbit's *The Story of the Amulet*, Max Beerbohm's "Seven Men", Virginia Woolf's *Night and Day* and John Collier's *His Monkey Wife, or Married to a Chimp*.

† Pieterkiewicz, like Angus, was the youngest son of elderly parents who died when he was in his teens and he linked this with creativity and unresolved anger.

There was the woman who, when asked not to eat oranges in the Library, replied robustly that she was not eating them but squeezing them on the books. There was the gentleman whose lack of personal hygiene finally compelled Angus to suggest that he should take a bath, an insult which was never forgiven, and which provoked years of angry mutterings about Johnstone-Wilson's own reach-me downs "paid for at the taxpayer's expense!" There was the famous Miss McDonald, who bicycled to the Museum from Highgate in her white Bermuda shorts, socks and plimsolls, regularly as clockwork, for nearly fifty years, always making for Seat J8, where legend had it that Lenin had once sat; she would report to Angus on the Chinese whispers of conspiracies that she believed circled around her daily. What she was working on, nobody quite knew, but it was said that she had announced she had given up her studies in Gaelic in order to translate Virgil into French as her war effort.* There was the woman who wished to be reassured that all the animals whose skins produced the pretty soft pale blue leather desk-tops of the refurbished Reading Room (redecorated in 1951) had died a natural death. There was the distinguished scholar who asked Angus's advice on whether or not a Preface was a Good Thing. There was the French gentleman who claimed to understand the language of the animals: when Angus asked him what they said, he had to confess that it was *"Rien que des bêtises"* . . .

And so on, and so on. Angus found it impossible to resist the anecdotes, even when trying to pay serious tribute to the library. (In a broadcast in June 1953, to commemorate the Museum's 200th anniversary, he rejected the view that his job was a mixture of "a tryst with ghosts, assistance at Mrs Jarley's waxwork show, and professional attendance at Bedlam" – but rejected it only to reinforce it.) He enjoyed the carnival aspects of his new position. He clanked his keys importantly, and was pleased when Readers whispered to one another about his growing notoriety. He was like a spider in the centre of his own web.

His domestic arrangements were also improving. He and Bentley Bridgewater had shared for a while a London *pied-à-terre* in Lambolle Road, Belsize Park, but on the strength of his published stories and his new contract with Secker & Warburg he began to look around for a place of his own. He wrote to Geoffrey Wright from Providence House on 3 July 1948:

. . . I have been to S. France and returned feeling better than for years. I am now busy looking around for somewhere to live in

* She died aged 82 in October, 1980, and received an obituary in the *Sunday Times* by Norman Maggs.

London – Mrs B does not feel she can manage to do full time work in the winter, so we are going to restrict to most weekends . . . I am not sorry really as the winter journeys are rather a strain. I shall get somewhere from roughly the first week in October either a room with kitchenette or a small furnished (or unfurnished) flat, the situation does not seem half as difficult as I expected. I don't quite know what B. intends. We are however giving up our room in Belsize Park almost immediately as it proves so very expensive especially when one or other of us is away, in any case with the evenings B spends at home he gets almost no use for his money. This leaves me somewhat high and dry for the next two months. I am writing to ask if for this limited period only (ie until October) there is a possibility that you or Kenward (I have no idea whether he is away from London then) rent a room to me for 3 nights a week (preferably at choice during weekdays, but if more convenient to you we could fix 3 definite days for each week). It would be a tremendous help until I definitely come to London, but I don't want to do this until the summer is over. I could not really afford to pay you more than £1.1 a week (7/– a night).I know you will say no if you prefer not – but it would not, I think, be likely to cause any difficulties, would be for a limited time only and would be of great service to me.

My regards to Michael
Wishes from all three of us
Yrs
Angus

And in December 1948, with Honoria Wormald's help, Angus moved into a one-bedroomed flat in Dolphin Square. His flat was 07 Frobisher House, and his rent was £112.00 a year; the lease was dated 24 December 1948. Here at last he had peace, privacy and independence.

To Angus, Dolphin Square was the height of chic. A large ten-storey red-brick block in Pimlico, it occupied over seven acres, had its own private gardens and some fine river views. The furnishings were Art Deco, there was a restaurant with an orchestra and a view of the swimming pool, and each room had a radio with a bakelite control which could be switched to the Home, Light or Third Programme. The décor reminded Angus pleasantly of his sea voyage to South Africa, and the nautical theme was echoed in the names of the houses: Grenville, Beatty, Howard, Hood . . . The block was prized during the war for its bomb-proof solidity: de Gaulle moved there in 1940, C.P. Snow and his friend Harry Hoff (the writer

William Cooper) lived there in its early days. Radclyffe Hall died in residence in 1943. It was and is inhabited by a wide range of characters – diplomats, politicians, con men, artists, spies, call girls, minor royals, and many others with good reason to wish for trouble-free, well-run anonymity. It seemed an appropriate place for an up-and-coming writer, and Angus liked it.

Angus had no river views: his apartment looked inwards, to the gardens, where he would sit outdoors and write, imagining with nervous pride that a thousand eyes were watching him, and wondering who that promising young writer could be.

This new apartment was visited for the odd night by Angus's young friend from the Museum, Anthony Garrett. This relationship developed, though not very rapidly, as Angus was still involved with Ian Calder. But Anthony was flattered by Angus's attention, and eager to profit from it: his first surviving letter to Angus (2 November 1947) is one of effusive gratitude for a heavyweight reading list – Montaigne, Pascal, Stendhal, Baudelaire, Gide. From the start, there was a strong teacher-pupil element in their friendship: Anthony, who had left Grammar School at the age of sixteen, was keen to improve himself, and Angus was a born teacher.

At this stage, Anthony Garrett would to an observer (and perhaps to himself) have seemed to be one of many young men circling round Angus. Douglas LePan, temporarily lured away from his close friends Denis and Patsy Barnes, was invited in January 1947 by Angus to a party at Honoria's in Dolphin Square. He remembers meeting there "two golden-haired boys", who seemed to him to represent an unnumbered succession of golden boys. This was not quite what LePan himself was looking for, and he did not return.*

But the boys were not unnumbered, and Anthony Garrett did not move on into oblivion. Nor, come to that, did Ian Calder.

Angus, even in the notoriously promiscuous world of homosexual affairs, seems to have found it almost impossible to let people disappear. He had a talent for getting himself involved, for taking an interest not only in the love object but in the love object's mother, father, brothers, sisters, uncles and aunts. Anthony Garrett found himself wooed not by a casual admirer or predator, but by somebody who wanted to know everything about him.

---

* Douglas LePan (b.1914) was born in Toronto. His works include volumes of poetry, *The Wounded Prince* (1948) and *The Net and the Sword* (1953): a novel, and memoirs. Late in life he surprised his readers by publishing a volume of homoerotic poetry as an elegy to a dead lover: *Far Voyages*, 1990, McClelland & Stewart, Toronto. (In Memory of Patrick Fabbri – 1948 Bordeaux – 1985 Montreal.)

★

Anthony Charles Garrett was born in London, at 35 Finchley Way, N3, on 20 July 1929, in the middle of a thunderstorm. His maternal grandfather had been a builder and undertaker in Old Southgate, but despite a potentially profitable contract with the old lunatic asylum of Colney Hatch he had gone bankrupt and departed in 1903 to the Gold Coast, whence he returned, remarried, and settled down to open a tobacconist's shop in Tankerton, near Whitstable, on the Kentish coast. His paternal grandfather, a commercial traveller and a drinking man, had died of cirrhosis of the liver in his fifties. Anthony's father, Charles Thomas Garrett, also had a drink problem, and was given to bouts of violent temper: he had left school at fifteen to become a bank clerk, had served in France throughout the First War, then married Jenny Margaretta Emery (always known as Margaret) in 1925 and settled in the newly developed suburb of Finchley where his three children, Genifer, Philip and Anthony were born. Tom Garrett survived the alcoholism, eventually becoming an inspector of Barclays Bank.

Anthony, the youngest, received the impression that his mother had not really wanted a third child, and that if she had to have one she would have preferred a girl.

The outbreak of World War Two found the Garretts on holiday near grandfather in Tankerton. They stayed there, letting the Finchley house to evacuees, preferring Kent to London despite the fact that the area became a Restricted Zone with barbed wire in the garden and anti-tank traps on the promenade.

Anthony gained a place in the grammar school, Simon Langton Boys' School, in Canterbury. His education here was disrupted by sirens and bombing, including some direct hits on the school itself and the neighbouring Girls' School – the upper end of Canterbury High Street was completely demolished. Many lessons, meals and sexual escapades took place in underground shelters. Despite this, Anthony achieved five passes (three with credit) in his School Certificate examinations in the summer of 1945, and a reference from his headmaster describing him as "a boy of excellent character . . . good ability and an intelligent interest in many subjects outside his ordinary School work". But he had not passed in mathematics, and therefore could not proceed to take Higher Certificate. ("I was never any good at mathematics" was to be his constant refrain.) Anthony applied for and obtained a job "as some sort of assistant librarian" at the British Museum at a salary of about two pounds a week (as he wrote to his sister Genifer Garrett). Anthony started work on 31 December 1945 – the day on which Angus first spotted him.

Anthony Garrett left school educated well below his ability, and with a nagging sense of having missed out. His letter to Genifer, dated 21 November 1945, is studded with self-conscious references to *Hamlet*, Tennyson, and the Subjective Idealists – what one might call a typical "undergraduate" style letter. He was only sixteen. He had vaguely hoped that the BM might give him a chance to pursue his interest in Chinese art and literature, but he found himself in what seemed a dead-end job as a "temporary attendant", until Bentley Bridgewater found him a post in the Director's Office where he spent his time issuing Readers' Tickets.

In London, Anthony lived at first with his Aunt Ethel in Arnos Grove, but when her son came back from the war Anthony moved for a while into the YMCA, before going back to his parents on their return to Finchley. The YMCA was a revelation. It was in Great Russell Street, a convenient two minutes walk from the Museum, and it had a pronounced athletic homosexual culture, with compulsory nude bathing in the pool and attendant goings-on in the showers: the YMCA motto of "By love serve one another" was variously and energetically interpreted by its members. Here Anthony, who had showed no interest in girls from the age of seven, took up with a musical young man called Bernard who worked for the Salvation Army in the Tottenham Court Road. They met in the swimming pool, and subsequently would meet for coffee of a morning in the Lyons café at the junction of Tottenham Court Road and Great Russell Street. Their relationship lasted for two years, and took in concerts and many religious outings – first to the Salvation Army, then, when Bernard became a Methodist, to Kingsway to hear Donald Soper and later to Central Hall, Westminster to hear Dr Sangster . . . "Bernard was not at all an intellectual, he didn't really want to discuss things, and our chief troubles came from that – We got on very well, but I was always expressing opinions and views without any rhyme or reason, and he didn't really like all that – why did it come to an end? I can't really tell you . . . we didn't part with any storm . . . it just stopped when I went into the army."[15] This was a good friendship, and Anthony felt he was fortunate to have met Bernard: Bernard was good to him and for him.

Angus Wilson and Bentley Bridgewater, however, opened a new world to Anthony Garrett. They offered not only meals at Fava's: they offered as much discussion as anyone would wish for, and a second chance of a higher education. They accepted Anthony as one of their own circle, introducing him to the Wormalds, Helen Pattisson, Ian Calder (who later coached him in those miserable mathematics), Perkin Walker, Forrest Fulton. They all encouraged this eager novice. Bentley wrote a reference to enable him to use the Royal Geographical Society library: both Bentley and Angus lent and gave him books. They were amused by his romantic narcissistic daydreams, but while they may have mocked, they did not crush.

This web of friendships might well have disintegrated when Anthony was called up for National Service in the spring of 1948, at the moment when Angus's life was moving into a new dimension. But Angus, unlike Bernard, did not let go. When Angus found that Anthony was to be stationed at the Intelligence Corps Depot at Maresfield, he encouraged him to call on Perkin's mother, Bump Walker – which, shyly, Anthony did, climbing over the fence into the garden of the Wilderness from the camp. Bump Walker received him with tea and sent him off with pots of jam. Then Anthony Garrett was posted abroad to occupied Austria (accompanied by a German dictionary presented to him by Bentley). This was a culture shock, and Austria was much less romantic than he had imagined. He was in the Intelligence Corps, and his duties were largely clerical. He found himself surrounded by public schoolboys from Eton and Sedbergh who spoke fluent German with no need of any dictionary. (One of these was Michael Swan, who became a friend of Francis King at Oxford and later of Philippe Jullian: he published *Ilex and Olive*: a *Journey through France and Italy* (Van Thal, 1949), *Temples of the Sun and Moon* (Cape, 1954) and *The Marches of El Dorado* (Cape 1958). According to King, he was the Bruce Chatwin of his day: one of several suicide attempts permanently damaged his health, and he eventually succeeded in killing himself.[16]) Garrett felt uprooted. Angus wrote to him, and Anthony Garrett replied. Angus sent Garrett an inscribed copy of *The Wrong Set*, and Garrett read it, thanked Angus for it, kept it.

22017442 Cpl Garrett, A.C.
68 FSS
British Troops Austria
9 May 49

My dear Angus,
    Knowing that I was on duty in the office this evening I considered that I had an ideal opportunity to write to you; the opportunity, however, was partially undermined by the OC's announcement that in all probability I would receive a female visitor during the course of my duty. This female, I am informed, is the daughter of an Italian police official with whom we have always had good relations, and she desires to learn English . . .
From all things in skirts, good Lord deliver us!

. . . May I offer my sincerest congratulations on the success of
your book? Had the critique in the Listener been of a book of
mine I should henceforth consider myself beyond reproach as a
brilliant writer. I have read, and re-read your stories, and each
time I have found more and more in them to admire. Crazy
Crowd, which at first I did not take to, I now rate as one of my
favourites; and so with several others – I find that my initial
reading was superficial and that I had missed the greater part of
their sparkling brilliance, I was too young to appreciate more than
a tenth of their meaning. That you 'can write as a duck can swim'
is a tribute obviously well-earned. May I thank you once again for
the copy you so generously presented me with? It is a privilege I
shall long remember and a volume I shall always treasure.

. . . the horror has just left me, after an hour's visit, during
which this letter lay dormant. Much to my dismay it was a very
pleasant female; extremely voluble and effusive, as will be
gathered from the fact that I have now begun to learn Italian! I
found her presence embarrassing, but not unpleasant, chiefly I
suppose because she insisted on paying me compliments upon my
'beautiful English' and ended up by saying that I was so humble
and yet so clever and mature. As you may imagine I am now
completely won over to her and have promised to lend her books.
I never could resist flattery!!

    Aufwiedersehn
     Yours
      Anthony

Angus was rightly proud of the Listener review (7 April 1949) for it was
by none other than Sean O'Faolain, himself a master of the short story, and
it praised the volume in the highest terms: ". . . a new writer of the first
rank has appeared on the horizon . . . He is a satirist with a lyrical touch;
trenchant, ruthless, often very funny, sometimes very frightening; and he
can write as a duck can swim. Naturally he is still uneven; one detects a
violent streak that sometimes betrays him into a melodramatic gesture; but
at his best he has already written some of the best satirical stories of his
generation . . . he is already completely déniaisé, though without, thank
goodness, losing his pity or his feeling. It may be this rare combination of
sharp wit and soft heart that makes one reader at least believe that this is a
man marked out for fame."

This is the kind of review a new writer dreams of, and O'Faolain was
echoed by many. The volume was favourably noticed (with occasional

murmurs about its malice and violence) in all the major London and regional papers.

Even *Under the Dome* astutely noticed it: "Again we see another member of staff seeking an outlet for his pent-up energies."[17] John Betjeman, Philip Toynbee and Frank O'Connor joined the chorus of praise. Despite the oft-repeated view that short stories do not sell, *The Wrong Set* sold out its print run of 2,000 within a fortnight, and reprinted in April, and again in June 1949. Angus Wilson was the talk of the town. He was snapped up by Spencer Curtis Brown, whose firm remained his agents for the rest of his life. He was photographed by Angus McBean for a glossy magazine, his name began to appear in gossip columns, he was quoted in reviews of books by others, he was himself asked to write reviews by the *New Statesman* and the *Listener*, he was invited to give broadcasts, and, at his own suggestion, he recorded one of his own stories for the BBC.* A new voice was heard. He was riding high. Writer and editor Kay Dick recalls his elation as he arrived on a visit to see her and her friend Kathleen Farrell at Great Missenden after hearing the critics praise him on the BBC. Robert Kee had spoken of the stories – and in particular "Raspberry Jam" – in the highest terms, recognising in them not only a "diabolic" cleverness, but also a form of poetry – "some infinitely gentle, infinitely suffering thing".

There were dissentient voices. The most decisive came from Elizabeth Bowen, who wrote of a talent misused, complaining of "an out-dated anger" – "the drunks and nymphomaniacs and sadists and have-beens who drool through these stories are no more funny than dead flies shaken out of curtains.

"What is more, they seem to have lived so long ago that they no longer matter: these stories *date*. If one is to be a satirist, one must be of the moment or of all time: it is fatal to fall between two stools. I do wish Mr Wilson could dislodge from his system the resentments of circa 1932; I wish he could eliminate from his style the over-thoroughness of a cement-mixer; and I wish he could realise that nauseating physical detail is, apart from other things, an offence against art."[18]

(It is not surprising to learn that this curiously violent attack elicited in turn an equally damning comment from Wilson on Bowen: he was to invoke "Mrs Thirkell and Mrs Miniver" when writing about her volume of short stories, *Encounters*,[19] a remark she understandably took long to forgive.)†

---

* His own reading of "A Visit in Bad Taste" was broadcast on 18 February 1951 on the BBC Third Programme.

† But all ended well: in 1956 she reviewed *Anglo-Saxon Attitudes* favourably, and wrote to thank him for his review of *Eva Trout* in the *Observer*, 26 January 1969.

Another female critic surfaced in Anastasia Anrep, an Oxford acquaintance from Somerville and a friend of Sonia Brownell, who met Angus in
the Salisbury pub one lunchtime: Anastasia Anrep had just read the stories
and hastened to tell Angus, with refreshing Bloomsbury frankness, that he
was "beating dead dogs". Angus seemed, she says, a little hurt.

Overall, in the general chorus of praise, it is remarkable how little critics
agreed about which stories were best. Few felt generous enough to give an
unqualified welcome, but there was no critical consensus about the
strength or weakness of individual works. Many remarked, almost as a
matter of form, on "uneven qualities", but few made an argued case.
Perhaps the shocking truth was that all of the stories were good.

*

The Wrong Set and Other Stories[20] consisted of twelve short stories (of which
three have already been discussed: see above pp.35, 84, 135). "Saturnalia"
is Wilson's archetypal South Kensington hotel story, set on New Year's
Eve, 1931, at the staff Christmas dance at the Mendel Court. The
characters, who have grown out of his schoolboy "Kensingtonian sketch",
include the plucky manageress, Stella Hennessy, carefully lipsticked in her
dove-grey tulle evening dress, desperate to keep her son at public school;
Claire Talfourd-Rich, the "injured wife", amusing herself with Tom the
porter; Sir Charles, a retired colonial governor throwing streamers at a
pageboy and crying out sadly in Greek; the drunken pretty waitress Gloria,
making up to Bruce Talfourd-Rich; and the dejected Grierson, medical
student from Barts, at the mercy of bandy-legged Bertha, the crazy
kitchenmaid. As in "Union Reunion", class differences are dissolved, but
only temporarily, in drink and sex: beneath the wild night of licence the
realities of economic survival hold all the characters in an iron grip. This is
the world which Maud and Willie and Viva King's mother inhabited, from
which Angus and Viva had fought to free themselves: a world of pathos
and black comedy, irregularity and pretence. It was a world which lingered
on for decades, despite Elizabeth Bowen's assertion that it was already dead
and gone: dead it might be, but gone it was not.*

"Mother's Sense of Fun" tells the sad story of Donald, struggling in vain
to free himself from the tyranny of Mrs Carrington, herself the
embodiment of the manipulative maternal passion – amusing, devious,
relentless, intrusive, unable to let her son speak or think or breathe for

---

* Elizabeth Taylor's *Mrs Palfrey at the Claremont* (1972) is a classic of the genre. Several of
Angus's friends found a bond in hotel memories: Glen Cavaliero's ever-quarrelling
grandparents owned a hotel in Eastbourne, about which he wrote a somewhat Wilsonian short
story, "The Wicked Mrs Berryman", published in *Encounter*, March 1982.

himself, yet dangerously capable of disarming and charming his friends. She is the emasculating mother, whose successful operations Angus had watched at first hand in Violet Bridgewater, Helen Pattisson and Molly Calder. Hostile though the portrait is, it nevertheless betrays a fascination: these women were as dreadful as Medusa if you were in their power, but if you gazed at them through a glass from an unfilial distance you could enjoy and survive. In later years, Angus was one of the first to recognise the social distortions that had made these women behave as they did: even here there is a lack of blame, a sense almost of admiration for the sheer energy and enterprise of motherly destruction.*

Another surrogate mother, Bump Walker, appears in "Fresh Air Fiend", which introduces the gardening motif which runs through all Angus's work. Miranda Searle, wife of an Oxford don, now a "destroyed beauty", is given over to histrionics, alcoholism and gardening in Somerset. (The West Country is always a bad place for Wilson.) Her garden is evoked in not wholly attractive detail, and Angus later wrote of Miranda's use for it as "an exercise in thwarted power": "The clumps of lupins were massed like an overpainted sunset – anchovy, orange and lemon against skyeblue – only the very tops of their spikes had been bent and hung like dripping candles. The crests of the delphiniums were broken too, and the petals lays around pale ice-blue and dark blue like scattered boat-race favours."

Miranda's precarious mental state is ascribed partly to the death of her only son (shades of "Union Reunion") in a car crash. An intrusive and unattractive young academic, Elspeth Eccles, is on a visit; she resents and fears Mrs Searle, whom she sees as a drag upon her husband, and the principal obstacle to his long-awaited edition of Peacock's letters. An attempt to force Mrs Searle to confront her own drinking and let some "fresh air" into the couple's marital collusion goes disastrously wrong: both women are humiliated, but it is Professor Searle who proves the long-term victim.

This story, with its careful dissection of the nature of domestic guilt and the fragility of human interdependence, has a more ambitious scope than some of the others, and suggests a novelist in the making: Angus himself saw that Miranda was something of a sketch for the wonderfully drawn Ella in *Hemlock and After*. His sensitivity to those on the edge of nervous

---

* Anthony Symondson spotted elements of the bossy though childless Honoria Wormald in Mrs Carrington: writing her obituary in the *Independent*, he buried in his text a more or less direct quote from "Mother's Sense of Fun" – "moving and looking like a young girl well into old age, full of charm, a delightful companion, investing the most ordinary event with a sense of adventure" (2 December 1991).

breakdown, and his description of the strategies they use to defend themselves and wound others, are strikingly deployed, and his interweaving of literary allusion with reality is also a pointer to the future: the reckless private lives of the Shelley-Godwin-Peacock circle are revealingly contrasted with the woolly timidities and heartinesses of Oxford. The story also, unhappily, proved prophetic. In *The Wild Garden* Angus was to say: "When I wrote this story I had never gardened, although it has since become my chief hobby. I had only one woman friend who was a devoted gardener at that time (1946). Had I been told that she resembled my character . . . I should have rejected the idea, and so I think would others who knew her. Ten years later when my friend died she had become an unhappy neurotic . . ."[21]

"Realpolitik" describes the machinations of a professional careerist, appointed director of a Gallery, who finds himself in conflict with its older, more cultured staff. This is Angus's first study of power and institutional behaviour, as observed at the BM and Bletchley Park, and the timelessness of its theme of management in dispute with scholarly expertise was to be vividly recalled in many of the controversies of the 1980s – including the reorganisation of the V and A and the London Zoo. It was a theme to which he would return.

"Crazy Crowd" is acknowledged by Rosemary Merry to be in part a portrait of Calder family life in the 1940s at the Red House in Mettingham. Scholarship boy and rising civil servant Peter is making his first visit to his girlfriend Jenny's family. The Crazy Cockshotts live in an early-Victorian house in Cambridgeshire, and pride themselves on their eccentricity and outspoken vivacity. Stepmother Nan is carefully disguised as a talkative American, Father is a tweedy, puckish antiquarian, Auntie Betty (who in real life painted and lived at Eastgate House, Bury St Edmunds) appears as the birdlike, gruff and kindly Flopsy, and Ian Calder is presented as the dazzling and perversely opinionated brother, Hamish, with whom Jenny's relationship is perhaps almost too intimate. The atmosphere of family jokes and self-congratulatory liveliness is sharply drawn, and so is the untidiness in which they all live: the sitting-room is cluttered with deep armchairs and sofas in faded flowered cretonne, with tables and stools, used plates and unused plates, "half-finished dishes of sandwiches, half-empty cups of coffee, ashtrays standing days deep in cigarette ends; even the family photographs on the mantelpiece seemed to be pushing half-finished glasses of beer over the edge. It was impossible to sit down, for the chairs and sofas were filled with books, sewing, workboxes, unfolded newspapers and in one case a tabby cat and two pairs of pliers."

But the story ends well, on an embrace: the Cockshotts win a degree of authorial approval.* This also was a theme which recurred in later work: the Crazy Family formula haunted Angus, for the Johnstone-Wilsons, like the Calders, were self-consciously crazy, and more manageable, perhaps, if seen in this mode.

The title story, "The Wrong Set", is a family comedy in a very different milieu: Soho night-club pianist Vi from Leicester, living in a bed-sit with wavy-haired, grey-moustached "Major" Trevor Cawston, thinks she ought to visit her nephew Norman, new to London on a University scholarship. Trevor, who is given to railing against Yids, Lizzies, the Labour Government, Mr Attlee and the Ballet, does not see the necessity, but Vi insists, and discovers that Norman is living in Kilburn with a staunchly respectable Labour-voting landlady, and that Norman has been with her sons to a Communist Party rally. The landlady dispproves of the CP, and so does Vi, but for opposite reasons. A row flares up as Vi expresses the view that Norman shouldn't have got himself mixed up "with a lot of reds and Jews" and later that night she appeases her muddled conscience by sending her sister a telegram (she is too drunk to trust herself to speak): "Terribly worried. Norman in the Wrong Set. Vi." The phrase reverberates.

"A Visit in Bad Taste" owes much to brother Fred – as, perhaps, does the wavy-haired Major Trevor. Its protagonist, Arthur, is visiting the cultured home of his sister Margaret and her husband Malcolm Tarrant after a spell in gaol for "offences against children": they agonise, not very painfully, about what to do for him. His criminal record they can almost excuse, by invoking Dostoevsky and progressive notions of penal reform, but his vulgarity is more than they can stomach: they tell him, indirectly, that he has to go, hint that he could go abroad or in some other way disappear. "Arthur sat, thinking – the colonies or suicide, neither seemed to be what he was needing."

★

Fred Johnstone-Wilson, the tragi-comic inspiration for this story, and, as we shall see, for fiction by another of his mercilessly observant brothers, had died of chronic bronchial asthma in Clapham, at the Montrose Court

---

* Rosemary Merry, describing the Calder household four decades later in her spacious drawing-room in Hartley Wintney, surrounded by deep armchairs and sofas in unfaded chintz, pointed proudly to her not-quite-overflowing ashtrays and to an upholstered pouffe, and cried "Look, that's one of the very pouffes!" She went on, with much laughter, to deny allegations of incest with brother Ian: Angus had certainly exaggerated all *that*, though they had been very close. Surveying her antiques and her paintings and her furniture, some inherited from Molly Calder, she sighed robustly and delivered her mother's epitaph: "Well, she was a very naughty lady, but she did have a good eye."

Hotel on Clapham South Side, on 2 August 1948. He was fifty-eight. His death certificate gives his occupation as unknown, but Bentley Bridge-water, who went with Angus to see the body and register the death, says that his room contained forged printed notepaper which suggested he had been borrowing money under false pretences. He had served a short spell in prison, probably in the 1930s, an event which appears in different forms in Colin's writings, in this story by Angus, and (more heroically, and much transformed) in *No Laughing Matter*.

What had gone wrong? Had Fred been over-indulged by grand-parents, neglected by parents, thrust out of the family nest too young by growing siblings? He had relied on his easy charm, and he had plenty of it when young. Was he work-shy, like his father? Did he feel the poultry business was beneath his public-school dignity?

Colin and Pat never forgave Fred. Winn, who had adored him, was already dead. And Angus seems to have written the anger out of himself. Nothing was left but pathos.

★

The remaining two stories in the collection, "Significant Experience" and "Et Dona Ferentes", deal with sexual relationships. The first flashes back from wartime to young Oxford undergraduate Jeremy's painful but instructive affair with an older woman in the South of France: it is set in a colourfully French landscape which Angus knew well from his visits to the Anquetins at La Ciotat. His own early sexual experiences were very different from Jeremy's, but the finale, as Jeremy, escaping forever from Prue and her demands, is pinched and teased and pursued through Marseilles by a mocking sexually ambiguous street child, has a ring of the vividly remembered.

"Et Dona Ferentes" is a more complicated, less smartly controlled piece. It is the only story in the collection with homosexuality as a dominant theme – and even here the homosexuality is repressed. Sven, a Swedish boy spending the summer in England on an exchange visit with the Newman family, deliberately provokes his host, forty-seven-year-old Edwin Newman, into acknowledging his own sexual feelings for him, though Newman draws back at the last moment. Despite his restraint, the implication is that his marriage will never be the same again. Sven, the wrecking force, has invaded the safe English countryside of picnics and family outings, where Edwin's mother is trying to blot out family dissension by reading *Emma* for the twenty-third time, and although he is forced to retreat, he has conquered.

As a story, this is one of the least satisfactory in the collection. It has too many characters, too much action for its length: the emotions are too ambiguous to be contained so neatly, and the narrative devices (which include a convenient thunderstorm) seem a little clumsy. Real memories of the Sussex downs had become muddlingly mingled with its ostensible setting in the Thames Valley. Angus had needed more space. As he soon recognised, there was a novel here waiting to be written.

OVERTURES FROM THE RIGHT SET

Some are spoiled by success. Others are improved by it. Francis King, who met Angus in the late 1940s, is emphatic that Angus blossomed in the warm sun of admiration. His tendency to waspishness lessened now that his natural sharpness was finding an outlet in fiction, and his tantrums lessened too. For the first time since the happy days at Westminster, Angus found himself the centre of attention. He enjoyed it.

He was stared at as he sat in enthroned in the Reading Room, and he was courted by the literary world. He had always been an asset at a party, but now he was no longer a social climber: he was a lion in his own right. Invitations from the Right Set, the Wrong Set, the Monde and the Demi-Monde poured in. He was seen everywhere.

Richard Wollheim spotted him first in the Museum Tavern across the road from the Museum, talking conspicuously in his high-pitched voice. Suddenly Angus had a powerful nosebleed and, dramatically, fainted. Wollheim did not at that time know who he was, but he recognised that he must be Somebody. They eventually met in less gory circumstances, probably at Viva King's, and became good friends, taking many a meal together, at home and abroad – the Queen's restaurant in Sloane Square was much favoured. Wollheim had been at Westminster and at Oxford some ten years later than Angus, and had vivid memories of John Edward Bowle, who, he claimed, had particularly disliked a fellow master called Claridge, and would exhort his pupils: "Boys, whenever you see Claridge, spit!" With such stories would he and Angus entertain one another.

Wollheim was the son of a theatrical producer and a Gaiety Girl. Stuart Hampshire's mother was also a Gaiety Girl. How pleased Willie Johnstone-Wilson would have been with his boy's new chums! Angus and Stuart Hampshire met at a *Horizon* dinner, in the large flat overlooking Regent's Park where Cyril Connolly lived in passing grandeur with Lys (nicknamed "Lend-Lease") Lubbock. Lys Lubbock was Alan Campbell-Johnson's sister-in-law; Alan had married Lys's sister Fay Dunlap in 1938, and Connolly had embarked on an affair with Lys in 1940. She had become an energetic hostess on *Horizon*'s behalf, introducing many of the rising literary and artistic stars of the day to one another; she and Connolly had given a cocktail party for Stephen Spender and Natasha Litvin when they had married in April 1941, and they had followed this success with many other parties. Elizabeth Bowen, A.J. Ayer, the Spenders, and Robin Ironside were among the regular guests at these events, and here Angus made the acquaintance of Stuart Hampshire. They took to one another. Angus was never very good at abstract thought and did not read philosophy, but this was no impediment to their friendship, as philosopher Hampshire loved to gossip: they talked people, parties and politics.

There were plenty of parties. Viva King carried on bravely: her salon was celebrated in the gossip columns, and on 30 January 1952 the *Sketch* reported that the house in Thurloe Square, "full of lovely and unusual things: antique musical boxes with figures which perform to the tunes, cases of Nevers glass figures, a famous Tiepolo over the fireplace", had recently attracted Mrs (Faith) Compton Mackenzie, Madge Garland, Mrs Christopher Ironside (better known as the dress designer, Janey Ironside), Lady Richardson with her sons John and David, Lord Amulree, and "Angus Wilson, whose acrid and penetrating short stories sting his readers to ecstasy." (The "famous Tiepolo" was, in fact, a Reynolds, of Joanna Leigh, Mrs R.B. Lloyd, cutting her initials on a tree.) Another party-giver was Lady Harris ("widow of a shipping magnate, 105 years old, hoaxer of the art world, with an ear trumpet", according to Wollheim) who would stand at the top of her staircase wearing a placard saying "I am deaf, enjoy yourselves!" Hester Chapman, biographer and cousin of Evelyn Waugh, gave parties, and her style amused Angus: "You can't have catarrh! It lacks panache!" was one of her remembered *bons mots*. Lady Hulton, the flamboyant wife of Sir Edward Hulton, offered Angus tips on social climbing, John Fowler (of Colefax and Fowler) and eye-surgeon Pat Trevor-Roper gave gay parties, Ivy Compton-Burnett gave tea parties. Edith Sitwell gave lunches at the Sesame Club, where the food surprised everybody by being rather good. Angus supped several times with Denis and Edna Healey in their attic bed-sit in Manchester Square: they had a mutual friend in Geoffrey Wright's friend, Kenward Knox, a communist from Ilkley.

Angus's own restaurant life grew grander, as he graduated from Ley-On's cheap Chinese and from Fava's (to be dubbed "Our Fava which art in Greek Street" by Charles Osborne, that clever young Australian who worked with John Lehmann) to Au Savarin, run by Mr Christie in Charlotte Street (chicken pilaffe, excellent fruit salads, Greek dishes and Greek wines). Au Jardin des Gourmets at 5 Greek Street was a long-lasting authentically French favourite and Angus became a regular, well known to proprietors M. Richier and M. André: here, for six shillings by 1953 prices, one could feast on a salmi of pheasant or *poulet poché au riz* or *crêpes de volaille aux pointes d'asperges.*[1] And there were increasing numbers of assignations at London's clubs – at the Reform with Francis Wormald,* at the Travellers with Philippe Jullian.

Philippe Jullian and Angus met at Viva King's – where else? – and embarked on a long and productive association. Both were at the beginning of their careers: both were ambitious: both were fascinated by the caprices of society: both had survived eccentric childhoods: both were capable of outrageous behaviour: both had a deep vein of melancholia: and both, oddly, were fond of zoos. They amused one another. Philippe managed to overcome his disapproval of Angus's politics and his ugly Dolphin Square apartment – *"cyniquement petit bourgeois: chambre nue, mal habillé, en rien esthète"* – and Angus in turn tried to forgive Philippe for his desire to rush over and introduce himself and Angus to his old friends Sir Oswald and Lady Mosley from 707 Hood, spotted dining in the Dolphin Square restaurant.[2] (Angus continued to refuse to meet the Mosleys, and turned down invitations to literary luncheons at which Lady Mosley was to be a guest.)

Jullian, born in Bordeaux in 1920, was the grandson of Camille Jullian, the French historian (1859–1933) and great-grandson of Eugène Azam, a distinguished psychopathologist and one of the founders of Bordeaux University. From this auspicious ancestry little good had descended to Philippe. The family fortunes had declined more suddenly than the Johnstone-Wilsons', and his parents had separated and divorced, a disgrace which turned Philippe, in his own eyes, into a social leper. To make matters worse, he had to wear spectacles, and spectacles lacked panache. But at least he got rid of the name of his despised father, André Simounet, and reverted, with his mother, to the distinguished name of Jullian.

As a young man, like all Bordelais with social pretensions, he had become passionately Anglophile, enraptured by his first boyhood visit to Cheltenham, enchanted by London Zoo and the Wallace Collection and a glimpse of the Queen in a white dress. (He was not so impressed by Ramsay MacDonald, *"un petit homme mal vêtu de noir"*). Returning after the war in October 1945, he found a London magically transformed, grand

---

* Francis Wormald's portrait by Hermione Hammond, donated by Angus, now hangs at the Reform in the Librarian's Room.

in its verdant ruins, a city which to his artist's eye ressembled Ancient Rome. He launched his gangling form upon London with vivacious energy, using invitations to the French Embassy from the well-connected ambassador René Massigli as a base, and soon found himself at home in both high and low society. He was an unashamed snob, fascinated by anything to do with what he thought was the aristocracy. "*Les gens distingués*" mesmerised him. But although eager to please, he was also willing to shock, and both in London and in Paris would embark on transvestite adventures which made Angus's Oxford tea party seem decorous. His pseudonyms included Mme Jacquemart-André, Mme Surgis du Passet, and Mme Ducottet de Chesouane, and in one oft-told anecdote he is said to have successfully passed himself off to the reclusive collector Cornwallis-West as a suspiciously well-informed French duchess.

Jullian was not only entertaining and audacious: he was also highly talented. His sketches and illustrations brought him many commissions in England. Norman Douglas, Beverley Nichols, William Plomer, Vita Sackville-West and Angus himself saw him not as a rival but as a potential collaborator, and he was to illustrate their works, though he is perhaps now best remembered in England for his illustrations to Proust. He illustrated Proust twice, once, privately, for the Duke of Devonshire, and again for Chatto & Windus, to accompany the Scott-Moncrieff translation. A generation of English Proustians were brought up on his images: Angus, writing in the *Observer* (10 September 1950), agreed with Chatto that Jullian might become to Proust what Phiz had been to Dickens: "It is not only the deadly satire which M. Jullian catches in his portraits of Oriane, Charlus, Odette and Albertine, but also their tragedy. It is not only the beauty and life of the 'Jeunes Filles' . . . but also their cruel fleetingness."

Angus's 1920's scrapbook, *For Whom the Cloche Tolls*, sprang out of a conversation at Viva's during which Angus, observing one of the faded beauties who haunted these events, described the dresses that his mother had worn. Angus's interest in women's clothing was less obsessional than that of Colin and Pat Johnstone-Wilson, and indeed than that of Viva King, whose description of her own wedding dress has a strange and fetishistic power. (She made it herself in her workroom: it was a dress of "a dark blue charmeuse, a material which reversed crepe or satin. It was made on the crepe side with trimmings and belt of satin. It had a short pleated skirt and the top, which bloused over the scalloped belt, almost to my knees, was open in the front to show a pleated silk chemisette and a Peter Pan collar in the new *bois de rose* colour which was a subtle shade of rosewood pink . . .")[3]

Angus could not rival this intensity, but he had an amazing memory for detail, and he and Jullian were well-matched. A contract with Methuen, dated 11 April 1951, offered Angus a fifty pounds advance on signature for "A Scrap Book of the Twenties". When the volume appeared, in 1953, it was to be greeted by the accolade of approval from those who might have remembered the period better than he. Betjeman testified to its accuracy (*Daily Telegraph*, 19 June 1953) and Cecil Beaton, himself one of the satirical targets, was lyrical about Jullian's illustrations: "With devilish relish, he shows us Maisie, dressed in a short sack of bead fringeing, barrel-shaped capes, heavily tasselled beach pyjamas, or Jazz-patterned Fair Isle sweaters, surrounded by Pierrot or 'Venetian' dolls, futuristic leather cushions . . . None of the appalling fads of the twenties escapes Mr Jullian's notice. The batik scarves, the tasselled necklaces, the geometric roses made of taffeta on a sausage-waisted Lanvin 'picture dress', the bowls of real flower-heads floating among wax water-lilies, the electrical fitment of 'modernistic' frosted glass in the Cannes casino, the mosaic of glass lamp-shades . . ."[4] With Jullian, Angus had relived his own boyhood: here are the musical songs and shows of the Twenties, the ballets, the stock market crashes, the cocaine: here are parodies of Bennett, Woolf, Huxley, Katherine Mansfield: here is Maud with her red hair – "My hair had a lovely auburn tinge then . . . and I always wore something green – if only a scarf or a handkerchief – to set it off."

(Edmund Wilson, deeply intrigued by yet hostile to English social life both past and present, much admired *Cloche*, and praised it highly to Max Beerbohm on a visit to Rapallo in March 1954: "When we were going, I told him that I wanted to send . . . Angus Wilson's *Cloche*, which I said was the best thing of its kind since Harold Nicolson's *Some People* – though I wasn't sure that Wilson hadn't invented a genre of his own . . .")[5]

★

In the autumn of 1949, while Anthony Garrett was still away in Austria with the army, Angus went to Paris for three weeks on leave. On 31 August 1949, he wrote to Philippe in Paris:

Dear Philippe,
    Did you get the 'Wrong Set'? I met a nice friend of yours – a Pole from Naples – recently.* Did you also hear anything from 'Picture Post?' or perhaps you didn't want to, anyway.
    Now, the people with whom I hoped to exchange a flat have

* This, presumably, was Kot – the beautiful blond newly-demobbed officer, Constantin Jelenski, with whom Jullian was much taken.

failed me, can you help me find a pleasant hotel (or other
accommodation) within English means for about 3 weeks from
25th September or four or five days later for about a fortnight or
three weeks. If possible I would like to find somewhere I could
write in the afternoons occasionally, i.e. with at least a comfortable
chair in the room, also, and most importantly, somewhere where I
can get a room for Ian who is going to join me for a week. Help
me, dear Philippe, to find such a place, and I will remain yours to
command for ever (Indeed I am anyway, but this could clinch the
matter.) I hope to see much of you in Paris, anyway . . .

Ian Calder did indeed join him, on 6 October, and no doubt Angus did
see much of Philippe in the moments when he was not listening to Ian or
working on his next volume of short stories and a biography of Zola
commissioned by Herbert Van Thal. But in January 1950 Anthony Garrett
returned from the army, and on 27 May 1950 Angus wrote again to
Philippe to say he was coming to Paris for 8 days on June 3rd, staying at the
Hotel Grand Saumur in the Rue de Bellechasse.

Ian is busy with lectures, so I am bringing to Paris (with Ian's
permission) a very nice boy called Anthony Garrett . . . Bentley
and Ian send their love, Love from Angus
P.S My book has gone into 4 editions in U.S.A.

Everything was going very well for Angus, as the proud claim of four
editions indicates. William Morrow had published *The Wrong Set* in March
1950, having paid an advance of five hundred dollars against royalties of 10
per cent and rising; an advertisement in the *New York Times* for the third
printing declared, "The *right* people are talking about *The Wrong Set*," and
added a quote from Edmund Wilson's review in *The New Yorker*: "After
Evelyn Waugh, what? . . . the answer is Angus Wilson, a master of
mimicry, rich in invention and wit."

But fame and fortune had not blotted Anthony Garrett from Angus's
memory, and Anthony, despite a new entanglement with a young Scot
called John, had not forgotten Angus. John the Scot was to cause many
moments of jealousy and drama over the next year or two: according to
Anthony, John was, like Angus, a fully-fledged anxiety neurotic. And then
there was Ian Calder, still very much upon the scene.

★

Ian Calder by now had moved to the University of Reading, where he was
working on a vast, ambitious and ground-breaking dissertation on the
works of the Elizabethan magus, John Dee. He had migrated there from

Cambridge via the Warburg Institute, where his work had much impressed the scholarly and fastidious Perkin Walker.* And at Reading, he had found himself at the centre of a lively group of young writers and academics.

This was a good time to be there. The young university had recruited from Oxford the young John Wain, described by Ian Calder in a letter to Angus as "rather striking – plus traits of beauty – in the young intellectual, poet, or undergraduate tradition of looks, long, lean, somewhat 'unfinished' strong features, huge luminous eyes, long lashed, carefully untidy, rather limp fair wavey hair . . ." Frank Kermode, fresh from the navy, was another rising star, and in 1947 the combative and brilliant Luigi Meneghello from the Italian Resistance arrived.† Meneghello developed a Department of Italian Studies, with the encouragement of English lecturer Donald Gordon. Gordon was another precocious academic (he became professor at the age of thirty-four) whose particular field was the interplay of literature, drama and the visual arts in Italy and England: he had close connections with the Warburg. Meneghello described him as "a kind of modern incarnation of a Renaissance humanist", with a marked physical resemblance to Erasmus of Rotterdam.‡

In the 1940s all was going well at Reading. Ian was to be seen shuffling happily around in slippers with a large suitcase containing apples, his spreading thesis, and bottles of beer, or lecturing in full spate to entranced students, running on for two hours without stopping. He was to be seen lying elegantly on the grass as Perkin Walker played tennis, less elegantly dripping blood as he attempted to open bottles of orangeade with his bare hands – characteristically thoughtful in providing them, characteristically thoughtless in forgetting to bring an opener, said Meneghello – "We drank blood and orange." Ian busied himself with the literary society, inviting speakers – Nevill Coghill, John Woodward§ from the Ashmolean, and Angus himself, to meet the students. "He paraded Angus, still

* Walker had transferred from University College to the Warburg at the personal request of Ernst Gombrich: Walker's colleague Dr Frances Yates also had a high opinion of Calder's work on the Renaissance.

† Luigi Meneghello, professor of Italian and author of novels *Libera nos a malo*, 1963, and *I piccoli maestri*, 1964.

‡ Gordon worked hard but published little; he was a depressive alcoholic homosexual, who eventually, after a series of more-or-less self-induced catastrophes, was forced through scandal into early retirement. He died a year later, on 22 December 1977, at the age of sixty-two.

§ Woodward met a fate as unhappy as Gordon's: after years at the Ashmolean he failed to get the job at Birmingham on which he had set his heart, and took to the streets, tramping from friend to friend cadging fivers, until his early death.

introduced as Johnstone-Wilson, as a celebrity," said Wain. Angus and Perkin became frequent visitors to Reading, and in 1951 Meneghello and his wife Katya borrowed, though Ian's good offices, Angus's flat in Dolphin Square – they were embarrassed to arrive upon his doorstep with "flowers for Mrs Wilson", Ian having been too polite to disabuse them of their misunderstanding.

Ian Calder was never quite to disappear from Angus's life, though he wandered off on unexpected courses. The relationship with Anthony Garrett, in contrast, intensified. Their trip to Paris in June 1950 was the first of many travels together, and Anthony's first visit to France. He remembers some details with an odd clarity – such as the fact that M. Lampacher, manager of the old-fashioned hotel, greeted Angus, bewilderingly, at breakfast on their first morning with the words "Ah, Mr Wilson, so your little holiday is nearly over!" Lampacher also annoyed Angus by insisting on speaking English to him, on the grounds that he had some English relatives in Sanderstead. Their bedroom was Zolaesque, with a patterned deep red wallpaper, and Monsieur Lampacher had decided the couple would require a matrimonial bed. (M. Lampacher's hotel was a favourite with writers from across the Channel and the Atlantic: he features in person, again showing off his English, in a short story called "Il Ploe:r da mo koe:r" [*sic*] in Hortense Calisher's collection *Extreme Magic*, 1964.)

Angus and Anthony saw the sights – Père-Lachaise and the grave of Oscar Wilde, Montmartre, the Luxembourg gardens, Versailles. They spent their evenings with Philippe Jullian and his friends. Paris was enjoying its first period of relaxation since the war, and the atmosphere was heady. Gone were the icy lodgings and the fuel shortages which had tormented the luxury-loving Jullian: the spring of 1950 was "*une suite ininterrompue de déjeuners, cocktails, dîners, galas et festivités diverses qui consacrent la résurrection de Paris après dix années d'austérité.*"[6] Jullian's set included the rich and famous (he was particularly devoted to Violet Trefusis and Nancy Mitford); the Proustian Yves Clogeson, faithful despite many a rebuff; and languid silk-scarved novelist Bernard Minoret, with whom he was to collaborate on a volume of literary and artistic pastiches.[7]

It was a new world to Anthony, with new rules. One evening he was detached from Jullian's circle by a wealthy American with an open Packard, with whom he spent the night in a room looking out over the garden of the Hotel Matignon: on his return to the hotel the next day, he found a little note from Angus, saying "Is it all over? I do hope you will come back. Love, Angus."* Was this note some kind of turning-point? Anthony was surprised by Angus's tone, perhaps by an awareness of his own irresponsibility, and by the concern of Angus's French friends, who turned on the American poacher with indignation. One did not steal from Angus.

Anthony also recalls that Angus was invited to visit Nancy Mitford, who was at this period comfortably installed in her apartment in the rue Monsieur. It had become one of the obligatory staging-posts for literary and not so literary tourists – she complained that everybody called on her, even total strangers – "I suppose it's the £25 [i.e. of travel-restricted money], they hope for a free glass of water."[8] Angus had made it clear that he was in Paris with a friend but she had replied with what seemed a very definite singular – no "looking forward to seeing you both". Anthony was relieved to be let off the Mitford conversation test, but he had unwittingly posed what became a problem for this arbiter of manners – what should one do about homosexual couples? "There is a new problem for the hostesses here do you have it? which is this. Chaps ring up and say can they bring their homosexual wives. 'You know Hans, you met him at so-and-so's' or 'Roberto who is staying with me' or one just said 'my partner' like a deb dance. Then these fearful gorillas appear. They have no conversation & are not even pretty or not to ONE anyway. Schiaparelli is quite firm & says no – what do you do in London?"[9] Nancy Mitford had no prejudice against homosexuality and many of her best friends were homosexuals – indeed she had drawn a notably sympathetic portrait of Stephen Tennant as the outrageous Cedric in Love in a Cold Climate (1949), a portrait which shocked her American readers – but the social niceties perplexed her, as they perplexed many. Angus was not perplexed. He expected Anthony to be treated as an equal partner, and would be offended or angry – sometimes conspicuously so – if he felt that Anthony was being neglected. (He quarrelled permanently with Philippe Jullian's picture-dealer friend, David Carritt,† later Director of Christie's, on this issue. Carritt arrived at a party at Dolphin Square, and was greeted at the door by Anthony: he brushed rudely past, and thereupon was booted out by Angus, who never asked him round again.)

Angus did not go in for secrecy or social segregation. British Museum

---

* This note does not survive: an envelope of the right period, long cherished, bearing the single word "Anthony", proved disappointingly empty.

† David Carritt (1927–1982), art historian and art dealer, Director of Christie's 1964–70.

colleagues from lower grades, like Alan Gray,* were pleasantly surprised by invitations to supper. If Jullian was a snob, Angus was, in theory and practice, an egalitarian. Everybody was asked to Dolphin Square.

Some of his parties were mixed, some were all-male. A young National Serviceman on leave, Michael Woolley, was taken to one of the latter by the Deputy Warden of Halliday Hall (a London University Students' Hostel, also known as Holiday Hell) and he remembers it thus. "Tony Garrett opened the door of a very crowded flat. The party was in full swing . . . Angus gave me a kind welcome and, tagging onto Arthur at first, I was soon airborne. The drink helped. Tony Garrett was leonine. That was the word for him. A large blond head, very good-looking, and a strong athletic body. Eventually people began to drift away and when only a dozen or so were left, Angus suggested we all go down below and have dinner in the restaurant of the block, where there was a Ladies Orchestra playing. We settled down at a long table . . . After dinner was ordered, a marvellous scene began when Angus invited the lady conductor of the band to come over to our table and meet Geoffrey Wright, the composer of 'Transatlantic Lullaby'. Angus was clearly on close camping terms with the girl and she gushed madly over Geoffrey before returning to her podium to swing instantly into that very attractive song . . . The girl crooner sang it straight at our table, and Geoffrey stood up to take a bow and to applaud the band." (This account, written in Lisbon in 1990, is probably a more authentic version of another story, which has Ivy Benson, the leader of the orchestra, recognising Geoffrey, striking up spontaneously with "his song", and then going over to greet him and Angus, whom she addressed as "your lovely wife" – leaving Angus in some difficulty as to how to leave the restaurant without causing embarrassment.)

The mixed parties and entertainments were very mixed, and became more so as the forties moved into the fifties and Angus's social circle continued to expand. Sir Edward Marsh was invited to tea, and got lost on the way in the vastness of the undistinguished blocks of the square: he arrived distressed, windblown, a tragic Lear-like figure with his hat and stick and monocle, after an unfortunate encounter with a suspicious female flat-dweller from whom he had had to ask directions. Hortense Calisher, whose first short story was published in the *New Yorker* in 1950, and who also lived for a while in Dolphin Square, was introduced to Angus by Emily "Mickie" Hahn (journalist, writer, and author of *China to Me*, 1944: married to the orientalist Charles Boxer). Hortense Calisher became a

---

* Gray worked his way up the hierarchy from the clerical to the executive grade, a feat impossible in earlier years, and praised Angus as one of the few executives to communicate across the frontiers. Interview M.D. 17 May 1991.

frequent visitor: she was in England on a Guggenheim grant and was happily discovering English manners and conversation, of which Angus seemed to offer a splendidly eccentric yet archetypal example. She particularly cherished, some years later, his comment upon a miscellaneous spread she had laid out in her rented house in Portugal Place in Cambridge, designed to cope with the uncertain arrivals of uncertain guests in uncertain weather: "Ah!" said Angus, conspiratorially, to Brigid Brophy, "a nursery tea!"

Then there was one young man who came to Dolphin Square and cast greedy eyes on Angus's guavas – he was indulged. Tinned stewed guavas were one of the new post-war treats, supplementing the brilliantly-coloured tinned mandarin oranges which had brightened many a wartime feast – Frank Francis's wife Kitty had always liked to pop some into her jelly to brighten it up. The guava was a peculiar fruit, of a pinkish-orange complexion and a rubbery texture, with conspicuous stones: it featured, not very attractively, in Angus's short story, "Who For Such Dainties?", which describes one of those disastrous meals of which Angus wrote so well – a meal of Rumanian stew enlivened with amusing plums, olives and figs to eke out the meat ration, which "had stuck to the saucepan and were burned", and guavas which were "dead and flabby", like the hostess's "own flat, pendulous flesh". (The title of this story, published in the *Evening Standard* on 2 September 1949, is taken from the sad song of the Mock Turtle in Lewis Carroll's *Alice in Wonderland*:

> Who for such dainties would not stoop?
> Soup of the evening, beautiful soup!

Carroll was to prove a useful source for Wilson titles and quotations, but the burned stew was probably taken from Angus's own experience, as several guests report on cooking crises at Dolphin Square.)

The Barnes, the Merrys, and the Davieses met at Angus's apartment regularly. Mary McCarthy and Rose Macaulay and the Wollheims and John Freeman and Cyril Connolly and Robert Kee and James and Jean MacGibbon were all invited. At one of the larger gatherings, critic and essayist Dwight Macdonald introduced himself, American-style, to Rose Macaulay, describing himself as an editor of the *Partisan Review* and founder of his own journal, *Politics*: she stared at him and said, "Have you come all the way across the room to tell me that? How kind." (And it was at one of Angus's parties in Dolphin Square, on 8 April 1957, that Richard Wollheim was to meet his second wife, Mary Day Lanier: she was Dwight Macdonald's stepdaughter.)

In the late forties and early fifties Tony (for so he now becomes in our story) was still living with his parents at 35 Finchley Way. But he was becoming a familiar presence in Frobisher. He helped Angus organise his social life – one of the tales he tells is of the day when he and Angus decided they needed some sort of bench for the hallway in the flat, where guests could leave their coats. Tony set off to Gamage's, where he spotted a suitable object, and tried to buy it, only to be told a lady had just rung up and ordered it. When he got back to Dolphin Square, there it was – purchased, as Gamage's had thought, by a Miss De Wilson. (No wonder Angus disliked the telephone.)

★

Angus, meanwhile, was hard at work on his next collection of stories. Could he do it again? His publishers hoped so. A letter from John Pattisson dated 16 November 1949 to Spencer Curtis Brown indicates that Angus was considered a valuable property. "Before discussing terms for this new volume, it is clear from your letter that I shall have to remind you of some historical background, for you say that in negotiating the first contract you 'gave us the earth'. The real facts were rather different and were nearer to our giving you the earth, for it was only because I told him that I felt an agent would be more effective in selling first serial rights of his new stories than we would that Angus went to you at all, on our recommendation. I know that you were recommended to him by others as well; but I am sure that Angus will confirm that it was my recommendation which turned the scale." (The advance went up from *The Wrong Set*'s £50 to £75 on a contract dated 23 December 1949.)

Such Darling Dodos, dedicated to "Mr and Mrs Pickering Walker", was published in July, 1950, to renewed acclaim. The repeated sentiment that "his second volume is no disappointment" must have come as a relief to one familiar with the dangerous habits of reviewers, who turn today on what they prized yesterday. Peter Quennell, in the *Daily Mail*, complained that he needed "a little more humanity", Stevie Smith found his interest in sinfulness "depressing", and Marghanita Laski curiously complained that "neither Mr Wilson or I are at college any more, and surely one has a right to demand that the ageing eagle shall stretch his wings a little?"[10] But the general consensus was that these stories were even better than those in the first collection.

Angus Wilson's work was happily controversial. Opinions were sharply divided as to whether he was moralist, satirist, or both. Was he a cynic or a disappointed idealist? Was he tender or cruel, acid or gentle? Was life really as macabre as his portrayal of it? Did he perhaps represent, enquired one American reviewer, the New Decadence?

George Painter wrote a long, thoughtful appreciation, coming down on the side of morality versus satire – these stories, he says, are all "about goodness".[11] Alan Ross wrote an equally thoughtful but less friendly piece. While admitting that it was unlikely that a better book of stories would be published in the year, he felt that Wilson appeared as a "contemptuous ringmaster" or a bayonetter of "dead corpses", with no respect for his characters.[12] This allegation was to be repeated by others, and indeed in later years by Ross himself: Wilson's sensitivity to such criticisms went deep.

C.P. Snow's review* sums up the salutary uneasiness unleashed by this new talent: "Part-bizarre, part-macabre, part-savage and part-maudlin, there is nothing much like it upon the contemporary scene. It is rather as though a man of acute sensibility felt left out of the human party, and was surveying it, half-enviously, half-contemptuously, from the corner of the room, determined to strip off the comfortable pretences and show that this party is pretty horrifying after all . . . Sometimes the effect is too mad to be pleasant, sometimes most moving; no one could deny Mr Wilson's gift."

What was there in Angus Wilson to create such a stir? John Osborne, who was to head the next new wave, remembered the "sensation" of Angus's arrival in the "post war literary vacuum" – "those ten years after the war were like a frozen waste, bland but frozen over. The whole nation was having a little lie down. Angus's cold eye was needed. He had a personal and an intellectual energy . . . He woke people up." His stories were in their own way as iconoclastic and irreverent as Osborne's plays were to be – for some years now the British had been congratulating themselves smugly on having won the war, and Angus exposed them to themselves as a nation of beggars, snobs, bullies, black-marketeers and hypocrites, ill-dressed, plain, timid, and adventurous only in pursuit of selfish ends: it was not a flattering portrait, but it made a change after all those patriotic war movies, those sentimental brief encounters, those novels about heroism on the high seas. He introduced new social types, types which had hitherto been politely ignored, or which had not existed – for society itself was rapidly changing, and he was its new chronicler.

Osborne was only one of many to respond to Angus's new voice. John Blackwell, who was years later to be Angus's editor at Secker & Warburg, recalls that for his generation Angus's writing "coincided with a feeling of, for want of a better word, rebellion". Wilson was a forerunner of a mood which produced such disparate cultural manifestations as *Rebel Without a Cause* (1955), *Rock around the Clock* (1956) and *The Wild One* (1954), as well

---

* *Sunday Times*, 23 July 1950. Snow was at the beginning of his career as a novelist. *Time of Hope* was published in 1949, *The Masters* in 1951.

as the anti-establishment protests of Kingsley Amis, John Wain and Osborne himself – yet Angus, unlike some of his successors, had first-hand inside knowledge of the great institutions which they came to mock and undermine. He appeared to Blackwell as a "fifth columnist prepared to chuck a grenade into the magazine while we were shaping up to fire slingshots at the battlements." He wrote with the authority of experience, from a familiarity with the old régime and its instincts for power.

★

Some of the themes of this new volume are familiar; almost all connect directly with the life. "Rex Imperator" is a portrait of life at Ashampstead: Rex Palmer stands for Captain Winn Johnstone-Wilson, surrounded by a collection of scroungers and spongers, and supported by a much-put-upon wife. "What Do Hippos Eat?" portrays another hopeless gentleman-scrounger, owing something to Willie Johnstone-Wilson, something to Fred. (The hippos themselves were observed on an outing to the zoo with George Painter.)* "Necessity's Child", the first-person narration of an imaginative child trying to protect himself through fantasy and story-telling, refers back to the theme of "Raspberry Jam", and evokes Angus's seaside memories of Bexhill and Eastbourne. Both "Learning's Little Tribute" and "Totentanz" attack the pettiness and narrowness of an academic and bureaucratic world familiar to Angus through Oxford, the British Museum, and his convalescence at St Andrews: Isobel Capper, with her desire to escape from the dowdy world of academe and to cut a dash as a London hostess, combines elements of Helen Pattisson and Viva King. (The idea for the plot had been haunting him for a long time: what seems to be one of his very earliest ideas for a story mentions "the crematorium ball".) "Mummy to the Rescue" revives Angus's obsession with the sinking of the *Titanic*, and "Sister Superior" is a black seaside family comedy of manipulation and misunderstanding, again with an underlying financial threat to the "good" sibling. "Heart of Elm" draws on Little Hadham and the death of Mrs Baker: she had died aged seventy on 25 March 1949 at Providence House, and Angus, Bentley Bridgewater and Ian Calder, her surrogate family, her "boys", had been shocked when her real family descended to claim the spoils.

This incident, and the character of Mrs Baker, continued to work on Angus's imagination: many notes concern her and the conflict between seeing her positively as a Wife-of-Bath, Rabelaisian figure or as something more brutal and sinister: she reappears in a television play, and there are

---

* According to Valentine Cunningham, an obsession with zoos was a feature of 1930s literature – *British Writers of the Thirties* (OUP 1988) p.86–90.

echoes of her in later novels. In *The Wild Garden*, Angus makes a connection between Mrs Baker's death and his mother's: he states that it "had something of the same traumatic suddenness for me as my mother's. I opened the door of her cottage one Saturday afternoon to find her lying on the floor in an apoplexy from which she later died."[13] (Tony Garrett, however, believes that it was Ian Calder who opened that door, and Angus admits earlier in the paragraph that he had, in the story, distorted his friends' reactions to her and her death, and confused them with his own.)

The most bizarre story in the volume is "A Little Companion", which again draws on village life. It is a ghost story: the intelligent, sensible old maid Miss Arkwright finds herself haunted by a vulgar sickly snivelling child. Miss Arkwright herself is drawn in tribute to the Jane Austen school of spinsterhood – good-humoured, ironic, Christian. The "one or two very fine old pieces of jewellery" inherited from her grandmother have a hint of Madge Gillespie, that sensible (though irreligious) schoolmistress in St Andrews. Miss Arkwright knows she is experiencing some kind of mental aberration, which her friends date from the outbreak of war, but which she herself dates back to 24 July 1936, her forty-seventh birthday.

Miss Arkwright, before the haunting, recognises herself and knows how others see her: she accepts her own place in the social world. The child is a creation which contrasts with anything Jane Austen could have drawn. (Jane Austen herself, in fact, had a mentally defective brother, banished forever in infancy from the family circle.) The appearance of the child disrupts her existence. Sensibly, methodically, she attempts to exorcise it, first through the Church, then through Christian Science, purgatives, spiritualism, psychoanalysis and travel. Eventually she learns to accept it and live with it. When he finally leaves her (having finally established himself as a "him" rather than an "it") she mourns his loss, and becomes a recluse.

What is the meaning of this little fable? Its use of the supernatural is unusual in the Wilson canon, though it may owe something to his admiration for Kipling. Its message – "common sense is not enough" – is commonplace, and the child may readily be seen as an emanation of Miss Arkwright's repressed sexuality, underemployed intellect, deluded faith, or false position in a false social structure. (It is a very working-class child, with common tastes, and when the London evacuees reach the village during the war their physical unhealthiness reminds her of "her lost one": one might note that during the war Bump Walker had at first taken in evacuees, but, unable to stand their behaviour, had converted her war effort into setting up a village nursery school in Maresfield.) But there seems to be more to it than that. The child connects with the urchin of

Marseilles that teases the young Oxford undergraduate Jeremy in "Significant Experience", and with the possibly imaginary orphan imprisoned by Mrs MacLachlan in Regent Street. What is the child? Is it Angus himself, abandoned and abused? Is it his sexual alter ego, perversely in love with the Cockney whine? Is it an illegitimate infant of the middle-to-upper-class realist tradition of English fiction, a bastard heir of Jane Austen, Galsworthy and Walpole?

"Christmas Day in the Workhouse" is more straightforward, and makes direct use of his wartime experiences at Bletchley Park.* It describes the social tensions and emotional frictions, the voluntary and involuntary cruelties of life at Bletchley through the experiences of Thea, an intelligent young middle-class woman from the West Country whose fiancé has been killed in a plane crash. Bletchley Park is disguised as "the Bureau", and Thea is the efficient head of a subsection. She observes with superior distaste the power and sex games of her Head of Section, the jumped-up Major Prosser, and allows herself, encouraged by a moment of intimacy, to dream of a closer friendship with the beautiful, blonde, remote Stephanie, who works in her section and whose photograph appears in the *Tatler*. The atmosphere of girlish boarding-school "crushes", of sad billets run by lonely widows, of ugly canteens and jolly home-made fun, is captured in chilling detail. The compulsory Christmas fraternisation has echoes, though in a very different setting, of the disastrous attempts at social mixing in "Saturnalia".

The story recalls a incident remembered by several of Angus's Wrens. Rosemary Merry wrote a poem about it.

> On Christmas day we rigged up paper chains,
> stole holly, planned a feast
> while you made ink-blot spiders from old charts.
> Governesses now, we gave you pens, of red and green,
> insisted on a message
> of hope and welcome.
> Unusually meek, engrossed in silent toil,
> an age went by until you waved writ large:
> "DEBENHAM AND FREEBODY".
> We pinned it up.
> It seemed to say everything, or nearly everything.[14]

The title story of the volume, "Such Darling Dodos", suggests, as did "Et Dona Ferentes", the potential of a novelist. The title has a double

---

* BP may have surfaced in a completely different form in the ghost story. Maybe Angus, like Virginia Woolf, had heard voices? He certainly dreamed dreams.

resonance, and a resonance beyond the story itself. So many Wilsonian characters, stranded helplessly by wave after wave of social change, seemed to be "dodos" – dodos like Maud, like Willie, like old-club-tie conman Fred, like the Firbankian brothers, like First World War hero Winn and his prep school.

There are two kinds of dodo here – the most obviously superannuated is Tony, a fifty-five-year-old corseted hair-netted aesthetic Catholic convert, who is visiting his cousin in North Oxford. His heyday had been the Twenties, whereas the cousin and her husband represent the intellectual progressives of the Thirties, with their Heal's furniture, their good causes, their photographs of themselves handing out mugs of tea on hunger marches. Robin is dying, very fast, of cancer, and Tony, alerted by an unusually emotional letter from Robin's wife Priscilla, descends upon them in the hope of precipitating a death-bed conversion. The comedy of mutual misunderstanding is beautifully judged, and suggestions of underlying tragedy – the pathos of Tony's life and his desperate and genuine reliance upon his faith, the subdued regrets of Robin on his approaching death, the self-doubt of Priscilla about her marriage – are inescapable. The story ends with a double take, as a much younger couple, invited out of duty to lunch, seem to reveal to Tony that they have more in common with him than with his worthy cousins. He is delighted:

" 'Poor Robin and Priscilla are extinct, I'm afraid.' He hadn't felt so modern since the first production of 'L'Après-midi'.

'They're dodos, really, but,' he added more kindly, 'such darling dodos.' "

Tony's revelation is an illusion, for the young Ecclestons do not represent a return to Tony's frivolous youth, and even he suspects that it would be unwise to press them too hard on their political opinions. They are hardly likely to prove supporters of Franco, even though they speak well of college chapel. A new age has arrived, and Tony, Priscilla, and Robin are all out of date. The Thirties dodo of North Oxford might seem one of those easy targets deplored by Elizabeth Bowen and Anastasia Anrep, but the species had an enduring fascination for Angus, and possessed remarkable powers of survival. (Such dodos are alive and well in North Oxford and other protected breeding-grounds to this day.)

Some have read this story as Wilson's dismissal of his own Thirties political illusions, but this seems unlikely, both from the tone of the story and its date – a date at which Angus was a member of the Labour Party, and himself committed to a vision of a brave new post-war world of drains, baths, refrigerators and national health. He seems to be questioning all "progressive" principles, be they adopted in the name of liberalism,

1 View of West Street, Durban, 1855

2 Angus Wilson's mother, Maud Johnstone-Wilson (*neé* Caney), Durban 1898

3 Willie Johnstone-Wilson with the young Angus (c. 1914)

4 Angus Wilson with his mother, at Bexhill, 1914

5 Angus Wilson with his brother Winn,
on leave at Bexhill, 1915

6 Angus Wilson, aged nine,
in a rickshaw in Durban, 1923

7 Angus Wilson with his parents (centre and right), 1929

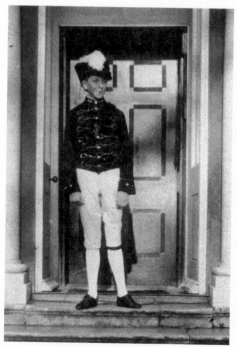

8 Angus Wilson as Sir Joseph Porter
in HMS *Pinafore* at Ashampstead

9 Angus Wilson with John Pattisson
in a Westminster school production, 1931

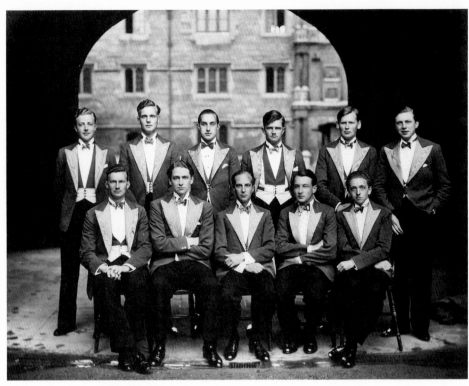

10 The Myrmidons at Merton College, Oxford, 1935
Back row: W.M. Moore, G.D. Leyland, S.C. Sleeman, R.C. Bewsher, C.L. Hall, A.M.S. (Airey) Neave
Front row: K.A. Merritt, J.S. Daniel, G.J. Barry, R.A. Lamb, A.F. Johnstone-Wilson

11 Angus Wilson (second right) with RN and WRNS at Bletchley Park

12 Angus Wilson with Geoffrey Wright
at Little Hadham

13 Angus Wilson
with Ian Calder

14 Angus Wilson with Bentley Bridgewater

15 Angus Wilson at Providence House, where his first stories were written

16 Angus Wilson with George Painter

17 Viva King

18 Forrest Fulton

19 Tony Garrett in uniform, 1948
(photograph by Bentley Bridgewater)

20 Ian Calder

21 Chris Arnold as an undergraduate

22 Perkin Walker

23 Angus Wilson on the steps of the British Museum, 1954
(photo Mark Gerson)

humanism or socialism. He was to revert to this theme again and again. Unable to take refuge in religious faith, unable to dismiss the existence of evil, he continued to probe questions of public and private morality. Committed reviewers – from either the *Church Times* or *Tribune* – tended to deplore his lack of moral centre. It was the lack of a centre that drove him on his quest.

Angus was old enough to remember the mysterious process of The Strange Death of Liberal England. He may well have read George Dangerfield's popular analysis, published under this title in 1935. Dangerfield's definition is suggestive of some of Angus's own arguments: "Liberalism, after all, implies rather more than a political creed or an economic philosophy; it is a profoundly conscience-stricken state of mind. It is the final expression of everything which is respectable, God-fearing and frightened. The poor, it says, are always with us, and something must certainly be done for them: not too much, of course, that would never do; but something."

★

Several models have been suggested for Robin and Priscilla. Was there a touch of the socialists G.D.H. and Margaret Cole, or of those liberals of the old régime, C.F.G. and Mrs Masterman? Were Beatrice and Sidney Webb at the back of his mind? Or was he thinking of donnish friends like Christopher and Helen Morris, now safely back from Bletchley Park and settled for life in Cambridge?

The Morrises were characters who popped up several times in Angus's fiction, teasing and pleasing the imagination partly because of their contradictions – he a scholarly historian and Kingsman who was also an athlete and a cricketing fanatic, she an austere and formidable pedagogue who was also an excellent cook and a generous hostess. (She wrote a life of Escoffier.) Friends spotted them in several stories. Mathematician Robin Gandy identified Morris with the husband in "Totentanz", who is given to "tobacco-jarred, golfy homeliness [and a] habit of pointing with his pipe and saying: 'Now hold on a minute, I want to examine this average man or woman of yours more carefully.' " Even more tellingly, Morris recognised himself as Robin the Dodo: writing to Angus (3 July 1969) on the publication of an omnibus reprint, he said "I am so glad that the Dodos got themselves in, as I always think they are Helen and myself . . ."

Was Angus perhaps attacking academic cosiness itself, the toasted-teacake warmth of that safe provincial world where E.M. Forster had at last found a permanent home? In *The Wild Garden*, Angus was to emphasise that his target in "Such Darling Dodos" was not so much false standards as insufficient standards. Robin and Priscilla are good but blinkered, and they lack "some deeper personal convictions, some poetry to illumine them when history has temporarily turned against them."[15] (The tide, by implication, will turn.) Like Dangerfield, Angus had lived through the inter-war rise of violent political forces. He had some hopes of the Labour Party and the New Men, as represented by Denis Barnes. But would they bring in a New World? He doubted. The old world seemed stubbornly – and dangerously – determined to survive. The dodos would not die.

A NEW AGENDA

In September 1950, high on the success of the dodos, Angus went off to see the flamingoes. He went with Bentley Bridgewater to the South of France, on a working holiday – doing research for his Zola book, and, as a postcard to Tony Garrett shows, writing more fiction. He wrote that he had started a new story about "real Myshkins and false Myshkins and who knows which is which which I hope will appeal to you. There is much else here of a very special kind that would appeal to you – perhaps later you will care to give ear to the Moor's exploits – only, of course, they're not exploits, just beauty seen. Have a nice holiday. J'attends te voir avec impatience. My salutations to my brother Scotland."

When he got back, Angus took himself off to the Garden House Hotel in Cambridge for a few days in November to finish *Zola*. (His old friend Humphry House, whose Dickens proofs Angus had helped to correct years earlier, bumped into him in the street and enquired what he was doing in Cambridge. "Writing a book on Zola," Angus replied. House replied "Oh, how wise that is! Every lane, every street here speaks of him."*) A letter to Pattisson about the money from *Zola* (earmarked for income tax) indicates that Angus viewed this task not wholly as a labour of love: "I am working, let me assure you, like a Trojan (curious phrase) . . ." (1 November 1950) Nevertheless, *Emile Zola: An Introductory Study of his Novels* was more than a pot-boiler: it was well received (save by those critics to whom any whiff of pscyhological intepretation was anathema) as a serious and timely attempt to review and revive Zola's reputation in Britain. It led to many requests for introductions to new translations (of *Restless House*, 1953; *Earth* and *The Kill*, 1954; *Zest for Life*, 1956), to reviews of any works dealing with Zola, and to lectures on French

---

* House credited "Mr Johnstone-Wilson of the British Museum" for correcting the proofs of *The Dickens World*, 1941. He died in 1955, aged forty-six.

literature: also to a friendship with fellow Zola scholar F.W.J. Hemmings, of Leicester University.

Zola was published by Secker & Warburg in February 1952 and by Morrow in the United States in September 1952: the original commission had been from Herbert Van Thal, but Secker & Warburg had taken over with a contract dated 24 April 1951 with an offer of an advance of £100. The contract for his next novel, already entitled *Hemlock and After*, was dated 12 January 1951, and it offered an advance of £250, half on signature, half on publication. The back of the original contract is covered in Angus's own financial calculations, totted up in purple ink.

Finding time to write became increasingly a problem. With a full-time job, a diary crowded with social engagements, and articles to be written, it was hard to carve out a space. There were emotional tensions too. Angus made another trip to Paris with Ian Calder the following spring (6 April 1951) leaving Tony in the company of John the Scot. This was almost immediately followed by a second two-week trip abroad, in May, this time to Italy with Tony. Was some sort of power struggle taking place? Angus and Tony flew to Florence and saw the sights, including Harold Acton at La Pietra, then moved on to Siena, Ravenna, Bologna and Lake Como.

Angus had already filled many notebooks with jottings for his next book, and in the summer he settled down to write it. Most of *Hemlock and After* was written, at considerable speed, during leave from the Museum in the August of 1951, in the home of Sandy Parnis at Thorley, near Bishops Stortford. It was very close to Little Hadham territory, and indeed had been the base from which Bentley Bridgewater on one of his bicycle expeditions had discovered Providence House. Crowscroft was a pretty thatched cottage, bordering a stretch of wild woodland, which Parnis had bought in 1937: he let it during the war, then returned to commute daily to the Treasury. He would leave in the mornings at 8.00, with Angus still in bed: Angus would get up and write in his dressing-gown. Parnis returned at 7.30, by which time Angus, sitting out of doors in the sheltered south-facing garden, had done a good day's work. There were visits from Tony, from Bentley (who would swoop upon the contents of the refrigerator like a gannet) and from neighbours Robert French and Montagu Turland, but overall this was a period of intense concentration.* Angus wrote, euphorically, to Pattisson, reporting on progress – "I have had a wonderful time . . . I have done Book II all but the last chapter and then there is an epilogue . . . About 70,000 words in all I should say. I shall be back at work

---

* Robert French worked with John Lewis, Montagu Turland as an architect with the firm of Casson-Conder. Always known as Bob and Monty, they were to become close friends of Perkin Walker.

tomorrow (3rd) but I am so deeply in that evening work will not be difficult." He adds that he does not know whether it is good or not but thinks it is "very interesting" and has "some very good characters". He expected to finish by the end of October.

The place of composition was appropriate, for *Hemlock and After* is a novel of village life. Angus had found Little Hadham and Simpson both fascinating and alarming. The plot centres on the problems caused by the bisexuality (in Angus's notes, the "queer marriage") of its protagonist, the Grand Old Man of Letters, Bernard·Sands, and on his conflicts at village level and finally beyond with fat and flowery Mrs Curry. She is one of the most memorable figures in Wilson's fiction: all sweetness and light and cosiness, she is also a procuress who deals in underage children. Jane Austen and E.F. Benson would hardly have recognised this vision of rural England, and at times the novel seems like a deliberate subversion of a particular genre of English fiction. (Angus says he chose respectable St Albans as the scene for a particularly unsavoury encounter partly out of mischief.)

There is a suggestion that Angus himself, as a homosexual far less easily disguised than Bernard Sands, felt that he might suffer from discrimination: it surfaces in a piece written years later about Hugh Massingham's novel about rural anti-Semitism, *The Harp and the Oak* (1945), which he had read in Little Hadham in 1946. He much admired Massingham's handling of the mindless persecution of Victor Abrahams and his wife Ilse by the villagers of Mandon; he saw it as a book that proved "how detestable is the naive belief in village natural warmth"[1] and concluded that while writing *Hemlock* "I was not wholly unaware that the homosexual scandal that the hero suffers in the novel came from my sense of the anti-homosexual prejudice in that village world. Yet, I must say that in those days it had not touched me personally."[1]

But it is probable that Angus himself not only feared the whispers, but had already had some direct or indirect confrontation. Mrs Baker and Val Graham Young had liked him – indeed Val, in her way, was in love with him – and Mrs Hill had cared for him like a mother, but there were others around who might have been less benign. In notes for a lecture on "Novelists: Deception and Reality" he mentions as the imaginative starting-point for *Hemlock* a neighbour just down the road in Little Hadham who said to him "I'm getting to know all your little movements, dear" – a remark which precipitated what he describes as a "novel of fear and conscience". Elsewhere he identified this starting-point as "a momentary powerful visual image of a fat woman and a thin man" – which again points at Mrs Curry down the road.[2] He admitted that Mrs Curry was one of the few characters in the book based directly on a real person, and praised Evelyn Waugh for guessing that this was a possibility – other reviewers, said Waugh, had too easily dismissed her as "preposterous".[3] Years later, when Lord Beaumont wrote (31 January 1977) to enquire if Mrs Curry had been in any way influenced by the portrait of the plump, slightly ridiculous, slightly sinister graveyard-haunting Mrs Sammile in Charles Williams' mystic village novel, *Descent into Hell* (Faber, 1937), Angus replied, ". . . I'm afraid the answer is 'no' for to my shame I've never read that book of Williams. Strangely, Mrs Curry was one of my few characters drawn from life as Evelyn Waugh alone in reviews guessed." Vera Curry, "an elephantine figure of Mabel Lucy Attwell chubbiness before her vulgar, picturesque, tea-cosy cottage", was based on a near neighbour in Little Hadham, a much-married lady from Devonshire connected with property, antiques and partridges: she was described by one of her descendants as a "devious old hag".

The lofty Bentley – a big man and above such things – always seemed sublimely indifferent to public opinion, behaving *en grand seigneur* as though it did not exist. Angus had a need to be liked and accepted – though, as Tony recalls, he would react with a display of exaggerated camp disdain if he spotted anybody staring disapprovingly at the middle-aged man dining in a restaurant with the fair-haired boy. (Angus looked older than his age; Tony looked younger. This did not help.)

Angus's relationship with Tony is clearly echoed in that of Bernie Sands with pretty young Eric Craddock. Eric is a would-be poet, who works in a bookshop and is dominated by his attractive, intelligent mother, a widowed Southern belle. The novel is dedicated "To Anthony, most gratefully", and Tony himself accepts the tribute – yes, he was a bit like Eric in those days, a daydreamer, full of fancy notions, only half-educated, narcissistic. (He had a lot to be narcissistic about.) But there are also hints of Ian Calder, The Wonder Boy, who, unlike Tony, had been very much on the scene in Little Hadham, and very much in Mrs Curry's eye.

Bernard, a prep-school master before his days of success, sees good educational material in Eric. This is a classic Socratic master-pupil friendship. Angus and Tony might laugh at those who used this model as a ploy in a YMCA swimming-pool game of seduction, but they themselves conformed in some measure to this version of the old, old story, although their relationship was also founded on powerful mutual attraction. But Bernard Sands is not Angus's attempt at a self-portrait. He is older than his creator, and more of an establishment figure. He is a married man who has long led a double life, and Eric is one of a succession of younger lovers. Bernard's position is complicated by his need to appear respectable – if his sexual preferences become known, he will prejudice his own good cause, which is the setting up and endowment of a writers' retreat at Vardon Hall. Private life threatens public good, and Bernard Sands, by a web of intrigue partly engineered by Mrs Curry, is made to appear as a corrupter of youth.*

Bernard believes himself to be a good man: the novel exposes the damage he has done. His wife, Ella, is a tormented neurotic: his journalist daughter is hard, bright, and emotionally vulnerable: his barrister son is an ambitious prig. By his own standards, Bernard has failed in terms of human relationships. Bernard himself, in a rather sudden epiphany in Leicester Square, comes to doubt his own motives, discovering in himself a sadism he had never acknowledged, which seems to undermine the very basis of his tolerant liberal humanism. His death leaves a legacy of unresolved moral conflicts and unanswered questions about crime and punishment.

(There is some evidence in the notes that Bernard's central recognition of his own sadism – as he watches the arrest of a young man for soliciting – was originally intended to be aroused by the arrest not of a stranger, but of Eric himself – a scene which would have had a different, more troubling and more powerful impact.)

*

Hemlock caused even more of a sensation than the stories. Far more explicit in its homosexual content and its treatment of sexual abuse, it was considered shocking – so shocking that Wilson's American publishers, Morrow, declined to take it, allowing it to be snapped up for Viking, via his old Reading Room acquaintance Gwenda David, now a publisher's scout, for an advance of $1250 against a royalty of 17½%. (Morrow were also to reject Mary Renault's *The Charioteer*, published in England by Longman in October 1953, because of its frank treatment of homosexuality.) Some public libraries refused to stock *Hemlock*, and there was a lively debate in the pages of the *Times Literary Supplement*, initiated by one Thea Hush who wrote on 30 January 1953 to complain that *Hemlock* was unobtainable through the Manchester Public Libraries, apparently on

* Daniel Waley (in a letter to M.D. 4 May 1993) suggests that the name "Bernie Sands" refers to the scorching fate of homosexual scholars and pedagogues in Canto XV of Dante's *Inferno*: J.H. Stape (*University of Toronto Quarterly*, 53, Summer 1984, 435–437) suggests that Sands refers to Bernard's shaky creed of "humanism": and Jay Halio makes a similar suggestion. Angus denied this when talking to a graduate student many years later, in the burning summer of 1976, but one cannot always trust an author's own denials: the subconscious makes its own connections. Can it be wholly a coincidence that Vardon Hall takes the name of a young American student/scholar named Bruce Vardon, who appears at some post-war point to have been passionately enamoured of Angus?

principle – the libraries stocked Miss Ruby M. Ayres but deemed Wilson and de Beauvoir "unsuitable". There was one letter of support for her, but Gilbert Benthall came back strongly, defending the public librarian's right and duty to ban absolutely any book "which he considers objectionable from a moral or literary point of view" (6 February 1953). The next week an ex-librarian, W.E. Simnett, wrote in to say that there was no conspiracy to censor, but a shortage of funds, and recommending that an eager reader could take the desperate remedy of buying the book. (This suggestion and indeed the whole discussion must have been very pleasing to Secker & Warburg.)

There is little in *Hemlock* now, post-Lady Chatterley, post-Lord Chamberlain, post-Wolfenden, to raise the eyebrow of a censor (although its themes remain stubbornly topical). Predictably, some reviewers disliked its subject matter: Stevie Smith bluntly stated that "perhaps the fact that the crux of Mr Wilson's situation is homosexual and its morals deviationist puts reviewers on their mettle to show how broad-minded they are."[4] The *Sphere*, more amiably, protested that there could be few English villages which harboured "so many drunks, homosexuals, blackmailers, procurers of little girls and general purveyors of evil". The reviewer of the *Seattle Times* longed for "some light tale of normal, sweet love" to rid itself of the bad taste. But overall, remarks about "unpleasantness" and "nastiness" and "unsavoury characters" were well offset by praise for Wilson's brilliance, wit, savagery, honesty, moral stamina (Pamela Hansford Johnson) and relentless courage (J.D. Scott). Somerset Maugham and Ernest Hemingway admired, and so did Tom Driberg and John Betjeman.

Wilson was acclaimed as the heir to Evelyn Waugh, even, more curiously, as an English Mary McCarthy. The *Times Literary Supplement* gave a long, serious lead review, and Arthur Calder-Marshall in the *Listener* implored the reader to buy it and read it many times. One who took this advice was Waugh himself, who claimed he read it three times: he wrote to Angus praising it, and then to Father Caraman, editor of the *Month*, offering to review it there. Caraman, hoping perhaps that Waugh's influence might persuade where Father Martindale's had failed, agreed. Waugh's article complimented Angus on his "sharp nose for class", wondered if he could be troubled by "remote dreams of the classless society", and concluded with the hope that Ella in her return to sanity represented the Saving Conscience.

Friends as well as reviewers expressed their support. Donald Gordon wrote him a letter of admiration and anxiety: "Bernard's catastrophe, from the crisis in Leicester Square, is brilliantly done. And I suppose it is acceptable that he, at this point, should discover, and fail to resolve, the problem of how to move into proper action on the basis of motives now known to be impure. But I think it was at the age of 20 that this problem suggested itself to me . . ."[5] Stephen Spender also wrote in appreciation – "Your novel is very good indeed, I think, and it has quite obsessed me for several days . . ." He declared it "a very moral book" but ambiguously so, and expressed unease about the "moral sweeping out of the stables and your leaning upon the judgement of a British court of law."[6] Rosamond Lehmann, Nancy Mitford, bookseller and novelist Martyn Goff, and many others wrote in support. (Nancy Mitford wrote saying that it filled her with despair as England had clearly changed so completely in her absence in Paris that she would never be able to write about it again.) J.B. Priestley, taking mild exception to the novel's use of his own name as a password for he knew not quite what (but suspected was somewhat unkind), wrote a robust letter of friendly protest, pointing out that Bernard Sands appeared too old, that the book was too short, and that he could have done with "a Proustian treatment of those London homosexual circles of which I catch only the rarest glimpses." He suggested lunch with him in his Albany flat, and Angus responded in a conciliatory vein – "My reason for mentioning your name was that the Vardon 'commuting gentry' have, in my experience, the tendency to view you as a 'dangerous radical' – their name for anyone who they would like to feel is on their side, but suspect is not . . . I admire your plays very much – 'Dangerous Corner' has a very special interest for me. Your politics I have always believed to be Liberal, individualist, Social Democratic – which would be my own – though such words no doubt cover great differences . . . Yes, 'Hemlock' should have been longer – there are so many reasons, none of course adequate excuses, why it was not. I did not think of Sands as 67, partly because I thought so definitely of Ella as in the fifties and nearly his age, partly because I wanted him to have only brushed the twenties and really come to notice in the early thirties, partly because he must have enough physical charm, as well as mental qualities to make Terence and Eric *pleased* to go to bed with him. 67 would be possible, but odd in the last case. Yours sincerely, Angus Wilson."[7] This exchange was the beginning of a long friendship.

Edith Sitwell also praised this "great, terrible, wise, tragic, far-seeing book,"[8] and she too invited him to lunch.

Hemlock was not only terrible: it was also extremely funny. Its portrait of the camp world of golden spivs, social climbers, interior designers and theatrical producers was sharp, exhilarating, and new. These were the young and not so young men who haunted Viva King's salon, and here they are on the page, brilliantly alive. There is darkness underneath, but the surface sparkles. The novelist Paul Bailey, himself once an aspiring actor, recalls the delighted shock of recognition when he first came across the moment at which the wicked and worldly producer Sherman Winter greets Bernard and Eric in a theatre bar during the interval of *Ghosts*: " 'Bernard my dear, Heaven!' Sherman's speech had not changed for twenty-five years. 'And with such beauty, double Heaven! Don't be cagey, dear, introduce!' " Bailey knew he was at last in a world without pretence. This was how things really were.

The darker side rang true, too. Wilson was not the first novelist to write about homosexuality, but he was one of the first to write frankly about such matter-of-fact but beyond-the-law matters as cruising and cottaging. The arrest in Leicester Square was new in fiction, but hardly new in life. It was recognised at once by those who inhabited this world. Alan Turing, who had met Angus not at Bletchley Park but at the Cambridge home of the Morrises, had read the short stories with admiration, and one of his own attempts at fiction shows a marked debt. In Turing's story, a young man called Alec is doing his Christmas shopping when he decides to make a diversion: "It was quite some time now since he had 'had' anyone, in fact not since he had met that soldier in Paris last summer." As he walks along Oxford Street pretending to look at cinema posters, he catches the eye of a young man. As, indeed, fatally, did Alan Turing, whose relationship with a nineteen-year-old Oxford Street pick-up, Arnold Murray, led to Turing's suicide.*

Angus explored new territory. Some, like Bailey and Turing, recognised the familiar: heterosexual readers discovered the strange. From either perspective, this was new ground. It had not been trodden and retrodden by generations of clumping moralising novelists. Here was freshness of insight and a questioning of sexual stereotypes: women as well as men welcomed this re-assessment of the normal. If some men weren't really "men", then, thank God, maybe women didn't have to be women. Angus extended the map of the human. Bernard Sands was simultaneously new in fiction and instantly recognisable as fact. It was as though we had known all along, but had not known we had known.

★

This was a moral arena where codes were not fixed. Homosexuals, living outside the law, had to create their own rules. Angus had his. He tended, for instance, to disapprove of homosexuals like Gide or Norman Douglas,

---

* This is reproduced by Turing's biographer Andrew Hodges, *Alan Turing: The Enigma* (Burnett Books Ltd 1983), p.448. The pick-up scene in fiction became increasingly acceptable: see also Martyn Goff's *The Plaster Fabric* (Puttnam 1957), which describes the meeting and friendship of a guardsman and a bookseller.

who married as a cover and then expected their wives to condone or even assist with their bizarre infidelities. He disapproved of Bernard because of the harm his hypocrisy had done to others. He admired those who knew themselves. Eric, like Tony, never doubts his own sexual nature: he is therefore in a sense morally "better" than Bernard's ex-lover, Terence Lambert, who is drawn into a heterosexual affair with Bernard's daughter which is clearly doomed. Bachelor barrister Hubert Rose is killed by an incestuous nostalgia and an interest in little girls. What are the boundaries, what are the rules, once one has stepped beyond the social norm?

Angus's redefinition of the homosexual and his exploration of homosexual society were to lead to a redefinition of society at large. His early work in the Fifties (often attacked as mysogynist) helped to clear the way for the Women's Movement of the Sixties.* It is perhaps for this reason that *Hemlock*, though ostensibly it deals with doubt and defeat, strikes a positive chord. It is a liberating book. There is Life after Hemlock. The implications are revolutionary.

Not all readers welcomed this new spirit. Some, like Bernard himself, feared anarchy if the thin ice of the old order were to crack. And anarchy is indeed unleashed in one of the book's fine set pieces, the disastrous public opening of Vardon Hall – an episode which owes much to the doomed fête at the beginning of Part Three of Dostoevsky's *The Possessed*. It carries to tragi-comic lengths the incipient mayhem that lies beneath the very British surface of "Saturnalia" and "Christmas Day in the Workhouse". After disruptions on this scale, what can be secure?

Some, however, considered that liberty in *Hemlock* had not been taken far enough. Could not a defence be made for Hubert Rose's desire for underage sex? Angus received one or two letters suggesting that there was no need to weep for the fate of such a child as fifteen-year-old Elsie Black whom Mrs Curry attempts to procure for Hubert Rose. Should one not rather condemn the public-spirited interference of Bernard and Ella that drives Hubert Rose to suicide? Had not Norman Douglas been a welcome and honoured guest at Viva King's? And why draw the line at little girls? Why had not Angus gone all the way and made Mrs Curry a procuress of little boys? In his novels C.P. Snow had clothed Bert Howard's seduction of schoolboys with heterosexual respectability, for what he thought were obvious reasons. But were they really so obvious? (And why, one may wonder, did Snow in *The Sleep of Reason* make his Moors murderers a lesbian couple?)

Angus's views on the age of consent are not wholly clear. One of the

---

* He was to lecture on this theme to the Albany Trust, in December 1964: "Literature and Sexual Freedom" now sounds like a prelude to the debates of the Sixties and Seventies.

most interesting – and disturbing – responses to *Hemlock* came from E.M.
Forster, who wrote from Aldeburgh thanking Angus for sending him a
copy, saying that he had rushed through it with excitement and
amusement. He found the orgy at Vardon Hall "wildly funny" – but:

> I found myself rather lost when Bernard died and my protection
> was invoked for the virginity of Elsie Black. 'Is Hubert so wrong'
> I began thinking – a shocking thought, but I had for so long been
> allowed to think nearly everything right. However there's Ella
> well and Hubert hanging and we must look out.
>
> One or two things puzzle me – it may straighten out at the
> second reading e.g. p.218 over half way down: the 'false note' in
> Ella's voice. I can't think what it is or means. At one time I
> wondered whether she was planning to make the omelette of
> toadstools. Then – much more important – I can't follow the
> reactions of Bernard in Leicester Square. His glimpse of his own
> sadism shatters him. I should have thought he would have known
> that it was there, and would pass; or even if he didn't know,
> wouldn't his general view of human nature – his own and others
> – anticipate cracks though which ugly things would peep from
> time to time? Yet the glimpse kills him."[9]

Angus's reply survives in an infuriatingly incomplete scrap, beginning
" 'lostness' that I recognise:

> All other activities are the people's own affair – minors even if
> they are considered as human beings, though I think most
> relations with uncomprehending minors would become difficult
> once one considered them as people. Ella, of course, though an
> excellent jolly good sort, sensible Social Democrat gardening
> gentlewoman is wrong because it's no earthly use sending people
> to prison and worse still driving them to suicide. All that I fear is
> left in my humanist world are the few influences Bernard could
> exert saving the boys from silly or corrupt liaisons by instilling
> them with humour and decency and getting his sister to stop
> teaching a subject (English Lit.) which should be real when she has
> no sense of its reality. A little, I agree, but all, I fear, that one can
> hope to – [page missing] – man. Maybe they would persist, but I
> think it would be a very great shock to me if I still wanted to hurt
> an attractive person when they were before me in actual distress
> and collapse Perhaps I am fooling myself here like Bernard. I don't
> know.
>
> Thank you for your interest which means a great deal more to

me that I should care to write down.

yrs sincerely,
Angus Wilson.[10]

This interchange was prelude to a long and complicated relationship between Forster and Wilson, whose concerns had so much in common, and who found such different personal and artistic solutions.

Ella Sands, the gardening gentlewoman who had bad dreams of tunnels, caves and icebound oceans, seems to have been partly inspired by Bump Walker. In 1979 J.H. Stape, who became one of Wilson's bibliographers, sent Angus a copy of his paper on *Hemlock* "The 'Possible Socrates' in Every Man's Breast" in which he discussed Ella's role, tending to see her less as a saviour than as one who betrays her husband's intentions and finally evades responsiblity for her own actions: Angus replied "If there is an ambivalence in my treatment of her it is because she was in some part based upon a very much loved surrogate mother, whose simplistic morality, however, was always deeply abrasive to me" (5 August 1979). The question of the morality of Ella's conduct – has she achieved good, limited good, nothing much, or positive harm? – remains unresolved.

(Ella's dreams, however, owe nothing to Bump, and everything to Angus's own nightmares of Scott at the Antarctic, of the sinking *Titanic*, of the cracking of thin ice, of Golliwogg at the North Pole.)

*

Others found other reasons to bridle at parts of *Hemlock*. Geoffrey Gorer conveyed to Angus his own appreciation and that of his friend W.H. Auden – but Auden had clearly cavilled at Terence Lambert's reference to his own favoured retreat of Ischia – "And then, of course, I can usually manage a tart's holiday at Cannes or Ischia. But I'm twenty-seven, Bernard, and I must get settled."[11] Angus apologised: "Thank you for your nice remarks about Hemlock and also for telling me of Auden's interest – I am sorry about Ischia but naturally know its reputation only through the mouths of young Americans and not from Auden's own lips."[12]

Forster, W.H. Auden, Joe Ackerley, Stephen Spender – an older generation was watching with interest, some admiration, and possibly some alarm to see what effect this middle-aged *enfant terrible* was going to have upon their world. Was he going to let all the skeletons out of the closet? Was anarchy really on the way? And if so, would they be able to enjoy it?

The young John Richardson also viewed Angus's novel with dismay. Many identified him as the original of Terence Lambert, rising star of the world of theatre décor – and Richardson himself, in a BBC programme (about *The Wild Garden* in 1963), volunteered that he had spotted himself as a victim. But at the time he found the portrait unnerving. To the reader, Terence comes across as strong, shrewd, witty, and sympathetic despite – perhaps because of? – his fixation on worldly success. Richardson did not see him that way, and a brief chill fell over the friendship.*

John Richardson came from a Wilsonian Kensingtonian world which he and Angus would mock together in joint flights of fancy. His father, Colonel Sir Wodehouse Richardson, had been born in 1854, ten years before Angus's father: he had served in Africa and Egypt. He met his second wife, Clara Crocker, in that archetypal Wilson venue, the Army and Navy stores: he was a director of the company, and she was working there as a photographer (or was she a piano tuner? – memories are vague). She was many years younger than he, and the daughter of a butler at Mentmore. He saw her, wooed her, and in 1923 married her; she promptly bore him three children – John was born in 1924, and a daughter Judy and another son followed. The colonel then died, in 1929, and Lady Richardson settled in South Terrace, just round the corner from Viva King, and took up bridge. For life, as it were.

John Richardson studied at the Slade, which during the war was evacuated to Oxford, and he first met Angus in 1941 or 1942 at John Fowler's in the King's Road. It was his first gay cocktail party, and the gay scene struck him with "all the shock of the familiar". Angus and Bentley Bridgewater seemed its personification – stilted, absurd, somehow inevitable. But he came to like Angus, and to admire his work: his review of *Such Darling Dodos* was complimentary, discerning in the stories "a potential novelist" and claiming that "Mr Wilson supports the true heart and 'the good scout' as ardently as he fights the two- or three-faced and the hordes of the pretentious."[13]

Richardson was soon absorbed into Viva King's salon. She changed his life. "Everything started for me there." His sister Judy also became an habituée, helping Viva to prepare the sandwiches (cream cheese, chives and paprika) and to mix the cup (soda, rum, ice and slices of orange): she

---

* Angus Wilson's letter to David Farrer gives a clear indication of Wilson's high opinion of Richardson's friendship:

    8 December 1963
    My dear David,
    I have only just today heard of the very friendly criticism of The Critics on the BBC of The Wild Garden. I don't often ask favours of S and W, but I would ask in this case that you should (unless it is economically impossible) give me an advert quoting them by name ie Karl, John R., Jack Lambert and Alvarez in the T.L.S. – The Sunday Times – and the Sunday Telegraph. It would give me a great boost of morale for my novel I'm writing . . . Forgive me for asking for this, but it would be a *great* personal satisfaction.

was also charged with sitting with Willie King while Viva was at the opera, and with trying to prevent him from breaking up Viva's parties.

There were rumours that Richardson had had a tragic love affair with a Slade student, Diana Bulteel. They had wandered dramatically round Oxford together, hand in hand, a Cocteau-esque couple, he wearing violet powder, she chalk white, with great black-rimmed eyes. Richardson had been denounced to the young woman's father, and she had been whisked home to Dartmoor, where she had died in 1948 in questionable circumstances – some said she had shot herself with her father's shotgun, but the inquest declared that she had died, accidentally, of Veganin.* Richardson by then had moved decisively into the gay world, where he met the implausibly wealthy art collector Douglas Cooper, a friend of Viva King's and the Wormalds, who was to whisk him away to an enchanted castle in France and, for a time, to a life of *luxe, calme et volupté*, surrounded by Picassos and Braques and Légers.†

For Angus, Richardson was a somewhat improbable hero of the post-war world: a Labour-voting son of Liberal parents, *déraciné*, bisexual, frivolous, scholarly, a little *fantaisiste*. (His cousin, the journalist Maurice Richardson, was a Communist: his sister Judy voted Conservative.) Angus romanticised John Richardson as a powerful portent of social change.

★

Britain in the late Forties was making a self-conscious bid for a post-war renaissance. First had come an exhibition by the Council of Industrial Design at the V and A in the autumn of 1946 called *Britain Can Make It*, in which John Richardson, Gaby Schreiber, James Bailey, Francis Wyndham, Geoffrey Bennison and all the clever young people from the Slade were involved. It had offered a socialist paradise of plastic macintoshes, pleated nylon taffeta dressing-table units, viscose and Viyella, spun rayon and seersucker, utility sheets and banister brushes. Mrs Barbara Castle and Mrs Madge Garland had joined forces with Sir Kenneth Clark and Basil Spence and Sybil Colefax to show Britain the way forward, and Nicolas Bentley's cartoons brilliantly captured the average family which would inhabit "the kitchen of a cottage in a modern mining village" or "the bedroom of a small house in an industrial town" – (he a railway engineer

---

* The Veganin had worked fatally upon "a weakened and debilitated physical condition" and death was given as due to misadventure. At Oxford, she had been fat: she had later, it seems, developed anorexia.

† Douglas Cooper (1911–84), art historian and lecturer at the Courtauld and the Slade, passionate and irascible advocate of Klee, Picasso, Gris, Léger, Miro. He inherited a fortune at the age of 21 and promptly began to collect the Cubists.

on night shift, ex-Eighth-Army, she a house-proud wife with five children.) Tribute was paid to the Single Woman in her kitchenette – she is a dietitian at a hospital, and an excellent cook, and as she is very modern she is portrayed smoking like a chimney while shelling peas. War had taught us the arts of peace: inflatable dummy tanks had produced the technology for rubber chairs, and Ack-Ack gun suits had been woven into Travella coats. Peggy Reekie at British Nylon was one of those who had been working on this transformation, and it had come to pass.

Inspired by the success of this exhibition, Stafford Cripps and Herbert Morrison dreamed up the 1951 Festival of Britain, which was to celebrate the centenary of the Great Exhibiton of 1851 and to restore to Britain the confidence of the Victorian era. In February 1952 the King died, and, auspiciously, in came a new Elizabethan age.

Angus wrote on the Coronation of Elizabeth II for the New Statesman in his new role of investigative social analyst: he spent the weekend in East Anglia, watching the ceremony on television in a draughty saloon bar in a Trust House hotel, trying to preserve his scepticism and his republicanism in the face of the "elaborate Byzantine grace" on screen. The outdoor dancing was rained off, but the dancers moved indoors with their piano and Angus fell asleep to the music of "Bye Bye Blues" and "Pat Him on the Boko". The pre-1914 generation, with their feeble attempts at "Knees Up Mother Brown", were drowned out by the young and Angus, being thoroughly modern, approved. The next day brought an excellent lunch at Long Melford, a pageant at Castle Hedingham, and Morris Dancing at Thaxted.[14]

Could Britain really make it? Was Britain really on the move? Some, including Michael Frayn, were to see the Festival of Britain as "a kind of elegy for Mr Attlee's Britain". The country had rejected the Labour Party and re-elected Churchill in October 1951, thus replacing Frayn's gentle ruminant "radical middle-classes – the do-gooders; the readers of the News Chronicle, the Guardian, and the Observer; the signers of petitions, the backbone of the BBC" by the "Carnivores – the readers of the Daily Express; the Evelyn Waughs; the cast of the Directory of Directors."[15]

Others saw the vote for the Tories as a sign of renewing confidence and affluence. What would emerge from this strange mixed land of commuting gentry in yellow waistcoats, schoolmasters in coloured braces, tweeded ladies flashing diamonds, Joyce Grenfell look-alikes and village children playing village sports? What was the future of Merrie England? Angus (but it must be remembered that he was writing for the New Statesman) made a telling point: while watching the fireworks display and the efforts of the local children to get past the police, he noticed "a line of dwarfs drawn up black and threatening on the edge of the common against the skyline. What could they be? Martians, no doubt. What better time and place for an interplanetary invasion? But no, I was informed that this was a nearby private school come to observe the pyrotechnics, drawn up at a safe distance from the town's possible infection. It cannot be said that the townspeople objected. They were used no doubt to the private school headmaster's medieval belief that they were infected with bubonic."

In 1953, Angus Wilson was one of many who hoped and believed that the next decade would see the end of private education and public schools. He had put his faith in the future, and in many interviews had advertised his support for the Labour Party. At the next election, in May 1955, the writer who had made his name as an analyst of social class would vote (unsuccessfully) for the classless society.

THE CLEARING IN THE WILD

Life after *Hemlock* glittered. Angus was more in demand than ever – as lecturer, broadcaster, pundit and guest. With the enthusiasm of a new star he accepted invitation after invitation. He went to Germany, Holland and Denmark to lecture and to talk about his work, which began to appear in translation. News of his gifts as a speaker spread, and henceforward he was to be always in demand, particularly from the British Council. He was courted by the bright undergraduates of the day: he presented a prize to Julian Mitchell in Oxford, and in Cambridge he addressed a gathering chaired by a yellow-scarfed and open-shirted Mark Boxer. This was on 9 October 1952, and Harry Guest remembers "A.W. read marvellously extracts from Such Darling Dodos and a Mrs Curry episode. I think we were all surprised at how old he looked – red face, white hair – especially as he made a point of saying he was 38. He was waspishly charming, answering questions with wit and no condescension. He claimed there was a great deal of moral conflict in his work . . ."[1] He read manuscripts (in Scandinavian as well as in English) for Secker. He lunched (but who did not?) with George Weidenfeld. With George Painter and Willie King he judged the British Museum short-story competition. (They did not even spell his name right in *Under the Dome*: did they really deserve him, he began to wonder?)

He appeared as himself in his BBC Third Programme Kensingtonian drama *Skeletons and Assegais: Family Reminiscences*, produced by Rayner Heppenstall, in which he revived the legend of Edward VII and the gilded nipples of Fred's mistress: this was perhaps the best of his attempts at original radio drama. Broadcast on 2 December 1952, on the Third Programme, it was also printed in the *Partisan Review* No. 9, Spring 1962. His second effort was *Left in the Middle*, directed by Louis MacNeice, broadcast on 23 April 1956: the text for this had to be extorted from him with menaces as by this time he was very busy with other commitments. It is a light-hearted satirical account of Francis Black, a young ballet-loving solicitor in the 1930s, who fights his way through the claims of pacifism and revolution to join the Labour Party. The third and last was a half of a six-part radio series, written with Christopher Sykes, *The Memoirs of Mrs Cramp*, advertised as a highbrow *Mrs Dale's Diary* (shades of those Westminster story-telling days): it was broadcast from 30 September–5 October 1956, featuring Patience Collier as the wife of an eccentric Man of Letters. The cast includes a redbrick novelist, a horsey daughter, a Betjeman-struck son, and a couple of operatic Italian servants.

As a critic, Angus was now more fiercely and less whimsically upon the warpath: he took on the old guard, cutting down reputations as he saw fit. Virginia Woolf had already come in (8 August 1950) for harsh treatment in a broadcast on "Sense and Sensibility in Recent Writing", in which he mocked her stream-of-consciousness technique and its content in a parody which brought her into the deadly company of Mrs Miniver* – he traced her influence through Elizabeth Bowen, Nancy Mitford and Angela Thirkell, and he deplored it. Leonard Woolf wrote to protest, in a letter "which seemed to me then to be charming reasonableness but was really, I think, patient disgust" – and Angus, who was radically to revise his opinion of Woolf's work, later wondered if it was not partly her dignified unwillingness to "join protests and march in processions" that had temporarily forfeited the admiration of his own generation: "She stood by her pacifist guns. And to my generation she lost all our sympathy by doing so."[2]

In another, mercilessly witty broadcast (22 March 1951) on "Broken Promise" he anatomised the failure of the novelists of the 1920s: he accused Compton Mackenzie, Gilbert Cannan, Frank Swinnerton, F.B. Young and even his old hero Hugh Walpole of shapelessness, cosiness, verbosity, indulgence: concluding "The old battered caravan of loveable, quarrelling middle-class families, of interesting Birmingham iron-foundry men or of Sussex farmers, of quaint old second-hand booksellers or troupes of actors with a special crazy wisdom, had only one road to take – the broad highway of the middlebrow novel."

This did not go down well with Compton Mackenzie, who also wrote in protest: nor did it go down well with the BBC, which made Angus promise never again to mention any living writer.[3] And Angus began to realise the pitfalls that awaited the satirist. He had offended his friend and hero John Richardson: would the publication of *For Whom the Cloche Tolls*

---

* Mrs Miniver was the middle-class heroine of newspaper articles and books by Jan Anstruther, and of a highly successful sentimental patriotic film in 1942 with Greer Garson.

lose him the friendship of Edith Sitwell? Simon Raven's review in the *Listener* suggested (though without naming names) that Edith Sitwell was the sibylline Sybil Clamber: Angus wrote in a panic to William Plomer (to whom the volume was dedicated) wondering if she had been hurt, and whether he should do anything about it. He greatly admired her, he said, and she had been very kind to him . . . what should he do?

The dedication to Plomer, as it turned out, had not been an entirely happy notion. It had been Jullian's idea, for Angus did not know Plomer, though he admired his work. The admiration was not wholly reciprocal: in a letter to New Zealand writer Frank Sargeson (August, 1950) Plomer declared that he did not like Wilson's stories (though he had taken the trouble of sending Sargeson a copy), and had not liked him either when they had met. There is, Plomer wrote, a fashion for him in New York, but the stories "seem to me the work of a hysterical misanthrope and mysogynist, screaming like an ape that can't get out of its smelly cage. But I shall go on reading him, for his cleverness."[4]*

However, the Edith Sitwell affair concluded satisfactorily: Angus received an appreciative letter of thanks for the copy which he had sent to her at Renishaw, saying it was a *"perfect* study of the age" – "How strange it is to look back on the behaviour of certain people in the 1920s. I think it explains the Maenads' orgies – a drunkenness brought on by the fumes of spilt blood."[5] She also invited him to lunch again at the Sesame Club in the company of Joe Ackerley, Rose Macaulay, Rebecca West, Rosamond Lehmann, John Hayward and Geoffrey Gorer, and unlike some of her lunches this one passed off without incident or recrimination. (It inspired a note in Ackerley's diary: "Afterwards Rose said that, for the second time, Rebecca West had remarked to her that it was extraordinary how like Angus Wilson was to Jane Eyre."[6] W.H. Auden, incidentally, always said that Angus reminded him of a governess.)

The meetings of celebrities are fraught with danger. It was Mary Lee Settle, American writer and frequenter of the Reading Room, who introduced Angus to Somerset Maugham. She had interviewed Maugham in his suite at the Dorchester in October 1953: she had been terrified, but Maugham had been kindness itself. When Maugham expressed his admiration for the works of a young man called Angus Wilson, she was able to claim that she saw him every day. A luncheon was proposed for 30 October, when Mary Lee Settle, high with excitement over the acceptance of her novel *O Beulah Land*, escorted Angus to the Dorchester.

---

* Angus sought Plomer's advice about a visit to South Africa, and gave a glowing review of Plomer's first novel, *Turbot Wolfe*, when Hogarth reissued it in 1966. (*Anti-Apartheid News*, February 1966.)

But she found another Maugham awaiting her. "He wore another face – reptilian, defensive, cold . . . His clothes were *de rigueur* for bankers in the city: the black jacket, the pinstriped trousers, the dead-white collar, the black tie with daring faint stripes. Outside of shaking hands, he never spoke to me but twice in the next two terrible hours. I had brought Angus Wilson into a literary lion's den. I was a Chinese go-between, nothing else. We all sat down on the two sofas. Searle poured martinis from a pitcher.

"I realised, of course, what had happened. Angus Wilson was a rival and a threat. I had not been. Wilson was, for that day, all the enemies that paranoid man had had to contend with during his later writing life. Unfair? Of course it was unfair. Wilson was and is the most generous critic and writer in England, more helpful to the young than Maugham ever thought of being, a fine stylist, a natural teacher . . . but on that day, as a new contender in that arena I did not yet know, he had to fight. I hardly remember Maugham taking his eyes off him. Question after question. There was not a leading writer who had visited his house in Cap Ferrat that Maugham did not destroy . . ."[7]*

Angus inspected the world of literary success with a sceptical interest, and noted its dangers. He also heard its siren voices. Old friends from the past – Peter Glenville, Frith Banbury, Terence Rattigan, George Devine – began to reappear and whisper of his old love, the stage, and his Oxford triumphs. Kenneth Tynan took him out to lunch. He was to be the target of one of the most successful lyrics in the 1954 July Cambridge Footlights, called "Putting the Cloche Back". Was it not time to make a theatrical comeback? There was big money in the theatre – more money than in fiction. Look at Somerset Maugham, look at Noël Coward. Come and meet Noël Coward, he will encourage you, he will tell you to burn your boats, leave your job, go freelance . . . (Noël Coward had read Angus's early stories and thought them "very fine indeed" (Diary, 23 June 1950): when they met at Hester Chapman's for dinner on 5 November 1952, he took "a great shine" to him.)[8]

The prospect of leaving the British Museum became increasingly attractive to Angus. (If he hung on there he might hope to be presented, after a lifetime's commitment, with a suitably engraved umbrella: Mr Ellis had received one in 1948.) On the other hand, he was not sure if he was

---

* In fact the introduction worked out more happily. "Willie" Maugham, Alan Searle, Angus and Tony became friends, dining together occasionally and exchanging cordial messages until Maugham's death in 1965. Searle wrote (8 January 1966) to Angus thanking him for a letter of condolence: "I have thought of you and Tony so often and with deep affection." Angus wrote an introduction to a selection of Maugham stories: *A Maugham Twelve*, Heinemann, 1966.

ready to plunge into the unknown. Unlike his father, he was not a gambler. He had no pension, and no security. But he could see that if he wanted to write seriously, he would have to take his chance and write full-time. He began to discuss the possibility with friends and colleagues.

Some – including, it is said, John Lehmann – urged caution. It was also said that Lehmann, the influential editor of *New Writing* and the *London Magazine*, had rejected Angus's stories, although he later claimed to have encouraged his career. The archives in Austin, Texas, support the gossip. Angus had written to *New Writing* in November 1947 offering three stories, all of which were rejected; he had thanked Lehmann for his criticism and written again in May 1948 asking for the return of the typescript of "Saturnalia". Angus's third letter bears the annotation "I cannot see *what* Connolly sees in this writer. I don't think the satirical ones are amusing and the serious story *Mummy to the Rescue* is just silly." The typescript had been returned. (But from 1954 onwards Angus was to write not infrequently for the *London Magazine* – his first piece, on Arnold Bennett, appeared in October 1954, and Lehmann regularly solicited Angus for more articles.)

Others had always had more faith in Angus, and argued that he was so well-established that he could not fail as a freelance. All remembered the anxiety and doubts he felt at this time. Part of him was a grasshopper, part of him a worker ant. He had seen all too clearly the fate of the grasshoppers in his own family. Fred Johnstone-Wilson had died in poverty. Clive had got himself involved with wild goings-on with Alan Rook up in a Jacobethan country house near Uttoxeter, and was soon to leave the country with Lucie and settle abroad on the tax-exile circuit. Pat and Colin were already in permanent (and less well-cushioned) exile. What would happen to Angus when winter came?

★

His own domestic life had calmed down considerably. Tony Garrett had left the Museum, and, after a brief spell in the Foreign Office, had decided he did not wish to pursue a career that would oblige him to spend much time abroad – and had become, somewhat late in the day, conscious of possible problems with security vetting. After dallying with the idea of trying to get into RADA or of applying for a post with the National Assistance Board, he decided to train for the Probation Service, and in 1952 was accepted for a course at the London School of Economics, where he began to study for a Social Science Certificate. All was set for an independent career which would allow him to spend time with Angus. And Angus wanted to spend time with him. He moved to a two-bedroom fllat in Grenville House, Dolphin Square, in the summer of 1952, at a rent of £142.00 a year, and Tony joined him there.*

Their relationship had moved on, from jealous scenes after watching *Sunset Boulevard* to letters about how to poach an egg. (Angus the pedagogue to Tony: "You put water in a frying pan with a little vinegar to stop the eggs from sticking to the pan – break an egg into a cup – then when the water in the pan is bubbling put in the egg – you will see it cook – if the centre is not getting cooked splash a little of the boiling water over it – then remove from the pan with the fish slice and eat. You wouldn't let me show, you ass." But the tables were shortly to be turned – within months Tony was writing severe notes to Angus to remind him to clean out the lavatory pan.)

Tony, coached by Pat Trevor-Roper, Michael Howard, and Bentley Bridgewater (in Betty Wilson's car), passed his driving test in 1952 and he and Angus took to pottering around the countryside in a little Austin 8 called OMP after its registration number OMP488 – they went to the Peacock at Baslow in the snow, to Simpson with Bentley, to Seaford to see Betty Wilson, to Long Melford to see Charles and Pamela Snow. They both enjoyed looking at buildings, guidebook in hand, and while Tony drove Angus would plot stories and novels in his head, picking up ideas for scenes and characters and names of characters as the landscape passed by. (Angus never learned to drive, as he never learned to swim.)

Tony was posted for field work to the National Children's Home in Harrogate in March 1953, and wrote regularly to Angus, describing the monstrous chapel, the furniture of his bedroom, and his work with the children – "The children are absolutely sweet, and for a large part of the time I find myself almost crying. It is so moving when the little girls and boys put their arms around me, kiss me on the mouth, and sometimes call me Daddy. I can see that this seems somewhat like Mrs Curry, but I can't put it any better, and it is just as simple and sentimental as that . . . I must say I am very glad that I am popular with the children, it would have been hell otherwise." He found OMP added to his popularity for he could offer people lifts and make himself useful. After his stint at the Home, Angus joined him by train in Leeds, and they went off together on a little tour of Northumberland. Tony received his certificate in October 1954, and, armed with glowing character references from Bentley Bridgewater and

---

* A draft settlement drawn up by lawyers in May 1952 attempted to establish a Trust Fund (with Bentley Bridgewater and Ian Calder as Trustees) which named Anthony Charles Garrett of 35 Finchley Way and Nicholas Davies (Angus's oldest nephew) as beneficiaries in the event of Angus's death. Tony did not know of this plan.

Francis Wormald, was taken on board as a Probation Officer in the Metropolitan Magistrates Court Area.

Angus and Tony were now spending most of their free time together, and we glimpse them, in January 1954, through the eyes of Angus Wilson's admirer Edmund Wilson. On Edmund Wilson's London visit (during which he found much to criticise) the two Wilsons met on several occasions, and talked literature and politics. Edmund Wilson noted that Cyril Connolly "evidently envied and resented the rapid rise of Wilson's reputation and his accelerating productiveness" and predicted hopefully that he would never be able to give up his job as a civil servant. On 11 January 1954, Edmund noted: "Angus Wilson came to dinner, with his 'friend', whom he asked to bring. The friend was a very good example of the current English pansy: good-looking, though a little bit dead, as they get; did not talk much, made a little shy, I think, by his position – like a wife who remains in the background. He is interested in prison reform. We both liked Wilson and spent a very pleasant evening with them . . . What made our conversation with them different from our conversation with other people was their interest in social problems that the literary world in general seems to have completely dropped. When I asked about such slums as Whitechapel, they told me I ought to go there to see how new housing exploits were being carried out in the midst of squalor. Wilson said (either on this or the following occasion) that, though he still wrote in terms of the social classes, England was heading for a classless society. He told Elena that he had stuck to his job at the British Museum partly because it was useful to him in enabling him to see a variety of types."[9] On a second meeting, after dinner, the Edmund Wilsons went back with the Angus Wilsons to Dolphin Square and spent an agreeable evening with friends and the editor of the *New Statesman*. Tony by now had been fully integrated into Angus's life. (Edmund Wilson ascribed Angus Wilson's "positive opinions" and his making his homosexual habits "a matter of principle" to his strong Scottish moral strain; Nadine Gordimer was to ascribe Angus's interest in social justice to his South African ancestry.)

Angus and Tony, during these years, made several excursions to France together, the dates of which are now lost and muddled beyond recall; on one of them, they visited Douglas Cooper and John Richardson in the Château de Castille near Avignon, where they lived in bronzed splendour surrounded by Picassos. A snapshot shows Angus in his bathing trunks, an arm slung round each of his hosts. Angus is thin and white like a crucified saint. Richardson and Cooper are both gleaming, burned dark by the sun and meals taken *en plein air*. Richardson thin and brown, Cooper fat and brown. (Tony had to retire into the shade: Angus loved the sun.) They talked of Zola and Cézanne, and slept in a room adorned with priceless Cubists: Angus nearly ruined a Braque with a mosquito spray. It was all very magnificent: a somewhat different life from the Reading Room and the magistrate's court.

They took another holiday in France with Patrick Trevor-Roper and his young friend Christopher Arnold. They travelled down the Loire Valley, where Angus had a frightful tantrum at Amboise, to Aigues-Mortes and les Baux, then up the other side of France through Andorra, where there was a crisis about food. ("There's *nothing* to eat in Andorra," Angus cried in despair after returning empty-handed from his daily task of purchasing the picnic: dinner in the hotel featured a vast mound of mashed potato, and perching upon it a few sausages.) Chris Arnold was much impressed by how expertly Tony calmed Angus down when he became over-excited. Tony had embarked on a lifetime of managing Angus.

Pat Trevor-Roper and Chris Arnold were, quite unintentionally, to play a decisive role in shaping the married life of Angus and Tony. Trevor-Roper, then based in London in a mews cottage behind his consulting room in Harley Street, had known Angus for years. Angus had also known Trevor-Roper's friend Alan Yorke-Long, who had spent much time in the Reading Room doing research for his book on Court Music.[10] Yorke-Long died in October 1952, at the age of twenty-seven, and after his death Trevor-Roper struck up a relationship with Christopher Arnold, whom he had met at Cambridge at a film society meeting.

Chris Arnold was a slightly built, vulnerable, intense young man. "Everyone wanted to mother him," except, perhaps, his own mother, a "bright, pretty, silly" much-married woman who lived near Stowmarket. His father had died in a Japanese prisoner-of-war camp. Christopher Arnold's great passion in life was to become a writer, a goal for which he longed with a peculiarly ardent intensity. Writing was in the blood. His grandmother, Lilian Arnold, had published several successful novels (including *Liege Lady*, 1902; *The Storm Dog*, 1912; *Earthquake in Surrey*, 1932); her younger sister published two novels under the pen name of Louise Valmer; and his father, John Arnold, had published thrillers. Chris Arnold felt he was destined to follow in their footsteps. He also passionately collected paintings and *objets d'art*. He was not in the Douglas Cooper league but his grandmother had left him some money and as an undergraduate he would wander into the Heffer Gallery in Cambridge and shake visibly with excitement as he contemplated a Graham Sutherland painting or a Bernard Leach pot. Thrift was not in his nature: he spent his inheritance, and he spent it partly on principle, for he was also a committed socialist, and the idea of inherited wealth displeased him. He wished to get rid of his money and be at one with the workers. For his National Service, he volunteered as a Bevin Boy, living in a Nissen hut and working in the mines in Sheffield.

In the early 1950s Trevor-Roper and Chris Arnold would spend weekends together in Suffolk ("the poor man's Wiltshire", according to John Davenport), in a little woodman's cottage with several acres of land. It was known as The Tin Shop. Chris bought it in 1954, and settled in there, digging the garden, chopping wood and writing his masterpiece. The land was let out to a local farmer. Just over the fields were two more adjoining flint cottages, knocked into one, which came onto the market: Trevor-Roper suggested to Chris that he buy them too, to protect his privacy. The cottages were in an appalling condition, overgrown, semi-derelict, with no indoor lavatory and no electricity. Cooking was done on a Valor stove. The previous occupants had not looked after the property (one of them was blind) and damp ancient medieval woodland had invaded it to the door. It seemed just the place for a sophisticated sun-loving metropolitan satirist like Angus Wilson, and there it was that Angus wrote his next novel.

Angus had decided he liked writing in the open air. He wanted to repeat the successful experiment of Crowscroft, where he had written *Hemlock* so rapidly, and Felsham Woodside was in some ways very like Crowscroft. It was beyond commuter territory, further to the north-east, near the villages of Bradfield St George and Felsham, and six miles from Bury St Edmunds. Angus had always liked East Anglia, with its large skies, its undulating landscape, its wonderfully refreshing absence of mountains. He and Tony enjoyed visiting The Tin Shop. When Chris Arnold suggested to Angus that he should rent the neighbouring cottage over the field, Angus agreed. And it was here, in 1955, that he wrote *Anglo-Saxon Attitudes*. He dedicated it to Pat Trevor-Roper and Chris Arnold.

Angus had decided to take the plunge and resign from the Museum. He left on 31 March 1955. He liked to say that he left on April Fool's Day. Pressed on by a desire to write a big novel, calmed by Tony's support, tempted by the owls and nightingales in the coppiced woods of Bradfield, he left the dome and the web forever. He said a fond farewell to George Painter, Tim Neighbour, Laurence Wood, Alan Gray, Audrey Brodhurst, and others whom he would continue to see intermittently for the rest of his life: to Bentley Bridgewater, whom he was to see nearly every week: and to various colleagues, some of whom he would be quite happy never to see again. The Director wrote, formally thanking him for his services, and wishing him well in the future. Seventy members of staff clubbed together to give him a fine collection of Blue Guides and Nagels as a leaving present, presaging a life of freedom and travel. Scotland, North Italy, Sweden and the Netherlands beckoned, to the tune of £17.13s od – the sum total of the collection. He left with a few hundred pounds in the bank, and no pension.*

Everything depended on the next novel. It was a sobering moment. They all got very drunk on gin and orange squash in water glasses at the farewell party in a small room just off the Reading Room. The cataloguers snoozed all afternoon.

★

Angus sits in his clearing in the wild, out of doors, with an exercise book on his knee, and writes. *Anglo-Saxon Attitudes* is a long novel, with a carefully articulated plot. It requires concentration. A scattering of letters between Tony in Dolphin Square and Angus at Felsham Woodside records its progress. At dusk, the wind howls like a radio horror play and the owl hoots. There are badgers nearby. A tabby cat with a white front called James (the first of many cats) adopts him. He hears the neighbourly sound of Chris Arnold chopping wood. A wet May turns into a golden June. Roses and Chinese peonies and scented stocks blossom. A red squirrel nibbles at the cherries. Sometimes Angus gets up and starts writing at six.

All is well back in London at the flat. Tony is working hard, and amusing himself of an evening (but not too much) with the Wormalds, the Barneses, the writer Angus Heriot, the composer and playwright Sandy Wilson – and John the Scot, now under Perkin Walker's protection. (Perkin has to lock the wine-cupboard door when John the Scot is around.) Tony dines in Sydney Street with the artist Barbara Robinson and her depressive husband Walter: Barbara has been painting a portrait of Angus.† Sad news comes through in July of the death of Bump Walker: she had died aged seventy of cerebral thrombosis on 15 July 1955, after a slow decline into the heavy drinking and neurosis so strangely foreseen in Angus's story, "Fresh Air Fiend". Angus had seen her in London at her home in Rutland Gate at the end of May, and then again on 5 July: Tony writes thanking Angus for his birthday present (a copy of Banister Fletcher's *History of Architecture*) and saying, "Perkin looks very shattered and several years older. I am sure it has affected him more than he could

---

* In June 1954 he had signed a contract with Secker for his next novel for an advance of £300; delivery of a completed MS "ready for press by May 17, 1954" was expected, but this date must have been a mistake for 1955 or 1956.

† According to Barbara, Walter Robinson's depressions arose in part from his Top Security work in British Intelligence abroad during the war and afterwards at GCHQ: a revealing sidelight on Angus's own condition. Walter Robinson is remembered for his translations from the Chinese of the poet Wang Wei, published in Penguin Classics.

ever acknowledge. He wants to come for the weekend, so I shall pick him up on Friday as soon as I can . . . I expected to hear from you yesterday. Did you get the shorts? Hope all is well, Love Tony."

But Angus continues to work. He shuffles off a BBC commitment with excuses, and carries on writing. Of an evening, he reads the Venerable Bede and a little Pelican on Roman Britain by the light of an oil lamp. He is well placed for the writing of a novel which deals with history and historians, for the woods around him – Felsham Hall Wood, Monk's Park Wood – once belonged to the Abbey of Bury St Edmunds, and the great stumps of ash and alder, still living, have been growing here for a thousand years. St Edmund himself, who was martyred in Norfolk in 869, and whose death gave rise to much legend, was enshrined nearby in the Abbey. Angus is surrounded by memories of the medieval past. He sees them every day. The woods are full of rare wild flowers, and great clumps of honey fungus flourish. He makes himself comfortable: he has invested in a gas cooker, a gas fire, and a gas cylinder, as well as a shelf for books and a deckchair. Somewhat to Chris Arnold and Tony's surprise, he manages not to set the cottage on fire. The Felsham Woodside experiment is working well.

By 29 April 1955, when Angus started to write, he had been planning the novel for months. His working method consisted of making notes in notebooks over a period of time, then putting them aside and settling down to attack the composition. (Years later, he was surprised to find that some of his 91 pages of notes were dated back as early as September 1954, and to discover that some of what he had remembered as raw material was hardly mentioned.)

The plot of the novel turns on an archaeological fraud which reveals layers of personal fraud and deceit. Angus was delighted to be able to use so much of what had seemed academic in a narrative that had all the suspense of a detective story. Here they all are, those scholars from Oxford, from the Museum, from the Warburg – some drawn affectionately, some with a cathartic indignation. Here are characters met on lecture tours of Denmark, in homes in the stockbroker belt, in pubs and louche boarding-houses in Notting Hill and Earls Court, in BBC studios and Bletchley Park and the offices of *Horizon*. Here is a novel with scale.

Archaeological discoveries and academic scandal had long fascinated Angus, and he had plenty of opportunities to study them at the Museum. He had been intrigued by the over-energetic cleaning of the Elgin marbles in 1938: gossip claimed that they had been scrubbed with scouring powder. Only the outbreak of war prevented newspapers from leaking the story and departmental heads from rolling. (Roger Hinks, Deputy Keeper of Greek and Roman antiquities, was left to carry the can, or so it was said: Hinks disappeared into the British Council, which saw fit, after the war, to post him to Athens. There, according to Francis King, he had his revenge on the marbles by insulting the Parthenon: "What is the *point* of the Parthenon, I keep asking myself. It's – it's just a marble table with too many legs.")[11]

Angus had followed with great interest the discovery of the Anglo-Saxon burial ship at Sutton Hoo: he listened attentively as scholars discussed the personalities of the archaeologists involved. (One of these was Thomas Kendrick, who in 1955 was the Museum's Director.) The Romano-British Mildenhall treasure, discovered in 1942, also in East Anglia, gave him great aesthetic delight. These matters sank into his imagination – though they did not appear in his notes.

What does appear (on page 59) is a reference to the Piltdown scandal of 1953, which revealed that a supposedly vital link in man's evolution had been forged by its discoverer in 1912. Angus heard first-hand accounts of this giant hoax, eagerly debated at meetings between staff of the British Museum Library and the Natural History Museum of South Kensington. He stored it all away for future reference, and his first idea for a plot was based on a group of professional forgers involved in the blackmail of an implicated professor. Although he abandoned the "crime story" aspect of this treatment, elements of it survived in the finished work.

The notes suggest sources for many of the characters in the novel, which was originally entitled *Perfect and Pluperfect* (or, for a while, *Saxon Side-Tracks*): the chosen title, *Anglo-Saxon Attitudes*, is taken from Lewis Carroll's *Through the Looking-Glass*, where the messenger to the White King falls into paroxysms of wriggling, hand-waving, eye-rolling attitudes as he feeds the King with ham sandwiches. Gerald Middleton, the protagonist, is a scholar of private means, in his sixties, unhappily married, estranged from his mistress, and no longer wholly engaged with his career. (He was originally called Medlicott, till a panic about a real Medlicott – W.N. Medlicott, who wrote on British Foreign Policy in the twentieth century – erased the name.) Angus himself later tactfully admitted some broad connection with "the brilliant, very delightful yet complex character of Sir Thomas Kendrick." Others have glimpsed some aspects of the background and even the physical appearance – handsome, heavy, sensual – of Perkin Walker. Chris Arnold thought that Ronald Searle's jacket design had a Perkin Walker look about it.

Ingeborg, Gerald's wife, went through many transmutations – from English Rosamund, to German Trudi, to Norwegian/Scandinavian Inge – but repeated references establish that she was in part based on Lisa (*née*

Balster), the German-born wife of the Labour M.P., Morgan Philips Price. Angus and Denis Barnes both knew her son, film-maker Peter Price, and visited him at his home at Tibberton Court in Gloucestershire: Tony remembers in Lisa some of the coy mannerisms attributed to Inge. Mrs Price's life, like Inge's in the novel, had been made difficult by nationality: born in Halberstadt near the Harz Mountains, she had worked with Rosa Luxemburg during the First World War, and then at the Press Department of the Soviet Embassy in Berlin. She met Morgan Philips Price in Berlin when he was special correspondent there for the *Manchester Guardian*, and married him in 1919. When he returned to England to fight the Gloucester seat in the 1922 election she had been ostracised as a Hun, and had again suffered discrimination during the Second World War. She fought against this, Inge-like, with a vigorous sweetness.*

Angus had strong views on Mrs Price, for she emerges with less credit from his notes than the character Inge does from the novel. He confessed in a lecture (delivered at a safe distance across the Atlantic[12]) that Inge had been modelled on a real person: he described with a vividly remembered mock horror finding himself alone with her in her large house in the country, at the age of thirty-five, when she said, "So sad that you are left here to talk only with the old woman. I will tell you a story about an elephant . . ." and had proceeded to address him as though he were a small child – an enormous blonde woman suddenly and implausibly starting to pretend to be an elephant. As he said, it made an enormous impression on him, and it was through invoking Mrs Price that Inge came to life. But he could not really dislike Mrs Middleton, grotesque though she is: he was at least as amused by his own creation as he was appalled by her, and there are signs that his attitudes towards Inge softened during the writing. Another character who improved steadily was Gerald's ex-mistress Dolly, widow of his old college friend, the original archaeological hoaxer: Dolly begins as hard, shallow and selfish, and ends up as something of a heroine. Was the Wilson imagination mellowing?

Gerald Middleton's son Robin, following in his father's footsteps, also has a mistress, the voluptuous Elvira Portway, whose phsyical mannerism (twisting her hair round a finger) and intellectual pretensions owed something to Sonia Brownell.

" 'It's just an English parlour game,' she said, twisting her hair with her fingers, 'and what's so *ghastly* is that it's got into our literature. It's all there in Morgan Forster and those people.'

---

* In 1970 she composed a note for her own funeral, hoping it would be "as cheerful as possible" with "a few nice memories, if any, (and) plenty of good drink . . ." She did not die until 1985, when she was nearly ninety.

"Gerald noticed that the more vague the content of her words became the more emphasis she laid on them . . ."[13]

Sonia Brownell, by now Sonia Orwell, noted the debt and was not pleased.

Robin Middleton's bourgeois, conventional, Catholic French wife, Marie-Hélène, owes something to Lucie Johnstone-Wilson. Ghosts of Naomi Mitchison and Jacquetta Hawkes lurk behind (very far behind) the historical novelist Clarissa Crane. Sir Edgar Iffley is Sir Frederic Kenyon. Two literary sources, Wyndham Lewis and T.E. Hulme, appear in Gilbert Stokesay, hoaxer, sadist, poet and essayist. A selection of older Wormalds and Crittalls loom in the the solid moneyed Middleton background. The Ladies' Lavatory Attendant from the Reading Room, Mrs Mainwaring, is transformed into Gerald's ex-charlady, the salacious Mrs Salad. A version of Ian Calder, "the maquereau intellectual", went into Donald Consett, Gerald's clever but unreliable son-in-law. Mrs Baker's predatory relatives, so salt-of-the-earth yet so mean, are worked into the blackmailing coachman and his daughter. A tantalising scribble suggests that at one point Angus had thought of marrying Gerald's younger son John Middleton off to Mary Lee Settle. The names of Clun and Stokesay come straight from a mid-April visit in 1954 with Tony to a *New Statesman*-recommended guest-house in Shropshire, and Canon Portway came from a tomb in Bury Abbey precinct graveyard.

The appalling Professor Clun, mean-spirited, bad-tempered, wife-bullying and austere, scored too many bull's eyes to count: every University department seemed to have one, and many were the letters that came in claiming to know him. (One suggested Dr Leavis, who was not known to Angus.) And there is a trace of John the Scot in the wild Larry Rourke – though Angus's attitude to John was no doubt coloured by jealousy, for Tony had been passionately involved with John, a tempestuous character who had too much in common with Angus for Angus to accept easily.

One of the novel's most memorable characters is Rose Lorimer, senior lecturer in medieval history, the rigour of whose scholarship had been affected by her interest in pagan survivals in Christian Britain, an interest disastrously stimulated by Stokesay's phallic hoax. (In 1912 he had inserted a little fellow with a big member into the newly excavated tomb of Eorpwald: this is the Piltdown-style fraud that Gerald feels obliged decades later to investigate.) Rose Lorimer is at once sublime and ridiculous: bizarrely dressed, eccentric, yet a true scholar, she represents a whole range of the academic oddity Angus had encountered so often in the Reading Room.

The notes suggest two originals for her, Jane Ellen Harrison and Margaret Alice Murray: two unofficial candidates, Frances Yates and Margaret Deanesly, have also been canvassed. Jane Harrison (1850–1928) was an eminent classical scholar and anthropologist of the Gilbert Murray-J.G. Frazer generation, and for many years a Fellow of Newnham College (where a striking portrait of her by Augustus John still hangs). Handsome and inspiring, she became a legendary figure: Virginia Woolf paid tribute to her as a pioneer feminist in *A Room of One's Own.**

Margaret Murray was alive and well and the President of the Folk-Lore Society when Angus was writing, and indeed she lived to be a hundred, publishing a triumphant memoir of her "first hundred years" in 1963. Her fields were Egyptology and witchcraft, and like Rose Lorimer she expressed herself interested in "the survival of pagan beliefs under a veneer of Christianity." She published many learned works, but achieved wider popularity with *The God of the Witches.* This was something of a flop (her own phrase) when it first appeared in 1933, but it achieved cult status as a cheap remainder during the war, and was reprinted by Faber in 1952. It puts forward her theories of pagan survival in the sacrifice of the Dying God: surely it was no coincidence that King Edmund was stabbed in Pucklechurch in May 946, that Edmund Ironside was killed in November 1016, and Rufus in 1110, and *all in a month in which one of the great Sabbaths were held?* William Rufus, Thomas à Becket, Joan of Arc and Gilles de Rais were all proposed as Divine Victims. This is very Rose Lorimer.

Margaret Deanesly (1885–1977) was a distinguished historian of the medieval church.† She had been drawn to convent life, but had impatiently jumped over the wall: with escaping hairpins, and eyes gleaming with eagerness at tales of rape and violence in the middle ages, she frequented the Reading Room, addressing friends and colleagues as "my little woolly lamb" or "my nasturtium". She had a Rabelaisian relish in the loves of others, and was heard to declare at a wedding reception "What a pity that nowadays we don't bed the bride!" As she grew older, "she became less able to distinguish fact from fiction" and her scrupulosity over fact went, one of her old acquaintances recorded.

Professor Deanesly's hairpins were not, however, as disordered as those of another celebrated scholar, Dr Frances Yates (1899–1981). Frances

---

* Woolf imagines herself looking out over the gardens of Newnham, glimpsing phantoms in the spring twilight – "and then on the terrace, as if popping out to breathe the air, to glance at the garden, came a bent figure, formidable yet humble, with her great forehead and her shabby dress. Could it be the famous scholar, could it be J— H— herself? "

† From 1942–50, Professor of History at Royal Holloway College, and then Birkbeck Lecturer at Cambridge.

Yates, the daughter of a naval engineer, was of independent means and spirit, and her unconventional career crossed many boundaries. She joined the Warburg Institute at the outbreak of the Second World War, and there became a close friend of Perkin Walker. (Indeed, some thought she was more than half in love with Perkin Walker.) She was not a medievalist, but a student of the Renaissance (she published important works on John Florio, Giordano Bruno, and the Hermetic tradition) and her interdisciplinary approach appealed to a wide general readership. But she did have in common with Rose a certain wild enthusiasm for and immersion in her period. Ignoring secondary sources, she sank herself into the mental patterning of the past. She carried about with her an aura of white magic. Like Rose Lorimer, Frances Yates was large and untidy. Generations of students bear witness to the awesome sight of her tottering dangerously on the top of a library ladder, her arms full of weighty volumes, or descending with an unashamed flash of pink knickers. Her appearance increasingly resembled that of Madame Arcati as played by Margaret Rutherford. Her combination of comedy and high seriousness appealed to Angus greatly.

Angus was much challenged by the narrative problem of combining his "straight" scholars with the marginal homosexual world of his sub-plot. How was he to introduce his lower-middle-class characters into the same frame as his professors? His notes reveal that he did not wish this novel to be "too homosexual" (had *Hemlock* gone too far that way, perhaps?) but on the other hand he did not want it to be too middle-class and Dorothy Sayersish. Gerald's son, John, a radio celebrity and journalist, is a homosexual of "a straightforward Freudian mother-dominated type", but various other types are drawn into the plot – John's rough trade Irish lover Larry Rourke, the sentimental landlord Frank Rammage, the sharp waiter Vin Salad, and the old-style platonic clergyman Canon Portway. Even more successfully than in *Hemlock*, Angus demonstrates the fictional advantages of a knowledge of a homosexual culture which cut across class. As the notes indicate, he had found within the ranks of the Museum itself, through his links with the homosexual fraternity, a wide social range. The Museum had been a microcosm. Somerset Maugham, writing to congratulate Angus on a "fine piece of work", commented particularly on Alan Searle's admiration for the authenticity of the low-life dialogue: "Alan says the Cockney dialogue is amazingly accurate and wonders how you acquired such a knowledge of it in the Reading Room of the British Museum . . ."[14]

Angus did not, however, regret his departure from the BM. As the words flowed, to a carefully planned schedule, he knew he had made the right choice. He hid away and worked, but his disappearance provoked pursuit. One day Ian Calder's mother Molly turned up unexpectedly, beat on Chris Arnold's door with a big stick, and demanded "Take me to Mr Johnstone-Wilson!" Tall, fat, alarming, and of a ferocious sweetness, she strode off across the fields and burst in on Angus just as he was about to write about Larry Rourke's urinating on Inge's carpet. Nancy Spain also pursued him: she sent six telegrams in two days, demanding his views on Science Fiction. ("Poor postman he was very sweet about it," Angus wrote to Tony.)

Then there were local engagements to contend with. There was Felsham Fête, the summer play at Nowton Court, the November fireworks at Nowton Court, the November fireworks at the Romans' cramming establishment. Friends came down for the weekend (Tony, Noel Sharp from the Museum, the faithful Bentley Bridgewater) and there were visits to town to see Willie and Viva King, Stephen Spender, John Croft, Cyril Connolly. Chris Arnold, easily depressed, needed encouragement, and so did various other young writers who had become his protégés. Meanwhile, the BBC was pestering him for scripts and appearances on a Brains Trust called "London Calling Asia". It was almost impossible to become a recluse, even if one lived in the middle of a field without a car or a telephone.

*

Nor was Angus very good at being a recluse, except when he was working flat out. The bright lights tempted him. In July 1955 he went up to town, like Frank Churchill, to have his hair cut, and heard some exciting news from his barber, Mr Teddy, in Monmouth Street. The Bristol Old Vic was thinking of putting on his play!*

This was *The Mulberry Bush*, which Angus had written back in 1953. It had been rejected, under its original title of *A Liberal Education*, by P.H. Newby at the BBC in February 1954, and it had also been turned down by director Frith Banbury, who thought it promising but seriously lacking in structure – too many arbitrary exits and entrances.† Peter Glenville up in Newcastle had responded with more enthusiasm: he wrote to say that he found it "extraordinarily stimulating" (apart of course from the impossible first quarter of an hour) and in March 1954 his company Hardy, William

---

* Angus to John Morris at the BBC, 13 July 1955: "Yes I am very ashamed but *honestly* I would have known *nothing* of the production of the play at Bristol had it not been for my hairdresser who got it from a customer!"

† Banbury tried to persuade Angus to work with a collaborator, Dido Milroy (alias Dido Merwin, cousin of Patsy Barnes and wife of poet W.S.Merwin). But Angus did not take kindly to this. Banbury (and Geoffrey Wright) continued to believe that Angus was basically lazy – he disliked rewriting.

Smith Productions bought an option on it as it was for the sum of fifty pounds.[15] He then sat on it for a year.

Mr Teddy's inside information proved to be correct, and the play was scheduled for production in Bristol in September. Angus was very excited. After a seemly delay he rushed off to Bristol and threw himself into rehearsals and rewrites. The director, André Van Gyseghem (who had come to an arrangement with Glenville over the rights), had a record of peculiar eclecticism: his credits as director included *Noddy in Toyland*, *Sailor Beware*, *Doctor Faustus* and *The Confidential Clerk*. He had been artistic director of the Nottingham Playhouse from 1949–51, where he had known Alan Rook and Clive and Lucie Johnstone-Wilson and partici- pated in the goings-on at Wootton Lodge: Alan Rook (a man of many talents) was closely involved with the Playhouse and had once appeared for Van as Hamlet's Ghost. Was it he who suggested *The Mulberry Bush* to his old friend?

Van Gyseghem as director struck Angus as a bit too close to the "overintense leftwing experimental theatre" school – but he thought Mary Hinton as the matriarch Rose Padley was going to be "superb". (Mary Hinton was the first wife of the eccentric rightwing anthropologist and eugenicist, George Pitt-Rivers, who wrote much on the science of population: born Emily Rachel Forster, she took her stage name from Hinton St Mary in Dorset where her husband continued to live with two subsequent wives. She was the mother of Michael Pitt-Rivers, who became the second husband of Sonia Orwell.) A letter from Angus to Tony shows considerable modesty about the play itself – the first act doesn't work, and some of the parts are badly written. But he is fascinated by all the stage-manager people, and longing for Tony to get there as early as he can. All the seats are sold, and the world and his wife will be there.

The play opened on Tuesday, 27 September 1955, to an audience which included Tony, Chris Arnold, and Bentley Bridgewater. Perkin Walker had been driven down cramped in the dickie of a car belonging to sociologist Michael Schofield. There was a grand turn-out of supporters, and everybody was in high spirits. Angus had written rather a pompous programme note about himself, speaking of "his conviction that the divorce between the stage and literature in England – so different to the situation in Europe – was very unhealthy for English writing and that anyone who could should try to bridge this gulf." The atmosphere in the auditorium and backstage was less solemn.

The reviews took Angus to task for "insufficient stagecraft", but praised most of the cast, which included Eric Porter, Derek Godfrey, Alan Dobie and Viola Lyel. And the play itself was taken seriously. Brian Inglis in the

Spectator called it "painfully credible" and Harold Hobson liked it. Richard Findlater hailed it in the *Tribune* as a "play that's fit for adults", and hoped it would be brought to London – commenting that it had been "turned down by leading London managers, who apparently prefer to lose their money on kitsch (home-made or imported)."

The reception was encouraging, and it was clear that the play had a future. But fortunately it was not upon the theatre that Angus pinned his hopes. His own future lay with the novel.

Anglo-Saxon Attitudes was about to be published, and it was on this, rather than on theatrical success, that Angus rightly pinned his expectations. Angus and his publishers hoped for great things. 13,750 copies were printed – a substantial figure for hardback fiction. The book appeared on 14 May 1956, and less than a fortnight later a reprint of 5000 was ordered. It was a Book Society Fiction Choice. The reviews, Fred Warburg wrote to Angus, were sensational. Forget the carping of the *Times Literary Supplement*, remember its article was three and a half columns long. "The picture could hardly be rosier" (23 May 1956).

THE RISE OF THE ANGRY YOUNG MEN

1956 was an important year for Angus. It was his first year without a regular income, and although he was in constant demand from newspapers and periodicals, reviewing could prove a serious distraction. He had by now established a long-term relationship with the *Observer*, for which he had first written, in 1950, on Scott-Moncrieff's translation of Proust: in 1955 he had written twelve *Observer* reviews, which was to prove a rough average for the next quarter of a century. But he had also in 1955 written for *Encounter*, the *Spectator*, *Evening Standard*, the *New Statesman*, and the *London Magazine*. This was a hard grind. It would be good to have a financial success on his hands, and *Anglo-Saxon Attitudes* was his bid for lasting freedom and independence.* But serious theatrical success also seemed a possibility. *The Mulberry Bush*, published by Secker in February, was chosen by George Devine to open his season of new plays for the English Stage Company at the Royal Court. The second play was Arthur Miller's *The Crucible*: the third was John Osborne's *Look Back in Anger*.

The London launch of *The Mulberry Bush* on Easter Monday, 2 April 1956, was not wholly a success. After all the fanfares about a revolutionary new Writers' Repertory Theatre, the reviewers were expecting something different. John Osborne summed it up: "As an opening production, heralding the regime of a new company, *The Mulberry Bush* must have been a keen disappointment to George. The indulgent memories of provincial bedrooms often fade on reviewers returning to metropolitan responsibilities. The critics who had already seen the play in Bristol complained that a new company should begin with something untried. It was indeed a tentative start, and timidity . . . was this time unrewarded."[1]

* In November 1954, Angus's accountants calculated his gross annual profit as £1449.4.8: the next year it was £1441.8.7: in 1956 it doubled to £3541.12.8. (The pound in 1956 was worth 10.85 times its 1990 value.)

It was a disappointment to Angus too. He and Tony escorted the fortifyingly decorative Rosamond Lehmann and Hester Chapman to the centre of the front row of the dress circle for the first night, which was also attended by family and friends – including Wollheims, Wormalds, and Warburgs. Angus later referred to the first night as "a disaster". But it was not as bad as that. Many wrote appreciatvely, including the powerful impresario Binkie Beaumont, with his eye on a possible future winner, who found it "a wonderful evening" of "real theatre".[2] The play had a strong cast – though inevitably, after the event, some said it was not as good as the one in Bristol. Gwen Ffrangcon Davies took over as Rose Padley, Rachel Kempson as the worldly and dying Cora, and Kenneth Haigh (soon to become Jimmy Porter) as Peter Lord. Kurt Landeck was played by Christopher Fettes, and Simon Fellowes by Alan Bates – the first time Bates had ever worn a dinner-jacket. (Rachel Kempson had happy memories of the production years later – 3 March 1982. She wrote to Angus about it.)

Angus had done a fair amount of rewriting, working closely with Devine's assistant Tony Richardson on the script: he excised one unnecessary character, and tried to tighten the action. He had worried about whether he would hit it off with George Devine as they both had "over-plus personalities"[3] but in the event they worked together well. And the reviews were certainly no worse than the first reviews of Osborne's play which was, notoriously, saved by the Sundays, when Kenneth Tynan and Harold Hobson both declared in its favour. Nor did the play disappear after this unfortunate London début: it was successfully revived by the Oxford Playhouse in November 1956, directed by Frank Hauser, with Frank Windsor and Avril Elgar as James and Rose Padley: Pat Keen, who doubled as Geraldine and ASM, recalls that Angus had not been crushed by his experience at the Court – on the contrary, he burst into rehearsals at the Playhouse with theatrical panache, and seemed to enjoy himself thoroughly – as he did at the after-the-show party given at Merton by Norman St John Stevas. St John Stevas, who was then working for Fred Warburg, and who became godfather to Warburg's wife Pamela when she was received into the Catholic Church, also remembered the occasion, and noted it in his diary: "Monday Nov 19, 1956. Felt nervous about the party, but in the event it was a huge success. The Prof [Professor Lindemann from Christ Church] came, Angus Wilson and Tony Garat, the Harrisons [the Warden of Merton and his wife], Levens [Daphne Levens was married to a Merton don and was a theatre freak], Roy Porter [the "camp" Chaplain of Oriel], Corbishley [Fr Thomas, Master of Campion

Hall] and quite a crowd. 'The Mulberry Bush' I quite enjoyed but not a good play."[4]*

★

But the differences between *The Mulberry Bush* and *Look Back in Anger* and their London reception were telling. Maybe Angus had rewritten too much? The Bristol version opened much more violently than the London version, with the excised character, a neurotic but hearty young woman called Wendy, yelling at the Oxford liberal Padleys that they are "hypocritical dirty-minded beasts": she turns on refugee Kurt with the lines "How dare you speak to me, you filthy little Jew? That's the sort of ghastly thing you Padleys did, saving filth like that from Hitler's ovens." All this was to disappear. The Bristol version had been angrier, and if anything slightly closer to the Osborne mood and therefore to the mood of the times. The Lord Chamberlain's Office, through St Vincent Troubridge, had expressed nothing but admiration for Wilson's play, describing it as "excellent" and comparing it to *The Wild Duck*,[5] and the re-write had pleased the Lord Chamberlain even more: Wilson had learned from the first production, and had "tightened and improved his dramaturgy throughout". No excisions were requested: the only query was of the word "godmongering", and that was allowed to pass.

(Osborne's plays, in contrast, invited numerous alterations. How could actors be allowed to deliver words like "ass-upwards", "shagged", "pouf", "turds", "balls" and "camp"?)

The harsh fact was that Osborne was in tune with the time: Angus and the Lord Chamberlain were not. There is something curiously old-fashioned about *The Mulberry Bush*. It reminded Van Gyseghem of Priestley's *Dangerous Corner* (1932), Frith Banbury of A.A. Milne's *The Truth about Blayds* (1921), and St Vincent Troubridge of Ibsen. This was not very modern. The play was an attack on do-gooding liberalism, and the plot dangled family skeletons. The Padley family is composed of Oxford dodos: the intruders are the "sensitive" and apparently silly ex-mistress Geraldine Loughton-Moore, who owes something to Val Graham Young: the rising civil servant Peter Lord, who owes something to Denis Barnes: and the outrageous and ungrateful Kurt Landeck (who was to elicit a sharp but not wholly serious protest from Arnold Simmel of Ashampstead). Angus, one feels, could have managed these characters better in narrative fiction: there is something about the theatrical form that dulls the edge of the satire. Even the sets are nostalgic. Originally the action

---

* St John Stevas also noted that he found Angus a dry writer "but a charming, human and fun person. He was devoted to Tony and made no bones about it which was ahead of his time."

was planned to take place in a country house in Berkshire, but we end up in the chintzy sitting-room of the Warden's house at St Roland's College, and the Master's Garden with its ancient mulberry tree imported from the prep-school garden at Ashhampstead – sets which belong to the dramas of an earlier age.*

Angus was quick to appreciate that something serious and interesting had happened at the Court. He urged Fred Warburg to go to see *Look Back in Anger* – "I do ask you to do so because altho' it can make one furious – it did me – one cannot understand the whole new generation ranging from Kingsley Amis and John Wain on the one hand to Colin Wilson on the other hand without studying John Osborne, I think. I must in the last event reject their standpoint but they represent a new and very powerful eighteen nineties up to date, and I don't think their rejection of all political, social etc standards is by any means a youthful phase-I think there will be a consciously philistine (Kingsley A) and partly Art for Arts sake, but always angry, rude etc. They, you know, are the only people who could and did take my character Kurt in the play as a hero . . ."

The Angry Young Man had taken up the baton from the Enfant Terrible.

*

In contrast, the reception of *Anglo-Saxon Attitudes* in May was highly satisfactory. It appeared in May 1956, with a dedication "For Chris and Pat", and was hailed as a major work of fiction, and a great advance on his previous work. Critics praised his large canvas and his technical bravura. Bernard Levin (*Books of the Month*) declared that "Few English novelists since Dickens have attempted a novel on such a scale": *Encounter* called it the book of the year: Mervyn Jones hailed Wilson's immense zest and energy – he is "the novelist we have been waiting for." Wilson, declares John Raymond in the *News Chronicle*, has come of age. No need to pay attention to Kingsley Amis in the *Spectator*, who thinks Gerald Middleton is "vaguely women's magazine" as well as priggish and indecisive, and concludes with the Olympian authority of one who has published one best-seller that the novel is "clearly a failure." Ignore the anonymous *Times Literary Supplement*, which also finds Gerald unsatisfactory and detects repeated patterns from previous works. (At least it liked Elvira.) And do not listen to Nancy Spain, who has decided that this "gay, spare-time writer has become a bit of a bore".[6] (She had her revenge for all those unanswered telegrams.)

---

* Angus observed that the conflicts between the generations in the play owed more to his memories of the 1930s than to the conflicts of the 1950s. "The emotional overtones . . . have their origins in the unspoken battles of my own youth." (*The Wild Garden*, p. 105)

Angus read the reviews with his usual attention. He was never to acquire the gift of ignoring them. On the whole, they were highly gratifying, and the coverage world-wide was immense. As Zola scholar F.W. J.Hemmings wrote from Leicester, it was "the most talked of novel since *Lucky Jim*" (27 May 1956). This was high praise, for *Lucky Jim* had had a particular vogue in Leicester, where the novel was recognisably set: academics there had had a happy party game, matching local personalities to fictional characters.

The hardback publication of *Anglo-Saxon Attitudes* followed closely on the heels of his first Penguin paperback, *Hemlock and After*, which had appeared a month before, in April 1956. *Hemlock* was now read avidly in universities, by young men doing their National Service, by common readers up and down the country. The possibility of a mass readership seemed more than likely.

★

Angus could afford to be generous to the Angry Young Man. Through Colin Wilson, Angus Wilson witnessed his birth. Indeed, he acted as midwife.

John Osborne claims the catch-phrase was first applied to him by the part-time press officer of the English Stage Company, George Fearon, who "told me with some relish how much he disliked the play and how he had no idea how he could possibly publicise it successfully . . . He looked at me cheerfully as if he were Albert Pierrepoint guessing my weight. 'I suppose you're really – an angry young man . . .' He was the first one to say it. A boon to headline-writers ever since."* Retrospectively, various writers were roped in – William Cooper, John Wain, Kingsley Amis, John Braine, Alan Sillitoe – but it was Colin Wilson and John Osborne, whose works happened to burst upon the world together, who caught the headlines.

Neither achieved instant success. Osborne had been working as a journalist (he launched his career on *Gas World*) and as an actor in provincial repertory, and had been trying to write plays for some years before he reached the Court. His first play, *The Devil Inside*, written in collaboration with his actress-mistresss Stella Linden, had an inglorious première at Easter 1950 in Huddersfield. From time to time Osborne resorted to odd jobs, as washer-up and waiter. *Look Back in Anger* was

---

* *Almost a Gentleman* (Faber 1991) p.20. The phrase was later said to come from a book of memoirs by Leslie Paul (Faber 1951) but it was not until *The Outsider* and *Look Back in Anger* that it gained currency.

rejected by nearly every theatrical manager in Britain, before it was finally accepted by Devine.

Colin Wilson's career had been even more irregular. He came from Leicester, where his father worked in a shoe factory, his mother in a hosiery factory. Despite showing promise at school (he says he was "teacher's pet") he got through a spectacular number of jobs, as well as getting himself dismissed from his National Service with the RAF after six months on grounds of "nervous instability". He worked in a tax office, on a fairground, as a builder, in a plastics factory, in a laundry, as a hospital porter-his CV was a classic of its genre. In 1951 he married a nurse from Leicester, but the difficulty of finding reasonable lodgings together in London eventually drove her back to Leicester with their baby son and gave him a lasting loathing of landladies. (These were the days of No Blacks, No Irish, No Students, No Women, and a shilling extra for every bath.) He meanwhile was trying to write, meeting other Soho writers, taking trips to Paris, joining an Anarchists' group, talking about Life, and doing all the other things that young novelists used to do. He spent Christmas of 1954 back in Leicester working at a department store; he now met Joy Stewart, a graduate of Trinity College, Dublin, who was to be his second wife.

Returning to London early in 1954, he decided to avoid landladies by sleeping on Hampstead Heath. He dossed down in a sleeping-bag with a waterproof cover, keeping most of his belongings in a large paratrooper haversack on the back of an old bicycle. By day, he went to the British Museum, where he worked on a novel about a serial murderer. He spent a lot of time browsing through old *Times* accounts of Jack the Ripper. He made Angus's acquaintance through a request at the central desk of the Reading Room for T.S. Eliot's essay about Joyce's *Ulysses*: two hours later Angus, intrigued, came over with the book, and asked Colin what he was working on. Colin said he was writing a novel with a mythical base, like Joyce, but using *The Tibetan Book of the Dead* as a framework. Angus expressed interest, and offered to read it.

Colin saw in Angus a published author, already famous, whose *Hemlock* he had borrowed from the public library on the strength of a review which had compared it to Oscar Wilde. He did not think much of it. Angus, for his part, saw a handsome and probably rather dirty young man from the provinces, duffle-coated, bespectacled, clearly intelligent, with a curious taste in reading-matter, possibly a little crazy (maybe a swine or an anarchist?) and certainly in need of a helping hand. Angus helped.

Colin Wilson finished the first part of *Ritual in the Dark* in December 1954, and gave it to Angus to read over Christmas. He then took himself off to a room in New Cross: winter and rough weather had forced him off the Heath. There, temporarily deprived of the company of Joy, who had left her Chalk Farm flat and gone home to her parents, he "got an idea for a non-fiction book about outsiders". When he returned to the Reading Room, he discovered that Angus had read his manuscript and liked it, but said that it needed a lot of work. Colin said not to bother, he had already started another book, of which he had already written a couple of chapters, and that he was going to concentrate on that.

Colin shelved the novel, and worked on *The Outsider*. He sent a section of it to Victor Gollancz, who responded with encouragement. Angus said he would like to see it too, and why not show it to Fred Warburg? A muddled battle ensued, in which both Gollancz and Warburg expressed interest and received copies of the text, which was finished in August 1955. Gollancz got the top copy, Warburg the carbon. Both said they were willing to publish. But Warburg wanted Colin to rework the central chapter on T.E. Lawrence, Nietzsche and Van Gogh, whereas Gollancz was prepared to take the manuscript as it stood. The top copy won. Gollancz (who dismissed Warburg and his rival offer as "an absolute disgrace – totally immoral") published *The Outsider* in May 1956. It was an instant and sensational success. It was dedicated to Angus Wilson.

But that was not quite all of the story. There was still the unfinished novel, for which Warburg made an offer. Angus, despite the Gollancz débâcle, continued to be supportive. He invited Colin to Dolphin Square several times: he offered to lend money, which Colin declined, and the use of his cottage, which Colin accepted. So, in the winter of 1955, Colin went off to Felsham Woodside to work, financed by a small weekly retainer from Fred Warburg. He was met by Angus and Tony, who settled him in overnight. In the morning they departed, after a long evening's conversation about good and evil and the novel on which Angus said he was working – to be called *The Goat and Compasses*. Evil, said Angus, was the deliberate inflicting of pain on a weaker person, for the sake of dominance. Colin said he agreed.

Colin Wilson was at Felsham Woodside for some weeks, and remembers vividly the thick snow, the smell of paraffin, the plod to the village for basic foods. He browsed through Angus's shelves of books – a complete set of Elek's Zola, some John Cowper Powys, and the hand-corrected proofs of *Anglo-Saxon Attitudes*. He was thrilled by the sense of being in on the literary scene – all those books sent for review or comment seemed then the height of glamour.

Over the fields, in The Tin Shop, Chris Arnold was also working away at his novel. The two young men, both in their mid-twenties, met over various pots of tea. Colin was not at all fazed by homosexuality, and indeed most of his works contain dissertations on the subject – one of the characters in *Ritual in the Dark* is a homosexual serial murderer.*

Colin was inquisitive about Chris Arnold's life – but Colin was inquisitive about more or less everything. They spoke of Sheffield and Leicester, of oysters and mussels. Colin Wilson, in flight from the proleteriat, voted for oysters: Chris Arnold, longing to be united with it, voted for mussels. (Chris Arnold always liked eating in workmen's cafés – a romantic habit Angus could not abide.)

Colin Wilson returned to London with his manuscript. Warburg would not accept it as it was, and said it needed more work. Colin quarrelled with Warburg, and transferred his allegiance to Gollancz. Fred Warburg was outraged, and when *The Outsider* was published to fanfares, his picturesque wife Pamela de Bayou arrived on Colin Wilson's doorstep, asking him to make it up with Fred. But it was too late. Colin had committed himself.

Colin Wilson's relationship with Angus remained friendly. In December 1956 he invited Angus to a joint celebration at his flat at 24 Chepstow Villas, Notting Hill, where he had managed to find an acceptable and accepting landlady. This was Bohemia. (Dylan Thomas was said to have lived there for a while, and so had the wild Scottish painters, Robert Colquhoun and Robert MacBryde.) Colin was in bottle-green corduroy trousers, a white sweater, and brown sandals: Joy was wearing a sleeveless dress of blue and gold. The L-shaped room was packed with Colin's Soho crowd of art students and would-be writers, reinforced by a scattering of the famous – Angus himself, Iris Murdoch, Stephen Spender, Herbert Read, John Osborne and Mary Ure. The young Lord Gowrie, fresh from Eton, was also there: he had met both the Wilsons in this Wilson era through the Eton Literary Society, to which both had spoken – Angus at first playing the outrageous queen, before settling down to a very friendly question-time. Angus and Gowrie subsequently met and chatted at various parties thrown by Colin, including this celebration, at which a pepped-up punch was served, dispensed by Colin from a large bowl. Colin, holding aloft a copy of *Anglo-Saxon Attitudes*, thanked Angus for all his help.[7]

Angus and his generation were to become heartily tired of being asked to pontificate about the Angry Young Men. (E.M. Forster refused to address the subject.) The Angry Young Men also got tired of one another.

---

* Wilson says in his autobiographical work, *Voyage to a Beginning* (1968), that he used to dress up in his mother's clothes, including her underwear, when he was a little boy, and that he managed to get out of the RAF by confessing that his sex-life had been permanently damaged by this: he brilliantly pleaded that his inefficiency at polishing floors was caused by "the emotional strain of living in close contact with so much male beauty."

Angus warned Colin Wilson of the dangers of notoriety, as newspaper interview followed newspaper interview. Colin was never out of the gossip columns, and as Angus predicted, the situation got out of hand. Tipped off by Joy's sister, who had been surreptitiously reading Colin's diaries, Joy's father arrived in Notting Hill with a horsewhip shouting that Colin was a homosexual with six mistresses. He tried to drag Joy away, and Colin called the police. By ill chance there was a witness, in the form of Gerald Hamilton (Christopher Isherwood's Mr Norris), who leaked the story to Fleet Street. Joy and Colin, pursued by reporters, fled in a blaze of publicity to North Devon and Cardiff (where they popped in on Kingsley Amis) and returned to yet more newspaper inches.

Angus invited Colin to lunch and told him sternly that all this kind of thing must stop. It would do his reputation no good at all, and he would cease to be considered a serious writer. Victor Gollancz agreed with Angus. Colin and Joy listened. They took themselves off to a cottage in Cornwall, near Mevagissey, which they rented for thirty shillings a week. And in Cornwall they lived eccentrically and happily forever after.

Angus resisted some temptations to sound off about the Younger Generation, but Colin Wilson was too good copy to waste. He appears in the story, "A Bit off the Map", first published in October 1957, where he is portrayed, partly through the eyes of an admiring young psychopath, as the mystical genius Huggett, leader of The Crowd. Angus felt nervous enough about the possible identification to send an advance copy to Colin along with a tactful invitation to a party on Monday, 8 April. Colin responded generously and with good manners: "It made me laugh enormously, and the portrait of the coffee bar intellectuals is altogether brilliant. I'm afraid Huggett will certainly be identified with me, & his doctrine of the Will sounds like me on my soap box (though its by no means what I believe) & Tristam whatisname with Conolly [sic], I suppose. But that cant be helped & I wouldnt have any of it cut. (PS I detest coffee bars and their types) Crack about weird surnames very funny! (Gorfitt!!) Only way I can retaliate is by altering so much that it ceases to be in the least like me. See you both. love Colin." A friendship was saved.

Angus's generosity was not always repaid. He complained that when his support of Colin Wilson reached the press, he became the target of every coffee-bar manuscript in London: similarly a generous review of a Science Fiction anthology in October 1955 brought him endless and sometimes crazy requests for endorsement from publishers and writers alike. But many were lastingly grateful for his help. John Bowen, who had been introduced to Angus's own work by Gore Vidal in 1952 while in America on a Fulbright, had published a first novel with Chatto & Windus in 1956, but Chatto had declined his second, *After the Rain*. Distraught, he had consulted Angus, who offered to read it, did so, and immediately telephoned to say "Don't worry, dear. It will certainly be published. If Faber don't want it, I'll talk to Fred Warburg." (Faber did want it: it was published in 1958, and Angus supplied words of praise for the cover.)

He also intervened on behalf of Chris Arnold. Arnold was delighted to have his novel published by Secker in 1957. *The Wedded Life*, formally dedicated to Pat Trevor-Roper but personally inscribed for Angus "with thanks for his continuous help . . . his understanding, his patience . . ." (22 August 1957), had a modest and deserved success: it is a low-key but atmospheric and carefully written portrait of life in Sheffield, seen through the eyes of a young married research scientist who becomes involved with a small-time criminal group. Nothing is exaggerated, and every detail tells. Its tone is very different from that of the messianic Colin Wilson. It was a promising début.

Another young protégé, Stuart Mitchel, was helped into print with a novel in a not dissimilar genre. Mitchel got to know Angus while himself working in the British Museum in 1949: in April 1950 he had been transferred to the Department of Atomic Energy, where he became a *cause célèbre* when his colleagues noticed that he openly read the *Daily Worker* and spoke up for the Soviet Union. He was suspended from the Holy of Holies on full pay while his case was discussed, then eventually re-employed at the harmless V & A, where he worked for three years before leaving the Civil Service for a career in teaching. This experience provided the background for his novel, *Clerks in Lowly Orders*.

Angus read the typescript in the spring of 1956 and responded with enthusiasm, writing several times with comments: "The dialogue is quite excellent and we are in an untouched (or almost so) social milieu which is excellent. *But* I do think it is all a bit cocksure and moralising . . . Are you both in London for Easter – if so we have dress rehearsals on Sat and Sun (7.30) If you want to come – come to the Court Theatre and say friends of the author. Angus."

"Friends of the author" – a proud phrase, and Stuart Mitchel responded with "hero-worship". This was the period when Angus was popping in and out of George Devine's court at 9 Lower Mall, frequented by Lindsay Anderson, Karel Reisz, Nigel Dennis and Bill Gaskill, and attending rehearsals of *The Mulberry Bush* in the church hall behind Peter Jones. But Angus found time for Mitchel's book: he recommended it to John Pattisson at Secker & Warburg, but Pattisson declined it, and it was taken up by Gollancz. "Occupational" books like Monica Dickens's *One Pair of Hands* were in fashion, and *Clerks* was well received: its portrait of the dull routines and petty conspiracies of office life was chilling, as were its revelations of the Cold War mentality of the 1950s. It revealed a drab world of tea-trolleys, McCarthyism, sexism and linoleum. It nearly got made into a film.

The grey, grainy weariness of the 1950s was at last beginning to brighten. The attacks of the Angry Young Men were greeted with almost hysterical delight, as the bombed landscape lit up in a blaze of invective. And there were other signs of rebellion too. The sexual revolution of the 1960s was on the way.

The works of Braine, Wain, Amis, Osborne and Colin Wilson were aggressively masculine and frequently misogynist. Womanising was a popular theme, even with the older and relatively respectable Cooper and Snow. Women's voices, in these post-war decades, were quiet and ladylike – still too much of the Mrs Miniver and Mrs Thirkell for Angus's taste. (Of Antonia White's *The Lost Traveller* he wrote "the middlebrow musquash fits Miss White all too like a glove" – *Listener*, 4 May 1950 – and in a review – *Time and Tide*, 5 July 1952 – otherwise full of high praise for his friend P.B. Abercrombie's first novel, *The Rescuers*, he had not hesitated to urge her to "clear her purely descriptive passages of a number of high class women's magazine clichés".) There was as yet little to signal the 1960s revolt of women against such categories and condescensions, but on another front protest was being organised, and impossible changes were being contemplated. John Wolfenden's Committee was beginning to receive evidence.

Hemlock and After had brought to public attention the existence of an area which many had chosen to ignore. It had admitted a new group into the literate consciousness. A respectable civil servant had written a book about a subculture which he appeared to regard as neither normal nor abnormal. It was illegal, and it was there. Could this be right? Had not homosexuals for too long meekly accepted their deviant status? Should not they, like the Angry Young Men, speak up?

Speaking up was not easy because it courted imprisonment. Many of the old guard were happier – and would have gone on being much happier – in a world of semi-secrecy, where nobody interfered provided you did not break society's unwritten rules. Sophisticated hostesses were accustomed to their useful spare men leaving dinner promptly in order to get to the pub in time for a pick-up, or to placate a jealous boyfriend left in purdah at home. All would be well if you stayed in your country cottage at the end of a long wooded lane or hid away in your villa on a Mediterranean or West Indian island. All would be well if you kept away from policemen in public

lavatories. The brave days of Bloomsbury's sexual revolution were over. It
was a Cold War truce.

Occasional incidents of victimisation reminded some of the true situation.
There were scandals, of which the suppression was sometimes more
scandalous than the offence itself. Tom Driberg (when William Hickey of
the *Daily Express*) was put in the dock in 1935 accused of "indecent assault"
by two pick-ups, and then acquitted. The details did not reach the press. Lady
Astor's son, Bobby Shaw, was similarly reprieved by a direct appeal to
Beaverbook. What was the point of having laws, if you did not invoke them?

In post-war Britain the law was invoked, and with increasing frequency.
Between 1945 and 1955 the number of prosecutions for homosexual
behaviour rose from under 800 to just over 2,500, of whom over 1,000 were
given custodial sentences. Sir David Maxwell-Fyfe, Home Secretary from
1951–54, was known to be keen on convictions. The disappearance of Guy
Burgess and Donald Maclean in 1951 stimulated homophobia as well as spy-
phobia. In 1953, Eisenhower's Executive Order banned homosexuals from
federal posts, and in the same year, after consultations with the FBI, a newly
appointed Commissioner of Police at Scotland Yard, Sir John Nott-Bower,
"swore he would rip the cover off all London's filth spots . . . For many years
past the police had turned a blind eye to male vice. They made arrests only
when definite complaints were made from innocent people, or where
homosexuality had encouraged other crimes. They knew the names of
thousands of perverts – many of high social position and some world famous
– but they took no action. Now, meeting Sir John's demands, they are
making it a priority job to increase the number of arrests . . ." (*Sydney
Morning Telegraph*, 25 October 1953).

The witch-hunt was on. McCarthyism had reached England. Gone
were the days when Frank Birch was hero. Homosexuality meant treason.
Members of MI6, including some of Angus's personal friends from
Bletchley Park, discreetly resigned or contemplated resignation. Fortu-
nately, the sheer ineptitude of the hunt soon produced an outcry of
revulsion not only from homosexuals themselves, but from other sections
of society. Certain well-publicised cases helped the cause. The suicide of
Alan Turing in 1954 passed more or less unnoticed, but not so the John
Gielgud case. Gielgud was convicted, in the autumn of 1953, for
"importuning male persons for immoral puposes" and fined ten pounds.
This was not well judged. Even more devastating was the Montagu case.
Here were martyrs. Brigid Brophy's view was that the trial of Oscar Wilde
had traumatised a whole generation.[8] Perhaps the Montagu case could be
put to service in healing the trauma.

The story of the case was told by Peter Wildeblood in *Against the Law*.[9]

He describes how he, Lord (Edward) Montagu and Michael Pitt-Rivers had been arrested in January 1954 and appeared in court in March 1954 on charges relating to a party in Dorset in the summer of 1952. They were convicted on the evidence of two of the party-goers, and they went to prison. This, society felt, was really going too far. What had these three done to harm anyone? What had been the motives of the tale-bearers? The law was an ass.

The case provided a focus for a disquiet which was already widely spread. The Church of England's Moral Welfare Council had prepared a pamphlet on the subject, and there were members of parliament willing to adopt the cause of reform. In August 1954 Maxwell-Fyfe found himself obliged to set up a committee under the chairmanship of John Wolfenden, to examine and report on the law relating to homosexual offences and prostitution – an unhappy conjunction of topics, some thought.

Setting up a committee was one thing. Getting evidence was another. By definition, anyone who spoke up from personal experience was in danger. Wildeblood, who was still in gaol, volunteered, and was told the committee would see him when he was released. Others – including Pat Trevor-Roper and Angus Wilson – were also willing to take this self-incriminating step. Nevertheless, the gathering of material was not easy. The subject was ill-documented and shrouded in secrecy. Not even the Private Case had many useful statistics. The sociologist Michael Schofield, writing under the pseudonym of Gordon Westwood (and there are many pseudonyms in the bibliography of this topic), had published one survey, *Society and the Homosexual* (Gollancz, 1952), and was at work on another, *A Minority* (Longmans, 1960): this was based on interviews – but how to find the interviewees? True, one contact led to another, and many talked willingly and with relief to someone they could assume was sympathetic. But what if he lost his address book and his contact list? Schofield went through elaborate security procedures with coded numbers and safe deposits, bearing in mind the testimony of one boy whose pub talk had been the source of a round-up by the police.*

Angus felt the wind change. He looked around him at the inhabitants of the queer world, and wondered. Attitudes towards risk and self-disclosure were fascinatingly diverse. Some homosexuals were defiant, cruising happily and dangerously through the nightlife of South Kensington or the

* It has been impossible, even with the assistance of the Home Office, to locate any evidence given by Angus in the Public Records Office (HO345, classes 1–11 and 17–20) or elsewhere, and the HO writes, "We are of the opinion that the evidence (if any) given by Sir Angus would have been in the strictest confidence and may have been destroyed." HO to M.D., 13 January 1994.

wastes of Tooting Common: others hated the promiscuous scene and were willing to give years of their lives to working for law reform and respectability. The literary world had its own extremes. At one end, there was E.M. Forster, venerated and almost sainted: at the other, the outrageous Angry Young Gay Dutchman, Gerard van het Reve.

Other countries, other laws. In Holland and Japan, in Morocco and Ceylon the rules were different. Peculiarly English was the compromise which enshrined Forster in King's, sat students at his feet, and set his novels for school examinations, while the MS of his Arcadian homosexual novel *Maurice* lay in a drawer awaiting its author's death. This made Angus feel uncomfortable. Universities often made him feel uncomfortable. He had been much influenced by Forster's work, and when invited by Spender to interview him for *Encounter* in 1957 he looked forward to the meeting. But the Great Man made him nervous. Angus drank too much of Forster's Dubonnet, and got the names of the trees in the courtyard wrong. He took against the dark brown of the chimney piece. He was worried by two small vases of petunias. He talked (and later wrote) about himself too much. The fourth paragraph begins, unhappily, "Although I had never interviewed anyone, I had often been interviewed . . ." – but he had not learned the correct lessons from his experience. He harangued his fellow-author instead of listening to him. In short, he wrote a self-conscious piece – the Christ Church interview pattern repeated. It is like a not very satisfactory short story, written in a tone of uneasy irony. He was not proud of it.

The explanation for this unusual uncertainty seems to lie partly in Angus's insistence that Tony Garrett be present at the meeting. Angus establishes early in the article that he was accompanied by his "friend". "I sat back in my armchair. The friend who had accompanied me sat back in the armchair opposite, ready to undertake the silent office of noting E.M.F.'s replies." And he concludes with the parenthesis "(I wish to thank Mr Garrett for his kindness in taking down much of the interview.)" Surely this is rather odd? One must conclude that Angus had taken Tony to King's and included his name in *Encounter* as a political act. Forster's life was concealed. Angus's was out in the open, and here was Mr Garrett to show it.

Angus felt a justified unease about this interview,* and Forster himself was caustic at the interviewer's expense, according to his friend and

---

* *Encounter*, November 1957: "A Conversation with E.M. Forster". Reviewing Forster's *The Life to Come & Other Stories* (*Observer*, 8 October 1972) he noted, "I am very conscious that my own interview with Forster . . . was highly unsatisfactory. There is a great deal in Forster's work and there was much in his personality to bring out the inept, the pompous & the insecure in near strangers."

biographer, P.N. Furbank. But Forster wrote pleasantly enough (if perhaps a little ironically) to Angus:

August 19
Dear Angus Wilson
I am charmed and much pleased by the enclosed. I suspect though that you and I are both too nice to evolve an interview of the 'memorable' type. Reading it over, I didn't see or hear the wheels biting, and wasn't left with the definite impression that I got from the Paris Review article. [This was a piece by P.N. Furbank and Francis Haskell, to which Forster had alluded favourably in his letter accepting the interview.] However Stephen didn't commission the normal article: he wanted two writers to be overheard talking about the work of one of them, if I understood him rightly, and this has certainly been achieved . . .

Angus's estimation of Forster's work, however, which had meant so much to him as a young man, began to decline: as the years went by, he came to admire Virginia Woolf more and Forster (except for the Forster of *Passage to India*) less. He became increasingly dissatisfied with Forster's *rentier* world and with its implicit snobbishness. The two men remained on friendly visiting terms but Angus on several occasions expressed a lack of respect for what he saw as Forster's lack of moral courage. Why could Forster not come out and declare himself as a homosexual? (He seems to have expressed this view as early as January 1954, according to Edmund Wilson's diary.) Angus had declared his probation-officer friend Tony Garrett. Why was Forster's policeman-turned-probation-officer friend Bob Buckingham kept so discreetly out of sight? Why had Forster avoided the issue of homosexuality when invited to make a programme on any topic of his choice with Lord Wolfenden soon after the Wolfenden Report appeared, when the subject was in everyone's mind? Could he not then have struck a blow for reform and hastened on the slow process which dragged on for so many years? People had to listen to Forster. Forster, of all the writers in England, had moral authority. He should have spoken up. Old age was no excuse.

★

But was youth an excuse for the *very* odd behaviour of young van het Reve? Even Angus sometimes thought Reve would go too far. And he did. (But, being Dutch, perhaps it did not count.)

Gerard Kornelis van het Reve was born in 1923. The son of a communist journalist, he was educated in Amsterdam and started to publish poetry when still very young: his controversial first novel, *De Avonden* (The Evenings), was published in 1947. It painted a grim picture of the dullnes of post-war Dutch life, was accused of Nihilism, and did not recive the recognition he felt it deserved. So he left small-minded Holland and came to England, hoping to make an impact here. He arrived in 1951: he had been married (in 1948, to the Dutch poet Hanny Michaelis) but soon abandoned the wedded life. In 1952 he embarked on a long homosexual affair with Wim Schumacher, later artistic director of the Dutch publishing house, Elsevir: they worked together as porters in the National Hospital in Queen Square, Bloomsbury. Strikingly handsome, charismatic, hard-drinking, highly emotional and excessive in every way, Reve inspired both rage and admiration.

He met Angus, by his own account, some time in the winter of 1952/3, at Dolphin Square. Angus encouraged him and recommended his works, without avail, to Fred Warburg. Reve needed friendship: the years from 1951 (when he published a work called *Melancholia*) to 1957 were largely unproductive and became known, when he achieved literary fame, as his *"Engelse grijze periode"* – his English grey period. But he was a dangerous protégé. At one point, the ever-generous Angus lent him the Dolphin Square flat, then suddenly panicked and asked Bentley Bridgewater to go round and check what was happening. Bentley discovered that Reve was sleeping in a sleeping-bag in the middle of the floor and cooking for himself on a primus stove in the sitting-room. Similarly, while living for a while with the painter John Minton in Allen Street, Kensington, Reve had insisted on cooking on a gas ring.

Reve was in every way an incendiary figure, increasingly intent on shocking the bourgeoisie. (The present author's letter to him requesting information was returned in a heavily singed and charred envelope.) One of his party tricks was the imprisoning of his own farts in a wine glass: he would release them to extinguish a candle. (This trick was recalled by Angus in one of the more extreme scenes of *As If By Magic*.) Another was to ask for a plate and some mustard, if conversation at table grew dull; he would then spread the plate with mustard, and lay his penis temptingly upon the plate . . . Such games, Angus feared, could easily go wrong. James Kirkup, another *enfant terrible*, recalled spending a drunken night with Reve in Dolphin Square: Kirkup and Angus had been to "some kind of international literary gathering" where they had both performed, and then Angus had put Kirkup in a taxi "with a mysterious young Dutchman, extremely good-looking, who seemed to have communist leanings, and who appeared to be living or staying with Angus. We drank a lot of Angus's liquor and I left as dawn was breaking, and Angus had still not returned. I could never understand what that was all about, though I suspect it was some kind of trick that people liked to play upon my innocence and naïveté in those days . . ."[10] (By his own account, Kirkup was in the habit of popping in at the BM in Angus's Reading Room days to borrow a pound or two from Angus to buy some brandy, so he might have expected an occasional act of retaliation.)[11]

Reve's career, in the 1960s, grew ever wilder. Like Kirkup, he managed to get his work prosecuted for blasphemy: he wrote of paedophilia, of perversion, of racism, of sado-masochistic orgies, in a high-flown pornographic manner which echoed yet exceeded Firbank, Céline, Genet, and the Book of Revelations rolled into one. In the early sixties students were to adopt him as a cult figure, after the publication of his *Op weg naar het einder* (1963: *Journey towards the End*). His Dutch prose was said to be sublime, and his fellow Dutchmen, after taking a deep breath, began to heap honours upon him. He became rich and famous, a cult figure. Yet, through all this, he retained a touching affection for staid England and his old-fashioned English friends. It was so easy to shock people in England.

Perkin Walker developed a particular affection for him, which began in the days of Reve's grey English obscurity. This reserved, scholarly, melancholic man led a double life. At the Warburg, Walker was famed for the regularity of his habits: as Anne-Marie Meyer, a close personal friend and Secretary to the Warburg, bore witness, his routine never varied. He worked the same hours, rested the same hours, took the same place in the canteen, day by day. Gombrich, who liked and respected him, would often join him for lunch and Perkin Walker would not utter a single word. Writing on the Decline of Hell and Unclean Spirits, he lived in a sort of hell of loneliness.[12] He believed all human love was transitory: its essence was its fragility. He fought against solitude by frequenting joyless noisy pubs, where he would sit in a corner reading a Greek or Hebrew text; by maintaining his close ties with Forrest Fulton and Angus; by playing in a trio or quartet with Gombrich, his wife and sister; by surrounding himself with what Chris Arnold called "a little homosexual republic". He formed a close non-musical trio with Bob French and Monty Turland, who stuck to him loyally through dark moods and fits of weeping. (When Bump Walker died, Gombrich said, Perkin wept for months.) When, in 1955, shortly before his mother's death, he left his tumble-down flat over a corset shop in Notting Hill, and bought a house at 2 Regent's Park Terrace, Bob and Monty moved out of their flat in Mrs Fulton's house and moved in with him (as, later, did Angus, Tony and P.N. Furbank): in 1962 they bought with him (and with another friend, Vernon Harrison) a house in the country. They were his jesters, his familiars, his family. They protected him from his nightmares.

The tall, narrow, four-storeyed house at Regent's Park Terrace (or RPT, as it was known) was to play an important part in the lives of Angus and Tony: somewhat ironically dubbed "The House of Love" by their melancholic and tormented friend Raymond Tyner from Georgia, it bore witness to many an emotional drama and entanglement, not all of them entirely loving. But Perkin Walker needed the drama. He observed at second hand, and the sight of Bob and Monty's quarrels and reconciliations, of Monty's occasional spat with Angus, afforded him some pleasure. Never drunk himself, although a heavy drinker, he encouraged, wittingly or unwittingly, the intoxication of others.

Gerard Reve might have seemed an uncongenial companion to those who knew only the Perkin Walker who spent his days with scholars like Gombrich and Frances Yates and Michael Screech.* But Reve called to Perkin's darker side. Reve was quite uninhibited about his own sadistic sexual interests, and Perkin was grateful to him for giving him "the comfort of realising I was not alone in having such inclinations."[13] Bob and Monty disapproved: they thought Gerard was wrong to encourage Perkin's interest in flagellation. But Perkin found Reve a liberation.

Reve was to spend a good deal of his time with his English friends, though it is not always clear why. One of his published letters to Wim Schumacher complains of "that sad, cold house of P's, the stink and noise of London, the tittle-tattle of homosexuals who thank God every day that they are still being prosecuted and not recognised as grown-up people, like on the continent . . ." He had cast himself in a bolder role, and was waiting for his moment of declaration.[14]

Between the extremes of Forster and Reve, there was a great deal of unoccupied territory. Angus, in the late 50s and early 60s, had many choices still to make. He had thrown in his lot with Tony Garrett, for richer, for poorer, in sickness or in health. Should he now opt for a respectable married life and a solid artistic career? Should he leave the ravings to the youngsters? The very title of his next novel, *The Middle Age of Mrs Eliot*, might suggest that he had moved towards such a decision. But it was not as clear as that. His novel in progress proved difficult, obstinate. He returned to short stories, but they also gave him a fair amount of misery. The way ahead was not obvious.

* Michael Screech: Rabelais scholar, Fellow of All Souls, and author of many studies of French Humanism. He was a close friend of Perkin's.

A FLIGHT OVER THE DESERT

1956 closed on a note of anxiety. Angus was struggling with a new volume of short stories, as well as a recalcitrant novel. In December he wrote to Fred Warburg "I am in a great deal of misery with my stories at the moment – some I have scrapped entirely, others I am rewriting. I am not wholly worried about this as I think I am pushing through to a new level as I did after Hemlock and as I must do before I tackle 'Goat and Compasses' which now assumes wider and wider proportions. All the same it is a period of creative hell – with long periods of sitting before blank sheets and desperate attempts to stretch my imagination until I feel it will snap." Fred Warburg wrote back on business matters and with comfort on 12 December 1956: "I now come to your own misery about which I can say nothing, for I can well understand its nature, and that there is no short cut through it to the other side. I have little doubt however that you will come through as you have done before . . ." And yes, he will reimburse the twenty pounds for the November publicity trip to Holland.

Angus and Tony returned to Holland for Christmas, to the liberating atmosphere of their mixed bunch of Dutch friends, most of whom Angus had met while on lecture tours – they included novelist Adriaan van der Veen and his American wife Jeanette, Airey van Nierop, and Henk van Gelder and his friend Christiaan Grotevoohl, who lived together in a handsome art nouveau house in the Hague. Henk was a financial director of KLM, and Christiaan (who was Jewish, and whom Henk had hidden during the war) taught the piano at the Concertgebouw. Shipping magnate Ludo Pieters from Rhoon also became a lifelong friend: he and his wife first met Angus when he was speaking in the bookshop of Voorhoeve and Dietrich in Rotterdam. Over the years, Angus and Tony paid many visits to Holland, and in turn had introduced E.M. Forster to their circle: Forster spoke in Amsterdam in June 1954 on *Passage to India* and had written (3 July 1954) to thank Angus for the introduction.

1957 began more locally with a speech on 10 January to the Hampstead Literary Circle, followed by a succession of social engagements with Frith Banbury, Bentley Bridgewater, Colin and Joy Wilson, Sandy Wilson, the Wollheims, Colin McInnes, Peter Wildebood and Ann Fleming.* Angus had become a welcome guest at Ann Fleming's salon, where he met Somerset Maugham and Peggy Guggenheim and Patrick Leigh-Fermor and Iris Murdoch and John Bayley and Arnold Goodman. He greatly enjoyed her wicked humours, and her table offered rich comic material – he would be seen egging on Connolly and Waugh to yet greater excesses of eccentricity, a Quilpish grin of delight upon his face. Like a naughty child he poked his stick through the bars and stirred up the old furred creatures and made them roar. Ann Fleming was an inspired and impulsive hostess: on some occasions guests would be required to speak in Latin, on others they would burst into spontaneous song and dance upon the table. (Iris Murdoch particularly loved the singing.) Ann Fleming found Angus wonderfully amusing: one note to him says plaintively that she was appalled to learn from Stuart Hampshire that Angus was about to go abroad – "I can't be a hostess unless you are a guest" – a remark which confirms Stephen Spender's view that "Annie needed a genius, and she wanted Angus to be *her* genius." At first she tended to ask Tony to "call after dinner" but gradually the pattern changed, and they both stayed with her at Sevenhampton on several occasions.

Working life was not so entertaining. In February 1957 Angus went off alone with his schoolboy's exercise books to Lewes, to Shelley's Hotel, which was owned by the uncle of his friend Angus Heriot: it was a pretty eighteenth-century building, with well-proportioned rooms and a cupola over the stairway, and the weather was mild enough for him to sit in the garden. He posted what was to be the title story of the new volume back to Tony to hand on to his typist Mrs Provis: he was "rather pleased with it", but other stories were giving him a headache. He was beginning to doubt whether he was a short-story writer at all. The new novel, with all its problems, called him.

He tried to shuffle out of engagements, but some claimed him: in early March he went to lecture in Belfast and Dublin, and in May there was a

* Angus met Ann Fleming through John Russell of the *Sunday Times*, who recalls that Ian Fleming put in a request to meet Angus. Russell arranged an encounter, and Fleming, who had "a genuine and deep awe of and respect for what he rightly regarded as 'real writers'," came along "with a glint in his eye and unwonted shyness." (Letter to M.D.) This friendship did not prosper, but Angus grew very attached to Ann.

long tour of Austria and Germany, followed by gaps in the diary that seem
to indicate more creative hell. He wrote in May firmly declining yet
another BBC request, saying he was "off to the country to start a new
novel." But was he? Letters to Tony from Felsham Woodside, written in
the summer of 1957, chart the struggle:

(4 June 1957) So far my mind has remained a blank with moments
of bright ideas which don't seem bright an hour later and I get fits
of terror about the novel – but I keep telling myself there is no
hurry and it is, of course, largely true. Will you bring clean sheets
when you come . . . Chris's is locked so I can't telephone. See
your Friday. Love Angus.

(Undated) After much agony, it looks as though I shall actually
start today . . . Chris was very helpful over difficulties I had with
the novel . . . It has been very nice here alternately hot and
refreshing rains and the birds and flowers have been superb.
Especially owls – a white barn owl in the early evening and later a
tawny owl that sits in your path like a little old woman. Oh dear!
The novel is going to be long, but it could be very good, I think
. . . I am going ahead, tho' still with great labour, no confidence,
and a pain in my tummy . . . perhaps you could ask Patrick W.
[his doctor, Patrick Woodcock] if he could let me have a very few
luminal tablets . . . *Esquire* are publishing 'Ten Minutes to Twelve'
in their Christmas number but not much money because it will be
after Viking publication and so by contract they take half.
However – its another step in the American march. If only I
thought I had a winner on hand now! By the time you get this
you will have been to Honoria's – don't drink the wine, I'm sure
it will be sour . . .

And again (6 July 1957): I have started the book but am not
very happy about it yet – still have a dead anxiety in the pit of my
stomach. The refrigerator is out of action . . . On the whole its
been hell . . . I long and long to see you. I thought of asking the
Barnes down but I can do nothing until the book is more
satisfactory – if it ever is –

The notebooks for the stories of the collection published as *A Bit Off the
Map* offer an insight into the kind of hell they had given him. There are
slightly desperate lists of titles (some never written in any recognisable
form) and many tottings up of word counts. (Angus always made fun of
Arnold Bennett's *Journals* with their smug mathematical and financial
calculations: perhaps they somewhat scared him.) In the event, he

completely scrapped a promising story called "Judas Jude" based on the visit to their Oxford son of a Norman-Morris-style Lancashire Jewish left-wing couple: he could not get the tone right. A fragment called "Dad's Dreams" and various other false starts also disappeared.

The notebooks for the novel also betray anxiety. He had planned a long novel set in a cathedral country town, the action centred upon the compulsory purchase of a public house called The Goat and Compasses. It was to involve a good deal of local politics, a subject on which he did considerable research, and a conflict (as he had told Colin Wilson) between Good and "the old goat" Evil. He drew charts of "golf course, wood, main road, and school": he planned murder and blackmail and a bogus Sister Philippa. Wormalds and Crittalls again provided inspiration. In the event, he wrote a solid Prelude set in 1947 which describes a middle-aged couple abroad, the husband in a state of nervous collapse, the wife attempting to calm him.[1] He is a Tory councillor, and he works for her father, the owner of a department store built up from humble beginnings. There has been some difficulty, and he is on the point of an angry resignation. Meanwhile, in Belgium, they move restlessly from hotel to hotel, and from tantrum to tantrum, amidst broken inkwells and embarrassing scenes. The fragment promises well, but it kept getting stuck. There was something deeply wrong with it. But what?

The letter to Tony of 6 July 1957 concludes by describing the nature of the problem: "the theme is acquiring depth, but I just don't feel the people to be alive which is not surprising as for the first time there are no semi-portraits. Its probably a sort of Deronda – an attempt to extend my character range beyond its powers – if only I thought there were a Gwendolen to offset the blankness. The trouble is that this country town setting, of necessity, means a realistic but seen from outside large canvas like A.S.A. or Hemlock, but the only really living character at the moment is concerned with my own hysteric fears and is of necessity an inside character. I dont yet see how to marry them without reducing the townspeople to puppets or the central figure (Bob Greenacre) to a cypher. And in the background looms Sister Philippa and the need to draw a truly religious person who is also a fake – and not fully to take sides. Oh dear! Well there it is . . . How did your ordeal in court go? I shall ring you up at Woolwich at 6.0 on Tuesday – I know no other time to get hold of you. Yours ever, Angus."

Tony wrote back soothingly from time to time. He had been to the Wormalds, he was reading Pascal, he had organised a discussion group with his fellow Probation Officers in the flat, he was working hard. Angus was not to worry. All would be well.

★

In the summer of 1957 Angus flew away from it all on his first Grand Tour of the East. The journey was to make a profound impression on him, and to alter the course of his fiction in more ways than one. He departed on 30 August for Tokyo, full of vaccines and armed with visas, as a guest of the 29th International PEN Conference, the first ever to be held in Asia.

Like most of his fellow travellers, he knew little about Japan, which was still held in a form of uncertain post-war isolation. He did some homework before he went: he reviewed (rather unfavourably) an anthology of Japanese Literature edited by an American, Donald Keene.* But one review does not make an expert, and he knew he had much to learn. So did they all. He travelled on the bus to Heathrow with Hungarian-born humorist George Mikes, on a hot summer day: Mikes told him that he was going to write a funny book about the whole of Asia, although he was also, more seriously, representing Hungarian PEN in Exile. (Mikes published his recollections of his tour of Japan, the Philippines, Malaya, Siam and India under the title *East is East* in 1958, with illustrations by Nicolas Bentley.)

Angus was strangely affected by the journey out, via Teheran and Karachi. It was his first long international flight, and flights were long in those days, with several stopovers: the water ran out on the first leg. He sent two postcards *en route* to Tony in Dolphin Square describing the flight over the desert – "more desolate than I could have conceived but there is a certain strange beauty to it . . . incredible miles and miles of rock mountains sand and snow and lakes . . ." He found it disturbing, almost as disturbing as those dreams of polar seas.

Japan received the delegates with massed cameras, flags and fanfares, and a coach which took them to the Imperial Hotel, a famous building (now demolished) described by Mikes as "Frank Lloyd Wright's practical joke", and by Angus as a monstrosity – Angus's passion for the works of Frank Lloyd Wright was yet to develop. On the long route to the hotel from the airport, the young Japanese guide chatted relentlessly in Americanised English to her exhausted group: most of what she said "was largely unintelligible and her manner was a travesty of 'peppiness' that reminded me of a film star of my youth – Clara Bow, the It girl."[2]

Angus and Stephen Spender were the stars of the British contingent.

* *Encounter*, April 1957, review of *Modern Japanese Literature*, by Donald Keene, Thames and Hudson, 1957. Angus found the introduction confusing, and in the fiction noted "an obsession with adolescent youth" even more marked than in European literature, and a lack of personal vision.

They were an odd couple, Spender tall, bony and gangling, Angus small, slight, and darting – but temperamentally they made a good match. Both were great talkers, and both had a keen sense of the absurd. Each found the other amiably dotty. There was to be much giggling, and some weeping.

The opening ceremony took place on 2 September, and the theme of the conference was "The Mutual Influence between the Literature of the East and the Literature of the West". There were various panels, on which Angus was always willing to leap forward: Spender was entertained by the confidence with which Angus came out with phrases like "Of course, we of the younger generation don't agree with Mr Spender" or "As a spokesperson for the younger generation, I would like to question Mr Spender." (Angus was less than five years younger than Spender, but often looked older and was white of hair.) But Angus spoke up in a more statesmanlike manner on several occasions, notably about the need for good translations of Asian literature, and the difficulties of attracting serious reviews for foreign works: his contributions were favourably reported world-wide, and greeted with "thunderous applause".*

There were the usual conference disasters. John Steinbeck was so unnerved by an Indian delegate who called for two minutes' silence that he took to his bed and stayed there, pleading a heavy cold. Alberto Moravia, who hitched up with Angus and Spender, proved to be a melancholy and world-weary figure who found Angus's jokes one of the few consolations for the crippling experience of having to sit so much upon the floor – he later wrote that Angus made everything seem "friendly and simple and gay: this doesn't happen very often in travels."[3] (Angus nicknamed him "Bruin".) One of the American delegates proved to be that very Donald Keene whose introduction Angus had found so unhelpful: fortunately, Keene was forgiving. "It was the most brilliant literary gathering, in terms of who attended, of any I have experienced. The British delegation included Angus Wilson and Stephen Spender, and I spent quite a lot of time with them both. For some reason that I have forgotten, I invited them and also Alberto Moravia to a Japanese meal that was not only perfect of its kind but served beautifully in a restaurant overlooking a lovely garden. But I remember most of all Mr Wilson suddenly saying, 'It's awfully good of you to eat with me!' no doubt referring to the review."[4]

Making contact with the Japanese themselves was not so easy. Keene was one of the very few to speak the language, and he found himself much

* Harold Soref, *Truth*, 4 October 1957. The *Bookseller* agreed: "the most useful contribution . . . appears, by all accounts, to have been made by Mr Angus Wilson on the subject of translations: and the Congress unanimously approved a resolution to the effect that PEN and Unesco should help to provide more Western translators." (21 September 1957.)

in demand for interviews. But both Angus and Spender were fortunate in their contacts. Spender made the acquaintance of Shozo Tokunaga, who became his translator: Tokunaga recalls that when he first met Angus in the hotel lobby "he looked so cheerful that, as I remember, I suddenly blurted to him: 'Hail to thee, Blithe Spirit! Bird thou never wert.' I don't remember anything else –."[5] Angus also met Kazu Serikawa, a modest and intelligent young Japanese student interpreter with exquisite English. Serikawa found Wilson and Spender enchanting and was overwhelmed when they invited him to join them for dinner – "that wonderful dinner and wine and talk over 'Scotch'." Angus helped him with his translation of John Horne Burns's *The Gallery*,* and Kazu Serikawa was to read Angus's work with admiration and understanding. He became his translator, friend, and negotiator in all things Japanese. (Angus recommended him for a Fulbright, which he did not get – the competition to get out of Japan was ferocious.)

Angus wrote to Tony:

(Wednesday September 4)
Imperial Hotel
Tokyo

My dear Tony – my very very dear Tony –
   As you see I miss you a lot and have felt very sick for you many times. It has been extraordinary so far like 3 lives in one week and when there are three weeks more to come I think of them with a mixture of excitement and of longing to be home . . . You must by now have got some postcards sent en route but possibly not one from here saying that I had changed my tour to fit in with Stephen S. and Moravia (of whom I have become a good friend) so that we take in a lot more of Japan – the Inland sea, the cormorant fishing, the seashore, a monastery in the mountains etc. This means that I will have only a few days in Bangkok and in Angkor Wat. I shall arrive in London on Thursday 26th September morning – it would be marvellous if you could meet me but I imagine court will make that impossible . . . My speech seems to have been a real success – the Philippines delegate when introduced to me today said 'Ah! Mr Wilson. The guy everyone is talking about' then hurried to Stephen and said 'You still write at all, Mr Spender?' As Stephen had pinched a very pretty boy from

---

* An evocative American portrait of Naples and North Africa during the last years of the Second World War. Secker published it in 1947.

under my nose last night he agreed that this was a fair revenge.
The most wonderful thing for me so far has been the Noh play –
simply incredible in beauty and movement. The geisha houses &
the incredible dishes (quail eggs in a monkey's paw with the roots
of a ginko tree!!) are exciting but rather exhausting. I have been
photographed about 100 times and given 35 interviews for the
press and seventeen broadcasts – its unbelievable. I was with
Stephen and Don Richie in a queer strip tease house last night
when word went round that we were Spender and Wilson –
every single person in the place asked for our autograph – its as
tho' all the teddy boys and [illeg.] hostesses of Tottenham Court
Road were to lose their heads over Mauriac and Camus. Philip
Hope-W[allace] has written to the M.G. that Spender and Wilson
have been given a reception that would be excessive for
Lollobrigida and Marilyn Monroe. Set against this is the boredom
of the speeches and the awfulness of the garden and cocktail
parties and my longing for you to be here. All my love, Angus.

Dear Tony,
    This is my last letter from Japan, as Stephen and I leave early
tomorrow for Bangkok (where a silent revolution has broken
out!) It has been a strange time of great interest in personal
contacts and in forming a picture of what Japanese society and life
are like. I think I have found out a lot – I am very much touched
by the Japanese themselves despite their inadeq[torn paper] . . .
corruptions etc. The countryside is very picturesque. (Pause here
while I did a lunch symposium for the highbrow Shin Chon and
then spent two hours with Stephen answering questions at the
Jesuit University.) . . . We have done our tour of the extreme
south – extraordinary eating and living and sleeping in the
Japanese manner in temples (impossible to sleep) The Osaka-Kobe
period was also very peculiar because I was involved with
Americans and the boy brothels (rather distressing) All in all I must
have talked to *hundreds* of people and really feel I know something
about Japan at any rate on the surface. Sad, kind, brutal, lovable,
tiresome lost people – I'm really very fond of them in a way I
have never been with any other foreigners – and yet life is madly
in the surface. The suicide rate here is very high – the population
is enormous and the poverty terrible – yet even so they are not
like the other Asians. They have a standard of living and they
could be very good people, I think. I'm longing for home, yet

enjoying this last part rather more because I see the end in sight. I shall not miss Japan but I shall miss many many Japanese people very much indeed . . . All my love I will write from Bangkok, Angus.

Air France. En Plein Ciel

My dear Tony,

We are now high up over Okinawa flying at 260 miles an hour towards Manila. The leaving of Tokyo was very distressing because the little boy (not really he was 18 but he seemed like a small boy) whom Stephen had taken on our holiday was in such great distress – I even feared he would throw himself over the rails. S. is distressed that perhaps he should not have made the holiday for the boy – but strangely altho' I am terribly worried about the way these Japanese boys get treated I do not feel this – their lives are so desperate and (—)'s pleasure was so great in the days he went around with us that unless they are never to have any happiness I do not see how this distress can be avoided. They are such a strange race – and the young people at any rate both boys and girls so desperately anxious to know what to do with their lives, so utterly dependent on every word from the West (and every word they hear is contradictory) that I have felt nearer to tears in these last few days for things which have nothing to do with myself than almost ever in my life. Then again there are some such intelligent and fine people of my age but all nicer people than we meet in Europe. Without you I haven't really enjoyed it and I know that such holidays don't work – but I would love to visit here with you one day – not in September when it rains so much (tho' now it is boiling hot sun) and not because of the buildings which are pretty dreary (the towns hideous beyond belief) nor even the wonderfully 'picturesque' countryside but simply because of the people – their beauty and friendliness and so on altho' there are many vile aspects of the social system and vile people who are responsible for them – and then again I must tell you that these people so charming etc are at the same time shallow and naive (which I would expect to hate) but they mean so well that one cannot dislike the shallowness. Finally they are cruel and brutal (some of them) and quite bewildered about this, trying to ignore any frank remarks about it because my mentioning their brutality is so rude of me and they

don't wish to notice my rudeness and when I press the question
giving absurd answers or their favourite philosophical statements
meaning nothing. Remind me to tell you about the Austrian
Ambassador and the grilled cat (it is a strange story) and there are
many other strange stories I have to tell you. It won't be long
now – grace a Dieu! All my love Angus
P.S. If it isn't absolutely fixed with Frith etc for weekend – do
nothing as I shall be v. exhausted. You can arrange for weekend
following. Has the New Yorker money come?

Erewan Hotel
Bangkok (21 September)
Dearest Tony,
    I don't know whether this letter will reach you before I get
back and in any case it must be short as I have to go to address the
students at the University. God knows what they will understand!
For here in this land (very beautiful, dirty, incredible from the
sexual standpoint) we are back in the 17C as remote from Japan as
Japan is from England. I am enjoying it all and looking forward to
Angkor, but *not* to the return journey – the clock keeps on going
back now so that altho' it happens to be only 24 hours to Paris
from here by air it is really nearer 36 and underneath my surface I
am *very very* exhausted. All these receptions, sight seeing etc and
here in Siam in intense, moist heat with no sun. No letter here
from you so I imagine my mail takes longer than I think. I can
only hope to see you at 9.15 at London airport on Thursday. I
will be some time in the Customs probably as I have so many gifts
given to me or bought (none really quite worth having.) I earned
over £90 in Japan and all expenses were paid for ten days of it –
even so I spent about £60 of my own money – so you can see
how fabulously expensive it is – here it is even worse! When they
are so desperately poor its no surprise they think us all millionaires
– and so of course most Europeans who travel here are. Well here
is the car to collect me. All my love, longing to see you, Angus.

    A scatter of postcards also records his hectic progress. He had sent cards
from Kobe (he found the background here "like some strange but slightly
sinister sexual fantasy"): from Kyoto (a typhoon): from Nara (teeming
rain): from Osaka ("Herewith a big Buddha . . . S.S. really a very sad, good
person – ditto Moravia)" and from Saigon airport ("the poorest pseudo-
French meal has just been served to us"). His head was turning with new
impressions, some of which he was to shape into two articles – one for

Encounter on the Japanese character and the tensions of the culture, one for *Lilliput* on nightclubs, neon and Noh.[6] In this, he admitted that he had found Japanese food a great problem, and Donald Richie, the American scholar who accompanied him and Spender on their temple excursion, records that Angus was as appalled by the frozen tofu as Spender was by the sight of a thin futon spread for the night on the hard tatami. He also recalled that Angus, who was sleeping in the same room with him in the temple, warned him: " 'I should warn you, my dear, something quite awful occurs once I drift off. The entire roof of my mouth (here he pointed) seems to fall down and interfere. A terrible noise, I am told. Of course, I have never heard it. I am asleep.' And sure enough, after a bit a terrible noise began. It eventually sounded scarcely human – more like a factory, a stern and clanking sound, the worst industrial excesses of the 19th century. And then I remembered that Angus had told me he wanted to do a life of Dickens."[7]

Richie also felt that Angus did not really like Japan – he was forever talking about home and Tony. He claimed that Nikko reminded him of his dining-room at home, with its red Chinese wallpaper – "Tony just hates it but I have something chinoiserie about me. That is why I like it here so much." Richie did not quite believe this: he felt that Angus was homesick. And during this "feverish, unbalanced" time Tony had written to him with calming details of home life: the garden was looking wonderful and he had staked the dahlias (but part of the hunt had been through the garden and broken the dahlias). Theatrical producer Peter Wood had caused a stir by coming down for the weekend to stay with Chris Arnold – Chris was thinking he would let rather than sell his cottage and had promised to think about Angus's lease. Tony has seen Perkin Walker, the Wormalds, John Croft – "I am missing you *very much*. I am sorry if I seemed cold before you left, but I didn't want to think too closely about your going."

When Angus returned to Felsham Woodside, he found that the novel on which he had been working so painfully had died. The deserts of Iraq and Persia and the gardens of Bangkok had killed *The Goat and Compasses*.

On his last afternoon in Thailand, Angus had checked out of the Erewan Hotel and was sitting resting and dozing in the garden of Bangkok resident Victor Sassoon waiting for his departure to the airport and his next flight. (Sassoon had settled in Bangkok in 1955, and his name had been given to Angus and Spender by Raymond Mortimer.) There, in Sassoon's garden on Soi 3, Sukhamvit Road, a gibbon played: Angus watched it, admiring its airy, weightless grace. He perhaps pondered a little on the "silent revolution" he had mentioned in his last letter to Tony from Japan, which had been supported by some of the senior students he had met at

Chulalongkorn University. On 15 September 1957 a mass rally against Field-Marshal Phibulsongram had filled the streets: Phibul, who had collaborated with the Japanese occupation after Pearl Harbor, and who had held power for a decade, had become an unpopular figure, particularly with the young – regressive and repressive, he was said to have introduced a rule that all women should wear hats, skirts, gloves and stockings, which had so incensed one of the princes that he took to taking his Great Danes for walks wearing hats. Phibul now fled to Cambodia and then to the United States, and his place was seized by another Field-Marshal, Sarit, whose reign was to prove no more democratic though (some thought despite him) economically more successful.

Angus brooded on Japan's impending economic miracle, on Thailand's impending transformation from Siam to modern Thailand. The gardens of Sukhamvit Road would soon be swallowed up in high-rise extravaganzas and massive traffic jams. And here, in this unlikely refuge, his next novel, *The Middle Age of Mrs Eliot* was born.

Mrs Eliot, like Angus himself though in more desperate circumstances, would gaze at the palm trees, the great massses of purple flowers, the orchids and bougainvillaea and gerbera and portulaca, and at the gibbon "that swung from one silvery arm to another along a wire, a rope across the garden." Her husband would be killed in an attempted airport coup, in an imaginary country very like Thailand. But she, like Angus, would return to England to work out her resolution there.

★

Back in England, the October publication of a new volume awaited him.[8] Unlike its predecessors, *A Bit off the Map*, dedicated to "Francis and Honoria", is an uneven collection, betraying the difficulties its composition had cost him. It contains some of the best but also some of the weakest of his short stories. Several of the stories had already appeared in periodicals: "A Flat Country Christmas" as early as 1950, under another title (as "The Old, Old Message" in the *New Statesman*, 23 December 1950): "Higher Standards" in the *Listener* (15 January 1953): and "More Friend than Lodger" and "Once a Lady" in the *New Yorker* (10 August 1957 and 31 August 1957). The *New Yorker* had the best of it, and although Angus never really liked the magazine – indeed, was often rude about it and its mystique – it was a good showcase and it paid well. (In a review of high praise for Hortense Calisher's stories, *In the Absence of Angels*, he had accused the *New Yorker* of "embalmed chic and blasé cockiness."[9])

The best of the stories – "A Bit off the Map", "More Friend than Lodger", "Once a Lady", "After the Show" – show a growing ability to handle complex plot and to speak in different voices. ("More Friend than Lodger" is a *tour de force* of dramatic monologue.) In contrast, the weaker of the group seem a little bored with themselves. "A Sad Fall" harks back to the Bletchley Park days of billets and evacuees: the violence of the action (a child falls from a roof while playing spy or detective) has a Forsterian arbitrariness that disturbs the reader in perhaps an unintended way. (But the theme of falling is prophetic.) "Higher Standards" returns to Simpson and the upwardly mobile schoolteacher daughter of landlady Mrs Hill, but the determined lack of sentimentality has an uncomfortable edge. This vein of material seems to have been worked out, or to need radical reworking. "Ten Minutes to Twelve", inspired by the 1956 Suez débâcle, is set on New Year's Eve in the home of the autocratic but senile Lord Peacehaven, and the symbolism of end-of-year portending end-of-class-power seems a little obvious: the story is curiously staid, unlike the notes for it (under the title "A Quarter to Twelve"), which promised something more bizarre and high-spirited, involving "a whole Annie Fleming group", a Home Secretary's mistress, a lot of hard drinking, and a beautiful pianist raped in a bath.

Angus had become dissatisfied with the constraints of the short story. He had produced some classics of the genre, and some amusing commissioned pot-boilers which he never wished to see collected – they had appeared over the years in *Contact*, the *Evening Standard*, *Homes and Gardens*, and other magazines, and some were to pop up again in anthologies and in radio adaptations, but they were not to be included in his own *Collected Stories*. Their subject-matter – threatening bailiffs in bowler hats, pretentious novelists, versions of his story-telling father, Cunard liner drownings, exorcisms of the late Mrs Baker, Jane-Austen-reading spinsters – had begun to seem repetitive. His fondness for neat double-edged titles seemed suspect to him. He had distrusted it in *Hemlock*, and was to make fun of it at his own expense in *The Old Men at the Zoo*. It was a pity to abandon good ideas like a Sunday supper scene called "Cold Shoulder", but he could surely aim higher than a life of phrase- and title-making.

Some of his friends disagreed. They insisted that at heart he was a teller of anecdotes, a writer of vignettes, and kept on telling him so, to his annoyance.

The new stories were well reviewed, and on the strength of the title story he was hailed by the *Daily Telegraph* as the Teddy Boy's anthropologist and "the nicest nasty writer after the war". "More Friend than Lodger" proved something of a test case: mis-read by many, it was picked out for special praise by the professionals. Some, however, were determined to cut Wilson down to size. John Metcalfe in the *Sunday Times* said he was grossly over-rated – no sign of growth, a surface scattering of topicalities . . . The readers at the BBC, who had been earnestly soliciting Pattisson at Secker for a sight of this fashionable writer's new volume, spitefully muttered out of his hearing that the stories were tedious, trivial and obvious.

Some reviewers urged him on to more full-length fiction. John Raymond, in a long analysis in the *New Statesman*, hedged his bets: he noted that only the title story is quite as brilliant as "Totentanz", but ascribed this to Wilson's growing benevolence and need to understand his characters more fully. "Personally, I am not among those who would prefer Mr Wilson to stick to the short story and eschew the novel; I believe that he is one of the few English writers living with sufficient energy and moral seriousness to re-vitalise the great tradition." Angus must have read this as a challenge.

He took on the great tradition. It was not easy. A letter to Richard Wollheim dated 21 January 1958 reveals the extent of his anxiety. (Wollheim remembers the occasion as fraught, and thinks it was one of several lunches or dinners organised by his art-historian friend Benedict Nicolson at Bertorelli's.)

My dear Richard,
    I am writing to you in great unhappiness. I had to leave the dinner because I was so upset. I am sure that when you said to me what you did about the short stories you did so in all good faith and it is I who am crazy to mind about it – *but* I am now struggling with a novel – I think it may be very bad (or it may not) but whatever it is costing me an agony so that I am often near to suicide. And for good or ill I depend on that now for existence. I don't know what to say because I value your friendship *very much* but feel that you are there judging everything so harshly (I am indeed aware that the stories have defects altho' they are not bad short stories either) and that *so much is expected* of one all the time makes me utterly miserable. I don't know what to say – because a friendship in which one cannot communicate is absurd between adults and yet I can't bear this criticism – it inhibits one from working for days. I did not mean to come this evening – alcohol and company at the moment terrify me, but Ben asked me especially to do so. But please don't take my feelings so lightly and what is so awful is that I feel you must say these things to others and that means all that goes on behind ones back. Well, there we are – at least I've written it. Yours, Angus.

"So much is expected" – this was a terrible cry. An undergraduate called Francis Hope wrote a piece in *Isis* about Wilson's work, duly forwarded to him while he was working on the new novel. Angus was eagerly read at Oxford, where the new 1958 Penguin edition of *Anglo-Saxon Attitudes* was widely admired by the young, and he had a large following amongst aspiring writers like Julian Mitchell, John Caute (who later wrote as David Caute), and Dennis Potter. In his article Hope praised not only the "brilliant exhibitions of virtuosity in catching or holding a style of speech" (as in "More Friend than Lodger") but also the underlying seriousness of his intentions, concluding "Angus Wilson isn't the only writer alive today who looks like saving the English novel from swamps of mediocrity, but he is one of them. If you want commitment you can find it in every line he writes; a strong moral conscience and strong left-wing principles are not less part of his make-up for the fact that some people are too stupid or too bigoted to see them. He also happens to be an extremely good writer; and that is always important."[10]

This praise from the young was very pleasant – but what a responsiblity! He felt himself charged by two generations to save the English novel. What yawning chasms of disappointment might lie ahead! No wonder he felt anxious as he worked on and on at *The Middle Age of Mrs Eliot*.

★

Angus was to tell his friends that he *was* Meg Eliot: "*Mrs Eliot, c'est moi!*", as Flaubert might have said. She was one of the three characters in all his works with whom he most closely identified.

Meg Eliot is a very attractive woman, but this does not prove that Angus's fantasy life revolved around the image of himself as a female beauty. (Bunny Roger believed both Angus and Frederick Ashton had this fantasy.) Gone were the days when he played at being Kiki in front of the mirror, or dramatised himself with "camel-hair coat held toga-like across the hips, now, Marlene Dietrich alighting from an airliner, coat collar gripped across the neck like mink."[11] His female identification went beyond transvestism and narcissism. In Meg Eliot, he showed his own strengths and weaknesses of character – her manipulative charm, her social skills, her self-satisfaction, her need for admiration, her misplaced pity for others, her nervous breakdown, her recovery, her courage. And Mrs Eliot had models other than himself.

His notebooks indicate his plan: the novel was to deal with pity and cruelty, and with the power of pity as a destructive emotion. There were to be not more than ten characters. Meg Eliot (originally Shenston) "must be a woman whom one can admire and love as well as pity and yet *none* of the others must be hateable": it was of the essence that she should suddenly fall from protected comfort into semi-poverty, while in a condition of social ignorance. She was to be a plucky widow (though nowhere does this reductive phrase appear), and she was clearly to be based in part on Helen Pattisson (who had died on 3 January 1956) to whose "loved memory" (along with her son John) the book was dedicated. It was a story of a descent from hubris to pathos, and much of its plot follows closely that of the self-delusions of Jane Austen's interfering Emma. Copious changes reveal that Angus had at various points intended that Meg Eliot's husband commit suicide (before the novel opens) as Helen Pattisson's had done (but in fact Bill Eliot is shot on a foreign airport): that she should have had two children (she is in the novel childless): and that she should take and eventually reject a lover from the world of the theatre (she remains sexually untempted throughout). Some ingredients remain constant, including the three "Job's comforters", in the form of her lame-duck friends: Poll, the merry King's Road slut; Viola, the gruff charity worker; and Jill, the proud and lonely Army and Navy Stores naval widow – three wonderfully realised portraits.

The character of Meg's brother, David Parker, developed gradually: he was to be a non-practising homosexual, living chastely with a wealthy High Anglican ex-Quaker ex-lover Gordon Paget, and practising a form of deliberate humanist quietism. (Francis Wormald was to see something of himself in Gordon, as well as something of one of Angus's brothers.) David and Gordon run, with a community of workers, a nursery garden in Sussex (Angus notes "Brighton – Eastbourne – Seaford – Alfriston . . . old England with a vengeance") and write together a series of books on gardeners. (Is this, Angus asks himself, "too queeny"?) The notebook contains a list of what seem to be possible models for David and Gordon: it includes the names Ian, Bentley, Perkin, Chris, Pat, Jack, Raymond and Bruce. (But one must always beware of Angus's notebook lists: one, at first sight a list of Subject Victims, is on closer inspection quite clearly a list drawn up for Party Invitations.)*

Gradually the novel shaped itself from its multiple sources. It became clear that Angus's recent journeys – the views of the desert, the tropical gardens and swinging gibbons of Bangkok, all of which he used dramatically – had somehow enabled him to write about England in a way

---

* I suggest Ian Calder, Bentley Bridgewater, Perkin Walker, Chris Arnold, Pat Trevor-Roper, Bruce Vardon. Raymond may be Raymond Tyner, an American academic who worked on his thesis on Francis Quarles in pre-war days in the Reading Room, and who maintained a long friendship with Bentley Bridgewater.

that he had found impossible in *The Goat and Compasses*. By going abroad, he had come home.

The composition was, inevitably, much interrupted. In an interview published on 16 February 1958 in the *Sunday Times* he claimed that he kept the Dolphin Square telephone disconnected between 9 am and 4 pm in an effort to keep to his schedule for what was then entitled "Mid-Term Report" — he aimed at 2,000 words a day. Nevertheless, the world broke in. In March 1958 he signed a letter to *The Times* drafted by the English lecturer A. E. Dyson in support of the recommendation of the Wolfenden Report (1957) and he was to be on the Executive Committee of the Homosexual Law Reform Society, founded in 1958 to urge the government on to action. The letter was published on 7 March, and its 33 signatories included several peers, two bishops, Noël Annan, A.J. Ayer, Isaiah Berlin, Jacquetta Hawkes and J.B. Priestley, and Stephen Spender.

(The campaign for Law Reform was conducted on many levels. Angus's fiction made its own contribution: David and Gordon could be seen as excellent prototypes of Good Caring Homosexuals — music-loving, garden-loving, law-abiding decent citizens, unlike the gilded riff-raff of *Hemlock* and the dangerous underworld of *Anglo-Saxon Attitudes*.)

★

Angus still spent time in Dolphin Square, rushing off to PEN meetings, dinners, the theatre, the BBC, and to encounters with Roy Jenkins and Hugh Gaitskell. (He had become an active and welcome supporter and member of the Labour Party.) But he was settling more deeply into Suffolk life. In April, Tony was transferred by the Probation Service at his own request from London to Suffolk: this meant less driving, less ferrying backwards and forwards of sheets, and less risk of Angus burning himself to death while waiting for Tony to come home at the weekend. (Once he had lit an oil lamp in an upper room to provide a welcoming beacon: by the time Tony got there everything was about to burst into flames.) It seemed a very good move.

Increasingly, Angus was to present himself as a country-dweller, as a man who loved his garden better than the literary life. If not quite David and Gordon, or David and Jonathan, he and Tony had worked out for themselves a harmonious pattern of living. The garden, by now, was looking good: Angus had reclaimed it from the encroaching wild, dug up all the gin bottles, indigestion tablets and bits of rusty bicycles with which his predecessors had loaded it, and planted it with old roses. An avenue of young maple, whitebeam, apple and plum trees now led up to the cottage across the fields — Mr Squirrel, the farmer, had voted against poplar because

of the long roots. The cottage itself sported glass cages of stuffed birds —
an owl, a parrot and a grebe — and yellow Chinese wallpaper. Tony was
to design a pretty little Gothic window for the larder, which soon looked
as though it had been there for centuries. Felsham Woodside was a safe
haven. They felt they were accepted by their neighbours: they had homosexual friends in Suffolk, but they also had many straight friends who did
not question their way of life. They had acquired a Welsh cat called Morgan, and a cleaning-lady called Mrs Revens. They were a household.

Mrs Eliot was finished some time in mid-1958. The summer was taken
up with visits — to Clive and Lucie in Nottingham, to Oxford and Cambridge for talks — and with visitors. They saw Jack Plumb, who had a
country retreat nearby at Westhorpe, near Stowmarket — one of many
of their Suffolk friends to inhabit an Old Rectory. (Despite past tensions
Angus and Jack maintained a close friendship, although observers say that
each always tried to out-talk the other.) They saw Tess and Victor Rothschild, who spent their summers *en famille* four miles from Felsham
Woodside at Rushbrooke. They saw the Blackburnes at Nowton Court:
Charles, Neville and Betty Blackburne, a formidable trio, ran a prep
school where Geoffrey Wright (another Suffolk weekender) had for a
time taught music. (Tess Rothschild was an old friend of the Blackburnes
and had appeared in the Marlowe Society's *Hamlet* with Neville: her
brother Andreas Mayor had been at Bletchley Park with Angus.) Angus
and Tony continued to make a new acquaintances in the neighbourhood
— painters, rose-growers, fashion designers, fishmongers, teachers, race-
horse owners, hoteliers, antique dealers, amateur Thespians, antiquarians.
Daphne and Graham Reynolds, Gerry and Mary Cookson, Roger and
Mary Gilliatt, Humphrey and Natasha Brooke, Martin and Jean Corke,
Norman Scarfe and Paul Fincham — all became close friends, as did Joan
Colin, who ran an excellent restaurant in Long Melford where they ate
many a meal and entertained many a guest.

On 8 September 1958 Angus was interviewed at the cottage by a young
Italian critic well versed in English life and letters, Alberto Arbasino: Arbasino's piece, "*Una giornata con Angus Wilson*", is a colourful account of
a country Wilson with cornflower-blue eyes, a celestial blue pullover, and
red socks, romantically ensconced in his little hut* amidst his dahlias,
lilies, marguerites and zinnias. But the interview was not horticultural in
tone. The great author, having established that he did all the cooking and
housework himself, rattled on at tremendous speed over a casserole of
grouse ("*Non ho mai assaggiato un piatto come questo*," Arbasino innocently
comments) about Tony and his work as a probation officer — no, Tony's

---

* Referred to as "*capanna*" and "*baracca*" in Italian.

charges are not all minors, one of them is a colonel of over seventy – about the free and easy bisexuality of the working classes, the intensity of three-way love relationships, Proust and Lovelace and Don Giovanni and Zola and society hostesses, T.S. Eliot and *The Middle Age of Mrs Eliot*. By this stage Angus had produced bottles of liqueurs and boxes of chocolates, and was busy dipping fondants in his cognac as he described his meeting with the Queen and T.S. Eliot at the British Museum, his impressions of Japan and Moravia, Terence Rattigan's opinion of *Hemlock and After*, the art of the short story, Stephen Spender, grouse-shooting, his four-year-long nervous breakdown, the woman who encouraged him to write "for the good of his health" ("*le fa tanto bene alla salute*"), his parents, his itinerant childhood, his insecurity, his preference for the novel over the short story, his vague plan to write another play . . . All this while eating and smoking, and scattering ash from his cigarette over the chocolates.

Arbasino concludes that this "extraordinary monologue, lasting several hours" went through three phases – the desire to shock, the conventional bit on self-defensiveness, and then "*questo scoppio di finta sincerità*" – this outburst of feigned sincerity. What was he playing at, the great writer? Was he playing tricks? Wilson went on to say that he was fed up with writing for the English press, which paid so badly, unlike the *New Yorker* . . . and ended, on Arbasinos's prompting, with an aria to teddy-boys, these sweet rustic Byrons with their jukeboxes and scooters and jeans and Coca-Cola, and the even sweeter Japanese teddy-boys playing their pinball machines . . . why didn't the English leftwing who so long to embrace the working class ever talk to people like this? It was a bravura performance, which Angus might well have hesitated to bestow upon an English journalist.[12]

★

Later in September Angus, accompanied by Tony, went to Poland to lecture for the British Council and to spend his non-convertible zloty royalties from *Anglo-Saxon Attitudes*. It was his first visit to what was then called an Iron Curtain country. They made many contacts and friends there, including the Conrad scholar Zdzislaw Najder.* But conditions in Poland were grim: on his return he told P.N. Furbank that people were sleeping fifteen to a room, and that the only thing that made life bearable was that homosexuality had just been made legal.

This visit was almost immediately followed by another long tour of

---

* Author of *Joseph Conrad: A Chronicle* (Cambridge University Press 1983). Najder was to earn the distinction of a death sentence from his own country when he began to work for Radio Free Europe. He became an accidental exile in December 1981 when martial law was introduced in Poland and he decided, finding himself abroad at the time, to stay abroad.

Scandinavia, Germany and Switzerland in October and November. It was pleasant to be in demand, but it was exhausting and not very profitable: these tours were largely unpaid. Angus lectured and lectured – on the Victorian novel, on the contemporary novel, on his own fiction. He wrote to Tony from Trondheim, Britannia Hotel, 2 November 1958:

> My dear Tony,
>   Its all an experience as they say, but not, I think, again.
> Especially when I see four weeks more ahead. The hotels are very comfortable, altho' unfortunately they were mending tramlines in Oslo outside the room at night so that I had to dope myself silly in order to sleep. The lectures were an *enormous* success in Oslo and also the broadcasts and I had an excellent press both in Oslo and Bergen . . . I get on very well with the Norwegians and they are kind and friendly (except the heads of the Anglo-Norwegian groups in places like Trondheim and Bergen who tend to be the local Maecenases (very rich and patronising) otherwise there would be no money to pay for the things) but one does not get very close to them (or rather tho' intelligent they do truly seem a bit dead and without charm – it seems unkind to say so when so many, I think, have felt that they have made a very close rapport with me) – but its not the sort of rapport made with the Poles. Nobody queer as far as I know but anyway I haven't time to find out because in Oslo I never had a minute to breathe – callers at 8 am and nobody stops talking until 2 am . . . I had a lot of pleasant moments in Oslo (the British Council people are delightful and the Ambassador a very nice funny man) but felt at the end of my tether with exhaustion.* Anyhow I can tell you much more when I see you – may the time pass as quickly as possible. Love to Morgan and Mrs Reavons [*sic*]. Look after yourself – all my love Angus.

Post cards followed – Stockholm pouring with rain, staying with a very kind but very neurotic consul straight out of *Mrs Eliot* in Hanover, desolate on Frankfurt airport en route for Munich, Berlin was wonderful, on to Zurich and the baroque cathedral of St Gall and the disgreeable Profesor Stamm in Berne, and on to Geneva, worried all the time about the *Mrs Eliot* reviews . . . – a crescendo of worries about *Mrs Eliot*, due out on 5 November.

Tony writes back with comforting news about the reviews, about sales, about Morgan. Morgan gets liver once a week, and is very purring and

---

* The British Ambassador was Sir Peter Scarlett, KCMG, KCVO, 1905–1987.

affectionate. Sales are good ("steady as a rock at 1,000 a month", Fred Warburg was to write to Penguin the following February, while negotiating an advance of £500 – a handsome improvement on the £300 accepted for *Anglo-Saxon Attitudes*). Tony is organising Angus's correspondence and a forthcoming Irish visit. Bentley is re-reading *Mrs Eliot* with great admiration, and so is Tony. The reviews have been excellent – even Metcalfe, who was so rude about *A Bit off the Map*, liked it, but Tony would like to write to them and to point out to them all how "courageous" the book is. Angus will probably think the *Spectator* review by Kermode the best he has ever had. Tony's life had not been entirely rustic – he has been to a not very amusing party at Perkin Walker's with Forrest Fulton in dark glasses, Geoffrey Wright, a frosty Parnis, and a character described as "the most pretentious snob that ever came out of the South . . . You were naughty to afflict him on B. and Perkin." Perkin Walker spent much of the party weeping in a corner.

The European press coverage of Angus's tour was extensive, and he returned at the end of November in triumph to the British reviews of the novel. The consensus was that he had grown milder (William Cooper, *News Chronicle*) and more constructive (Francis Wyndham, *London Magazine*): Frank Kermode found the closing scenes between Meg and her brother magnificent and placed Wilson squarely in the "great tradition of moralising novelists." The *Times Literary Supplement* concluded at great length that the book was "a brave and memorable mistake" but kindly thought his move from Gogol to George Eliot had possibilities. Anthony Quinton in the *Observer* misread the book (as did many) by assuming that Meg had been "happily married", when one of the main points of the carefully constructed plot is her gradual discovery of all the unhappinesses the conventions of marriage had concealed. Angus had perhaps been a little too indirect in his narration, had expected more alertness from his readers. But these were pinpricks. *Mrs Eliot* joined *Dr Zhivago* on the best-seller list, and it gained him a new (and arguably more female) readership – a useful addition to his following, as women are believed by the book trade to be the most committed purchasers of hardback fiction. Angus himself certainly believed that *Mrs Eliot* had increased the numbers of his female admirers. (When Audrey Brodhurst saw Angus carrying a copy of his rival, *Dr Zhivago*, she asked him what he thought of it. "Rather soupy," he replied.)

He was particularly pleased by a letter from Tim Neighbour, who wrote that he (and Bentley) thought the new book his best. Neighbour wondered if critics would be disappointed by its more sombre tone: "No reviewer would have spotted how *Mansfield Park* improves on *Pride and*

Prejudice." Neighbour had much sympathy with David's quietist outlook, and (à propos of the nursery garden) had, according to P.N. Furbank, long been trying to curb Angus's obsessive "flower snobbery". (Angus thought Perkin Walker's taste in roses *very* vulgar.) Many of Angus's circle saw something of Perkin Walker in David, somewhat to Angus's surprise – he had intended a life-denying portrait of a man deliberately content with the second-rate. But Perkin (who never recognised himself in the portrait) – Perkin, with his long silences, his string quartet, his tolerance, his generosity, his Sussex Wilderness – had invaded the book, and had brought with him a powerful undertow of affection and respect.

Angus's Westminster friend Richard Gorer also suggests himself to the reader as a model for David. Richard had become a horticulturalist and plantsman in Kent, and his brother Geoffrey had a fine garden at Sunter House near Haywards Heath where he indulged a passion for rhododendrons. Richard Gorer had lost touch with Angus after school, but met him and Tony at least once during the 1950s with his friend and neighbour Jocelyn Brooke: over lunch they spoke of Tony's work as a probation officer, of Jocelyn Brooke's editing of Denton Welch's journals, and of Cyril Connolly's "slightly tiresome fragment of a novel which he had titled *Shade Those Laurels*. I believe it is a quotation from Pope, but Angus thought it more likely that it was spoken by someone arranging decorations for a function and instructing his assistants to bring up the hydrangeas and shade those laurels . . ." (Richard Gorer questions Angus's horticultural chronology: the monstrous rhododendrons bred by Tim Rattray in David's nursery belong to the beginning of the century, as in the mid-fifties breeders were concentrating not on size but on new colours and smaller plants suitable for smaller gardens – but he adds that "To a certain extent Angus was prophetic as recently the American breeders have turned again to very large flowers.")*[13]

★

Angus returned from his Scandinavian tour to triumph but not to tranquillity. The hysteria of his *cri de coeur* to Wollheim found an echo nearly a year later in a letter to Pamela Warburg from Dolphin Square:

  12.Dec.58
  2 Grenville House
  My dear Pamela,

---

* Gorer (as well as contributing to *Groves*) wrote books on gardening in collaboration with his friend Thomas Rochford, but he says that he did not start publishing until the 1960s. The Connolly fragment was published in *Encounter*, March 1956, so the lunch should be dated pre-*Mrs Eliot.*

When I lunched with Fred today, he reminded me ever so
tactfully that I had not answered your kind invitation to a party
next week. I was appalled by my bad manners and in my distress
said that of course I would come. But I'm going to ask you & him
to excuse me. I haven't been to a London party for nearly two
years now and I have a real horror of doing so. If I could bring
myself to look at the literary world en masse it would be because
it was your party but I hope you will forgive me if I don't make
any exception. It is my fervent hope that I will not have to go to
an English literary party again in my life tho I have little hopes of
fulfilling it.

Yours ever, Angus.

This emotional letter illustrates the fact that Angus was on good personal
terms with the Warburgs. He got on well with Fred Warburg, and wrote
him long, chatty letters as well as despairing ones.* Fred Warburg had
managed to offend Angus, however, by his remarks on *Mrs Eliot* (for which
he claimed to have invented the title, not liking the pun in Angus's second
choice, *Change of Life*): he had rashly criticised the nursery garden
descriptions as excessive. He was forgiven for this, but the editing of
Angus's work was thenceforward handed over to David Farrer, who had
to exercise a fair amount of diplomacy – Angus was never easy to edit, and,
as Angus himself wrote to Hemmings, he could not punctuate "for
toffee". But, as he also insisted to Hemmings, he set very great store by
shape – "what is most important to me is a certain shape that I gradually see
– often I feel it dominates my work and robs it of life, but it is nevertheless
absolutely vital. This shape demands for example that there should be so
many side plots . . . to create balance and often for this reason I conceive
that new characters are needed. I am excited by giving these 'extra'
characters needed for balance a special paradoxical existence – eg we all
know the good-hearted tart and the tweedy country girl who loves
animals but is sexually afraid – let us try a country woman who under
sexual shyness has a nymphomaniac disposition but by virtue of her
breeding, her tweediness attains a decency not to be found in the ordinary
tart. Such paradoxes I enjoy assembling and using in the novel's shape – but
it often happens that when I have 'created' these impossibilities, I find they
are portraits from life – this happened twice in Hemlock, once in my play

---

* Frederic J. Warburg had been at Westminster (which he loathed) from 1912–17, and had
followed the traditional Westminster route as an exhibitioner to Christ Church, Oxford: he
served in the First War, then went into publishing, taking over Martin Secker's assets and
forming the new company in 1936. He was an adventurous publisher: his list included Stefan
Zweig, Rayner Heppenstall, Robert Musil, Orwell and Moravia.

and not until the whole thing was in proof did I see that my created
monstrosity was someone I knew."[14] This emphasis on shape he reiterated
in a piece in *Queen* (15 March 1960), in which, in dialogue with William
Sansom, he said "Though I am not proud of the shape & structure of my
sentences, I am rather proud of the putting together of the whole book.")

Warburg's stylish second wife, dress-designer and amateur painter
Pamela de Bayou, was an exotic to delight Angus's heart and pen:
outrageous, malicious, fast-talking, she loved scandal and gossip. Angus
enjoyed her. He particularly relished her story about cheetahs' piss: she
claimed to have seen a woman walking two pet cheetahs along on leads on
a marble pavement in Verona, and had gone into raptures over the
aesthetic effect of their green urine upon the Italian marble. On another
occasion, even more implausibly, she related to Angus that she had sat next
to André Gide at dinner, and he had found her so irresistibly attractive that
she had been pinched "black and blue" by the end of the meal. (Others
relate that she claimed her assailant was Thomas Mann, but Angus and
Tony understandably preferred the Gide version.) Angus enjoyed these
highly-coloured tales, but at times they were too much for him: another
party at St Edmunds Court, St John's Wood, was more than he dared face.

David Farrer, who had accompanied Angus to Stockholm in the
autumn of 1958, also became a close friend. Like John Pattisson, he had a
long association with the firm. The son of a successful barrister, he had
been to Rugby and Oxford – a History Scholar at Balliol, and a member of
OUDS. During the war he worked for Beaverbrook, on Tom Driberg's
recommendation, in the Ministry of Information. On his mother's death,
he invested capital inherited from her in Secker & Warburg, and worked
there for the rest of his life. He was not exactly a literary type – more of a
punter, really, a Garrick Club man who liked his gin and tonic, his red
wine, his cigarettes. Or so he chose to present himself, although this
exterior concealed a sharp critical intelligence and a conscientious
professionalism. A steady heavy drinker, a lunching publisher, a lonely
homosexual (or so speculated one of his authors, Melvyn Bragg) who
envied Tony and Angus their happy domestic life.

Farrer was to edit Angus's next novel, *The Old Men at the Zoo*. Hitherto,
for good or ill, very little editing of Angus's work had taken place – he had
received almost random comments from Fred Warburg and Spencer
Curtis Brown, which he did not always take well. He did not like revision.
He had not enjoyed rewriting *The Mulberry Bush*, and although he solicited
advice from Somerset Maugham about writing plays (Maugham replied
that he put in too much, and had too many characters) and was in receipt of
a useful work from Peter Glenville called *How not to write a Play* by Walter

Kerr, he was not very good at taking suggestions from others. The editing of *The Old Men at the Zoo* was to prove no small task. And the years of its composition brought quite unexpected problems for him and Tony.

A FLIGHT FROM THE VILLAGE

Angus was so busy during 1959 that he hardly knew where he was. Sometimes he wasn't there at all. He rushed around the countryside and around Europe talking here and talking there and talking everywhere – Yorkshire in January, Ireland in March, France and Switzerland in April, Switzerland again in August. The Irish trip took in Cork, Dublin and Kilkenny, but Belfast was called off at the last moment because, as the *Belfast Telegraph* drily remarked, "it was only after studying a road map that he discovered that the distance between Belfast and Kilkenny was rather more than he imagined, and could not be done in time."[1] It was so easy to get in a muddle. In Grenoble in April he began to lecture, as usual in English, but the students cried out "*Français! Français!*" and thumped their desks angrily. Obligingly, he instantly began to address them in fluent French. (No wonder the British Council appreciated him.)

He was still reviewing busily: in January alone he wrote four pieces on the theatre for the *Observer*. His 1958–9 theatre pieces included three on pantomime: *West Side Story* (loved the Sharks and the Jets, hated the lovers); Willis Hall's *The Long and the Short and the Tall*; Shelagh Delaney's *A Taste of Honey*; and Sandy Wilson's *Valmouth*, which he found "a sorry piece of English amateurism" after the professionalism of *The Boy Friend*. (Sandy Wilson was offended and wrote in protest to the *Observer*: but the two Wilsons were later harmoniously reconciled in Bury.) In March, a cool piece on *Nabokov's Dozen* appeared in the *Spectator*. Angus had signed the group protest letter which appeared in *The Times* on 23 January 1959 on behalf of *Lolita*, but the short stories he found full of "cosmopolitan glitter, the small change of competent short-story writing" and his last paragraph on this "bargain basement collection" is telling: "I cannot forbear to advise all ambitious young writers to look at Mr Nabokov's bibliography at the end of the book. This account of the successful publication of these stories is a lesson in how to make the most lolly out of your work."[2]

He tried to keep his own lolly under control: with a careful eye on the Inland Revenue, he set up a special arrangement with Secker and Curtis Brown whereby he received his money in rationed instalments. But it was a bit of a treadmill: if only, he wrote to David Farrer, he could get more occasional TV appearances – "for example on the Brains Trust, only I don't know how to set about crashing the gates." And when he was asked, he often had to decline: he turned down innumerable broadcasts.

In March, he sat for his portrait to Colin Spencer in Felsham Woodside, at Alan Pryce-Jones's request: the drawing – of a noticeably plumper, pullovered, country Wilson – appeared in the *Times Literary Supplement* on 15 May 1959. The country image was reinforced by the sight of a large goose egg in the kitchen – Spencer, not yet a gastronome, was astonished by its size. Spencer wrote to his Australian lover John Tasker:

"Croydon
31.iii.59
. . . I was afraid he might not be very nice but I was quite wrong
and I'm completely converted to him. He lives with someone
who is younger and a probation officer, they've been together
about ten years and are charming. They're buried in the country
in a flint cottage enclosed in a garden like a parcel. He is wickedly
funny telling the most detailed sagas about literary windbags and
being marvellously vicious about them. I told them all about you
and how wonderful you were, and he gave me a copy which he
signed of the last volume of short stories . . . and bought a drawing
I'd done of him.*[3]

Colin Spencer married later that year, on 2 October 1959, to John Tasker's distress. Spencer saw his marriage in part as a "rebellion against what society did to gay people." Ian Calder, The Golden Boy of the Little Hadham Experiment, was also to marry this year.

*

Ian Calder's metamorphosis had been strange and unexpected. He had finished his dissertation in 1952, then had suddenly decided to become an actor. (His dissertation remains unpublished, but was a valuable resource to other scholars for years.) Tempted by what he considered his own great success in various amateur Shakespeare productions at Reading, he had

---

* Spencer found Tony on this occasion rather alarming: "he stared at me all the time with a kind of basilisk look. Many years later, of course, I found him an absolute sweetie."

thrown away his promising academic career and his pension and headed for the stage. (John Wain, at the same period, took a gamble and left Reading to become a full-time writer.) Ian Calder's friends dutifully attended his appearances at Reading (as Polonius, he trembled throughout) but thought he was crazy to take the thing seriously. He would not listen to reason – and anyway, what right had Angus to give advice? Had not Angus himself risked security for art? (Meneghello recalls that Angus's attitude was of "amused tolerance".)

Ian Calder appeared as *The Jew of Malta* at Toynbee Hall in an amazing performance which his friends remember to this day with a mixture of horror and admiration: the intensity of his desire to perform and his lack of trained professional talent appalled them. They had good cause to fear. He sold everything he had, and took off for the life of provincial repertories and theatrical lodgings so well chronicled by John Osborne. Then he returned to London in 1956, where, unable to find paid work, he appeared for a while with Valery Hovenden in the Hovenden Theatre Club, playing Mr Punch in her summer shows in the parks, and other more classical parts in her stage productions.

Valery Hovenden was a character before her time, running a fringe theatre before the fringe had been invented.* Herself a professional actress and drama teacher, she had taught the RADA overflow (the Preparatory Academy), and had concluded that what many young actors needed was a theatre where they could work and train, combined with a showcase where they could display their talents. Energetic, untidy and well-connected, she put on productions of a wide variety of plays – rare eighteenth-century comedies, new translations from the Greek, musicals, new dramas – first in private homes, then in the basement of an art gallery in Lisle Street, and eventually in her own tiny premises in Garrick Yard in St Martin's Lane. She attracted some interesting talent – Ann Jellicoe, James Kirkup, Margaretta D'Arcy, Edward Petherbridge, Bernard Kops, Lindsay Kemp, and Charles Osborne were all at one time associated with the Hovenden Players. (She reminded Osborne of Judith Bliss in *Hay Fever*.) Amongst her protégés were Ian Calder and Patricia Taylor.

Ian Calder appeared in several productions in the late Fifties – in some Housman plays, in a new translation from Aristophanes, as a tribune in *Coriolanus*. And in the summer of 1958 he appeared as Antipholus of Syracuse in *The Comedy of Errors* with Pat Taylor as his Dromio. This was performed in the Garrick Yard, and also as part of a Theatre Festival at the

---

* Valery Hovenden (1902–92) was married to an Irish engineer, John Henry Woulfe Flanagan, who translated several Greek classic dramas for her under the pseudonym of Dionysius McDuffy. He died in 1956.

George Inn in Southwark. After the show there were many drinking sessions in pubs, and nine months later, Antipholus and Dromio were married. Ian Calder proposed to his Dromio in the interval of the Folies Bergères.

Pat Taylor was a dark, gamine girl, aged twenty-four. Ian Calder was thirty-five, but he still looked like a boy – a beautiful boy. They were both stagestruck. It seemed like a fairy story.

Perkin Walker, Bentley Bridgewater and Angus had been shocked by Ian Calder's decision to become a strolling player. His marriage was another cause for wonder. This was not the first time he had been involved with a young woman – there had been the strange case of Antonia Bracken, daughter of his secretary at the Warburg, a promising young schoolgirl musician whose cause had been taken up in 1950–51 by Calder, Perkin Walker, and André Mangeot, all worried that she was suffering from serious parental neglect. Molly Calder found her precocious (and threatening) but Rosemary and her husband Ian Merry liked her very much and took her under their wing – she was always running away from home to be with them. Was Angus jealous of Ian Calder's concern? Possibly. (Toni Bracken had married from the Merrys' flat in Eccleston Square in 1954.)

Angus, Bentley and Perkin felt protective about Ian Calder. One became accustomed to young men growing up and growing away – it was a common pattern in university life, where much-loved protégés would regularly abandon their mentors for marriage, causing intense but usually short-lived pain. (The pain often dissolved into a family friendship, with the older man transformed from Lover into Uncle: there were even benefits, in the form of hot meals and invitations to Christmas.) But Ian Calder's sudden engagement to Pat Taylor came as a surprise. Rosemary Merry doubted if Ian could be serious, and assured her future sister-in-law that he didn't really mean to get married. Molly Calder was amazed: he had preferred another woman! We do not know what were the thoughts of the Reverend Bill (Ronald Bain) Calder, the new Rector of Martlesham in Suffolk – he too had gone through a metamorphosis, from headmaster to cleric, and was not well placed to exert the authority that he had never had.

And so they were married, on 4 April 1959, by the Reverend Mr Calder himself, at Christ Church, Woburn Square. Bentley Bridgewater was best man, and Denis and Patsy Barnes, Bob French and Montagu Turland, and many others of the supporting cast were in attendance. Viva King, bundled into the back of a taxi with Violet Bridgewater, was heard to refer to the affair as "this marriage of midgets". The reception was held at the

Hovenden Theatre Club, and then all the rout repaired to chew it over at Perkin Walker's place at 2 Regent's Park Terrace.

What did the future hold for this doll-like couple? They were like twin figures from an Iris Murdoch sibling romance. They did not seem to be made for the real world. Pat Calder had acquired three fairy godfathers – Perkin, Bentley and Angus – who would watch over her married life. Would their supervision be benevolent or malign?

Some thought Angus was angry about the whole business, but Pat Calder felt he was relieved that Ian was finally rescued from Molly. Tony maintained that Ian – who had patiently coached him in maths for a Civil Service examination, as he had coached Antonia Bracken for her School Certificate – had a natural generosity of sexual temperament, a natural lack of guilt and possessiveness. Ian Calder was dangerous to nobody but himself.

★

In August 1959 Angus gave up the Dolphin Square flat. He had been spending more and more time in Suffolk, when he was not dashing round the Continent. Every summer brought more local commitments. There were parties and plays and pageants and meals at Long Melford: there were visits to Aldeburgh and their local stately home, Ickworth – a must for all weekend visitors. Once they even went to the races with Peter Jenkins's uncle, Cyril Croger, the gay fishmonger of Bury. Every year the summer cast list swelled – historian Michael Howard, Jack Plumb and his friend Neil McKendrick, the Annans, Victor and Tess Rothschild and their family, Paul and Celia Jennings, the Wollheims, Stuart Hampshire, Stuart's brother Peter and his wife Eve, the Wormalds, the Romans, Sir Malcolm Bullock, the Cockells, the Blackburnes, the Brookes, the Corkes, the Cooksons, the Christopher Morrises, the Reynoldses . . . Perkin Walker and Forrest Fulton came with their Danish friends, and artists Richard Chopping and Denis Wirth-Miller would pop over from Wivenhoe. Occasionally Angus and Tony saw Cedric Morris and his friend Lett Haines, who lived together at Benton End, where Morris painted, cultivated irises, and encouraged a generation of talented young artists. Spencer Curtis Brown had an antique home in Suffolk, where he entertained in lugubrious style, waited on by an old couple. And this year Bentley Bridgewater came for five weeks in September; sometimes there seemed no reason why he should ever go.

(Bentley Bridgewater was not really a country lover: of an evening, after dinner, he would wander in the dark down the long muddy avenue of trees through the fields to the road "just to see if anything was going on".

Nothing ever was, but old habits died hard. And when Angus proudly came up to his bedroom one morning to show him a live mole in a saucepan he was horrifed. Bentley did not share Angus's taste for the wild.)

They paid some return visits – one to the Priestleys in the Isle of Wight. The Priestley friendship, since Jack's challenging letter about *Hemlock*, had flourished: Angus and Tony stayed with them several times, and Jack and Jacquetta Priestley had dined with them and Bentley in Dolphin Square – a somewhat wild evening, Jacquetta recalled, as Jack had arrived late after drinking slivovitz at the Czech Embassy. Dinner was late, the fowl in tatters, and Jack glassy-eyed – Priestley had written to apologise and they had all got on even better than before.[4] This was a strange quartet, but they had much in common – Jacquetta's first husband, Christopher Hawkes, had worked before the war at the British Museum in the Department of British and Medieval Antiquities, and as an archaeologist herself she was intrigued by the personalities in *Anglo-Saxon Attitudes*. And she and Jack Priestley gave full support to Homosexual Law Reform – indeed the Albany Trust was named after their rooms in Albany, where the group first met. Angus, for his part, admired Priestley's sound humane political views, respected his broad canvas as a novelist – and envied his apparently effortless success in the commercial theatre. (It also has to be said that Jack was a gift to a mimic: Angus loved to do his Priestley.)

Angus and Tony also visited Clive and Lucie Johnstone-Wilson again in Nottingham, and listened to Clive's stories – Clive had moved out of Alan Rook's enormous pile, Wootton Lodge (too many dramas, Lucie didn't like it), and into a nice suburban home with a garage with a glass door – "What's the point of having a Jag if the neighbours can't see it?" Wootton Lodge had been the reverse of suburban – a magnificent five-bayed late-sixteenth-century mansion, with balustrade, fluted Ionic columns, and extensive landscaped gardens, it was described by Pevsner as the most fascinating house in Staffordshire, "a compact building of calm perfection". Little calm had it known with the Rooks and the Johnstone-Wilsons, and possibly not with its previous occupants, Oswald and Diana Mosley, who had lived there for four years from 1936: when Clive and Lucie left, Alan Rook and his mother rattled around in its beautiful empty vastness before Alan Rook bought Stragglethorpe Hall near Grantham, where he cultivated his own vineyard. (Stragglethorpe, Mrs Rook wrote to her sister-in-law, was "much smaller, it only has seven bathrooms": it was to feature thirty years later in the 1994 TV adaptation of *Middlemarch* as Stone Court, the home of Mr Featherstone.[5])

Clive was running the Skinner and Rook coffee-and-walnut-cake shop, a famous and fragrant Nottingham rendezvous, affectionately remembered long after its disappearance. The brothers spoke of Pat and Colin, and their restless wanderings. Clive was not very sympathetic to their difficulties. He was busy minding his own business.

And Angus was busy minding his. In September he started plotting a new novel, filling his exercise books with ideas. He got depressed by it, but that was only to be expected. Everything else seemed to be ticking away satisfactorily. His own TV adaptation of his short story, "After the Show", with Jeremy Spenser in the lead as Maurice, the young Jewish boy learning sophistication through an encounter with his uncle's suicidal mistress, was shown on 20 September in ABC's "Armchair Theatre" slot: Angus was photographed at rehearsals with director Ted Kotcheff. The play was on the whole well received; Keith Waterhouse in the *New Statesman* said it was a delight, and the *Sunday Times* commented that this was the time of all the Wilsons – Woodrow, Jumbo, Sandy, Colin, Angus, Edmund . . . (Hermione Baddeley, who played the grandmother, surprised Angus by some of her lines, which he could not quite recall: she said to him in a break "You wrote some lovely words, dear – I didn't say many of them, but I knew you wouldn't mind.")

There was no Harold Wilson as yet as Labour Party leader (he was elected leader in February 1963 after Gaitskell's death), but Angus Wilson gave his public support for Labour for the forthcoming October election: he had written for the Fabians, and appeared in *Forward* (10 July 1959) under a massive headline in Francis Williams's column – WHY ANGUS WILL VOTE LABOUR – which quoted him as saying that the new "meritocratic society, with all its new social snobberies, its *Daily Express* for romantic glamour thrown around careerism [*sic*], its expense account hypocrisies and its committee and board room intrigues is, of course, as much a gift for a satirical writer as the old and co-existent class system. But the satire has become more tragic because it threatens to deflect a better world back into the old, wasteful, silly, snob paths." (But for all that, on 9 October 1959 "Supermac" Macmillan and the Tories were elected with an overwhelming majority.)

This autumn, a South African relative (W.H.Caney) died and left Angus £1,119.3.0: Angus set up a company called Angus Wilson Ltd, and in November, for £927.5.10, he bought a new car in part-exchange for his old one – this was an Austin Westminster in Bermuda Blue, and on his accountants' advice he bought it outright instead of on the hire-purchase system. He gave Gerard Reve some money to enable him to fly back to Holland to his mother's deathbed. Angus was feeling comfortable financially, and morale was high; his total income this year was to be just over five and a half thousand pounds, including the Caney windfall, and an untaxable £175 for winning the James Tait Black Memorial Prize for *Mrs Eliot* – this was more than two thousand pounds up on his 1958 income. Despite defeat on the political front, all seemed to be sailing calmly in the right direction, but as he struggled with the complexities of his new plot, a storm was brewing. It broke at the end of the year.

★

Angus and Tony had made their home in Suffolk. They felt at home there. It came as a shock to them when they discovered that there had been gossip. Tony's job was at risk.

With hindsight, perhaps there had been warnings of trouble. Towards the end of 1958 Tony had written to Angus to warn him about his affectionate messages – "please be careful on your postcards and telegrams – 'love' – 'missing you' etc – all very welcome – but Mr Parrish [the postman] gives me such coy looks now I don't know how to face him!!" And others picked up undertones that perhaps Angus missed.

Some time in 1959 a young Indian student and aspiring playwright doing his A-Levels at the Romans's school at Felsham House made his way across the fields and arrived, hours late for his appointment and caked with mud, bearing a manuscript of Nordic gloom and youthful megalomania: he was well received by Angus, though Tony warned him that when Angus was working on a new novel "You can't go anywhere near him, he's like a tiger." Adil Jussawalla later reflected: "Angus wasn't Mr Romans' kind of writer and I don't think the people of Felsham cared for the person they had in their midst. He seemed to have been seen as a deserter from the British Museum and perhaps his homosexuality, which I wasn't aware of then, was a further cause for suspicion and mistrust. Perhaps more people knew about it that Angus realised. I was shocked to hear about it from one of the Mahdis who were also students at Felsham House: shocked and indignant . . . Angus got along well enough with Mr Romans but I think he held his wife Laura Romans – a woman of great charm and beauty – in higher esteem. He spoke warmly of her on several occasions and to this day I wonder if he modelled any of his characters on her . . ."[6]

In a small community, anything could give rise to gossip. Angus and Tony were to look back in dismay at an innocent interview in the *Tatler*, published on April Fool's Day 1959, with photographs showing Angus as a helpless and harmless-looking solitary country gentleman – hoeing, watering his seedlings, cooking himself scrambled eggs. But one photograph showed him at work, sitting in the study before a bookcase full of books, reading and smoking in the proximity of a table with a bottle of gin, a bottle of martini, and a lemon. The text is brief and innocent: it mentions that Angus Wilson chose Suffolk "for its open skies and wide landscapes", that he liked writing out of doors, that he had just won the James Tait Black Memorial Prize, and that he liked the Somerset Maugham oriental look of his stripped lath walls and wallpapers and Cambodian souvenirs. It concludes: "A habit of industry, cultivated as deputy superintendent of the British Museum, remains with him. Work begins at nine, and goes on until three or four. He completes each book with the firm conviction that he can never write another. But Angus Wilson has published a book a year since 1949 and his next will be under way before the month is out."

Tony and Angus chose to lay a great deal of blame for what was to happen on that bottle of gin. They made a scapegoat of it. Had it not, they wondered, hinted at decadence? The Suffolk neighbours were *Tatler* readers, and like the voluntary spies of Little Hadham they did not miss much. One way or another, tattle – the more distressing because anonymous – circulated, and it came to official ears that Anthony Garrett, probation officer, was living openly with a known homosexual. He was summoned in the first week of December, 1959, by the Chief Probation Officer. He wrote to him three days after this interview:

Dear Mr. Hodges,

I am appalled by the malicious lies which you reported to me on Thursday. As I told you I am seeking legal advice. Meanwhile, so that I can make things clear to the lawyer when I see him, I should like answers to the following three points: firstly, among how many people in your estimation has this malicious gossip spread? Secondly, as far as you are aware, what are the things they are saying? And lastly, when did you first hear any of this gossip?

I think you should know that I propose in the near future to speak to my referee Mr Charles Blackburne about this matter.

I do hope I made it clear to you how much I value your goodwill. I know the whole thing must have been very distressing for you.

Mr Hodges replied that after his confidential interview he did not propose to discuss any of the facts any further.

This was a disturbing and potentially serious situation. Despite the Wolfenden report and the changing climate of public opinion, prosecution was not unthinkable – or so Secker's lawyers thought, who, unnervingly, asked them if their passports were in order. Was Angus about to become another Oscar Wilde?

Tony had been told that he could continue to work in the Probation

Service provided that he stopped living with Angus and moved forty miles away. His professional integrity was not in doubt. He declined the compromise, and on 25 January 1960 he resigned – his resignation to take effect from 1 April 1960. He gave his reasons:

> For many years past I have acted in a part-time capacity as Secretary to Angus Wilson: his commitments in the University and British Council lecturing field, his television and other literary work have greatly increased – so much so that he feels he needs a full-time secretary. Since this work with him is of great interest to me and may well involve trips abroad, possibly to America, I feel that the opportunity of working with him is one I do not wish to miss, though it may be in some years time I would think of returning to the Probation Service.

His resignation was accepted "with the greatest regret" and the Secretary to the Probation Committee concluded "I haven't the slightest doubt that from all I hear of your excellent work in Suffolk your return would be welcomed and I should be most happy to support any application you may make for another appointment in the Service if that would be your wish."

Further civilities, of a slightly more than formal nature, were exchanged over the next few months. But the die was cast.

How did this all come about? Friends and foes produced their own versions – Angus and Tony had been seen arm in arm, they had been seen kissing in the wood. (Some thought it was all a Tory plot: Angus, as we have seen, had declared his support publicly and in print for the Labour Party in the last election, and this was a deeply conservative county.) But who *were* the foes? They were never to find out, and Tony still refuses to spread the damage by speculation. One neighbour says she believed the whole affair began quite innocently – somebody at a party had said "Isn't it wonderful that now two men can live together so openly?" – or something to that effect – and the whole sorry story had unrolled from there. Whatever its origins, in carelessness, malice, or genuine if misplaced zeal, the disaster was long remembered in the neighbourhood.

It was perhaps more shattering to Tony than he realised. He developed a stammer, which was with him for a year.

He had valued his career. It had satisfied his need to do something for others. He had worked hard to achieve his qualifications, and had surmounted the obstacles of interviews – he rightly suspected that his sexual orientation was recognised by some of those who taught him at the London School of Economics. He had been good at his job. He could not talk football with young offenders but he made up for this by a self-effacing sensitivity, by a genuine desire to help, and by an appreciation of the problems of late developers – he had seen himself as "a boy at the back of the class". He had worked hard in Suffolk, driving home late two or three nights a week after home visits, bumping around over seemingly endless distances in all kinds of weather. It was a vocation as well as a job.

Others had been interested in his work. Angus had used details of his social service training for the background of *Mrs Eliot*, and Terence Rattigan had consulted him about the probation service for a play. (This conversation had taken place at a party of Baroness Budberg's: as Rattigan and Tony talked, she came up and said pointedly to Rattigan, "I do hope you're not being bored," a remark that Tony did not forget.) Janet Jenkins, sister of journalist Peter Jenkins and daughter of a local pharmacist, remembers hearing Tony talk with enthusiasm about his career at her school, St Felix's, in Southwold. Ben Duncan, a young "red hot Marxist" American from the University of New Mexico studying at Oxford on a scholarship in the 1950s, remembers his first meeting with Angus and Tony, at a tea arranged by John Woodward: the thrill of meeting Angus was overshadowed by meeting "this glamorous, beautiful, marvellous man" who talked so modestly about his noble occupation. But Tony brushed aside the questions of Ben Duncan and his friend Dick Chapman. He never sought the limelight.*

Tony threw in his lot with Angus. It seemed he had no choice. In so doing he sacrificed his independence, not only financial but professional. What he had written about Angus's need for a secretary was true, but others could have played that part. (Tony has remained a two-finger typist all his life.) Had the malicious gossip never reached the authorities, there seems no doubt that he would have continued to work in the Probation Service.

The affair was distressing on many levels. Some friends indicated that they supported Tony "even though he ought to have known better" than to enter such a risky area – implying that they believed his interest in his job was not wholly altruistic. This Tony found hard to forgive. He recalled an evening in the mid-fifties when he and Angus and Frith Banbury had been dining with Banbury's friend the writer Sewell Stokes. (Stokes had published an amiable interview with Angus on 18 December 1953, in *John o' London's Weekly*, in which he said that Angus "might be cast by a film director as someone attached to the retinue of Marie Antoinette.") Stokes had worked as a prison visitor, then as a probation officer for four years

---

* Ben Duncan published *The Same Language* (Faber 1962): a memoir of Oxford days, and *Little Friends* (Faber 1965): a novel. He had a career in advertising.

during the war, and had published a light-hearted volume of memoirs about it.[7] Over dinner Stokes made fun of the service, but had then written Tony a penitent letter saying he was sorry he had gone over the top, and wishing Tony well in his career.

Not everyone was so sensitive.

Some good came out of it all, perhaps as a result of a kind of shock therapy; worried about their health, and possibly their finances, Tony and Angus stopped smoking this year. They did not yet give up gin. (And at some point, Tony records, Angus gave up biting his nails, and grew immensely proud of their new length.)

It was painful to think that stories were spreading amongst those who seemed so kind. Suffolk was no longer such a friendly spot. Was it really the right place for them, this old-fashioned county with its hunt balls and its Conservative Club and its old rectories and old lime kilns? Martin Corke, one of the closest and most loyal friends of their Suffolk years, recalls that when he first moved there many people still changed for dinner as a matter of course. Dodos, and not very darling dodos, some of them. Angus recalled Hugh Massingham's treatment of village prejudice in his novel, *The Harp and the Oak*, and his own treatment of the theme in *Hemlock*: twenty years later he was to write: "By the sort of paradox that I think governs the relation of the events of life and the working of a writer's imagination, when, some years later [ie after *Hemlock*], I was made to feel cruelly the workings of that anti-homosexual prejudice – so akin in its depth and contagion to anti-semitism – it did not, in all the pain it caused, involve my literary imagination. I had imagined and written about it before I had experienced it."[8]

Fact had caught up with fiction. Perhaps it was time to move on? Maybe a retreat to the anonymity of Dolphin Square would be safer? Maybe they should never have given up their London flat?

★

The New Year opened defiantly with a party at the cottage (attended by a shy young Australian academic called Vivian Smith, who spend the night on the floor) and more agonising over the novel. (Smith was introduced to Angus by Richard Brain of the Oxford University Press and *Times Literary Supplement*. Brain was also a good friend of Bentley Bridgewater.) The novel was continuing to cause Angus great difficulties. In December 1959 his notebooks record that he was still unsure both of plot and characters. "7.12.59 Still with us as problems Q's wife family etc . . ." Should he write in the first or third person, he wondered? He discussed the growing monster at length with David Farrer and Fred Warburg, and eventually settled on a first-person narration – a decision which was to create more difficulties. He wrote to Fred Warburg on 6 January 1960 that his title would be *The Old Men at the Zoo*: he hoped to get "a substantial amount on paper before I leave for a 3 week lecture tour in Italy on Feb. 29th. And then to finish May some time I should hope." (This was wildly optimistic.) "Now as to coming up to London I should like to postpone it until I've really got going – partly because I don't want to give up a day (I've cancelled 2 TV appearances & a talk at PEN) . . . Partly this last stage before one starts to give birth makes one horribly anti-social as I'm sure you know . . . I have been asked to lecture at Los Angeles next October and shall probably go for about 8 weeks to California, Texas, the South and round to New York."

They did meet, however, and Fred Warburg wrote to him on 22 January 1960: "I thoroughly enjoyed our talk yesterday, the longest and least interrupted we have had for God knows how long. I cannot tell what use these conversations are to you but to me they are invaluable and I hope that when I am back from New York we may meet irregularly, say once a month, if convenient, for a free-for-all-conversation . . . before closing, may I express the hope that your complicated affairs will in the end work out satisfactorily." David Farrer, at the end of March, wrote that he was sure Angus was "right to stay on in Suffolk at present – the more I see of Tony the more I like and admire him." They were keeping a close watch on their troubled author and his valuable companion.

Angus tried to turn down all engagements to work on the novel and regretted some of those he accepted. (In January he wrote six reviews.) In his three weeks alone in Italy he went to rainy Milan, snowy Bologna, Rome (where he met Saul Bellow, and went on a night tour with Moravia), Naples (Vesuvius was disappointing – "*E' stato deluso dal Vesuvio*," declared *Il Mattino of Naples*, 3 March 1960), sinister Venice (where he dined with Peggy Guggenheim) – it was all very hectic. A postcard from Venice to Tony thanking him for his letter continued "Silly of me about Perkin's card; I forgot the publicity of his house. Sorry about my cards, but you once said they were too profuse. I'm longing to be back – yet it has been very interesting – Venice is marvellous but no minute to myself anywhere. I think about the novel when I can – but its not often. Only 2 more speeches now. A." Tony wrote to Angus about his television viewing – "Arnold Wesker on TV seemed like John trying to flirt with Alan Bullock and Norman Fisher and Peter Hall (who looks exactly like Ivor Jones) all at the same time; and they all seemed like Perkin trying to quieten him down." (4 March 1960)

Hysteria at this time was never far below the surface. On 5 April, back in

London, Angus had one of his frightening outbursts at a PEN dinner at the Café Royal, at which Moravia was a Guest of Honour: Angus felt himself ill-placed at table and stormed away, thereby offending Dr Ivan Morris, his Japanese wife Ayako Morris and Jintaro Kataoko, a former host in Japan. The PEN officers who became embroiled in the incident, David Carver and Helen Rogers, cannot have been very pleased about it either. Angus had been seated not at the top table but at Table E between Mrs Morris and Natalia Ginsberg, and had been overheard to say to Mrs Morris, when she asked him who the other guests were, "Oh, no one here is of the least importance," and then, "No, I agree with Moravia; PEN is not worth bothering about. This is the last time you'll see me at it." He had then, or so it was reported, said, "This is not good enough," and left. Morris expressed a desire to challenge him to a duel, but instead wrote a letter of protest, and the next day the whole affair hit the headlines in the *Evening Standard*, one of whose journalists had been witness – "ANGUS WILSON WALKS OUT", it declared in bold type and explained that, "The top table was weighted with writers – Rosamond Lehmann, Storm Jameson, Signor Moravia, Denise Saurat, Douglas Young," and that Angus left in protest as "the dinner rattled on without him."

Angus was contrite, but not abject. He wrote to Alan Pryce-Jones, President of PEN, on 8 April, saying:

> My dear Alan,
> Thank you for your kind and friendly letter.
> The manner of my protest on Tuesday night was most unfortunate – and I can only plead that I was very overtired. I feel most strongly that I owe an apology for my rudeness to Mrs Morris (Ivor Morris) and to Signora Ginsberg who were seated each side of me. I also should like to express my regrets to Helen Rogers for any embarrassment I caused her at the time . . .
> If the manner was unfortunate, the matter still remains in my mind. P.E.N. is above all an organisation of writers and should set the respect due to writers of some distinction above everything else. Particularly in this country when disregard for this has been so inimical to the arts. I am, I hope you know, not an arrogant person – there are great numbers of writers who had they been present I should have considered to have precedence over me (a table full of English writers alone at the very least). As far as I know none of these distinguished colleagues of mine (except Rosamond, yourself and Margaret Storm Jameson) were present on Tuesday; if they were – and I did not see them – they should have been at the top table. You say 'inevitable guests' but I cannot

understand what inevitable guests of minor literary stature should have precedence over established writers. Not, of course, the persons but to honour the craft.

I hold this matter to be of the greatest importance and clearly my views on it are different from those of the P.E.N. administration, I feel therefore that I must resign. When you put my resignation before the Committee, I should be grateful if you would give them the reasons that I have set out here.

Please also express to David the pleasure I have had in my relations with him and my regret that the difference seems to me too important to be passed over.

Yours ever,

Angus.[9]

PEN was as dismayed by Angus's threat to resign as it had been by the original incident, and tried to cajole him to withdraw it – John Raymond wrote to him saying that PEN needed its Netherlands nonentities and paying members with porcelain teeth and blue rinses in order to function at all. Angus's protest had in effect highlighted one of the persistent problems of the hybrid nature of PEN – partly a club, partly a charity, partly an organisation campaigning for writers in prison and against censorship worldwide. Inevitably some writers felt some of its meetings degenerated into pointless cosy happy-family gatherings: to other members, it was precisely this social aspect (in a notoriously lonely profession) that was most valued. These points were made to Angus, and he was persuaded: he remained a member, and continued for many years to attend meetings and to lecture for PEN around the world.

But the episode betrayed the fragility of his confidence at this period. It was a nervous time. Martin Corke thought that Angus and Tony were still very frightened about the possible consequences of the probation-officer row: in June Tony drove over to Linstead, to deliver a bundle of their private papers to the home of Philip and Sally Toynbee, who were living in a remote cottage set in the sugar-beet fields.[10] (The Toynbees had had their own Suffolk difficulties: neighbours had not taken kindly to Philip Toynbee's anti-Suez position in the *Observer*.)

Angus and Tony got their American visas in July – but the problem of American visas was to surface worryingly in later years. The summer of 1960 brought the usual succession of visitors: a clever young graduate student from Cambridge called Michael Tanner was invited for the night and was left to browse among the books when Angus took himself to bed early, and during the night Tanner was disturbed by the eerie sound of jackdaws in the rafters. The following weekend brought American

Dickens scholar George Ford and his wife Pat for a lunch of salmon and Pouilly-Fuissé. "Some talk and then a drive to see three wood-roofed flintstone churches . . . back to cottage for a high tea and home by 9.30 to Liverpool station. Angus looked immensely improved from 3 years ago; rosy, happy and exuberant. Talk flowed. Both men are superb mimics." (One of the people they mimicked was Noël Annan.) They also talked of the Dordogne, of Japan and Stephen Spender, of a nasty Polish professor, of Dr Leavis and J.B. Priestley. They reminisced about the Reading Room where they had first met, and talked of the not disconnected topic of the new novel about the zoo. "At the end of our visit Tony had become a little moody, but Angus was flowingly genial. Tony tells me that Angus is almost unbearably happy in the mornings, when he writes, and collapses about 4 pm!" [11]

Angus kept on at the novel, and also somehow managed to write a television play for Sidney Newman at ABC: it was broadcast in November, directed by Ted Kotcheff. *The Stranger* was set in rural East Anglia and was based, like "Heart of Elm", on the death of his landlady Mrs Baker: the central figure was a lodger, and his brutal treatment by the old woman's family after her death "is shown as a direct result of his carefully fostered innocence."[12] The lodger, Mr Milroy (played by Peter Sallis) was another bird brutally thrown out of its nest by an invading cuckoo – but, as in Simpson, the aggressor is in fact no cuckoo but the legitimate heir. Angus the murderer-author, in preparation for his autobiographical Ewing lectures in California, was already busy digging for the corpses he had buried so carefully.*

The Stranger is an effective piece, and was well received: it deals once more, as did *Hemlock*, with the newly relevant theme of village small-mindedness, but it also sheds light on Angus's view of himself as a perpetual spoilt child. (Angus was variously seen – and saw himself – as "an old head on young shoulders" or "an overgrown baby".) Mr Milroy is the much-petted forty-eight-year-old bachelor lodger of Ruby Blacker, described in the stage directions as "Mrs Blacker, formerly Mrs Merkins, seventy-five or so; the heroine; a handsome, stout, life-loving old woman who has seen service with all sorts of people and learned from it. Has the measure of the

---

* "Any author, I am sure, is aware at times of how strangely his own material has rearranged itself; and like a murderer who has hidden a body most skilfully, even dissolved it in the most artistically effective acid, he always envies a little the detective-critic who is on his trail. After all the murderer-author could tell you how it all happened – if only, that is, he could remember." From a lecture, "The Novelist and the Narrator", delivered in Lausanne, August 1959, at a conference organised by the International Association of University Professors of English. Published in *English Studies Today, Second Series*, Francke Verlag, Bern (1961). This lecture is a rehearsal for the Ewing lectures, which in turn became *The Wild Garden*.

hardness of the Blackers, and fond of the Merkins; but above all devoted to Mr Milroy."

The events turn on the family's celebration of Mrs Blacker's first great-grandchild, and the family's jealousy of Mr Milroy's place in her affections: during the party she has a severe stroke, and the pretences of goodwill almost instantly degenerate into suspicion when Mr Milroy offers to look after her as they all seem too busy. The Blackers at first accept his offer, but soon cluster for the spoils, and when she dies Mr Milroy is immediately evicted, as they go through the cupboards looking for money they think he or she has hidden. To compound his humiliation, they discover in his bedroom, amongst his encyclopedias and books on natural history, copies of girly magazines and pin-ups – an echo perhaps of Val Graham Young's wrath at Angus and Bentley for their copies of London Life. He denounces them somewhat melodramatically for their fear of "anything that's different, anything that doesn't fit into your little schemes of making more lolly and getting on and having good positions" – and the play ends, and Mrs Baker of Little Hadham is once more laid to rest.

★

On 18 September 1960, Tony began one of his intermittent attempts to keep a Journal. (Angus never even tried – the nearest he got to recording daily events or emotions was in occasional jottings in the notebooks for the novels.) The 1960 Journal reveals that Angus and Tony spent much time discussing work in progress. It also records that they went to Thornham Parva Church on Francis Wormald's recommendation – they were great church-visitors, and in 1956 Angus had written to Nikolaus Pevsner begging him to hurry along with Suffolk. Thornham Park was the right place to go, for the visitors' book "showed very recent visit by Frederick Ashton and William Chappell* and many others from London smart set." 22 September saw the end of the book in sight and £350 unexpected royalties from America. The next day they went to see a Charlie Drake film "and both laughed a great deal":

> But on way home – discussing a party – I suggested asking Alison
> Walter and her husband, but A. said he felt more hurt about her
> than anyone. Neither she nor any of the local Labour Party had
> made any contact since the election after all he had done for them.
> He wondered if it was the trouble or just bad manners. He was
> very depressed before dinner about the shape of the novel: the
> new men protagonists not in evidence early enough. We discussed

---

* William Chappell (1908–1994): dancer, stage-designer, director, librettist.

— Morgan crunched a mouse all through our dinner.*

Saturday 24th September. We saw Elmswell church, a very splendid tower and position — and a fine Elizabethan monument to Sir Robert Gardener — a Viceroy in Ireland.

Sunday 25 September. All still going well with novel, but Angus has run out of sleeping pills and finds it difficult to get to sleep . . . We are both very troubled about the news and I particularly find it difficult to tolerate the endless speeches of Eisenhower and Kruschev promising total disarmament when their actions mean total war. They both look revolting.

Monday 26th September. Angus spent many wakeful hours going over his past — his mother's death then father's, and all his breakdown. Apparently not tensely but purely factually . . .

And so the journal continues, with descriptions of the novel's progress, of dinner at the Angel in Bury St Edmunds, the writing of an article on Dickens ("which he much enjoyed") and the planning of a London party before their departure — "an amusing session putting down names and crossing them out again."

Wednesday 28th September. Angus completed his article at 7.30pm. We ate sole fillets and apples. He read something about Snow and as usual became depressed, so we diverted in re-arranging books. I left some old suits in the Probation Office — my successor seemed very low — his caseload has risen above 60.

Thursday 29th September. We both had very good partridge. I typed A's article, and he went on with the novel. He is anxious to begin on the Englanders rule by tomorrow — then to leave off while Bentley is here and devote all of three or four days to his American lectures. Chris has been at home but we have seen nothing of him. He is said to be typing upstairs . . .

Friday 30th September. Bentley arrived long very complicated route on his cycle.

Sunday 18th October. We went to strong drinks with Chris — he was very pleasant and there genuinely seemed to be a change in his attitudes. Bentley said afterwards it was a pity we didn't get more of his views on Perkin — but this was largely because Bentley was too impatient to wait for Chris's stammer to pass . . . we discussed Perkin endlessly and then nuclear war.

Monday 19th October. A very busy time and both of us beset with colds. But it looks as though the book will be finished.

---

* Macmillan and the Tories had won the General Election on 9 October 1959.

Angus sneezing and blowing his nose like a foghorn next door. Last week he wrote at night for the first time. Perkin came for the weekend.

The party was held at Perkin Walker's house at 2 Regents Park Terrace, on the evening of the 20th.

Friday 21st October. A mad rush to complete the novel, and then a party in London last night. I delivered the novel this morning and we caught our plane. A terrible flight – three hours late – very cramped and felt like death all the way. However we were met at the airport and taken to a comfortable hotel . . .

This was their first trip to the States. After a year overshadowed by "the trouble" it felt like a deliverance. Angus's next novel was to show America as the fantasy safe haven, the dream escape. Aeroplane journeys had already been used by Angus as a symbol of hope and renewal. This journey, cramped as it was, had none of the horrors of the flight over the desert. He and Tony, like Isherwood and Heard before them, had got away together to a new start.

★

California lived up to their hopes. The temperature was in the 80s, and there were swimming pools and parties everywhere. The hired car, picked up from Wilshire Boulevard, turned out to be an enormous Chevrolet automatic with powerful brakes that nearly shot Angus through the windscreen: "When I hit them, Angus hit the roof," remembers Tony, accustomed to English brakes where full pressure did not up-end the car. In this thoroughly American vehicle, they took themselves to Sunset Boulevard and Sunset Plaza and Beverley Hills and the Santa Monica Waterfront. They were entertained by Christopher Isherwood ("a superb house overlooking the Pacific", but Chris was sad because Don Bachardy was in New York); they met old friends Tony Richardson and Lesley Blanch.* Stars and starlets glittered upon them. Isherwood took them to a lunch party for fifty in a ranch-type house perched on a hillside, with separate tables and gay umbrellas on a terrace by a pool. It belonged to British-born producer Anatole de Grunwald. As Tony recorded, "I only saw slowly who they were – Jean Simmons, Lawrence Harvey, John Mills, Terry Rattigan. And producers – Arthur Freed and Daniel Selznick. Leslie Blanche and George Cukor emerged as the people with the best manners.

---

* Lesley Blanch (b.1907), romantic orientalist, author of *The Wilder Shores of Love* (1954) and *Pavilions of the Heart* (1974).

Everyone seemed happy and prosperous – steak and kidney pie and champagne for lunch."

After this glamorous debut, they found their first lunch with faculty ("a canteen queue-up") at the university a bit sticky, but Professor Hugh Dick, who showed them over the campus, was "sweet, charming and helpful". Angus delivered the first of the three Ewing lectures on Monday 24 October, and it went well. They found the Ewings themselves a somewhat alarming couple. Dr Majl Ewing had been Professor of English at UCLA since 1930 and Head of Department for several years. He was married to a wealthy Southern Californian, Carmelita Rosencrans, daughter of a Civil War commander; he was a collector of antiquarian books, a gardening enthusiast, an Anglophile and Beerbohm scholar, and his wife's riches had allowed him to cultivate his gardens and to endow the named lecture series, which was inaugurated in October 1956 by Marianne Moore. Angus and Tony found the large Ewing house a little sinister and inhospitable but Dr Ewing and Carmelita were renowned locally for their elegant dinners and receptions, for their "His and Hers" Rolls Royces (and their modest Thunderbird for marketing).*

Angus and Tony spent their free time in Los Angeles dining with professors, talking politics (a Presidential election was imminent) and visiting the sights – they went to Hollywood and Forest Lawn Cemetery, and Tony also visited the probation department. On the 28th a friend of the Wollheims, Ivan Moffatt, took them to lunch at Twentieth-Century Fox Studios. They dined that day with the Hacketts, friends of Frith Banbury, and met Edward G. Robinson, with whom Angus had a long conversation. Christopher Isherwood was also there: he went back with them to their hotel and sat "high" on the bedroom floor and talked and talked.

With Professor Dick's help they had fixed up a lecture tour which would take them over thousands of miles and to several universities in the next two months. They set off up the coast by car to Palo Alto (filthy food, a gale, and a temperature like Seaford) and San Francisco, where there was thick fog on the bay and the hills were terrifying. (Both Angus and Tony had increasing tendencies towards vertigo.) Angus visited the zoo, Tony the probation department. Then on to Death Valley, through snowstorms and great heat – there the car broke down, "fortunately only 50 feet from a garage . . . It was strange to see that they were trying to grow a lawn in the valley. A most remote and desolate place – but with wild life. Then an exhausting drive in the dark to Baker – a messy grouping on a main

---

* Ewing lecturers included Katherine Anne Porter (1959), William Golding (1961), Helen Gardner (1966) and Leslie Fiedler (1972).

highway near a vast naval station." Then on again, back to the relief of palm trees and San Diego – Angus wanted to see the zoo but had to make do with the whales and porpoises of Marineland. "We went for drinks with Ada Nisbett.* Then on to George Cukor for dinner – a very comfortable house with some good paintings and filthy food . . . much too much drink." After dinner Cukor insisted on showing them his bedroom "which was the size of three apartments, with a bed to match. Mr Cukor said 'When I lie on that bed, I can get rid of what I don't like just with a button.' Then he demonstrated his remote control button on a giant TV screen."

The next lecture was in Iowa City. They flew from San Diego to Chicago, and were delayed overnight by a snowstorm. There was a moment of panic in the darkened bar of the hotel where they were staying, when Angus found his hand baggage had gone missing, and with it the sleeping pills on which he was still heavily dependent. The taxi driver was despatched to a night chemist to try to procure some, but meanwhile the airport telephoned to say the case had been found and was on its way. A bar waiter brought this good news to a delighted Angus who, in his relief, tipped him a hundred dollars, mistaking, in the gloom, a hundred-dollar bill for a five. Angus had thought the bar waiter seemed very pleased, and Tony, checking Angus's monies later, found he had good reason to be.

Eventually they arrived in Iowa City on 7 November. Their first impressions of a town which was to become very familar to them were disappointing. The academics all seemed very gloomy, particularly Paul Engle, the director of the famous Writers' Workshop. Engle was the biggest man in Iowa City, responsible for attracting there innumerable famous writers: Iowan born and bred, he had been transplanted from the cornfields and lumberyards of his native state to Oxford as a Rhodes scholar, where he had been at Merton at the same time as Angus. He had studied under Blunden, rowed on the river, written poetry, and become Europeanised. He knew Angus's work, and had written a very favourable review of *The Wrong Set* in the *Chicago Tribune*. ("The most delightful and disturbing book of stories I've seen in a long time. They have that startlingly accurate insight into human weakness, and that easy skill in revealing it, which occasionally terrify.") In *Hemlock*, he might have recognised in Bernard Sands's attempt to establish a writers' colony at Vardon Hall a satire of some of the difficulties which he had triumphantly surmounted in Iowa City. For the Writers' Workshop was a success.

Engle's private life, however, was tempestuous, and he had a way of contracting out his social obligations. On this occasion novelist Vance and

---

* Ada Nisbet, b.1907, Dickens scholar.

his wife Tina Bourjaily had been selected as hosts for the visiting celebrity, and Engle took Angus and Tony to the Bourjailys on the evening of the Nixon-Kennedy election contest. They dined on pheasants, elaborately prepared by the obliging Tina, and garnished with a fan of tail feathers. She had shot the birds herself. The pheasants were followed by fresh raspberries from the Bourjaily farm.

As the evening wore on and the election results began to indicate that Kennedy might win (as he did) a narrow victory, spirits rose. Kennedy's success was a good omen for Angus's Iowa connection. Angus and Tony remained a little puzzled by the seriousness of the artistic workshop atmosphere of the University – they visited a sculpture class, and saw a small dramatised piece from one of Bourjaily's novels – "very emotional and method. Like group psychotherapy" – and were baffled as to whether Angus's own lecture had gone well or not.

On Wednesday, 9 November 1960, they took a bumpy flight to Chicago, and there Tony's journal ends. He did not have time to chronicle their rapid onward progress – the Moody lecture in Chicago, followed by Columbus Ohio, Kenyon, Yale, Harvard, Rochester, New York, Baton Rouge, New Orleans, Nashville, Duke, and back to New York in mid-December. Angus and Tony were impassioned tourists: from Rochester, they crossed the border to see the Niagara Falls from the Canada side. Then they flew home to spend Christmas in Kent, Tony with his parents, and Angus in Dover with Jeanne and Glyn Davies and their children, putting up in a nearby hotel for peace and quiet because he was so exhausted – and he needed to recoup for his next long trip. At the beginning of January he would be off again, to revisit South Africa.

The journey made them friends of America for life. They were to dissent on Vietnam, but always dissociated themselves from anti-Americanism – sheer envy, Angus considered it. They had been enchanted by the freedoms and oddities of the country – by the pelicans and rattlesnakes and sea-lions, the big cars, the big-bottomed ladies playing bowls, the public parks, the sprawling diversity. They met an extraordinary mixture of people, from the films stars of Hollywood to Eudora Welty in Jackson, Mississipi, from George and Pat Ford in Rochester who fed them pumpkin pie for Thanksgiving to James Purdy (whose first book, *63: Dream Palace*, Angus had admired); Purdy offered them a break from the cocktail-party circuit by taking them to an old ale house near the Bowery, some off-limit drinking places, and the Night Court. And they met Yukio Mishima and Edmund Wilson.

Of the latter, Angus wrote: "We first met, when in 1960, on a first wonderful dreamlike tour of the United States, beginning at Los Angeles, I reached Cambridge, Mass., to lecture at Harvard. He had booked a room for me and my friend at a small hotel and we went to dine with him and Elena. Their courteous friendliness and hospitality were more than I'd ever anticipated – and Edmund's solicitude about the hotel was touching. We spent a long, gently boozy, talkative and delightful evening, in which, as I remember, although he was a most argumentative man, he genuinely seemed to consider everything I had to say about the States, about which I was brimming over, although it all must have been weirdly naive. Indeed he was the only New Englander or New Yorker who heard with patience, though not without doubts, my paeans of praise for Los Angeles with which I had fallen in love . . ."[13]

(This was not, as we have seen, their first meeting: Angus wrote this tribute some years later after Edmund Wilson's death, and would appear to have overlooked their earlier London encounters in 1954. According to Edmund Wilson, one of the subjects discussed on this occasion in 1960 was Henry James's underwear: John Betjeman believed he was in possession of this, but Edmund Wilson told Angus that the garments he owned had belonged to James's nephew Henry.[14])

The American euphoria was soon dispersed not only by the very different shock of South Africa, but also by the considerable task of reworking *The Old Men at the Zoo*. David Farrer had written to him in America with pages of commentary on the typescript. (Angus had written back saying that he and Tony never wanted to come home.) There was much still to do. But before he settled down to the zoo, he had to face South Africa.

*

He had been commissioned by the new *Sunday Telegraph* to write two long pieces, one to appear in their first issue, and he set off on on 2 January for a three-week visit. He flew to Durban, via Khartoum, Nairobi and Salisbury, and also visited Johannesburg, Pretoria, and Cape Town. Everywhere he met and interviewed dozens of people – Durban relatives (a family reunion at Kloof, with a barbecue round the pool, produced 55 from several generations), Black Sash supporters, African leaders, academics, farmers, editors, businessmen, Tony's brother Philip Garrett, Tony's aunt at Stellenbosch. He met Alan Paton and Nadine Gordimer: Alan Paton gave him tea on the stoep of his beautiful home, as Angus recorded years later in 1980 in a tribute in the *New Republic*.[15] He spoke at PEN and did countless interviews for newspaper and radio. He visited a Children's Court, which provided the setting for an unpublished short story.[16] He was entertained by political activists George and Betty Sacks and by Randolph

Vigne and his wife: Vigne recalls:[17] "Douglas Brown, who was assistant editor and whom I had known when he was Daily Telegraph correspondent in South Africa, asked me to contact Angus, which I did at his hotel. I think we met a night or two later at George and Betty Sacks's and I offered to drive him wherever he wanted to go in the Cape Peninsula . . . He said he wanted to visit a black township, and to meet some young Afrikaners. I drove him to Nyanga West (now called Gugulethu), a ghastly 'site and service' scheme (i.e. Build your own shanties and we'll supply electricity, running water and standpipes). I vividly remember taking him to see Mr and Mrs Majija in their shanty, where we had tea. Majija was a Liberal Party activist, from a Transkei chief's family, and his wife a sterling woman but with very little English. Angus put on his best 'Labour toff being chummy with working class family' manner, complete with faintly cockneyfied touches to his accent. He was particularly cosy with Mrs Majija and they enjoyed his visit though in class terms they were not blue collar, cloth cap or other English equivalent. His personal warmth came through and he spoke glowingly about them when he had left. But he was right that he would have had to learn a lot about black South Africans to have written about them."

Despite the wind of change forecast by Macmillan in Cape Town almost exactly one year earlier in February 1960, it was also difficult to meet real Afrikaners, but Angus managed to spend some time with the daughter of Afrikaans poet Uys Krige, and her farmer husband: also with Gerhard Krone, who had married a schoolfriend of Vigne's sister.

Angus chose to write about white society and white attitudes, on the grounds that he did not have time to explore the black community. Inevitably he was criticised, by white and black alike. The Caneys were offended by his remarks about naive South African taste – "Regency stripes and Spanish ironwork grilles" – and the world of "morning tea, tennis, swimming, gossip, bridge, dancing, and so on, varied by the occasional charity committee or flag day" which they had generously shared with him – but compared with the savagery of "Union Reunion", they had little to complain of. The Black Sash, the Women's Anti-Apartheid protest group, sent him a letter thanking him for publicly acknowledging their existence and advertising their views. Equally inevitably, he would be drawn when back home into the growing Anti-Apartheid movement, to which he gave considerable time and support.

The family members he met included Uncle Wakes, who was now aged 90: he opened a hooded eye at Angus like an old tortoise and said "Don't write anything that's bad for trade, boy." Cousin Guy McDonald, whom he had known in his innocent schooldays on the Berea, was there, and so was Gavin Jack, the charming *bon viveur* and second husband of his cousin Betty, whose hospitality Angus was on several occasions to return in England. (Jack wrote about food and wine, and ten years later he composed a complimentary piece about L'Escargot in Greek Street.)

It was extraordinarily – everyone told him unnaturally – hot for most of his visit – 110 degrees and humid, he wrote to Tony, which made sleeping difficult. And it was strange to see the family again after so many years. He had written to Guy McDonald on 12 December 1958, on some family matter concerning an Aunt Mary – "I know, of course, that you and Leo will do whatever is right, but I should not wish you to think that silence on my part due to ignorance and distance was a measure of any lack of feeling. It is difficult to imagine anything that a woman of her age would want that could not be got in Durban, but if for some reason there should be anything I can get here, please advise and I will be glad to send it to her.

"I travel about a good deal nowadays as a reasonably successful author. Last year I went all over Asia. I keep on hoping that circumstances will take me to Durban, but so far no luck. I should like to see the family and to meet the vast younger generation. Do please remember that if anyone is coming over at any time I shall be glad to see them and do all I can to entertain them ... I am as my literary reputation may have told you the least sentimental of persons, but the collapse of the family (in Europe at any rate) is one of the greatest evils of this time, I think, and I should be pleased to strengthen what family ties I have. Forgive this personal rambling but the occasion to write to anyone in my mother's family seldom arises, Yours sincerely, Angus." Memories of his mother must have returned to him strongly on this pilgrimage, now that circumstances and the *Sunday Telegraph* had brought him back to his youth.

But he was also anxious about the present – anxious about gathering material he could use, and anxious about the revisions which would be awaiting him. While he was away Tony read the novel and sent encouraging responses to it and good reports of their cat Morgan. But they both knew the novel needed work and they had booked a visit to Sicily in order to concentrate on it without interruptions. There were also worries looming on the domestic front – Chris Arnold was planning to sell his cottage, and they were not sure what would happen to theirs.

Angus came back to England at the end of January 1961, and turned in his articles in the first week of February. He and Tony then flew to Naples on 7 February, having shipped their car out. (It arrived late, and they had to bridge the gap by hiring one.) They had booked themselves into a hotel in Ragusa but as Angus complained "it had a garden the size of a pocket handkerchief," they moved on to the quiet out-of-season Albergo dei

Templi above Agrigento where they both settled down to work – Angus rewriting *The Old Men at the Zoo*, Tony typing up his corrections. A photograph in the local paper, *Cronaca di Agrigento*, shows them both sitting in the sun on the hotel terrace, with notebooks upon their knees: the commentary reports that Angus Wilson is finding inspiration in the land of Pirandello, and that his *"fedele segretario"* Mr Garrett, who interests himself in juvenile deliquency, has not yet met any Sicilian gangsters.[18]

★

The Old Men at the Zoo had been through many manifestations since its gestation period in 1959. The earliest notebooks bear little resemblance to the finished work. Originally Angus seems to have been planning another "swindle" or "forgery" novel, with a cast of crooks – a black comedy with echoes of Conrad's *The Secret Agent*, Mann's *Felix Krull*, and Gide's *Les Caves du Vatican*. He wanted " a very tight plot with plenty of action". The narrator is to be "a neo-moralist", commenting on an action involving a character called Quentin – a name with which for years he had had a curiously unconsummated love affair. (At one stage he even wrote "Notes on *Quentin* character (I don't like this name).") There are miscellaneous notes on John Edward Bowle, Fred Johnstone-Wilson and his mistress with gilded nipples, Alan Bullock, Ann Wormald, Pamela Warburg, the Constantine Fitzgibbons, Spencer Curtis Brown, J.P. (= Jack Plumb, or John Pattisson?) and many others: also on the Chamberlain-Hitler plot of 1939, Munich, the Harrod-Cherwell theme, and the possibility of a science-fiction treatment.

At some point this mass of suggestions crystallised into plot. The Old Men emerge, from the caves of the British Museum – Marsden, Ellis, Thomas, Witney* and Forsdyke, all listed in Angus's notes. So, too, do some of the Old Men of Bletchley Park. The narration will cover "Outbreak of War, Phoney War, Air Raids, Sieges and Blockade, Occupation and Liberation": the opening will be the "amber warning" that the Museum received on 23 August 1939, and the subsequent evacuation of the treasures of the Library/Zoo. Angus drew largely on his own memories of appeasement and war: but chose to set the action (he claimed for libel reasons) in the future, in 1970, as a non-nuclear European War breaks out. He also had at the back of his mind memories of the personal lives of many of the Museum staff – one had a mistress who was killed in the blitz, another lived as a quiet fussy recluse. He used them and rewove them all.

---

* J.H. Witney joined the staff of the British Museum as a Boy Clerk in 1896, rose to be Museum Secretary in 1940, and retired with an OBE in 1946.

The story is narrated by Simon Carter, Secretary to the London Zoo, whose position and character owe a little – though not, finally, much – to Bentley Bridgewater. The uxorious Simon, aged thirty-five in the final draft but considerably older in earlier versions, has an American wife (whose character also underwent many revisions) and two small children. Some of Simon Carter's adventures, such as the uncomfortable train journeys with guard and railway detective were imagined from Angus's own journeys to Aberystwyth: ". . . from crevices and doors freezing draughts sped down my back and crept round my ankles. I sat on my air cushion on the minute wooden seat that was hinged to the wall of the van; I clutched the thermos of rum and coke that Martha had made up for me; and I dozed on and off as it seemed for hours. It was the third journey I had made since a fortnight earlier the escape of a skunk had led the railway authorities to insist on the presence of a senior officer with every trainload of beasts. They agreed it was a futile precaution, but it satisfied the insurance law."(p.150) Others, such as the devouring of badger flesh as Simon escapes the conflict, took off into the future.

The plot, once formulated, was carefully and methodically shaped. Angus had always loved zoos, and now he let his natural curiosity run riot, joining the Zoological Society as a member, consulting Victor Rothschild about animals and animal diseases, enlisting Bentley Bridgewater's assistance in discovering what had really happened with the evacuation (particularly of dangerous species) from the zoo during World War Two, devising a Nature Reserve that would be a grander version of Whipsnade. His knowledgeable interest in birds and animals, one of the more unexpected traits in his character, had led him to many zoos at home and abroad, and was to lead him to more: he had delighted in the walrus of Hagenback Zoo in Hamburg, in the enchanting "rather small, plump, Marc-like brown" tapirs of Fleishhacker Zoo in San Francisco. It is hard to work out quite why he was so fascinated by the world of the wild, and he himself seemed vaguely puzzled by his own passion – was it those early readings of Kipling and *The Swiss Family Robinson*, or that exotic black mamba encountered in Natal, that had captured his interest for life? Both he and Mrs Eliot had been moved and in part mesmerised by a swinging gibbon in Bangkok: here in his new work Angus was able to evoke a fantastic world of seals and lynxes, of butterfly gardens and badgers, of lemurs and lorikeets. The bibliographical classifications and departmental power struggles of the British Museum were transferred to a new and moving arena – yet one to which Angus also had a complex relationship.

One of the recurring motifs of his work, from "Raspberry Jam" and *Hemlock* onwards, had been the cruel wanton destruction of innocent creatures – a theme born perhaps from an innate sadism, or perhaps from its intimate reverse, an over-sensitive affection?

(One oddity of Angus's attitude to animals continues to perplex – although he loved to watch them free and in the wild, and would, like Simon Carter, have wanted to enjoy them in a vast natural reserve, he also, like his character Sir Robert Falcon, Curator of Mammals, felt a strong affection for the old-fashioned architectural features of London Zoo, regardless of the inevitable constraints and suffering of the animals on display. His delight in the human crowd on display at the zoo competed with his interest in the animals for their own sake. In an essay entitled "Confessions of a Zoo Lover", first published in *Holiday*, USA, June 1964, he attempted to explain his own pleasure in zoos, describing his parents' incomprehension at his boyhood delight – "If only we had known some distinguished explorer or naturalist, preferably one who had been knighted, my parents might have seen the whole thing differently. I wish that we had. It would have been both 'suitable' and exciting to have been the director of a vast national zoological park. However . . . I should have been content to have been the humblest stuffer of exhibits in the Natural History Museum.")[19]

On the military front, he consulted Michael Howard, then at London University, who drew up for him a four-page document on "The War of 1971", discussing the premise that "Britain's withdrawal from NATO" had made the war inevitable – the traumatic loss of Gibraltar and the running down of Britain's conventional forces had led to the Treaty of Zürich, signed by Ian MacLeod . . .

All this was fun, and the novel grew. But when David Farrer and Spencer Curtis Brown had read the hastily delivered copy, in November 1960, they had reservations. Both of them wrote to Angus in New York more or less simultaneously. Yes, they admired the virtuosity: the opening (the keeper's death by giraffe-kick and his subsequent funeral) was fine, the move to the park at Stretton was fine, but there were confusions, inconsistencies, longueurs – and above all they could not bring themselves to like Simon Carter. They had been able to be "involved" with Mrs Eliot, but Simon repelled them. He is vain and unlikeable – "at least three-quarters a shit". (Farrer also noted, in an internal report, that the role of the newspaper tycoon, Lord Godmanchester, was not clear.)

Angus wrote back strongly on 28 November to Farrer and Pattisson: he accepted some of their points but "I am a little more concerned about David's view of Simon – yes and no, but I do mean him to be a man of subtlety, who sees everybody's point of view and beyond it and who (in a time of violence) tries to maintain feeling, intelligence and a certain distance from events — it's, of course, the impossible dilemma of liberal man in the modern world and it ends in ones being associated with 'a bad period' and even to 'being something of a quisling', but the dilemma is a real one and if Simon comes out badly, it's perhaps because anyone who doesn't blow their own trumpet is at a disadvantage in the 1st person. Before your and John's letters arrived there was one from Spencer in which he described Simon as a 'vain man who found moral scruples to justify his lack of sensible planning', this so annoyed me that I sent a fierce cable, subsequently modified by another. As if life (especially in times of revolution and war) can be 'sensibly planned' by anyone who sees even a *quarter* of what's going on! But there you are . . . For the rest I do agree and I'm only so pleased that you think it potentially a considerable novel because I am rather proud of all the active second part – Harriet, Leonard F., Matthew's death, the badger feast, and the Englanders in their greenhouse. I've got nearer here to fusing the social novel with the allegorical one than ever before and this is increasingly what I feel I must be after."

Angus stuck to his view that a narrator need not be lovable, but nevertheless had to sit down in Agrigento and work on major revisions – some suggested by Farrer, some by his own second thoughts. He also had to cope with many pages of detailed suggestions for cuts and hints on how to make Simon Carter seem less "priggish" or "prissy". He did his best to oblige. Some characters disappeared altogether. Lady Godmanchester's description was altered so that Lady Hornby, the wife of one of the trustees of the Wallace Collection, would not recognise hersef too easily. Should the word "fuck" go from p.289, in order to appease Boots and Smiths? (It stayed.) By early March, having moved on to Erice from Agrigento, the work was more or less completed, and he was prepared to leave final adjustments to Farrer – though still worried that his American publishers would remain "completely mystified" – "I think I have done all I can to it, or wish to do."

After the mildly digestible Mrs Eliot, *The Old Men at the Zoo* proved as unpalatable to some of its readers as it had in its first version to Angus's publishers. The violence of the action – those worrying deaths of animals, the bestiality of the Director's daughter who has sex with her pet Alsatian, the gladiatorial confrontations in a demoralised post-war Britain – was disturbing to many. The British did not wish to see the besetting sins of themselves and their old men – "obstinacy, vacillation, wishful thinking or even plain blindness to change" – exposed, when they were still congratulating themselves on having won the last war. They did not wish to be reminded of the past opacities of Munich, of the changing and diminishing role of Britain in Europe. They did not wish to contemplate the paradox that "insight is incompatible with activity and yet that activity's failures are too often the results of lack of insight." The past had been pinned down with medals. Why question it? Why ask if it could all happen all over again – and, if it should, why speculate on the unheroic role one might be called upon to play?

The novel was published in September 1961. Some agreed with Viva King, who wrote saying it was "too depressing" – though she was thrilled by the portrait of Willie King as Matthew Price, the dandy curator of birds. (Willie King had died in 1958.) Victor Rothschild wrote from Jamaica with praise and one or two small scientific emendations, to say that it had made him feel "like a rabbit in front of a rattlesnake." Ian Norrie in Hampstead thought that it was his finest book and Angus was a prominent guest at the official opening party of Norrie's new High Hill Bookshop premises on 18 September: Angus arrived clutching a large plastic bag full of mysterious objects, and was photographed chatting to Olivia Manning. (Manning was not one of Angus's favourite people, though he relished her particular brand of exaggerated pessimism: his many encounters with her were distilled into his story of her arriving delighted for a party at Regent's Park Terrace full of the – luckily erroneous – information that "Secker and Warburg have gone bankrupt! Ruined, ruined!") She doubtless had little good to say of his novel, but Edmund Wilson thought *The Old Men* one of Angus's most successful performances and "all too much like what is going on over here".[20] But Jovan Hristic in Belgrade thought that Simon Carter was worse than self-righteous, and assumed he was intended as an Eichmann figure.

The reviews were what is called mixed. John Wain in the *Observer* praised its "sheer energy and unexpectedness" but many predictably found Simon Carter priggish, while the *Times Literary Supplement* priggishly commented on "an unpleasant recurrence of unnecessary and therefore ostentatious nastiness" and "the sporadic (and unnecessary, and pretentious) inclusion of the now statutory four-letter words".[21] Some found the idea of a non-nuclear war in Europe innately implausible. (Nobody commented on Angus's prophetic vision of a Europe torn apart by local nationalist violence and simultaneously occupied in large areas by nostalgic theme parks. Such things had not yet come to pass.) There were many serious accounts – from V.S. Pritchett, Raymond Williams, Raymond Mortimer, Anthony Burgess, Francis Hope, Nigel Dennis – but the two reviews that seem to have registered most with Angus were those by John Mortimer (in the *Spectator*) and Penelope Mortimer (in the *Evening Standard*). John Mortimer's piece accuses the novel of "pontificating" and its talented author of becoming too serious and self-important. Penelope Mortimer's piece was less respectful. She declared the novel to be "a blunder, a work of gross artistic tactlessness which it would be kinder and possibly wiser to overlook." She proceeded to make fun of the plot and his post-Chatterley vocabulary, and concluded that this was a "dull, pathetic and charmless novel."

Angus was offended. What seemed like a joint attack from a husband-and-wife team was calculated to upset a writer with any tendencies towards paranoia. (Had they been talking about him, laughing about him? Of course they had!) David Farrer was also outraged. He considered the *Evening Standard* review libellous and wrote off to its editor indignantly – an extreme and unusual step for any publisher to take. He saw the unseen hand of the paper's proprietor, and his own one-time employer, Beaverbrook. Beaverbrook, he assumed, had perhaps been less than pleased to hear that he had appeared as the power-besotted and warmongering Lord Godmanchester, and had wanted revenge.

The character of Godmanchester, like that of the zoo's director Leacock, had been through many alterations during composition, and had in fact ended up more sympathetic and idealistic, as well as older, than was at one stage planned – but nevertheless there was enough in him to alert the reader to a Beaverbrook connection. John Bowen's review in *Punch* on 4 October was, apparently fortuitously, accompanied by a caricature of Beaverbrook: this was one of a series of sketches of press barons (Cecil King, Lord Astor, Laurence Scott) by the cartoonist Atchison, and had no connection with the text. But the unlucky conjunction did not help. The story reached America, where the *New York Times* (30 September 1961) mentioned the "furious criticisms in Lord Beaverbook's newspapers of Angus Wilson's newest novel" and whether they were linked to "one Lord Godmanchester, who seems to remind them of someone." (Far less reasonable was the connection, made by some, from the sheer coincidence of names and one or two physical characteristics, of Godmanchester with Lord Goodman – Angus had the greatest respect for Arnold Goodman, and Goodman for Angus.)

The Mortimer attacks brought forth a staunch ally in the form of Evelyn Waugh, who wrote in at length to the *Spectator* on 13 October, praising the novel and defending its realism: "If I read him right, Wilson is concerned with what might have happened, rather than what will happen . . . He required a war for his plot and the war he has given us is what many Englishmen feared at the time of Munich." (Waugh had also written privately to Angus "I am impelled to write you a fan letter . . . I have always admired your writing but hitherto with a small reservation of sympathy. This book seems to me to be faultless."[22]) But overall, the reviews damaged sales, which were never as good for this novel as for most of his other titles. They worried Angus, as all reviews did. And many of the American critics, as he had predicted, were baffled: Edmund Wilson got the point, but to many his European war seemed as fanciful and remote as had the Second World War itself.

The most bizarre response came from brother Clive and Lucie, now living as tax exiles in Torremolinos. Angus had dedicated the book to them, and Clive rang up in agitation on publication, saying "My dear Blond, both Luce and I are delighted with the dedication, but friends round here who take the English papers are saying that the book has rude bits in it, and that could make things difficult with the ex-pats here. So Luce and I wondered if you could undedicate it, please?"

SPEAKING OF EVIL

The writing of *The Old Men at the Zoo* laid to rest some of the nagging questions about the past. Angus was never to return with such intensity to memories of the muddles of the Museum, the codes of the Civil Service, and the power struggles of Bletchley Park. But other ghosts were waiting for him, and they would take longer to exorcise. His friend George Painter was half way through his magnificent biography of Marcel Proust. Angus had reviewed the first volume in the *Observer* in September 1959, under the headline "Fulfilment in Time." Painter, despite the Old Men at the Museum, had found fulfilment in this work. Angus's own great work of Time Regained lay in the future. But he received an intimation of the task that lay ahead when he and Tony left Sicily in the spring of 1961.

They had planned to drive home from Sicily to Spain, taking a holiday in the Algarve on the way: they drove up the coast, through Amalfi and Naples, and then put the car on the ferry. After Cadiz and Seville they made their way to the Algarve, but the hotel they had booked was full of elderly English ladies knitting, so they moved on to Lisbon, arriving on 6 April 1961. Here, with some difficulty, they managed to track down Colin and Pat Johnstone-Wilson, living together in genteel penury in the diplomatic quarter in the Rua da Lapa – two elderly English gentlemen, with their adored dog Tiho and their cleaning-lady. Pat was giving English lessons at the British Institute, where Angus was to lecture on 11 April. (The British Institute, established in 1938 by the British Council, was the first of its kind.) Colin, who now called himself David Johnstone, was giving private lessons. Both had dropped the Wilson from their surname, thus giving rise to the belief that they and Angus were only half-brothers.

Angus was now a celebrity. He swept into Lisbon on the winds of fame. This annoyed Colin, who, when asked if he was Angus Wilson's brother, would always reply "No, Angus Wilson is *my* brother." He had reasons for envy which Angus did not yet suspect. Angus was also still a man of the left. Colin and Pat, devout Catholics both, living peacefully under Salazar, had moved steadily to the right – in Colin's case, to the extreme right.

The devoted couple had led a strange life since the tea rooms of Pevensey. They had both departed for Yugoslavia before the war, Pat in July 1936, and Colin a year or two later. Pat had taught English in Split, and they had both later taught in Dubrovnik. Pat was rumoured to be a British spy, and Split, in these pre-war years, was full of intrigue and a cloak-and-dagger romanticism. He was said to be a fast friend of a Mme Granickarsky, who was spying for the German consul: they attended all the concerts together. With his long cigarette-holder, his long umbrella, his long scarf and his hat, he was a familiar figure in the beautiful Venetian-Gothic streets of Split. Rebecca West, travelling through Yugoslavia in 1937 with her husband, had an introduction to him there, and it is surely he that she describes under the pseudonym of Philip Thomson in *Black Lamb and Grey Falcon*. (She changed many of the names for publication in 1942: "If I were to name any of my friends, this might add a last extravagance to their sufferings.")[1] "Philip Thomson teaches English to such inhabitants of Split as wish to learn it. He is a fine-boned, fastidious, observant being, very detached except in his preference for Dalmatia over all other parts of the world, and for Split over all other parts of Dalmatia. We had morning coffee with him, good unnecessary elevenses, in the square outside our hotel, a red stucco copy of a Venetian piazza, with palm trees in it . . ." They talked about Split and its characteristics, about Serbs and Croats, and about "that pretty dark woman crossing the square" whom Mr Thomson claimed as one of his star pupils.

"Later we lunched with Philip in a restaurant which though small was not a mere bistro, which was patronised by handsome and dignified people who were either professional or commercial men."

Later over dinner Rebecca West and her husband discussed Philip Thomson with a local Professor: Thomson was to call in at ten, having been unable to dine with them because he had to give a lesson.

" 'I hope you will like him?' she enquired.

'I have not met him,' said the Professor, 'but I know him by sight, and I am sure I will like him.' 'Yes, he has a charming, sensitive appearance,' I said. 'It is not what I mean,' said the Professor. 'I am sure I will like him because he is a very pious Catholic. I have noticed that he is most pious in his observances, and during Lent I have gone into my church several times, and found him praying like a little child.' And when Philip Thomson came in he greeted him with a special confidential and yet reticent friendliness, as if he knew they had in common certain experiences which, however, cannot be shared."

Little remains of these sunlit years but this record and a few boxes of postcards and photographs of cypress trees and cafés and balconies and sailing boats and bronzed young men smiling on the beach. (There are many photographs, indeed whole albums, of handsome Bill, at sea and on land: and several of swarthy Emerico.) Colin, as his notebooks record, looked back to Yugoslavia as to Arcadia – though he nearly killed himself there one day when, smartly putting up his umbrella, he walked out of a first-floor window, mistaking it for a door, and fell down the cliff outside. (He said the umbrella saved him.) The pre-war idyll came to an end, and some time after 1940 the brothers fled the turmoil. Angus's old school friend, William Deakin, was to play a major role in British intelligence in Yugoslavia in the war-time struggle, but Pat and Colin went East, like Olivia Manning and many others, to Egypt – and then on to India.

In India, the brothers made their way to Bombay, where they both found work. Pat taught first in a school, and by March 1941 Colin had found a position as Company Secretary with Phipson and Co. Ltd, Bombay, a business which dealt in Wine and Provisions. He was to remain there for twelve years, making his retirement speech on 1 November 1952 (regretting that in all these years he had not learned Mahrati – had he known how long he would be staying, he said, he would have applied himself to the language. . . .) Some time in 1941, Pat applied for a post as private tutor to the son of Princess Abida Sultaan of Bhopal. Bhopal was an important Muslim state, some five hundred miles north west of Bombay, and she (separated from her husband) was looking for a male tutor to succeed two governesses – a Miss Wilson, who had carelessly allowed herself to be mauled by a panther and who had fled back to Bournemouth with 53 wounds upon her body, and a Miss Grumley, who had married an officer. The Princess and Patrick Johnstone had taken to one another at once on their first interview in Bombay. She describes his expression of astonishment at seeing, not a bejewelled and beveiled Indian lady, but an active young sportswoman in trousers and bush shirt: he looked so shocked that she stuck her tongue out at him, and he returned the compliment. After this curious exchange they became firm friends, and he accepted the post of tutor to her seven-year-old son Prince Shaharyan Mohd Khan and his two young companions, one Muslim, one Hindu.[2]

Pat Johnstone remained with them for three years, becoming almost one of the family: he took to wearing Indian clothes (a loose white kurtha and pyjama-style trousers) and became a familiar figure at Noor-us-Sabah, with his striped umbrella and his endless supply of cheap cigarettes. (The rumour reached Ashampstead that Mr Pat had become a Muslim.) The three boys loved him (and still speak of him when they meet today); he was an excellent teacher, firm, fair, egalitarian, enthusiastic, teaching them the geography of Africa, reading to them from Dickens, and instructing them in table manners fit for a duchess. "Imagine yourself sitting next to a duchess at dinner," he would exhort them. "How will you entertain her?" And, when they were naughty or rude, "I don't think the Duchess would like *that*."

Princess Abida had happy memories of him. He was a loner, interested neither in the English community nor in Indian shooting parties; he would sit for hours with a pack of cards happily telling the fortune of one of her aunts who came out of deep purdah specially for him. Of an evening he would amuse them all with wonderful imitations of her purdah relatives. He was the soul of courtesy, never touching alcohol in her presence, and showing always the greatest respect to the Muslim religion. He did not go to church himself – he never asked for the car to attend services on a Sunday, unlike his predecessors – but she felt he had a religious spirit. He was unworldly, unambitious. Cheap cigarettes were his only extravagance, and he gave many of those away.

Why was he in India, and not fighting for his country? She wondered, but did not care to probe. She speculated that he did not approve of the war – deeply pacifist, he was also pro-Irish (she believed he had Irish blood) and felt that this might have influenced him. He had no desire to return to England. He did not like the formalities of the British expatriates in Bhopal, and indeed seemed to get on better with one of the Germans there. When Colin visited, they were all happy, for Mr Johnstone was happy then, and they would laugh and laugh.

When she decided to send her son to boarding school, Mr Johnstone moved on (with an excellent reference) to become the tutor of another young princeling, His Highness the Raja of Rajgarh, in nearby Indore.

A curious document, dated 13 August 1947, sheds further obscurity on Pat's wartime movements. A communication from the Political Agent in Bhopal to the Secretary to the Resident for Central India, Indore, it concerns a small amount of money due from a Mr Wilson deposited in Bhopal in January 1944. It appears also to involve a Mr Johnstone, and to be related to money (£111.9.7) advanced to one or the other or both of these gentlemen by His Majesty's Government "as an evacuee".

Pat's Will is a more comprehensible document: it was made on 28 May 1949 in Bombay and drawn up by Colin's close friend the advocate Mr T.S. Hegde. In it, he leaves everything to Colin, who is to arrange his funeral "according to the rites of the Roman Catholic Church in a Roman

Catholic Cemetery", with a Solemn Requiem Mass. Here he describes himself as Patrick Francis Johnstone Wilson commonly known as Patrick Johnstone. That seems clear enough, but even here there is an oddity. For Patrick was baptised Patrick Boswell, not Patrick Francis. An elusive, evasive, protean couple, these brothers.

They left India for Portugal in the early 1950s, not long after Independence. Pat, according to Princess Abida, at first attempted unsuccessfully to invest his small savings in a tea-room in Alassio on the Italian Riviera. Colin taught for a while in Angola – he later wrote to Angus that he had returned to Lisbon in 1952 because of a duodenal ulcer. Angola, a Portuguese colony, was Graham Greene territory. It was the desolate land where many a Catholic teacher or missionary was washed up on a far shore.

Angus had not lost touch with the brothers during these wandering years: Pat at least had returned to London and visited him in Dolphin Square and the British Museum. In July 1954 Angus had given Pat and his ex-employer the Princess a guided tour of the Department of Printed Books and had delighted her with the speed with which he was able to locate the three-volume autobiography of her grandmother. Young Shaharyan also met Angus, and was impressed by his much-loved tutor's famous brother – about whom Pat had never spoken while on Bhopal. By this time Pat had already been settled for a couple of years in the Rua da Lapa at Lisbon, where Colin, after his Angolan adventures, was shortly to join him.

And there Angus found them, in the spring of 1961, as he embarked on a mini-lecture tour of Lisbon, Porto and Coimbra. They had made a life in exile for themselves in this right-wing tax haven, in a country which, like Spain, was still avoided on political grounds by many visitors from the rest of Europe. They were thin, and they were poor, and they were shabby, but they had survived. Pat was still much loved by his pupils, and their narrow house, in a street on the steep hillside above the Tagus, had charm: there were fine views down over the city and the British Embassy towards the wide river. They lived quietly, and kept themselves to themselves: old friends from Yugoslavia and India wrote to them – and Princess Abida, on her way back from a spell as Pakistan's Ambassador to Brazil, had made a special stop to spend a week in Lisbon with her son's old tutor. He had shown her around, never introducing her to anyone, seeming as content with his pupils, his cats, and his brother's company as he had been in India. The Johnstone brothers did not see many people. There was a British colony in Lisbon, which would gather for tea at the handsome British Institute in the Rua Luis Fernandes where Pat taught: the tea-room, with its fine stained-glass windows, was a popular rendezvous, and Mr Johnstone was a familiar figure renowned for his old-fashioned courtesy. Rachel Gardner, Angus's old friend from Westminster days (now Mrs Brewis), remembered meeting "both the Mr Johnstones on their morning walk, when we would greet each other somewhat formally" – her husband was then in the Embassy at Lisbon.[3]

The brothers did not mix with the gay community in Lisbon, some of whom Angus and Tony got to know well, nor did they drink in the red light district near the British Council: they did not frequent Serafim's bar and tiny friendly restaurant, which Serafim had been running since 1947, but many an omelette Javanese was served up there over the years to Dickie Wyatt of British Petroleum, to David Ponsonby, water colourist, to Johnnie Cobb and Johnnie Weyman and David Duck and Michael Woolley and Mike Eltenton and the heavily bearded and whiskered Vasco Freitas Simoes, whose obstetrician father was reputed to have delivered all the crowned heads of Europe. The brothers were on the fringes of this gossipy, ingrown expatriate world of teachers and Embassy and British Council folk – the names of some of the Lisbon Players from the Repertory Theatre were recorded in their address book – but they did not mingle much.

Despite his long years of exile, Colin had not forgotten his origins. He had always considered himself the family historian, and from his meagre resources he sent a small yearly cheque to the Borough of Kingston for the upkeep of the Caney grave where his grandfather and mother were buried. (Portuguese burial customs appalled him: they lacked respect.) Despite his difficult temperament he had tried to keep on good terms with the family, both in England and in South Africa, and Angus could all too easily see why. Angus was worried by the brothers: they were clearly living very near the edge. Pat came up to the hotel in Sintra where he and Tony were staying and mentioned financial difficulties. Once again, the Johnstone-Wilsons were borrowing money. The small Caney legacy of 1959, in which both they and Angus had had a share, had not lasted long.

It was a warning, and Angus registered it. But meanwhile, he flitted on – through Spain, scattering lectures here and there as he went, from Madrid, to Seville, to Valencia, and then on again via Barcelona to France for a holiday. He sent a postcard from Madrid to nephew Nicholas saying he had just had too much for lunch, and asking him to tell his mother Jeanne that he had "met the uncles after all in Lisbon": he sent another to niece Penelope promising to find her a Spanish doll in Valencia or Seville. (Some of Angus's travel expenses in Portugal and Spain were met by the British Council: Tony's were paid from the profits from the American lecture tour.) He and Tony returned on 17 May 1961, to a garden waist-high with weeds. He settled back in to the cottage, awaiting the September publication of *The Old Men at the Zoo*, and filling in the summer by writing a television play and thinking about the Northcliffe Lectures which he was committed to delivering that autumn.

The Invasion (at first entitled *Operation Take Over*) is a light-hearted satire on the complacency of the rural England in which he still found himself, despite the Probation Office scare, deeply rooted. It involves the invasion of earth by Martians: their arrival goes unnoticed by the local community, which is far too involved with its own parochial affairs and disputes to look up or listen. Only two schoolboys, playing with their television sets, pick up the messages, and like Cassandra, they are ignored. The idea for the play clearly sprang from Coronation Day in Suffolk and the vision of those alienated prep-school boys hanging around on the fringes of village life – a theme of England divided, un-selfknowing, trapped in the past, unable to meet the future. It is a social comedy rather than a work of science fiction, and Angus and Tony enjoyed tossing ideas for it backwards and forwards between them.[4] (Some say Tony's contribution consisted of more than the odd line, but Tony dismisses this.)

The Northcliffe lectures were a more earnest and solitary undertaking. These were not to be the entertaining and discursive chats which had proved so popular round the world, but serious discussions of the theme of Evil in the English Novel. The task hung over him during a summer of parties, Aldeburgh, visitors, and meals at Long Melford. These lectures, like *The Invasion* and *The Old Men at the Zoo*, were to tackle the theme of rural innocence, of rural ignorance, of Town *v.* Country, of Felsham Woodside *v.* Dolphin Square. In them he was to pursue, though less autobiographically, some of the themes adumbrated in his Ewing lectures.

Publication of *The Old Men* in the autumn was accompanied by a round of parties, interviews, television appearances, invitations to speak to Fabians and to appear on Brains Trusts. At this period publishers and the media were comparatively restrained in their demands that authors become salesmen for their own books, but the pace was beginning to quicken. Angus rushed around obligingly, from Amsterdam to Toynbee Hall, from Manchester to Lime Grove, from Teddington to George Weidenfeld in Eaton Square, from Bush House to bookshop. Suffolk was more peaceful, though reporters fought their way through the bushes to interview him even there. But there he could enjoy what at times seemed to be the Good Life. Suffolk was an escape from those London literary parties about which he had written to Pamela Warburg in such despair – those parties which, he knew, tempted him into hysteria and malice. If he buried himself more deeply in Suffolk, would he become a better person? Or would he become a complacent narrow-minded provincial bore?

*

Although Angus always readily admitted that he had no training in and no capacity for abstract thought, this did not prevent him from metaphysical brooding. The nature of evil preoccupied him. His mother's denial of it, as a Christian Scientist, had seemed to him wrong: he was himself to ascribe his concern with the theme to her refusal to consider it. He had attempted to tackle it in *The Goat and Compasses*, and had given up. Now, with the Northcliffe Lectures, he would approach it from another angle.

The lectures were given in November 1961 on four separate evenings at London University. In them, he ranged from Richardson's *Clarissa*, through Jane Austen and George Eliot and Trollope and Dickens, to Henry James, John Cowper Powys, Ivy Compton-Burnett, Graham Greene and William Golding. His general thesis was that the provincial English novel of manners was inadequate to the violent age of Buchenwald, and that the English had tended to lock themselves in a citadel of false security called country life. They refused to believe that evil or violence could invade them or their land. They lived in willed ignorance, and their novelists encouraged this. Hence, he suggests, the comfort drawn from Jane Austen and E.M. Forster, the bewilderment that greeted a writer of ideas like Powys, the outcry against his own "evil" characters, Hubert Rose and Mrs Curry, the horrified reaction to *The Old Men at the Zoo* which said "These things could never happen here."

Angus believed that evil did exist, and that it existed in a dimension beyond right and wrong. He believed this, that is, until he was asked to point a finger at individuals. Even his fictional characters he could not bear to condemn outright. He gave them justifications, explanations. They had had an unhappy childhood, they had been put upon by society, they had been abused. Try as he would, he could not quite incarnate evil. Even Mrs Curry was on one level excused. He could create nasty characters, violent characters, dangerous characters, but the humanist in him kept providing them with an escape from judgement.

He was aware of this inconsistency in himself, but nevertheless he kept on trying to assert the existence of the dimension of evil. This was not only a reaction against the creed which he believed had killed his mother: it was also a reaction against the particular cosiness of English fiction. The writers whom he most admired – Kipling, Dickens, Waugh, Powys, Dostoevsky, Zola, De Montherlant – all recognised the potential savagery of human nature. What Angus could never tolerate was a false optimism. Yet he himself had an unusually developed capacity for seeing the good in the most unlikely people. His tolerance, like Forster's own, was immense.

The Town-Country theme in his "Evil" lectures was one which continued to preoccupy him. It went to the very heart of the conflicts of his own nature and his own decisions. Tucked away in Felsham Woodside, he composed his speeches on why it was wrong to elevate country living as an image of the Good Life. He himself needed this retreat: yet he also needed, desperately, to get away from it. There was no stasis to be found. Village gossip had ruined Tony's career, yet Felsham Woodside remained their refuge. It was a troubling paradox.

The delivery of the lectures placed him firmly in the most exposed of arenas. They were open to students and the public, and they were filled to overflowing. Some had to wait outside and listen to them relayed on a loudspeaker. They were acclaimed as a theatrical *tour de force*. Stuart Mitchel attended, and recalls the immense excitement of the occasion, and his pleasure when Angus spotted him and waved to him through the milling crowds as he made his way to one of the smart dinner parties that succeeded each event. Fred Warburg's recollections were equally enthusiastic, and he claimed that when he asked Angus if he could have the typescript of the talks with a view to publication in book form "he looked at me blankly. 'Typescript?' he said. 'What typescript? I had no typescript.' He had delivered an hour-long lecture at the rate of at least 150 words per minutes (that is, very fast) in all some 9,000 words, with the aid of nothing but three or four sentences scrawled on a sheet of note paper."[5]

This was only a slight exaggeration, for there was indeed no typescript – the notes were far more copious than Warburg describes (pages of handwritten and typed outlines, many quotations) but the delivery was impromptu, and it is clear that Angus made additions to accommodate the audience and his own last-minute thoughts even as the series progressed. This was how Angus performed best – he could speak at length and to time on television without consulting notes, a prospect daunting even to experienced broadcasters. When, on occasions, he found himself tied to a written text before a formal audience, he tended to be uncomfortable, to mix up his papers, to lose his momentum. His style depended on a continuing surge of power. Mildly resisting Warburg's notion of printing the lectures in book form, he warned that "tho' I say it myself I *am* a rather impressive lecturer and maybe a little of the enthusiasm must be given to my delivery and not to the matter . . ." (9 November 1961). This energy would carry him on, after the event, to a dinner with Wollheims or Gaitskells or Annans, where he would continue to sparkle.

And then he would collapse, and Tony would have to rebuild the fortifications around the citadel. It had become a pattern.[6]

The Albany column in the *Telegraph*, reporting on the first talk on 5 November, praised Angus's "bucolic energy" and said he had "the build and ruddy complexion of a farmer", a description which deeply puzzled Angus, who saw himself, at least on such occasions, as a metropolitan intellectual standing up for high culture. Had he really taken on so much local Suffolk colour since 1955? He worried about this remark for years, and referred to it in many a lecture to come.

*

Angus did not publish another book until 1963, but he took on many journalistic enterprises, some of them abortive – at the end of 1961 he went to the Channel Islands for the *Sunday Telegraph*, which never published his piece.[7] Colin Wilson, writing to his old champion in 1960 and again in 1962, expressed astonishment at their joint survival as freelance writers: "Above all, I hope youre managing to live comfortably off writing now. In the old days, I used to think of you as a wealthy writer – as no doubt my friends think of me now! Now I wonder how on earth you manage to live on one book a year." And again: "How on earth do you manage to live? I always wondered. In the days when I first knew you, I thought of you as the wealthy author; but since then, I can't imagine how you manage to publish so few books and still keep from starving!"[8]

Angus was still maintaining a steady flow of reviews and occasional pieces – an article on Envy as one of The Seven Deadly Sins for the *Sunday Times*, a list of "Things That Had Angered Him" for *Encounter*.[9] His dislike of anti-Americanism featured in both pieces, and it was a theme to which he would return over the years: he had already published a piece in *Esquire** in which he discussed the different forms which anti-American-ism took in Britain (the Left took issue with the US on McCarthyism, the Right on Suez, while a neighbouring retired army officer in Suffolk had expressed a desire to "exterminate the Yanks" at a local airbase). In *Encounter*, he deplored the "Double-talk" of the *New Statesman* over communist countries and its persistent snide references to the United States. It was a subject on which he felt strongly, as he had done even before America had offered him those happy months of escape from persecution: American Ben Duncan noted that Angus was wholly free from the vulgar prejudice that portrayed all Americans as vulgarians. Fifteen years on, the subject still preoccupied him: while dining with the Hampshires in Wadham in Oxford in August 1979 an accusation from

* "Aftermath: Americans in Britain", March 1960.

Stuart Hampshire elicited from him a written protest (of which he kept a copy) in which he said, "I daresay you were teasing me, but I was surprised when you said you thought that I had always been anti-American. From my brilliant filing system I turned up the enclosed; this was written two years after my first visit to the States, when I lectured all over the country . . . How do these falsities get about? Is it because I have little connection with the New York intellectual world? I lectured in New York twice a long time ago, and I have reviewed infrequently for the New York Times, but nobody has asked me to do anything else there, and I *have* been invited to many other places . . ." (2 August 1979). (Hampshire's reply makes it clear that he was not wholly convinced – surely Angus's attitude must have changed? Angus, for his part, clearly did not want to perpetuate the notion of any prejudice on his part against the States, on which he came to depend for part of his income. But he also genuinely enjoyed his visits.)

In January 1962 Angus took on a new commitment. He was recruited by Francis Wyndham as television reviewer of the smart new *Queen* magazine, an old glossy revamped on "aggressive and stimulating" lines by Jocelyn Stevens.

He did this for the money. Famous he was, wealthy he was not. *Queen*, like the *Observer*, offered regular payments, and he could watch television comfortably at home in the cottage.

Reviewing for *Queen* was fun. His début was announced with a splendid snowy January photograph by Norman Parkinson, and Wyndham gave him a free hand. Angus could watch what he liked and say what he liked about it. He watched a women's magazine soap opera called *Compact*, and pop singer Adam Faith and the Archbishop of York, and Katina Paxinou as Mrs Alving in *Ghosts* ("quite superb") and John Freeman's famous *Face to Face* series of interviews, and *Panorama*, and Cleo Laine, and Lotte Lenya (looking a bit like Iris Murdoch, he thought), and the popular police drama series *Z-Cars*. He expressed strong views on wildlife documentaries – high praise for David Attenborough, a dislike of the facetious diaologue that American programmes provided – the "O.K., when officer owl turns his back, you sneak right past him" school of soundtrack – and he was not too keen on the whimsical Armand and Michaela Denis rolling their French R's over giraffes and zebras. He sounded off about his love of the music of the twenties, and the days when he collected cigarette cards of Rudolf Valentino. He informed the reader that although he did not support CND, was sceptical about the USSR, and liked the US, he would have to change all these views if he were subjected to any more crude anti-Soviet caricatures by Constantine FitzGibbon. He watched afternoon television, which reminded him of the miserable days between Oxford and the British Museum when he sat in the cinema eating double-decker sandwiches and watching Ruby Keeler. He praised *That Was the Week that Was* and *Your Life in Their Hands* and Harold Pinter. He was nothing if not eclectic.

And he told the reader all about his travels – he had just got back from the Berlin Wall where he felt like a pop singer, from Vancouver where everyone talked about Buddhism, from Rome where he had met a lot of intellectuals who despised television ... In short, he wrote about whatever came into his head. Wyndham did not try to edit his discursive and entertaining copy. It arrived in longhand, but it was always on time. (Editors at the *Observer* were sometimes less tolerant, and made vain efforts to tidy Angus up.) In all, Angus wrote nearly forty pieces in 1962–3: quite a useful sideline.

His underlying anxieties about security were reinforced even as he embarked on this project. In January 1962 came the news that his brother Pat had died suddenly in Lisbon, on the second of the month. And he had died seriously in debt. Pat's visit to the hotel in Sintra in April 1961 had been made in desperation. Things were worse than he had said.

Colin's response to Pat's death was one of grief combined with a desperate desire to raise funds to cover the cost of the funeral, to pay off Pat's debts, to keep himself afloat. Angus responded instantly; Clive characteristically delayed; the nieces and one or two of his dwindling handful of old friends helped out, with ten pounds here, twenty pounds there. Winn's widow Betty Wilson sent a generous widow's mite of ten pounds. On 19 January Colin wrote Angus a Dostoevskian 24-page letter full of anguish and what sounds like remorse, thanking him for money, for the announcement in *The Times*, for putting his name closest to Pat's in the announcement. (It had bidden farewell to "Patrick Johnstone, much loved brother of David Johnstone, Clive Johnstone-Wilson, and Angus Wilson" – no wonder the Brits in Lisbon and the Khans in Bhopal had been puzzled by Johnstone-Wilson family relationships.) Colin asked Angus to have a mass said in Bury St Edmunds, which Angus did. And Colin continued to hymn Pat's goodness and tenderness, to bewail the hell of their childhood – "a tragedy for them and for us too that Father and Mother ever married ..." – to regret that the Congo war had prevented him from going back to Angola to work and to save money, to deny that he had dominated Pat. He had not invited Angus to his home in the Rua da Lapa the year before because it was too shabby, he had not come to Sintra to beg with Pat because his absence made "one less to pay for". The burial and funeral had cost £115.00, for a permanent drawer in a stone tomb –

otherwise the remains from a municipal plot would have been disposed of
after five years – a repulsive notion. The cross had been of violets and
narcissi.

This, and many other many-paged letters that poured from Colin/
David over the years, made hard reading for Angus. Pat was the one he had
loved but Colin continued to haunt him. At the end of the year, in
December 1962, after another appeal for funds, he wrote:

13 December 1962

My dear David,
I had thought that my silence spoke my inability. But it was rude
of me and I apologise. I have had to buy my house or have it sold
over my head and in addition I have had a temporary setback
because "The Queen" in which my television articles appear is
now to be a fortnightly and not a weekly. I, therefore, must make
economies. I shall send you £50 in early June without fail. I am
sorry I cannot promise more or sooner, but, to be honest, I am
much alarmed by the economic trends of this country (and for all
the bursting opulent appearance of W. Europe – Europe
generally) not now but when the bubble bursts in say 7 years time
and, for the first time, I feel that I must put every penny by for the
future.
    I am very sad to hear of your heart trouble. As a family perhaps
we all give a greater appearance of health than is justified by our
medical histories. Look after yourself.
    If when June comes I can manage more I shall do so – but £50
I certainly shall. I am going to Jane for Xmas . . .

★

As Angus informed his *Queen* readers, he was in constant demand around
the world, and translations of his work continued to appear in many
languages. Berlin and Beirut called for him, Venice and Vancouver insisted
upon him, and he fitted in the Balkans, Edinburgh, Frankfurt and
Formentor – all in one year.* And in January 1962 he also managed to get
to a bookseller's meeting in the Midland Hotel, Manchester.

This provided an opportunity to catch up with his old friend from
Merton, Norman Morris, who was by now a considerable figure in

---

* The dates are impressive. In 1962 he was in Berlin from 20–24 January, in Lebanon,
Turkey, Greece, Yugoslavia and Italy from 7 March to 29 April (car serviced in Venice with
19,361 miles on the clock), in Formentor from 30 April to 10 May, in Vancouver from 10–19
July, in Edinburgh from 18–25 August, and at the Frankfurt Book Fair from 20–21 September.

Manchester local government and in the University Education Department. But one of the things that Morris remembers most clearly from this
visit was Angus's emphasis on his money worries: Angus said he made his
living from articles and reviews, not from fiction. He also told Norman
Morris with relish that he was on his way to visit the Duchess of
Devonshire. He was proud of the range of his social acquaintance. And,
indeed, he and Tony went straight on from Manchester to Chatsworth,
where they spent the night of 12 January, entertained by the Duchess.
(The Duke was not at home.) Tony's principal memory is of restraining
Angus from singing loudly in the bath

> Now 'arken you Dukes and you Duchesses,
> Now listen to what I've to say
> Be sure that you owns all you touchesses,
> Or you'll join us in Botany Bay!

and of the Duchess on the telephone, declining a neighbouring friend's
suggestion that she should invite Cyril Connolly over for the evening:
"Oh no, I don't think so, we've got quite enough inties here already."
(The Connollys were not to be indefinitely postponed: Cyril and his wife
Deirdre appear in the Visitors' Book for 14 and 15 January 1962, along
with Eddie Sackville-West.) Later that month Angus paid his flying visit to
Berlin, where he appeared to vast crowds in the Kongresshalle and was
interviewed and photographed for every major newspaper. Most of his
works had already appeared in German, and *The Old Men at the Zoo* was
due out later that year. (This series of literary events included appearances
by Nathalie Sarraute, Henry Miller, Michal Butor, Max Frisch and Eugène
Ionesco – the Top League.)

More low-key was his visit in early February via Birmingham University English Club, where he renewed an aquaintance with Malcolm Bradbury, to Bangor University College Club, where he met for the first time
the critic A.E. Dyson, editor (with C.B. Cox) of *The Critical Quarterly*,
and renewed an acquaintance with Malcolm Bradbury, rising star of academe. He was to see much more of both of them. On the way back, he
and Tony paid a visit to his longtime hero, John Cowper Powys, now
living in seclusion in Blaenau Ffestiniog. It was a poignant encounter.

Life had not been wholly gentle to this old man, who in his eccentric
prime had galloped wildly through the United States, teaching and
preaching from mountain and prairie. Now he lived in semi-poverty,
semi-forgotten, with his faithful American friend Phyllis Plater. Angus's
notes on expenses for this meeting justify the visit rather bleakly – he had
gone, he informed his accountants, to pay homage but also with a view to

writing an obituary (Powys was nearly ninety) and "to see if he was in need."

Angus had admired Powys's work for many years, since he had discovered *A Glastonbury Romance* in 1932, and he and George Painter had talked much of him in their Museum days: Angus later passed on his enthusiasm to others through reviews and articles and introductions. His admiration was shared by spirits as diverse as J.B. Priestley, Wilson Knight, George Steiner, Iris Murdoch and Colin Wilson. Angus was deeply impressed and influenced by Powys's resolute idiosyncracy, by his sense of the living past and present, by his interest in evil and perversion (and the torture of animals), by his delving for the sources of the sadism which he believed to be in us all – and by his bold, Russian handling of vast, chaotic crowd scenes, to which the fête at Vardon Hall was a tribute. Angus saw Powys as a British Dostoevsky, bursting out of the bonds of the English provincial novel. With Evil fresh in his mind, he went to visit the man who had looked it in the eye.

He had been invited many times. Years earlier, he had sent Powys a copy of *Hemlock*, and the two had embarked on a correspondence (on Powys's part, increasingly illegible).

Powys had written to him

> "Let dulness hold dénouement back
> Till of suspense there is no lack."

and had continued "You speak of my influence as a novelist on you – O O! but for *every Muse's* sake be *careful just there* as to which 'little me' it is who is playing the Bee in your Bonnet! Let it I implore you be the Bumble Bee of *Longueurs!*" Angus had taken this enigmatic advice to mean that in order to achieve Powys's own heightened level of tension and fantasy he had to abandon the epigrammatic brevity of his short stories, to risk longueurs – and to leave the British Museum. He thanked Powys for helping him to this decision. A later letter from Powys, dated 30 June 1955, thanked Angus for his article in the *Observer* (26 May 1955) on *A Glastonbury Romance*:

> I Waterloo Blaenau Ffestiniog Merionethshire North Wales
> This is only a wretched scrawl of thanks my generous friend Angus Wilson but I felt (as not only the *ladies say*!) I *had* to write to let you see that your old partner in the difficult art of trying to make fiction more like truth than it generally is and yet not less strange and weird than truth can be *didn't miss last Sunday's Observer*! If ever you can steal off in a car, driven by a skilful friend or by 'thy *wone* self' I beg you must *come through* this absolutely

crazy 'town in the clouds' which I am convinced is far more like
that town in Aristophanes 'Birds' than *any place* in any other
country (save possibly Tibet!) Its a real *authentic* and *realistic*
Nephelococcygia and this no exaggeration – And though there'd
be no 'putting you up', as they say, in *this* house – we *could* give
you directions, clear and candid, where you *might* get a good bed!
– Anyway since this an answer of gratitude to all you wrote in last
Sunday's paper you must *not* think of replying. Yours ever
J.C.Powys.

Seven years later, on 9 February 1962, he and Tony made their way to
the strange slate town in the hills.

"It was, of course, wet and misty, but, as we descended the hill of
Blaenau Ffestiniog, it ceased to pour waterspouts. Only behind the strange
little terrace of Waterloo, which J.C.P. had already warned me was no
terrace but one house made into two, did water pour down the slate
quarries and grey boulders that formed the background to the small,
regular-styled house. The scene blended the world of the country lodgings
of *Wolf Solent* with the most dramatic John Martin scenes from *Porius* –
and, to my pleasure, the *Porius* was uppermost. It was exotic and domestic
. . . the room was small but very warm and full of objects and furniture that
gave an exceptional sense of being part of the owners' lives and histories.
On a bed in a recess immediately ahead of me lay John Cowper Powys.
That wonderful, delicate, handsome, boyish face of a nonagenarian sage
and wizard (a photograph of which covers one whole door of my cottage
home) was seen in profile, his hands cupped on his chest. It was hard not to
expect to find his feet crossed, so like some great crusader's figure whose
mane of hair had escaped from his helmet did he seem. Yet the room was
vibrant with his life." (One of the objects was a carving from Africa of male
and female organs combined "sent by his brother Lulu from Africa – 'while
that is in the house, my friend, all is happiness.' ")

The meeting went well, although Angus in his nervousness felt he
talked too much (as he had with Forster): when Tony tried to check
Angus's outpourings, Powys "cried delightedly 'Well done, my friend,
well done.' Yet I do not believe I fool myself when I say that he succeeded
in making me feel, as he had often said in his letters about my radio talk on
his work and reviews of it, that there was a close tie between us."[10]

It was a significant encounter. Powys represented *par excellence* the
lonely road. He had accepted no compromise, from the world, from
publishers, from readers. He had remained himself. And despite the
difference of their sexuality (Powys was passionately heterosexual) he had

accepted Angus more wholly than Forster, more evidently a natural ally, had done.

Powys had achieved a noble dignity amongst the bleak landscapes of hell. But the road of excess does not always lead to the palace of wisdom.

*

The excessive Gerard Reve was apparently as reckless of public opinion as Powys himself, although he exposed himself to it more wilfully. And he, too, was fascinated by evil.

Reve was, and continued to be, an extreme case. Most of his friends were remarkably tolerant of his Bad Child behaviour.* One of its worst (and potentially most dangerous) manifestations was a short novella he wrote in the summer of 1960, at the time of Angus and Tony's troubles: called "A Prison Song in Prose" and eventually dedicated "to Angus F. Johnstone Wilson in gratitude", it was published in a limited edition in 1962, but circulated earlier amongst friends. It is an illustrated porno-graphic fantasy, and it describes the activities of Tony G –, a cruel and feared officer, in an eighteenth-century house used as an incarceration centre for delinquent youth. This must have seemed poor repayment for lending Reve the fare to attend his mother's deathbed in September 1959, and Angus was not amused. Nevertheless, although both he and Tony were highly sensitive to tactless remarks about Tony's resignation, Reve was forgiven. Like Genet, he was licensed to go too far.

In February 1962 Angus and Tony held their most notorious party at Felsham Woodside. It was what Bloomsbury would robustly have described as "a buggers' party": Norman Scarfe the historian commented more elegantly that it was "not a grey suit party" – and, as an aside, that it was "the days of the twist". There was music and dancing in the clearing in the wild, as professors and antiquarians and eye-surgeons – well, one eye-surgeon – mingled with friends from Bury and the villages around. Here Wim Schumacher, Reve's lover for ten years, met local boy Mike Goodall: carried away by the excitement of their mutual discovery, they cracked the marble table upon which they were sitting. Michael Tanner remembered that there was "a lavish spread like a wedding breakfast" and the whole thing made him feel so un-urbane that he left at 11 p.m.

Perkin Walker with his London flat-mates Monty Turland and Bob

---

* David and Mary Lodge were coerced by M.D. into attending a reading by Reve in Birmingham on 20 November 1992. Mary Lodge commented that he was a Bad Boy trying hard to shock. It has to be said that with some he succeeded, though Simon Westcott, at this point helping Drabble with her research, and who had also been taken on this outing, had by now become accustomed to Reve's prose and pose.

French and another friend called Vernon Harrison had recently purchased a near-by retreat in Essex where they too could lead their own lives and hold their own parties in private. They had found The Chase, at Sible Hedingham, in September 1961: like the cottage at Felsham Woodside, it was secluded, overgrown and secret. They transformed it into a comfortable home, where they entertained guests ranging from scholars from the Warburg (Frances Yates, Michael Screech, the Gombriches, Anne-Marie Meyer) to Crittall relatives, from local tradesmen and shopkeepers to George Coulson and his friend Thomas Hutton of Bletchley Park days, from Bob's brother Lieutenant-Colonel John French and his wife Sheila to musician Imogen Holst. Forrest Fulton, much loved by them all, was a frequent guest, and so was the provocative Reve. Perkin Walker cooked, carved the roast, poured strong drinks, and cultivated his roses. (*Hideous* roses, said Angus: strong and disease-free, retorted Perkin.) Perkin Walker felt himself happily and safely surrounded by an eccentric extended family.

The Chase was a theatrical household, full of colourful talk and containable drama. The annual drag ball, based on the theme of Du Maurier's *Rebecca*, was a highlight of the gay season, and it would make Perkin laugh until he wept as he saw The Chase transformed into Manderley.* Bob and Monty loved the theatre – as, more surprisingly, did Sandy Parnis. (Bob French, whose family lived in Thorley, had been in pantomime in 1951, the year when Angus wrote *Hemlock* at Crowscroft, and Sandy Parnis had worked on the lighting. Bob French kept up his theatre interests all his working life.)

The Chase was for week-ending, but the purchase of Felsham Woodside was to commit Angus yet more irrecoverably to Suffolk life. Negotiations took place in an unlikely manner. Christopher Arnold had disappeared to Majorca in 1960, then had come back, sold The Tin Shop, and spent the money on going off to the Lebanon in September 1961 with a new boyfriend from Helsinki who had a job at the American University in Beirut. There Angus caught up with him in March 1962 while on a British Council lecture tour. Angus wrote back to Tony on a postcard from Baalbek "This is really very fine but perhaps Byblos of which I can get no card is better. Very full programme – all great success and very interesting. Strange with Chris but he was very charming and says yes about house. On to Damascus tomorrow. Looking forward to seeing you in Belgrade . . ." Tony wrote back (16 March) "*Hooray* for the cottage –

---

* I have tried to avoid too much anachronistic usage of the word "gay", but have at times found no elegant alternative. The word was needed and therefore it was coined.

Mrs Revens and I were celebrating today – probably prematurely, but hooray."

Beirut was only the beginning of a tour that took Angus back through Damascus, Turkey and Greece. In Greece he met Robert Liddell, Cairo-educated novelist and friend of Ivy Compton-Burnett, who was lecturing from the British Council in Athens, and poet John Holloway, then Byron Professor at the University of Athens. (Years later, Holloway was to act as poetry adviser for Angus's anthology, *Writers of East Anglia*.)

Then Angus went on to Yugoslavia, where Tony met him with the car in Belgrade. They travelled on together, part work, part holiday, meeting writers and publishers, and spending Angus's blocked Yugoslav royalties. *Anglo-Saxon Attitudes* had been translated into Serbo-Croat and published by Prosveta in 1961: the sum of 283,500 dinars had been deposited in the Jugoslav National Bank, and was awaiting collection. (There were 2,100 dinars to the pound, with the rate moving in their favour, Tony noted in his pocket diary: the conversion came to about £135.) A contract for *The Old Men at the Zoo* was drawn up in November 1962, partly as a result of this encouraging visit, promising to pay £239.11s.8d. on signature for an edition of 5,000 copies.

Angus sent postcards to nephews and nieces from Dubrovnik, Sarajevo and Mostar. To Penelope Davies, from Dubrovnik, 10 April 1962: "Uncle Tony and I drove thro' this very wild part of Yugoslavia where there are hardly real roads and most people are dressed as in the picture you see – they are Mohammedans. We are going to an even wilder part – Montenegro – after we leave Dubrovnik."

He also found time to write from Opatija in Yugo-Slavia (*sic*) at more length to Vivian Smith, thanking him for a perceptive review of *The Old Men at the Zoo*, and to Leonard Woolf about Virginia Woolf – a letter which marks another interesting landmark on his long journey from near-dismissal and parody of her work in his broadcast of 1950, through a belief that none of her novels stood "in the front rank" (review of *A Writer's Diary*, *Observer*, 1 November 1953) to the profound admiration of his later years.

Leonard Woolf had been reading the British version of Angus's much reprinted essay which originally appeared as "If It's New and Modish is it Good?" in the *New York Times Book Review*, 2 July 1961,[11] and had written to Angus to question what he read as an assessment of Virginia Woolf as a novelist of "feminine hyper-sensitivity" who dealt primarily with "the personal relations of human beings as individuals": Leonard Woolf suggested that at least in her later works she was concerned to connect individuals to "reality" – "the relation of friendship, love, life, death to 'reality'".[12] He concluded that her only really great and successful novel was *The Waves*.

Angus, whose article had already advanced far along the road to admiration, wrote back on 17 April 1962:

Dear Mr Woolf,

We did, as a matter of fact, meet for a few minutes with Morgan Forster at King's before a feast. I am deeply touched by your appreciations of my work, especially as I am someone whom criticism (as of my last novel) casts into utter despair.

My wish to reassess your wife's work grows each year. She had so much influence on me when I was an adolescent that I was bound to react violently when at the late age of thirty six I first began to write. I agree with your assessment of her novels, but I am sad that you should leave out 'Between the Acts' which for me is really the most exciting experience of all, for it gives me the wit and the traditional formal surface of 'Mrs Dalloway' or 'The Lighthouse' and yet is shot through with the perception of 'The Waves'. I gave recently four lectures on 'Evil in the English Novel' at London University (I shall hope to summarise them in 3 shorter talks on the third) and the stamping beast of 'The Waves' and the rape image in 'The Acts' took up much of my third lecture with Forster's demons and caves . . . [Angus proceeds to discuss the different limitations of George Eliot and Dickens, and concludes] one thing I am sure that your wife was right to attack utterly all the self conscious plain manism of a writer like Bennett. One must be as clever as one can be, but, alas, also know that the novel is an art and not an intellectual exercise . . . Please excuse my rambling reply but I have been wandering for weeks partly lecturing, partly living from my earnings in Y–S which cannot be brought to England and the change of scene from Damascus upwards through Turkey, Greece and Y–S have bemused my brain. Yours very sincerely, Angus Wilson.[13]

Angus's relationship with Virginia Woolf – a writer notorious for producing extreme swings of critical reaction even within the same reader – was to continue to develop, and his notes for his later novels are studded with references, quotations, echoes: her influence on him was very great. On plain man Bennett, his opinion did not vary. He did not care for his work (though he claimed to have read his *Evening Standard* articles with pleasure as an adolescent) and dismissed it harshly (with the exception of *Riceyman Steps*) in an essay in the *London Magazine* in October 1954: he reiterated his dissatisfaction in 1974 in a long article in the *Times Literary Supplement*.[14] Bennett, he concludes, was so warped by "the Wesleyan ethic that had greyed and calloused the world he was born into" that his whole personality was warped, sexually and artistically, by his "endless, extravagant search for happiness and an endless, backbreaking load of work to pay for that extravagance." Bennett tried to be fair to the dull Midlands, and by failing to hate them sufficiently, he was unable to bring them to life. Fairness, Angus believed, was not enough.

It is interesting to note that Angus had instinctively preferred, although his mature judgement could not continue to admire, Galsworthy and Walpole: one might perhaps suspect that his ear was simply not tuned to the bass intended tones of the deep, unfair hatred which runs through Bennett's treatment of the Potteries. (Angus did not much care for Balzac's provincial tales, which Bennett greatly admired.) Bennett was too provincial for Angus's sympathies – provincial through and through. And yet Bennett plagued him a little, and irritated him more than seems necessary. There was something unsettling about that stoic slog and grind, coupled with that desire for yachts and Monte Carlo and the Savoy Hotel. ("Baby wants to go to Monte Carlo.") Bennett was extravagant. Angus Wilson was to be accused of extravagance. Virginia Woolf led a more quiet *rentier* Sussex-Bloomsbury life and despised the vulgar show. Wilson partook of both natures. And he partook, also, just a little, of the nature of Hugh Walpole, whom he described as "Mr Facing-Both-Ways" in the *New Statesman* (15 March 1952): "He adored every aspect of success, yet he was constantly aware of the ridicule or contempt it might bring. When he was knighted, in 1937, he wrote in his Journal: 'This is a dangerous proceeding and there will no doubt be some mockery – "Just what he's always wanted" "The sort of writer they would make a Knight of!" . . . I must confess that since Scott I can't think of a good novelist who accepted a Knighthood – Kipling, Hardy, Galsworthy all refused. But I'm not in their class, and range with Doyle, Anthony Hope and such . . . Besides, I shall like being a Knight.' "

*

Meanwhile, plain Mr Wilson journeyed on, from Yugoslavia to Majorca, where he was to be one of the judges of the new Prix Formentor. It was a demanding itinerary he had set himself.

Tony had resisted suggestions from George Weidenfeld and Weidenfeld's publishing associate and fiction editor Barley Alison that he should sit in on the judging sessions of the Formentor, preferring to wait at a distance while Moravia, Butor, Carlo Levi, Henry Miller, Hans Magnus Enzensberger and others fought it out. The British contingent included Nigel Dennis, Peter Quennell, Melvin Lasky (of *Encounter*), Francis Wyndham, and Weidenfeld himself, who had been one of the group of publishers to set up the prize. No prize is thought worth its investment without scandal, and the Formentor provided plenty. James Baldwin was said to have flown in by helicopter, tried to award the prize to Katherine Anne Porter, failed, and flown away again in disgust. Carlos Barral (of Seix Barral, the Spanish publishers) arrived with a black eye, having been roughed up by the Spanish police, who kept a most unfriendly eye on the whole proceeeding and tried to ban all Spanish reporting of it. George Weidenfeld said that the conference was disgraced by the presence of four secret policemen wearing shiny blue serge suits permanently in residence. The Formentor was described as a junket and a circus by most of the journalists who went off to the luxury hotel in the sun to cover it, but some of those who attended encountered political censorship first-hand for the first time.

The awarding of the prize also caused a stir. There were, in fact, two prizes, one the Prix International for an established writer, the other the Prix Formentor for an unknown. The French canvassed for their *nouveaux romans*, the English for V.S. Naipaul, and Angus also spoke up for the Japanese and the Turks: John Cowper Powys, fresh in Angus's memory, was sent the consolation prize of a telegram from the judges congratulating him on his approaching ninetieth birthday. The Prix International went to a young West German political novelist, Uwe Johnson. This was acceptable, but there was an outcry when it was discovered that the prize for an unknown had gone to a twenty-five-year-old Italian called Dacia Maraini who was known to be Moravia's mistress. Maraini went on to refute the cynics with a distinguished literary career, but at the time the Italian press was in the most enjoyable uproar, as Alberto Arbasino reported to Angus: Moravia found himself denounced as a Lost Leader and reproached by his oldest friends for letting down the image of Italian fiction abroad. He ran out of the final press conference at Einaudi's crying "This is an organised lynching!" The situation was inflamed by gossip about his wife, Elsa Morante: her handsome young lover, a neurotic naif painter, had just committed suicide in New York, and she had taken to drugs for consolation.

Angus and Tony returned to England on 10 May, having driven back through France. Angus had been away from England for more than two months, and in July he was off again to Canada after many a lunch and dinner, including a large drinks party on 6 June, given by writer Robert Rubens in his first-floor flat in Holland Park. Rubens was then assistant editor of Joe McCrindle's *Transatlantic Review*, and he had written to Angus asking if he had any short stories available: Angus had responded by offering the script of his radio play *Skeletons and Assegais*, and he and Rubens had met after one of the lectures on Evil in the autumn of 1961. They had gone back to McCrindle's flat in Ennismore Gardens, and Angus had handed over his typescript; then they had all three talked about books and writing – how good to talk seriously, Angus had said. Yet here he was, not at all serious but on his best party form, on Derby Day, with a cast Rubens was proud to have assembled, for this was the first big literary party he had ever given – the guests included Patrick Kinross, Andrew Sinclair, Doris Lessing in an offwhite basket-weave suit, and Muriel Spark, who had come straight from the Derby – she was dropped off at the door by publisher Alan Maclean. Angus, standing on the balcony overlooking the garden on this beautiful summer evening, had entertained the whole gathering with a high-spirited fantasy about what would happen if the balcony collapsed – he had his listeners enthralled.

But before Angus disappeared once more to foreign parts – to a conference in Vancouver on "East-West Dialogue" which seems to have had a high Buddhist content, and a very noisy Indian in the hotel bedroom next door – the domestic arrangements of both Angus and Tony assumed a new and long-lasting pattern. From 1 June 1962 he and Tony began to rent rooms in London from Perkin Walker in his house at 2 Regents Park Terrace. Since they had given up the flat in Dolphin Square, they had begun to feel the need for a London base, and Walker provided one on easy and friendly terms. They paid him £14 a month. Their apartment was at first on the second floor (they later moved to the top) and they shared a kitchen and bathroom with other tenants. It was a tall building, with handsome sash windows, on a terrace set slightly back from the main road and separated from it by a row of trees: it was well placed between the park and Camden Town, and within walking – and howling – distance of the zoo.

When Walker had first bought the property in 1955 the area was not at all smart, and still bore signs of war damage and post-war drabness. Now it was on the cusp between fashionable renovation and the perpetual and seemingly unalterable dreariness of Camden Town: the Sixties phenomenon of fashionable NW1, portrayed by cartoonist Mark Boxer, was on the way. Perkin Walker favoured a particularly gloomy and noisy Irish pub with dreadful Irish wakes on Camden High Street, but there were other more cheerful places to eat and drink – Angus and Tony regularly patronised Trattoria Lucca round the corner on Parkway. 2 Regent's Park Terrace itself was to house many of Walker's entourage: Bob French and

Monty Turland, who had lodged with Mrs Fulton in Ladbroke Grove, became permanent fixtures, and P.N. Furbank was also a long-term resident. (Forrest Fulton complained that all his friends were being swallowed up into the House of Love at RPT.)

The neighbours were agreeable. On the terrace lived the V.S. Pritchetts, the A.J. Ayers, the Claus Mosers, and other congenial friends who were to become familiar with the sight of Angus bounding down the front steps, singing along the pavement, or looking about for someone with whom to swap his latest stories. Jonathan Miller, Alan Bennett and the Tomalins were all near by in Gloucester Crescent. The area was crowded with satirists busy satirising one another – all in the most amiable and liberal-minded, indeed occasionally self-congratulatory way. There was good material here.

Meanwhile negotiations for the Suffolk cottage also proceeded satisfactorily. These, which had been broached in Beirut with Chris Arnold, were held up for a while by worries about damp, by a question of a hanging mortgage dating back to 1937, and by the drawing up of an agreement with the farmer, Mr Squirrel, who rented the field. But eventually all was sorted out, and Angus bought Felsham Woodside for £1147.13.0. in the autumn of 1962.

For the first time Angus found himself a property-owner. He would always be on the move, but he would always have somewhere to call home. He continued to flit from conference to conference, from continent to continent, but Felsham Woodside and Mrs Revens stayed where they were. It was a modest security his parents had never known.

THE CONFERENCE AGE

Gerard Reve, the *éminence noire*, was very much in evidence in the summer of 1962. He was staying on and off at The Chase at Sible Hedingham with Perkin Walker, Bob French and Monty Turland, and planning to accompany Angus to the Edinburgh Festival in August. Was this, one might wonder, wise? Should not a distinguished man of letters choose his company more carefully? J.B. Priestley, smelling trouble from afar, gave Edinburgh a wide berth, and later wrote to Angus to congratulate himself upon having done so. But Angus was less cautious.

This festival was to prove a turning-point in the literary history of the 1960s. Literary manners would never be quite the same again.

The age of the conference had dawned. After Tokyo and Berlin and Formentor and Vancouver and Edinburgh, conferences and festivals followed in unending succession: writers who had been cooped up during the immediate post-war years by political and financial restrictions were longing to stretch their wings and see the world. Even so, Edinburgh, the city of John Knox, seemed a curious place for declarations of sexual freedom.

All began mildly. On 16 August, Reve took the night ferry from The Hook to Harwich, and then caught the train to Stowmarket, where Tony met him. On the 17th they all dined decorously at the Old Vicarage with Martin and Jean Corke, and the next day, driven by Tony, they set off early for the Athens of the North. They had a pleasant journey, in holiday mood, taking lunch at Wentbrigge and spending the night in a hotel at Otterburn. The hotel reminded Angus of a mental hospital, but not even this dampened their spirits. They arrived on the Sunday, and dropped Gerard Reve off at his hotel while Angus went to attend a PEN meeting.

This was the sixteenth Edinburgh Festival, but the Writers' Conference was the first of its kind. It was organised by the young publisher John

Calder, with the help of Sonia Orwell, and it was widely and hopefully predicted that it would be a flop. In the event, several of the boasted big names failed to show – Sartre, Duras, Sarraute, Robbe-Grillet, Butor, indeed the entire French contingent did not make it: nor did Nabokov, Ehrenburg and Moravia. Neither did Norman Miller, whose solidarity in defection was triumphantly reported by the French newspaper *Combat* (3 September 1962). However, both Henry Miller and Norman Mailer turned up, so perhaps his composite ghost was not much missed. Others present included Mary McCarthy, Rebecca West, Lawrence Durrell, Kingsley Amis, Muriel Spark, Alexander Trocchi, Hugh MacDiarmid, Hal Porter, Kushwant Singh, Stephen Spender, Angus Wilson, van het Reve, and an audience of two thousand. It was an explosive mixture. (Angus was nervous about meeting Mary McCarthy, with whom he had recently had a "great coolness" prompted by remarks about her novels in a review of her essays in *Encounter*, June 1962:[1] he had accused her of "intellectual exclusivism", to which she would probably not have objected, but then had added in a more or less off-hand way, "She has written novels and they are not very good. She engages in general journalism and often . . . she is dull." This was harder to forgive, and Angus's admission, a year later in a letter to Mary McCarthy's editor Barley Alison (30 August 1963) about *The Group*, that the coolness was "only just patched over" at Edinburgh seems to imply the opposite – clearly their disagreement was still fresh in both their minds.)

The meetings took place in the vast McEwan Hall, with Malcolm Muggeridge – who claimed not to read novels – presiding over a kind of Roman holiday, where writers happily butchered one another as a spectator sport. The discussions (some hastily rearranged in the absence of the French) covered topics such as "Differences of Approach", "Is Commitment Necessary?" and "Censorship". As Neal Ascherson was to conclude, it was all more of a "huge, entertaining, elusive performance" than a serious debate.[2] Writers sounded off in all directions. Scot abused Scot, the turbanned Singh* deplored Western decadence, and Rebecca West wept to find herself sharing a platform with a pornographer. Angus Wilson, in a striped shirt and turquoise blue tie, declared that the future of the English novel lay with none other than Ivy Compton-Burnett. (His old friend Ivy was in her late seventies.) Mary McCarthy firmly said nonsense, and dismissed the French *nouveau roman* in its absence as literary

---

* Kushwant Singh, b.1915 in the West Punjab, and educated in Delhi and at King's College, London, had published short stories and several novels, including *The Mark at Vishnu* (1950) and *I shall not hear the Nightingales* (1959), and was shortly to receive a Rockefeller Foundation grant to study Sikh history and religion.

dressmaking. A respectful silence fell when a message was read out from Alan Paton in South Africa regretting his involuntary inability to attend. One American delegate, Niccolo Tucci, was told (by Angus, in the chair at this moment) that he was so boring he would have to sit down. Henry Miller said he had come to see Scottish paintings and the city of Edinburgh, and why bother talking about the novel as it had already been dead for a hundred years? Muriel Spark was ticked off for saying she had come to have fun and meet people. Norman Mailer added to the drama by arriving late to announce in mid-conference the birth of a baby daughter in New York. Both on and off stage discussions were animated and uninhibited. John Bowen, trying hard to chair and control a BBC radio programme *New Comment*, found himself noisily shouted down by his guests, writers who sensed that for once they had got the upper hand. The anarchy of the Vardon Hall disaster was in the air.

One of the most deliberately sensational contributions came from van het Reve. On Tuesday, 21 August, the second full day of the conference, he rose to his feet, enraged by a speech on "homosexuality, lesbianism and sodomy" from Trocchi, and asked for permission to speak as a homosexual writer.[3] This was the first time he had made such a statement in public – and it was intended to be very much in public. His remarks were widely reported, although many of the English papers referred to him merely as "a Continental writer" – an anonymity galling to one who set so much store by Fame and Genius. But they were reported only because he persisted. Spender in *Encounter* (October 1962) commented: "The press undoubtedly contributed to the success of the proceedings by reporting such spicy items as van het Reve's confession that he was a homosexual, and Norman Mailer's casual aside that Alexander Trocchi took heroin; though I should add that the confusion of the Scottish nationalist debate was such that when, on the same day, Mr van het Reve made his announcement, it was received with sympathetic applause from the audience, and without astonishment, as though he were speaking as one other representative of an oppressed minority (perhaps from some remote Hebridean isle). He had to make his confession again the next day to provoke any reaction from the audience, any report from the press. In the long run it acted as a Time Bomb which may yet blow up any future Edinburgh Writer's Conference."

The homosexuality debate continued, as well as rows about nationalism and drugs. J.R. Ackerley wrote to William Plomer that Henry Miller "talked about practically nothing else but indecent *graffiti*" and that Rebecca West "remarked that there should be two conferences, one for those who wanted to talk about the novel, and one for those who wanted to discuss homosexuality."[4] Kushwant Singh declared that no homosexual could know true love, which enraged Angus as well as Reve: Angus went so far as to say, in the John Bowen programme, that although he had enjoyed meeting Trocchi, he had come to hate some writers, "like that Indian Kus Wat Sing or whatever he's called". To Reve, Edinburgh was an important turning-point that pushed him towards the next – and, at last, triumphant – phase in his career. For others it marked another step in the slow march towards homosexual law reform. Various commentators suggested that reports from the conference should be sent to the Director of Public Prosecutions, to prove how innocent and harmless public debate on this issue was, and how little shocked had been the good folk of Edinburgh.

(The Vassall affair broke that autumn: George Vassall, a clerk at the Admiralty, who had a flat in Dolphin Square, was charged under the Official Secrets Act with passing on secrets: it was alleged that he had been vulnerable to blackmail because of his involvement in homosexual parties in Moscow. Almost exactly a year later, in August 1963, Angus was to be one of those who contributed to send a wreath to the grave of Stephen Ward, who committed suicide in the wake of the Profumo scandal, with a message describing him as "a victim of British hypocrisy".)

Reve returned to Holland, to write the work that made him the hero of Dutch youth. Angus, more soberly, went on with Tony in their Austin for a tour of Scotland, joined in Edinburgh on 25 August by nephew Nick Davies – "a charming companion", Angus wrote to grandmother Betty Wilson in Seaford. They travelled from coast to coast and Angus saw, for the first time, the family graveyard in Dunscore and the house at Stroquhan. They went to Iona and Loch Ness, and dropped in on Bunny Roger in his home in the west, with its magnificent garden, its aviary, and its nursery puddings. The tour was not an unmixed delight, as Angus reported to his *Queen* readers: the anti-English mood engendered in him by the Edinburgh conference had been reinforced "by the sight of innumerable English middle-class families (Ford Consul to Jaguar, with here and there a Rolls) braving out the Highland rains and mists with Bloody Marys and games of rummy in a series of very expensive, inadequate hotels from Killiecrankie to Inverness and Oban and down . . . I haven't toured at home for ten years and I shan't do so again for even longer." (What had this to do with TV? His link was daringly tenuous. He declared that the sight of Signor Piero Orsini telling Ludo Kennedy on *Viewpoint* about England's slums and how novelists ought to write more about them had almost driven him back into chauvinism. Had Moravia and Pasolini, he asked rhetorically, managed to raze the slums of Naples

and Palermo, or reduced the gross materialism of Milan? But the sight of
the English in Scotland had reconciled him once more to Abroad . . .)

For the rest of the year, Angus remained very busy – indeed,
overworked, as he told Anthony Thwaite in October, while apologising
for a telegram cancelling an agreement to write a review – "I'm helplessly
acquiescent on the telephone."[5] He went to the Frankfurt book fair,
celebrated the birthdays of J.B. Priestley and John Cowper Powys and
Madge Gillespie, and introduced Günter Grass at the German Institute,
dining with him after the event at La Speranza. (This event prompted an
anxious letter to Farrer written on 19 September – "I suppose Grass will
speak in German – or will he? And shall I understand him, if he does? I
hope so . . .") He dined with Jack Plumb and John Petch and Ann Fleming
and Richard Wollheim, spoke to the Hull English Club (where he met
Philip Larkin) and the Cambridge English Club, went to Rome and was
presented at Garzanti by Moravia, was endlessly interviewed, agreed to
appear on various TV programmes, and wrote a piece about the British
Museum. But he was not writing a novel. The somewhat disagreeable task
of shaping his Ewing lectures into publishable form was looming over him
– there had been compaints from the University of California Press about
the delay of the manuscript, reminding Secker & Warburg that the terms
of the lectureship had required a text and that the stipend was handsome:
"But at this late date I am afraid that Mr Wilson's ardor has cooled and, of
course, the fee has long since been squandered," wrote an editor on 17
July. With all these pressures, there was no novel in sight, nor any time
even to think about one.

Then suddenly, out of the blue, in the first week of December 1962,
came a quite unexpected invitation. He received a letter from Ian Watt
asking him to consider joining the University of East Anglia as a member of
the English Department.

*

When this invitation arrived, the University of East Anglia did not exist.
An appeal for it had been launched in 1962, and Norwich City Council
had donated the site of a golf course at Earlham – a good 165 acres. The
Chancellor-designate was Viscount Mackintosh, the Vice-Chancellor
Frank Thistlethwaite. Denys Lasdun was commissioned as architect to
begin work on designs for the new buildings.

UEA was one of several new universities going up at this expansionist
period – Sandy Parnis, who had been Cambridge University Treasurer
from 1953–62, had now been transferred to the University Grants
Committee to look after their development, and was spending much time

tramping through muddy fields in gum boots on sites from Stirling to Guildford, from Warwick to Bath. He also tramped around the golf course outside Norwich.

There were some early difficulties with Lasdun, who seemed a little slow with his plans: the committee was said to be on the point of ditching him when it suddenly woke up to the fact that one of the reasons why Lasdun was hard to get hold of was that he had also been commissioned by Olivier to design the National Theatre. Impressed, it stuck to its first choice.

Frank Thistlethwaite had taken a combined degree in English and History at Cambridge, where one of his friends and fellow undergraduates was Ian Watt. When Thistlethwaite came to making appointments for his new university, he thought of Watt, who had a considerable reputation as teacher and critic. Watt's sociological/historical interests appealed to Thistlethwaite, who hoped to make UEA as decompartmentalised, as inter-disciplinary as possible. Watt's best known publication was the classic work on English fiction, *The Rise of the Novel: Studies in Defoe, Richardson and Fielding* (1957), which was required reading for all students of literature. Watt, who had just completed ten years at Berkeley, accepted the offer to become the first Dean of English Studies. He in turn began to assemble a supporting cast.

Newly returned from California, with an American wife, Professor Watt had learned American ways, and thought it would be a good idea to introduce a creative writer into the Department. He asked around amongst his friends, and learned from P.N. Furbank that Angus Wilson lived in the neighbouring county of Suffolk, not too far from the designated golf course on the outskirts of Norwich, that he had a reputation as a speaker, and that he was sociable and easy. He didn't like poetry, Furbank said, and was not an experienced teacher, but perhaps that would not matter? (Angus did not dislike poetry, but he was reluctant to deliver judgements on it, and it is fair to say that Painter had struggled in vain in his BM days to persuade him to appreciate Rimbaud – "arrogant nonsense" had been Angus's verdict.) On the whole, this seemed promising, for there was only a part-time post on offer, and it seemed possible that it might suit Wilson well. To both Watt and Thistlethwaite, the fact that Angus had a degree in History, not English Literature, counted as an asset. Watt wrote, outlining his proposal, and reminding him they had met once in Grantchester with Nick Furbank about ten years ago. Angus expressed interest, and on 18 December he arrived in Norwich for a preliminary meeting.

The surroundings were not auspicious. Ian and Ruth Watt were living temporarily in "a repellent apartment" with green over-stuffed chairs in Unthank Road, above a dentist's surgery. Angus had to run the gauntlet of a corridor of grinning dentures and a strong smell of chemicals to reach the Watts, but he found a civilised and charming couple – handsome, travelled, sophisticated. (Ian Watt was half French: he had been stationed in Bury St Edmunds during the war, before departing for the River Kwai). Watt described what he had in mind, and Angus listened patiently. Then he asked his own questions, the first of which was "Would the position be pensionable?"

Watt was surprised to find a well-known novelist worrying about this, and replied that although it would be, the amount would probably be derisory. But the question showed, Watt thought, that Angus was seriously considering the offer.

Tony had been waiting below with the car, ready to carry Angus away. Over the next ten years he was to spend much time waiting with the car in Norwich.

Angus's decision was announced – and widely reported – in January 1963. *The Times* wrote "The appointment is to be of a new kind. Mr Angus Wilson will be available to encourage and criticize the work of student writers as well as to assist in the development of the cultural life of the university. He will also be taking part in the regular teaching of the school of English Studies."[6] Angus would have the rank of senior lecturer, would teach for two terms out of three, and his salary would be a thousand a year "with F.S.S.U. benefits".

Another of Watt's early recruits to the department was thirty-four-year-old A.E. Dyson, from University College, Bangor, already known to Angus as a committed worker for Homosexual Law Reform. This was to be a brave new university, not one modelled on the past, and the emphasis was on innovation. New ideas were welcome: Nicholas Brooke, from Cambridge (where he had known Ian Calder) and Durham (where he had taught Lorna Sage), was attracted by the idea of experiment and "the big empty field" – and depressed when, within a year, he heard someone talking about the "traditions" of UEA – it was to escape from all that that he had gone there in the first place. The balance was hard to strike. Dyson was to endure a certain amount of teasing from his students about his association with C.B. Cox and the Black Papers on education, which were not widely seen as representing the avant-garde: in an autobiographical note in a UEA "Who's Who" published in 1977 he was to comment "Described in late 50s as 'extreme left-wing', as a result of part in campaign for homosexual law reform, in early 70s as fascist monster, effete aristocrat etc. as a result of modest musing on education in *Black Papers*."

Conservative Norfolk might seem an unpromising part of the country for a social experiment: it was alleged to be even more set in its ways than neighbouring Suffolk. (Lady Marjorie Erskine, daughter of the Fourth Marquess of Bristol, retorted to Angus's quip that social life in Suffolk had got stuck in 1854 by saying that Norfolk was still living in 1754.) The University had warm support, however, from Sir Edmund Bacon, Lord Lieutenant of Norfolk, who was keen on the project. Stradbroke of Suffolk was less encouraging and continued to complain about the absence of a chapel. And the Watts did in the event find Norwich uncongenial: their American-reared children found the schools old-fashioned, with too much sport and religion, and after a couple of years the whole family flew back to California, where Watt became Professor of English at Stanford. But by then, the university was in full working order, and had begun to move into its permanent home.

The first undergraduates were to due to arrive in October 1963, and Angus would throw himself into his new career with all his usual vigour. It gave him a new lease of life.

★

On other fronts, life and work in his fiftieth year remained fragmented. In February 1963 he went up to the Harrogate Festival and appeared at a literary luncheon with Monica Dickens and Stephen Potter. After feasting on toasted grapefruit, apple omelette, and Penguin Pie he gave local colour by speaking about his step-grandmother Alys, she who was said to have died in her bath in Harrogate, watched by her parrot. His notes read:

Her parrot – two views.

My own memory.

Should I investigate?

No.

This was probably the correct conclusion, in view of the fact that she died in Harrow.

Later in the month Angus went again to Italy, with Tony: they stayed in Rome at the Hotel River on the Via Flaminia. He met the leaders of the Communita Europea degli Scrittori, lectured for the British Council (in Rome, Milan and Naples), listened to a good deal of literary gossip and quarrelling, and worked, sitting in the sun in the Borghese gardens or on the Pincio, on the text of his Ewing lectures. They were still provisionally entitled "Speaking about Writing", but on 4 March he wrote to Jay Halio (the first American to publish a critical volume on Angus Wilson's fiction) that he was hard at work on his "little book" and perhaps it would be called

"The Wild Garden"?*[7] He managed to finish it, and to get the manuscript typed while he was there. He renewed his acquaintance with Arbasino, and various friends from back home and down under caught up with them – Charles Blackburne flew out to join them for a holiday and Terry and Joanna Kilmartin (whose son Christopher was at school with the Blackburnes at Nowton Court) were also around. Vivian Smith and his wife Sybil from Tasmania were in Rome, and happened to notice that Angus was billed to give a lecture: they attended it, were impressed by the vast audience, then met for a drink at the Canova. Angus and Tony were sitting in short sleeves in the sun, although to the Smiths it seemed bitterly cold.

Angus did not think so: he sent a postcard of the papal guard to Nicholas Davies saying "Rome is beautifully hot now and if it wasn't for having to see too many people and do too many things I should be in absolute bliss – as it is I'm in bliss – love to you all, Angus." Charles Blackburne spent ten days with them in Italy, and Angus and Tony showed him the sights. Charles was much impressed by their knowledge of paintings (they made a detour to Arezzo), by Tony's command of petrol-station Italian, and by Angus's dashing appearance upon Italian television.

One sortie abroad leads to another, and the Italian venture was to take him, that August, on a delegation to the Soviet Union. But before then, he fitted in more of the domestic round. He dined with Ann Fleming and went to *Don Giovanni* with the glamorous Mostyn-Owens – the lean and erudite William Mostyn-Owen, art historian, was married to writer Gaia Servadio, one of the chief ornaments of George Weidenfeld's many parties. He sat between Mrs Aarvold and Miss Charlotte Halliday at the Lord Mayor's Midsummer Banquet at the Mansion House. (He behaved himself on this occasion, and did not storm out because he was not seated on the Top Table: his reward was that his photograph appared prominently in the press coverage, along with Sidney Nolan, Fenella Fielding, Barbara Hepworth, and many other newsworthy guests.) He went to a May Day party of Geoffrey Wright's in Holland Park and during that summer he and Geoffrey were to work together on a long-cherished project of producing a musical version of "Totentanz" – as "The Dance of Death" – for television, which they delivered to Curtis Brown in September. (There was some interest in this from Sydney Newman and

* Jay Halio: *Angus Wilson*, Writers and Critics Series. (Edinburgh and London, Oliver and Boyd 1964). Halio had first come across Wilson's work in 1959, had read A.O.J. Cockshutt's essay on it in *Essays and Criticism*, January 1959, with which he had disagreed: he responded in an essay in *Modern Fiction Studies* (West Lafayette 1962), and had gone on to study Angus's work in depth. They corresponded but did not meet until 1967.

Peter Luke at the BBC, but eventually, in 1964, both the BBC and ABC turned it down – "A little far out for us," apologised ABC.) On 2 May 1963 he delivered the Leslie Stephen lecture in Cambridge, choosing as his subject Samuel Richardson, a novelist whose influence on both English and European literature had, he considered, been far more profound than was generally recognised – he was to teach his works with unfailing persistence and against some resistance for years to come. He spoke at Eton College and at the Arts Theatre, and whisked off to Munich to give a reading of two of his short stories for British Week. He mourned the death, on 17 June, of his old hero John Cowper Powys, with his "great, handsome, white-maned head, a sort of stricken Minotaur", and his extraordinary fictional "world of sudden gatherings of human beings – battles, pageants, brothels, fêtes – in which weather, scene, the very mineral substance of the earth, add a whole other dimension to events such as can be found in no other novelists' imagination."[8]

John Pattisson came to stay for the weekend of 20 June and was taken to Aldeburgh to see The Beggar's Opera: this visit was followed a month later by one from David Farrer, who in his letter of thanks mentioned "problems" with Pattisson, who was letting work get out of control – Farrer suggested it was time for Pattisson to leave Secker & Warburg and seek a career elsewhere. Angus, with some prompting from John, was to take his old friend's side: he wrote to Fred Warburg on 1 September 1963 that Pattisson had had many personal difficulties culminating in the recent death of his brother, and surely his long service with the firm required patience with his "nervous troubles"? Could not some treatment be found – "if not by orthodox psychologists then by hypnosis or other modern medical treatments"? Angus had not forgotten his own debt to the Pattisson family.

Angus and Tony saw the Osbornes, the Priestleys, Jack Plumb and Ian Calder. They saw Angus Davidson, translator of Moravia, whose brother was now curator of Ickworth. They saw a performance of Cymbeline at Nowton Court. Paul Binding, an Oxford undergraduate and a great admirer of Angus's work, was invited over to lunch: he arrived by train and taxi with his friend Jonathan Gili from New College. (Both young men were in love with a young woman from Ruskin called Phillida: Jonathan Gili was to marry her.) Binding had impulsively telephoned Angus the year before, giving his own name as Simon Davenant, from a public call box outside the Sheldonian – the curiously memorable number, Rattlesden 200, was in Who's Who for all to ring – and had engaged Angus in a long conversation about his short story, "Et Dona Ferentes". (Angus had talked about its connections with and foreshadowing of the themes of

Hemlock.) Later Binding had written, confessed his true identity, invited him to his twentieth birthday party in London (cancelled by snow and ice) – and now here he and Jonathan Gili were, enjoying steak and zabaglione, at the very table of The Master. (Binding identified strongly with the Wilsonian Home Counties world of middle-class neurosis described in Wilson's fiction – his own father had endured an alcoholic breakdown, and his mother, who died of cancer, had been a reader of Angus's novels, and had a connection with Perkin Walker's family.)

Angus's own career as official teacher of undergraduates was fast approaching, and he attended preliminary conferences of the English board at the Athenaeum and in Norwich. (He had already volunteered a course on Dickens and Dostoevsky.) Then there was a lecture at the King's Lynn Festival, graced by the Queen Mother, who came over from Sandringham. And then, after dining in the Albany with John Richardson, he was off to Leningrad. He flew off on Saturday 3 August 1963, eight days before his fiftieth birthday. The company was to be as mixed as it had been at Edinburgh the summer before. And this time, the French did not fail.

*

The flight to Leningrad was not direct. The British contingent flew via Hamburg and Helsinki, changing planes twice. Communications with the Soviet Union were not easy, and despite an official policy of "peaceful co-existence" Soviet writers remained in deep Cold War cultural isolation. The conference had been organised by COMES – the European Community of Writers – as an attempt to build bridges across the ice. (The Community was founded in 1958 by the Italian writer Jean-Baptiste Angioletti: it called itself "a free association of anti-fascist and anti-racist writers" but its agenda in Leningrad was intended to be strictly non-political.) So off they went, William Golding, John Lehmann, the Catholic journalist and editor Bernard Wall, Angus Wilson, and the Irish writer Kate O'Brien, for several days of "Round Table" discussions.

The visitors were housed in luxury, in a decaying nineteenth-century hotel with enormous red-curtained bedrooms, huge desks, and heavy reading-lamps of marble and brass: William and Ann Golding's room was so vast it contained a grand piano on which he would play "The Mountains of Mourne", hoping that Kate O'Brien could hear its comforting tones echoing through the walls. (But the rooms were so huge and the walls so thick that no sound reached her.) Six days were spent in Leningrad, discussing the state of literature at great length and with many pompous generalisations. The French were well represented, by Nathalie Sarraute, Robbe-Grillet, Sartre and Simone de Beauvoir. (She was

dubbed Simone de Bandeau by Angus, after the turban-like scarf she wore
– James Kirkup, who translated her *Memoirs of a Dutiful Daughter*, more
unkindly called it a Stakhanovite turban, and claimed she wore it to
conceal her large ears.)[9] The Italians sent Ungaretti and Vigorelli; the
Germans young Hans Magnus Enzensberger whom Angus had met at
Formentor: and writers from several other European nations attended.
The Russians provided their usual party hacks, and one or two writers of
more distinction – including Ilya Ehrenburg, aged seventy-two, and
Alexander Tvardovsky, aged fifty-three, both of whom spoke up for
freedom. (It is to be hoped Ehrenburg had not seen Angus's review of his
"monster novel", *The Ninth Wave*, which he described as "895 pages of
such deadly boredom", sentimental, disingenuous, and undigested.)[10]

The Soviet Writers Union continued to condemn Modernism as it had
done for decades. It also condemned decadent strip-tease and sex. There
was little sign of a thaw here. De Beauvoir, in the last volume of her
memoirs, *Tout Compte Fait*,[11] recalled that she and Sartre had hoped for
some kind of cultural *rapprochement* in the autumn of 1962, in the wake of
Pravda's publication of Yevtushenko's poem, *Stalin's Heirs*, and *Novy Mir*'s
publication of Solzhenitsyn's *One Day in the Life of Ivan Denisovich*, but that
hope had been dashed by Krushchev's subsequent violent denunciation of
formalism and abstraction in art. A speech of twenty thousand words
delivered in March 1963 had defended Stalin and fired "broadsides" at
Ehrenburg, Nekrassov and Yevtushenko. Now, in the summer of 1963,
Soviet aesthetics were as entrenched against Western artistic experiment as
ever, and "ideological coexistence" was condemned as undesirable and
impossible: de Beauvoir found the opening session of the congress
"strange and disconcerting".

The tone of the other sessions was in fact more moderate: but there was
no dialogue whatsoever between the East and the West – it was as though
neither listened to what the other was saying. On the Western side, the
French had a good deal to say, and they defended the *nouveau roman*: on the
Eastern side all the speakers with the exception of Tvardovsky, Ehrenburg
and two or three others proclaimed their faith in a literature that should
"help to beautify men's lives".

Angus had arrived armed by his conviction that the British and the
British novel were peculiarly insular, but after hearing the French
contingent talk endlessly about continental literature he began to feel the
British were not so bad after all, and leapt to his feet with an impassioned
defence of the English novel. It would be a tragedy, he thought, if the
oppressed young Russians were to move straight from the monolothic

culture of social realism to the monolithic culture of Robbe-Grillet. Long
live variety, and down with ideology.

The final press conference in Moscow, on Friday 9 August, took place as
a nuclear test ban treaty was being signed in the same city by the
Americans, the British and the Russians. As several delegates pointed out,
the writers did not seem to resolve their differences quite so well. The
official Soviets stuck to their party line, earning a reprimand from Sartre,
up to this point suspected by many of being too pro-Soviet: if you dismiss
Joyce, Kafka and Proust, he said, why bother to meet to discuss the novel at
all? The informal meetings had been useful, everybody agreed, as
everybody on these occasions always does, but there was nevertheless a
depressing sense of *impasse*. Only growing affluence, Angus believed,
would change Russian attitudes.

Sunday, 11 August 1963, was Angus's fiftieth birthday. He spent it with
the other delegates on board ship, cruising the Moscow waterways. The
English were suddenly very popular because of the test ban – which de
Gaulle, to Sartre's disgust, had refused to sign. News of Angus's landmark
anniversary had got around, and his health was proposed by Aleksei
Surkov of the Writers Union, who then made the surprise announcement
that Angus, John Lehmann, Sartre, de Beauvoir and several others had
been invited to visit Krushchev in his villa at Pitsunda in Georgia on the
Black Sea. They were flown out the next day at dawn, and driven to the
Soviet leader's estate through lush subtropical scenery: there they were
received by Krushchev himself, who appeared suddenly "like a silent-
footed, lumbering bear or even more a giant panda", dressed in wide beach
trousers and a Russian blouse.[12]

Nikita Krushchev had been in power since March 1958, when he had
replaced Bulganin: he had only just over a year to go, before being himself
ousted by Brezhnev. He had made himself into a character for the Western
press; homely, wise-cracking, full of peasant wisdom. The reality was not
quite so benign, and the writers found it hard to make out why they had
been summoned to his presence. The whole occasion was marked by a
curious and uneasy mixture of lavish hospitality and deliberate offence.
John Lehmann, as British representative of COMES, spoke, as did one or
two other delegates. Krushchev then harangued them all as capitalist
writers and described Stalin as a pioneer of atomic détente. He made no
concessions to western European literature and its heretical views on
freedom of speech and thought: there could be political compromise over
peace, but no compromise in the war of ideas. His arguments, as they came
over in translation, were inconsistent, but his delivery was strangely
impressive. He listened to the "capitalists" in non-committal silence – "as

though a baby had learned calculation" – and they listened to him politely – until the whole performance was suddenly broken off, with a wonderful smile, and they were free to bathe and to lunch sumptuously on caviar, smoked salmon, trout, duck, and many fine wines, as their host brightened up at the arrival of his old friend Sholokhov, doubtful author of that famous work, *And Quiet Flows the Don.*

They were not all appeased by the beauties of nature, the thoughtfully provided bathing suits, and the caviar: de Beauvoir did not forgive having been made to leave Moscow at seven in the morning on an empty stomach, to find not even a cup of coffee on the plane. It was all very well being greeted everywhere by flowers, but *on ne peut pas manger les fleurs*, she complained crossly to Angus. In her memoir she records that she was faint with hunger by the time she arrived at Krushchev's place, and when food did arrive, she was not pleased to find dessert accompanied by a forty-five-minute rendering of a satirical poem in Russian by Tvardovsky. The guests sat in silence, "profoundly bored", while their host incomprehensibly chuckled.

It had been a disconcerting experience, in which Krushchev seemed to have been eager to discompose them, and they were even more puzzled to find the meeting reported favourably in the press. Forces were at work behind the scenes which not even experienced travellers like Sartre could interpret.

The super-delegation was then whisked ministerially back to Moscow, but getting home again the next day was not so easy. Angus and Lehmann were supposed to fly to Heathrow via Vienna, but were turned back at Kiev. Angus on his own initiative discovered there was a KLM flight from Moscow to Amsterdam and pleaded his friendship with a Dutch KLM director. Thus he got tickets for the two of them, and also, politely and helpfully, for two hopefully attendant Indians who were also trying to get to London. They confirmed the anti-Indian prejudice aroused by Kushwant Singh by delaying the plane with difficulties over their baggage. "John said to me, you know, this is a lesson to you not to be kind all over the place, this really has been insufferable – but I realised that for me it wasn't kindness, it was really politeness . . . it was impossible for me to be anything other . . . I *am* a polite person."

Angus wrote up his reactions to the trip on the plane on the way to Amsterdam. He noted that neither his novels nor Golding's had yet appeared in Russian, and concluded "perhaps they'll even translate their guests' books now, who knows?"[13] But privately he suspected they would not, because of their Victorian "moral puritanism" – and they never did, or not in any official version. (His works were however the subject of much critical commentary, notably by Professor Valentina Ivasheva, a worrying advocate, and his study of Dickens eventually appeared in a pirated version in 1975.)

Almost immediately upon his return he was interviewed on tape by Kay Dick, who came to stay in Felsham Woodside on 15 August 1963, fresh from a suicide attempt following the break-up of her relationship with Kathleen Farrell. He was full of memories of Russia, and chatted about them, the writers he had met, the contrasts between Russia and America, his fears of a new moral puritanism, the Indians on the airport, the non-recognition of the existence of homosexuality in the Soviet Union, the death of Stephen Ward, the forthcoming publication of *The Wild Garden*. (Stephen Ward's suicide had prompted a note to Angus from E.M. Forster, dated 10 August – "I rather envy you joining with younger writers in their protest against British hypocrisy. Even at my age I would gladly have added a petal to that wreath.")

The Russian visit had been immensely stimulating – Angus told Fred Warburg (perhaps in the heat of the moment) that these twelve days had been, for him, the most important of the last decade. It is clear from the tape that, paradoxically, it had set his mind to work in a new direction on the novel he was beginning to plan. This was to be one of the most English of his works, yet at this stage it had, in his imagination, a distinctly comparative flavour. It was to deal with the life of an Englishwoman of sixty, but she was to be contrasted with others – perhaps with a Russian, an American, a South African woman? Was it to be about insularity, perhaps?

★

The novel developed against a background of distracting activities. Americans arrived, including Dwight and Gloria Macdonald on 17 August. (Gloria professed herself delighted by the mugs hanging quaintly from the cottage beams in the kitchen: Dwight brushed aside her enthusiasm brusquely – "Gloria, we don't *have* beams" – and carried on talking politics.) Angus was drawn into the appeal for the restoration of the derelict Theatre Royal in Bury St Edmunds, and Tony had his own theatrical interests, appearing with panache in September in a production at Nowton Court with, according to Angus, a bird of paradise in his hat.

September also brought E.M. Forster, on the 19th: he wrote the next day with thanks for "a delightful outing. I hope that it may occur again or that I may be able to show some competent hospitality over here. The roses all slept splendidly and are now busy perfuming the suite. With all kind wishes, Morgan." (It is pleasing to note that Morgan the novelist met Morgan the Welsh cat.) October brought Edmund and Elena Wilson for lunch: Edmund Wilson was in pursuit of his Kimball ancestors who came from the villages of Rattlesden and Buxhall. He recorded, "They have a snug cosy little nest in the country in a little dark flint-covered house, surrounded by a partly wild garden, where roses and other flowers are still brightly blooming – one still alive white lily, of which they are very proud. The house is full of stuffed birds . . . Excellent lunch of pheasant, 'overcooked' potato chips, red wine, and a special 'sweet' made by Tony."[14] Wilson was pleased to find Kimbles and Kemballs in the local telephone book, and a marble plaque with the name Kemball in the entrance of the church at Buxhall.

And in October, the first students (eighty in all) arrived with fanfares at the University of East Anglia. Angus loved them and they loved Angus. He wrote a piece for the *Express* called "Looking Forward to Life with the Young Ones" (in which he said that he saw them as his bridge to the future).[15]

The spirit of those first years at UEA was improvisational: the new university, with its new agenda, had attracted pioneers rather than conformists. (Some claimed that for them this simply meant that it did not require a Latin O-Level.) Students, staff and builders invented the university as they went along, and Angus joined in happily as the 1960s got under way. He was all for experiment. In an interview in the inter-university magazine, *U*, published at the beginning of the next university year, Angus, wearing a "ritzy" red leather tie, mildly deplored the current student habit of partnering off and settling down: the "married state", he said, was not "the best for studying, which demands solitude and privacy, as well as a wide social life in which ideas and opinions can be exchanged with many others."

★

The students represented the future: *The Wild Garden*, published by Secker on 11 November 1963, and by the University of California Press in December 1963, looked back into the past. The writing of it had initially been a chore: Angus had had to dispense with his lecturer's ad libs and edit out some unguarded comments on Mrs Curry and Mrs Price – possibly identifiable to a British readership, and possibly libellous. But he had eventually become seriously engaged with the book as a book, and he was pleased with it. This exploration into the springs of imagination was, he recognised, an un-English enterprise. Writers in the 1950s and early 60s were not accustomed to standing up in public and talking confessionally about themselves and their work: the Edinburgh festival had marked a new departure. Angus worked hard on the thesis from which he took his title, which elaborated the view that his writing sprang from the opposition between two polarities – the "garden in the wild" of his pioneering South African mother, and the "wild garden" of his Scottish gentry father. The town-country opposition explored in his lectures on Evil was here developed further, and his use of gardening as a metaphor. He was also peculiarly frank about the sadistic impulses in his own nature, about the breakdown at Bletchley Park, about his inability to write about his mother's death, about his father's eccentricities. (An expanded extract about his father had appeared on 8 September in the *Sunday Telegraph*.)

He seems not to have anticipated the resistance that critics and friends might feel to this frank revelation of the precariousness of literary creation and the personal nature of a writer's raw material. He must have recalled the naïve hostility that some reviewers expressed towards his discussions of Zola's relations with mother, wife, mistress, children and creativity. Some seemed to think that a work of art had no connection whatsoever with its begetter, and that tracing links between life and work was an illegitimate occupation. Did not the New Critics insist that the words on the page were all, and that nothing existed beyond them? Others who knew better did not deny links, but questioned the wisdom of letting the public know about them. Why give away trade secrets?

The double attack – on content and decorum – was unnerving. Some of the reviews were good, and friends wrote in support and appreciation: Malcolm Bradbury in the *Listener* (28 November 1963) praised its luminous intelligence and its ambiguities – but Bradbury had already acquired an un-English interest in creative writing and the creative process. Angus had opened an autobiographical Pandora's box, and found himself unexpectedly accused of "comic self-importance", and of being "embarrassing" and "reverent" about his own work. The volume appeared at the same time as *Writers at Work: The Paris Review Interviews, Second Series* which on the whole was slightly better treated.[16] (An interview with Angus, by Michael Millgate, had appeared in the first Secker volume in 1958, reprinted from the *Paris Review* no.17, 1957.) It is hard to escape the impression that one of Angus's offences lay in dispensing with the helpful interviewer or interpretative critic, and doing it all for himself. There were several cracks suggesting he was in effect writing a PhD thesis on his own work, and perhaps foolishly queering the pitch for a future autobiography.

The two pieces that annoyed him most appeared in the *Times Literary Supplement* and the *Sunday Times*. The *Times Literary Supplement*, in a piece headlined "Getting Themselves Taped", anonymously commented: "Mr Wilson does not tell us whether he wrote out his three Los Angeles lectures beforehand or whether his little book (which 'came out' of them) was worked up from recordings of the lectures. Mr Wilson is certainly known to be a dauntless improviser, with all the speed if not quite the weight of Sir Isaiah Berlin. Probably, lecturing from notes, Mr Wilson improvised largely, playing for laughs to a sympathetic audience of old ladies, having wilfully misunderstood the nature of his assignment," and goes on to suggest that there must have been some "hotness under the collar" in Los Angeles as Mr Wilson described his feelings towards other boys at school.[17]

It is not clear why the *Times Literary Supplement* assumed the University of California to be populated by old ladies, nor why the West Coast compatriots of Baldwin, Burroughs, and Ginsberg were supposed to be more prudish than the British: but the reasons for Angus's indignation are clear enough, and he wrote in defence of his weeks of work in Rome. He protested against the slur on his professionalism, concluding "As part of my livelihood is gained from university lecturing, may I ask your reviewer for a clear apology for these baseless surmises?" He got a rather unclear apology: "I'm sorry that my remarks, intended to give an impression of the style of Mr Wilson's lectures, should have been considered a reflection on the seriousness with which he undertook his particular assignment."[18]

Connolly in the *Sunday Times* was dismissive.[19] He said that the portrait of Angus confronting a microphone on the cover looked like a small sea-lion in Marineland, and that he had not been able to get beyond page 80. This was infuriating rather than damaging, and Angus wrote back saying that Connolly, on the Penguin cover of *Enemies of Promise*, looked like a warthog. Honour was satisfied, after a schoolboy fashion.

It is clear that many critics, comparing *The Wild Garden* and the volume of *Paris Review* interviews, preferred the apparently no-nonsense (and deeply evasive) approach of Hemingway: remarks such as "I suppose there are symbols since critics keep finding them" or "When I am working on a book or a story, I write every morning as soon after first light as possible. There is no one to disturb you . . ." were quoted with approval. The honesty and self-doubt of Angus's account were disturbing, as perhaps was the subtlety of some of the connections he made. How could a critic ever hope to track down the murderer-writer if the writer were as elusive and self-concealing and self-knowing as this? Angus had exposed himself to hostility, and not only from the public.

Some were supportive, particularly the professionals – Priestley wrote praising his "ingenuity and frankness" and William Golding on 5 November wrote in fellow feeling: "You read so easily, slipping into the eye and ear, I think we both came up against the end of the book, like skaters hitting the barrier; and only then realised what horrible times you'd had, yet described so lucidly. One can say nothing, nothing – only wonder again at the toughness of the psyche, who should properly be allegorised as an old boot, rather than the delicate winged thing with the lamp. Reading your frank and acute self-analysis put me out of patience with my own shoddy Ewing lectures and more than ever determined not to publish them." (He never did: neither did Marianne Moore publish hers.)

Other reactions, while friendly, were disquieting. Spender wrote telling Angus to pay no attention to Connolly, but went on: "Of course, in publishing this book you stuck your neck out to be struck by rival egos. However, you are universally admired, liked, respected. I realise this from everyone I have ever heard talk of you . . . Of course your book is a bit maddening. One loves the straight autobiographical bits. Also anything you write about other writers is illuminating. But when you write about your own books one feels 'Oh I do wish aunty would sit down and tell us another story instead of telling us her old stories' . . ."[20]

And Perkin Walker, to whom the book was dedicated, wrote saying the Walker family did not deserve the unqualified gratitude and affection with which Angus had regarded them. "I ought perhaps, when you showed me the extract, to have encouraged you to be more harsh about my family and me. There was a very nasty side to our affection for you – at times at least, regarding you as a very amusing clown or freak who could be treated, and sometimes was, as less than a person. I still feel very worried about this . . ." The beloved surrogate mother Bump Walker, who had died in July 1955, had made fun of Angus: so had the whole family, as Angus now discovered. He was looking back to a Garden of Eden that had never been. Angus had been a better friend to Perkin than Perkin had ever been to Angus. Perkin was ashamed. "You have been overgenerous," he wrote.[21] Angus was sensitive to all these criticisms. He wrote to George Ford on 2 December 1963, "I have had a violently hostile reception for it here on the whole – it transgresses all the English rules about reticence and vulgarity etc. etc." – an exaggeration, but with some truth in it.

Another crack opened in the thin ice of his confidence. Spender generously assured him he was universally liked and respected. His students seemed to admire him and to enjoy his seminars. But what lay beneath these appearances?

In The Wild Garden, he wrote of his terror of the sea, his mother's fascination with shipwrecks, his inability to swim, and his night-time fears of being sucked down into icy water like Mr Astor, who went down on the Titanic. (The story of Lady Duff Gordon, whose fate he does not mention, had also impressed him and possibly his mother – Lady Duff Gordon's survival, and that of her husband, in highly dubious circumstances, had caused a scandal in the press – they were said to have refused to pick up other *Titanic* victims, although their lifeboat was far from full. She had been a fashionable dressmaker: one of her clients was Ronald Firbank's sister Heather.) This fear of drowning in arctic wastes, which Angus had given in *Hemlock and After* to Bernard Sands's wife Ella, came in part, he said, from "a picture of Golliwog's head appearing above the ice, entitled 'Golliwog at the North Pole'." He had forgotten the name of the children's book in which this appeared: it was in fact *Golliwogg's Polar Adventures*, by Bertha Upton, with pictures by Florence K. Upton, first published by Longman in 1910. This popular and lively work related in verse the hazardous expedition of a golliwog with his crew of doll companions to the pole: the pictures of Golliwogg marooned on a sinking ice floe surrounded by barking seals, or capsized by a ferocious tusked walrus, are horrifying, as is an eerie picture of the little ghostly crew pulling its sled through a thick grey fog. Golliwogg's appalled round black face, with its round white eyes and round red mouth, encircled by a white circle of fur, is like a terrible parody of a baby – a helpless baby struck by permament fear.

Angus could not look back on his childhood or his early years with any complacency. He had tried, in *The Wild Garden*, to exorcise some of his memories, including those of Bletchley, but he knew that he had not wholly succeeded. Perkin had reminded him of what lay beneath the ice. Angus knew that one day, like the doomed characters of the Ibsen he so admired, he would have to dive further into that dangerous darkness.

HAROLD WILSON'S ENGLAND

Late Call, begun in the summer of 1963 and published in November 1964, is the most deeply English of Angus Wilson's novels, deliberately confined to one country, almost to one location – the New Town of Carshall. Sylvia Calvert, his elderly heroine, is also deeply English. Yet much of the book, paradoxically, was written abroad. On the last day of 1963, Angus and Tony set off for Morocco, taking their notes and working manuscript with them.

They loved Morocco. They set off armed with guide books and advice from Roland Gant about how to poison their enemies with chopped-up cat's whiskers; Gant's uncle Edy Legrand had illustrated a classic French work on Moroccan life and manners, and Gant himself had once witnessed the Blue Men bringing 4000 camels into Gouilimine. Angus and Tony flew to Tangiers, where they met the resident expatriate American novelists Paul and Jane Bowles – Angus had written to Paul Bowles in August 1963 announcing his plans to visit Morocco, and now he and Tony were entertained in Tangiers in the company of "a princess and her husband" – should they, Angus later wondered, have offered the princess a lift in their taxi after dinner? (Don't worry so much about other people, Tony told him.) They hired an Opel car and travelled on to Rabat, Casablanca, Agadir and Essaouira, admiring on the way jackals, camels, nesting storks, and a boy with a dancing bear. They settled for sixteen days in the Grand Hôtel du Sud in Tafraout, consuming carefully itemised and modest quantities of chocolate biscuits, coffee, tea, wine, Alka Seltzer and petrol – British travellers were still on a tight budget, and many items in Morocco, like postage, proved unexpectedly expensive. Tony wrote from Tafraout on 8 January to thank the Bowleses for their hospitality, reporting on their travels: "We spent a night at El Jadida in the Marhaba Hotel in the kind of loathsome luxury we hope to avoid in future. A beach hotel set in a large private park, miles from the town and people, with an expensive hush of cultureless riches. In great contrast to the Des Iles at Essaouira . . . At Gouilimine we saw the market and snake charmers, and a comic in a large crowd did an imitation of two French people making love, and then of us doing the twist much to the delight of the crowd. I think I was more upset than Angus who just laughed gregariously. This is certainly the oddest landscape we have seen and the sunset lights are superb . . ."[1]

Ten days later, on 18 January 1964, Angus wrote to Fred Warburg saying that he found himself in "a sort of Shangri-La – nearby is a fifteen mile long valley of palms and almonds and apricots (just coming into blossom) where are the villas of many of the rich shopkeepers of Casablanca – they leave their wives and small children and visit them once a year. We go there to write in the afternoons as a distraction – the children run up to the car and sing (I think that's what they're up to) and thousand hidden women's eyes peer at us from the house . . . A few old retired grocers live there all the time and have invited us in for tea and mutton fat (not somehow my favourite meal – it's like the White King's hay and ham sandwiches). As to the hotel (Tony and I are both reading Dostoyevsky & so are constantly saying "as to the so and so, your excellency") it is vast and set up like a fortress – very comfortable (with limited but pleasant Moroccan (not French) cuisine) save for the cold of the nights – only a few other guests ever appear (usually two English or Swiss or Americans each night) and they go on next morning. The staff – indeed all Moroccans – seem to me delightful – friendly, kind, gentle and a bit inefficient. We have rusticated long enough and shall go on for two weeks to Marrakesh in a few days time to a hotel also with gardens and balcony so that we can continue our beaverlike daytime work, but perhaps distract ourselves a little more in the evening and eat Frenchwise. Then to Essaouira (Mogador) by the sea which we saw on our way down and adored . . ." (Angus wrote a travel piece on "The Old Lady of Mogador" about an elderly Morocco-born piano teacher, Miss Broome, whom he had visited: it was never published, but the Mogador setting was used to powerful effect in *No Laughing Matter*. The idea of the Ideal City or the Planned Utopia – of which Mogador presented a magical example – greatly interested Angus, as it had interested Perkin Walker's Crittall grandfather.)

They moved on, via the Hotel Marhaba in Taroudant, to the Hotel Majestic in Marrakesh, where Angus sat up on the roof in the full sun to work. On his winter travels abroad, he was often to be discovered on rooftops amidst flapping laundry, like an industrious Mr Toad disguised as a washerwoman: apart from the pleasure of the sun on the skin, it was a way of avoiding those inquisitive small children. Tony, shaded, did the typing, as he had done in Agrigento. Together they made good progress. Here Angus put together the autumn's research – a letter from the Ministry of Pensions on the long-term effects of poison gas, a letter from Viva King about fashions in underwear and sunbonnets in 1911, a suggestion from Patrick Woodcock that his elderly heroine's health problem should be high blood pressure, advice from Ian Merry about the kind of technical education one of the Calvert grandsons might need. The weather in the novel's Prologue (set in the hot summer of 1911, when Sylvia Calvert was a child) had been carefully checked against the meteorological records, and, in the blaze of North Africa, Angus wrote about the heat-wave in England two years before he was born. A hint that he was thinking of Betty Wilson and Winn's war wounds while writing of Sylvia Calvert appears in a postcard to Betty from Marrakesh: "I'm really in love with Morocco – we have 80 degrees of sun with these lovely snowy mountains in the background." On the first of February, 1964, on the hotel roof, he recorded "Problems in mid Chap 5". But he pressed on.

It was not all work. There were diversions and excursions and emotional dramas. In Essaouira, they became deeply entangled with a handsome young Moroccan, who had been working at the Hôtel des Iles, and who had been seduced into dreams of the grand life by distant memories of the legendary visit of Orson Welles and the film crew of *Othello*. (This disruptive visit was still vividly remembered in the town in 1994: the film had appeared in 1951.) An indiscretion had cost him his job at the hotel, and he had been brutally sacked with a note in French from the manager saying he had been dismissed "*à cause de scandale*". Angus and Tony befriended him: according to Tony he was "a lost shepherd boy". He attached himself to them as companion and guide in Essaouira, and when they departed for Marrakesh he pursued them with letters and requests for money. The requests continued (and were occasionally met) over years: letters and cards variously addressed to "*Cher amis*" or "*Cher Taouni*" or "*Cher Père Felsham Woodside*" or "*Cher Monsieur Wouilsson*" trickled in until the late 1970s, along with information about his health, his hospitalisations, his bad leg, his work plans, his unemployment, and his brother's funeral expenses. Tony and Angus were to send not only money (several small donations of eight or ten pounds) but also clothing (waist 28 inches, inner leg 24, outer leg 36, seat 34 and a half . . .). A photograph, dated April 1973, shows a proud and adult Ahmed in a Moroccan jellabah, cigarette in hand, posing over the corpses of four large wild boar. He was clearly pleased with his own progress, for he annotated it "*Regardez la différence de ma photo avant et maintenant faites la différence.*" This tragi-comedy ended happily.

In Marrakesh they met more sophisticated friends in the form of Philippe Jullian and Angus Heriot.* (Jullian was scathing about the unspeakable vulgarity of the Belgian hotel manageress, who had placed in the lavatory a sign in pokerwork which read

Ici tombe en ruines
L'architecture de la cuisine.)

Heriot was a historian, novelist, opera-lover, dilettante, and a friend of Mrs King – " dear, sweet enchanting old Etonian" according to Tony. His was to be a life of unfulfilled promise, a life that did not quite happen. On 26 January 1964, shortly after greeting Angus and Tony's arrival with delight, he killed himself in a car crash on the road from Marrakesh to Casablanca. Was it a suicide? Heriot had been involved with a Moroccan boy, and had hired a car, perhaps to meet him, had driven through torrential rains, had lost control of the car, and thus had died. He was in his mid-thirties. Philippe Jullian was desolated. So were they all.

Angus Wilson wrote a brief obituary note for Angus Heriot, published in *The Times* on 10 February 1964, paying tribute to his overflowing wit and fantasy, his "fascinating books" on such subjects as the Castrati in Opera and French Revolutionary Naples, his Firbankian flow of sheer funniness in half-a-dozen languages. It was a bitter loss of a young writer who might have achieved something remarkable. Angus Wilson became involved in protracted negotiations to prolong Heriot's afterlife by the publication of his last unfinished work: these came to nothing.

*

Angus and Tony returned to England via a brief visit to Tangiers, where they met Veronica Tennant, her cousin David Herbert, and Paul and Jane Bowles. They also met Jane Bowles's Berber friend, who cooked for them but did not speak a word of English and thumped their plates down in front of them with alarming force. They flew home on 27 February 1964, and delivered the typescript of *Late Call* in April. The response from publishers on both sides of the Atlantic was enthusiastic. Thank goodness, wrote David Farrer to Tom Guinzberg at Viking in New York, this was a saleable novel with human sympathy and likeable characters. There was a little checking for libel but otherwise all seemed set for autumn publication.

Angus, meanwhile, returned to meetings of the Bury Theatre

---

* Angus Heriot (1927–64) lived in London with Neil Macmillan in Manchester Square: they frequented Viva King's salon, and Macmillan had published a murder story in 1954 called *The Other Side of the Square* which used Viva's house as a setting. Angus reviewed it in the *Observer*, 6 June 1954. Heriot's first novel, *Orphan's Progress*, was published by Secker in 1957.

committee, lunch at the zoo with Melvyn Bragg, and a day or two in the London Clinic in May to have a bladder problem checked. Spring and summer brought the usual round of visitors, including Anne Wollheim (now separated from Richard Wollheim). Richard Wollheim, for no good reason, felt that Angus and Tony took Anne's side in the separation, and now saw less of Angus. (It had been at a party in Dolphin Square in 1957 that Wollheim had first met his second wife, Mary Day Lanier, whom he married in 1969.) Tony appeared as Bottom in the Nowton Court production of *A Midsummer Night's Dream*. Michael Tanner went with Angus and Tony to hear Britten's *Curlew River* at Orford Church but was unfortunately convulsed with giggles as they sat in a row immediately behind Britten and Pears: they went back to Felsham Woodside to recover over a high tea of ham and eggs.

There were many interchanges about a possible visit from John Osborne and Penelope Gilliatt, following Angus's request (immediately granted) to quote from and use *Look Back in Anger* as a theme in *Late Call*: Osborne said they would be delighted to come. ("What kind of people have you got? Will leave selection to you. Local queens, husky market gardeners, or Lady Christian Scientists would do fine."[2]) The Osbornes had to cancel once, for a trip to California (which Osborne said he loathed), but they rearranged the date and eventually spent a pleasant weekend at Felsham Woodside in late September: Osborne remembers that they went on a Sunday-morning tour of grand neighbours in grand houses, spreading the Gay Gospel, and lunched at Joan Colin's restaurant in Long Melford. There was still much talk of Tony's having lost his job, but Osborne did not recall that he demanded a horse, as Tony had nervously anticipated that he might. (At some point, Angus had visited the Osbornes in Sussex, where he was very rude about the Sussex countryside and insulted the tea roses, according to Osborne.)

On the public front, Angus attended a large Anti-Apartheid rally, addressed by Wedgwood Benn, on Sunday, 14 June 1964 in Trafalgar Square. The new Africa was emerging: Kaunda became the first President of Zambia in August, and Ian Smith arrived in London in September for talks on UDI in Southern Rhodesia. It was time to apply pressure. Angus had already put considerable energy into the cause: he signed the "Playwrights against Apartheid" boycott declaration in June 1963, and had spoken at another huge Trafalgar Square meeting in November 1963, along with Barbara Castle, Humphry Berkeley, Mervyn Stockwood and Vanessa Redgrave.* At one of the Trafalgar Square rallies he was

---

* In November 1965 Angus attended (with Iris Murdoch and Prof. Wedderburn) a press conference supporting a controversial academic boycott and he wrote for the AAM news sheet.

Mummy would say all that about his having to learn to take a joke and about his being highly strung and where could he have got it from, not from her. ~~Should not have feared,~~

~~But Johnnie feared not, to have feared,~~ like many children he did not fully estimate ~~Luckily~~ Anna's design in changing the conversation ~~without Johnnie's being involved~~ was effected ~~but therefore without~~ Johnnie's being involved. The topic of the old ladies at the farm became a general one, and although many of the things the others said made the little boy bite his lip, he was able to go on drawing on his knee ~~without being involved~~ with the feigned abstraction of a child among adults.

"My dear," said Grace to Dorothy "you really must meet them. They're the ~~most~~ wonderful pair of freaks. They live in ~~a~~ great barn of a farmhouse. The inside's like a museum, ~~my dear,~~ full of the most terrible junk mixed up with some really lovely things all mouldering to pieces. The family's been there for hundreds of years ~~out of you f~~ and they're madly proud of it. They won't let anyone do a single thing for them, although they're both well over seventy, and of course the result is the place is in the most frightful mess. It's really rather ghastly and one oughtn't to laugh, but if you could see

25 Inside Angus Wilson's cottage
at Felsham Woodside: the study (*top*),
sitting-room (*centre*) and dining-room

26 Mrs Revens
at Felsham Woodside

27 Morgan Forster the novelist meets
Morgan the Welsh cat, Felsham Woodside,
19 September 1963

28 Angus Wilson at work in Felsham Woodside
the photograph that appeared in the *Tatler*, 1 April 1959
(photograph by Kurt Hutton)

29 Angus Wilson in France
with (left) Douglas Cooper
and (right) John Richardson, 1952

30 Angus Wilson
with Tony Garrett
on holiday in France, 1950s

31 Angus Wilson at Christ's College, Cambridge,
with (left to right) Neil McKendrick, Sir John Plumb and Tony Garrett

32 Angus Wilson and Tony Garrett (photograph by Cecil Beaton)

33 Angus Wilson aboard the *Maxim Gorky* on his fiftieth birthday,
with William Golding (11 August 1963)

34 Angus Wilson and Tony Garrett
with Dutch literati, Amsterdam, 1960s

35 Angus Wilson with Dr Anne Thomas in her home
at New Vernon, New Jersey, 1983

36 Wilson Knight, Angus Wilson, Colin Wilson and Glen Cavaliero at the
John Cowper Powys Conference, Churchill College, Cambridge, September 1972

37 Angus Wilson as Orator at the
University of East Anglia

38 Pat Johnstone Wilson,
Angus Wilson's brother, in Lisbon

39 Colin (David) Johnstone Wilson,
Angus Wilson's brother, July 1966

photographed in the company of his old friend Alan Gray from the British Museum and Gray's black lover Lionel Davies, who met Gray after the failure of Gray's marriage and rescued him from the cruising grounds of Tooting Bec. (Gray remained on good terms with his former wife and family.)

Alan Gray and Lionel Davies were summer visitors at Felsham Woodside in 1963: the August of 1964 brought another fighter against apartheid, Randolph Vigne. Vigne, who had been so helpful during Angus's 1961 visit to South Africa, was now on the run, and he talked Southern African politics non-stop for two days in the blazing Suffolk sun. Angus told Vigne that he thought the days of communism were numbered, in South Africa as elsewhere – and Angus, with J.B. Priestley, was to part company with the Anti-Apartheid Movement as he increasingly perceived it as a willing instrument of Soviet foreign policy.

The memory of last summer's visit to the USSR had faded somewhat, according to a letter to Anna ("Nyuta") Kallin of the BBC Third Programme – Angus wrote to her from Morocco saying Russia now seemed very far away. She had been trying for months, since October 1963, to set up a programme in which Angus and C.P. Snow would discuss the Soviet Union, which the Snows had visited as Sholokhov's guests immediately after Angus's visit with COMES. Snow had received an honorary degree from the University of Rostov-on-Don, in polite exchange for the one he had bestowed on Sholokhov as Rector of St Andrews: Pamela Hansford Johnson's novel, *An Impossible Marriage*, had been translated into Russian. Angus had written to Anna Kallin saying that the idea would interest him, as he respected Snow's views more than his fiction: but that he did not think that Snow himself would agree to the proposition, as they had had a difference of opinion at a party of Jack Priestley's. (Pamela Snow had criticised him for being unfair about Snow's novels: Angus, for his part, confessed to Fred Warburg that Snow gave him nightmares.) Unfortunately, Snow eventually said he would be delighted to discuss Russia with Angus, and in April it was Angus who had to withdraw.*

Anna Kallin did not mind much. Relentlessly, she pressed Angus to come and talk about Morocco, about his new novel, about *anything*. Bravely he declined: he managed to do no broadcasts until the autumn, when he contributed to a radio portrait of Graham Greene and was himself

---

* Angus and Snow met amicably as fellow-speakers at Jack Priestley's seventieth birthday celebration at the Savoy on 14 September: this did not prevent Angus from continuing to snipe at Snow's reputation.

the subject of a similar portrait (broadcast 7 September 1964) in which
Joanna Kilmartin described how he had taught her how to cook carrots
(with sugar, in a frying-pan). Angus himself declared on this programme
that he was "sometimes enormously happy" but was also subject to
"extreme depressions, insomnias, and so on and so on . . . if I'd given up
writing I'd be a deeply embittered person . . ." He said that he was very
glad he had left the British Museum: he still had long bouts of worry about
security, but at least he was *not* embittered. He said this with much
emphasis.

V.S. Naipaul was in the chair, and he and Angus talked a little of Kipling,
Naipaul comparing Angus's early stories to Kipling's *Plain Tales from the
Hills*: Angus admired Naipaul's work, had strongly supported it at
Formentor, and was to continue to offer encouragement. They had met
several times on similar occasions: on one of them, in a hospitality room at
the BBC, Naipaul had been speaking about his dislike of promoting his
own works, for which he was attacked by BBC potentate, Grace
Wyndham Goldie: Angus sprang to Naipaul's defence. (On a subsequent
meeting, Angus had explained to Naipaul his own attitude to publicity –
"With me it's the old actress thing really: there are all those lovely people
out there: you reach out and make contact with them."[3]) Naipaul recalls
that Angus himself had been complaining not about promotion but about
his teeth – the twenty-nine-year-old Naipaul tried to console the forty-
eight-year-old Wilson for their loss by urging that they had served him for
a long time – a remark he was to remember with some chagrin.

Angus took the young Naipaul out to lunch at the Jardin des Gourmets,
and once invited him to a dinner of grouse which the vegetarian Naipaul
could not eat. Angus talked to him of South Africa, and on one occasion
burst out to him in a violent attack on Indians – he loathed Indians, Indian
piety, Indian sanctimoniousness. He did not count Naipaul as an Indian, he
said, but as "a negro from the Caribbean", and therefore exempt from his
criticism. (Were the words of Kushwant Singh still rankling, or the
memory of that maddening Indian in the next room in Vancouver who
had talked loudly on the phone every morning at 4 a.m. to somebody in
Bloomington?)

★

Through early September 1964, Angus and Tony lay low in Suffolk before
disappearing to Northern France for a short holiday. The weather was not
perfect, and Angus's temper was short – in Peronne after a tiring drive he
left the restaurant in a rage after insulting a widow's dog, then had to return
for humble pie as there was nowhere else to eat. They came back to an

autumn of teaching, theatre and library committees, literary lunches and dinners, TV appearances, speeches here and there, and a narrow Labour victory on 15 October 1964. There were plenty of invitations coming in – would Angus like to lecture at Rutgers or at the University of Southern California, would he like to do a British Council tour of Algiers and Tunis in the New Year? (Yes, he said, to the last of these, full of his new enthusiasm for North Africa: but the British Council had to cancel because it had forgotten about Ramadan.) He began to wonder if his teaching at the University of East Anglia, which he greatly enjoyed, might perhaps begin to interfere with his earning capacity as a freelance. He was finding himself obliged to turn down some lucrative offers.

He also came back from his French holiday to three publications, two in the same fortnight – *Late Call* on 9 November 1964; *Tempo* on 16 November and a revised reprint of *Zola* in December. *Tempo*, celebrated by a candle-lit party at the Cheshire Cheese, was not a very worrying matter: a short illustrated text, published by Studio Vista, it discussed "the impact of television on the arts." It was an efficiently-executed pot-boiler, and Angus expressed to his friends the hope that he would not have to write many more of such works: it had earned him £500.

The reception of *Late Call* was a more serious matter. How would the critics and readers respond to his first novel for three years?

★

The heroine of *Late Call* seems at first reading to have little in common either in character or circumstance with her creator. The novel breaks new social ground, and its main emphasis is set firmly in the present of the 1960s – a world of New Towns, comprehensive schools, nuclear disarmament, social workers, television soap opera and automatic ovens. Sylvia Calvert is the retired manageress of a South Coast hotel, but she comes from a different social drawer from the Kensingtonian manageresses of Angus's youth. She is the daughter of a poor and unsuccessful East Anglian farmer, married to a veteran ex-ranker invalid-scrounger Captain from the First World War: she has worked her way up from scrubbing floors to middle-class respectability, and her only surviving son, Harold, is the absolutely modern headmaster of a comprehensive school in a New Town in the Midlands. His three children are also working their way up through the social system. This is not a family in decline, like the Johnstone-Wilsons, but a family in the ascendant.

Yet this novel too contains an exploration of the past. As Sylvia Calvert struggles to understand the new technology and new attitudes of the *Look Back in Anger* generation, she is forced to re-examine her own brutalised childhood and sense of worthlessness, and she suffers a near breakdown as a consequence. The commonplace trauma of retirement – she has retired early through ill health – is described with sympathy, and her breakdown – like that of Meg Eliot and Angus himself – is a creative breakdown. She is able to use it to come to terms with a new role. During her illness, she is, like Meg, haunted by a sense of her own uselessness. Unlike Meg, she has had children, but two of those are dead, and she feels herself redundant in a world where grandsons as well as granddaughters take turns at cooking the evening meal. She has hideous visions of herself as fat, ugly, sprawling, fit only for the knacker's yard, and is haunted by stories about the murders of old women. Age is unnecessary, she fears.

Did Angus too, at Bletchley Park and now in middle age, suffer occasional spasms of terror about his own superfluity? Was there an undercurrent of anxiety in him about his own social role? What were his feelings about his childlessness, about the strange lack of reproductive energy in the whole of the Johnstone-Wilson family? (The Garretts too, one might note, were not reproductive: Tony had no children, and neither did his brother Philip or sister Genifer.) Were his novels a sufficient justification for his life? Should he not take on yet more and more compensatory social obligations, more and more good works? And if he did, would they kill him as a novelist?

*

Angus always said that the plot of *Late Call* came to him from the fleeting image of a stout elderly woman leaning on a gate and staring out from the New Town of Stevenage over the desolate wastes of rural England. "The idea of 'The Midlands' struck chilly upon her; looking before her at the vast fields, she imagined them stretching on and on across the middle of England. She saw them as one huge ploughed plain and herself on an endless, lonely walk across it, rather as in the far distance she could see a solitary tractor at work, its sole moving companion a flock of rooks and seagulls that fed in its wake."[4]

This is Bletchley Park territory once more, and here is another Midlands breakdown.* Sylvia Calvert, like Angus at Bletchley and Little Hadham, tries to wear herself out in body and mind by tramping pointlessly for longer and longer distances. Meg Eliot had her breakdown in the very English, very middle-class-gentry South Downs (which Angus too had walked in his own depression). Sylvia's takes place in a bleaker landscape.

---

* Bletchley was designated a New Town Development Area in a White Paper published on 19 March 1964: a decision that led to its being surrounded by the myriads of mini-roundabouts of Milton Keynes.

Meg Eliot in early middle age was handsome and physically fit. Sylvia, in her sixties, is overweight and has high blood pressure. Angus himself looked both ways.

Angus had researched his New Towns and his comprehensive schools and his local politics. For a subplot which turns on planning permission for a piece of land called Goodchild's Meadow, he re-utilised the local government material he had assembled for *Goat and Compasses*. He also made forays to Harlow and Basildon, and talked to architects, town planners and educationalists who worked for the new egalitarian classless society of Essex man. The buildings of the University of East Anglia rose from the mud, and new shopping centres opened up and down England. Angus welcomed the future. But at times it all seemed very heavy going. The earth looked raw. The mud clung to the boot.

Late Call took him into an unfamiliar social world – there are no hostesses, no acrimonious academics, no mandarins or playboys or dandies here, although there is one homosexual Calvert in the rag trade, who moves in a camp Carshall the others never see. Most of the characters are serious, ordinary, hard-working. The action, apart from the Prologue, is seen consistently through the eyes of Sylvia, an intelligent but uneducated woman little practised in self-analysis, although she is a shrewd (if inexperienced) observer of others. Yet Angus makes this world wholly convincing in its own terms. He satirises its obsessions, but appears to find it as absorbing as do its inhabitants. Technically, the work is a *tour de force*.

His entrée was partly through the democratic medium of television. He had been watching professionally for some time now ("marooned," as he once wrote, "in darkest East Anglia").[5] *Tempo* dealt with television treatment of the arts, but Angus was equally fascinated by the broad spectrum of lower-middle-class viewing. (He loved Cliff Michelmore and the *Tonight* programme.) Sylvia is addicted to a family soap called "Down Our Way", which she attempts to use, not always successfully, as a point of contact with her grandchildren and her acquaintances in Carshall. The unrealities of the soap family are contrasted with the real and uncomfortable family dynamics of the Calverts. Harold's wife, Beth, has recently died of cancer: this is not the kind of event that took place in early Sixties popular viewing (when the very word "cancer" was banned from women's magazines). And Sylvia reacts indignantly when one of her favourite "village novelists" tries to introduce a more sombre note in the form of the spinster-heroine's mild heart attack. This is not what she expects from light reading. But when the reading gets *too* light – the boss anonymously paying for the convalescent secretary's romantic holiday and declaring his passion for her – Sylvia is also unsatisfied. The pastiche of popular culture, as one would expect, is accurate, sometimes prophetic, but Angus is making a serious point about escapism, social bonding and the lies we live by.

There were dangers in both subject-matter and technique, acutely spotted by Colin Wilson who felt that Angus verged on soap opera, and who objected to his cosy and overfamiliar use of his character's Christian names: a fair objection to one who had made fun of Colin Wilson's own persistent use of eccentric surnames. Angus shared these worries: his planning notebooks record anxiety about the "Mrs Dale's Diary" and "Booth Tarkington" aspects of his project, and he admonished himself with the word "Beware!"

Angus had few identifiable real-life models for his Carshall cast. Country living had introduced him to Mrs Baker and Mrs Hill, and to Mrs Revens, about whose family and affairs he now heard much, as well as to the Corkes, the Cooksons, the Brookeses, the Gilliatts, and the various co-patrons of the Bury Theatre Royal fund. But neither group fitted the New Town model. Perhaps Tony's mother, Margaret Garrett, had supplied some hints. Mr Garrett, himself a war veteran, may have spun some of Arthur Calvert's yarns. Tony had kept on close terms with all his family, and took his mother on a holiday every year, of the sort that might well have delighted a Sylvia Calvert – a week in a well-vetted hotel in the Cotswolds or the Lakes. Angus knew both Garrett parents well, and there was an unspoken recognition of Tony's relationship with Angus. ("Thank you for lending me Tony," Mrs Garrett wrote to Angus, after one of these outings with her son. "Thank you for the lovely gift of pepper pots," wrote Angus, after one of his birthdays.)

Elizabeth Smart said that Angus told her that Sylvia Calvert was modelled on his own mother, but as the venue for this confidence was a publisher's party (at Ye Olde Cheshire Cheese, to celebrate *Tempo*) perhaps this should not be taken too seriously.[6] It seems unlikely.* But other friends and family members may have come in useful. Both his nieces, Jeanne and Sybil, had married men far removed from the Johnstone-Wilson mould. Jeanne's husband, Glyn Davies, was a Senior Customs Officer who shared Jeanne's love of the theatre, and became a keen and skilled amateur film-maker, successfully adapting some of Angus's short stories – indeed, he and Jeanne had first met while indulging in amateur theatricals. Sybil's husband, Richard Scott, whom she had met through Angus and married in 1948, was an engineer, whose career took

---

* But he did tell Jay Halio (11 April 1980) that though there was much of Mrs Garrett in Sylvia, there was also a little of his own mother – or at least of her predicament: what was a woman to do with the last years of her life?

him and his family to China, India and the Far East. Sybil, like her mother, was a talented painter, but she did not move in artistic circles. Was there a touch of Winn's widow, Betty Wilson, in Sylvia? Betty, like Sylvia Calvert, had been called upon late in life to earn her own living, and had shown an unexpected independence in her retirement in Seaford.

The Scott and Davies nephews and nieces were a little young to suggest much of the personalities of the adolescent Calverts, but Angus knew them well, and through them the problems of the educational system, the rapidly changing world of the teenager. He was a conscientious and affectionate uncle, who not only peppered nieces and nephews with postcards but also took trouble to learn their interests and offer help as they grew older. He took an interest in the children of his friends: he would talk to them for hours, and he and Tony were famous for their delightful gifts. Celia and Paul Jennings, who asked them to Christmas parties at East Bergholt, remember their arriving one year with what looked depressingly like a book, but, more excitingly, turned out to be a large box of chocolates disguised as a book.

Mark James, the young schoolteacher friend of Michael Howard, thinks he may have played a part in the creation of Sylvia's grandson Mark, the Aldermaston marcher. (Angus himself was never a member of CND: in reply to an invitation to address a local group he wrote, "I am of course deeply & inevitably concerned about this question but I have never been associated with the campaign or its aims & methods.")[7] Penny Corke (now Penny Turner), daughter of Martin and Jean Corke, believes she inspired the authentic horse-talk of young Judy Calvert, the talk which so annoys her egalitarian father, Harold. Penny was brought up with horses: her father, unlike Harold, was a rider and a huntsman, and at the age of seven she herself had been blooded in Bradfield Woods. She lived in her jodhpurs and for her pony. Angus, who did not really approve of the hunt, and who complained when hounds raced through his garden (and on one occasion into the cottage), would listen to her for hours as she talked about her pony Edward. He would settle her down by the fire at the rectory, and encourage her to chat. It was years later that she realised – and he confessed – that he had been using her as a source. (*Late Call* was dedicated to her parents, Martin and Jean Corke.)

Yet again, the ever-useful Denis Barnes must have come in handy, for he was not only an offspring of the old grammar-school regime, he was also an architect of the new. His team was on the move. Harold Wilson was elected a month after the publication of *Late Call* on a manifesto of "purposive planning" and public control of steel, water and building land. Reform was to be powered by the white heat of a scientific revolution, triumphantly announced a year earlier at the Labour Party Conference in Scarborough. Angus's novel apppeared at a good moment. It captured the optimistic spirit of its time.

But the optimism was shadowed by doubts from the past. Angus's short story, "A Flat Country Christmas", somewhat resembles *Late Call* in background: it describes two young left-wing couples on Christmas night, 1949.[8] The Slaters (he overworking as he tries to struggle out of the Technical Grade to an Inspectorship) live in a bungalow on a new housing estate, "so almost in the country", with a view of "flat marshy fields, broken here and there by a muddy stream or a huge oak in the last decay of majesty"; their friends Sheila and Eric, she rich Guildford, he ambitious educated Cockney, live nearby in a small Edwardian house with a derelict conservatory. They dine together, deplore the lack of social activity in the area ("you'd think there'd be a dramatic society or something"), discuss devolution and the last war, and then in some desperation play a game of looking for the future in a mirror. It all goes wrong when Ray Slater says he can see Nothing, and bursts into tears.

What survives best in the story is the sense of almost intolerable strain. This generation, which had fought in the war, which had clambered up the ladder of educational opportunity, which had cross-married and kicked away the conventional supports of class, was still having to struggle night and day for survival. The past was being demolished and falling into disrepair all around them: the present was shapeless, lonely, naked, raw: the future was, perhaps, a blank. Angus knew several young couples who had worked as hard as this and perhaps had been brushed with this fear. Would their lives ever brighten, would their gardens ever mature, would their dreams of a better and fairer society ever be fulfilled, or were they doomed to the friendless housing estate for life? *Late Call* is in part his answer. And it is at least moderately confident.

*

Angus awaited the reception of *Late Call* with his usual anxiety. When it came, it was encouraging. Monica Dickens liked it very much, and so did Madge Gillespie, who wrote "I am old fashioned you know and can't appreciate all you write, but this I really found quite to my taste." Betty Wilson also wrote from Seaford, and amidst bits of family news (including the latest about the fate of Pat's one-time tea room) commented "I personally think it your best, except for your short stories." Did they represent a new, more broadly based middle-class readership? His publishers hoped so.

Most of the reviews were all they could have hoped for. Many mentioned a new "compassion", and Christopher Ricks in the *Sunday Times*, John Gross in the *Observer*, and Francis King in the *Sunday Telegraph* all gave high praise. Angus must have been particularly pleased by a long, well-informed, well-written analysis in the *New Statesman*. It was by Francis Hope, the young man who had expected so much from Angus, and who was not now disappointed. Hope, one of the most perceptive critics of his generation, had appreciated precisely the magnitude of the task Angus had set himself in writing about a society "with no conventional foundations or landmarks", and concluded that he had succeeded brilliantly: he also, with a characteristically prophetic insight, looked forward to the effects of Angus's interest in Dickens, theatre and mimicry on future fiction. Another young man who much admired the novel was Michael Ratcliffe, who did a sympathetic radio interview with Angus on the Third Programme about it.

Not everybody was won over. Arthur Calder-Marshall in the *Financial Times* mentioned the dreaded *Mrs Dale's Diary* and John Daniel in the *Guardian* roped in H.E. Bates and the Larkins. The *Times Literary Supplement*, which had been fairly rude about most of Angus's previous novels, now decided that he was not as good as he had been, and that Sylvia was a bore. The word "sentimental" surfaced here and there, as Fred Warburg tactlessly pointed out in a letter of congratulation. Angus cannot have been very pleased by the success of Snow's *Corridors of Power*, which also appeared that season, and was reviewed in tandem in some papers; it stayed longer in the best-seller lists. The proximity of Christine Brooke-Rose's post-catastrophe novel, *Out*, was more congenial. But Angus scored well in the "Book of the Year" choices, and Warburg assured him that he was "a top novelist from egghead to pop levels" and was reprinting:[9] Edmund Wilson wrote saying both he and Elena had read the book with great enthusiasm – "The use of the Prologue is masterly and I don't remember anyone else's doing anything like it in the way of changing the reader's perspective."

In this, Edmund Wilson showed more percipience than many. Some simply failed to connect the Prologue with the text at all, and others came up with the irritating old cry that it was as good as a short story, and would work better on its own. The allegations against Angus's lack of structural sense can at times be re-interpreted as his readers' failures in structural reading. The episode of the Old Woman's Story, also praised by Edmund Wilson, caused even more difficulty than the Prologue: the confused monologue of this slightly dotty and meaninglessly cultured European was intended by Angus to contrast the fruits of stupid highbrow reading with those of intelligent lowbrow reading, and may have owed something to his impatience with the high-flown platitudes of the French delegation in the USSR. Some readers were unable to make any sense of it. Was the failure theirs, or his?

Some six months later, in the spring of 1965, *Late Call* appeared in French, as *L'Appel du Soir*, published by Stock. Angus must have arranged for a complimentary copy to be sent to Henri de Montherlant, whose work he greatly admired, and with whom he had been in mutually pleasing correspondence a year earlier over his favourable *Observer* review of de Montherlant's extraordinary black comedy, *Chaos and Night*, excellently translated by Terence Kilmartin. De Montherlant wrote to thank Angus for *L'Appel du Soir*, in a scarcely legible letter dated 21 July, 1965:

Cher Mr Angus Wilson

Au moment d'ouvrir votre livre le désir m'est venu de le lire en anglais. Pouvez-vous dire à votre editeur à m'en arranger un exemplaire? Et, bien entendu, sans vous embarrasser de l'exécrable habitude français de dédicace.

Merci

Croyez au grand plaisir qu j'en ai . . . m'agréez, cher Monsieur . . .

H. de Montherlant

There is something peculiarly pleasing about the notion of this poorly-sighted alleged misogynist attempting to pick his way in English through the English adventures of Sylvia Calvert in a New Town: he undertook the task conscientiously, helping himself out occasionally ("*je l'avoue à ma honte*") with the French version. He wrote to Angus on 10 September 1965 to say that he was frequently interrupting the progress of his own novel to read *Late Call* – "*C'est un extraordinaire dépaysement pour un écrivain français, en train de créer son monde français, d'entrer dans le vôtre. Il me semble que vous avez voulu écrire la tragi-comédie . . .*" – an exercise the wisdom of which he questioned. Why make the effort to enter into the idiocies of the lives of others, he asked.

De Montherlant himself was nearing the end of his tether. The book on which he was working at this time was probably *Les Garçons* (1969): on 21 September 1972, he was to shoot himself. Angus met him only once, in his Paris apartment on the Quai Voltaire: Angus was offered a sweet liqueur cordial upon arrival, at ten thirty in the morning, and was moved by it to compliment M. De Montherlant on the beauties of his *anti-chambre*. "*L'anti-chambre!*" de Montherlant had protested. "*Ce n'est pas l'anti-chambre, c'est le salon même.*"

De Montherlant could hardly have been more unlike the majority of

Sylvia's admirers. But there were many of these, and there were, through a successful television adaptation shown in March 1975, to be more. Tony and Angus could conclude that *Late Call* and the Moroccan experiment which had helped to create it had been successful. They decided to return to Morocco again the next winter, after spending another Christmas *en famille* in Kent.

AT HOME AND ABROAD:
THE GLOBAL VILLAGE

Late Call had extended Angus's middlebrow readership. But unlike Hugh Walpole and Compton Mackenzie he had not settled for "the broad highway of the middlebrow novel".[1] He remained an adventurer.

On 2 January 1965, after a quiet family Christmas in Kent, Angus and Tony had an adventure which nearly prevented them from getting back to Morocco at all. As Tony drove back from a lunch party, the car skidded off the road on black ice. The car sustained nearly three hundred pounds worth of damage, and Angus sprained his arm quite badly.

They had been lunching with Richard Chopping and Denis Wirth-Miller, an artistic and Bohemian couple who were in those days famous for drinking: they lived in a house on the quay in Wivenhoe, near Colchester, and were friends of Francis Bacon (who also lived for a while at Wivenhoe), John Minton (with whom Gerard Reve had shared a flat for a while in 1952), and the Roberts MacBryde and Colquhoun. Chopping designed book jackets for Ian Fleming's thrillers and had proposed a jacket for *Late Call* which never materialised: he and Wirth-Miller had worked together to illustrate several pleasant works such as *Butterflies in Britain* (1945) and a charming children's Baby Puffin book of chopped-up people, *Head, Bodies & Legs* (1946), but they also represented the side of Angus's life that had been deliberately excluded from *Late Call*. (Angus had at one point thought of setting a scene with the gay grandson, Ray Calvert, in London, but had decided to stick with the unity of place.) Denis and Dicky, as they were known, thrived on scandalous behaviour: they knew everybody in the gay overworld and underworld of East Anglia as well as in Soho, and they were generous hosts – perhaps too generous. They went in for flyting matches: they would quarrel vociferously in a stylised manner which some found amusing, others appalling. Their relationship endured through many storms.

Angus and Tony saw something of them in the 1950s, and the friendship had been renewed when Angus read the typescript of Richard Chopping's novel, *The Fly*. (Chopping excelled in insect drawings: the fly was his trade mark.) This was definitely one of Chopping's unpleasant works: it was a scatological and audaciously squalid tale of office life, with a central conceit of a ubiquitous, voyeuristic fly, and it was published, not unsuccessfully, by Secker & Warburg (to whom Angus recommended it) in January 1965: Angus's copy bears the inscription "To Angus without whose help and advice this novel would neither have been finished nor published – from Dicky with love and gratitude. December 1964." Fred Warburg had referred to it dubiously as "a remarkable and rather revolting book whose sales possibilities are hard to estimate," but in fact it did rather well, and reprinted.[2] Secker & Warburg were also to publish Chopping's second novel, *The Ring*, in 1967: in his rather equivocal report Angus noted as an aside, ". . . I have something of a distaste for the male sexual organs and found my distaste clothing itself in the excuse that I was bored by the constant repetition of the crotch motif." (Fred Warburg replied that this was "quite one of the most brilliant reports I have ever read from you or anyone else . . .")[3]

Having more or less recovered from this New Year accident, Angus flew off alone from the black ice of Suffolk to Lisbon, where he had arranged to see his brother Colin/David. Colin was still living in dignified poverty and by now, since Pat's death, in intense solitude in the Rua da Lapa, teaching a few classes, worrying about his duodenal ulcer (aggravated by a diet of "kangaroo and zebra, alias veal"), and deploring the Labour government back home. The cranks, he said, had taken over from the crooks, and he had heard that the Cromwell Road was full of Kaffirs: what would Tillie Frank have said? Angus had received a half-hearted offer to stay in Pat's room: the house had no central heating, Colin threatened in his letter of invitation, and as the Lisbon winter was bitterly cold, Angus would really be better off in the small hotel of a French Jewess he knew . . .

The two brothers, who on one level hardly knew one another, talked and talked. They reminisced about their childhood, and Colin reminded Angus of the Earls Court Exhibitions which the family had visited – there had been one on the theme of the Wild West, and Willie had been very fond of a song about Buffalo Bill, but neither of them could quite remember the words.

In Lisbon, Angus also had a rendezvous with John Croft, his old friend from Bletchley Park days, who was to share the first part of the working holiday in Morocco. (John Croft was not introduced to Colin.) Angus and Croft were due to fly to Casablanca, where they would be met by Tony with a hired car. This elaborate plan nearly failed at the first leg, as the car ferry from Gibraltar was delayed, but after many troubles with customs and insurance Tony managed to get to Tangiers where he went to bed with a heavy cold and de Sade's *Juliette*. The next day Tony noted in his diary that it was "pissing down with rain", but after a five-hour drive he managed to meet Croft and "Willy" (as he now privately called Angus) at Casablanca airport.

An American translation of de Sade, in four volumes, was to be their holiday reading, and de Sade's endlessly repetitive descriptions of "reciprocal friggeries" caused much mirth. Angus had recently reviewed a version of *Justine* edited by Hull Walton, in which he had wondered when English readers would ever be allowed to encounter unexpurgated versions of *La Nouvelle Justine, Les 120 Journées de Sodome*, or *La Philosophie dans le Boudoir*. De Sade, he claimed, had a small nugget of originality in a mass of chaotic pseudo-philosophy: he alone had perceived the dangers of nascent eighteenth-century humanitarianism, he alone had seen that "to weep excessively at some one else's pain was very close to enjoying the spectacle."[4]

The following morning the trio set off for Marrakesh, where they spent several days sight-seeing: amongst the sights were Stephen and Natasha Spender, who were "edgy about T.S. Eliot" over dinner, but much jollier over breakfast.

They then drove off across the Atlas mountains, crossing them without difficulty, and reached Ouarzazate, only to break down completely on the way to Ksar es Souk. There were no reliable mechanics around, and a high wind was blowing across the desert. John Croft hitched a truck lift back to Ouarzazate, where he organised a search party to rescue Angus and Tony from the jackals and the cold night. They all returned to Ouarzazate and were stranded there for a few days, waiting for mechanics or spare parts: it was during this stay that Croft witnessed first-hand one of Angus's outbursts, when he "verbally savaged, in a torrent of French, some man who had jumped the queue at the hotel desk. Underlying the friendly open exterior that Angus habitually presented, there was an element of hysteria . . . and of sadism . . ."[5]

The car fixed (though not very permanently) on they went, to Taroudant, Tiznit, and Tafraout: things looked up, and Angus was enchanted when they reached the Southern States after the desert. In Essaouira they were met by a *"très chique"* Ahmed, who was "obviously very pleased" to see them, and then by a feverish Martyn Goff, also very pleased to see them. (Goff, who had written a fan letter to Angus about *Hemlock*, was at this stage still a bookseller: he became Director of the

National Book League in 1970, and went on to achieve a high profile as promoter and manager of the Booker Prize.) Goff was so sick that he had left his holiday reading (Doris Lessing, not de Sade) behind in Ouarzazate: he was running a high temperature and arrived at the Hôtel des Iles more or less slumped over the wheel. Angus and Tony rescued him and found him "a proper doctor" – the fear of finding himself at the mercy of a wild witch doctor had been making him feel even worse.

Ramadan ended on 3 February, and Angus and Tony were entertained by Ahmed's family and received by the Calif. They also made the acquaintance of a new young Moroccan, Mohammed from Larache, who was to prove even more persistent (and who, says Tony, was "much more fly") than Ahmed. Then it was time to settle down to work, time for other visitors to depart. Angus started to write an *Observer* review of *The Letters of Charles Dickens, 1820–1939*, edited by Humphry House's widow Madeline and Graham Storey: he was also beginning to have ideas for the new novel as he went back over those conversations about childhood with Colin in Lisbon. The call of the past was strong, and Angus was reduced to tears by a report that the Trocadero was closing down. He was also distressed by a "silly letter" from David Farrer hoping to see the new novel "soon": Angus wrote back saying that he needed time, needed money, and why hadn't *Late Call* sold more copies? (The word "silly" was applied by Tony, in his pocket diary: both he and Angus no doubt understood well enough that publishers felt obliged to keep on making encouraging noises, lest they be accused by their sensitive authors of indifference or neglect, but nevertheless at times these well-intentioned attentions struck Angus unhappily.) On 17 February he developed a high temperature: was it malaria, typhus or anxiety? On 28 February they had had to send an SOS to Perkin Walker asking him to leave ten pounds cash for them at Regent's Park Terrace to await their return: travellers' allowances were still restricted and they were running out of cash.

They remained in Morocco for another two weeks, travelling a little, working a little. On 11 March they found themselves in Tangiers, where they spent five days, and dined with Veronica Tennant and Jane Bowles: Paul was away, but Jane generously helped them out with their currency problems. (Years later Angus repaid the generosity by visiting Paul Bowles in hospital in London with piles of books.)[6] Tony, in his letter of thanks written from the Rock Hotel in Gibraltar, gave her their Suffolk address, and said that if she lost it, she would find it in the Penguin edition of Beckett's *Malone Dies* which they had left behind, and Angus added a postscript – "Thank you and all the others for so much friendliness and hospitality to us – if the Moroccans have all the beauty, at least the European and American residents have a great deal of charm –"[7]

They got home on Wednesday, 17 February 1965, but David Farrer's hope that Angus would come home with a finished typescript was very wide of the mark. Angus's next novel was the most complex and ambitious of his career, and it took him many months to write. But he had, despite the setbacks and the anxieties and his painful arm, enormously enjoyed the trip: he wrote to Philippe Jullian saying he had "adored it" – so much so that he and Tony were thinking of buying a house in Morocco. Martyn Goff thoughtfully sent them an estate agent's list, with tempting properties in Tangiers ranging from two thousand pounds to an architect-designed bungalow for twelve and a half thousand – but this was to remain a pipe dream. Other Moroccan plans – to write a guidebook to the country, to write a life of the romantic French general Lyautey – also came to nothing.

Angus returned to a mass of unanswered correspondence, eager students, a new car (another Austin Westminster, this time in Blue Royale), a dinner of jugged hare with George Coulson and Thomas Hutton, and a visit from Yukio Mishima. Mishima, whom Angus had first met in 1960 in New York, now arrived somewhat improbably for a night at Felsham Woodside and lunch at The Bull in Long Melford with Gerard Reve. It is not easy to imagine this Japanese exotic in Suffolk. Mishima wrote an exquisite letter of thanks in a fine clear hand:

A whole day you kindly gave me in Suffolk is absolutely unforgettable. Completely relaxed, I enjoyed your enchanting talk and restful atmosphere of country. Through our common *virtue*, I did not feel any language barrier between us in spite of my poor ability to speak English. It was a wonderful meeting of a great bird in England and a little strange bird from Far East.

Your friend Mr Trevor-Roper was very kind to me and gave me nice interesting views in London. Please send my thanks to him.

I am very grateful for Tony's excellent hospitality. I believe he is a seldom man who knows penetratively how a lonely traveller feels and how he could be entertained.

I have thousands of words I still would like to talk with you, but I am irritated that my writing never follows quickly my own real feeling. Hoping enthusiastically to see you again, yours sincerely, Yukio Mishima.

March 31,65.

According to Trevor-Roper, the interesting views were of the gay night life of London, or such as, on request, he could summon forth: he feared it might have proved disappointing after the notorious gay bars of Tokyo. That seldom man, Tony Garrett, remembered the visit vividly, and years later wrote his version in his Journal for 1979: "7 October ... Found life of Yukio Mishima. Remembered his staying with us in country and how reserved yet with inner calm, and then lively and amusing – ? to me in morning, wanted us to go to bed together, but would make no move because it might be insult to A. Incredible lunch at Long Melford (? others there) anyway Yukio, A. and Gerard van het Reve – 3 prima donnas." He also recalled that the night before, after Angus had gone to bed, the vain and body-obsessed Mishima had raised his kimono to display his legs, and had said "My legs! What can I do? Chest of strong man. Legs of old maid."[8]

Mishima himself gave an account of his visit in a newspaper article for *Mainichi*: he recorded that he and Angus had talked largely about English manners. Angus had said that "while in Victorian times men used to retire from the dinner table to a room by themselves and drink for two or three hours to get dead drunk, reluctantly returning to join the women folk, these days they were becoming meek, returning after only thirty minutes; that in his childhood it had been the etiquette in English middle-class families to leave some food unfinished on the plate for the benefit of the poor ..." Talk had moved on to the aristocratic airs and social respectability of John Gielgud, and to Kabuki actors in the Meiji era. Mishima said he had enjoyed it all immensely.[9]

Angus was back from Morocco in good time for the April opening of the Theatre Royal in Bury, and crowned his years of fund-raising by luring Sandy Wilson down for a night in May to see an amateur production of *The Boy Friend*. Sandy Wilson stayed the night at Felsham Woodside: he had forgiven Angus his bad review of *Valmouth*. Angus and Tony gave a drinks party for him at Sunday lunchtime, and invited many of the local theatre supporters to meet him.

These theatrical activities were both a pleasure and an anxiety. Angus, as a Suffolk celebrity, had become much involved with the Restoration Appeal, as had several of his close friends, including Martin Corke, a director of the Greene King Brewery which owned the building. The Theatre Royal, designed by William Wilkins, architect of the National Gallery in London, had originally opened in 1819, and had closed in 1925: for years it had been used as a barrel store. It was now restored to its Regency splendour, but only after years of time-consuming committee meetings. Various local dignitaries and stars of the theatre world – the Duke of Grafton, Lord Euston, Mrs Ironside-Wood, Miss Pleydell-Bouverie, the Tudor-Craigs from Ickworth, Tess and Victor Rothschild,

Frederick Ashton and Benjamin Britten – gave their names and money to the cause, and some of them gave their energy as well. From 1960 onwards Angus had attended meetings at The Dog and Partridge, the Westgate Brewery Board Room, the Guildhall and the Shire Hall: he wrote letters to Nikolaus Pevsner and Binkie Beaumont, negotiated a connection with Cambridge-based Prospect Productions, and eventually enlisted support from Jennie Lee, as Arts Minister, and Lord Goodman at the Arts Council. He was a member of Prospect's Advisory Council from 1963. He used his contacts conscientiously, and conjured up John Gielgud, through his friend Patrick Woodcock, to give his *Seven Ages of Man*.

It was not all plain sailing: there were storms in teacups, backstairs squabbles, resignations, tantrums, and some of the meetings conflicted with Angus's teaching days at UEA. Letters about Bury theatre politics and finances had reached him even in Essauoira. But by and large, the Appeal was a triumph, and for years Angus and Tony remained closely connected with the theatre. Actress Maria Aitken (daughter of Sir William Aitken, MP for Bury 1950–63) remembers that when she was appearing at the Theatre Royal in *The School for Scandal* she was taken out to tea at Felsham Woodside, and was courteously received by a mauve-haired Angus Wilson, who held court without rising from his chair. It was a magisterial, formal tea: Tony hovered helpfully with the sandwiches. She took it that Angus was one of the fixed sights of the Suffolk double-barrelled theatre circuit – indeed, she seems to recall that one of the Pope-Hennessys had something to do with the introduction.

But despite their close involvement, Angus and Tony declined Olga Ironside-Wood's invitation to appear together there in Robin Rook's production of *Hamlet* in the autumn of 1966. Angus would have appeared as Polonius, Tony as Claudius: an opportunity missed.

Olga Ironside-Wood of Clopton Hall, renowned for her production of *Murder in the Cathedral*, was a well known enthusiast. There was a keen amateur group in Bury, which included Joan Jenkins, her brother Cyril Croger, and John Petch: the last two names recur frequently in Angus's diary. But the most prominent figures in this scene were Charles and Neville Blackburne, famous for their Nowton Court productions, of which Tony was becoming quite a star. Originally performed in the open air at the Court, some eventually transferred to the restored Theatre Royal. Angus much enjoyed them, and told Neville and Charles that watching the boys in Shakespeare was not like watching children at all, but like watching a play through the wrong end of a telescope – perfect but miniature. Over the years, however, Angus became anxious and jealous – "restive" was the Blackburne word for it – if Tony spent too much time on rehearsals: Angus did not like being left alone to fend for himself in the cottage for too long.

The three Blackburnes were well known in Suffolk. The family came to East Anglia in 1936 when their father, previously a canon of Winchester and an Archdeacon in Surrey, was appointed Dean of Ely: Neville was at Winchester, Charles at Charterhouse, and both went to Cambridge, where they were members of the Footlights, and they had many friends in the professional theatre. In 1946 Charles and Neville founded the preparatory school at Nowton Court, near Bury: Martin Corke's mother had discovered the building for them. Charles ran it, Neville was known as the "*éminence grise*" behind it, and Betty, a large and at times – at least to small boys – terrifying bulldog of a woman, was matron. The writer and journalist William Chislett remembers his time there with great pleasure: Betty's gruff and brusque battle-axe manner concealed a shy vulnerability and a great kindness, and she was a great help in crises. All three Blackburnes were very fond of children, and took them very seriously. Chislett recalled seeing both Angus and Tony at High Table for dinner, and on at least one occasion (in July 1965) Angus presented the prizes. The school laid a strong emphasis on the arts – as well as the celebrated dramas, there were also Thursday-evening opera sessions with a score round a gramophone, and much encouragement to read adult fiction. Sherry was served of an evening to thirteen-year-old boys: Nowton Court was a Cambridge college in miniature. Tess Rothschild, who had played Gertrude to Neville's Player Queen at Cambridge, thought highly of it, and so did the Kilmartins.

Chislett described the Blackburnes as "a very Ivy Compton-Burnett sort of family": they talked a great deal about "what Daddy would have done" and "what Daddy would have thought". (Daddy had died in 1951.) Some thought they took eccentricity too far – what kind of parents would entrust their children to this strange trio, to this gloomy Gothic ivy-shrouded pile hidden amongst dripping conifers? – but others remember sunlight and music, with birds tapping at the window and rabbits and squirrels on the lawns. The Blackburnes provided a cultivated oasis in a somewhat philistine county. In 1952 Neville had published a book called *Ladies' Chain* (about "famous women of the eighteenth and nineteenth centuries" – rather a Willie Johnstone-Wilson title), and he wrote a life of Crabbe, *The Restless Ocean* (1974), which Angus reviewed favourably. Neville also complied an anthology about children in Dickens, a subject on which he and Angus could talk for hours. Tony and Charles exchanged over the decades many letters and postcards with excruciating schoolboy jokes which tickled them both. ("What do you get if you pour hot water down a rabbit hole?" "Hot cross bunnies.") Notes on Betty Blackburne and Blackburnes in general can be found dotted through Angus's notebooks: they were a wonderfully stimulating mixture of personal oddity and archetypal Englishness. They were also loyal friends in times of trouble: with them Angus did not have to sparkle all the time.

Tony, this summer, appeared as Boyet in their production of *Love's Labours Lost*. In July Angus attended another school performance – the end-of-term Election Dinner at Westminster, where he dined on Roast Aylesbury Duckling Bigarrade and Japonaise Salad, and saw the boys deliver their traditional after-dinner Greek and Latin epigrams. He was not on this occasion alluded to by name in the verses, as were the Liberal lords Byers and Rea, Sidney Bernstein of Granada Television, and one or two others; this distinction was yet to come.

★

Television, as it happened, was a subject that now much preoccupied Angus; it was responsible for some of the delay in the progress of his next novel. He was no longer much interested in writing original television drama: his last attempt, "Come in out of the Cold", about two penurious students who pass their honeymoon in a Common Cold Research Unit, was dropped by ATV at the outline stage. (The plot was no doubt inspired by Forrest Fulton, who ran such a unit without, alas, discovering a cure.) No, it was as a "personality" that he was now in demand. He had been wooed by Huw Wheldon and Melyvn Bragg at the BBC, and by Lew Grade at ATV. Bragg, who was about to publish his own first novel, *For Want of a Nail*, with Secker, had made a film about Angus at the cottage for a series called *The Writer's World* in which Angus had talked about his work with Hans Keller and Robin Ironside.[10] Angus had appeared on many literary chat shows, including *Not So Much a Programme, More a Way of Life* (where he had been very funny at the expense of Snow) and *Take it Or Leave it*. The latter, on which he appeared six times in 1965, was a potentially humiliating BBC2 quiz, devised by Brigid Brophy, in which a panel of authors was asked to identify passages by unnamed writers. Each passage would be read aloud, then each panellist would be asked to suggest an author. The joy for the viewer lay in watching experts like Cyril Connolly, Anthony Burgess or John Betjeman make hopelessly inept guesses, or fail to recognise a piece from a book they had reviewed the week before. Passages chosen were sometimes easy, sometimes obscure to the point of torment: on one occasion one panellist had not only not read any of the books, she had never even heard of any of their authors.[11] The joy for the performer lay in the fee (money for jam, said Betjeman), the

BBC hospitality room (in those days generously stocked), and the amusing company. Mary McCarthy called it the best literary club in London: it was a place to meet old friends, to make new, to repair old friendships. Connolly, an obsessive bibliophile, arrived one day with a pile of Angus's first editions in dust jackets for signature: the sea-lion obliged the warthog, but muttered to Melvyn Bragg afterwards that Connolly had *hated* the books, he was just a *collector*. Connolly, it was said, liked the make-up, which was as lavish as the drink, and would keep it on at the end of the show. Elizabeth Jane Howard, despite the enthusiasm of the make-up artists, always looked particularly elegant.

Angus was good at this kind of game, and appeared to enjoy it. But he was cautious about more serious propositions. On 19 March 1965 he turned down an invitation from Huw Wheldon to present a new BBC2 arts programme: Wheldon thought his refusal might have been connected with a nervousness about his own homosexuality. Would a public TV slot oblige him to compromise his beliefs, to moderate his manner? According to Melvyn Bragg, Wheldon, although he disliked "what he considered arty-farty folks", had assured Angus that this would not be an issue, but Angus had nevertheless declined. This account forms an interesting sequel to a story in *Sex and the British* (Michael Joseph 1993): Paul Ferris writes (p.159) "A man of Wilson's sexual character was not seen as a fit and proper person to appear on television. When an item about him was proposed by a producer for the BBC arts programme *Monitor* in the late fifties, Huw Wheldon, an aggressive heterosexual who understood the BBC mind, ruled that 'we can't have someone who's overtly queer on the programme'." Tony Garrett's view, conversely, was that Angus had had serious reservations about becoming a TV personality, and had resisted Wheldon's offer of an office, secretarial assistance etc: his view was that if he wasn't good at it, it would be a waste of time, and if he was good at it, it would be a worse waste of time, and would effectively destroy his career as a novelist. The correspondence on this matter supports Tony's view. (Ferris's index melodramatically refers to this incident under "Wilson, Angus, blackmailed", which somewhat overstates the case.)

Nevertheless, later that year, Angus agreed to appear as an interviewer for ATV in a series called *The Reputation Makers*, produced by Colin Clark (a son of Lord Clark). In this, he talked to influential critics – Penelope Gilliatt, Cyril Connolly, Milton Shulman, Kenneth Tynan, Robert Pitman, Donald Zec, Philip Purser. The programmes went out on Sunday afternoons from November to January, and Angus was acclaimed as a "first-rate interviewer . . . urbane and knowledgeable" – Peter Black said he was "as good as Muggeridge". But Angus was not happy with this role,

despite the chorus of praise and despite the fee of a hundred and twenty-
five guineas a programme. It worried him, Tony thought. It was stressful,
time-consuming, and it kept him away from his new novel, *Laughing
Mirrors*, which included a satirical portrait of a 1960s cynical Muggeridgian
TV personality . . . A second series with Clark in November 1966,
interviewing figures from that newly-defined body called "The Establishment", was less successful, and Angus abandoned this high-profile role
with relief. But he did not abandon television as a medium: some of his
most dazzling solo performances were still to come.

★

Deciding which invitations to accept and which to refuse grew no easier
with the years. Angus would have found it hard to cope without Tony,
who wrote many letters a week, most of them politely rejecting speaking
engagements. (Some of his correspondents wrote back to that nice Miss
Garrett, thanking her for being so helpful.) And when Angus did agree to
appear, he would be pursued after the event by letters from a delighted
Literary Committee Secretary asking for a text to publish in the group's
newsletter. All this involved yet more correspondence, explaining that
there was no text. Like most occasional lecturers, Angus tended to re-use a
basic lecture structure, filling it for each new occasion with new bits and
pieces, new local references, an update on the literary scene – the last thing
he wanted was to see all this in cold print. But explanations and apologies
nevertheless had to be politely proffered, again and again. It was all very
distracting. He would have to get away.

A brief visit to Czechoslovakia in September 1965 for a conference in
honour of Capek in Karlsbad proved neither restful nor enjoyable. Angus
spent much time in Suffolk signing letters of protest about censorship and
harassment of writers in Eastern Europe and the Soviet Union, and this
new glimpse behind the curtain did nothing to reassure him. The
atmosphere there struck Tony (who drove out to Prague to meet Angus) as
"horrible": they were both oppressed by the grim-faced party hacks. At
one point Angus, who abhorred a silence, found himself stuck in a lift with
a group of grey suits and trilbies, and was provoked to burst into brave
British song:

> Daddy Neptune one day, to Freedom did say,
> If ever I lived upon dry land,
> The spot I should hit on
> Would be little Britain –
> Cried Freedom, "Why, that's my own island!"

Nobody smiled.

Angus was becoming familiar with what he had described as "life at the Communist top – the heavy banquets, the bonhomie, the drink, the carefully dowdy sexy women, the threats veiled in joviality, the chauffeur-driven car"[12] and was planning his revenge in fiction.

He had other trips lined up. He was committed to appear at the Adelaide Festival the following spring, and worked in an invitation to speak at the American University in Cairo on the way, followed by some free time during which he could perhaps get on with the novel – Egypt, like Morocco, might prove congenial to work. He felt, perhaps, a slight self-consciousness about these winter trips – in a short piece written in 1965 for a UEA magazine called *Decanter* he noted that "all round me, and increasingly as my winter trip abroad becomes a regular event, neighbours, friends and literary colleagues say, 'So you're going abroad again this winter, it seems,' and all the guilts and shames that I once felt about my book on Zola now gather around my winter visit to Morocco. 'What do you find to do all that time?' or 'I don't think I could use all that much holiday,' are the usual follow-ups . . . 'Writing' is not real work, abroad in winter in shameful luxury. Holidays were once sinful, foreign holidays more so; times have changed, but at least we can keep *foreign* winter holidays on the index."[13]

Not everyone envied him. It must have been while he was working out this 1966 itinerary that he met Dadie Rylands* one day in King's Parade in Cambridge: Rylands politely asked how Angus was and what he was doing, and Angus replied at length – he'd just been to Morocco and Poland, would soon be off to Egypt and Australia, the year after that to America . . . Rylands, who spent most of his very long life in the same beautiful Carrington-decorated rooms in King's College, looked at Angus coolly, said "You must be mad," and walked away.

Angus and Tony took off, full of cholera injections, in early January, 1966: Angus spoke to the University of Cairo in defence of homosexuality and Virgina Woolf. (His views on Woolf, as we have seen, had changed very considerably since his dismissive BBC broadcast in 1950, and continued to change.) There he encountered some old acquaintances, Alex and Jean Kern, American academics from Iowa whom he had met some years earlier in August 1959 at a conference in Lausanne (where Angus had delivered one of his most memorable lectures on "The Novelist and the Narrator"). Jean proved a friend in need, for she had got to grips with the system in Egypt, and conspired with another faculty wife who

---

* George Rylands (b.1902), Fellow of King's, Shakespearean, theatre director and don, was for many years the power behind the Cambridge Marlowe Society and its traditions of verse-speaking.

spoke Arabic to procure for Angus and Tony a temporarily vacated "luxury houseboat" with a cook and servants. There, once more installed in the sun amidst the flapping laundry, Angus sat down to write, stirring Egyptian scenes and memories of Suez into the thickening *roux* of his novel. The house boy prostrated himself upon the deck and prayed to Mecca, and Angus scribbled away. Philippe Jullian and his Danish friend Bent Mohn paid a visit, and there were excursions in a little open red Triumph sports car loaned by the President of the American University: red being the royal colour, Angus was cheered or booed as a friend of Farouk wherever he went. But the main agenda was the novel. It was slow. He was still jotting away in his notebooks the following October.

On 16 February 1966 Angus flew from Cairo to Sydney via Singapore, and Tony set off to drive back overland to England. In Australia, Angus was fêted and celebrated until he was quite worn out. He gave dozens of speeches and interviews and press conferences, he opened exhibitions, he sparkled at parties. In Sydney he stayed at the Belvedere Hotel in King's Cross, and wrote back to Tony with his first impressions – terrible crosswinds, a bad landing, then pouring rain, sporty ladies, menfolk slightly tipsy in seaside blazers, cocktail parties, TV appearances, a barbecue on the North Shore, a PEN dinner at Ye Olde Crusty Tavern, a specially illuminated duck-billed platypus – "I told the Sydney Sun reporter that my childhood dream had been to see these creatures – normally nocturnal they will be activated by day for my benefit – so is all vestige of a childhood dream banished – I wonder if Caligula and Nero felt like this? Sorry to be so bitter, I'm not really, it's the pouring rain in temperature of 94 and the near accident flying . . . No diarrhoea here, a lady told me – so the gripes I have are something else. Love to all who need it and especially you. Angus. PS The only queer dinner has been cancelled because of more important engagements. (Dated 19(?) Saturday night, 12 midnight.)" (*sic*)

(Peculiarly revealing is that hastily scribbled comment on "a childhood dream banished" – he was tasting here the bitter sweets of fame and success, the emptiness of gratification, all summed up in a photograph of him holding an unhappy playtpus, aroused for his delight but clearly undelighted and undelighting. The zoo could never deliver all it had once promised.)

Other letters followed, reporting glorious weather, keen readers, but feeling "a bit overkeyed up and and trying to calm down". (When he dined with Patrick White he later felt contrite for having broken out into "angry sharpness with a chic librarian queen".) He was driven to Canberra in a car that skidded into a gum tree, then flew to Melbourne where he declined an invitation to play in a literary cricket match, then on to

Adelaide, then back to Melbourne to address universities – "a Red Queen whirl." He reports feelings of physical tension and exhaustion: he might survive but his suitcase was about to collapse under the strain. He had done no work on the novel except for one morning at Canberra House, where he stayed with Sir Charles Johnstone, High Commissioner and translator of Pushkin.

In Melbourne, he stayed with an old friend of Bentley's from Bletchley Park, Michael Sinclair-Wilson, who had undergone a mysterious meta-morphosis from aspiring ballet dancer and linguist to husband, father of two sons, and Academic Warden of the University. His wife Helen had also been at BP, where she worked for Frank Birch and became an officer in the Wrens. Sinclair-Wilson had studied classical Chinese at King's: he then acquired Japanese and Malayan, and worked for years in Singapore before making his way to in 1963 to Melbourne, via Bentley Bridgewater's sponsorship – there was some story of a train, a taxi and a bottle of brandy which had convinced Sinclair-Wilson that he would never get to the job. But there he was, and there, in the bath of of the Warden's Residence, was Angus, loudly splashing and warbling songs from Doris Day. "Helen and Mick," he wrote to Tony, "have been immensely kind to me. I am rather in love with this country . . ."

Travel had gone to his head, and he made wild plans for taking Tony to Australia next winter. These plans alternated with bouts of homesickness – "my heart is is with you and the cats and Mrs R and so on. What about your parents I wonder? But what's the use of worrying it never was worthwhile . . ."

He flew on to Hobart in Tasmania, writing his speech for Adelaide in scribbled biro in an old exercise book on the plane: he stayed there for a few days with Vivian and Sybil Smith. Smith had kept in touch with Angus since their early meetings in England, had reviewed his books perceptively – particularly *The Wild Garden* – and now was able to offer Angus a small interlude of recuperation in his hectic programme: while with the Smiths Angus sat in the garden, corrected the proofs of an introduction to *Oliver Twist*, and worked on the novel. Angus loved Tasmania – the geraniums made it seem like the Riviera after the tropics. He bought a new suitcase ("Give the old one to the nuns," he told Vivian) and was taken to Port Arthur, the old Tasmanian convict ruin which he found a compelling mixture of beauty and horror: he declined to descend the 200 steps to the bottom, pleading vertigo – an increasing problem. Sybil Smith, who was four months pregnant with her first child, had been nervous about the visit of this eminent guest, and had rushed out and bought a new spare bed for him, but in the event they found him easy and undemanding: he had seemed to enjoy everything, particularly meeting the students at the two parties they had arranged – though they remember that he fretted a little about not having been at his best in some of his Australian interviews. They noted that he was far more knowledgeable about Australian flora and fauna than they were themselves.

The Australian journalists did not complain about Angus: they found him a delight. "You just start him off and he'll go on for hours," said *The Bulletin*.[14] But he could not relax and take his success easily. The crowning ordeal of Adelaide still loomed. As Guest of Honour he had to open the Festival, a ceremony which he performed on Sunday, 13 March 1966. He spoke about conferences in general, about private and public art, about the limits of international "mateyness" and the menace of "a sort of international airport art which by trying to meet all kills all".

He spoke, also, about censorship in many countries, all of which he knew at first hand – Portugal, Spain, Poland, South Africa, and the Soviet Union. The poet Yevtushenko, one of the few Soviet writers allowed to travel, had been eagerly awaited in Adelaide, as rumours of his non-appearance proliferated: but he made it. Angus wrote to Tony (14 March 1966) of Yevtushenko's coming "into my room with a blonde pick-up (a nice Australian girl) and waking me so that I screamed but being awfully nice with a bottle of champagne at 4 in the morning . . . I think that my visit has been a *succès fou* tho' not, of course, the great public triumph of Yevtushenko (he is, by the way, quite wonderful when he reads his poems). And I have been woken up to so much that the awful nag of my novel untouched is slightly stilled. Oh how I long to be in England again! I wish, too, I didn't have this growing thing about flying . . ."

(The Yevtushenko incident he was to revise and reinterpret in his mind: years later he said that he had spoken of state interference in the arts "as part of a general charge, saying, perhaps a little unfairly, that I felt sure that he would agree with the general charge against regimes that behaved in this way. He brushed it to one side as a mistaken judgement. Now, early in the morning, about one or two a.m., he chose to get a Russian-speaking Australian girl to tell me that he absolutely agreed with what I had said, but could not say so in public. I might perhaps have let it pass, had he not insisted on saying a number of times that he loved so much to see me because I reminded him of his Father. He hoped, the interpreter said, that I should forgive him for not having spoken out publicly, and would I show my friendship by joining him in a glass of champagne. I said, roughly, I remember, 'No, I damn well can't. Why does Yev think it worth his while to wake me up with all this rubbish? Take him and the champagne away.' It was not kind, or understanding, but I don't regret it.")[15]

Tony wrote to Angus with good news. The University of East Anglia had decided to make Angus into a Professor, in a Chair of English Literature "personal to himself", as "an appropriate recognition of the very real position you have established in the University as well as in the world of letters" – so wrote Frank Thistlethwaite. Angus had been sounded out about the possibility of this appointment in December, and had made demurring noises – was he really a proper critic? Would the title make him look pompous and ridiculous? But when a firm offer arrived, he was delighted. And he was also delighted to hear that he had been elected to the Athenaeum.

Tony wrote of home affairs – the Blackburnes had invited him to be in two more plays, the winter jasmine, cyclamens and crocuses were out, the cats were well, he had dined with Perkin Walker, accompanied by Bob and Monty, who are like "Perkin's Ka's – his Egyptian shadows." Angus had had enough travelling, and longed to be back: he flew home via Bangkok (where he purchased some curtain material) and returned with roaring high blood pressure, utterly exhausted. He had to rest and diet. Several interviewers in Australia had commented on his "pink face", which they attributed to the unfamiliar sun, and Angus himself had made his old quip about "looking like a red-faced farmer" – but this time there was a more sinister cause for his bucolic appearance. (Angus tended to ascribe this simile to a member of an audience in Poland, but it seems more likely that it was remembered from the *Daily Telegraph* in November 1961 – and, in characteristic style, turned by Angus into his own joke.)

His blood pressure was not improved by Fred Warburg's demands for the new novel: Angus said he could no longer teach, write novels, review once a month for the *Observer* and act as reader and adviser to Secker at the same time. From the last of these roles he resigned, writing to Fred Warburg on 2 April 1966 (in a letter which also mildly complained that no copies of *Late Call* had been available in Adelaide): ". . . I found no time at all during five weeks of Australia to write any more of my novel, although I made a good deal of progress in the houseboat in Egypt. Now that I am returned I must give my time and energies solely to the novel apart, of course, from my duties at the University – where you may perhaps have seen I am to have my own chair from August 1st next – and my monthly obligation to the Observer. For this reason I am going to suggest that we bring to an end my advising and reading duties for Secker and Warburg. They have of course never been onerous, for you have been modest in your demands. But extra work is extra work, and I do not feel that I can be at the ready to advise when you wanted, as the job certainly requires, while I should be fully intent upon this new difficult novel. I shall therefore consider the £75 I received today as my last quarterly payment from Seckers for these advisory services. Of course if there are any particular points on which my advice can be useful, not entailing any detailed reading, I shall always be glad to offer my services in friendship."

*

Shadows of mortality overcast the spring and summer. Robin Ironside had died in the late autumn of 1965 (and what to do about his boyfriend?): Somerset Maugham, George Devine, and Evelyn Waugh followed. In June the stout black-and-white Morgan was found to have inoperable cancer and had to be put to sleep. Betty Wilson died in July, and Angus and Tony attended the funeral in Seaford, where she was buried in the churchyard on the hill with Winn and Angus's father. (Georgina, Sybil Scott's daughter, recalls Angus's particular kindness to her on this occasion.)

Visitors from Poland, Romania, Russia and California reached Felsham Woodside, and had to be entertained. The Priestleys also arrived, inviting themselves to stay after Aldeburgh, thus claiming a return for the weekends Angus and Tony had spent with them on the Isle of Wight and at Kissing Tree House near Stratford – though Jack Priestley hastened to assure Tony that he did not need any fancy French food, but would be much happier with a plain pork pie. Jacquetta remembered the cottage as "rather uncomfortable and very charming", with difficult stairs: she admired the old roses, in particular the Moyesii and the Climbing Guinée, of which Angus was particularly proud, and which he had recommended all over Australia.

Angus spoke here and he spoke there. He attended a Foyles' Luncheon at the Dorchester given, rather surprisingly, in honour of Maurice Girodias of the Olympia Press: he addressed the Suffolk Poetry Society on what they wrongly thought was the poet Robert Bloomfield's anniversary: he did a Holiday Books programme about Waugh's *Gilbert Pinfold* with Julian Mitchell and Eleanor Bron for the BBC: he agreed to give a series of lectures in the Midlands in the autumn. He was now a member of the new Literature Panel of the Arts Council, and requests from indigent and unpublished writers became even more frequent than they had been in the past. He finally declined to edit or introduce Angus Heriot's last unpublished novel. His own novel was more or less put on hold. Tony appeared as Horner in *The Country Wife* for two weeks at the Theatre Royal in August, and in September 1966 Angus and Tony took the ferry to Denmark for a working holiday, but the crossing was rough and it rained a lot. In Copenhagen Angus saw Villy Sørensen, the Danish writer whose work he had admired and recommended in England. (He had first met Sørensen on 28 February 1954, while giving a lecture at the British Council in Copenhagen: a volume of stories, with an introduction by Angus, was published in 1956 by Secker, and the friendship had been maintained.) Angus did not make much progress with his work. He came back to a term's teaching, more meetings, a students' party. At the end of September, he wrote to the impatient Fred Warburg that he hoped to finish a first draft of his novel "by about the first week in November, but I trust you do not think from this that it would then be available: first, it must be typed; then I must read it through and revise it; and then it must be re-typed."

He hoped he might deliver by Christmas, but he did not. He would have to go abroad again, to revise in peace. In the New Year he and Tony set off with manuscript and notebooks for the Middle East. Angus lectured for the British Council (on television and the arts) in Amman, visited Petra and Jerash, and in Jericho he settled in the Winter Palace Hotel, where he could sit and work in a banana grove. The hotel had been recommended by Val Graham Young's brother, Major Robert Young, who farmed at Letheringham, near Woodbridge; Young was a keen Arabist who knew the Arabian peninsula and its language and peoples well, and his recommendation proved a happy one. In Jericho, Angus found an oasis of concentration. The end of the new novel – an Arab ending, as it proved – was at last in sight.

21

THE FREEDOM OF THE SIXTIES

Late Call had been a product of the sober Sixties. *No Laughing Matter*, although set in the past, was to be a product of the swinging Sixties. By 1967, nobody could ignore the swing, and unlike Philip Larkin, Angus embraced the new age. His hair grew wilder, as did that of his students: he wore Moroccan shirts, and on occasion beads. The sexual revolution was all around him, and he was interested in the experimental relationships of both students and faculty at the University of East Anglia. At the Arts Council debates about the drug culture were bubbling; in the fringe theatres, happenings were happening. (Angus Heriot, with Bunny Roger's friend Georges Garcin, had tried to organise a happening – "*un événement*" – in Paris, but it had never quite happened.) Literature was winning the battle against censorship: the presence of Girodias at a luncheon of Christina Foyle's would have been unthinkable a few years earlier. In 1965 Ken Tynan had said "fuck" on television and the walls had not tumbled down – though three years later the cause was still having to be defended, when the Third Programme cancelled a talk by David Caute about Norman Mailer because it contained the shocking word. (Karl Miller managed to slip it into the *Listener*, in a protest letter, signed by Angus, amongst others.[1]) Angus, working on his new novel, had realised that anything – well, almost anything – was about to be possible.

The contrast between Angus Wilson and Larkin is illuminating. Angus had visited the University of Hull in November 1962, where he had struck Larkin as prematurely aged – "a small bunchy little man looking every minute of his 60 years (he is 49), full of energy (the ineluctable quality) and also full of the kind of crappy theorising about novels I seem to remember your reporting from Charlie Snow . . . he said he was trying to turn *Totentanz* into a musical. Cor! Coaargh! Cuh! . . . he is more like Harry

Hoff than anyone else I have ever met. So there you are! I have a good mind to turn queer, & cable the decision to my parents."[2]

Larkin's sex life, as has been recently revealed, was less than fulfilled, and early photographs of him have a disturbing sexual ambiguity. His famous use of the word "fuck" was in a revealingly asexual context – "They fuck you up, your Mum and Dad." His political opinions became increasingly reactionary as he recoiled in horror – sometimes in mock horror – from the march of what others perceived as progress. Angus took the other route. Still Bowle's adventurous pupil, he was as determined as ever to be in the vanguard. If he made a fool of himself at times, well, never mind.

UEA was a more adventurous university, by design, than Hull. Its very motto was "Do Different". Students and staff considered themselves unconventional, creative. Out on its own East Anglian limb, it hoped to avoid the worst of the North-South, Redbrick-Oxbridge divide: yoghurt-eaters in Jaeger scarves mingled with Mancunian addicts of chips, peas and tomato ketchup. Students were discovering their own sexuality in an atmosphere of unusual freedom and tolerance. Bisexuality was permissible, homosexuality quite chic, and the coupling of students with teachers was not greeted with excessive alarm. Jonathan Courage, one of Angus's students, was attracted to UEA in the first place because he knew himself to be gay, knew also that Angus Wilson was, and knew that Peter Pears and Britten lived not too far away – maybe the climate would suit? Peter Conradi, one of the first to get a First, gradually discovered that he was gay while he was an undergraduate: Angus's understanding and advice were – and remained – important to him over the years. Rose Thomson married a fellow student, John Tremain, in 1971: her novels were to explore questions of gender and identity. Maggie Reed and Peter Humm married, and divorced, but both still unite in talking fondly of Angus's generosity to them as a couple – he lent them his Regent's Park Terrace flat, took them to the theatre, fed them their first snails, gave them introductions when they went to Poland, urged them to spend his blocked zlotys there. The handsome, radical, maverick Simon Edwards, expelled from Wellington, was almost extravagantly heterosexual, yet was to exert a strong pull on Angus's imagination: he too became a lifelong friend, bringing a puzzling succession of wives and girlfriends to admire the guru. Edwards's own father had been very absent: Angus became a father-figure "of anarchic authority". A generation of young people were attracted into Angus's circle. This was not only the university which was to produce Malcom Bradbury's History Man: it was the university of Ian McEwan, Snoo Wilson, Jonathan Powell, Jonathan Raban, Clive Sinclair, Alan Tuckett. There was much to watch.

Angus was a responsible teacher, punctual and attentive, marking papers conscientiously (and some said over-generously), encouraging the shy, the silent and the dim to speak up. His lectures and seminars were brilliant events, and in the early years they were always crowded – indeed, the seminars had to be rationed. A talk by him on Firbank or Henry Green or Compton-Burnett could empty the bookstore of copies of their works. His reading lists were anarchic – he jumbled extracts from George Orwell with Lewis Carroll's descriptions of Humpty Dumpty, and recommended Meredith, Zola, Diderot and Richardson, in a manner that defied Leavis's attempts to define a great tradition. He talked not only about a writer's achievements, but also about his or her intentions – what had Woolf been trying out here, what had moved Dickens to return to this theme? What were their technical problems, how had their lives shaped their work, their work their lives? He spoke as a writer, about colleagues, introducing anecdotes about Norman Mailer and Saul Bellow and Leonard Woolf as he talked, making his students realise the continuity of past and present, of effort and achievement. His views changed over the years – everybody noticed his growing admiration for Woolf, his diminishing admiration for Forster. His gossip about Bloomsbury was enthralling.

He got to know his students individually, inviting them with Tony two by two to lunch at a hotel or pub in Norwich – "it must have cost him a fucking fortune," Simon Edwards realised in retrospect. There he would ask them about themselves and their families – Rose Tremain's mother, Peter Conradi's grandmother, Simon Edwards's stepfather – all were discussed and filed away. He made heroic efforts to memorise names – a handwritten list of students is annotated with mnemonics such as "long hair", "+ baby", "Tennessee" and "red beard" – with one afterthought about a Brian – "apologise to him for calling him Kelvin." He and Tony gave a students' party each summer, to which they invited also a selection of their own friends from the neighbourhood – a characteristic menu for 38 offered 12 lettuces, 5 cucumbers, 12 lbs ham, 11 bottles champagne, 28 punnets of strawberries and six medium chickens. One year Tony added to the list the postscript "This was only just enough" – the young had healthy appetites.

These occasions were remembered with rapture: Angus in a white suit and brightly coloured shirt and tie would sit on a bench in the garden in the perpetual sunshine while rotating acolytes sat at his feet and listened. But Angus listened too, and watched – catching the changing fashions, as hippies and gipsies and beaded nymphs and satyrs adorned his woodland and disported on his little lawns. Faded jeans, jumble-sale evening dresses, tattered shawls and granny spectacles – he watched them all with amusement and amazement.

Was there a downside to this, a sinister side? Were some excluded from the magic circle? Pamela Aubrey (now Schweitzer), one of his most able students, thought that he did have favourites – "Oh Peter dear, what a lovely tie, do come and sit by me!" – but that he was scrupulously fair to all. Angus was, Simon Edwards thought, perhaps a bit "looksist" – he liked the handsome and exotic of both sexes.

What did Angus get out of all this? Were the students, as he had hoped, keeping him in touch with Youth? Did he want to purchase their love and admiration with champagne and strawberries and theatre outings?

Occasionally he drew a firm line. When Michael Schofield asked him to sign an advertisement in July 1967 in favour of the legalisation of cannabis, Angus took advice from medical friends on its long-term effects, was told that cannabis could lead to "heroin taking", and declined to give his support. Unlike some, he did not give his name to every "progressive" cause. For those who did, it was a period of increasing anxiety, as authority was increasingly challenged. In December 1967, Brigid Brophy resigned from the Arts Council Literature Panel in sympathy with Barry Miles, who had been dismissed from the panel earlier in the year on the grounds that his fortnightly magazine, *International Times*, was promoting psychedelic drugs. Some admired her stand, others mocked it. In her letter of resignation, interestingly, she specifically linked the common practice of illegal drug-taking with the recently legalised practice of homosexuality: where were the barriers to fall next?[3]

Unlike some of the teaching staff, neither Angus nor Tony made sexual approaches to any of the students. Allegations of "gross moral turpitude" were not unheard of even in this liberal atmosphere, but Angus and Tony were untouched by rumour or scandal. ("Would that *Tony* had harassed *me!*" one of them was to cry in later years.) Paradoxically, it was the ordered nature of Angus's domestic life, his happy marriage with Tony, that appealed most strongly to the young. UEA was full of paradoxes.

Lorna Sage, who came there as a young – a very young – assistant lecturer in 1965, describes the atmosphere in the 60s as "very camp". She and her first husband, Victor Sage, had both graduated, with Firsts, from Durham. Vic, as all his students called him, taught the Gothic novel, looking uncannily like a werewolf as he did it. Lorna found herself taking over Ian Watt's teaching of the eighteenth-century novel. Watt had disappeared back to the sun of California: "instead of chain-smoking Ian Watt the students got chain-smoking me." Durham had been solemn: UEA was the reverse. It was committed to the contemporary. There was a cult of beauty, and a lot of humour, cleverness, smartness, sexual experimentation and screwing: it was never as political as its neighbour, Essex (though there was an occupation of the Arts Block in 1968, and a demo against Princess Margaret). Lorna, a vicar's granddaughter, escaping from a disapproving provincial family on the Welsh borders, threw herself into this new world energetically, working her students to death in order to keep a step ahead of them, and thriving on the heady atmosphere of sexual and every other kind of ambiguity. They all read William Empson: the more meanings the merrier. They read *Lolita* and *L'Histoire d'O*. Lorna had fallen in love with her tutor, the handsome Nicholas Brooke in Durham, and her students now fell in love with her. (The blonde blue-eyed Lorna was, says Tony, "the prettiest young thing in the world.") And for Lorna Sage, Angus represented the road to survival through this unsettled world. He could live with frenzy. He turned anxiety and competition and uncertainty into pleasure and excitement. He could ride the tiger.

★

1967 was a year of dramatic significance for British homosexuals. In July, the Sexual Offences Bill received the Royal Assent. The stigma of illegality was at last to be lifted from adult consenting homosexual acts in private. The first battle in what was to prove a long campaign had been won. Not everybody approved: Angus's own MP, Eldon Griffiths, had refused to support the Bill. He did not approve of the permissive society. Amongst his reasons were his belief that "there is already too much sexual licence in society and I see no reason why Parliament should remove the existing deterrent" and "It is no excuse that because we cannot stop homosexuality that therefore we must legalise it. We cannot stop many kinds of abuse and prurience, but that is surely no reason for writing them in to the statute book as permitted by the law of the land." (This is from an undated leaflet sent to his constituents.)

Angus had supported reform for years. He had spoken at the Albany Trust in December 1964, and had agreed in principle in 1965 to take part in a debate on the motion that "the homosexual should be left to his own devices" at the University of London Union. (He had to withdraw because the date clashed with his teaching commitments.) He was a member of the Executive Committee of the Homosexual Law Reform Society, with Leo Abse, Jacquetta Hawkes, Norman St John Stevas and Jeremy Thorpe. The memory of his and Tony's troubles of 1960 had not entirely faded: there was always to be a nagging worry, a slight sense of insecurity – and despite it, because of it, Angus continued to involve himself with the cause.

The homosexual community was divided in its attitudes to reform. Many of Angus's contemporaries stuck to the line that it was better to say as little about the matter as possible. Why provoke one's neighbours? Why rock the boat? Others were slightly disapppointed by the removal of the thrill of being beyond the pale. Conditioned to a life of cruising and cottaging and rough trade, it was hard to be allowed to settle for tame respectability. (This was said to be Francis Bacon's attitude.) Their sexual inclinations had been formed in another climate and they could not adjust.

Angus struck out for disclosure, and made increasingly harsh judgements on those who did not. He spoke sharply about closet queens, although in private life he was a friend of many. Yet he himself occasionally fell short of the high moral standards of others: Antony Grey, who had devoted his life to the cause, was to be much saddened when in July 1970 Angus felt he had to revise a book review to take out all overt references to his own homosexuality.

Angus was as brave as most, and much braver than many. He was well placed to be so, some argued. A distinguished writer, internationally famous, he could afford to take a few risks with his reputation. But he had also a yearning for respectability, a desire to be recognised as a useful citizen and public servant. It was a fine balancing act.

The noisy and very public politics of the 1960s were for ever calling on writers to make "commitments", as the Thirties had called on the writers of Angus's youth. Bowle's introduction of Heard and Huxley and Gandhi had not been forgotten. Angus became involved in many other causes. In 1963, on 23 October, he had flown to Paris for the day on a secret mission for Spanish Amnesty, concerned with the persecution of the miners of the Asturias. On 7 June 1967, at the outbreak of the Arab-Israeli war, he withdrew his signature from an advertisement calling for "whole-hearted support of Israel", "as the situation has now changed and action must be conducted on many different fronts – ceasefire, frontiers, United Nations Policing etc."[4] (Elsewhere he wrote sympathetically of "Arab grievances".) Ever since his 1961 visit to South Africa, Anti-Apartheid continued to claim his attention: in July 1967 he wrote protesting about the withdrawal of Athol Fugard's passport. All these matters, and many others, consumed time and thought. He never answered lightly, except on odd occasions: it was a relief to be able to refuse to contribute to a book on the monarchy because he had "not enough interest in the subject".[5]

(Nadine Gordimer, interestingly, attributes some of his public spirit to his South African background: "I wonder whether his strong social conscience, and the activity which arose from it, even manifest in his choice of a life partner, was not influenced by his consciousness of what he had absorbed and what had continued grotesquely in South Africa?" She had first met him on his South African visit and they continued to meet occasionally in Suffolk with Anthony and Sally Sampson, who had a cottage at Walberswick: "The Angus/Tony house was so lovely, sheltering, with a marvellously tended garden, and yet it was in no way a retreat from reality. Perhaps that's it – Angus always kept the tension alive between the solitary pursuit of the writer and the involvement with harsh reality. He clearly regarded Tony's work as important as his own . . ."⁶)

But the tension could cause anxiety, and the great *Encounter* scandal could not be dismissed as easily as the monarchy. This blew up in May 1967, over revelations in the American magazine *Ramparts* of the CIA's secret funding of *Encounter* through the Congress for Cultural Freedom. Angus, who had been writing irregularly for *Encounter* for years, was naturally drawn in. Both sides appealed for his support – the *Partisan Review*, which attacked the funding, and *Encounter*'s supporters, Max Beloff and D.W. Brogan. Stephen Spender and co-editor Frank Kermode both resigned, but Melvin Lasky agreed to stay on, and was joined in August by Nigel Dennis. There was, Natasha Spender wrote to Sonia Orwell, an atmosphere of "intrigue and hysteria".⁷

Angus refused to support Beloff and Brogan. He wrote privately to Beloff saying that he did not believe that *Encounter* could recover its reputation under the same editors. "It must be and seem to be quite free of all its previous commitments. This may be unjust or even illogical but what is important is the continuation of a first rate paper and nothing else." Much as Angus disliked British anti-Americanism, much as he deplored what he had seen in the USSR and Eastern Europe, he could not accept the CIA's covert methods of discrediting Communism.

It was a sorry affair that caused distress to all involved. Spender said that he and Kermode objected to having been "misled, I for fourteen years and he for two, by our CCF American colleagues, and to having consequently in good faith defended *Encounter* upon information now shown to be untrue."⁸ (Lasky wrote a long, personal and anguished letter to Angus from the airport on his way to the University of Michigan, protesting his own integrity, saying that he had never censored or doctored the views of his contributors, that he had never published any article of which he was ashamed, that he had actively sought pieces against the American involvement in Vietnam and against the "illegal and immoral intervention" of the Bay of Pigs. He questioned the motives of the *Partisan Review*. And why single out *Encounter*? Were there a not a dozen other European magazines similarly implicated? Could he come and talk about all this with Angus as soon as he got back from the States?)[9]

Being a Man of Letters and a Moral Authority, particularly in the rapidly shifting moral landscape of the 1960s, could become a full-time job. It required vigilance, diligence and quick footwork. But in fiction, Angus could escape the constraints of public accountability, and write from the depths. In fiction, he could be his own disreputable self.

★

No Laughing Matter, written amidst flapping laundry in Morocco and on the Nile, and in the banana groves of Jericho, was delivered in March 1967. At one stage entitled *Child's Play*, at another *Laughing Mirrors*, the title finally chosen (under some pressure from Fred Warburg) was invented by Tony. (Curiously it echoes, though none of them were aware of this, the title of a sketch written by Hermione Gingold for the *New Ambassadors Revue* of 1941, in which Frith Banbury had appeared with Charles Hawtrey.) The book was unlike anything Angus had done before. It was at once carefully structured and boldly experimental, private and public, personal and panoramic. It spoke with many voices, yet it was unmistakably the voice and vision of one man. It was very long, and Angus thoughtfully provided a synopsis to help his publishers and agents through the plot. (This, together with a long letter from Angus to David Farrer, are reproduced as Appendix 1: they offer a clear illustration of Angus's methods of construction, and also of his working relationship with David Farrer.)

It is the story of the Matthews family, from before the First World War to a finale in 1967, and it covers a little more than the whole lifespan of Angus Johnstone-Wilson. Angus drew heavily on his own childhood, convinced by his deepening appreciation of Dickens that this, for him, was the true source of imaginative power. Conversations with and letters from Colin in Lisbon had revived forgotten or repressed recollections of his parents, his step-grandmother Alys (and that peculiarly memorable parrot), his brothers and their dressing-up games, Ashampstead and the Kensington hotels, Fred's prison sentence, the days when Colin and Pat trolled the Dilly, the days when he lay alone as a petted and neglected schoolboy and stared at the shapes in the ceiling. From this rich and at times high-smelling compost of the past grew amazing blooms.

The Matthews family, like the Johnstone-Wilson family, consisted of two feckless parents and six children. The mother, known as The Countess (or Cuntess, by implication, as one of the sons points out), is physically unlike Maud, for she is dark, slim, and gipsy-like, but she shares some of

her characteristics – a histrionic streak, a fondness for dress, an impractical-
ity, a refusal to accept unpleasantnesses. The father Billy Pop, spoiled son of
Pater and Mater, and a failed Edwardian essayist, is another resurrection of
Willie – self-pitying, gambling, scrounging, charming, running off to the
Club for a Dover sole when life at home becomes disagreeable, packing his
bags to leave forever, but back in time for supper. Their relationship is full
both of sparring contempt and enduring affection, of cruelty and
sentiment: the nature of marital complaisance is brilliantly captured. (It
may also owe something, the notes suggest, to the relationship of Molly
Calder and her husband.)

Angus set himself problems with the size of the family. Six principal
characters in a narrative (as in a biography) are hard to control. But six
siblings, he decided, there had to be, in fiction as there had been in life. The
oldest child is called Quentin: at last Angus had found a place for a name
which he had tried out in so many ideas for stories. (Why did it attract him
so much? Are there echoes of Cuntess here? Grandmother addresses her
favourite, familiarly, as "Quintus".) Quentin was, like Fred, farmed out to
grandparents as a child for financial reasons, and educated at Colet Court
and St Paul's: like Winn, Quentin was wounded in the First World War.
In other ways he resembles neither – although, like Fred, he is a
womaniser. The second child, Gladys, is the fat music-hall comic of the
family: the third, Rupert, is the spoiled but self-knowing handsome
mother's darling: the twins, Margaret and Sukey, are sharply contrasted,
the first all ironic intellect, the second all domestic cosiness: and the baby,
Marcus, rejected by his mother, is the spiteful wit and aesthete of the
family.

Here was a formula for another loveable Crazy Crowd novel, a danger
of which Angus was all too keenly aware – the eccentric Matthews, herded
together like a heap of kittens in their narrow house in Victoria, battling
against parental selfishness, a dwindling fixed income and genteel penury,
and finally, in their different ways, winning through. The left-wing
Quentin becomes a successful and cynical journalist and TV figure (clearly
based on Malcolm Muggeridge), Gladys a well-turned-out business-
woman, Rupert a famous actor (the notes suggest Michael Redgrave as an
original), Margaret a famous novelist, Sukey a headmaster's wife and
mother of three, and Marcus a dandy, designer, collector, and philanthropist. But Angus's awareness of the dangers of the genre lead him to subvert it
in the most unsettling and powerful way. Through pastiche, through
parody, through self-mockery, through bitter distortions and savage
theatrical improvisations, the Matthews come to life on the far side of
realism.

Angus had learned from Dickens, and he had learned from Woolf. *The Waves*, Virginia Woolf's own group portrait novel, similarly springing from painful childhood memory, had shown him that one could free oneself from conventional narrative and, if the writer's emotion were strong and dark enough, the reader could follow the subconscious pattern of the dream. (Angus worried that Woolf would influence him too much: in his notes he wrote that he must avoid comparison with *The Waves* for "my purpose is other".) Dickens had taught him the powers of exaggeration, of expressionist violence, of caricature. Welding these two, and adding his own particular brands of accurate mimicry, macabre humour, and intense social curiosity, he produced a novel which both in form and content was uniquely his own. For he is far more worldly than either Woolf or Dickens: his narrative reaches down into the psychological depths, yet manages to reach up into the world of politics, finance, and social change, and to show how the one grows from the other.

The novel was published in October 1967, when Angus was already safely out of the country teaching in Berkeley, California. This family saga was, appropriately, dedicated to his niece and her husband, Glyn and Jeanne Davies (the dedication reads "For Glyn and Jane").

Angus, as ever, had done his research, consulting Michael Levey at the National Gallery for the background and tastes of Marcus's lover and protector, the wealthy Jewish collector Jack; consulting the Home Office about women's prison dress for the scene when Gladys does time on behalf of her fraudulent lover; consulting Viva King (now running an antique shop in Sloane Square) about *art nouveau* and period furnishings; asking J.C. Trewin and actor friends for period plays to parody, for actors' memoirs to consult; writing to Michael Havers about fraud cases and points of law;* consulting the *Tangiers Gazette* for details to fill out the historical backdrop to Marcus's Moroccan idyll. Despite the efforts of a professional researcher, he never discovered the original of the song about Buffalo Bill that Colin thought he remembered, but there were fifty years of family legend and stories to draw upon – Aunt Alys's parrot appears upon the shoulder of Aunt Mouse, Winn's wound on Quentin's shoulder, Nurse Sopp's recipe book (and even a mention of her eggless cakes) is discovered in the kitchen of No.52, Winnie the Wolseley breaks down on Porlock Hill. Marcus's experiences as rent boy recall the stories of Pat and Colin: Ashampstead surfaces in Sukey's small ingrown prep-school world: Split and the coast of Yugoslavia in the 1930s are seen through the eyes of Margaret, and revive memories of Pat's meeting with Rebecca West. And

---

* Michael Havers's son, the actor Nigel Havers, was at school at Nowton Court.

Angus used his own recollections, becoming again the grubby Westminster schoolboy taunted in the street with cries of "Nancy!", the squeaky-voiced youth wrapping himself defiantly in dreams of glamour in his overcoat, the young man complimented on his cooking by his working-class lover from over the river – a nostalgic evocation of Charlie, the blackmailing butcher's boy.

The Mastermans recognised elements of their own chaotic house at 46 Gillingham Street in the portrait of 52 Gillbrook Street, a house "long in the same family" with its dark kitchen, its coal hole, its area into which passers-by vomited, its background noises of quarrelling prostitutes and drunks. Bunny Roger acknowledged a reference to his own stylish designer parties in the décor of Marcus's green balls in Hampstead: Wendy Charles (by now Wendy Rintoul) recognised the descriptions of the anti-Fascist demonstrations and the Tooley Street march. Literary detectives spotted parodies of Shaw, Maugham, Coward, Rattigan, Chekhov, and Beckett/Pinter – parodies that were to involve Angus's conscientious Japanese translator, Kazu Serikawa, in much hard work.

More recent experiences were seamlessly interwoven with the historic Johnstone-Wilson past: we find the scenery of La Ciotat, Mogador, and the houseboat on the Nile. The eerie experience of visiting the Soviet Union in the summer of 1963 is cleverly set back in the 1930s as Quentin, a fellow traveller, senses that much is being hidden from his delegation. The student generation of the 1960s appears as a hitch-hiking travelling caravan of great-nephews and great-nieces. The wheel comes full circle, as Sukey's retired schoolmaster husband watches the Forsytes on television – the Forsytes whose saga Winn had read aloud to Angus.

But the great triumph was not in the detail: it was in the vitality and passion of the whole. All the characters are fully realised in time: their hopes, fears, successes and failures are charted with compassion but without the sentimentality which the format might have induced. The Countess and Billy Pop, on mock trial for cruelty and neglect, are forgiven, but their offences are not condoned. The six children survive, but they cannot break free of the family web: the force of heredity, of environment, of sheer habit is given its full and frightening weight. They are always being tempted back into regression: their weapon of humour is destructive as well as defensive. It is no laughing matter: their regressions "are conditioned by the very ancestry they seek to reject".[10]

Angus had tried to pre-plan, in a schematic way, what qualities in each would be destroyed by the particular comedy of each: Sukey, the whimsical, would lose love: Margaret, the coolly ironic, would lose her sensibility (and stiffen into a dead marriage): Gladys the clown would lose her self-esteem: Rupert, the master of sentimental comedy, would lose his honesty: Quentin the satirist would lose his integrity: the malicious Firbankian Marcus would lose his gaiety. Angus identified most closely with Margaret and Marcus, but they do not fare very much better than the others – though he did worry that he had been soft on Marcus. He wrote to Drabble on 21 October 1968: "Margaret has so much of me as has Marcus that it's hard for me to judge whether I have sentimentalized but I think not Margaret tho' possibly Marcus a little."

Is there an element of wish-fulfilment in this re-creation and expurgation of the Johnstone-Wilson family romance? One of Angus's notes reads "How much is it a family of AWs manqués that I am attacking?" and the question is relevant. The Matthews are notably more successful than their originals. Fred's prison term had been served for far less creditable reasons than those of Gladys. Pat and Colin had failed. Winn had served honourably in the small world of Sukey Pascoe, but worldly-wise Clive had prospered more mysteriously and possibly less respectably than Gladys before her fall. Only Margaret/Marcus/Angus had been recognised by the world. The Johnstone-Wilsons, as a family, had failed. The Matthews survive – although it is interesting to note that only two of the six, Rupert and Sukey, produce children. Like the Johnstone-Wilsons, they are not a reproductive clan.

It is hard to avoid recognising an element of fantasy in the resolution of Marcus's story – when Marcus's lover and protector Jack dies, Marcus goes off to Mogador and sets up a non-profit-making scent factory to provide employment for his Moroccan ex-lovers and their vast extended families. How nice it would be, if all the Mohameds and Ahmeds and their successors could be set up in one big happy family, benevolently protected, and loving their protector! As Wilson Knight rightly guessed, Morocco had worked upon Angus's imagination, providing a version of Arcadia or Utopia, as Dubrovnik had provided long ago for Pat and Colin. (G. Wilson Knight had written to Angus on 29 March 1965: "I wonder if your visit to Morocco will lead to some large work like Anglo-Saxon Attitudes or The Old Men at the Zoo?")

Not even Angus's many layers of irony can conceal his doubts about this ending: one early note reads "Marc – spy or fantasist? A dandy must not use a rusty spike – bleeding to death in 1968 when we leave him." And apart from the practical implausibilities of such a utopian scheme, there were psychological obstacles too. As Angus was eventually to admit, while confronting a similar moral/artistic problem in a later work, his real-life dandy heroes were never political. Art and morality could not be forced to mix.

In this novel, Angus confronted the whole of his own biography. He looked unflinchingly at his parents and his brothers, yet his glance did not wither them. They remained lively enough. By the mid-sixties, when he began the book, he had reached a sense of personal equilibrium, of creative calm and courage which enabled him to look back at the monsters without fear. Like Marcus, he could enter the cramped bedroom of his childhood, and outstare its horrors. The prison could hold him no more. He was no longer lonely, no longer on the brink. The novel is at times violent, at times dark, and always uninhibited in expression (here the Sixties had brought freedom to explore and to speak out), yet it gives less sense of emotional vulnerability than its predecessors. It has no undertow or groundswell of breakdown and panic. There are moments of despair, when Margaret contemplates suicide, when Gladys faces disgrace, when Quentin realises his intense loneliness – but they are swept away by a confident energy.

Had Angus, perhaps, put *everything* in this book? Had he used it all up? Were there any dark corners left in which the little snakes of plot could breed?

The most vulnerable of the Matthews is the motherly Sukey. She lacks the armour of irony, and therefore she is the most ridiculous. She rarely rises above a self-protective whimsy. Yet she suffers the most: she gives all her love to her youngest son, the whimsically named P.S., and loses him. Angus at one point doubted if he could get inside her character, though his notes say she was based on "many women I have known". (One surprising note of a possible – and very far removed – original is Nancy Mitford, whose "English" comedy had, to Angus, a certain desperate pathos.) Of Sukey, he wrote to Julian Mitchell: "the aura of 'The Waves' was so great that only after the book was complete did I realise that the country/children needing sister had been called Susan and so that no one would think I was aspiring to compare I changed her name to Sukey (even so I had to let the Countess call her Susan once – as tho' my debt to V.W. must be owned somewhere[11])." (Mitchell, in a letter dated 20 October 1967, had said that the novel reminded him of "Virginia Woolf at her best".)

Interestingly, Sukey's tragic dénouement takes place in the West Country. There she retreats (like one of her models, Ann Wormald) to save her boys from the bombs of the South Coast: there she learns that her beloved son has been killed in Aden: there she takes refuge chatting to God in church, remembering walks with P.S. up Porlock Hill. Sukey had dreamed of a clean and happy home in the Quantocks when cooking in the filthy basement of No. 52: when she gets it, it is invaded first by Jewish refugees (shades of Arnold Simmel) and then by death itself. Billy Pop and the Countess also die in the West Country, at Exe Grange, a residential hotel in Devonshire, killed in a Baedeker raid.

Is there some link here, conscious or unconscious, with that fateful holiday at Watchet, the summer before Maud's death? This would seem fanciful were it not for a note apparently made while Angus was plotting his first novel, *Hemlock and After*. In a list of what seem to be possible "ideas" or "psychic moments" which he may have been planning to weave together, Point 9 (out of 30) reads "Mother and me on the road from Porlock." What happened there? Was Maud, like Sukey, "taken short": did she, like Sukey, ring on the door of a dilapidated old rectory covered in ivy, receive no reply, and in the end have to "go in the bushes"? (p.461) Or was Maud perhaps, walking up a steep Somerset hill with Angus, her youngest, her own P.S., taken short in another way – short of breath, panting from the asthma which was so soon to kill her? Had a return visit to Exeter, for research, in December 1966, revived some rare memory of embarrassment or intimacy? Whatever happened, Angus never forgave the West Country. Had he truly been interned there during the war years in a camouflaged mental hospital (at Exe Grange? at Holne?) he could hardly have disliked it more.

*

Angus spent the autumn of 1967 teaching in California. Towards the end of August he flew off to speak at a summer school for mature students (code-named Methuselah) in Santa Cruz. Here, despite "all the symptoms you can imagine, including an itching bum and insomnia", he found a superb house, a delightful campus, and quantities of peaches. He was joined by Tony, who had been spending a week or two with his parents in Tankerton and appearing in a Blackburne play. (There was some anxiety about visas: would Tony get through immigration all right on his own? Angus himself had difficulty filling in his forms, and had been sent like a naughty boy to the back of the queue.) They took a short break, driving up the coast to see the sea-lions at Point Wilson, and then settled back for a semester's work.

No Laughing Matter had been received with great enthusiasm by Warburg, Farrer and Spencer Curtis Brown himself at Curtis Brown: it was also well received by the critics, even by the *Times Literary Supplement* (at the anonymity of which Angus had recklessly sniped, under the cover of Margaret Matthews – her hostile reviewer, she speculated, was "a well known face, no doubt, red and blustering or white and smirking, seen very often all smiles behind a cocktail glass"). The only "snide" review, wrote Angus to Farrer, seemed to be Nigel Dennis's, though he was sorry Francis

Hope, and some of the "boys", seemed to have missed so much. (It was a diffucult book to review in a weekly column.) Warburg was in raptures, assuring Angus that he deserved the Nobel prize. But still the book did not sell. Despite the reviews, despite being the most talked-about book in London, it reached only 8,000 copies, not the 15,000 that had been hoped for. Agent chastised publisher, publisher snapped back at agent. But so it was. Why? What was to be done? How else was money to be earned?

Angus was still suffering from hypertension, and trying to take life in California easily: he was on a diet – no spirits, no carbohydrates – and had lost a stone and a half since his return from Australia. He pleaded ill-health as an excuse for not attending his American publication in New York. He was upset by a remark of Secker's new publicity manager, Jeremy Hadfield, who had told *Smith's Trade News* that he hadn't been helped "in his promotion task (of NLM) by the author going off to America. 'You must have personal appearances these days to get into the big time,' he says . . ."[12] Angus wrote back indignantly, saying he had done his very best to oblige before leaving, and that anyway he was under doctor's orders. Everyone apologised (an "idiotic paragraph", wrote Farrer) and Angus did his best to forget the stresses back home – though he cannot have been pleased when Fred Warburg helpfully wrote suggesting that Angus's next novel should be "if not short, then shorter".[13]

The Californian sun suited him, and he had a beautiful view over the bay from his comfortable suburban house in San Luis Road. There was a resident cat called Walker. (He had left Felsham Woodside and his cats in the care of Julian Mitchell, who was honoured by the offer but found the cottage was too lonely and the fire smoked: Mitchell was charmed by Victoria, who tried to share his bath, but less charmed by Giuseppe, who presented him with the tail and two paws of a squirrel. Mrs Revens, Mitchell noted, had extraordinary eyes – but he did not note, as did some visitors, her extraordinary resemblance to the Queen.)[14] The young people, revolting *en masse* throughout America, did not revolt against Angus. He lectured on Dickens and his fear of mob rule as seven thousand pale beaded and bearded students demonstrated on the campus against the Vietnam draft in a temperature of ninety degrees. He sympathised with them as they tore up their draft cards, though he wrote to Fred Warburg that nice though they were, *they* were not the "beautiful people" – the beautiful people were the black tanned surfies, the idle children of the rich bourgeoisie, who lay around on the beach all day and were probably Fascists to a man . . . His own seminar students were well-read and interesting, though he was a little alarmed by two Chicago Aristotelians – "just as bigoted as Leavis's followers". And love to Pamela, he hopes she is less depressed. (He wrote to Julian Mitchell that the Chicago Aristotelians should be condemned to reading Lytton Strachey for ten years to cure them of their smug "18C and 19C pietism".)

Their visit was enlivened by Ann and John Dizikes. Ann, the daughter of Christopher and Helen Morris, was now married to historian John Dizikes, a founder member of the new university at Santa Cruz – and they were "enchanting", Angus had written to Tony. Angus was to dedicate to them an American collection of his short stories, published as *Death Dance* by Viking on 9 May 1969. John believes that this gesture was made because when he saw them that year they were much preoccupied with a tragically short-lived spina bifida twin, born in 1966, and that he wanted to express his concern and affection: Ann says no, "we just had a lot of laughs and he enjoyed being with us."

At the end of the semester at Berkeley, Angus and Tony drove through a snowstorm to Dallas, then on to New Orleans for Christmas, where they stayed in the Provincial Hotel, visited the My-oh-My Club, and were entertained by Clay Shaw, a wealthy homosexual business man famous for his hospitality. (He was later to feature prominently as a suspect in one of the Kennedy assassination conspiracy theories, the brainchild of local district attorney Jim Garrison: the appearance of Angus's name in Shaw's address book, along with the names of Frith Banbury, Sir Michael Duff, Lord Edward Montagu, Steven Runciman and others, was fearlessly exposed by the English investigative magazine *Lobster* in November 1990: *Lobster* also reports that Tony Garrett was "a schoolmaster who was sacked when the nature of his relationship with Sir Angus was discovered by the school's governors.")

The trip to Mexico and Trinidad proved immensely enjoyable. The Hotel Montejo at Merida in Yucatan was delightful: one of its eighty-year-old guests was to be seen on the patio chuckling over a copy of *No Laughing Matter*. (Less tactful were the four people who, as Tony wrote to his mother, asked Tony if Angus was his father.) Angus wrote from Yucatan to thank Fred Warburg for his congratulations on his CBE, announced in the New Year Honours list – Tony said the consul-general had telephoned Angus from San Francisco to see if he would accept, and upon learning that it was a higher honour than Muriel Spark's, who acquired her OBE the year before, he gleefully agreed. (He had overtaken Spark, and caught up with Spender, who had received his CBE in 1962.) The award honoured not only Angus's distinction as a writer but also his services to literature, as unpaid ambassador for the British Council, and as a member of the Arts Council. He was to take his niece Jeanne to the palace with him in the spring to receive this honour: the photograph of them standing smiling side by side shows a remarkable family similarity. They look like brother and sister.

Angus was on top of the world, and he was taking the Mayan ruins by easy stages. He and Tony both loved the rainforest, the parrots, the decaying splendour of the old mansions. They hoped to see an ant-eater or perhaps a kinkajou. Then they went on to Port of Spain, Trinidad, where they stayed with Stuart Hampshire's brother Sir Peter, the High Commissioner, and his wife Eve: they survived the cocktail parties, met Norman Parkinson, and admired the scarlet ibises. A snapshot shows Angus wading in the sea in his rolled-up trousers dragging a huge piece of seaweed. He looks ecstatically carefree and happy, as though childhood itself had been redeemed by the catharsis of the novel: the beaches of Bexhill, the waves of Watchet were all forgotten and forgiven in this island paradise. They then flew on to Martinique for another week (the island on which the Empress Jospehine and Madame de Maintenon were reared, as he wrote reminding Neville Blackburne) where they admired and photographed a plaque which announced that *"Nulle terre française ne doit plus porter d'esclaves."* Then home, after a couple of nights in Lisbon.

Angus returned to a lunch and a dinner on 7 February 1968 with UEA colleagues Colin Clarke and Nicholas Brooke to catch up with the university news, and on 24 February he lunched at Yaxley with George Coulson, Thomas Hutton and John Croft on Finnish ham, salami, dates, lackschinken, olives, cress and marinated tomatoes, followed by poached trout, boiled potatoes, chived salad and lemon sorbet. (According to Coulson and Hutton, who kept a food diary, Tony would arrive on these occasions with "a half bottle of champagne for Angus".) Friends old and new lay in wait, and so did piles of letters. On 21 March Angus lunched with the Queen and dined with John Croft. In the midst of all this, he was planning a book on Dickens, toying with possible offers from Hollywood, and attending meetings at the Arts Council. He was full of confidence and energy. It was all going to be all right.

Television producer Julian Jebb, another of the clever, slight, amusing and ultimately tragic figures who have featured in this narrative, was in negotiation over one of Angus's most interesting television performances. The subject was to be sexual revolution. Jebb stayed at Felsham Woodside in the spring, to talk the project through. The theme was not to be the legalisation of homosexuality, or the sexual permissiveness of the 1960s, but the relationship between the sexes. In it, Angus was to pick up one of the themes of his Albany Trust lecture – the social distortion of women in a male power structure, and their revolt against it in literature. This theme has become so familiar that it is worth recalling that in 1968 feminist criticism had not been invented. The proto-feminist novel of the 1960s (Lessing, Weldon, O'Brien, Forster, Duffy, Dunn, Plath) was popular, but there was as yet no body of critical work to describe it: Mary Ellmann's attempt to do so, *Thinking about Women*, was the first of many, and it was not published until 1968. Angus was scenting, in his own new freedom from constraint, a shift of opinion that would change many lives in the next decades. His argument was presented as a plea for a united front.

The programme was filmed in May, as the student barricades went up in Paris, and transmitted on 10 September 1968. The air was hot with revolution, but Angus was one of the few to spot that sexual revolution was an essential item on the agenda. And by revolution, he did not mean perpetual revolution and perpetual warfare. He meant an irreversible redistribution of power. In Paris, women were still offering sex and sandwiches. Despite the revolutionary relationship of Sartre and de Beauvoir (and Angus had strongly defended de Beauvoir from urbane philistine mockery in Santa Cruz) the French remained paralysed by archaic notions of gallantry, romance and submission. Angus perceived that we needed a new agenda.

He had begun to provide it in his fiction. Now he gave his analysis of the situation as he saw it, as he had observed it in UEA and Berkeley and in the fiction of younger writers, and in the unfulfilled lives of Bump Walker and Helen Pattisson and Clara Matthews the Countess. Behind his protest hovered a host of smiling silent talkative amusing witty sacrifices to sexual stereotyping and sexual distortion – Forrest Fulton, Angus Heriot, Philippe Jullian, Julian Jebb, James Mossman, John Minton, Keith Vaughan, all suicides who would bleed in the dark wood of the suicides: and the self-destroyers, Robin Ironside, John Woodward, Perkin Walker, Ian Calder, Bert Howard . . . (John the Scot, who died young, was, according to Chris Arnold, one of the saved: he had pulled himself together and was teaching in a language school in Spain when he was accidentally drowned.) And women too had suffered – the death of Virginia Woolf had shocked Angus greatly even before he had learned to admire her work.

Angus's Albany Trust lecture on "Literature and Sexual Freedom", delivered on 17 December 1964, and chaired by J.B. Priestley, had swept through a vast range of material. He discussed Richardson's *Clarissa*, to him a key text which exposed the way in which woman was seen as prey – hence a milestone in women's emancipation. He moved on to the bifurcation of Richardson's influence. In France the novel of de Sade, Diderot, and Laclos flourished, the novel of seduction, cellars and country houses and quasi-religious ritual and masturbatory fantasy, the novel of the pretty body chained in the dungeon. (Angus's paperback New English Library copy of Diderot's *La Religieuse*, translated by Marianne Sinclair (1966), is very heavily annotated – it is clearly his UEA teaching copy, for he had read the novel in French during the war.) In England, in contrast, sex in the novel ceased to exist. Which was more revolting, de Sade or the death of Little Nell? Angus deplored the "angel" virtues and qualities that men have imposed on women and which he had exposed in his fiction – coquettishness, smother love, cock-teasing – and went on to discuss homosexuality in literature through the ages – gay frolics in the *Satyricon*, Christian rejection, Chaucerian contempt, Smollett's view of it as a dirty joke, Balzac's macho criminal-hero Vautrin, the mawkish schoolboy dreams of Hugh Walpole and Forrest Reid, the Proustian and Wildean obsession with the working classes, Carpenter's manly clasp of the hand, Gide's sad blind alley in Algiers, John Rechy's City-of-Night obsession with he-men and leathers and his "disgusting adaptation of shameful anti-woman hatred." It was a bravura speech, in which women and homosexuals were equally seen as victims of a puritanical patriarchy.

The 1968 broadcast picked up the baton from the Albany lecture. Here, he argues that women in literature had been protesting against their oppression for centuries: he begins with the two Richardsons, Dorothy and Samuel, and gallops through Austen, Meredith, and Woolf, and on to Katherine Mansfield, Rebecca West, Elizabeth Bowen, Rosamund Lehmann, Jean Rhys, Elizabeth Taylor, Doris Lessing, Muriel Spark, Iris Murdoch, Penelope Mortimer, Edna O'Brien, Brigid Brophy and Margaret Drabble. He argues for a new equality, a new "merged and fluid" concept of sexual identity: get rid of the ideas of the victim and the chase, get rid of the necessity of pain and destruction in love, get rid of sadistic pleasure, opt for more respect for the individual, for more tenderness. He uses a quote from Jean Rhys to suggest that "if the sexual revolution that is being sought by the younger generation doesn't come about, if it peters out or fails, then I do think we may get a sort of Black Power position amongst intelligent women. And if that happens, writers like myself who have tried to enter into women's characters and feel compassion with them, we are exactly the people who will be treated as the Black Power people treat the white liberals. There will be no more time for us. Women will demand from men the same violent response in turn. It will be a world of Strindberg, a world of Montherlant, or a world of Osborne's Jimmy Porter. Women's reply will be total war of an Amazonian kind."[15]

Fred Warburg loved it all and wanted to turn it into a book. Perhaps it would, with Evil, make a nice little volume? The BBC loved it, and wanted him to make another programme about the British Museum, about Dickens and Dostoevksy, about politics and art, about more or less anything he fancied. Angus toyed with ideas and rejected them. There was, as usual, far too much going on – students writing for references, students sending essays, students at parties, parties in London, parties in Suffolk. In August, he wrote to Frank Thistlethwaite handing in his resignation at UEA – it was all too much, and he would leave at the end of the summer of 1969.[16] (He was cajoled out of this decision by Nicholas Brooke on the understanding that he could cut down his teaching to one term a year – the summer term – for the same stipend.) There was a tour of the Midlands, a trip to Belgium, a convocation at Norwich. Patrick White came to stay for the night in September, followed by Bentley Bridgewater. Hampshires, Corkes and Cooksons clustered. Angus jotted notes for ideas for stories in the back of his tiny pocket diary, along with nursery notes about clematis. Should he or should he not attend a conference on Obscurity? He taught *The Waves*, *Great Expectations*, and *Between the Acts*. He ate too much: his weight was creeping up again. But how to control it, with all these lunches and dinners? On 13 November 1968 he was Guest Speaker at the Bury St Edmunds Art Society Dinner, where he gamely made his way through Lobster Tails, Asparagus Soup, Norfolk Turkey with Brussels Sprouts, Buttered Carrots, Game Chips and Chipolata, Roast *and* New Potatoes, Pineapple Sundae, biscuits and cheese, and a cake shaped like an artist's palette bearing 21 candles. He spoke about drinking brandy with Krushchev and a dinner of raw bullfrog. (Nobody seemed to know on which of his travels he had been offered this.) He was thanked by Air Vice-Marshal S.F. Vincent, CB, DFC, ASFC, DL.

And on top of all this junketing, there was the Arts Council. He took his job as chairman of the Literature Panel very seriously indeed.

22

TOURING

Angus was recommended as Chair of the Literature Panel by Lord Goodman, who was very happy with the appointment, for Angus proved a suprisingly sound committee man. Not only was he good at steering cheerfully through choppy ideological water: he also came up with practical ideas for encouraging writers. Some panel chairs were to give up on the whole business: not so Angus. He believed public money could be spent usefully, and he listened carefully to new suggestions. (As early as February 1963 he had been in correspondence with two teachers at the Royal College of Art, novelist Ann Quin and aspiring novelist Paddy Bowling, about the possibility of setting up a writing school: nothing had come of the project but Angus had expressed interest in it.)

The notion of Writers' Tours came originally from Julian Mitchell, who was earning his living as a freelance writer and broadcaster: he appreciated the difficulties that authors had in meeting readers, and proposed that groups should be sent off to visit the regions. Angus and Goodman both approved. Bursaries and prizes had attracted contrasting accusations of "old boy's network" and "sheer lottery": journalists complained if the Council favoured the experimental in the shape of Alan Burns or Christine Brooke-Rose, or the classical in the form of V.S. Naipaul. Tours would spread its favours more broadly. Wilson would lead the first, to North Wales: Mitchell the second, to Lancashire. A group of four writers would visit each region, where evening appearances with discussions and readings would be arranged. During the day schools and colleges, libraries and bookshops, would be on the itinerary.

In April 1968 Angus had received a letter from J.O. Jones, Secretary to the North Wales Association for the Arts, asking if he would be willing to visit various literary groups in the area. Angus wrote back saying that he was too busy, but that he felt such groups could be encouraged: and here, in the spring of 1969, came the opportunity.

Angus chose for his pioneer group Christopher Logue, Nell Dunn, and Margaret Drabble. Drabble had been reading Wilson's work since the late 1950s: she does not think that the first time she met him and Tony in person was at the Jardin des Gourmets in Greek Street, where Angus invited his flock on 28 January 1969 for a conference to describe his project, but it may have been. If they had met before, it had been at some large publishing occasion.

Angus in his role as leader was on top form. He was hospitable and professional: he made us all think it was going to be a great lark as well as hard work. (The pay was one hundred pounds a week, plus expenses – he himself took no fee.) One would never have believed from his cheerful and expansive manner that earlier that month he had been worrying about giddy spells, dizziness, ill-fitting teeth, fears of imminent death in the small hours, and that he was afraid to consult his doctor Patrick Woodcock for fear of hearing the worst: that he was anxious about his Dickens book, and had lain awake for hours wondering whether he had mortally offended Michael Howard or David Farrer . . . He seemed to be on the crest of a wave, still riding high on the success of *No Laughing Matter*, which had been everybody's Book of the Year. (Was this historian Michael Howard, or the other Michael Howard at Cape, whom he had recently met? Tony's Journal note does not make this clear, but it was probably the historian. However, this spring there was much activity in the publishing world: Cape made an unsuccessful bid for Secker & Warburg, and Spencer Curtis Brown was edged out of power. Angus was wooed by Deutsch, Hamish Hamilton, Blond, Collins, Cape, Longman, Michael Joseph and Gollancz.) Here at dinner at the Jardin was the jolly Angus, the one that was to be heard on Desert Island Discs in February, chattering happily away about Nellie Wallace and Edith Sitwell, Fats Waller and Alice Faye. He appeared to forget anxieties in company.*

He took us seriously and listened to us all. Nell Dunn and Drabble had both published several novels, and Logue was well known as a poet of the counter-culture, but we were very much his juniors: he never let us feel this. He seemed to find us as entertaining as we found him. There was a sense of excitement and anticipation. Writers on the whole lead solitary

---

* Angus's choice of records was eclectic: Nellie Wallace singing "The Blasted Oak", Fats Waller with "My Very Good Friend the Milkman", Alice Faye with "Rose of Washington Square", an extract from Britten's *The Turn of the Screw*, and extracts from Weber's *Oberon* Overture, Mendelssohn's 4th Symphony, Handel's *Messiah*, and Mozart's *Don Giovanni*.

lives: he had devised a scheme which let us out of the study and the kitchen, and sent us off on a spree.

North Wales was perhaps not ideal territory for an outing in March, but nothing deterred the little band. Off they went, through all weathers, through rain and snow and ice, driven by Tony and J.O. Jones round hairpin bends on steep mountainsides. They ventured boldly into draughty libraries where many a solitary librarian sat patiently amidst her quiet stock, they chatted up sixteen-year-old schoolboys in Welsh-speaking schools, and they were asked (by customers at W.H. Smith's) where the greetings cards were kept. It was heroic.

The travellers assembled on Sunday, 9 March 1969 at The Bulkeley Arms Hotel, Beaumaris, on Anglesey. Some travelled by train via Crewe: Angus and Tony went by car, spending a night on the way in Shrewsbury, and arrived to find an encouraging telegram from Julian Mitchell:

> "He who would valiant be 'gainst all disaster
> Let him in constancy follow the master."

Angus, unusually, started brief diary notes (in an exercise book full of Dickens jottings) at the beginning of the trip: at Beaumaris at the end of the first day he jotted down:

> Tony heard a porter tell Mr Jones in Welsh that Hutchinson the Maoist was loose – or rather Pwyllch ddrybrrau Hutchinson pride brannei Mau Tse Tung and so on.
>
> Hutchinson said – 'that's a liberal cliché, Logue.'
>
> I failed to recognise Mr Bradbrook, apologising for Hutchinson, 'We've done everything we can to keep him. We gave him no degree.' Mr Jones told us, glowing with pleasure, 'that there was so much noise of dogs and children that I don't suppose any of the BBC recording can be used. None at all.'
>
> A man arrived out of the blue and kissed Margaret D., saying 'Maggie, what are you doing here?' To which Maggie replied very casually, 'I'm on a writers tour of Anglesey' as tho' she did it every month. The man then claimed to know me, calling me 'sir' and told us about Welsh people in Patagonia.* Christopher then said wrongly but firmly that Patagonia was between Argentine and Bolivia. At the school a little boy stared at me very fixedly and then said gravely 'Do you still write what you want?' And when I answered repeated his question as 'Do you write for the

---

* This was the actor Kenneth Griffith, with whom Drabble had appeared in a TV programme: he played Sir Thomas More, she his daughter.

money?'

A lady said she'd enjoyed the occasion because she hadn't heard any good talk for twenty years.

Tuesday, Holyhead and Llangefni

The school – I felt that, tho' the boys and girls were the most important thing (and as a boy told me later at an evening meeting I had got something across to them) the teachers, too, at the luncheon (the trifle!!!) were getting something out of it. The reactions of the deputy head (scripture) towards a year's (or term's) revision at Keele were very good – his dislike of the degree to which the University was cut off from the Potteries from indeed, life, was excellent. He (with scripture in mind) saw the whole academic community like the Greeks to St Paul who had reduced truth to a niggling needle point. The deputy head woman teacher Mrs Heaney (English but twenty years in Anglesey) was very friendly and kind, but she had a definite bright head relationship to the pupils – And how indeed with such a building and such numbers can it not be so? It's easy enough for Christopher viewing everything revolutionarywise to say the buildings don't matter, but they do matter to overworked, over administered teachers. And Nell, too, feeling the head wasn't interested in her visit doesn't perhaps see what mountains of work the man has which allows for no possibility of an interest in anything else (tho' the man may very well be a philistine bastard). The deputy head (man) told me that all the 6th who will administer people have no time to take part in the community studies because of exams. As a result only people who profit from the connection with 'people' are those who will be 'people' (and not administrators) themselves. So it goes on. The bloody system – so much for Angus Maude and Tony Dyson and Kingsley Amis.

Nell set the subject beautifully and it led to a real revelation of what writers *were* rather than what they do (my approach). The deputy head woman who liked me in the morning didn't like this – probably personally but perhaps because pupils were there.

Here the journal ends, no doubt petering out under the pressure of travel. Oddly enough Drabble, almost as careless a diary keeper as Angus himself, also tried to keep a diary for this week, but she has carelessly mislaid most of it: all that remains are two pages which she copied out as an offering for a Birthday Book for her publisher George Weidenfeld. They read:

March 10, 1969 Beaumaris.

Waking up in a place seen only by dark, to open the windows
to a lovely pale mountainous view across the straits. I was up first
in the morning. I had no engagement so I put on my boots and
walked along the beach – it was very muddy and my feet sank in
and after the mud there were vast stretches of muddy mussels, and
I began to get quite nervous, crunching all these almost animate
objects with my boots. After an hour I sat down by the concrete
edge to read my book (The Last Post, Ford Madox Ford). A van
drew up and some men got out – all but one of them marched off
with a bucket to pick shellfish but one of them came and sat down
by me and asked me if I was enjoying my book. Then we sat in
silence and then I asked him what the men were picking, and he
said winkles. I remembered a thing I read in the paper about
winkle picking dying out because it couldn't be mechanised, and
one man (in East Anglia, I think) said 'Of course you can put posts
in the water and the winkles tend to climb up them, and then you
can pick them off easier, but you can't call that mechanisation, can
you?' After a few words more the winkle man said would I like to
go into Beaumaris and have a drink with him and I said yes, so
characteristically got out of my intended walk. He drove me back
and bought me a Guinness. He had six children, he said, and six
brothers and sisters, and six men to pick for him – he owned a
winkle business.

March 13, 1969 Colwyn Bay

Angus Wilson emerging from the technical college said 'This is
very like the nineteenth century, talking to a large number of
people in a building and then coming out into the snow.' I
thought this very funny and still do.

And there Drabble's fragment ends.

Clearly Drabble had the first morning off, but after that the pace
increased. The next day was spent in Bangor, where the group dispersed to
various venues during the day and met for an evening event in the
University College Refectory Lounge: the next day took in Llangefni,
Holyhead, Menai Bridge and Amlwych: Wednesday took them to
Llandudno, Llandrillo-y-Rhos and Colwyn Bay: Thursday to Wrexham
and Llangollen: and the grand finale was in Mold. It was exhausting, and it
was sometimes hard to find points of contact. The filmed versions of Nell
Dunn's works were familiar to some schoolchildren, and others recognised
Drabble from her recent TV appearances on *Junior Points of View*, but often
they had to start from scratch. Many school dinners and high teas were

eaten, many hands were shaken, and one or two insults were traded: the group was heckled one night as "a gang of bourgeois intellectuals", but Logue at least knew how to give as good as he got. (Angus on Logue, over some dispute about bacon at breakfast: "Funny how you left-wing chaps are often a bit sharp with the waiters . . .")

Logue shocked a few members of the audience and J.O. Jones himself by reading aloud a poem about a sergeant of the police who fell madly in love with his fourteen-year-old daughter:

> As she came through the bedroom door he grabbed her,
> ripped off her knickers,
> and fucked her and fucked her until he came,
> screaming:
>> "Let punishment come from Above,
>> for there is none on earth!
>> Let it fall on my stinking wife!
>> She is to blame for everything!"
>> (*New Numbers*, 1969)

Angus, as I recall, did not bat an eyelid as he listened to this: he stood by his troop. On a milder note, he himself surprised his fellow travellers by announcing one night that the theme for the evening's reading would be Death: he read from the scene in *The Middle Age of Mrs Eliot* where Bill Eliot is shot and several older people came up to him afterwards and told him they had found it "very helpful". (Nell chose friendship as her theme: Drabble forgets what she chose.) The question of women's writing also arose on several occasions, and Angus valiantly defended his own position as a Writer who Understood Women, and a defender of "the noble washers-up of life".

It was tiring, hectic, non-glamorous, and very stimulating. There was little time for sight-seeing, though one day Tony managed to charm open the seasonally closed gates of the house of the Ladies of Llangollen, and the watercolour views over the sea from Beaumaris, agreed Nell and Angus, were like a Boudin. They visited a friend of Angus's who had a Gothic cottage with ogee windows and wrote television plays in Welsh. Angus seemed to know or to make friends with such unlikely people, and all week he kept up an endless flow of informative and entertaining chatter. Nell Dunn, at this period, was wearing a Sixties scarf around her brow, which prompted Angus to a delightful aria upon the *bandeau* fashionable in the Twenties, and the Kensingtonian girls who had worn it through the Thirties, unaware of its loss of chic: how strange, how pleasing, he declared, to see it back in fashion again. To one like Drabble, who had so admired *Such Darling Dodos*, this was a historic moment. Less historic, perhaps, but equally fascinating, was Angus's remark, after blowing his nose heartily one morning, that his nurse had told him always to *blow his nose before coming down to breakfast*, as all the best people did.

In Llandudno the team was inspected by Charles Osborne, late of the *London Magazine* and now with the Literature Department of the Arts Council, who was able to report back to Eric Walter White at head office that it had all been a great success: it was now up to Mitchell, Adrian Henri, John McGrath and Iris Murdoch to carry on with the good work in Bolton and Wigan later in the month. (Eric Walter White wrote to thank Angus, adding that Tony had done "a superb job as general secretary, chauffeur and so on".)

But Angus had had enough of trouping in the cold and the wet. He rushed to Paris for the day on 18 March 1969 to talk about *No Laughing Matter* in French for Stock, his French publishers, and had then planned to take off for Cyprus to finish his Dickens book in the sun. Air strikes prevented him, and he and Tony found themselves flying off at the last moment to a hastily rearranged break at the Libyan Palace Hotel in Tripoli, and a hastily arranged lecture at the National University. The weather was poor and the public parks uncomfortable, but Angus managed to write on the balcony, and was to be seen correcting his MS in the Café Aurora in Cathedral Square. The ruins and the hoopoes were wonderful, and he was pleased to explore another North African country. From Libya, he sent postcards of thanks to his Welsh troupers. To M.D. on a card of Leptis Magna he wrote: "Apuleius was tried for witchcraft (or wizardry, I suppose) at Sabrata to which we went yesterday and Septimus Severus was born here – so! As you see we never got to Cyprus and only by devious routes here because of all the strikes. This was just to thank you so very much for all you did in Wales. Love from us both, Angus."

And then back to his Dickens.

★

The World of Charles Dickens was delivered in May 1969, and published a year later, to coincide with the Dickens centenary. It was an illustrated biographical study, packaged by George Rainbird and published by Secker & Warburg: it was dedicated to Betty, Charles and Neville Blackburn (*sic*). (Angus was never very good at spelling, and sometimes mangled even the names of his best friends: the Wollheims gave him lasting trouble.) Angus had admired Dickens all his reading life – he was introduced to his work when he was a boy by Fred's wife Winnie – and had championed his cause long before Dickens gained academic respectability. The idea for a full-length book had been germinating for years.

One of Edmund Wilson's earliest letters to him compliments him on a Dickens article – "I was much interested in it but rather sorry that you hadn't dealt with the subject on a larger scale."[1]

Angus had published several pieces on Dickens, including afterwords to *Great Expectations* (Signet 1963) and *Little Dorrit* (Signet 1963) and a foreword to *Oliver Twist* (Penguin 1966); he had lectured on him at UEA and discussed him in seminars, learning much from his students' responses: and he had protested vehemently against Leavis's as yet unlifted censure of Dickens's work, which he felt had done so much to dim his reputation and delay reassessment. (The Leavises were to publish their revised opinion in the same centenary year: see below.)

It is easy to see why Angus admired Dickens. Dickens's sense of the comic and the macabre is echoed in Angus's own work, along with his powerful mimicry of speech patterns and idiosyncracies – both shared a particular passion for the Cockney. Both drew heavily on memories of a childhood that had seemed unpromising and insecure. Both came from families which had pretensions to gentility and below-stairs connections – Dickens's grandmother had been housekeeper to the Marquis of Crewe, Angus's father had been born in The Grapes, and his maternal grand-mother had been a barmaid in Lincoln. Dickens's father was imprisoned for debt: Angus's was lucky to escape bankruptcy. Dickens had had a severely curtailed education: Angus was the only one of six brothers to have been lucky enough to go to university, and Pat/Colin/Marcus Matthews had trolled the Dilly, a fate worse than Dickens's bitterly remembered spell in the blacking factory. Neither Charles Dickens nor Angus Johnstone-Wilson had, at an early age, expected to escape: although, unlike Angus, Dickens was to make his mark as a writer at a very early age, Angus writes sympathetically about the agonies of a young man sitting for three years in the mournful Doctors' Commons as a junior clerk. The "verbiage and dusty ceremony" of the law filled Dickens's "youthful, ambitious, impatient soul" with contempt: three years seemed "a lifetime when one is suffocating with unfulfilled ambition."[2] (The British Museum had been more congenial than Doctors' Commons, but Angus implies a parallel.)

And there were other similarities. Like David Copperfield, Angus charmed his way through school by telling stories, staving off ridicule by the force of his imagination. Angus had been Daisy to the Steerforths of Westminster. (Steerforth, not surprisingly, was a character whom Angus particularly admired, as a perfect illustration of flawed dandy charm: Benjamin Britten had suggested to him the summer before that he might like to write a libretto for a Britten opera based on the Steerforth/Little

Emily/Lowestoft plot of *David Copperfield*, a notion full of interesting possibilities which was never pursued.) Both Dickens and Angus mined their own childhood: both had bad dreams which took on the vivid quality of nightmare hallucination; both as young men trapped by circumstance walked and walked to exhaust themselves and their demon. Both had an underlying violence – in Dickens converted into violent bonhomie, and in Angus into social display. Both were histrionic, with a theatrical flair, and enjoyed performing and reading from their own works. Both had "an almost childish aural delight in verbal eccentricity of any kind" (p.185). Both had a sadistic streak in their creative imaginations – expressed in Dickens largely in his obsession with murder and capital punishment, in Angus largely in the many macabre scenes depicting the deaths of the very animals which he so loved to watch alive.

Angus does not insist on these cross-references, and his book is unmarred by the occcasionally obtrusive personal reminiscences that surface in his journalism – one of his very few "first person" comments refers to the possibility that Dickens was positively stimulated by his failure with his brainchild, the *Daily News* (p. 199). (Perhaps one also detects a personal note in his exculpatory comment on Dickens's problems in the United States – "American stresses and accents to an Englishman can seem like a relentless machine" – p.166.) But a reader aware of Angus's recent delving into the past for *No Laughing Matter* cannot fail to see connections. Predominantly, perhaps, there is the theme of the thin ice of financial insecurity – the miseries and pretensions of Dickens's parents, and the shaming spell in the Marshalsea Prison, followed by the grinding hard work by which Charles kept his own family in comfort. Again and again Angus reminds us that successful Victorians like Trollope and Thackeray paid for their triumphs in heavy labour and ruined health, and that many of the lesser figures, like Cruikshank and Phiz, went to the wall, ending their lives on Civil List pensions. Angus writes with respect of Dickens's attempts to raise the status of his profession, of his concern for colleagues who had fallen on hard times. He writes most perceptively of Dickens's portrayal of the child – the theme of one of his most successful set-piece lectures, and a theme which links with his own sources of inspiration. ("Dickens and Childhood" and "Dickens and the City", linking Dickens to Dostoevsky, were two of his best performances: the first grew from a seminar on the Concept of Childhood in Literature, with reference to Wordsworth, Henry James, Meredith, Kipling, etc. Dickens and James as little boys lost but determined to survive in an adult world clearly struck a chord with him.)

Angus sympathises with Dickens's social preoccupations – his desire to extend his range to include the whole range of British society, his refusal to patronise or sentimentalise or try to "improve" the working man, his instinctive radicalism on most public issues. Dickens's concern about slum clearance was to be directly woven into Angus's next novel, which has many Dickensian links and echoes.(One recalls his early interest in this theme, expressed in 1954 to Edmund Wilson.) While he was writing about Dickens, Angus was meditating on many features of his own career. Why was he, Angus Wilson, although so highly praised in his own country and abroad, not a great popular figure as Dickens had been? Why had he not acquired a broader base of readers? Was this some fault in himself, or was it to be laid to the charge of history, of the universities, of television, of Dr Leavis, of his own homosexuality? This was a theme to which he would revert many times over lunches with younger novelists like Michael Moorcock and Maureen Duffy, who themselves suffered a sense of marginalisation.

Not unconnected with this subject was his pleasure in noting that Dickens, like himself, found it difficult to write about the English in England, and that increasingly he too had liked to work abroad. He states that Dickens found travel abroad "an absolute necessity to the development of his fiction world of England" (p.146) and traced his journeys to Lausanne and Genoa and Boulogne and Paris with a sense of justified fellow feeling. If the most English of Englishmen needed to travel, why should not Angus Wilson follow his example?

The book, which contained dozens of carefully chosen, captioned and integrated illustrations, was a great success: it was well targeted at a non-academic readership. Angus rejected the Leavisite view that *Hard Times* was the great novel: highest in his own canon stood *David Copperfield*, *Bleak House*, *Dombey and Son*, *Little Dorrit* and *Our Mutual Friend*, with a special affection for *Great Expectations* – "What larks, Pip" was one of his own favourite catch-phrases. He glosses over none of the great failings, attributing Dickens's notorious difficulty with female characters to his early disaster with Maria Beadnell: had she and her family not played him false, he suggests, Dickens might have been as great as Shakespeare.

Publication in 1970 was to involve Angus in a great deal of junketing. He lectured on Dickens here and he lectured on him there – at Birkbeck and Keele, at Harrogate and the V and A, in Switzerland and in Paris, on television in a one-man special for Julian Jebb. (The habit died hard: he even lectured on Dickens when he was meant to be talking about Shakespeare in Stratford-upon-Avon.) He was photographed and he was interviewed, at Felsham Woodside and in the Ritz. Suited by Moss Bros, he went off to the Midsummer Banquet at the Guildhall: he attended a service at Westminster Abbey with the Queen Mother, and drank wine with the Dickens Fellowship at Dickens House in Doughty Street. He lunched at the Dorchester with Christina Foyle where he addressed a clutch of ambassadors, Edith Evans, and several hundred guests: he lunched in Bristol with Robert Speaight on Soup Copperfield and Grapefruit sans Pip and Iced Pickwick Syllabub. Dickensians from the world over, including friends from the US like George Ford and Ada Nisbet, and Sylvère Monod from Paris, clustered in London, and were taken to lunch at the zoo or tea at the Athenaeum. (One of his favourite stories was of the American academic who, when asked why he insisted that *Pickwick Papers* was his favourite of the master's work, had replied "Because it's so – so Dickensian!") It was exhausting, and he developed asthma in response.

Letters of congratulation on the book and the television performance poured in – from J.B. Priestley and David Cecil and Tony Dyson and Paul Bailey and A.S. Byatt and Philippe Jullian and Mary Renault and Robertson Davies, from Perkin Walker (who particularly appreciated Angus's treatment of violence, murder and punishment and his account of Dickens's tendency to regard "evil as a kind of substance"[3]), and from Val Graham Young (who commented that Bentley had just moved into a Dickensian address in Doughty Street). Gladys Turquet was one of many to declare it his masterpiece. Barbara Hardy, Arnold Kettle, Philip Collins, and Kathleen Tillotson gave it the seal of scholarly approval. Felix Aylmer, who remembered Angus from the Reading Room, where he had tried to solve the Edwin Drood mystery, wrote in appreciation. Anthony Storr wrote asking him about Dickens's obsessional behaviour.* Some wrote kindly pointing out his errors: Madeline House, whom he had taken as his guest to the Guildhall Banquet, spotted quite a few, and a family connection wrote in to correct his spelling of Dickens's daughter – Mamie, not Mamey, please. Edmund Wilson noted a Catermole for a Cruikshank in the attributions. Vic Sage challenged Angus over environmental determinism (Dickens's, Zola's and Angus's own) and found the text somewhat impersonal: John Croft did not much care for the illustrations. L.P. Hartley wrote in sympathy with Angus's review of the Leavises' book on Dickens, which Angus had found simultaneously important, brilliant and odious: the Leavises, Angus noted, had swung round from opposition

---

* Angus replied: "Firstly, I think that his dictatorial mania for orderliness contributed very greatly to the break-up of his marriage. Secondly, it is true that Dickens corrected his work very much more as he grew older; I suppose this might have been connected with his obsessive desire for order, but more likely, I think, that as most writers find, he found writing more difficult" (10 August 1970).

to sympathy so sharply that they now veered towards the partisan. He quoted Leavis's own dismissive words on Dickens as entertainer from *The Great Tradition* and continued: "This verdict did a very great deal to retard the recognition of Dickens's genius, since the reputation of the Leavises is (contrary to what they appear to think from their Mrs Clenman wheelchair) rightly immense." Hartley enjoyed all this very much.[4]

Angus heard from old friends and made new through Dickens, who had himself valued friendship so highly: chief among the new was Michael Slater, lecturer at Birkbeck and editor of *The Dickensian*. Slater had been an undergraduate at Oxford, where he had found his enthusiasm for Dickens a little before its time, but he had persevered. He met Angus in 1969 through his own involvement with the Dickens Centenary Exhibition Committee: they lunched together at the Rembrandt Hotel, and took to one another at once. Slater, who greatly admired Angus's novels, was pressed into reading the typescript of Angus's work on Dickens, and was to remain a loyal supporter on all points of Dickens scholarship.

Angus and Michael Slater had more in common than their love of Dickens: they shared a gay ebullience. Slater was shortly introduced to Tony, Angus to Slater's more extensive circle, which consisted of three other characters – the quiet John Grigg, John's friend Choon, and the dashing Q. Many a merry evening did this little group dine and wine together in what Slater liked to call his little Bloomsbury grotto in Ridgmount Gardens. Slater was, like Angus, a first-class lecturer and raconteur, but conviviality rather than competition reigned at their meetings. (One of Slater's finest stories, a rival to Angus's own set-pieces, concerns a Japanese Dickensian whose miniature "Gadshill" Slater had visited in Japan.)

Over the next few years Slater and John Grigg were to make many visits to Felsham Woodside, returning on one occasion with their arms full of roses which, Slater wrote, "would certainly, were I Japanese, make me think of the Tower of London, Grasmere, Land's End, the National Portrait Gallery, Edinburgh Castle, Baden-Baden, the Tuileries, Helsinki Railway Station, San Marco, and goodness knows what else."[5]

(Was Angus a little galled when his Dickens book won the Yorkshire Post Prize, presented in January 1971? Did not his novels deserve as much or more? What price popularity?)

★

In the summer of 1969, with the Dickens typescript safely delivered, Angus threw himself into the usual round of work and play – there was a trip to the Stratford Poetry Festival, students came and went, there were lunches and dinners with Tynan and Wheldon and Ann Fleming and the Egyptian Ambassador and Cecil Roberts and John Betjeman and William Plomer and Michael Holroyd and Jonathan Raban and Simon Edwards and Malcolm and Elizabeth Bradbury. Charles Osborne and his friend Kenneth Thomson came to Felsham Woodside for a weekend, and so did critic Jack Lambert with his wife Catherine. Niece Jeanne and Angus's great-nephews came to stay: they behaved better than Ivor and Keith (who deserved a double exclamation mark of horror in the diary for their bad behaviour: they provoked Angus into throwing a cup of coffee at them). Julian Mitchell and his handsome new philosophical friend Richard Rowson came for a night to entertain and "mind" Angus while Tony was away visiting his mother.

In June, Angus appeared for the first time at UEA as Public Orator, gloriously robed in Cecil Beaton-designed purple and gold academic dress. (Beaton had done a splendid and theatrical job for the university: degree ceremonies glowed with emerald and salmon and magenta, and the registrar wore a surprising triangular mortar board which suggested a setting for *The Magic Flute*.) This was a task that he took seriously for the next few years, writing many letters to friends of the honorary graduands, and mastering arcane subject-matter in order to give substance to his orations. This year he was on safe ground with Sir Nikolaus Pevsner, Sir Hugh Carleton Greene of the BBC, and Robert Wyndham Ketton-Cremer, historian and owner of the great Norfolk country house, Felbrigg: he had to work a little harder to sound *au fait* with the careers of Professsor Charles Coulson, mathematician and theoretical chemist, and Sir Alec Issigonis, designer of the Morris Minor and the Mini. But to each he brought a personal touch and a note of genuine interest – as he was to do with the familiar (Frances Yates, Robert Lowell, Denys Lasdun, Jack Plumb, Harold Pinter, Freddie Ayer) and those who represented worlds far from his own. (Issigonis inspired a heartfelt hymn to the delights of democratic motoring.) The second group included Sir Gordon Cox of the Agricultural Research Council: Professor Cyril Clarke of "rhesus baby" fame (whose doctor grandfather, Angus cheerfully informed the congregation, had been murdered by a patient whom he had committed to the local asylum): and Sir Frederick Dainton, Yorkshireman, chemist and public administrator. With each he found points of contact, and from some he drew ideas for fictional characters. His annual performance was a great success, marred only by a tendency to talk very very fast and an at times incomplete control of the microphone.

The job brought some unexpected side benefits. Patrick Gordon Walker, to whom Angus had written for personal memories of Greene, responded with a story about a cricket match at Woburn Abbey and the disastrous news of the fall of Singapore: a note had arrived from Bush House asking how to handle it, and Greene "looked at the note and said: 'Lead the news bulletin with it' and went on with the game." Walker added, in a postscript, referring to that long-ago Christ Church interview for the lost Hinchcliffe Scholarship, "What a mistake JC and I made!" This was very satisfactory.

Public Lending Right, PEN, and the Arts Council claimed too much of his time, and he resigned a year early from his position as Chairman of the Arts Council Literature Panel, rebutting *Private Eye*'s suggestion that this was because of "adverse publicity" – on the contrary, he told the *Sunday Times* in August 1969, he had been an unqualified success.[6] Who was to succeed him? Would Roy Fuller do, they wondered, or was he too square?

Two non-events also occupied some of his time: in this year of *Oh! Calcutta!* Tynan had the idea of publishing with Grove Press a volume of self-addressed erotic fantasies by well known writers whose names would be published *en bloc* but not attached to individual entries. It was to be called "For Myself Alone" and Tynan would approach James Baldwin, W.H. Auden, Gore Vidal, Tennessee Williams, William Burroughs. Angus was at first tempted, but eventually fought shy, pleading that he did not usually have words for his fantasies: also "the smallest speculation . . . would identify me and, for a thousand different prejudices, disgust a thousand different readers – and unfortunately I don't have so many thousand. That is the crux really: I make no compromise in my novels, but outside I am not rich enough (indeed I am poor) to be able to take the risk of losing the small following I have especially as with approaching old age, I shall need all I can hold.

"It is cowardly; or rather it's prudential which is the same thing. But the risk to my security is greater than my estimation of the value of the enterprise – although I do think it a very interesting idea . . . Only I . . . can know what would be in my contribution (if it were honest and anything less would be a kind of child's cheating at cards) and only I can know how little it would do for public eyes."[7] Tynan responded in a friendly manner, adding that he had found the French and the Americans less concerned about the project – "I wonder why?"[8] (The volume never appeared, but Tynan was a great preserver of archives, and all correspondence relating to this abortive project is now deposited at the British Library, to the potential future embarrassment of some of his would-be contributors.)

Then there was the row over the Harrogate Festival: one of those many time-wasting storms in a teacup that plague affable celebrities. Publisher

John Calder, who was running the show, announced that Angus would be present. Angus had never said he would appear: indeed he had promptly declined in April. Nevertheless, he was now being billed as a star, and friends and acquaintances wrote to him telling him how much they looked forward to seeing him there. Angus wrote to Calder to remonstrate, and received not an apology but pressure to appear. Angus remonstrated again, and the pressure increased. If Angus's name had been used in error, surely he could do the decent thing and save other people's faces by turning up? Anyway, it wasn't really Calder's fault: it was the fault of the Festival organisers. This attempt to pass the buck did not pacify Angus, who made the *Yorkshire Post* print an apology.

★

On 23 September 1969 Angus fled far away from these irritations to the Far East. He was on his way to Japan, and was to travel on to a working holiday in Ceylon, then on to India.

This was his second visit to Japan, where he was to be unpaid ambassador at British Week in Tokyo, along with the Festival Ballet, Princess Margaret, a Henry Moore exhibition, Cliff Richard, Harry Wheatcroft and the sword of Sir Francis Drake. He flew over the North Pole and landed in the Hotel New Otani in Tokyo for a busy week of yen-raising. There were interviews, speeches, signings and cocktail parties. There were also unnerving encounters with old friends.

Japan was less of a culture shock than it had been in 1957, though it was still a land with "an incredible, frightening sense of ambiguity", a gentle, civilised, superbly hygienic society in which one could nevertheless meet a rat at large in a grand restaurant in Osaka.[9]

Angus was by now even better known there. Two collections of short stories had already appeared (1960, 1968), and a translation of *Anglo-Saxon Attitudes*.[10] It was pleasant to see Kazu Serikawa again: Kazu was hoping to tackle the difficult task of translating *No Laughing Matter*. Angus chatted on to interviewers about whatever came into his head – his last novel, Dickens, the British Museum Reading Room, William Burroughs. He saw Mishima on 27 September, who had kept the evening free for him, writing to Angus in July "I have been spending so many puritanical years that I am now quite ignorant about night-life in Tokyo; so I think I'd better consult with Tex to entertain you . . ."[11] Since his peaceful visit to the nightingales of Felsham Woodside and the night spots of Soho, Mishima had travelled far along the path that was to lead him to his spectacular death by hara-kiri on 25 November 1970: Angus found him much changed.

At this dinner there was also present a young Japanese actor, Yoshi Oida, and an American, Weatherill or Weatherby, who acted as interpreter. (This was probably Meredith Weatherby, who translated some of Mishima's work; his father had founded the Weatherill Publishing company.) Oida at this stage spoke little English, though he had already worked for a season in 1968 with Peter Brook in Paris. Trained in the classical Noh tradition, Oida knew Mishima well, had done body-building with him, and had been directed by him to commit suicide as a Syrian soldier in Wilde's *Salomé*: he and Mishima often talked of suicide. On this evening, Oida recalls, Angus was in high spirits, telling funny stories, "singing for his supper", as he put it, and after the meal they went on a round of bars and clubs. Did they meet there James Kirkup, whose poem "Gay Boys" celebrates this underworld? Did they see there the passion-less dancers,

> Their pale monkey faces mischievious and pure
> Beneath the hair's black tomboy fringe . . .?[12]

Angus stored it all away in the memory bank, along with the rat.

(His recollection of this meeting, written years later for his introduction to his collected travel writings, seems at odds with Oida's account: "On my last visit to Tokyo [Mishima] gave a banquet of fine splendour for me – dishes flown up from the far South and flown down from the far North – hostesses of exceptional beauty and careful naivete – but all threatened throughout by his own mood – this was the first inkling that I had of what was to be his tragic and horrible end. It seems that some remark of the English Ambassador about Japan's insufficient concern for the happiness of dogs had enraged Yukio. He ordered me to go to the Ambassador and extract an apology. I had a heavy programme and a short visit, and I said I could not do what he asked. In the end Yukio said abruptly, to one of his friends, 'Get Angus Wilson prostitute.' Then, he turned on leaving the room and added, 'A very cheap one.' His mood, let me say at once, was full of rage, not of laughter. It was unpleasant and I was sad to lose a friend.")[13]

More disturbing than his meeting with a changed Mishima was a meeting with the much altered form of Ian Calder, whom he had not seen for some years. Ian Calder had abandoned his stage career and was working as a television officer for the British Council. He had been posted to Teheran and Ghana, and was now in Tokyo, where he stayed for two years, with Pat and their two young children, Jason and Cressida. (The Uncles had responded differently to the Calder family: Perkin Walker warned Pat not to read *The Lord of the Flies* while pregnant: the agnostic

Angus declined to be Jason's godfather: Bentley Bridgewater agreed to be Cressida's godfather.) Ian Calder by now was drinking heavily, some said uncontrollably, and had put on a great deal of weight: Angus was shocked by his appearance when they met at a British Week dinner party. Worn down by two hours of watching Japanese dancing in royal company, Calder did not seem to make much sense. They met again, more quietly, and one evening Angus babysat for Cressida and some of her friends while the Calder parents went out to one of the week's innumerable functions. On another occasion in this hectic visit, in a speech delivered in Calder's presence, Angus paid tribute to Calder's encouragement and influence in early days.

But he was worried. Ian looked dreadful. Angus met Pat privately for breakfast and asked if there was anything he could do to help, and he later wrote asking the same question of Ian's sister Rosemary Merry. (Rosemary was not wholly pleased by his attempts at intervention.) What could be done? Ian Calder was launched on self-destruction. (He was shortly sent back to England with a British Council minder to be dried out.)

Angus felt he had failed here, but he fulfilled his official duties honourably, and the British Council pronounced him "an unqualified success". But it was all very tiring: he sent a card to Tony saying "I feel tired and dizzy – probably temper. I made them send me home by special car from a boring ceremony. I'm so longing for Ceylon – only 3 weeks – but 3 weeks of this!"

Japanese protocol was simultaneously baffling and demanding: according to Harry Guest, Angus caused offence twice on this visit, once by failing to turn up at an evening of concrete poetry with poet Niikvai Seiichi, and again by expecting the seventy-year-old Nobel prize-winning novelist Yasunari Kawabata to wait on him in his hotel, instead of calling on him in his home. To Guest, international etiquette seemed clear: to Angus, perhaps not.[14] Angus had clearly intended no discourtesy to Kawabata, for in a lecture on "Is the Novel a Doomed Art Form?" which he delivered on 29 September 1969 at Sophia University he had woven in several graceful allusions to his work, including a flattering comparison to Woolf's *The Waves*, "one of the finest novels of 20C England": he had valiantly tried to connect European and Japanese fiction, but had inevitably found himself wandering back from Tanizaki, Kawabata and Dazai to Beckett, Robbe-Grillet, Grass and Golding.

Tony wrote to Angus on 26 September, apologising for a hectic drive to Heathrow – "it was most unlike my usual efficiency in getting you to the airport an hour or so before time" – and reporting that he had been by himself to see *Edward the Second* at the Mermaid ("Gaveston was good, like a beautiful hairy monkey") and had bumped into Martyn Goff and his friend Peter, who took him off to supper – he ends "A man sat next to me in the theatre. We exchanged some words about the play.* Then he spoke again after the interval, when he said I like it all so much because it stinks of paranoia and I am paranoid. 3 minutes later he suddenly got up and left. I don't think I helped much.

I will write again to Hong Kong. Look after yourself. Love T

PS I have just seen the dentist Mr Watt. He had a dream in which he, I and Tony Storey were smuggling gold, then Tony S. strangled me. A typical small town dream, I suppose."

On 6 October 1969 Angus flew off to Hong Kong, where, again, he was to lecture for the British Council. He stayed in the comfortable Repulse Bay Hotel, recommended by Suffolk neighbour Freddie Fox, "with as beautiful a view as man could ask – miles of smooth pale blue ocean with shallows and deeps marked in shadow and large turtle shaped green islands humping out of the water at irregular intervals as far as the eye can see." There were flamboyant trees in flower, hibiscus, dragonfly, and unknown blue-green birds. The hotel was a treasure house of the 1920s: would it survive, he wondered? (It did not.) A friend of a friend threatened to ring him about "picking up on the beach (!!!) I hope he doesn't because at the moment after all the exhaustion and million impressions and thousands of people of Tokyo and Kyoto – and the sheer awful noise and confusion of modern Tokyo – and the difficult nuances of all the Council people and Embassy folk – and the tragic horror of Ian and Pat – and all the travelling . . . I really don't feel like moving from here (except I've just had to move out of the sun) – tho' no doubt I'll feel more energetic later and will do Macao and Botanic Gardens but I don't think I'll fuss with Dick Wells's island. Anyway Terry has sent me Dickens – so now I have 3 reviews to do and must get on with Joyce Carey [*sic*] – . . . I'm longing to see you. If Kandy is half as good as this it'll be fine. Love Angus."[15]

He did get to Macao, and he also managed to see his niece Sybil and her husband Dick Scott, who were stationed in Hong Kong – a less distressing encounter than that with the Calders, although he always found it a little curious to be addressed as Uncle Angus by a couple who were nearly his own age. And then he hopped on, for more lectures in Kuala Lumpur and Penang, and then on to Colombo, where he was to be reunited with Tony.

Tony flew out on 19 October, with a stewardess who thought he was

---

* This was a Prospect Theatre production by Toby Robertson with Ian McKellen as Edward and James Laurenson as Gaveston.

Dutch and a lot of Ghanaians: they stopped off in Bahrain, then on over the Empty Quarter to the paddy-fields and palms and orchids of Ceylon. There Tony spent a few days alone waiting for Angus's arrival, suffering from "muddles and depression" and anxiety about arrangements for the holiday ahead – the hotel staff were friendly but there was nowhere to go in the evenings, and increasing anxiety and panic about the weeks ahead overcame him. "Awful apprehensive feeling in tummy. It has been too long away from Willy, and foolish not to arrange some means of communication." On 22 October Angus's plane from KL to Colombo was delayed by two and a half hours, and Tony felt conspicuous hanging about on the airport, where he was questioned "in oblique but friendly way" by the airport police. But then, there at last was Angus, looking well, having lost weight, but exhausted. Back at the hotel Angus slept and slept, while Tony continued to panic about plans: he was not happy about the travel agency which was supposed to be looking after them. Things did not look up until the next day, when they went to the zoo. They pronounced it "excellent", and were charmed by a notice which announced

> If you with litter will disgrace
> And spoil the beauty of this place
> May indigestion rack your chest
> And ants invade your pants and vest.

In the evening they were greeted by the British Council representative – the charming and reassuring Bill McAlpine and his wife Helen, famed for her marvellous parties. Russell Bowden, ex-actor and now British Council librarian, also proved a great help: he sorted out their complicated touring muddles in half an hour, says Tony.

Gradually they both relaxed, as they began to take in the extraordinary beauty and varied wild-life of the island. The Isle of Spices, shaped like a tear in the Indian Ocean, was still a paradise, and almost as exotic as it had been at the beginning of the century, when young Leonard Woolf had encountered its "infinite variety" of "flat, dry, hot low country", thick jungle, brilliant, luxurious fountains, and its "dazzling world of sun and sea."[16] Its colours and scents reminded Angus of the intense sensuous experiences of his Durban boyhood. Woolf (whose glowing and vivid descriptions Angus and Tony had read with admiration) had impressed the local population with his 90 volumes of Voltaire and his snake-devouring wire-haired fox terrier called Charlie: the inhabitants of Colombo were newly impressed by the modern technology of science-fiction writer Arthur C. Clarke, wrapped in a slipping sarong though clinging to the cuisine of his native Minehead. Clarke had lived there happily for some years, surrounded by the extended family of his friend Hector Ekanayake, once a flyweight boxer and now an expert in underwater diving. Here, perhaps, a Marcus Matthews could live in a little untroubled kingdom of his own, with an air-conditioned library, a glass-bottomed boat and a satellite dish.

Angus and Tony stayed comfortably in a house in Model Farm Road in Colombo which belonged to the stately Mrs Wijesundera. The political troubles that were to engulf Singhalese society in the Insurgence of 1971 had not yet broken out into widespread violence, and Angus and Tony moved happily through crowds of exotic people with names which at first seemed unpronounceable, and made friends in the mixed local and expatriate community: Wilhelm Charig, a business man of German background, became a good friend, and introduced them to his circle. They ventured into game parks where they admired lorikeets, barbets, cormorants, pelicans, chameleons, bee-eaters and snakebirds. They encountered buffalo, crocodiles, elephants, the indefatigable Sir Mortimer Wheeler, and Anthony Powell and his wife, whom they bumped into at the famous Rock Fortress of Sigiriya. (She was matier than he, Tony recorded, and she and Angus talked of Ivy Compton-Burnett while refusing to follow Sir Mortimer, group leader, as he marched the rest of his troops to the sheer and terrible top of the rock.)

After the social round of opera and British Council parties in Colombo, and a meeting with a former Prime Minister (Sir John Kotelawala), they set off on a rough ride to Kandy in the centre of the island, where they stayed for some time, visiting the Botanical Gardens (pronounced superb), and making excursions to temples and shrines: the religious rituals astounded and impressed Angus. It was in the Chalet Guest House in Kandy, amidst the fine old Dutch furniture, that Angus came across "a 1930s book, the memoirs of Lady Addles, or something like that, and all about her love affairs"[17] which sowed the seed of an idea for the next novel – could he perhaps write the comic quest of a Lord Pangbourne in search of his Dream Boy, condemned to everlasting absurdity?

In Trincomalee, they sought in vain not for the Fairest Youth but for the grave of Jane Austen's admiral brother Sir Charles Austen (which lies, a friend later wrote, by the Outer Maidan, near the resthouse): on the way from Jaffna to Anuradhapura they gave a lift to a memorable swami, who crowded into the back of their small car and smoked cigars. The swami suggested that they stop at a lorry park to break a lucky coconut for Ganesh, the Elephant God, as all the lorry drivers were wisely wont to do: they neglected this rite, and thirteen miles ahead the bald tyres of the car submitted to two punctures. (The swami, though small, was plump.)

Driving in Ceylon was full of hazards: on another occasion, as they were driven through the jungle by the Secretary of the Wildlife Society in a Japanese jeep of which neither he nor Tony could master the reverse, they encountered an enraged elephant upon the narrow path. The tracker leapt out to try to calm it by tantric spells while the Secretary executed a four-point turn. Angus, completely unperturbed, continued to chat happily to a Sri Lankan dramatist who had come along for the ride.

Guaribala the swami was to prove the germ of inspiration for a character in Angus's next novel. The swami's own life, as recounted by Russell Bowden, was highly implausible: homosexual and of German-Jewish origin, he and his brother Malte Schoenfeldt had both fled the Nazis in 1934, and the swami after various adventures had arrived in Ceylon, where he had developed a passionate interest in Hinduism and Buddhism. The British had interned him and his brother during the war in their vast camp at Dehra-Dun in North India, where he had continued to study oriental religions, ordering books through an obliging Red Cross: he had then returned to Ceylon to live in a sacred cave at Ella with a son of the late Governor-General of the island, Lord Soulbury.

The swami's brother became a Buddhist monk with begging-bowl, and Guaribala by 1970 was a fully-fledged swami, in loincloth and white wrap, living in poverty in an ashram in a fishing village and indulging, when he could, his love for Hennessy brandy and fried prawns: twice a year he would walk barefoot through the snake-infested jungle to a holy shrine. On other occasions he appreciated a lift in the British Council Jaguar or a night on a British Council floor. Was Guaribala a fraud? His brother sometimes said so, but others took him quite seriously. Angus noted him, talked to him, visited him in his ashram on the shore, and stored him away. He would come in useful one day.[18]

Back in Kandy, Angus and Tony met up for the New Year with the Priestleys, who had consulted them in advance about the trip, writing from England to know whether they should come out. Like Arthur C. Clarke, who served Angus and Tony toad-in-the hole, Jack Priestley did not approve of the Singhalese food – doll's dinners, he growled. He was disgruntled. Luckily Priestley cheered up as they all saw the New Year in together on a starlit night with fireworks over the lake: Priestley bid a happy farewell to the "silly sixties" and hoped that the 1970s would bring an end to "all this satire".

*

In the first week of the new decade, Angus lectured in Colombo, made a final round of parties and theatres, was depressed and read Burns. (Robert or John Horne? His diary note does not say.) On 5 January 1970, he and Tony flew off to Madras, leaving the Priestleys to a fortnight of torrential rain, mould and a balcony black with ants and drowned caterpillars: Priestley had unpleasant memories of Ceylon, where sullen boys had thrown stones at him while he painted, where he felt that "the abominable cruelties once practised in Kandy had poisoned the air." Unlike Angus, he never felt the slightest desire to return.[19]

Their Indian tour, which began in Madras, took Angus and Tony on to Pondicherry, Bangalore, Mysore, Cochin, Goa and Bombay. Angus lectured many times for the Council, was interviewed by the press, met local writers, saw the sights, had indigestion, and was, as ever, cheered by the wild-life and the bird sanctuaries. On 23 January they flew back to England, dined with Perkin Walker, Bob French and Monty Turland in London, then went back to Suffolk, where Angus took to his bed for for a week with bronchitis. He was utterly exhausted.

Engagements were cancelled, and all he felt up to was a mild diet of Blackburnes, Corkes and Cooksons. When he was on his feet again, he and Tony both went to the Hospital for Tropical Diseases for a check-up. The weather did not help. In February 1970 there was much snow, and Angus seemed worried and silent, uncheered by Tony's offerings of oxtail, baked ham, boiled lamb and caper sauce. He was struggling with an introduction to *England*, a book of photographs by Edwin Smith (published by Thames & Hudson, 1971), but broke off to chat about Viva King and Leonard Woolf. Viva's memoirs were on the way: she wrote to him to complain that "all the dirt" seemed to be crowded into the extract chosen for pre-publication by *Nova* in February.* Angus and Tony were marooned and cocooned at the cottage, and when they broke out things did not go well. An excursion to Leicester Uiversity to speak in a seminar in early March proved disastrous: they were stuck in a snowstorm overnight at the Wellingborough Hotel in Market Harborough, where Angus tried to sleep on a sofa amidst the noisy shouting and singing of stranded travellers.

Meanwhile, the 1970 Dickens centenary activities (described in the previous chapter) threatened concentration on the new novel. Most of the spring and early summer was taken up with them, and it was not until July that Angus found time to think seriously about the plot of his next work. He read up on Hinduism in the breaks from lunching and dining with the Nolans and with P.N. Furbank, with Californians and Japanese, with James Mossman and Rosamund Lehmann, with the Hampshires and Angus's old Oxford friend Stuart Daniel – a reunion that did not turn out

---

* *Nova* was a new-style woman's magazine which dealt frankly with women's issues: its literary adviser was A.S. Byatt. The extract, "Viva! Viva!", appeared in February 1970.

too well. (Tony missed the way, they arrived late, and Mrs Daniel attacked Angus's novels – never a good party trick.) Angus and Tony went to see *Oh! Calcutta!* in July at the Round House, and spent a few days in Yorkshire with Perkin Walker in August after the Harrogate Festival: they stayed in the Midland Hotel in Skipton, which was to emerge, fire escape and all, in vivid unexotic detail in his next novel. Angus renewed his contract with the *Observer*, declined Giles Gordon's suggestion that he stand as a Public Lending Right candidate in the next election, declined to sit on a Home Office committee on privacy, refused for the second time to deliver the Clark lectures, declined tours of Italy and Israel, encouraged Jonathan Raban to apply (successfully) for an Arts Council grant, appeared on *Any Questions* in Ipswich where he enraged a listener by praising Samuel Beckett, and upset Antony Grey, as we have seen, by his second thoughts on a review about Montgomery Hyde which he had written for the Albany Trust's journal *Man and Society*: Grey had greeted the "explicit" article with delight in a letter dated 13 July 1970, but Angus wrote on 31 July that he had with deep disappointment "felt forced to remove all wording that openly declared me to be a homosexual". He said that he and Tony had agreed to brave "possible distress to his elderly parents and my family, embarrassment with acquaintances, the University etc . . ." but could not risk the possibility of being refused an American visa. "I won't go on apologising. You may be shocked by my backsliding but I simply cannot afford it . . . Yours in sadness, Angus." Grey ("A good man if ever there was one," said Jacquetta Priestley) wrote back saying that "There could scarcely be a more poignant and pointed commentary upon the degrading state of affairs we are all still left with, after the ten years' effort for reform."[20] (Angus had written a piece for the Albany Trust's Journal, *Man and Society,* published in Spring 1963, on "Fallacies about Homosexuality", but he had avoided any personal references.)

In September Yoshi Oida from Japan came to visit Felsham Woodside in his kimono: he was taken to The Chase to see Perkin Walker, who spoke to him never a word, and Tony showed him Cambridge in the pouring rain while Angus talked John Cowper Powys to Powys enthusiast Glen Cavaliero.* (A John Cowper Powys Society had just been founded, in which Angus was to play a lively part.) Oida was in England with Peter Brook's company:† Brook had now formed the International Centre for

* Glen Cavaliero (b.1927), poet, critic and teacher, and author of *John Cowper Powys: Novelist* (Oxford 1972) and *The Rural Tradition in the English Novel 1900–1939* (Macmillan 1977).

† Oida became a leading member of Brook's international team: in the next few years he travelled the world, appearing in Iran, Africa and India with *Orghast, The Birds,* and the *Mahabharata*. See *An Actor Adrift,* by Yoshi Oida with Lorna Marshall (Methuen 1992).

Theatre Research, and Oida had returned from Japan to join him. Felsham Woodside, with its cold salmon and hollandaise sauce, was a pleasant interlude for an actor adrift: Oida was driven back to London by Peter Shaffer, and stayed in the flat in Regent's Park Terrace. Angus and Tony laid on a welcoming drinks party for him there, on 28 September. Jonathan Courage, now himself an actor, was invited: so was Harold Acton.

Tony, who had never been to Japan, had a curious entanglement this same year with very different young Japanese – an affair not perhaps worthy of the cry of "*grand danger de mort*" with which Marcus and his lover Jack in *No Laughing Matter* would alert one another to impending sexual danger, but unsettling, nevertheless. Fuji was a young lad adrift in Piccadilly, whose ambition was to own a sauna bath back home: in February 1970 he picked Tony up, took him back to his room in Half Moon Street, and unveiled his plans to him while enjoying "fast sex" and eating plums and pickled onions to the sound of military music. This did not prove quite the casual encounter it might have seemed: in February 1971 Fuji wrote to Tony, enclosing a photo of himself in leather at Zürich, and requesting money in order to get himself to America to open a massage parlour. It is a desperate letter: even more desperate were Fuji's return visits in 1973 (with high boots, make-up, stockings and wigs – he came for plastic surgery) and in 1975, for a sex-change operation at Charing Cross Hospital, which he told Tony would cost him £1,200. His family had cast him out: he did not know if he was a boy or a girl: everyone despised him. He talked of suicide. A lost boy.

There were many such – Ahmed in Morocco had survived, but Mohamed from Larache, who had got himself to England with a great deal of help from his friends, was continuing to prove a worry. He had made an English girl pregnant: should he leave her, marry her, take her back home to Morocco? Would his work permit be renewed and what would he do if it wasn't? Both Angus and Tony did their best to advise: Angus wrote to the young woman in April 1973 warning her that life in Morocco would be very difficult for her – "I wonder if you have any idea of what the life of a woman is in a Moslem home – even a home like Mohamed's which (I have not been there) I imagine is more up-to-date than most. You would be with the women of the family I think all day long . . . to be honest the person I have most sympathy with is the child to come who deserves all you can both give." Angus told Mohamed not to marry her unless he loved her, he told her not to marry him unless she loved him, he advised her on the kind of work (a bar? a restaurant?) she might hope to find if she had a baby to support on her own. The plight of the single parent – not unknown amongst his UEA students – suddenly struck him forcefully. It was all a muddle and cost many hours of correspondence. (Mohamed to Angus May 1970: "I love her and she love me but! . . . I am sorry about what happened to you since you lift me at Market Harborough.") In the end, he married her, but they did not live happily forever after: in four or five years he was writing for advice about divorce, although still in close contact with both wife and son.

And after Mohamed came requests and appeals from the young Italian in Cairo, the prostitutes in Japan, the boys in Ceylon who wanted jobs in England or on board ship, the Indian boys who wanted to train as musicians, the youth in Lisbon who wanted to be a male model, the boys who simply wanted foreign postage stamps . . . Most of them wanted visas, work, money, shoes, overcoats. Could they become hospital porters or hotel receptionists, could they train as vets in Berlin or Amsterdam, could they become film extras? They thought Uncle Angus and Uncle Tony were millionaires and could open every door.

The lost boys haunted Angus. Through them, he glimpsed a world of unutterable woe. He had exorcised his own childhood: what of theirs? In them one could glimpse "that knowledge of finality that we may catch for a moment in the passing glance of the destitute, the wrapped-up bundles on the pavements of Bombay, the despairing lost souls of early morning railway station waiting-rooms, the meths drinkers on the benches of Camden Town, the winos of the Bowery, the white-faced shaky youths who emerge from the Piccadilly Gents after a fix."[21] The Lost Boys infiltrated his new novel which was beginning to crystallise: would it be farce or tragedy? As yet he did not know. He wrote to Philippe Jullian that it was to be "a pederastic Mr Pickwick." To Valerie Shaw, a young academic who had been writing about Mrs Eliot and Late Call,[22] he wrote in June that he had been busy promoting Dickens ("when a book 'does well' it seems that promotion becomes doubly necessary") but was about to start a new novel, and her article had encouraged "my always dubious self confidence. My real trouble this time is a feeling that I must expand my material both to include the new (ie younger) England and to take in the impact or failure of impact of the rest of the world upon England (something brought home to me by my wide travels in these last years) – how much has my 'experimental' side ie parodies and general stylization been a result of seeking some escape from a certain narrowness of world and theme imposed upon me by former rigid standards of realism in detailed observation and mimicry of speech? How much if I lose these, do I have anything I have to offer? Here's my dilemma and your article helps me a lot to decide . . . All this, too, to be reconciled to making a living, saving something for my old age and to leave to my dependent friend without whom I could have written nothing – these are my dilemmas. But on the whole, I enjoy life very very much – and in a slightly macabre way look forward to the agony of finding out whether or not I have another worthwhile novel before me. Please forgive the somewhat Oxford Group intimacy of this letter – but so few seem to care about my work, let alone understand it, that you unleash something by your own perspicacity and sensitivity. Very gratefully yours, Angus Wilson."

And at the end of September 1970, he set off to Lisbon with Tony to face the agony and write the novel in peace.

★

One of the major distractions from which he sought refuge was the curious affair of the Famous Writers School. In June of 1969 he had received a letter from an American writer called Gordon Carroll, asking if he would be interested in becoming involved in the setting up of a school to teach writing, on the model of a project already prospering in the small town of Westport, Connecticut. Angus had replied cautiously, and had at once written to his agent Richard Simon at Curtis Brown asking "Is it a respectable thing, I wonder? Would it be financially worth while? Would it involve an enormous amount of work? Can you help me?"

At first sight, the project seemed attractive, and at least one of the names on the letter-heading of the original invitation was familiar – he had met Professor Paul Engle on his lightning trip to Iowa City in 1960. But what *was* the Famous Writers School? It seemed to be a kind of correspondence course for aspiring authors, and it offered good money to its Guiding Councillors – two hundred and fifty pounds a month for a possibly renewable six-month advisory period, and a free trip to Connecticut to see what was going on there. A European branch had been established in Munich and opened in July 1969, nine years after the parent organisation was founded: expansion was on the agenda. The aim was to "develop self-expression, not only in educated people but in any who demonstrate by means of a careful test that they have aptitude to benefit from the thorough instruction offered by professional writers and editors."[23] Members of the "guiding faculty" would be active participants and would share in the company's profits. They would also, of course, lend the whole enterprise respectability.

Angus agreed, for a trial six-month period from 1 January 1970, to be a member of an Advisory Board. The others who signed on were Nigel Balchin, Richard Gordon, Tony Gray, Michael Holroyd, Alistair Horne, Angus McGill, Frank Muir and Elizabeth Taylor – a group chosen to represent journalism, biography, history, the novel both serious and comic, crime fiction, the short story. Some of them did get to Connecticut, in December 1969: they investigated what went on in the box-like offices on the edge of the pretty little town, and reported back home that many alterations would have to be made to make the enterprise suitable for British consumers. New textbooks would have to be written, and something would have to be done about the fact that most British housewives, a large part of the target clientèle, did not possess typewriters.

The team met on the afternoon of 7 May 1970 at the Stafford Hotel, after a good lunch, and discussed premises, grading, tutors and fees. Angus was elected Chairman of the Guiding Council, and Nigel Balchin was Chairman of the committee. Each writer agreed to contribute a chapter to the proposed textbook on some aspect of his or her own craft. All seemed set for further meetings, when ten days later came the news of Balchin's sudden death at the age of sixty-one. A lot of quick rethinking had to be done.*

Angus, as senior novelist, was clearly in line for promotion, but he happened to be safely abroad at the time, promoting his Dickens book in Switzerland. The dumpy, hospitable and engagingly absent-minded Christianna Brand,† who had appointed herself hostess to the group, summoned an emergency meeting at her home, and Balchin was replaced for a while by Stephen Watts. (She complained that Angus claimed he had gone off to a monastery, but answered her distress calls on the notepaper of a very posh Swiss hotel.) It was not only Balchin's death that had rattled them. Not everyone was pleased with the way Carroll kept referring to black people as "coons": was he really the kind of chap they wanted to work with?

They were right to be anxious, for very soon the whole enterprise, at least at the American end, was blown apart by that dangerous and highly professional investigative journalist, Jessica Mitford. Her lethal attack on the Famous Writers School was published in the *Atlantic* in July, but rumours of its contents were already circulating. She had had difficulty in placing her piece – the *Atlantic*, *McCall's*, and *Life* all expressed interest but they were afraid of offending the Famous Writers and losing valuable advertising revenue. The story was too hot to handle. The *Atlantic* eventually agreed to honour its own original proposal, and her article,

---

* Nigel Balchin (1908–70) had worked as a psychoanalyst in the personnel section of the War Office: he was a well-known screenwriter, playwright and novelist, author of *The Small Back Room* (1943) and *Mine Own Executioner* (1945), which portrays a psychoanalyst as hero.

† Mary Christianna Brand (1907–88) well-known crime writer, Chairwoman of the Crime Writers Association 1972–73, and author of *Cat and Mouse* (1950), *Death in High Heels* (1954), and the Inspector Cockrill series.

which had swelled from a projected seven hundred words to several thousand, appeared and caused shock-waves of horror that finally drove the whole enterprise into bankruptcy.

Jessica Mitford had been alerted to the misdemeanours of the FWS by her husband, lawyer Bob Treuhaft, who had been approached by a seventy-two-year-old widow who had regretted being talked by a sharp salesman into paying 200 dollars towards a 900-dollar contract with the School. (He got her money refunded, after a considerable battle.) Closer examination revealed that FWS's advertising was highly misleading and its assessment of potential clients totally inadequate, and that the personal involvement of its Famous Fifteen was minimal. Mitford interviewed Paul Engle, Mark Wiseman, and, most devastatingly, Bennett Cerf, Chairman of the Board of Random House, humourist, popular columnist and TV personality, who admitted that the School's success was due to a "very hard sales pitch and an appeal to the gullible." He begged not to be quoted, but she quoted him. She discovered that FWS had many subsidiaries worldwide, in the form of correspondence schools, Linguaphone, speed reading – and that it was planning "an invasion of Great Britain . . . as soon as the English prove themselves worthy of it by stabilising their currency situation."

Mitford was extremely proud of this hard-hitting piece, which created a scandal and a fracas throughout the media. She rejoiced in the fact that for once something that she wrote actually had an effect. She had bought shares in the company, partly in order to monitor its fortunes, partly to console herself if it wickedly continued to prosper: when the stock was finally wiped out, in May 1971, she was delighted.

Less delighted was the British team back home. What to do next? What on earth had they got themselves mixed up with? Of course they had not been planning to pocket money and eat lunches for nothing: they had already written their contributions for two textbooks on the *Principles of Good Writing* and were intending to keep a close eye on developments. The British school would be completely different, with different advertising and different customers. Their contracts had been renewed for six months on 30 June 1970, just before the story broke to the public. Would their names, like that of the villainously smiling Bennett Cerf, now be dragged through the mud by an avenging Mitford? They heard stories that a similar exposé was plannned in the UK by a British journalist. It was all very uncomfortable.

Angus and Frank Muir flew off to Munich in May on a fact-finding mission to look at the project there, to see what was really happening. Gordon Carroll ("a rather gentle soul", according to McGill) was hauled up for investigation by Angus on 16 June. Angus McGill was so worried that he flew back from holiday in Provence to attend a meeting at the Stafford Hotel on 20 August: this was followed by a gathering at Christianna Brand's. They were reluctant to see their work go down the drain, but deeply worried by their position. They continued to meet, through the rest of the year and the spring of 1971, at the Stafford and at Brown's: these gatherings were highly entertaining, indeed at times "an irresistible hoot", agreed Muir and McGill, but it became increasingly clear that as the mother ship sank, their own little bark would founder. And so it did. The International Writers' School, British branch, never opened. Its two expensive-looking textbooks were printed but never published: Angus's contributions included an entertaining piece about clichés, a denial that fame and money are the chief spurs to effort, and an analysis of *Mrs Dalloway*, chosen as "the book that more than any other has helped me to enlarge my craft." (The suggestion that each counsellor should choose a book that had a particular influence and write about it came from Angus himself, in April 1970.) But the volumes, with the enterprise, sank without trace. Gordon Carroll, writing to Holroyd in 1973 from one of his subsidiary companies, mourned the days when he had flitted in and out of Heathrow like a James Bond character: "What a shame that IWS was destroyed by a blend of corporate chicane [*sic*] and larceny! However, it's all best forgotten."[24] And they all did their best to forget. Carroll moved on, into Brightly Coloured Books as Decor and Heritage. Angus still had faith in the possibility of encouraging creative writing, but clearly the IWS was not the way.

23

MAGICAL MATHEMATICS

By the time Angus and Tony settled in Portugal in September 1970, Angus had accumulated a sprawling pile of notes which had to be squeezed into the seething, many-peopled mass of *As if By Magic*. They took rooms at the sixteenth-century newly-converted hotel of Quinta das Torres at Azeitao, between Lisbon and Setubal, and found it ideal for writing – sunny, with an enormous sitting-room, and a terrace overlooking a lake. They went on excursions and saw friends from the gay expatriate community: they visited the zoo, and basked in the lush tropical vegetation of the hothouse of the Estufa Fria in Lisbon. They saw Colin, still in the Rua da Lapa, but now accompanied by a cat called Feb, instead of a dog: Colin had once disapproved of cats, but he had become as devoted to Feb as he had been to his much-photographed fluffy dog Tiho, and wrote many a letter to Angus describing Feb's charming behaviour – a capitalist cat, exacting in his ways, who purred upon a special cushioned chair in his master's bedroom. At one point, Colin wrote to Angus, Feb had decided to change his name to Amin. The name-changing habit was catching.

(P.N. Furbank had visited Colin in Lisbon in July 1968, bearing a flame-coloured pullover as a gift from Angus: Colin had said of his little brother, as Angus had predicted he would, "He is a dear boy, but he forgets my age," and had continued to Furbank over lunch in the Rua Garrett, "Tell me, what sort of things does Angus write? Oh, they're novels, are they? I *never* read novels." Colin was nothing if not devious.)

Furbank fared better than another emissary (identity unknown) dispatched a year or two later by Angus: Colin wrote indignantly "I am afraid I was rather rough with him – He turned up one Saturday evening and . . . just would not credit that I had no knowledge of your whereabouts and seemed obsessed by the idea that I had you hidden in my wardrobe. He said he had met you on a train to Norwich . . . he came back

ANGUS WILSON

three more times as well as phoning insisting that you were in Lisbon . . . I got so tired of him that I finally sent him off with a flea in his ear – he was not a very encouraging person in fact rather scruffy I thought – but then its the fashion amongst the very young to look like a doss house. I think he said his name was Lopes but I'm not sure . . ." etc. etc.

In Azeitao Angus settled down to work, and by the third day of their stay, Tony noted with relief, he had written fifteen pages – but was depressed because although he was very pleased with the plot he felt his characters were dead – "don't know what they are going to do next." This was a long haul: a year later, Angus was writing semi-apologetically to David Farrer, explaining that the novel was breaking new ground and was taking even longer than anticipated. So much for Warburg's hopes of a shorter book next time.

The new novel sprang from Angus's world travels, and he had worked hard to provide a structure which would give them a narrative meaning. He had corresponded with Fred Warburg about steroids: with Solly Zuckerman (whom he knew through both the Zoological Society and UEA) about pesticides and population increases: with the John Innes Institute about agrarian developments: with Forrest Fulton about electron microscopes and centrifuges. He had consulted Patrick Woodcock and neurologist Roger Gilliatt about cortisone. (Roger Gilliatt was the first husband of Penelope Gilliatt: he was now living in Suffolk with his second wife Mary, journalist and expert on architecture and décor, and a generous hostess who invited Angus and Tony to many a dinner party.) He had written to Kazu Serikawa about Japanese revolutionary students and Yukio Mishima's followers. He wrote to Nadine Gordimer asking if she knew an African version of the Damon and Pinthias (sic) legend: he wrote to Patrick White asking for recommendations of Australian homosexual novels. He collected pictures of manatees and dugongs, studied protein plant breeding papers from Sweden, and read up works on Hinduism and Mesmerism and St Francis Xavier. Rice, sorghum, maize, sesame and rape filled his dreams.

It was Zuckerman, himself no stranger to the trials of the scientific humanist conscience, who came up with the suggestion which proved most fruitful. Angus had asked for ideas for a scientific discovery that could go wrong and plague its inventor's conscience: Zuckerman replied "I am wondering whether the best illustration you could use would be say a plant geneticist who, during the course of some enquiries into the factors on which the protein content of some leaf crop depended, discovered a means whereby it multiplied the productivity of a particular plant, say four times" – a development which would result in "masses of uneducated peasant farmers" being thrown out of work. And thus Magic Rice and its creator, Hamo Langmuir, were conceived.

This was Angus's most picaresque book, and its travels covered continents. At some point he decided to omit Australia, Africa and the Caribbean, but he included Morocco, Japan, Malaysia, Sri Lanka and Goa, as well as many English locations and a university campus not wholly detached from UEA. ("Who *is* UEA?" pleaded Viva King, in one of her letters of this period. Readers of *Magic* happily identified it by the boot-polish tin lids that served as ashtrays, by the babies conceived from D.H. Lawrence seminars.) The novel was composed in Ceylon, India, Portugal (on two separate visits), Ireland, Italy, Iowa, Kuwait, Italy again, and Austria. The novel embodies displacement.

It is also the novel in which Angus decided to confront the subject of sexuality. He had reached the age when perhaps he could recollect the past with tranquillity and without too much embarrassment. *No Laughing Matter* had been explicit: this book would be more so. And it would take on not only the homosexuality of his frustrated young-middle-aged hero Hamo (=Homo) Langmuir, but also the changing attitudes of the sexual revolution that he saw around him. Hamo's sidekick Errol, the Sam Weller to his Pickwick, would be casually randy, sleeping with a girl in every port. Hamo's god-daughter Alexandra Grant – a narrow-bummed, boyish student – would represent the extreme emotional and sexual confusion of the liberated 60s and 70s. And other forms of sexuality would be represented throughout the novel – the homosexual marriage, the male prostitute, the lost boy, the ageing queen, the heartless pederast, the sentimental pederast, the closet clubman, the colonial Uncle.

Sexuality at UEA had, as we have seen, been rampant and openly declared. The atmosphere had been highly charged, as Lorna Sage, Alan Burns, Ian McEwan and many others bore witness. Angus had watched with fascination. Part of him disapproved, part of him applauded. Were the young really different today? What kind of retrospective light did they cast over his own sexual history? Did his own experience make any sense in this new dawn?

The shock of his encounter with the youth of UEA had been reinforced at the Arts Council, where the question of drugs was frequently raised. Lord Goodman remembers that Angus's attitude towards the little magazine *Ambit*, which had encouraged drug-taking, was more tolerant than his own, but Angus, as he indicated to Michael Schofield in July 1967, was wary even about cannabis. In the cause of duty he had visited Jim Haines's Arts Laboratory in Covent Garden and inhaled its potent atmosphere: he tried to understand youth culture: he gave his own money to support *International Times* and *Black Dwarf*, and he knew that some of his students smoked pot and ate hash cakes. His interest in science fiction had been renewed by a friendship with Michael Moorcock: he warmly advocated Arts Council support of Moorcock's magazine, *New Worlds*. For his novel, Angus deliberately set himself the task of researching the young – he investigated them, Jonathan Raban noted, almost as though they were a different species, poring over articles about the Occult Sciences, Atlantis, Tolkien-mania, and LSD.

(Was this a mistake? Was he perhaps too *respectful* to Youth? Had he had children of his own, might he have been more dismissive?)

He knew there were links between the generations, but it was not easy to make them. In Morocco, many people smoked *kif*, and Paul Bowles – himself no chicken – had written stories inspired by it. Morocco was now on the student trail – the third generation of Matthewses in *No Laughing Matter* had got there, and so did Simon Edwards and Peter Conradi – but Tangiers, with its population of ageing tax-avoiding right-wing expatriates, was hardly a city of the young, and drugs were no new phenomenon. Was there not a link back to the Bright Young Things of the Twenties? Clive Johnstone-Wilson, according to Angus, was on cocaine all his adult life: from infancy Angus had shrewdly observed the mysterious "little white powders". Could he tie together all these observations, all these wanderings in time and place? He would try.

*

One of the most unorthodox sexual relationships in the novel is the three-way sexual relationship between student Alexandra and her two lovers; the dandy Rodrigo and serious bearded Northern Ned. (Conradi is convinced that Roddy is in part a portrait of Simon Edwards, inadequately disguised by blond hair, but Angus always denied this.) This experimental trio inevitably recalls the Little Hadham Experiment of Angus, Bentley Bridgewater and Ian Calder, to which it bears far more resemblance than it bears to the stock theme of the Eternal Triangle. The partners here, as in a homosexual trio, are as nearly equal as the author can make them. Nobody or in turn everybody is the jam (the raspberry jam?) in the sandwich: nobody – or in turn everybody – plays gooseberry. When Alexandra becomes pregnant, the child is to be the child of all three. The emotional mathematics of the situation, revived by that sad sighting of Ian Calder in Tokyo, are explored in the novel by Angus – as is its secret, frightening sexual compulsion, which so alarms Alexandra that she is forced to run, and run, and run again. It is as though Angus is determined to look at the worst implications of liberation, to be as unafraid as he dare before the unspeakable. He has decided to open up all the dark places of the imagination and the fantasy (as he refused to do for Tynan) and to see what lies there. (Early in 1973, writing on *Edwin Drood*, Angus was to suggest more forcibly than in his Dickens book that the creative imagination may be sinister as well as liberating – and that in his last work it had become so for Dickens. Dickens found violence, sadism and murder in the "treacherous, colourful Oriental source" of Jasper's opium-inspired dreams: Dickens had "become very mistrustful of fiction, of the art he practised, of the fancy and the imagination as weapons on behalf of the Good Life."[1])

Even more disturbing than the troilism of his three students are his detailed descriptions of Hamo's farcical failures in his global search for the Fairest Youth in the World. (Hamo too is haunted by mathematics, though not by multiples of three – measurements of chest, waist, hips and legs promise to provide his magic.) When we are introduced to Hamo Langmuir – whose ancestry of landed Scottish gentry suggests the background Angus might have known had the Johnstone-Wilsons hung on to Stroquhan – he is suffering from a form of emotional and physical impotence as a result of the break-up of his relationship with his one-time lover, schoolteacher Leslie (who is Alexandra's uncle). Leslie has, simply, grown too old to be sexually attractive to Hamo. Hamo now finds he can have sex only with those with whom he has no emotional involvement. He can settle accounts with money, but not with love.

The emotional aridity of his life, glimpsed although misconstrued by his god-daughter Alexandra, was something which Angus had observed many times in the homosexual world. He had witnessed the tragedy of the man who is attracted only to sexual objects of a certain age, and who is therefore doomed to lose them: the novel confronts the dilemma boldly, as his friends did in life. Some entered open marriages, maintaining emotional and domestic fidelity with a younger partner, but enjoying sex on the side. Some condemned themselves to loneliness. Some paid for sex and surrounded themselves with a circle of comrades. Some encouraged a succession of boys or young men, and offered friendship long after the younger partner had ceased to be of sexual interest. Some got knocked about by rough trade. Some died.

There were many dark possibilities here. Angus was to find that what shocked many of his readers was not Hamo's homosexuality – we had come to terms with that by 1973 – nor even his preference for young men, for Angus goes out of his way to emphasise that, unlike some of the characters in the book, Hamo is not technically a pederast and does not "like chicken".* It was Hamo's emotional coldness that shocked, his mechanical pursuit of casual sex which he thought he could satisfy with money. (He is, as it happens, a wealthy man.) Homosexuals were if anything more offended by this aspect of his behaviour than straight readers. Hamo was letting the side down.

And he is, it must be said, a curious hero. Conspicuously tall, moustached, curly-haired, old-fashioned in manners, fondly revering the memory of his soldier father, idealistic and hopelessly clumsy, with his accoutrements of highly-polished brogues, monogrammed hair brushes, silver shoehorns and trouser press, he is Angus's attempt at a Holy Fool, an Idiot. He is hardly calculated to appeal to the young reader. He is a clubman and at times a prig, and he is as disgusted by the sexual appetites of others as they are by his. Even his loyal and tolerant companion Errol misunderstands his tastes. Angus knew that this was dangerous territory, but did he know *how* dangerous?

The tragi-comedy of human sexuality is joined to a complicated plot about science and magic, about global responsibility, about Oriental materialism and Western occultism: the book demands to be read not only as a picaresque farce but also as a meditation on the war between Evil and Reason. How, then, to adjust to its passages of knockabout slapstick, of vulgarity, of cruelty, of horror?

There is much in Hamo that cannot be identified with Angus: nevertheless, he springs in part from Angus himself. The notebooks make this inescapably clear. "Of course, in a horrible sense this Asian trip is my Asian trip – health being substituted for sex – but one may think that the proof of the pudding will be in the eating – so whether I can do the book will tell equally about Hamo and me. Does my necessary confusion about his subject reflect (unnecessary?) confusion in me about writing?"

Again, we are reminded of Dickens, with his health failing on his last ill-advised reading tour of the States, on his frenzied itineraries around Britain. Angus had lain awake in hotel rooms round the world, alternately sweating and freezing in uncontrollable air-conditioning, appalled by nightmares when he slept. A kind of Gilbert Pinfold unreality had overwhelmed him at times – perhaps, like Waugh's and Pinfold's, aggravated by too many of those ever-needed sleeping pills. He had been praised and fêted, but at the same time he had been prey to anxiety about failing creative powers. He was getting older and short of breath, and he was no longer confident that the imagination was Good, not Evil. In

---

* Is he perhaps an ephebophile – defined by Mishima, after Magnus Hirschfeld, as one who likes young men between the ages of 14 and 21? See Yukio Mishima, *Confessions of a Mask* (Peter Owen 1960).

Hamo, he created a character of personal and professional integrity who found that evil came from good. His Magic Rice destroyed the lives of smallholders on poor land all over Asia. Hamo, says Angus in one of his notes, "seems to believe that he has lost powers by collapse of his sex life – it seems more likely, I fear, that he has lost powers."

The novel has many "set-pieces", and (unlike earlier works) it invites itself to be seen as a series of linked episodes. One of the most striking of these is the scene of the Uncles in Borneo – French, Dutch, Danish, English, German – with their schoolboy protégés – Master Cambodia, Master Burma, Master Hong Kong, Master India. Hamo is taken to a fourteenth birthday party at the Club of the Uncles, complete with monstrous iced cake, games of forfeits, crackers, cricket, farting and fornication. It is an elaborate and brutal parody of colonial penetration, based in part on de Sade's *120 Days of Sodom* – the celebration takes place at a hillside fortress which has been cut off by floods for 120 days at a time. Hamo is disgusted not only by the tone of the vast overweight Uncles, at once brutal and boyish, but also by their sexual tastes: the boys are all far too young for him, and he in turn is found disgusting when he shows an interest in an old young man of eighteen.

It is an extreme scene which examines the arbitrary and often ludicrous nature of sexual attraction and perversion: the overtones of "exotic and arcane mystery, initiation and rite" are explored and yet mocked. The Dutch Uncle, a Petomane and master-farter like Gerard Reve or the peasant Jesus Christ in Zola's *La Terre*, performs a gross and elaborate party trick: "Jonkheer Kerkelyk van Enkhuijsen rose to his full six foot height at the head of the table, turned his back upon the assembled company, let down his trousers and underpants: and from his enormous hairy arse emitted in rapid cannonade fourteen farts that resounded across the delicious cake, putting out the candles, giving an acrid turn to the cloying flower scent. A roulade of fourteen farts so consistently sustained in both force and note was an achievement that roused excited clapping from the boys and a warm shower of compliments even from the sophisticated grown-ups. Little Ian Wong, in whose honour the feat had been performed, buried his smooth saffron face in his white shirt to hide his delighted blushes . . ." (p.165)

The child victims in de Sade's elaborate fantasy come to extraordinarily unpleasant and violent ends: these little victims survive and prosper, backed by the patronage of their rich uncles. (Interestingly, in his book on Zola Angus had linked Zola with de Sade – both had a strong obsession with certain primary numbers and their various multiplications – in de Sade "almost to the point of insanity".[2]) Nevertheless, Angus was aware that in passages like this he had broken several taboos at once, and as publication drew near he became not a little apprehensive. This moment was, however, still a long way off. The preliminary assault on the text in Azeitao in 1970 was to be followed by eighteen months of frequently interrupted work.

★

Angus returned to a hectic autumn of lecturing, wining and dining. He lectured on Dickens in France and Virginia Woolf in Newcastle and Dickens in Keele. He entertained Americans and Indians and Australians and British Council representatives from all over the world. On 7 January 1971 he went up to Leeds to receive the Yorkshire Post Literary Prize for his Dickens book – two hundred pounds and an illuminated scroll – and returned to dinners in London with the Nolans and John Croft, the Pritchetts and Margaret Drabble with her first husband Clive Swift, who was like herself a keen admirer of Wilson's work. (Drabble and Swift think this is the first time they entertained Angus and Tony: Swift kindly recalls that Drabble was less flustered by the occasion than he had expected.) On 9 January Angus and Tony at Regent's Park Terrace gave a party with an oriental flavour for Roger Eliot, who had been Angus's host in Hong Kong: it was attended by Monty Lo, a Hong Kong Chinese antique-dealer friend, and by Harold Acton, who spoke fluent Mandarin, and who wrote from the Stafford Hotel on 16 January to say how much he had enjoyed meeting "a Chinese boy whose name, alas, I forget" and how much he had been charmed by Julian Mitchell's "Cleopatra" (Richard Rowson, a dark-browed, dark-eyed oriental beauty from Lincolnshire) "but all were charming and stimulating to me, also Furbank and the passionate Proustian. Believe me, I was quite sincere, when I expressed my deep admiration for your work, even in collaboration with Philippe Jullian! I return to Florence happier for having seen you again, so flourishing and fruitful. Yours ever, Harold." On 29 January, Angus spoke at a celebratory luncheon at the Criterion for Bloomsbury bookseller Ivan Chambers, whom he had known since Museum days, and dined that night with David Farrer at the Garrick, to report on progress on the book. On his return to Felsham Woodside, he was immediately driven away by the excessive telephoning engendered by a postal strike which had begun on 20 January: he disappeared by himself to Ireland to write.

From 31 January to 21 February he stayed in Kilkea Castle ("Modern Comfort in Historical Surroundings") in County Kildare – according to Colin the land of his ancestors. He claimed that the only other guest was King Boris of Bulgaria. He worked away at *Magic*, sketching in scenes between Alexandra's parents and Hamo on the backs of menus. While he was away the Public Lending Right debate received new impetus by the publication of Richard Findlater's symposium, to which Angus had contributed a fighting introduction, sub-titled "A matter of justice".[3]

The Famous Writers row rumbled on, and on his return Angus accepted a new public post, succeeding Mark Longman as Chairman of the National Book League. His old friend, the smartly-dressed, entrepreneurial but innocently idealistic Martyn Goff, was now Director of the National Book League, and the moving spirit planning the Book Bang which was to take place in Bedford Square in May – a fortnight's carnival-cum-exhibition with tents, performers and signings, which Angus opened, sharing the honours with Coco the Clown.

When he was around, Angus found it difficult to refuse invitations, and in early March he disappeared once more to Portugal with his novel and Tony, this time to a rented villa in Azeitao: Perkin Walker came to stay with them for some of their six weeks, and much shocked the Portuguese woman of the house by his battered footwear. In mid-April, Angus was back to dinner with Julian Mitchell in his home in Christchurch Street, to dinner with Paul Bailey at L'Escargot – very much the favoured restaurant at this period. On Saturday 15 May he attended the annual dinner of the Society of Civil Service Authors at Church House in Great Smith Street, in his capacity as the Society's vice-president: he had inveigled both Margaret Drabble and Christianna Brand to attend as guest speakers, and watched with a kind of delighted alarm as Christianna Brand was thrown off course during her proposal of a toast to the society by an intervention from the floor by a member whom Brand had supposed long dead, and about whom she was about to tell an amusing anecdote. ("She never quite got back into her stride," Angus commented afterwards to Drabble, with sympathetic satisfaction.)

The summer term's teaching beckoned, and with it came a lunch in Norwich on 25 May 1971 with a creative writing student called Ian McEwan, whose work Angus thought promising. The Creative Writing programme was new at the University of East Anglia, and McEwan was its first and at this time its only student. He had arrived in 1970, aged twenty-two and fresh from a good degree at the University of Sussex, and had been handed over to Angus by Malcolm Bradbury: Bradbury, off on a sabbatical for the summer term of 1971, had read his stories and approved them, and McEwan was allowed to submit them in place of an MA dissertation.[4] (David Lodge was the external examiner.) McEwan was the guinea-pig in a very successful experiment, and gave impetus to the UEA course, unique in Britain.

The course was supported and in part funded by Joe McCrindle, patron and collector of the arts, and editor of the *Transatlantic Review*, who favoured experimental writing and wished to encourage it in Britain: he was an admirer of the work of B.S. Johnson and Alan Burns. He could draw on money from a fund called the Henfield Foundation and, in conversations with Bradbury, McCrindle had shown interest in funding a Creative Writing Fellowship at UEA: the first Henfield Fellow, Alan Burns, was appointed in 1971. Bradbury's enthusiasm for the teaching of creative writing, which he had seen as a possibility in the United States (though he had not at this stage himself taught creative writing there), had been foreshadowed in his warm review of *The Wild Garden* in 1963: and as a novelist himself he had been eager to introduce other writers into the Norwich campus, if only to prove Roland Barthes wrong – the author was not dead, as Barthes had announced in 1968, but alive and well and enjoying himself. Angus himself had taken writers touring the regions, to show that they were real people: Bradbury would put them in touch with students.

Bradbury himself was now well established at UEA, though he had also embarked on his international career as peripatetic professor: he had launched the successful new American Studies programme at UEA in 1966, and got his chair in 1970/71. But he and Angus had known one another for years. They had first met in a pub in Bury St Edmunds when Bradbury was still an undergraduate at Leicester, and Angus was already "old and white of hair and famous": they had met again in the British Museum in the 1950s, and as we have seen on Angus's visit to Bangor in 1962, when Bradbury was on the faculty there. Their relationship had its professional tensions and perhaps its rivalries, and their teaching methods, Bradbury recalls, were very different – Bradbury stressing technique, Wilson instinct and themes – yet both worried that too much literary theory could perplex and destroy the creative talent, and both were anxious to break out of the old academic structure. (The American Studies programme was in part Bradbury's response to the restrictions of his own course as a student at Leicester.)

Creative writer Ian McEwan was certainly alive and well, and he made a great impact on his fellow students, on the Henfield Fellow Alan Burns, and on Professor Wilson. Here, thought Angus, was youth – long-haired, bespectacled, brilliant, alarming. McEwan and Angus became friends for life: McEwan and his friend and fellow-student Jon Cook invited Angus and Tony round for a meal of roasted duck in their student flat without furniture, and Angus responded with many invitations to Felsham Woodside. McEwan attended the annual student summer party on June 13 with a neurotic hippie beauty straight out of the developing pages of *As if By Magic*. (Angus was to write to Alan Ross at the *London Magazine* this summer about McEwan's work – with a letter proudly dated "11.8.71 – My 58th birthday" he enclosed "for the interest of your editorial staff a piece written by one of my students at Norwich which seems to me to have great virtues . . . to have an opinion from one of your editors if you think it at all worth encouraging would be of great service." His letter concludes with a complaint: "could you *please* ask your distribution department *what* has happened to my subscription? I have received *nothing* since April/May and since I have spent a good deal of such little life as I pass in literary circles praising London Magazine it seems a little hard . . ."[5])

Angus's social life was nothing if not mixed. A characteristically crowded June day (23 June) included lunch at Brown's with Alex and Jean Kern, by now old friends from meetings in Lausanne and Cairo, to plan a house swap in Iowa for the autumn, and dinner at L'Escargot with Patrick White and his friend Manoly Lascaris. (Angus and Jean Kern were exactly of an age, she a handsome white-haired Anna Massey, he a white-haired Margaret Rutherford: Angus liked to say they were twin spirits.) Two days later he was back in Suffolk robed in purple to present an honorary degree to his old friend Frances Yates, whose work on the occult had been much in his mind during his own work on *Magic*. They made a splendid couple, also twin spirits – *both* of them, as several members of the congregation commented, looked remarkably like Margaret Rutherford.

Visitors continued to pour in, and on July 26 Kazu Serikawa arrived from Japan. Angus and Tony met him in London, gave him dinner at L'Escargot (introducing him to Francis Bacon at the next table) and took him to a party at George Weidenfeld's in honour of Harold Wilson. Serikawa was most impressed. (Wilson was at this point Leader of the Opposition, having lost the election of 19 June 1970: the Labour Party was returned to power in March 1974.) The next day they dined at the Athenaeum, and after two more days of sightseeing in London Serikawa went to stay at Felsham Woodside for several days: he was working on a translation of *No Laughing Matter*, and needed help, particularly with the passages of pastiche. The large cast list also presented a problem, which Serikawa solved by using eleven different colours in his text – purple for Marcus, red for the Countess, blue for Quentin, pink for Sukey . . . It was a long, two-year task, which he was already half way through. (When the translation was published in 1972, it received much attention but did not sell as well as he had hoped; the shock change in the exchange rate of the yen against the dollar in August 1971 had more or less doubled the price of books in a year.)

It was not all work; they were soon on friendly terms. "Call me Angus," Angus urged him, and he became thenceforth Kazu. It was Serikawa's first visit to Europe, and he soaked in the atmosphere of the world he had so far known only through fiction. (In his text, he used one or two footnotes and inserted a few explanatory phrases: he had also made good use of the British Council library in Tokyo, and of its helpful librarian, Derek Cornish.) Angus and Tony took him around East Anglia, showing him Ickworth, the church at Woolpit, and Ely cathedral, introducing him to friends and neighbours, feeding him at the Angel Hotel, at Long Melford, and at the cottage on poached salmon, gammon, and roast beef. (Serikawa recorded that the salmon was boiled, but Tony says it was poached; this is one of the few occasions on which Serikawa's English needed emendation.) Then they put him on the train and off he went back to London, the British Museum, a tour of Shakespeare country, Harrods, and the theatre: he stayed in their rooms in Regent's Park Terrace.

In late August, after entertaining the Sinclair-Wilsons from Australia, Angus and Tony went off to Italy for a brief holiday in Milan and Turin to gird themselves for a long visit to Iowa City.

*

They left for America on 16 September 1971, via a four-hour wait in Chicago to Cedar Rapids, the home of Quaker Oats: its small airport was a short drive away from Iowa City. They had arranged to exchange Regent's Park Terrace for the Kerns' house on Ridge Road, up above the small town and the wide river. Here, in Iowa City, they had watched the Kennedy election and Angus had lectured on Virginia Woolf. And here, now, in the University's Special Collections, were Angus's manuscripts. Safely packed and shipped by Quaritch, they had preceded him: after lengthy negotiations, including abortive overtures from the University of Texas in 1964, they had been purchased by Iowa in 1968 via the agency of Franklin Gilliam at the Brick Row Bookshop in Austin. The price agreed was 30,800 dollars, a sum that was to be spread over four years. Many boxes of notebooks, manuscripts, letters and typescripts had been despatched: this was a boom period in American investment in British manuscripts, and many writers were making similar sales.

(Logue was full of good advice about the MSS market: on the Welsh tour he had pressed upon Drabble a poem written on the back of a Ladies Sanitation Bag, and urged her to keep it as it would no doubt increase in value.)

Angus was already well known in Iowa, and he settled in for a long stay. The Kerns' house proved ideal: large, attractive and comfortable, it had a sloping garden in wild woods full of deer and dogwood, and a basement suitable for student parties. Angus could write in the open air, by the bird-feeder, watched, as he liked to claim, by a Wilson thrush. (Angus took delight in all the Wilson birds, named for the great eighteenth-century American ornithologist, Alexander Wilson – Wilson's phalarope, Wilson's warbler, Wilson's plover, Wilson's snipe . . .) It was a friendly community: neighbours would pop over the undemarcated garden boundaries with cookies to sustain him during composition. Distances were small: the air was good.

(The energetic Kerns found Regent's Park Terrace equally convenient – so near the Park, Camden Market, the British Museum – and Perkin, Nick Furbank and Bob and Monty were so friendly and hospitable – though there were disdavantages to a shared kitchen and bathroom. *Who* kept eating the eggs and apples and drinking the orange juice? Was it that shy and quiet Nick Furbank? Though come to think of it, although shy, Furbank was not exactly *quiet* – he had quite a gift for letting doors bang!)

Angus wrote optimistically to David Farrer that his teaching load in Iowa would be light – only two evenings a week. He was clearly trying to appease Farrer over the delays in the long-awaited novel, for he added "to be away from the constant demand on my benevolence in reading other peoples ms and supporting good causes, will be a great relief. I think I shall be able to go ahead much more rapidly."[6]

Nevertheless, not all was rosy. An embarasssing incident immediately upon arrival had to be laughed off: it reminded them forcibly that this was the Midwest, not the West Coast. Jack Leggett, director of the Writers' Workshop, met Angus and Tony at the airport at Cedar Rapids and drove them to a party in their honour at the University Athletics Club. To his horror he saw as he approached that the letter G had been removed from a huge electric sign which had been designed to say WELCOME ANGUS WILSON. Leggett apologised for student humour, but Angus brushed it aside: Tony, who noted the event without comment in his journal, says that he seemed not to notice it much. ("He could assess and absorb these things," said Tony. "Even his explosions were a kind of protection." Tony also noted that the incident was not an example of student humour: the culprit turned out to be a member of the faculty.) The person who perhaps relished the incident most was Roy McGregor Hastie, a dark-spectacled half-Romanian Charles-Osborne-and-Larkin-hating poet and academic: he was of the opinion that Angus was not happy in Iowa. (A resident of Merano, McGregor Hastie was in Iowa as Visiting Professor and Hill Foundation Scholar: he founded the Bilingual Text Series there.)[7]

He wrote: "Like Larkin, he was always envious of people with earned higher degrees. He was a great grumbler but a good lecturer. The coeds loved him ('That cute accent!') His colleagues found him rather a b-ore. He was always trying to get himself an honorary degree (again like Larkin) or fellowship, or anything, and he was avid for money, like Dryden. He was also always job hunting. I hear they invented a professorship for him in Essex or somewhere . . .

"I feel sorry for the old queer really. In the UK, as you know, Tony and he were coddled in a nauseating English way ('Arent they sweet?') but he got rougher treatment in the Midwest."

Fortunately for Angus and Tony, this account is at odds with others. It is true that Tony's journal records a few grumbles – Angus had depressions, sometimes total depressions, about his novel, and could not work out how to finish it. (On Monday, 25 October 1971 Tony's diary reads "I suggested culmination at Goa to shorten and in partic to reduce scenes requiring new invention all time. Received very well.") Occasionally Angus met people who, as he wrote to Tom Rosenthal, who had taken over at Secker, were so "rebarbative or so stupid that one will wake up at 3 and lose an hour's sleep in rage or dismay." Tony became used to listening for Angus in the night, as though he were a restless baby. Some of the food was "filthy", even at so-called gourmet restaurants – you could be persuaded to drive seventy miles of an evening for a meal that was not worth eating, and get back exhausted at three in the morning. But overall, as Angus also wrote to Rosenthal,[8] the visit was proving useful, and he was finding teaching creative writing "infinitely more rewarding than academic teaching." He found his students "fascinating", and they liked him. Most people did indeed find him and Tony "cute" – "Fascinating old bird, isn't he?" remarked one student to Tony after a lecture, and one interviewer described Angus as a true leprechaun.[9]

Angus and Tony liked Iowa City, which was finely situated on the Iowa River, and architecturally more interesting than many small Midwest towns; it had originally been intended as the seat of government of the territory of Iowa, but that honour had passed to Des Moines, and the old capitol building had become the site of the University of Iowa in 1857. This imposing edifice, built in local limestone in the Greek revival style, now dominated the town, where other buildings had espoused the Italian Mediterranean, the English Gothic, the Colonial Revival, the Prairie Style, and the Modernist; there was much here to delight and surprise the eye. Angus and Tony loved the surrounding countryside with its pretty villages, churches and old farm buildings. They explored the surroundings of Coralville Lake, frequented by woodpeckers, fox-squirrels, tree-nesting ducks, racoons and opossums: they drove themselves to the soft green

Amish Country, where the Amish people rode in carriages and still ploughed with horses – it was like stepping back into the nineteenth century, Angus said, you could imagine Madame Bovary bowling past. They went on longer trips, to lecture at more or less neighbouring universities: they reached Madison, Detroit, Ann Arbor, and Southern Illinois. (When the Kerns returned they were somewhat surprised by the mileage on their car, which had been thrown in as part of the deal on the house.) In Saginaw, Michigan, they paid a friendly visit to Raymond Tyner, who was in need of friendship: Saginaw was the birthplace of manic-depressive poet Theodore Roethke, whose father had owned acre upon acre of greenhouses there, and it had driven Roethke slightly mad – many of his poems contemplate its small-town horrors and delights, culminating in a pub ballad written in 1961, "The Saginaw Song" –

> In Saginaw, in Saginaw,
> The wind blows up your feet,
> When the ladies' guild puts on a feed,
> There's beans on every plate,
> And if you eat more than you should
> Destruction is complete.[10]

Not all the Midwest was as charming and graceful as the landscape round Iowa City. (Visiting Saginaw years later with Bentley Bridgewater to see Tyner, young Ian Munday was driven to an aria of despair about small-town life worthy of Roethke himself.)

But in Iowa City, the lucky migrating birds Angus and Tony made friends, renewed frendships. The beautiful Tina Bourjaily, who had cooked for them on Election Eve, cooked for them on many other occasions. She and her husband Vance owned a farm a few miles out of town, where she surrounded herself with horses, ponies, cats, and King Charles spaniels: there were barbecues in the woods where wild turkeys and deer roamed and, for the brave, there was swimming amongst the fish and beavers in the lakes. Generous, cheerful, shrewd, and very know-ledgeable about the landscape, she represented the best in American hospitality: and her hospitality was often much imposed upon. She recalls Angus, at a barbecue, gnawing happily with his not very satisfactory teeth at a large lamb chop.

Others at Iowa knew Angus through his work: Frederick McDowell had written about the Wilson Papers, catalogued for the University Library by Sharon Graves in 1968, and he was to write perceptively about the later novels. (He asked if he could sit in on Angus's Dickens seminar with the students: Angus hesitated, for fear that the presence of a senior academic might inhibit students, but consented.) Then there was Paul

Engle, the uncrowned king of Iowa City, and his second wife Hualing Nieh. They were an imposing and powerful couple. They had met in Taiwan in 1963: Hualing Nieh, herself a writer who had already published nine books in Chinese, had visited the International Writers Workshop in Iowa and had stayed on, becoming an eminence almost as well known as her husband. Engle had founded the Writers Workshop not long after his return from Oxford, and over the years had attracted to it many of the most famous writers of the day – Robert Lowell, Robert Penn Warren, Kurt Vonnegut, Saul Bellow, Nelson Algren, W.D. Snodgrass. It was here, on the programme, that Hortense Calisher had met and fallen in love with her second husband Curtis Harnack, whom she marrried in 1959. Engle had presided over many meetings and introductions. He was a great salesman and fund-raiser: his poetic role as heir-apparent to Walt Whitman had suffered from his entrepreneurial activities, but he and Iowa City had prospered. He was known as a Robber Baron and a tough fighter, and his ambitions had grown with the years. He had travelled or sent emissaries all over the world – to Eastern Europe, Russia, Asia, Africa, South America, China – recruiting support. (Was he a spy, some wondered? Were some of his writers spies?) He was not universally liked or admired; many resented his dominance, and faculty wives complained that they were expected to do his entertaining for him. It was said that the head of the English Department, John Gerber, did not always see eye to eye with him: there was often friction between the Workshop and the Faculty. Both Engle and his wife were shrewd operators: he had been obliged by law to retire in 1967 as Director, but she had continued to work as Assistant Director, and he had remained a Consultant. The Engles did not lose control.*

Angus and Engle got on well enough, and Angus enjoyed his teaching, but the novel continued to nag, there were *Observer* reviews to fit in, and there were lectures at other universities. Angus had accepted many engagements during this autumn – perhaps too many? The mileage mounted on the Kerns' car, and stress mounted in Angus. It broke out at the end of November, in Philadelphia. The preceding days had been bad – sleeplessness, a long and searching interview with Fred McDowell,[11] arguments in seminars, and worries about agents and publishers back home – Richard Simon was leaving Curtis Brown to set up on his own, should

---

*Paul Engle's end was as dramatic as his life: he dropped dead at O'Hare airport in Chicago in March 1991 as he and Hualing Nieh were about to catch a plane to Poland. He disappeared as they were waiting in the lounge for their flight: she assumed he had gone off to the bathroom or the bar, but he did not return. Searching for him desperately, she found he had collapsed while trying to buy a magazine. The scene is oddly reminiscent of the sudden death of Bill Eliot on the airport in Angus's fictitious Eastern country in *The Middle Age of Mrs Eliot*.

Angus go with him? (He did not.) And he had indigestion from too much to eat at too many thanksgivings dinners. In short, as Tony noted in his journal, "plans for quiet restful days before Philadelphia and NY fucked up."

Angus had been invited to lecture at Temple University on 29 November 1971, and the following day to speak to the St Andrews Society at its annual dinner. From Philadelphia, he sent a cheerful postcard to Tony's mother showing the house where Mrs Elizabeth Ross made the first American flag: he wrote "We are here in Philadelphia – made a speech at the University this morning and tonight at a Scottish banquet! So far as I know I dont have to wear the stars and stripes. Tony bears me up. We left Iowa in snow but here is only a very wild wind. A beautiful town. On to New York. Only 2 weeks to home, thank Goodness. Angus."

Tony had a lot of bearing up to do and had also done much of the research for the Scottish address – he found helpful quotations from Burns and Scott – but it was up to Angus to provide the substance and to add the anecdotes and to sparkle for an audience. It was a nervous strain, and the sight of the Flow Chart, with its details of the timing of the pipers, the haggis, the procession with the Rams Head Snuff Mulls Small and Large, the meal, the many toasts, and, not quite finally, the Speech (to last from 9.32 to 10.13 precisely) was enough to make a less experienced performer faint. During the afternoon before this ordeal, Tony took Angus on a calming visit to the Philadelphia Institute of Arts, but Angus took it into his head that a group of giggling schoolgirls was giggling *at him* – and maybe they were, for he was a striking figure. He flew into one of his frightening rages. He had to explode, he became hysterical. He calmed down in time for the evening, and his speech – which embraced the lost domain of the Johnstone-Wilson estate and St Andrews in the war, as well as Scott, Burns and Fenimore Cooper – was excellent.

Nevertheless it was a nasty moment. Small wonder then, that when they met Jack Plumb in New York at the Algonquin on 1 December, Tony declined Plumb's offer to be shown round New York by Plumb while Angus went off to lecture at Yale. No, said Tony, he would go with Angus, and stay in a nearby motel. Seeing all those Viking people in New York had been tiring enough – though Peter Kemeny was a sweet chap and they had been pleased to catch a fleeting glimpse of Angus's old heroine Anita Loos in a restaurant. (Angus had long admired her classic work, *Gentlemen Prefer Blondes*, first published in 1925, and references to her and her heroine, Lorelei Lee of Little Rock, recur in his work and correspondence.) But Angus was tense in New York. Tony felt he had better stick with Angus. Plumb thought Angus was being possessive. Tony thought Angus needed protection.

Angus and Tony flew home on 18 December 1971, and spent their quiet family Christmases in Kent. The Iowan break had not been quite as peaceful as they had hoped. But the money had been good, and they had a new car waiting for them to cheer themselves up — a light blue Citroën super saloon with charcoal trim. (They traded in their old Capri.) Ian McEwan, remembering the Citroën in later years, said "I always thought they must be millionaires. I thought they were amazingly rich."

★

1972 dawned gloomily. Angus was suffering from a bad cold, bronchitis, urinary problems and worries about the book. The damp of Felsham Woodside did not help. "Oh to be out of England!" he wrote to David Farrer on 21 January. He had only been back for a month. He took himself off to the London Clinic for X-Rays and blood tests. He wondered if he had been taking too many barbiturates.

There was much to be gloomy about. The weather was terrible, the miners were on strike, there were coal shortages and threats of electricity cuts. Industry went on a three-day week and householders were asked to heat only one room. Jack Plumb wrote from New York saying he had been in hospital for surgery and had to cancel a trip to California. Nobody was getting any younger. The wife of friend and neighbour Douglas Blyth had died in December. On 11 January 1968 Francis Wormald had died, aged sixty-eight, after a long illness bravely resisted with the aid of faith, Honoria, homeopathy, St Thomas's Hospital, and his many old friends. For one living all his life, as Patrick Woodcock had put it, "on borrowed time", he had not done badly. More distressingly, a fortnight earlier, on 27 December 1971, Forrest Fulton had also died, at his home in Gower Street. The certificate gave "bronchopneumonia" as cause of death, but his friends said it was suicide. (There was a post-mortem.)

Fulton had ben unhappy and unwell for a long time, emotionally isolated, tending to get mixed up with the wrong set whenever he came out of his laboratory. Not even the camaraderie of Perkin Walker, Bob French and Monty Turland had been able to save him. His death, like Alan Turing's, was ambiguous: his mother believed it was due to some accident with photographic equipment which had affected his lungs. Others thought he had become dependent on the drugs to which his profession made access all too easy. There was a dignified Obituary Notice in the *British Medical Journal* 8 January 1972, describing his work on the antigenic structure of rickettsiae, scrub typhus, and the influenza virus: it concluded

"Fulton was a man of culture and exceptional mental ability. He had read widely, had studied philosophy, and was an admirer of Proust. In the teaching of his students, he took endless trouble, and they in turn responded by their devotion to him. A lonely man, he mixed little with his colleagues and made no intimate friends at the school [of Hygiene and Tropical Medicine]. He shunned scientific meetings, kept out of the limelight, and confined himself largely to his laboratory and the classroom. The last year or so of his life was clouded by ill health. Apart from recognition by those around him his intrinsic worth was shown only by the high quality of his published writings. An outstanding man with an original mind of a quality seldom met with, his loss to the school will be great and to medical research even greater."

Angus grieved and wrote letters of consolation to the family: Mabel Fulton wrote back, in a hand shaking with arthritis, thanking him for his "kind and helpful" letter, and for the lovely flowers, and telling him she had a nice snapshot of Angus and Forrest sitting in her garden. This was unusual: in most group photographs, Forrest was to be seen, in dark glasses, just slipping out of the frame. And now he had slipped away forever. Fulton's had been a sad and unfulfilled life. He had been held in great affection by his close friends, but had never found the companionship he needed. His fate worked on Angus, as he worked out the tragic dénouement of his lonely scientific protagonist, Hamo Langmuir.* He was thinking, also, about the fate of the lonely self-styled Baron Corvo: the publisher Cecil Woolf had sent him Rolfe-Corvo's *Venice Letters*, a mildly pornographic and erotic correspondence with the generous Mr Fox which deals largely with Rolfe's relationships with young men in Venice and Burano: Woolf had asked Angus to write an introduction, but Angus had declined, writing on 30 December 1971 to say he was just recovering from Iowa and bronchitis, had read the letters, and thought them "very fascinating. He has an honest diction like Norman D[ouglas] and hated humbug (although this, of course, is a very useful line for the totally selfish). He seems at once likeable and intolerable, but not pitiable except in the purely material economic sphere. As to his boys, youths would be better, my impression is that, like many people of all sorts of sexual concerns, he wanted a body without personal commitments and yet also a person, a human being. In short he wanted, I suspect, to love and be loved only when he wanted it. The distaste for younger boys because he couldn't see their faces when he was having sex with them is very significant here. The

---

*Forrest Fulton's odd name came, by odd coincidence, from his grandfather Sir Forrest Fulton (1846–1925), who had been junior counsel for Robert Ross in Ross's action for libel against Lord Alfred Douglas, November 1914.

eyes mean that [they] are in bed with a particular person, not just a body. Considering all his difficulties not least of which was lack of money and a room to take them back to – he managed fairly well and respected the boys in a way that satisfies his need for their being real people. Had he had money he probably would have been generous to them, but then again he might not. Mr Fox, however, seems a very likeable man and one can't help disliking some of the tricksiness with which Corvo tried to get the sustenance he so desperately needed from him – as if Mr Fox could go to bed with two Italian boys in an English seaside hotel! And Corvo must have known that.

"What does concern me however is what on earth you could want me to say in a Preface. The above horse sense reflections of another homosexual are hardly very penetrating nor would they take long to write. My impression is that any preface by me would be a silly attachment of a name . . ."*

Forrest Fulton, Baron Corvo, Hamo Langmuir – Angus brooded on them all as he recovered from his bronchitis.

*

Angus did not have to endure the misery of an English winter for too long. He was booked to go to Kuwait in late February 1972 for the British Council. Meanwhile, he dined with Angus McBean, stayed one night in Oxford with Stuart Hampshire at Wadham and another at Merton, spoke at the Oxford Women's Luncheon Club, visited Avebury for *Magic* research, lectured at the University of Kent, and saw the old crowd in Suffolk. He accepted a C.Litt. (the highest award of the Royal Society of Literature of which he had been a Fellow since 1958), and the Vice-Presidency of the Campaign for Homosexual Equality. He was also forcing his way through the novel.

On the night before he departed for Kuwait, he dined at the Escargot with Fred Warburg. They had not seen one another for a long time. Warburg, who had retired as executive chairman the previous April, wanted to talk to Angus about the second volume of his own autobiography, and, as he put it, had felt "shy" about contacting him: he had been supplanted rather more rapidly than he had expected by Tom Rosenthal, who had lost no time in building up a friendly relationship with Angus. His career as a publisher, Warburg wrote a little plaintively, was

---

*In the event, Woolf wrote the Preface himself, using (without acknowledgement) some of Angus's points and some of those of Alan Munton, who had written an MA thesis on Rolfe's *The Desire and Pursuit of the Whole. The Venice Letters* was published in 1974 by Cecil and Amelia Woolf.

over. In fact, he was still working at 14 Carlisle Street, but had been moved into a back office; Angus appears to have been one of very few confidants – perhaps the only one – to whom he confessed a sense of chagrin at this displacement. To others, Warburg appeared as sprightly, elegant and confident as ever, still sporting his crisp Homburg and his silver-topped cane.

The years were rolling by. Angus had been in Iowa for David Farrer's anniversary of 25 years with the firm. A young Australian called Peter Grose was about to replace Richard Simon at Curtis Brown. There were new faces everywhere.

Angus flew away from all this to Kuwait, probably with some relief. He was there from 25 February to 10 March, while Tony set off alone to France and Italy. At least Kuwait was a change. He stayed at the Hilton, on the Corniche near the American Embassy: he sent a postcard to nephew Mark Davies commenting that "affluence amid miles of desert sand is an interesting human problem." At Kuwait University he found large rigidly segregated classes of pampered young people with very diverse linguistic backgrounds: he spoke to men and women, separately, on the Modern Novel and the Victorian Novel. He also gave public lectures on Dickens and on "Being a Writer". One of the only two Westerners on the staff was a young American, Robert Lambert, educated at Rutgers and Yale, who had combined an itinerant teaching career with attempts to write fiction fusing "the genres of the academic novel (*Lucky Jim*) with the erotic realism of *Fanny Hill*. (I term the works *punography*.)"[12]

One day Angus and Lambert were whizzed off in a Mercedes to the Gazelle Club by Professor Widad Hamd Widad: Angus, according to Lambert, shocked her by declaring that he loved only those of his own sex, then proceeded to entertain them with stories of his childhood and the royal family. He said he had travelled with Prince Charles in a helicopter, or something to that effect. He also entertained Lambert in private (or was it the other way round?) with stories about sex, masturbation, and room stewards. Lambert found him *very* frank and uninhibited – for an Englishman.

While in Kuwait, Angus was also (rather like royalty) taken on a tour of a desalination plant, and on a boat trip to Phaelicia Island which boasted an ancient, phallic rock with magical fertility powers. Science and Magic met in this surreal trip, and no doubt they reminded him of the unfinished novel.

On Friday 10 March he flew from Kuwait to Rome, to be met by Tony with the car. They drove first to Viterbo to try to find a quiet place to write, but were driven away by noisy hunters with dogs and socks and

feathers in their hats, who were intent on destroying all the songbirds of
Italy. On they went, via Gubbio, where the hotel was fine but *In Restauro*,
to Ancona on the Adriatic coast, where they settled at Portonovo di
Ancona in a hotel called the Fortino Napoleonico. They were the only
guests, the sun shone, and the food was simple and good. Angus's jottings
are a clear guide to progress: in fiction he moved from Goa to Swami to
Boy's death to Elinor's Rape to Hamo at the Dam to Main Goa Scene,
while in fact he took excursions to Loreto and Rimini and the Botanical
Gardens. Then he and Tony journeyed back slowly, moving north via
Vicenza, Padua, Innsbruck and the baroque churches of Ulm, as the plot
moved on towards the Finale. The book was finally finished at Colmar,
where both Angus and Tony were lastingly impressed by Grünewald's
extraorinarily powerful Issenheim altarpiece of the young, wild-haired,
distraught Saint John comforting the swooning Virgin. At Metz Angus
made a scene in a restaurant – he ought to have been feeling calm, his task
completed, but he was still tense, became very angry when he was not
served promptly, and shouted both in English and in French. Tony calmed
him down, and the two well-travelled companions (Pickwick with his
Weller? Hamo with his Errol? Maugham with his Haxton?) moved on to
Lille and Montreuil (some exhausting English people in the hotel) and set
off for England from Calais on 10 April 1972. They had made it. The term
at UEA began on 17 April (with Anthony Thwaite as the new Henfield
Fellow) and Angus had a date with the Duke of Edinburgh and the
National Book League on 27 April.

*

Not all was gloom and doom on the home front. At least the gay cause
seemed to be prospering: Angus encouraged it by sending £20.00 to *Gay
News*. Suffolk gastronomy was also doing well. Earlier in the year Robert
Carrier had moved into the newly-restored Hintlesham Hall and Angus
and Tony became regular visitors at his restaurant, entertaining Sandy
Wilson, Bentley Bridgewater, David Farrer and many others there,
lunching with Carrier himself, and attending a huge lunch party thrown by
Chopping and Wirth-Miller – guests included Francis Bacon, Muriel
Belcher, and Angus McBean. In London, L'Escargot was rivalling the
Jardin des Gourmets at this period in Angus's affections – this year he had
already lunched and dined there with Penelope Gilliatt, Simon Edwards,
Monty Turland and Bob French, Fred Warburg, and Philippe Jullian. On
2 May he lunched there with the good-hearted South African gourmet
Gavin Jack, who sent him a copy of an appreciative radio broadcast he had
transmitted on Radio Port Natal – Jack mentions The Bunch of Grapes in

Shepherds Market, Wheelers in Old Compton Street, the Ivy, and concluded "lastly I am going to finish with a restaurant which is a very old friend of mine and that is the Escargot Bienvenu in Greek Street. This was the haunt during the war of the gay young men and women who belonged to the French section of that formidable organisation, SOE, and many were the members of this who, just before parachuting into France to the Maquis, dined at the Escargot. On this occasion I had luncheon with one of the most famous and certainly in my opinion the best writer in the English language, Angus Wilson. It was a gay and to my way of thinking a most stimulating meal. The conversation was as good as the food and that is saying something." (In a covering note, Jack apologised for his prose, but promised that "it sounds reasonable on the tape" – and hoped to be able to see Angus soon in South Africa on Kipling matters: clearly the new use of the word "gay" had not yet reached Durban.[13])

The summer's social life was as brisk as ever. Michael Slater and John Grigg came for a weekend and went to the Maltings to see *The Turn of the Screw*. Nephew Mark Davies came to stay. John and Ann Dizikes from Santa Cruz were in England in June and went to Angus's annual summer party, which was crowded with students, and attended by Thwaites, Cooksons and Viva King – a splendidly heterogenous mix. An Iowan creative writing student, brought up in a funeral parlour in Savannah, turned up in Norwich and was entertained for two or three days. Raymond Tyner arrived on leave from Saginaw and was pronounced by Honoria Wormald to be as nutty as a fruitcake. Cecil Roberts, a relatively new friend, had a splendid eightieth birthday party thrown by Hodder & Stoughton at the Savoy at which this one-time runaway best-seller raised a cheer when he mentioned Public Lending Right: he spoke brilliantly, without notes, for a full ten minutes. (Being eighty needs a lot of stamina, he had written to Angus, in one of his many chatty letters.) And on 15 June there was the presentation of the C.Litt. to Angus, Lord David Cecil, L.P. Hartley and Cyril Connolly.

This was a comic-macabre occasion. The award was presented at the Royal Society of Literature by its President, Lord Butler. Of the five grand old men lined up for the photocall, Angus and David Cecil looked the most nearly normal. Butler got all the citations wrong and praised Angus for his translations of Zola, Connolly for his novel *The Unquiet Grave*. Hartley, swelling, portly, and moustached like a gentleman of another age was nervous in case he had to sign something, and in the end Butler had to yell at him "Come on, Leslie, come up and get it!" The ceremony was attended by Connolly's brother-in-law and Angus's old friend from

Museum days, Anthony Hobson, who, with his wife Tanya, dined with Angus and Tony after the event: Angus talked a lot about the new novel.

In early July, Angus and Tony went off for a short holiday to France, and stayed in a château hotel south of Bordeaux: it was expensive and a baseball team arrived and devoured all the puddings. (Angus loved his pudding.) They sent a cheery postcard to the Blackburnes showing the Parc de la Garenne, Nerac-en-Albret, the supposed scene of *Love's Labours Lost*, in which Tony had appeared with such éclat: they said they were enjoying the pleasant rolling countryside. But they were also nervously awaiting the official response to the typescript of *As if By Magic*. David Farrer's report (dated 10 July 1972) differs somewhat from his letter to Angus (also 10 July 1972), but both betray anxieties. For internal consumption, Farrer expressed doubts about Hamo – he was "not convinced" by him – and found the plot far too rambling and self-indulgent, too much like a travelogue. He was worried about hostile review coverage, and says he would have "read the riot act" about the script to any author other than Angus – meanwhile he would do what he could to persuade him to make revisions and cuts. (Nobody else, he implied, could even go that far.) He found the whole thing uncomfortably similar to *The Old Men at the Zoo* – a novel he had never liked, and which had not sold well either.

To Angus, he wrote more diplomatically – it was "most ambitious" – "a wealth of superb scenes" – "very moving" – but was it not a little sprawling? was there not too much parenthesis? and would readers be able to understand all the references to Tolkien and Hobbits? Tom Rosenthal, writing a fortnight later, echoed both enthusiasm and doubts – extraordinarily moving, intelligent and humane, etc. etc. – but what about cutting down the Japanese-American banquet and the university seminar?

Angus could read between these lines. He wrote a long defence and explanation of his book (reproduced as Appendix 2) in which he shows how deeply he had considered and plotted the work. Small points he would let go: he stuck to his thesis. He was willing to work on the text, but only up to a point. He still hoped and believed that he had written, if not a perfect then an important work, and that he was proving that he could "really deal" with the young of today.

Would *Magic* have been a better book had Angus had a stronger editor? Tony sometimes thinks this might have been so. Many of Angus's friends, as has been noted, believed that Angus was essentially lazy and disliked rewriting, but the evidence does not wholly support this. He did revise much of his work, and thought hard and long about structure, excess, and indulgence, as his letter to Farrer proves – although he admitted he could neither spell nor punctuate. Lazy he was not. He came to suspect that one of his problems with writing for the theatre and for television was that he got too much embroiled with listening to advice and ideas from directors and actors, and that he would have been wiser to stick to Jack Priestley's principle of ignoring everything that went on betweeen the first rehearsal and the first night. Clearly Farrer, old friend and professional editor though he was, was out of sympathy, in this novel, with Angus's intentions: why listen to him, then, on points of detail? It was a dilemma. Angus knew himself to be more than ever on his own. If he altered too much, he might spoil a masterpiece. On the other hand, he knew from Farrer's response and his own misgivings that he was courting disaster.

His doubts about the book's reception expressed themselves perhaps subconsciously in his comments to Philippe Jullian and to Julian Mitchell, to both of whom he had defiantly described the plot as "pederastic" – and again, to Philippe, as "scandalous". He was not naive enough to believe that this theme would not raise a flutter of protest. Indeed, his choice of descriptive vocabulary itself had an awareness of provocation, for his hero Hamo is not technically "pederastic" in the sense of "boy-loving": Hamo is attracted, unlike the Uncles, by post-pubertal young men, and the Fairest Youth whom he seeks is, unlike Elsie Black in *Hemlock*, well over the age of consent. Angus perhaps chose the word "pederastic" out of what Tony saw as an occasional self-destructive desire to shock the self-consciously broad-minded – a desire to *épater* not *le bourgeois* but *la bohème*. "Pederastic" is a word of dubious meaning and history, often used with derogatory intention in the general sense of "homosexual", and used by some with the deliberate intention of suggesting that all homosexuals are lovers, abusers and corruptors of children; the novel is itself an attempt to define and describe widely differing forms of homosexuality, including that form which is associated with boy-love (as praised and practised in Ancient Greece) to which the terms pederasty or paedophilia might more properly be exclusively applied. Sir Kenneth Dover, in his book on *Greek Homosexuality* (Duckworth, 1978, p.16) addresses the semantic confusion, stating that in Greek homosexuality "the reciprocal desire of partners belonging to the same-age category is virtually unknown" and that the younger, passive partner was known as "*pais*, singular: *paides*, plural" – a term which embraced boy, child, daughter, son and slave – and related to no definite age group, though the "*pais*" was often a fully grown youth. Angus was certainly aware of the contentiousness of the term, and, Tony suspects, used it somewhat contentiously.

The book was dedicated to Nicholas and Pamela Brooke, perhaps his two closest friends at UEA: Nicholas greatly admired (and understood) Angus's work, but clearly Angus had written a somewhat diffident letter about it to them both, for each wrote separately to him in June 1972 assuring him that its shocking contents would not shock them. What could he do, in the end, but back his own judgement? It was a high-risk book, and it would have to take its chances.

*

One can, however, detect an undercurrent of anxiety as 1972 rolled on. In September Tony took a Cordon Bleu cooking course in Marylebone: he found he was twenty-five years older than the thirty-five girls in the class, but this did not deter him from putting in a good attendance and learning to make a good *béarnaise*. You could never have too many strings to your bow. Business affairs seemed to be progressing satisfactorily – *Cloche* was to reprint, *Dickens* was doing well and appeared as a Penguin in September 1972, offers to talk about Dickens continued to pour in. Angus was already planning a biography of Kipling, but this project was being kept under wraps. A French edition of *Dickens* by Gallimard (without the illustrations) appeared in November, and Angus went over to promote it and himself: his novels were much admired in France, and his fluent if idiosyncratic French made him a pleasure to interview. His old friend Sylvère Monod, a Dickens scholar whom he had known for years, was delighted to welcome him there, and delighted to learn that Angus had just been appointed Chevalier de l'Ordre des Arts et Lettres. In Paris, Angus now always stayed in the quaint and modest little Hôtel Racine, near the Odéon: it was, said Monod, "staid and Victorian", but they loved Angus there. (Monod had met Angus at the Lausanne conference in August 1959, and had been deeply impressed by him as a lecturer; he had invited him to speak at Caen, where he had been equally impressed by Tony's tact as friend and chauffeur. Unlike L.P. Hartley's friend, who on a similar occasion had arrived unexpected, late, and drunk, and talked incessantly throughout dinner, Tony had simply melted quietly away when he felt he was not needed.)

In September, Angus attended a meeting at Churchill College in Cambridge of the John Cowper Powys Society. Fellow Powys fans – George Steiner, Glen Cavaliero, Colin Wilson, Wilson Knight (all the Wilsons) – gathered to praise this eccentric genius, who had written with such passion of sadism and primroses, of mysticism and cups of tea, of mob hysteria and lonely recluses, of prophecy and vivisection and provincial life. Powys provided the clearest possible example – as both warning and model – of the high-risk writer. Dickens had taken risks and won millions of readers. Powys had taken risks and won a small cult following of devotees. Powys had ignored editorial advice and common sense alike, writing vastly long novels of which most were out of print for much of the time. (Angus wrote an introduction to a reprint of *Weymouth Sands* for the Rivers Press, 1973). Powys had never done anything to promote himself. His subject-matter was unfashionable and audacious: his books were unsaleable. Angus greatly admired him. Angus conducted a seminar on that dark-age novel of Arthurian and Mithraic legend, *Porius*, and three days later went off to dine with Mary Gilliatt and Princess Margaret. (Mary Gilliatt was plotting a book about Suffolk architecture in which Angus's cottage was to feature.)

Underneath all this activity, he was not well. Julian Mitchell wrote in his diary for 22 September 1972 "Saw Angus and Tony outside the London Library – Angus complaining of exhaustion, but bursting with apparent health as usual, very manic. People kept rushing out of the London Library having heard him talking in the square. He's very much *loved* – I think he finds he gives out so much, it *is* exhausting." In October Angus had to cancel, on Patrick Woodcock's orders, a month's lucrative teaching at Hollins College, Virginia: he sent a telegram pleading "nervous exhaustion", and returned the tickets to BOAC for a refund. On 6 October he wrote to Mitchell apologising for cancelling a dinner date at the last moment: "The truth is I have been badly overworking . . . and I'm alarmed at social occasions for fear I'll weep or get angry and weep (two different things). However, I'm recovering. We're off to Cyprus for five weeks. When I return please show your forgiveness of me by dining with us, Angus."

And off they went, to a flat in Kyrenia, where they were happy for a while until they got bored. Then they flew off to Rome for a week. After that came the Dickens trip to Paris, then another spell in hospital. On 4 December 1972 Angus had written to Alan Williams at Viking in New York largely about alterations to the American dialogue in *Magic* and cuts made with the help both of Tony and David Farrer: he had mentioned in passing that he was "under the tiresome threat of a prostate operation." He went in hospital on 14 December for tests, and was out in time to give lunch to visiting Leggetts from Iowa on the 16th. He was suffering from insomnia, headaches, bad dreams: Tony was worried about him and about his own parents, neither of whom was well. The tests proved negative – no prostate operation – but in February 1973 Angus told Peter Conradi (now teaching at the South Bank Polytechnic, and busy enlisting support for his new gay magazine, *Lunch*) that he was suffering from diverticulitis. (*Lunch*, a monthly magazine founded in 1972, had featured interviews with Maureen Duffy, Alan Brien, David Hockney and Jimmy Savile: it was also to interview Reve, Isherwood, Beverley Nichols, Robin Maugham, John

Schlesinger, John Bowen, Julian Mitchell and Margaret Drabble. Many of these pieces came about as a result of introductions from Angus, who nevertheless firmly declined to be interviewed himself, telling Conradi that although in principle he wanted to help, he feared for his reputation: a repetition of the hesitation he had displayed to Antony Grey.)

Angus was trying to start work on a new Kipling project, but it was difficult to concentrate. It is hard to avoid the suspicion that apprehension about the publication of *Magic* hung over him like a black cloud. The arrival of Alan Williams from New York and a dinner to meet him arranged by Gwenda David did nothing to cheer him up. They all said the book was wonderful, amazing, astonishing – but did they mean it? Tony was finding Angus difficult. They went to the Victoria and Albert in January, and Tony, fresh from the dentist (and full of painkillers) remarked to his journal "A. jabber jabber every item." With Angus it was mania or depression and not much in between.

Publication for *As if By Magic* was scheduled for the end of May 1973. Secker & Warburg hoped to sell 10,000 copies: they printed 12,000. A curious uncertainty hung over the book. Angus was marking time, with a Foyle's luncheon, a lunch with the Queen Mother and Lord Zuckerman, with dinners with Michael Howard and the Kilmartins and Jonathan Miller and Richard Wollheim and Peter Conradi. (He had consulted Miller about mesmerism, a strand of sub-plot in his novel.) A whole generation of graduates from UEA had gone out into the world and was pressing him for references, for lectures in their institutions. (Some of them were already divorced and remarried.) Michael Howard's friend Mark James wanted him to go and speak at Clacton, Maggie Humm would have liked him to talk to her students. Angus had drinks with Madge Gillespie, who was still going strong in Holland Park. The National Book League was quite time-consuming, and here was the Royal Society of Literature asking him to be a Vice-President – how could he refuse? He spoke to the John Locke Society at Westminster and to librarians in the Stationers' Hall. William Chislett, old boy of Nowton Court, came to stay, and there was lunch with Rosamond Lehmann, the Hampshires and the Blackburnes.

An *Observer* (21 January 1973) review of three Suffolk books by three Suffolk men – Ronald Blythe, Norman Scarfe and Neville Blackburne – involved him in a confrontation with the Lord Lieutenant of the County, the Earl of Stradbroke: Angus had mentioned, *à propos* of Crabbe, that the climate and soil of Suffolk could "sour and embitter", a remark to which Stradbroke had taken strong exception, writing to the Pro-Vice-Chancellor of UEA from Wangford that it was hardly fitting to employ as professor somebody who was so rude about the county. A palliative reply had been sent, and all had ended well, with an invitation to lunch. But such incidents *were* a little souring and embittering – time to get away again, perhaps.

His state of mind and health at this time is revealed in a long and very frank interview with Michael Moorcock, made at the Athenaeum on 10 March, and published in *Books and Bookmen* in May. In it, Angus talked about his work processes, his teaching, his finances, his lack of a sense of his readership, his search for and use of new experience: the piece ends with a strong declaration of his own unhappiness. His early writing had come out of the shriek of hysteria: he no longer needs to shriek on paper, but he still feels within himself the "moan of a very great unhappiness". He concludes "It's clear to me that I shall go through the rest of my life having various sorts of apparently physical ailments which have to be examined to be found inorganic. Maybe one may, one day, be organic, but at the moment they've always been inorganic and they assume different forms. As I pursue one, it goes into another form, and they are all anxiety things. Whether writing helps any longer I rather wonder."

It was more than time for another break. And off he and Tony went, this time to Venice. They had tried to rent an apartment, as they had done in Portugal, but failed, and ended up rather more expensively in a suite in the Palazzo del Giglio for a month from 14 March. The service apartments belonged to the Gritti Palace Hotel, the old Palazzo Pisano, by the landing stage of Santa Maria del Giglio: some of the apartments looked over the Campo Santa Maria del Giglio, others over a small quiet backstreet. Tony shopped and cooked for breakfast and lunch, trying to avoid the tempting cakes of one of the most expensive and alluring pasticcerias in Italy, the Marchini on the Calle de Spezier: amongst other delicacies it sold liquorice wheels which reminded them of the giant curled volutes of the Salute. They ate their dinner in a little restaurant nearby and spent much of their days giving rein to their growing passion for architecture: the marble jewel-box of Santa Maria dei Miracoli they thought one of the most beautiful churches they had ever seen, and they paid their respects to the charming creatures – dragons, basilisks, dogs, badgers – which enlivened the Carpaccio frescoes in San Giorgio degli Schiavoni. They visited the Gesuiti and the Gesuati and the Frari, they admired the Titians and Bellinis, they inspected the great renaissance tombs of the doges in SS. Giovanne e Paolo. Angus made notes in his tiny pocket diary on the Doge's Palace, wicked nuns, Tintoretto, and the father of Monsignor Giuseppe. They lunched with Freya Stark, and they dined with Peggy Guggenheim: she lived with her little dogs just across the Grand Canal, at the other side of the traghetto from the Gritti. Once they tried to return her hospitality by taking her out to an artists' restaurant of her own choosing on the Giudecca – they walked for miles and miles and were all out of breath and when they got there she didn't eat a thing. They were invited by a contessa or two to meals and drinks, and found themselves, as Tony later put it, "on the fringes of Venetian society, and were sad therein."

Angus lectured on 10 April 1973 at the University of Venice, under the auspices of Professor Perosa, on "Dickens and the City", weaving in graceful allusions to his predecessor's visit to Venice in the winter of 1844 – Dickens had stayed at the Danieli, and had been much moved by the glories of Saint Mark's, but equally impressed, as he wrote to his friend John Forster on 11 December, by Venice's secret underworld of "wickedness and gloom – its awful prisons, deep below the water; its judgement chambers, secret doors, deadly nooks . . ." It was sometimes warm enough to sit out on the little terrace to work: it was there that Angus wrote an interesting and largely appreciative review of Brigid Brophy's eccentric book on Firbank, *Prancing Novelist*[14] – in which he chided her for not knowing who Lady Duff Gordon was – had the woman never heard of the sinking of the *Titanic*?

He stored away his impressions of baroque and rococo architecture for future use, and also the views of the misty lagoon in the fog. But even here he could not relax. His urinary troubles returned, and a paranoid worry about Malcolm Bradbury began to develop – he had to teach a seminar on creative writing called "The Writer's View of Fiction" with Bradbury the following term, and felt that their critical approaches were miles apart. ("Doctor Tony," Angus wrote to Farrer, had very wisely suggested that the best way to cure himself would be to read all Bradbury's novels: he sent off for a set.)

And even in Venice *Magic* would not leave him alone. Letters went backwards and forwards between Angus, Secker and Viking about proofs, cuts, corrections, Japanese and American spellings, publicity appearances in England and Holland. (The Americans wanted "black ladies" for "negresses".) A photograph by Tony of the Abbé Faria inducing an Indian woman to levitate was chosen for the book jacket: at least that seemed to please everybody. (Angus and Tony also used this photograph for their Christmas card this year, to the bewilderment of some of its recipients: what *was* the woman doing?) Then there was the question of the party. What should they arrange? Just in case the critics were vile, would it not be better, wrote Farrer, to arrange for a small private family party at the Garrick with the Rosenthals and the Groses – then "we can all cry violently on each others' shoulders."[15] Yes, Angus agreed that would be much better.[16] There could be a bigger party a fortnight after publication if things went well – but "if, which I don't believe, it fails badly, then what's the point of a wake? Please don't either you or Tom think I'm ungrateful, but you know how much I can shine if the sun shines but how I like to keep the rain under my own umbrella.

"Oh! the marcheses and the principessas and contessas we endure – and the shit their dogs make on the pavements – but it's a world I've never been in before – a principe, hearing we lived in Suffolk, asked if he knew David Suffolk with whom he had hunted in Leicestershire – 'I imagine Suffolk must be his place, tho' I've never been invited there for the shoot.' A Marchesa told me 'What's happened to Dickens' England, in those days the writers heaped their cruelties at the scum – the Fagins and the Sikes – now it's supposed to be clever in London to make fun of good breeding. My god!'

"But it's all so beautiful and so much to see – you can escape the principessas and their children's nannies – one 'a treasure from England' is called Nanny Honeybake – and the tourists (even the Japanese) and the dog shit and get to wonderful forgotten, half poor quarters of the town with half forgotten Carpaccios in the churches and only cats. Love, Angus."

Was the anxiety over the novel linked with the anxiety over Malcolm Bradbury? Possibly. Jonathan Raban speculated that UEA was not good for Angus's work or for his own assessment of himself – the university was full of "fierce young smartyboots": the Brookes (ironically about to go through a divorce) were his only real friends there: "the young" were into movies, not novels: and Angus had become "a fantastic, but lonely, ornament to the School of English and American Studies."[17] Lorna Sage saw it differently: she thought UEA had contributed a new freedom and power to his writing. But whichever was right, it was clear that Angus was nervous about the birth of his book. He put a good front on it, returning to England for appearances at Ilkley Festival, where he spoke on Dickens, and at Birmingham, where his fellow guest was Monica Dickens. Tactfully he complimented Birmingham upon its fine Botanical Gardens. Then there were interviews with Philip French, Wilfred De'ath and many others. He turned down innumerable invitations to speak, citing research on Kipling as his reason. But he seemed to have a strong feeling that trouble was on the way.

★

The fears were self-fulfilling. His agents and publishers did their best to protect him, but when the reviews came out, in the last week of May, Angus would not be comforted. He never learned not to read his critics (though he had, way back in October 1963, asked Curtis Brown not to pass on rejection slips and adverse comments). Priestley stayed away from his own plays: Betjeman advised authors to leave the country when they had a book about to appear.[18] Angus stayed to face the music.

The first reviews were not good, but they were not nearly as bad as Angus felt they were. True, Francis Hope in the *Observer* began damningly – "I wish I liked this book more" – he found some of it embarrassing and self-conscious and pronounced the whole "a miraculous mess", both prodigal and prodigious: but he also praised the wild risks taken "at a stage when most writers of his eminence are nursing their proved abilities and repeating themselves on carefully chosen ground."[19] Martin Amis, in the *New Statesman*, in a piece that gave Angus deep and lasting offence, came very near the bone when he said that Angus's portrayal of the young was hilariously inaccurate: he somewhat priggishly recommended him to return to the novel-of-manners: "like his beloved Jane Austen, he needs only a small vista for that rheumy but unblinking eye."[20] But Amis takes him seriously: he dismisses the book, not the author, and John Gross, months later, wrote from the *New Statesman* saying that he was sorry if the review had caused distress, but that Amis had a high estimate of Angus's work, and had written in good faith. (Could Amis have suspected something of his father, Kingsley Amis, in the portrait of Alexandra's second-rate novelist father Perry, with his red-faced Francis Bacon cardinal's shriek? Was he also suggesting that his own *Rachel Papers*, published in this same year, would be a better guide to the students of the 1970s?)

Auberon Waugh in the *Evening Standard* found the novel overloaded and overly academic, but his remarks, from a critic so notoriously haphazard, now seem quite mild.[21] The *Times Literary Supplement* found it bookish and too full of quotations. Michael Ratcliffe was respectful but lukewarm and so was David Holloway. John Bayley and Francis King were interested, impressed though not wholly satisfied. Tony Palmer in the *Spectator* accused the book of "truly mind-boggling condescension" towards the young, and more astonishingly, read it as "a dogmatic but straightforward plea for scientific autocracy" – a message almost impossible to wrest from the novel, though pardonable, perhaps, on a hasty reviewer's first reading. He also accused Angus of mannered élitism, intellectual arrogance, and a cultural acceptability that guaranteed his sales.[22] (Would it had been so, thought Angus and Tony.)

Such were the rewards of trying to see the point of view of the young. It was not a very pleasing response. Peter Grose, in his robust Australian manner, called the reviewers pompous shits, and Tom Rosenthal wrote an outraged letter to Tony Hern, editor of the *Evening Standard*, protesting about his reviewing policy in general and, in particular, his allowing Waugh to repeat his insults over two weeks. Angus told himself and others that it was all "spiteful hatchetry" and urged Seckers to make sure that Viking saw the better articles and interviews. He had to keep on smiling for the press. The party at Tom Rosenthal's on 13 June was not a wake, but it was a group of carefully selected friends and sympathisers – Jonathan Raban, Rosamond Lehmann, Julian Mitchell, Patrick Woodcock, Perkin Walker, John Bowen, David Cook, Margaret Drabble, Bentley Bridge-water, Peter Conradi, John Pattisson . . . Mitchell noted that Angus was tense and shouting a lot: that Tom Rosenthal was claiming that the bad reviews were due to envy and spite: and that there was much discussion of the wills of Noël Coward and L.P. Hartley, both recently deceased – had Coward left anything to Patrick Woodcock, and why had Hartley left so much to his eighty-five-year-old sister? Conradi noted that Angus was in a state about something that Malcolm Bradbury was writing on him for the United States, and had to be calmed down by Raban: also that he had become involved in a lengthy and not wholly pleasing discussion with John Bowen about the East India Company, a subject about which Bowen happened to know a good deal – more, on this occasion, than Angus. (Drabble noticed nothing of all this: she was at this stage convinced that Angus was far above the pinpricks of reviewers, and seems to have spent much of the evening talking to Tony about how to prune honeysuckle.)

A visit to Holland and the land of Reve was a relief after the British reception: a photograph in the July *Bookseller* shows a seated Angus surrounded by five smiling men and one smiling woman, all in Dickensian mood, glasses of wine in hand. (Angus himself is looking slightly more elder statesman: Tony looks down proudly but perhaps a little anxiously?) And some of the American reviews struck a more generous note: Edmund White, at the end of a thoughtful piece in the *New York Times Book Review*, concluded "He cannot banish odd, mind-catching, exquisitely human details from his book. If too much humanity bulging out of the frame of a narrative constitutes an artistic problem, then it is an enviable problem indeed." Angus had betrayed his anxiety about the American reception in a letter to Jack Plumb: "I was very much touched and pleased by your letter about 'Magic'. Apart from a few discerning reviews, it has been a dismal disappointment, and there have been a few so spiteful that it was impossible not to be hurt. Especially because those already coming from Germany, Scandinavia, Holland etc have (even when very critical) been so different in tone. This, of course, is called 'continental pomposity' but I do not think England is better for its self congratulatory brutal philistinism.

The anti-homosexual prejudice I expected, but I had not realized that 'professor' was such a dirty word in modern Fleet Street . . . I very seldom ask favours but I should be forever grateful to you if you could drop a word in American circles (eg New York Review of Books or anywhere else – it comes out there in October) that the reviews are not all there is to be said. The preliminary interest there has been so good that I do want it to be judged on its merits there and not by the British envious. The US market is just getting going and is very important to Tony's and my future. Sorry to ask favours . . ."[23]

Was it true that the British reception was motivated by envy and spite? Not entirely. Rereading the book now, it does seem that Angus had at times miscalculated. His ear had at times failed him: his mimicry was not exact. His American mystic hippie, Elinor, convinces from a distance, but not at close quarters: the selfish fecklessness of the hippie community and its disastrous effect on the local communities (in Morocco, in Goa) upon which it preys are brilliantly diagnosed, but the group's mood is not captured from within. They are seen – and well seen – from afar, a ragged cast of extras. The grotesque quasi-religious cults and cult leaders of the 1970s, 80s and 90s have gone further than anything Angus invented, and his tragi-comic swami has a true whiff of giggling mystic charlatan evil – an evil which J.C. Powys would have recognised – but the swami too we see from afar. Ned and Rodrigo, of whom we see much more, are really not quite up to the twenty-four-year-old Martin Amis benchmark of sharpness. It was true that students in the 1970s spent a lot of time reading Tolkien (did not statistics, indeed surveys at UEA itself, *prove* this?) but perhaps they did not read him either as gullibly or as ironically as Angus suggested.* After all, Angus himself at sixteen had devoured Aldous Huxley, Heard, Bertrand Russell, Roger Fry and Freud . . . No, he had not got the young quite right. Raban, in an interview in the *New Review* (1 April 1974), commented that Alexandra's sensibility "is as remote from that of her Hampstead parents as a tribal African's." This, too, is part of the problem. Angus recognises that Alexandra is created by revolt against Perry and Zoe, but the nature of her rebellion is less accurately charted than that of Judy against headmaster Harold in *Late Call*. Angus had tried too hard to like Alexandra, to make her into a positive moral force.

*He tries to cover himself against this allegation (p.79) when Ned says, "But that's the whole point of The Lord of the Rings. It's a kind of play on a grand scale. You don't take it seriously. Least *we* don't. We're not *science* students or engineers and that, are we, Roddy?" But this explanation is itself something of a giveaway. A survey done by Eric Homberger at UEA in February 1972 had indeed listed Tolkien – along with Orwell, Nabokov, Heller, Hesse and Greer – among authors read voluntarily by students.

Nor had he got Alexandra's maternal feelings quite right. He had tried to project himself into the body of a young unmarried mother and had studied the woman's novel of the 1960s, but his phrases about the blissful cowlike contentment of motherhood struck no chord with the young woman writer by the washing machine, who was filled not with cowlike contentment but with rising irritation.

The third generation of teenagers in *No Laughing Matter* had been funny and well-observed, rightly bewildered in a comedy of mutual misunder-standing between parents and grandparents – but they had been seen through an adult lens. By closing in on the young through those dangerous fictional binoculars, those binoculars the gift of which had lured one of Hamo's Fair Youths to his death, had he attempted the impossible? (Binoculars, or field glasses, as Forster called them, also played an important role in the events or non-events of the Marabar Caves in *Passage to India*: had Angus consciously or unconsciously produced this echo?)

He wondered. It was a setback. He resigned himself, as he wrote to Jullian, to the fact that this was a book for the few. He accepted that the coldness and greed of Hamo's lust – what P.N. Furbank was to describe as the "awful and disastrous *mechanicalness* of his kind of 'Platonic' fixation" would repel many.[24] (Furbank in fact found the treatment of the theme "very original and very important", or so he wrote in a letter of commentary to Angus on 11 December, in which he also expressed doubts about Erroll's limp jokes and "Leporello" role. Angus replied on 19 December: "I am greatly pleased that you saw the trouble I had taken with the organization and that the mechanical quality of Hamo's life comes over. I'm not quite sure what you mean by tone. I'd like to talk to you about it. Probably some of the Alexandra stuff is not as funny as it could have been and also the last part of Hamo – tho' I hope the Swami and Elinor are. They might both have come over to readers as more agreeable if they had been funnier. As to Erroll, Sam Weller took over too much – and altho Mr Pickwick and Bertie Wooster are models as well as Juan and Myshkin, I tried to do too much with Erroll. I wanted to suggest that the Sam Wellers are only as nice as their masters allow them to be and that the comic Mark Tapley line imposed on them destroys them but *also* I wanted to give Erroll a genuine visual sense which revels in the sights of Asia whereas a very strong part of Hamo's failure and deadness lies not in a failure of heart but a failure of eye – except for boys' shapes.")

Angus knew that despite the reservations of critics and readers there was much in his book that was good: the Uncles in Borneo and the Japanese brothel were superb set-pieces, and his meditations on global misery, technology and the green revolution were surely of relevance in this increasingly global decade. Had his reviewers simply missed the point? It took John Updike another ten years to identify the rise of the global novel, and Lorna Sage believes that the book was before its time – its carnivalesque, flamboyant qualities would have been better received if reviewers had been able to invoke Bakhtin. Maybe she was right. As it was, there were readers who liked it the best of all his works, readers who discovered him through this one novel. Charles Blackburne admired it, preferring it to *Hemlock* and *Anglo-Saxon Attitudes*, and Anthony Symond-son thought it his best, though on reflection he was sorry that Angus had softened towards the end and redeemed Hamo and Alexandra: "Angus was always better at bad people than good . . . Some people have a vocation to be atrocious and it does them no good if they are given soft centres."[25]

Jack Plumb wrote telling him he had enough creative power for ten novelists and praising his "comic, tragic, despairing scenes", and Glen Cavaliero greatly admired the Powysian wildness: Norman Scarfe and many others wrote ticking off the reviewers. Such letters are not always much comfort to the author. Raban wrote saying some of his colleagues made him ashamed of his trade, but he admitted that the book was "an absolute bastard to review" – so large and complex, such technical scope, such puns and parodies and devastating use of farce.

In October Angus received an innocent fan letter from a stranger which gave him great pleasure. Lord Egremont of Petworth (who, as it happened, proved to be a cousin of his old friend Elizabeth Wyndham from Bletchley Park, and himself an aspiring novelist) wrote saying he had read *Magic* and recognised in Alexandra many girls he had known at Oxford: but he had been particularly enchanted by the farcical episodes in Ceylon, where Hamo, disguised as Doctor Malcolm (another UEA in-joke here?) pursues a beautiful houseboy. He had laughed aloud so much on the aero-plane to Italy that his neighbour had asked " 'Did you often do this?' The answer was: 'definitely not.' "[26]

So: some had understood. Some had understood it all – the farce, and the underlying strain of unallievable sadness and anxiety which he had confessed to Moorcock. Angus had never shared Hamo's life of habitual repression, "the generalized habit of wary concealment" (p.245) that distorted the lives of many homosexuals: he had boldly and at some cost ignored the sensibilities of his Suffolk neighbours. Nevertheless, there were points at which he identified with his protagonist.

"Honestly," says the cheery Erroll to Hamo at one point, "you're hopeless."

"Yes," said Hamo, "I am of that sad class." (Penguin p.302)

24

IMPROBABLE NONSENSE

The publication of *As if By Magic* caused intense psychological strain. Some think that Angus never recovered. But on the surface, the wounds healed. As Golding had said, the psyche was stronger than it seemed. Angus applied himself to his Kipling research and his summer term of teaching. And on Midsummer Day of 1973 the woman who had been in part responsible for his career of anxious triumph came to supper. If Sonia Orwell had not been his champion, he might now have been approaching an embittered but pensionable old age at the British Museum instead of drinking champagne in a Suffolk garden.

Sonia Orwell's own career after Orwell's death in 1950 had been fraught. In 1958 she had married Michael Pitt-Rivers, son of actress Mary Hinton and one of the victims of the Montagu case, but the marriage had not lasted and she was on her own again. Remembering the old days on *Horizon*, she decided to forget her irritation about her appearance in *Anglo-Saxon Attitudes*: she had expressed a desire for a rapprochement with Angus to her friends Daphne and Graham Reynolds. The Reynoldses – she a painter of delectable still lives, he the authority on Constable at the Victoria and Albert Museum – had been weekenders at Rougham in Suffolk, then settled permanently at The Manse in Bradfield St George, where they were among Angus's nearest neighbours. But they had known Angus from long before his Bradfield days; Graham remembered Angus from the BM ("that testy elderly female voice in the Reading Room") and from Viva King's salon. Daphne Reynolds had met Sonia Orwell at a private view in London, in the days when Sonia was riding high on Orwell's royalties, and they had become instant friends. So the Reynoldses were able to bring Angus and Sonia together, and they had met several times in Suffolk.

Now, on 30 June, Sonia Orwell was invited to supper at Felsham

Woodside with her friends John and Hilary Spurling. It was a magical evening.

John Spurling was the Henfield Fellow at UEA that summer, and Sonia Orwell had come to stay with him and Hilary: perhaps she had suggested taking them over to see Angus and Tony, or perhaps Angus had got to hear that she was there and had invited them? Nobody can remember – nor can the Spurlings remember how they all managed to squeeze into their green two-seater Morgan sportscar. (John Spurling was certainly driving, but perhaps, he thinks now, he was driving Sonia's car?) In one vehicle or another the Spurlings, their thirteen-month-old daughter Amy, and her godmother Sonia, set off across the hot flat biscuit-coloured East Anglian plain in what the Spurlings thought was excellent time – "Sonia, always phenomenally punctual, when not early, was having to contend with two ingrained latecomers" – but alas, Sonia's fears were fulfilled, and it grew later and later.

"After a while we seemed to be lost as well – & were all starting to feel fractious, when suddenly the balloon appeared, motionless in what had by now become a pale, still, midsummer twilight: a tiny striped balloon with a basket beneath, suspended far away against one of those vast skies that always fill three quarters of the landscape in those parts. Hot air balloons were rarer then than they have since become, in fact this was the first I had ever seen outside a picture book. It seemed quite unreal, coming from nowhere, as if by magic . . . we felt he himself had somehow conjured it up or sent it as a signal that we were on the right road at last."[1]

The Spurlings were gardening people, and Hilary's chief memory is of the roses – "striped, streaked, deeply scented towsled masses of shell-pink, apricot, carmine and claret-coloured roses with lovely names, all of which Angus told me for the first time (I have grown many of them since in memory of that strange and magical excursion). I remember especially his Cuisse de Nymphe, a tall graceful virginal white rose flushing as it opens a most sensuous pink, and the pleasure Angus took in its prim English name, Great Maiden's Blush. I remember too the way the wood breasted up against the garden hedge . . ."

The light died slowly, the birds sang, the cat played in the greenery, the baby slept, and they drank and talked as the hot-air balloon floated for hours overhead. They stayed late, going inside at last into the cottage "where the windows were so low you had almost to kneel down to look through them." It was an enchanted evening, and so Angus too remembered it: "Everything was so good and my gratitude and love for her seized me, but what could I say? And then quite suddenly, across the sky as we drank champagne, floated a vast striped balloon. We had never seen one there before and have never seen one since. But I could tell from her expression that the whole incident had taken her in delight away from the tensions that so preyed upon her . . ."[2] It had all been a rare treat, wrote Sonia more chummily, such fun to be gossiping again, and both Angus and Tony had both been on terrific form!

And so they both continued to appear to be. The weather was glorious and the landmarks of summer passed – Angus presented an Honorary Degree to Jack Plumb, speaking warmly in his oration of Bert Howard, and Plumb seemed moved to tears. Angus also gave an Honorary Degree to French novelist Claude Simon, whose work was then little known in England: UEA picked a winner here as he was to win the Nobel prize, and Angus, although Bradbury recalls he was initially less than enthusiastic about Simon's work, wrote an oration which much pleased Simon himself.[3] Honoria Wormald, still talking all the time of Francis Wormald, came for the night. Monty Turland brought his parents to tea; his father, unlike Hilary Spurling, found Angus's garden "very worrying", not at all like his own. They dined with Gerry and Mary Cookson: Mary's daughter Grania Caulfeild had in 1970 made a dazzling Trollopian marriage to Hugh Cavendish of Holker Hall in Cumbria, and there was much talk of Hugh and Grania. (Mary Cookson's mother, the lovely Lady Murphy, had been *delighted*.) And on 19 July, after lunch with Kipling contacts Mr and Mrs Arvind Mehrota (pronounced "most pleasant"), Angus and Tony set off to Salisbury Festival. Unlike Ilkley and Birmingham, this was an upper-crust, glitzy affair.

Angus had been invited by novelist Elizabeth Jane Howard, then married to Kingsley Amis: Amis himself had also been persuaded to appear. The trip tied in visits to various old acquaintances. First they spent a night with Cecil Beaton in his miniature mansion of Reddish House at Broadchalke, where they found a festival party in full swing – Stephen Tennant, the much-photographed golden boy of Beaton's youth, now with hennaed hair and a bald white patch, was much in evidence; he had contributed an exhibition of magenta sailor boys from Marseilles, on show in the Vestry of St Thomas's Church.* Lord and Lady David Cecil were there, with Rachel Trickett, Patrick Procktor (who had painted Salisbury cathedral specially for the occasion) and Lady Diana Cooper with her little Doglet. The Countesses of Pembroke and Westmoreland strayed upon

---

* Angus visited the Stephen Tennant exhibition: "They were all explicit scenes of sailors in the South of France, crowding public lavatories, picking up men in the street and other naval activities. The Vicar appeared and was introduced. He turned to me and said, 'So glad you are enjoying Mr Tennant's lovely paintings. He has such a lovely way with colour, don't you think?'" *Serious Pleasures: The Life of Stephen Tennant* by Philip Hoare (Hamish Hamilton 1990), p.368. From AW letter to Philip Hoare, 30 May 1988.

the lawns. It was all very grand and very Hampshire-Wiltshire. (Tony, spotting a copy of Angus's novel, pointed at the portrait of Angus on the jacket and declared proudly "That's *my* photograph" – Oh, how unfortunate, was all Beaton said in reply.) Angus and Tony admired the Gwen Johns and the Augustus Johns and the rococo busts and the French eighteenth-century furniture (though Angus was not very interested in furniture): there was a great deal of expensive and elegant clutter, and what they really liked were the tall white Charles Rennie Mackintosh chairs in the Winter Garden and a couple of fine art-nouveau brass candlesticks.

The next night, Angus and Tony moved on to stay with Anthony Hobson, who lived with his wife Tanya (half-sister of Connolly's wife Deirdre) in a handsome old house at Whitsbury. Hobson had known Angus since BM days: like Connolly, he was a serious bibliophile and book collector, and Angus was on several occasions to consult him about the valuation and location of maunscripts – his own and Kipling's. Hobson was not only a collector, he was an eagle-eyed reader: one of those readers whom writers fear and need. He would write to Angus pointing out mistakes in the ages of his characters, in the chronology of his events, in the spelling of his foreign expressions. And he was always right. (He had also dared to challenge Angus, over lunch in Scott's in April 1968, about why he had written *Tempo*: for the money, Angus had robustly replied.)

Hobson and his family lived in style. Tony and Angus had been to stay with them once before, in the summer of 1968, when Angus had chatted on over a large lunch about Christian Science, turned giddy on a walk to the church, and then fallen asleep for the rest of the afternoon. (Over dinner he had revived to talk of Oxford, and how he had wasted his time there in giggling.) On this visit, there was less time for chat, as Angus in his bright blue bow tie had to lunch with the Amises (he pale and yellow-eyed and not best pleased, Tony felt, when Tony attacked "the schoolboy sadistic eroticism" of Ian Fleming's Bond books) and then to lecture on Dickens in St Thomas's Church (fee one hundred pounds). But they enjoyed meeting the growing Hobson children, and admired again the fine demesne and its beautiful garden – all on a much grander scale than Felsham Woodside. (The Dickens talk was a success, according to Tony – not very well attended, according to Hobson.) Then they moved on, to a monastic night with Pat Trevor-Roper and Raymond Mortimer at Long Crichel* – seven men at lunch, Tony wrote in his card of thanks to Tanya

---

* Long Crichel, seven miles from Wimborne, is a Queen Anne country house bought as a weekend retreat in 1945 by Edward Sackville-West, Desmond Shawe-Taylor, Eardley Knollys and Raymond Mortimer: after Eddie Sackville-West's death in 1965, Pat Trevor-Roper became a part-owner.

Hobson. Then on again, to Ann Fleming's, where her son Caspar was playing cards with his friend Randall Keynes: they all played the dictionary game after dinner. Then home, via Compton Beauchamp, Faringdon, and lunch with Iris Murdoch, John Bayley and Francis Haskell. It was a tiring four-hour drive.

Depression set in on their return. The tour had been fun, but everybody else seemed to be living in such grandeur – Angus was worried about his stomach, his eyes, his Kipling book, and the fact that there was no money coming in. Three days of deep gloom followed, while Angus wrote letters and tried to clear the decks for work. He had already written twice this summer to brother Colin in Lisbon, who was complaining of ill-health: Angus had described his own itinerary, and continued "There is an insanity about these festivals but they pay well and, owing to the bloody critics, my last book will do no more than moderately well – though we have high hopes of America where at least they don't want every book to be about the Home Counties or NW3. My chief sin, I think, for many of them was writing about Asia. 'Mr Wilson should remember that Jane Austen produced her delicious comedies without stirring from the rectory garden.' However I'm in very good health to come up to my sixtieth birthday so chasing from Salisbury to Kings Lynn to Edinburgh to address cultured ladies in strawberry pink hats made of old knickers doesn't get me down as much as it might have done a few years ago when I had that high blood pressure. We have had a glorious summer and the garden has been enchanting – rose and clematis of every kind. I am busy trying to decide on my next book – I want to do one on Kipling but his daughter who has all the rights to quotations is very difficult, as I hear, and I shall have to use all my tact and so on if I wish to pursue the scheme. University term is over now – I only teach in the summer as you know – and we wind up with a ceremony when I, in purple velvet (almost dying of the heat) have to act as Public Orator . . . this year Lady Murphy who is getting very peculiar said in the loudest of voices from the front of the hall holding 700 people 'Look at the dear public orator with his little peek a boo face –' "

101 other letters waited, as he told Colin, and he plodded dutifully through them. A champagne dinner with lobster and the Zuckermans on 25 July, as a prelude to the King's Lynn festival, perked them up a little: the next day Wilson and Zuckerman put on a good double act. Zuckerman took the chair; Wilson talked about his grandmother.

Tony disappeared to his family for a fortnight: Angus had to look after himself. He spent some time in the BM and the London Library with Kipling, but then ran away to Scotland with Bentley Bridgewater. They hired a car, and toured – they went to Edinburgh, Oban, and Ayr, and spent a night at Steven Runciman's imposing fourteenth-century border castle at Elshieshields. This was once a Johnstone stronghold, but its watchtower had been turned from a fortress into a magnificent library. Runciman recalls that Angus did not seem very interested in his own ancestry, and did not bother to revisit the tombs of the Johnstone-Wilsons at Dunscore, although they lay so near: perhaps he had written them out of his system with *No Laughing Matter*.

★

In September, Tony and Angus took a joint holiday to Angus's old haunt, the South of France. They departed for Calais from Ramsgate on 11 September, the day after Jack Priestley's seventy-ninth birthday party, given for him by George Rainbird at the Savoy. Angus, who delayed his departure date to be at the celebration, spoke warmly of Jack, and (prompted by Jacquetta) praised his neglected offspring *Over the High, Long Wall*. Things were going well for Priestley – a revival of *An Inspector Calls* at the Mermaid had brought him a standing ovation (he did occasionally, it seems, risk dropping in on his own plays) – and Olivier was planning to direct *Eden End* at the National. Jack and Jacquetta both puffed contentedly at their cigars as Jack's praises were sung.

In France, Angus and Tony spent their first night in Ham, a place which peculiarly appealed to Angus. "Ham," he would say, with satisfaction, as he sat in the car rolling towards it through the passing landscape. "Ham . . ." (They dined on langoustines and pigeon.) They had lunch with Philippe Jullian and Bernard Minoret at Jullian's Moulin at Chaumes on the second day – the Moulin was almost as crammed with antiques and paintings and *objets de vertu* as Runciman's castle. Then on to Bourges, and to Vichy where they tasted the warm and musty waters, and finally to Salier, where they settled for a week. Quite a colony of migrants was gathering in the neighbourhood – they saw novelist David Hughes and his wife Mai Zetterling, they saw Hiram Winterbotham and Patrick Woodcock, and lunched with Wendy Rintoul and Sally Graves (now Sally Chilver, who had a house near Apt). They saw flamingoes, marsh harriers, sand martins, bee-eaters, storks. (Did they recall Jean Corke's face as Angus had tried to persuade her one evening over supper that the only way to see flamingoes was to creep up upon them pink and naked in the dawn? For a glorious moment she had been quite taken in.) They revisited the old emotional lodestones – Aigues Mortes, Montpellier, Arles – then moved on to Vence, where they dined on 20 September with brother Clive and his wife Lucie. Clive, noted Angus, looked utterly unchanged, which made Angus feel a hundred years old. Then back via Cluny and Compiègne to London, to launch an appeal for for the NBL. (Angus had already signed hundreds of letters for the Appeal: he received some dusty answers. Patrick White, who had just won the Nobel, said he was sick of being touched for money, and Jack Priestley said why not get the money off the publishers. They were the ones who made the profits – what had the NBL ever done for him or Angus, he would like to know? But Rattigan sent £200.)

The autumn brought visiting American and Japanese professors. One Japanese professor, carried away by excitement, kept calling for "More wine!" and devoured an enormous fish for lunch that Tony had hoped would also provide for their supper. It brought feasts in Oxford and in Cambridge and ambassadorial lunches in London. Charles Dickens and Peter Grose, PLR, CHE and the East Anglian Writers, Corkes and Gilliatts and Dior designer Jorn Langberg all made claims upon them. Angus appeared on platforms with Rebecca West and Corelli Barnett, with Frank Muir and Iris Murdoch, with Angela Huth and Michael Holroyd: he promoted Powys and reviewed Cecil Beaton. In December, a wave of justified rage swept through him when he read a *Sheffield Morning Telegraph* review of Mary Gilliatt's book on renovated houses in Suffolk.[4] His own cottage had featured pleasantly, with photographs of the flint walls, the crowded bookshelves, the Chinese wallpaper, peacock feathers and stuffed birds: Mary Gilliatt tactfully praised his "pleasing mixture of periods". But her subtitle, "The Second Home from Cottages to Castles", led the *Telegraph* into a characteristic fit of northern indignation, which confused Angus with the commuting inhabitants of the "Gin and Jag" belt. "May I point out," wrote Angus, "that I have lived and worked in my cottage for 20 years. I rented it until I was able to buy it. It has taken me many years to restore its dilapidated condition, to add sanitation and electric light. As well as living and working in Suffolk, I have involved myself in local life . . .

"Mine is not a second house, I have no yacht, and I don't drink gin. I don't know the circumstances of the others who appear in the book, but I do know that they have restored attractive country buildings, and in many cases they have saved them from destruction. I think this is a good thing to have done."[5] The *Telegraph* printed the letter.

If he was in fighting form, this was just as well. In November, Tony was in hospital for minor surgery. Tony's mother was unwell: his father had died this year. (Gerard Reve wrote in sympathy, telling Tony to take a lot of Vitamin B.) And on 16 December 1973, as Tony went back into hospital again, Colin Johnstone-Wilson died in Lisbon, at the age of seventy-six.

★

Angus received the news just as he and Tony were about to go to Holland for a recuperative Christmas with their Dutch friends. He placed a notice in *The Times*, requested masses to be said in Bury, cabled Clive at Torremolinos, and wrote at once to the British consul, enquiring about the funeral (which had already taken place at the Roman Catholic municipal cemetery at Benfica), asking that the maid's wages and Christmas bonus be settled at his own expense if necessary, and asking that all private papers and photographs found in the flat in the Rua da Lapa be preserved.

Colin's life had been bleak, and its effects, which eventually wended their way to the auction rooms of Lacy Scott in Bury St Edmunds and the cottage of Felsham Woodside, were poignant. Colin's epitaph from the head of the Caney clan in Natal was brief: "This is sad news about Colin, alias David. He never appears to have been a happy man and this quick death is a great relief."[6]

Clive seems not to have responded very promptly: Angus pursued him with letters as he flitted from Torremolinos to Madrid to Cannes, but Clive had got into the way of thinking that all news from Colin was bad news. Angus had to bear the full burden, yet again, of a brother's death. The British consul, R.S. Webster, could not have been kinder: he went to great trouble to describe the funeral to Angus – it had been attended by friends and pupils, and by the vice-consul – and to oversee the listing, valuation and packing of his goods. It was discovered that Colin had died intestate, and Angus instructed various items to be given to local charities in Lisbon. The consul battled bravely with the strict export regulations, and eventually two trunks and a suitcase were shipped out in June 1974 to London on an Ellerman steamer, the *City of Oporto*: they contained sundry items such as silver pepper-pots, a silver napkin ring, two silver cigarette-boxes, and some gold crested and initialled cufflinks. A medley of Indian brass bells and tortoises, a Buddha, and some porcelain figures remained behind for disposal in Lisbon. The maid agreed to look after the cat. The consul paid the final chemist's bill out of Colin's small estate. There was no money left to speak of – Angus had lent him money during the year for hospital expenses, and now requested that what was left should go to the maid.

One of the trunks that made its way to Bury contained Colin's papers and photographs. Angus had written to Clive that, with Clive's agreement, he very much wanted to have them: "There will I am sure be photographs which will be helpful to me with my autobiography – I have so few family pictures . . ." And here indeed were some family images –

Mother in an oval frame, baby Pat with curly hair upon a beach, double-breasted Pat on a terrace in Yugoslavia, Pat with his long cigarette holder at a café table. There were unlabelled Victorian gentlemen who could have been anybody or nobody. There were also whole albums full of bronzed sailors in the Arcadia of Dubrovnik. (Angus worried about how to contact Colin's old friends there: the links were so slender, would anybody remember?) There were many, many portraits of the beloved dog, the beloved cat. There was a tiny little book of nursery rhymes dedicated by Colin "with best love to dear Tiho – the dearest, cleverest, most perfect dog" – Bombay, 1944, Price One Rupee. There were home hints from *The Lady* of 1926, and letters from Caneys in South Africa, and letters from the loyal Mr Hegde, Advocate, in Bombay. There were photographs of handsome Indian princelings in full imperial dress. There were Christmas cards and photographs from old pupils. There were pictures of Pat, smiling gently, growing thinner and more white-haired. There were religious cards and souvenirs and prayers and devotional exercises. There were police passes for Split and vaccination certificates for Angola. There was Nurse Sopp's recipe book. There were receipts for Pat's funeral expenses, and the little black-ribboned key to his burial place: there were records of the small sums paid out so regularly over the years for the upkeep of the Kingston family grave. There were address books with old addresses of Angus at Providence House, of Fred and Winn, of Rebecca West Andrews, of Princess Abida, and of that beautiful benevolent guardian angel, Susan Lowndes Marques, who lived at Monte Estoril and kept an eye on all the English population of Lisbon. There were quotations from poems by Emily Brontë and A.E. Housman: there were poems he had written himself. There were rambling, barely legible diaries, about family matters – Aunt Alys, Mother, baby Angus, the Guv.

And there were the novels. Colin had never told anybody about the novels, but here they were – hundreds of pages of typed and jumbled copy, weighing more than a stone. One, called *Frail Sanctuary*, is set by the blue Adriatic and moves, it seems, to India: its heroine appears to have undergone an accident not unlike the one that nearly crippled Colin when he walked out of a first-floor window in Split. Another, *This Stranger is I?* assures the potential reader that it is approximately 100,000 words long, and that it is "not a novel for adolescents of any age or either sex. None of the characters is homosexual, nobody uses obscene language, nor has the dictionary been ransacked to delight the reader with the author's erudition." The style echoes Trollope, Meredith, Austen, with melodramatic touches from the Brontës. "Christine Sinclair, childless widow of a lawyer whose briefs had left her with an income comfortable enough to

live where she pleased with a margin for fun had, by the force of Hitler and
the aggravated insistence of the British Consul, been uprooted from settled
idleness and delightful careless enjoyment of life in a small mid-European
town to the intense discomfort of keeping house for her brother in
Bombay, endured by the both under the burden of conscience that
inspired them with the quaint and irksome illusion that it was the duty of
the one to look after the other . . ." etc. etc. They are literate, somewhat
stilted, and unremarkable.

But the fragment called *No Man Goes Alone* is a different matter
altogether. It has been dragged up from the Johnstone-Wilson communal
memory, passionate, angry, rapid, fluent: it is another indictment, from
beyond the grave, of Willie and Maud, of Billy Pop and the Countess.
Here they both are, and here are the Scottish estate and the Scottish
pretensions, here is Fred Johnstone-Wilson (now Douglas) in the dock,
here is Winn (relabelled Hugh) with his lovely red-gold hair, here is
Colin's admission that "I was odd man out in Mother's affection." It is like
a first or variant draft of *No Laughing Matter*, shocking not only in its
content but also in its talent. Peculiarly vivid is the portrait of Fred –
despised by Colin, loved and admired by Winn, and ruined by his doting,
carefully manicured, selfish grandmother Tillie Frank. Tillie is actually
named as Tillie in the text, in a parenthesis, but Fred is disguised as
Douglas, his father Willie as Charlie: "Douglas the eldest of us all we
particularly disliked even to sneaking on him when we saw him with the
fisherman's daughter . . . Douglas followed his father's footsteps but
without the cunning and yes ability that kept Charlie's neatly shaped feet
with the aristocratic insteps clear of any mud . . . Douglas with his fine
athlete's figure and good looks that infatuated silly girls, his air of good
breeding that dazzled lonely plain faced women yearning for the glamour
of an escort in evening dress who knew his way perfectly through the
intricacies of an elegant and expensive à la carte, his charm that was bait to
every shark that propped up a West End bar slaking Douglas's vanity with
just one more round of flattery till the barman's called Time Gentlemen
and Douglas stood alone in the Dock all money spent, all charm rent . . .
shorn of all pride before the judge's stern words . . ."

Here rises up from the grave Fred Johnstone-Wilson, who had died in
gloomy shabby solitude in Clapham in 1948, and who inspired several of
Angus's stories. Alas, poor Fred, and alas poor Colin Johnstone, he who
claimed he never read novels, he who would say "Am I Angus Wilson's
brother? No, *he* is *my* brother."

Did Angus ever read these pages? Tony thinks not. Did Colin ever tell

Angus of them? Tony thinks not. They lay untouched, until a grateful biographer searched them for clues, and found them.

*

The new year of 1974 opened in uncertainty. For months Angus had read, talked and dreamed of Kipling, and now it seemed that his premonitions about this book too would be fulfilled. Early in January, he heard from Tom Rosenthal, who had approached the agency of A.P. Watt on his behalf, that he could neither have access to Kipling's papers nor assume permission to quote from Kipling's published works: Kipling's daughter, Mrs Bambridge of Wimpole Hall, was proving as difficult as her reputation. (She it was who had prevented Lord Birkenhead from publishing his biography, completed in 1948: it was published after his death and hers in 1978.) In vain did Rosenthal protest that he was shocked that so distinguished a writer as Professor Wilson should be treated in this way. Mrs Bambridge was impervious to distinction. Angus would have to think again, and so would his publishers. (Mrs Bambridge had imposed the most exacting conditions and unfortunate financial agreements on Birkenhead, and then had refused him permission to publish during her lifetime; as Angus was to write in the *Observer*, when he reviewed this suppressed work, it contained none of the scandals that readers had expected. But Angus did have some sympathy with Mrs Bambridge's view that Birkenhead was "ill-suited by his social and aesthetic sympathies" to understand his subject – Birkenhead wrongly saw Kipling, in Birkenhead's own words, as "a hearty extrovert in the locker room of a provincial golf course".[7] Angus knew already that this would not be his own vision, were he to be allowed to pursue it – but how to persuade Kipling's daughter of this?)

Rosenthal came up with a stop-gap idea of a *Collected Short Stories*, to be published in the spring of 1975, and a suggestion for a new work of biographical essays to be called *Eminent Edwardians*, but Angus did not take well to either – nor to a slightly later suggestion of a book on Edwardian England to be called *Blighty*. He told Tom Rosenthal that his American volume of twenty-five short stories, published in 1969 by Viking as *Death Dance*, had had poor sales and attracted adverse comment from three directions – some had said the stories were brittle and overrated, others that they were dated, and yet others that they were wonderful – "how superior to all these novels he writes now – why *doesn't* he stick to stories? I don't want to write stories now and haven't since A Bit Off the Map – so the last type of comment is far from helpful."[8] Although he had long resisted the suggestion of writing more stories, it seems probable that this response was reinforced by reading John Bowen's too-perceptive review of L.P. Hartley's *Complete Short Stories* on 13 January 1974 in the *Sunday Times*: "Short stories are tricky, treacherous little objects, and dangerous for a novelist. Either he will write excellent short stories, as Angus Wilson has done, and then they will be bound together like twigs of birch and used to cane the novels, or else they may be as excessively bad as the short stories of E.M. Forster, and anyone happening upon them first may need considerable persuasion to try the novels at all . . ." Angus's disaffection with the short-story form was expressed later this spring in response to a questionnaire from a French scholar, Claire Larrière – he told her that he did not wish to recall any of his uncollected stories ("in any case, they are at the most 2 or 3"), that the short story seemed to him less concerned with the author's view of life "which makes novels, but rather with bits of life that have hit the author" – and his final message seemed to be "I do not wish to say that I shall not write any more short stories – if fragments of the modern world appear to give a more telling response to it than any one connected statement, I shall do so – *But* my concern *technical* is for the novel and it is as a novelist that I think of myself. A novelist who began late with much fragmented life to put on paper so he began with short stories." (He listed Kipling, Gogol and Babel as the greatest of short-story writers.)

He had no wish to go back in time, to fragment. His aim was to connect, to interpret. No, he told Tom Rosenthal, with whom he had dinner on 5 February, he had no immediate need of money: he was going off to Rome to lecture and to think about some fictional ideas which needed time to grow and expand. It was very kind of Tom Rosenthal and David Farrer to worry about him, but he would disappear and brood. Rosenthal asked him while he was away to think about the possibility of a *World of Anthony Trollope*, or possibly a *Politics and the Novel*. Angus said he would think about it, but probably he did not think about it very hard, for he had never much liked Trollope's work: writing for the *Library Association Record* (Vol 63, No.9, September 1961) he had said "I read all Trollope during the war and, though some of it was rewarding in a rich, damp, plum cake sort of way, I shall not repeat the dose. I do not care for such intrusions of style as Meredith forces upon us, but I like less such intrusions of lack of style as Trollope grinds away at his readers." But he did write a book which bore some resemblance to Rosenthal's *Blighty* proposal – for Methuen, not Secker; this was *The Naughty Nineties*, published in 1976, a short text with illustrations, in which he gave rein to his obsession with his father's Edwardian youth.

This winter he also fitted in a quick lecture or two on Dickens – one, on 7 February, for the Dickens Fellowship Annual Dinner, followed on

Saturday, 9 February by another at Eastbourne, full of references to his own South Coast childhood. He had a meal in Covent Garden with George Sacks (whose wife Betty, after a long letter of praise of *Magic* written from hospital, had recently died), met Tim Neighbour for a drink at the Athenaeum, and then, on 25 February 1974, set off for Italy.

Tony drove him down, via nights in Joigny and Orange, to meet Clive and Lucie for lunch in San Remo: Angus was tired by the journey but lunch passed off well. Clive and Lucie's only worry seemed to be what would happen to Minette, their Yorkshire terrier, if anything happened to them. Angus and Tony drove on, with a break in Lucca, to Rome, where they settled for three weeks, in a flat at the Palazzo al Velabro, Piazza Bocca della Verita. They wandered around, enjoying the Forum and the Palatine in fine weather, thinking about new work, and seeing crowds of people. (On 3 March a DC-10 crashed on a flight from Paris to London, killing all 344 passengers: one of these was Francis Hope, who had hoped for so much from Angus Wilson.)

One of the ostensible reasons for their visit was that Angus needed to build up relationships with Italian publishers, who had not yet made an offer for *Magic*. Feltrinelli had published *No Laughing Matter* in 1969, but since the violent death of Giangiacomo Feltrinelli in March 1972 there had been silence.* The death of Feltrinelli had in itself given rise to interesting speculation: this left-wing millionaire had blown himself up while trying to fix a bomb to a high-tension electricity pylon outside Milan. Political tension was high in Rome: rumours abounded in an atmosphere of threatened violence that Angus was to store up for future use. Rome was a city of extremes; here they met right-wing marquises and left-wing booksellers, Muriel Spark, Gore Vidal, David Lodge and Brian Glanville. They missed Anthony Burgess, who sent an apology to say he was trying to write a novel about Pope John, but their inexhaustible and prolix correspondent Cecil Roberts was there, in the Grand Hotel, whence he had penned them many a saga of comic misfortune: now he entertained them non-stop for three-and-a-half hours with his usual scandalous tales of aristocracy and royalty, this time with the addition of the Duke of Kent and hints of a Royal Romp. He should have died at seventy, Roberts declared at the end of this vivacious monologue. (One of his favourite stories was of going into a bookshop in Surbiton and asking for a copy of his latest novel: "No, sorry, sir," was the reply, "we've had no demand for Cecil Roberts since his death.")

The selection of Italian and other nobility that Angus met on this visit —

* Garzanti had published his earlier work, including Eugenio Montale's translation of *Hemlock and After* – *La ciauta e dopo* – in 1956. This version was reprinted in 1993.

Marina Emo, the Marquise de Riencourt, Prince Romanoff – stuck long in his memory: they were all so deeply bored by life, they found everything so boring. The conversation turned to travel, and they had all been everywhere – Paris, New York, the West Indies, Mexico – and everywhere had been "so bo-aring". Others had better conversation. Ivar and Jorn Langberg, the Suffolk exquisites, were in Rome, and Angus and Tony dined with them: so too was Nicholas Brooke, with whom Angus talked incessantly of Kipling. And Angus wrote to Muriel Spark from his hotel thanking her for recommending to him Clough's "Amours de Voyage":

> Palazzo al Velabro, Friday
> My dear Muriel,
>   How much I have enjoyed Clough! The two voices are so splendidly sustained. The wit of the picture of tourism and the combined horror and wit of the treatment of the French invasion and the death of the priest are superb. But its the extraordinary capture of the growing malaise of the 19C that is its supreme success – that search for faith, that fear of the fatness and solidity of the bourgeois ethic which paralysed the moral will of the most sensitive and educated people of the time. I do not see how it could be done better. Thank you for bringing it to my attention.
>   It was very kind of you to entertain Tony and me and our Danish Dior friends. We all enjoyed ourselves greatly. Do let me know when you come next to England and allow me to entertain you. Love, Angus.[9]

(Jorn Langberg remembers his amused discovery on this literary occasion that writers, like fashion designers, talked so much shop.)

Those polished Italian intellectual Anglophiles, Alberto Arbasino and Masolino D'Amico, were at hand with all the literary gossip: so were Moravia and Dacia Maraini. Angus and Tony took a night off (Tuesday, 26 March, warm and sunny) to visit Gore Vidal in Rapallo: Angus had vertigo as he looked down at the bay from Vidal's clifftop eyrie. Angus lectured for the British Council on Dickens, was photographed and interviewed. Tony watched him anxiously. How was he going to feel, deprived of his Kipling scheme? Would he get down to work? He seemed to be sleeping well, and had no ailments, although he was biting his nails to the quick as he had done as a boy.

On 13 March, Angus dated the notes for an outline of a new novel, which by Thursday 21st was entitled *Improbable Nonsense*: 29 handwritten pages bear witness to his preoccupations. The presence of Kipling broods over all, but Kipling is matched by a composite dame who was to be the protagonist – an extraordinary, somewhat sibylline mixture of Ivy Compton-Burnett, Rebecca West, Margaret Rutherford and E.F. Benson's Lucia – shall she be actress, scholar, teacher, writer, spy? Shall she be called Iris, or Elspeth? Shall she be subject to violent subversive fits of what Angus calls "Stalkyism"? Are her powers real or false? "*Deceiving elf,*" reads one of his asides, and "Prospero" another: he was worried that his own fancy could not cheat as she was wont to do, and that his powers were waning. Why had he been *quite so fascinated* by the Abbé Faria's raising the Indian woman in a trance? Had he himself tried and failed to emulate Dickens in his successful mesmerising of Mme de la Rue in Genoa? He feared the death of magic.

This, he announces in his first sentence, is to be his W.W.J.W. book – his tribute to Winn Johnstone-Wilson. His protagonist is a figure out of Kipling, a wounded hero, a war casualty. There will be a background of war, fascism, treachery: a conflict between well-heeled Darwinian pessimism ("rich Crittalls" again) and the depression. Liberalism will die the death once more. W.W.J.W. will run a coypu farm in East Anglia, not a prep school, but we must have not have too many tortured animals. The ghosts of brother soldiers, of right-wing Henry Williamson (he must re-read) and Edmund Blunden (who died in Suffolk on 21 January of this year), would hover: so would Leonard Woolf and that old-style gentleman and despiser of women, Cecil Roberts. He would weave in the Catholic pessimism of Evelyn Waugh, of Christopher Sykes, of his two brothers. His brothers – had they, he wondered, found in the jungle a "freedom from themselves, their history, their tiredness, a kind of basic empty peace?" Or were they "the sort of tail end of aesthetic romanticism?"

On all this he brooded, and on violence, sadism, right-wing heroics, and the difference between Kipling, Sapper, *Z-Cars* and James Bond. He would use the Wilderness at Maresfield again, filled with Gropius refugees: he would weave a spy plot around them. He would revisit Eastbourne, and place there a mystic medium with a message. The old memories pulled. Gogol, Dickens, L.P. Hartley. Ivy Compton-Burnett returned again and again: he had been talking about Ivy to Hilary Spurling, and the strange hidden life of her family, soon to be revealed to the world in Spurling's biography, was much on his mind. Was she sibyl or charlatan, witch or fraud? There would be a scene in Rome. "A book hardly funny at all. Grim," he notes. It would have a prologue set in 1927, along the lines of the prologue to *Late Call*, then Three Chapters, then Rome, then Three Chapters, then an Epilogue.

It was never written. Little sparks from it flickered up in Angus's next and last novel, but *Improbable Nonsense* remained in its notebook. For he discovered that, despite alarms, he could proceed with his biography: Michael Horniman, who handled the Kipling estate at A.P. Watt for Kipling's daughter Mrs Bambridge, had been persuaded that Angus's portrait would be sympathetic, and had convinced Mrs Bambridge herself of this. She had now withdrawn her original objections, and Angus was free to proceed with Kipling – or Kippers, as Tony now called him – with enthusiasm.

★

Angus and Tony drove back to England at the end of March 1974, through the St Bernard tunnel. Term began at the end of April, as the Portuguese dictatorship ended in a relatively bloodless coup – Europe seemed to be swinging to the left, which would have displeased Colin, and made Angus worry about whether life was going to get more and more expensive. (John Cobb wrote from Lisbon saying that "after a life-time of being govern(ess)ed, it left one feeling a bit like a small boy being sent off to school for the first time without Nanny to hang on to. She may have been a bloody old bitch, but at least she was familiar! . . . I should have said I was sorry to hear of your brother's death. So I was in that it severs one of your links with Lisbon, but from his point of view he has been well spared the present atmosphere of uncertainty which couldn't possibly make for a happy old age."[10]) Angus settled down to his teaching: this summer he planned to give a series of lectures and a seminar on "Kipling and his Times" at UEA, to fit in with further research. The seminar was conducted jointly with historian Dr Richard Shannon, biographer of Gladstone and friend of Peter Conradi: together Angus and Shannon drew up a reading list of Kipling prose and poetry, of works on Imperialism, the Liberal Empire, Chamberlain, Milner and Rhodes.* Angus found the historical perspective and the responses of his students useful, but Shannon felt the seminar did not really work – the historians liked it, but it was difficult, even for Angus, to persuade 1970s literature students to see Kipling's writing in perspective.

Kippers dominated Angus's life for years to come and an invitation to open an exhibition on 24 May at Penshurst Place to coincide with the publication of Ann Thwaite's biography of Frances Hodgson Burnett was made to serve the cause. Angus lunched with Lord de L'Isle, said many pleasant words about Ann Thwaite's book, and then was driven off to see Kipling's old home, Bateman's, at Burwash. The landscape of Sussex had

---

* Richard Shannon and Peter Conradi shared a cottage in Radnorshire, which Angus and Tony visited in 1976.

always moved him: he pondered the paradox that two of the great writers of his youth and of the century, Virginia Woolf and Kipling, had both lived in it, loved it, and found one of their greatest delights in motoring through it – yet would have had nothing to say to one another had they met. Near contemporaries in time and space, they inhabited different political and social worlds.[11] He wondered why he himself felt so strongly about both of them. Woolf was becoming increasingly fashionable, riding high on the tide of feminism, but Kipling, although much read, lay buried deep in a pit of critical neglect. Could he resurrect him? In September he planned to pursue Kipling to Vermont, to see what clues the landscape there might hold.

Spring and summer passed, bringing a return visit from the Hobsons and an oration at UEA about Harold Pinter, whose work Angus had long admired: this was their first meeting, and the prelude to a long friendship. Summer also brought Yoshi Oida, who was about to start rehearsals for Peter Brook's *The Ik*: he breezed through and spent an evening with them in London. Poor tabby Giuseppe, a gift from Juliet Corke, fell ill and had to be put to sleep. *Late Call*, adapted by Dennis Potter, was being filmed by the BBC, but strike action caused delays, depressing Angus and annoying Tony. It was a difficult time for the new Labour government and for publishers. Earlier in the year there had been paper shortages; television programmes had ended at 10.30 p.m.: and inflation reached 16 per cent in June. When Angus and Tony visited the Priestleys at Kissing Tree House at Alveston in July they talked a lot about money worries and were unkind about Harold Wilson: it was left to Paul Johnson, visiting for lunch, to defend him. Ann Fleming, at tea at Sevenhampton, seemed less preoccupied by money, though she had worries of her own. Something was going seriously wrong with her son Caspar, who was there with an "about-to-be-ex-girl-friend".[12] Angus and Tony drove home, taking drinks on the way with Robert Heber Percy and Sir Michael Duff, and lunch with Haskells and Hampshires: there was much talk there of Caspar Fleming, who was a depressive, and caught up in the drug scene.

At dinner at Julian Mitchell's in Christchurch Street the following week Angus entertained the company (Alfreda Rushmore, Polly Toynbee, Peter Jenkins) with imitations of Stuart Hampshire and Cecil Roberts. "Since his Stuart was exact, I now feel I know Roberts too. [Angus] said he was so disappointed by the reception of his last book, which *was* bad, he's thinking of writing no more novels, but he said it with no conviction. He and Peter had long gossip about Bury St Edmunds – Angus was delighted when Peter acknowledged that Angus had helped to get his first article into the *New Statesman*. Angus had told me this before Peter arrived, so the pleasure was general – Angus felt appreciated, I mean, and I was glad Peter admitted his debt."[13]

After a trip to lecture for the Open University in York, which Angus bravely delivered while feeling very sick from the poisoned pâté of a dinner in Selby, they settled down to an August in Suffolk, interspersed with visits to London to libraries and the Public Record Office. Tony went off to Paris for a few days towards the end of the month, and in his absence Angus had dinner with the Reynoldses – was this the occasion on which he invited them over to the cottage and cooked for them "chicken with all the trimmings", proving he had not yet lost all his old culinary skills? The Reynoldses were so accustomed to seeing Tony doing everything – opening the door, pouring drinks, making introductions, popping in and out of the kitchen, serving the meal, while Angus talked and talked: it was a change to see Angus in charge. Stuart and Renée Hampshire were not exposed to home cooking; Angus met them for dinner in The Limes at Needham Market. Then came Jane and Glyn Davies, who had stayed for a few nights in the flat at Regents Park Terrace: they stayed at Felsham Woodside for a couple of nights and were treated to dinner at Hintlesham and a visit to Framlingham: Tony reappeared, and on 3 September he and Angus flew off to Marseilles for a short holiday.

They arrived in humid cloudy weather, and were hit by torrential rain at Avignon, but the weather picked up and they enjoyed warm sunny days in Uzès, staying at the Champs de Mars ("good and cheap") and visiting Patrick Woodcock who had a house nearby. They admired swallows and butterflies, and took themselves to tea with their old friends Barbara and Walter Robinson and their children at Vic-le-Fesq: the boys were delighted by Angus's chatter about Dickens, and he promised to send them a copy of his book. (Barbara Robinson was convinced that Angus hated being a professor and that academic life was very bad for him: he should have stuck to being a creative writer, she continues to maintain. Angus in turn said that he hated the name of the place where they lived, and Walter Robinson admitted that Vic-le-Fesq did sound like something out of Dante's *Inferno*. Angus also took against the name of the Hampshire village where Rosemary Merry lived: he did *not* like the words "Hartley Wintney", he informed her.) Once more they went to see David Hughes and Mai Zetterling up the valley, and then took themselves back to London on 10 September, to prepare for another departure. On 19 September 1974, after dining with the Kilmartins, they were off to Toronto, on the first leg of another long visit to North America.

★

They stayed four days in Toronto, visiting two zoos, one closed and one open, eating a fish in a bun and some *crème de menthe parfait*, driving by the lake, and spending most of the rest of the time in the library working on Kipling. Kipling then led them on to the Houghton Library in Harvard, to Salem and Ipswich, to Bangor and Bowdoin College in Brunswick, Maine, where Longfellow and Hawthorne had both studied. Here Angus gave a lecture on 26 September and ate some Maine lobster. Then they drove to see Kipling's house, Naulakha, at Brattleboro, and back over the Green Mountains to Wilmington and Bennington, and on to their destination, Johns Hopkins in Baltimore, Maryland, where Angus was to be John Hinkley Visiting Professor.

This Kipling research was at times highly agreeable – they enjoyed seeing the paintings of Kipling's uncle, Edward Burne-Jones, at Wilmington, and Angus was surprised by how much he liked the New England scenery. He had thought of himself as a West Coast man, and had dismissed those who extravagantly praised the reds and yellows of the maples – but here he was, admiring the enchantment of the landscape, fascinated by the small spa town of Brattleboro with its evocative main street, impressed by the elegant colonial-style home of Kipling's in-laws, the Balestiers. Kipling's own home, Naulakha, designed by the architect Henry Rutgers Marshall, raised interesting queries. It was here, in his early married life, that Kipling had developed his hatred of journalists, his obsessive need for privacy: here he had tried – and failed – to seclude himself from the world. He had rejected the easy-going American hospitality which Angus himself had claimed to find so agreeable after the "daunting privacies" of an England hidden behind hedges and fences.[14] Yet Angus himself lived in a hidden cottage, lost in a dark wood.

At Johns Hopkins, he gave lectures on "Dickens and the Law" and "Kipling and the Law", and taught a course on "Children in Fiction" (Dickens to William Golding, taking in *Peter Pan* and, of course, Kipling's *Kim*). Many times he invoked the useful and still powerful name of his old friend Edmund Wilson, who had taken Kipling seriously as a writer when few would; Angus was much influenced by (though he did not wholly agree with) Wilson's influential essay, "The Kipling that Nobody Read", initially published in the *Atlantic Monthly* in February 1941, and reprinted in *The Wound and the Bow* the same year. It was not easy to interest American students in Kipling; students at UEA had reacted against him because they did not like his politics, whereas American students did not even know what his politics were – the history of the Empire and the British colonies meant nothing to them. Despite this, Angus managed to enthuse some of them with his own love of *Kim*, and over the years collected a large file of "Student Reactions" to the novel. (And one American reviewer of Angus's biography, Sam Pickering, writing in 1979, in the *Sewanee Review*, had fallen so much under Kipling's spell that he extravagantly declared that "Kipling's India is not today's India, but it is probably the only India most of us can imagine. Mahbub Ali, Hurree Babu, the Eye of Beauty, Lurgan Sahib, Sir Purun Dass, Kaa, Shere Khan, Bagheera, and the mugger of the Mugger-Ghat will remain vital long after Indira Gandhi is forgotten.")

From time to time Angus mentioned, a little uneasily, the initially disconcerting news that back home Kingsley Amis was also working on Kipling – on a picture book for Thames & Hudson, to appear in 1975. Kipling had had some strange admirers and critics, ranging from T.S. Eliot to Noël Annan (whose view of Kipling was too sociological-historical for Angus's taste), and Angus continued to be intrigued by the mystery of Kipling's complex, problematic personality. He was still worrying about it long after he had published his own book.

Angus remained at Johns Hopkins through the autumn, though he and Tony made a few excursions – they spent one weekend in October at Assateague Island, Virginia, on a nature reserve on the Atlantic Ocean, bird-watching. Angus also dashed off from time to time to lecture on Dickens and Woolf in Delaware and Sweet Briar College and Atlanta and the University of Pennsylvania, to research in the Pierpont Morgan Library, the Library of Congress in Washington, and the Princeton University Library. He dined with many librarians, and ate better lunches, he was later to record, in library canteens and restaurants in the United States than he had ever enjoyed in his BM days.

He and Tony lived in a high-rise apartment overlooking the town: Angus praised Baltimore, with its leafy open suburban lawns, its colourful markets, its restored downtown buildings, its stoneclad houses on Federal Hill, its Catholic basilica, its Latrobe building. The harbour (the second largest international port in the United States) was disappointingly far away, but the enormous ships and the waterways fascinated him. He liked the Sandy Point park and the Druid park with its fountain and reservoir and the Matisses in the Walters Art Gallery. But, he warned them all, he "despised" cold weather – he would be off before the winter set in.[15]

South they went, on 30 November, to Miami, and drove through the Everglades in the sunny 70s, then they flew on via three island stops to Guadaloupe, with its humming-birds and tree-frogs and ferns, its crab and goat cheese and coconut rum. They stayed there a week, then flew on to Lisbon (Tony had discovered you could do all this for the same price on the same ticket) where they stayed until 16 December.

On Tuesday, 10 December 1974, after visiting the zoo and Belem, Angus was "very happy and confident", but the next day, after a trip to Setubal and changing the hotel room because of noise, he had become depressed, had decided Kipling was no good, and that he might as well commit suicide. Tony took him off to the Estufa Fria and the Galeria Nacional to cheer him up, but his journal does not record whether or not this worked. Angus, as usual, was up and down day by day. Was he brooding a little on the fate of Cyril Connolly, who had died on 26 November 1974, and died, moreover, in some financial difficulties, leaving a widow and two small children? Their relationship had never been close, but Angus had always acknowledged the debt he owed to Connolly, and Connolly had acknowledged his acknowledgement: on 6 September 1973 Angus had written Connolly an unusually emotional letter, regretting his inability to attend various seventieth birthday celebrations for Connolly, and declaring that but for *Horizon* his own writing might have petered out "as the unfertilised hobby of a man who was looking for some means of self expression but never found it. This is a difficult moment for me, because the coincidence of the largely very dismissive and hostile reception of my last novel which I thought and know to be an intricate and interesting work with my sixtieth birthday has made my never very strong self assurance slump heavily and cast a temporary question mark over the writing which I know is the centre of my life. But I know that my life would have been emptier and more futile if I had never written and I think I have contributed much that is worth having done. *None* of it could I have done without your encouragement and I must be only one of many . . . Enemies of Promise echoes in my mind almost every day. I came in at a time when your work had borne its fruit and for a while my energies were all bent to restating the extraordinary and modern qualities of Dickens, of Meredith, of Richardson (all mistakenly taken to be some allegiance of mine to 'traditional' literature) but that work too it seems to me is now done. I have in these last years been fighting a hard battle to tie this extraordinary 18/19C to foreign literature that is our heritage from you. Alas, this fight is never done. To read Auberon Waugh's clever philistinism – 'all bores and foreigners like Zola, Conrad, Proust, Musil, Gide and Mann' – is to feel that a tedious old tidal wave which has threatened again and again is once more looming up, scummy and dirty with pebbly sand, to frighten us like so many Cnuts. But as it comes up again and again in new guises, we have in all you have done and written an enormous strength to draw on to fight their self satisfied chauvinist humour, their fear of greatness, and their hatred of difficulty.

"All this, I fear, is like the ramblings of some disgruntled clairvoyant lady

– but it is intended to tell you how much you have done for English Literature and to thank you personally for all you did for me and to wish you a very happy birthday. Angus."[16] Connolly had replied on 17 September 1973 sympathising with the bad reviews of *Magic*, complaining about hatcheteering journalism, and ending "PS You keep thanking me for publishing you – how do you think I felt when your first stories came in – an editor's dream – profoundly grateful."

Beneath these civilities, however, lay mistrust. Connolly, despite his editorial delight, had not really liked much of Angus's work ("too much vinegar, too laboured for me," he had written to Evelyn Waugh)[17], had been jealous of his success, and had not cared for his portrait as the ageing, cultured and womanising critic Tristram Fleet in "A Bit off the Map": Angus was well aware of all this, and had not quite forgiven Connolly's insults to *The Wild Garden*. Nevertheless, they were old colleagues, old comrades in arms against Philistia, and Connolly would leave a gap. (Michael Holroyd, dining with the Quennells and Lady Diana Cooper on the night of Connolly's funeral, recalls that Peter Quennell paused in the midst of carving the roast and said, carving knife and fork suspended in mid-air, "This is Cyril's first night underground." The words seemed to surprise him as much as they surprised his guests.)

There was no way but forward. Angus and Tony enjoyed their Portuguese break, meeting friends – John Cobb, Richard Wyatt, David Ponsonby. The architecture, as ever, delighted, though the food was not always all that could be desired. But perhaps they were lucky enough to dine on Lampreys in Bordelaise sauce – a somewhat fantastic dish which Angus was to contribute to a cookery book edited by Gillian Vincent in aid of the National Book League.[18] "Lampreys are strange primitive fish – like vertebrates with gills, fresh water and akin to eels. The sauce is made from their blood, red Bordeaux wine, stock, shallots, herbs etc . . . The only disadvantage I know of is that it is at its best in Portugal, which although architecturally splendid is otherwise gatronomically poor. You might, however, be lucky enough to combine it with excellent sucking pig in a Portuguese restaurant . . ."

On their last day, Angus and Tony went up to lunch at the hotel-palace at Seteais (named for the "Seven Sighs", said to have been heaved at the sight of the architect's bill) – the hotel where Pat Johnstone had come to meet them on his last mission before his death. Then back they flew on 16 December 1974 to London, Suffolk, the doctor, the garage, and Christmas in Kent. On 30 December, back in Suffolk, they dined with the Cooksons, Lady Murphy, the Reynoldses and the Rowleys. (Sir Joshua Francis Rowley was Vice-Lord-Lieutenant, later Lord-Lieutenant of Suffolk.)

The next day Angus was very greatly cheered by a letter from a young academic called Jaidev in Simla, praising his handling of Asian problems in *Magic*. Maybe he could make sense of Kim and Kipling after all. He must go back to India to find out.

25

IN SEARCH OF KIPLING

India was scheduled for early March, 1975. The biography was moving slowly along in Angus's head and in jottings in notebooks and diaries: on 9 January 1975 he went to the BBC TV Centre to record a television discussion for the *Book Programme* about Kipling with John Gross, and the following week he took himself off to Oxford to work in the library at Rhodes House and spend a few nights with Stuart Hampshire in Wadham. (He liked to tease Renée Hampshire about her good causes – currently gypsies and contraceptives for dogs: she enjoyed his teasing – "joshing", the Hampshires called it.) He had given up the hope of revisiting South Africa and retracing Kipling's footsteps there, but India and Pakistan were a necessity, and he prepared his trip carefully. (Mary Renault and Tony's sister-in-law Nancy Garrett were to be enrolled as volunteer research assistants on the South African front.) He dined twice with Alan Ross, who provided useful contacts and addresses – one of the names Ross gave was that of the Indian writer Dina Mehta, who had published a couple of stories in the *London Magazine*.

Angus put Kipling out of his mind for a while when recording a BBC radio programme and dining with Paul Bailey: they talked about their admiration for the late Henry Green, alias Henry Yorke.* Bailey was planning his biography, a project he eventually abandoned in despair. Despair attached itself to Green and all his works: in 1970 Angus had sounded out the possibility of offering Green an honorary degree, but his wife Adelaide Yorke wrote to Angus declining it on his behalf because he

---

* Angus participated in a BBC Radio 3 appreciation of Green's work, "Drawing Tears Out of the Stone", broadcast on 28 December 1975: he reviewed *Nothing* in the *Listener*, 4 May 1950, and a reissue of *Blindness* in the *Observer*, 28 August 1977: "Like Mrs Woolf, he walked on the thinnest of ice, on the cliff-edge of despair . . . he transformed his desperate tight-rope walk into a wonderful ballet of dancing words."

would never be able to get to the ceremony – he was too frail for public appearances. (He had died in 1973.) And on the way back from a rather fraught dinner with Bailey and his friend David Healey, Tony was given a blood test by the police at Notting Hill: luckily he was under the limit. Perhaps the alcoholic and desperate Green had infused his spirit into Tony's driving for the evening. (Conradi, another guest, does not remember the evening as fraught, but he does remember a brief attack upon Angus from Healey, along the lines of "Why do we all have to get dressed up when *you* come to dinner, Duchess?" – an attack to which Angus "listened attentively and spaciously, and which he used as a cameo in *Setting the World on Fire*".)

There were other minor distractions from Kipling. In January Angus dashed off his text on *The Naughty Nineties* for Methuen, and wrote an *Observer* review of *The Letters of J.R.Ackerley* in which he protested strongly against the necessity of loneliness in the homosexual life – perhaps all the more strongly in that aspects of Hamo in *Magic* had seemed to reinforce the stereotype. " . . . too often the pathos of the draughty, dismal filling-in-time life seemed wilful – searching for the ideal lover among young men who had been prejudged insufficient, allowing the inevitable boredoms, trivialities and shabbinesses that attach to all social life to enlarge into a general misanthropy, taking a highly fastidious and stern demand for craftmanship in the arts into wider spheres of life where it could only exclude variety and therefore impoverish experience . . . At the time I thought him guilty of wilful living suicide, and to some extent I still do."[1] ("Any outlawed world is a tragic world," he was to say of the homosexual life to Christopher Bigsby in 1980.)[2] How well some of these phrases might have applied to himself, had his life turned out differently – had he stayed on, for example, at the BM. On 31 January Anne O'Donovan, one of that earliest band of assistant temporary cataloguers, had a party to celebrate her retirement from the Museum, and a week later Angus lunched with his old friend and ex-colleague Alan Gray: he was spending much Kipling time in the Reading Room and Manuscripts Room, where he also renewed his friendship with Audrey Brodhurst.

The month before his departure for India was crowded: he and Tony dined with Sonia Orwell and the Corkes and museum director Carlos van Hasselt, and went with Jeanne and Glyn Davies to see Emlyn Williams do his one-man Dickens. Angus lunched with Lord Longford, and made a welcoming speech at the Dickens Birthday Dinner at the Washington Hotel in Curzon Street. (Angus was President of the Dickens Fellowship from 1974–75.) On 25 February he delivered the text of a children's story, "The Eyes of the Peacock", commissioned by William Feaver for the

Sunday Times[3] – it is an architectural and aesthetic fantasy, set partly in
Venice, and a foreshadowing of his next novel: its peacock feathers and
child's-eye sense of exotic adult mystery owe something to Angus's
meditations on the wonder of little Rudyard Kipling as he entered the pre-
Raphaelite treasure house of The Grange, in Fulham, where his uncle,
Edward Burne-Jones, offered such Arabian delights. (This story also
contains yet another crack at anti-aesthetic Exmoor.) Feaver (himself the
father of several children) commented in his letter of acknowledgement,
28 February 1975 "You were, I imagine, a most precocious child . . . "

Then there were interviews to publicise the strike-delayed BBC2 four-
part adaptation of *Late Call*, a production which received considerable
tabloid coverage thanks to the appearance of Dandy Nichols as Sylvia
Calvert – the sixty-seven-year-old actress (who, like her character,
suffered from high blood pressure) was famous as the "Silly old moo"
married to Alf Garnett (alias Warren Mitchell) in *Till Death Us Do Part*.
Late Call was shown in March and was on the whole highly praised.
Dennis Potter's adaptation was first-class, and Dandy Nichols with her
little grim self-deprecating smile was superb – solid, funny, touching, stoic,
and totally convincing. She wrote to Angus saying how very much she had
admired his work ever since she had first read *The Old Men at the Zoo*, and
how much she enjoyed the part – she had had more letters about it than
about anything she had ever done.[4]

But while Sylvia Calvert charmed the nation, Angus and Tony were far
away in Bombay. They left on Monday, 3 March 1975, after a night at the
airport hotel, and checked in the next day in a temperature of 70 degrees
(they were fond of recording the temperature) at the Taj Mahal Hotel. A
busy programme was lined up for them, of British Council lectures,
interviews, and visits to Kipling shrines: over the next six weeks they
travelled thousands of miles and met hundreds of people. Tony had taken
his Pentax camera, and was carefully recording all the Kipling sites. (He got
into trouble with his filter, but most of the photographs were remarkably
successful.) The grand tour took them through Delhi to Varanasi, to holy
Sarnath, to Allahabad, and by train to Lucknow: then on to Agra, the Taj
Mahal, Bharatpur, Jaipur, and back to Delhi. (In Delhi, they met Ruth
Prawer Jhabvala and her husband.) From Delhi, they went on to
Chandigarh and Simla, Amritsar and Lahore. In Lahore, they visited the
Shalimar gardens and Angus predictably burst into song – "Pale hands I
loved beside the Shalimar," he chanted, surprising the other strolling
sightseers as much as, all those years ago in the village of Simpson, Bentley
Bridgewater had shocked Angus's landlady Mrs Hill. From Lahore, they
went on to Peshawar, saw the Kohat Pass where Kipling's drummer boys

had drummed, then eventually made their way back, by Udaipur, to Bombay.

It was an epic and expensive journey which Angus enjoyed enormously. It was not without its dramas – missing baggage, trouble in hotels, encounters with gunsmiths and mystics and border guards and thieving monkeys – but they survived, leaving behind them a trail of enthused academics, aspiring novelists, Kashmiri poets, urgent booksellers, eager writers of dissertations. Angus's prejudice against Indians, formed in Tokyo and reinforced at the Edinburgh Festival through his encounters with Kushwant Singh, had been dissipated, though there had been some bad moments – in Simla Angus had a fearsome row with a young Sikh manager at the Oberoi Clarkes Hotel because he had to struggle, puffing and panting, up a steep flight of steps to the hotel, only to find that the driver could have taken the car up and avoided the climb: Angus was out of breath and had not reckoned with the effect of the thinning air. After the row, during which Angus threatened to report the smiling manager to the Viceroy, Angus calmed down and apologised – unnecessarily, in Tony's view.

Angus was much pleased by the way that Indian readers had reacted to *Magic*: one of them wanted to translate it into Urdu, and Jaidev of Simla was to write a paper comparing it with Dostoevsky's *Idiot*. Angus had worried that he might have caused offence – as he worried that he had caused offence in Ceylon, whither he was shortly to dispatch his nephew Mark Davies on a yet more epic journey.

Angus wrote about his adventures for the *Observer* Colour Supplement,[5] giving a colourful and on the whole light-hearted account of his travels: there were several stories that he loved to retell, particularly that of the Maharajah hotelier who insisted on ringing up in his presence the Chief Minister of Himachal Pradesh to announce that he had a professor at his hotel to whom special attention must be given in Simla – "He is rather old and probably bogus. And at the moment his face is covered in mango." After this, to entertain them, the Maharajah stood on his head, did a brief sword-dance, and displayed to them the contents of his laundry basket. (Angus's rendering of this episode was one of his best turns.)

But there were other episodes, less public, that did not make their way into his official account, nor into Kipling. In Bombay, he met Colin's friend, the advocate Mr Hegde, who over the years had been sending thin blue airmail letters of continuing adoration to his old hero, with details of his business affairs and his growing family. Another strange encounter was with Adil Jussawalla, poet, teacher and journalist, who had first met Angus fifteen years ago when he arrived muddied through the fields from his crammer's at Felsham Woodside: here he was again, polished in Bombay, with his wife Veronik, inviting Angus to an elegant little party and interviewing him the next morning (still a little affected by the party) for a magazine called *Debonair*.[6] They talked furiously, Angus spilling out his stories of mysterious India – there was this boy with a monkey, he kept pushing it into the sea then feeding it bananas – *why*? – and rattling on about Chaucer, Kipling, *Magic*, Hamo's homosexuality, *Little Dorrit*, de Sade. Jussawalla assured him that the Singhalese house of the frantically up-to-the-minute Jayasekeres in *Magic* was completely plausible – it could have been a household in Bombay. They talked and talked. The gulf had not been impassable, Jussawalla concluded in Forsterian style. And at the end of their conversation, Angus suddenly asked, "Why did you marry?"

"The expected reponses bubbled up to my head in surprise. Love, need . . . but also something Wilson had written in *The Wild Garden* about 'the necessary twin hells of solitude and society', an ambivalence that left no one alone.

" 'There's an ambivalence,' I said.

" 'Yes, you're quite right,' he said, brightening up. 'At my own university, I'm much more attracted to the girl students than to the boys. The boys grow such awful beards these days.' And there was a final earnest smile."

Jussawalla went down the steps of the hotel, hearing the "high distant overtone of perpetual woe" that Hamo heard as he travelled the world – and as he listened to it, suddenly, fresh from the sea, ran five young men with Hamo's perfect measurements – height 5'9", waist 24", hips 35", chest 30". "Not one but five young men, the water still running down their chests and arms. Hamo might have laughed. In this matter of his requirements, five is as good as none. But they were part of his quest, and he had drowned. They were no part of mine. Laughing, they walked by the sea, I back to the bar."

Also in Bombay, Angus met Dina Mehta and her husband Keki: she was overwhelmed by the torrent of his conversation as he sat in the lounge of the Taj, his white hair ruffled by the breeze from the Arabian Sea. He talked and talked, mainly of Kipling, but also commented on her own work, which he had read with interest – she was touched by "a certain painstaking courtesy of approach to the work of new writers". She and her husband showed Angus and Tony round Bombay, "cruising past gorgeous old heavyweights like the Victorian terminus, the Old Secretariat, the Law Courts, the Prince of Wales Museum and so on. They hugely enjoyed the Gothic turrets and Saracenic domes and Italianate galleries before we bought them home to meet our two daughters, and then to the Bombay gymhkana for an early dinner. Everything about the Gym, its furnishings and trophies and the building itself brought to Angus echoes of a past era. He observed everything: it was as if he had a window within him that he never closed. We said goodbye to them on the steps of the Taj Hotel and I remember asking Keki as we drove off, 'Do you think we'll ever see them again?' "[7]

(She did: her husband did not. Keki Mehta died suddenly of a massive heart attack in January 1976, leaving his wife to appreciate all too well the accuracy of the psychology of Meg Eliot. But she was to see Angus again, in England and in India.)

This journey had been of the greatest importance to Angus. He had been able to see for himself the places that had formed Kipling's imagination, so that when the time came he could write of them with a first-hand intimacy. He had seen the Delhi Gate at Lahore, "still today a tattered, blotchy, rubbish-filled nook and cranny" (p.60), where Kipling as a restless young reporter had explored the native underworld. He had seen the big gun, Zam-Zammah, outside the Museum, and Tony had taken a photograph which showed three boys at play around it just as they had been in the days of Kim. He had seen Mrs Hauksbee's Simla, with its "balconies, fretted wood, tiled roofs, corrugated iron roofs, fresh paint, dilapidation, all close-packed, all tumbling down the hillside like a large damaged layer-cake" (p.85) and he had identified the house, Northwood, where Kipling's room had been raided by monkeys. He had seen Lurgan's house in Simla, and the new Gaiety Theatre, and the Mall: he had been to see the school at Lucknow where Kim had been educated, and assured himself that Kipling himself could not have been there or he would have described its rococo architecture more vividly. He had seen the Grand Trunk Road, with its bobbing vultures, its perching scissor-beaked drongos, its Moghul milestones. And, perhaps most memorably of all, he had seen the ruins of Chitor, one of the inspirations for Kipling's cobra-haunted Cold Lairs.

*

Angus and Tony left India on Tuesday, 15 April 1975 at 01.00, and despite a diversion from Beirut to Kuwait were back in the cottage by 5.00 p.m. on what was, in principle, the same day. It was a triumph. Angus returned with temporarily renewed confidence, and was at once sucked back into public life. On 23 April, St George's Day, there was a large demonstration in Belgrave Square in favour of Public Lending Right. Angus turned out with his placard, wearing a bright purple sweater purchased earlier that morning – London struck chilly after India. The square was crowded by hundreds of protesters representing the Society of Authors, the Writers' Guild, the Writers' Action Group, and themselves: Kingsley Amis, Brigid Brophy, Maureen Duffy, Antonia Fraser, Elizabeth Jane Howard, Frank Muir, Dilys Powell, Ted Willis, Francis King with his Staffordshire bull terrier – there they all were, calling out for justice and a loan-based scheme from Hugh Jenkins, the bearded Minister, who braved the lions and threw them scraps of hope from a small podium. The event received a lot of coverage: *Private Eye* conceded that Angus Wilson looked "rather sweet waving a little piece of cardboard with all his demands on it."[8] (It said "WRITERS' GUILD OF GREAT BRITAIN DEMANDS PLR NOW!")

There was a reception at UEA for the new Henfield Fellow, Derek Mahon, on 8 May, the day on which Angus purchased a new pair of glasses – "old pair presumed thrown on compost heap", Tony solemnly entered in the accounts book. Angus spent the summer term teaching his "Children in Literature" seminar: he also entertained visitors from California, Atlanta, Japan, Heath Hurst Road, Regent's Park Terrace and Doughty Street, many of whom had invited themselves. He lectured on Dickens at Broadstairs after a feast of roast turkey (17 May) and he embarked on reading dozens of books for the Booker Prize.

He had agreed to chair the judges, and books began to pour in. The sight of them caused a great dip in his self-confidence. He wrote to Alan Ross in mid-August thanking him for all his help with the Indian trip "which was one of the happiest things of my life", but saying that since he'd got back he had been "overworked, horribly poor, depressed and frightened by the future."[9] He took up the theme again with Julian Mitchell, whom he met by chance in the London Library on 7 September – Tony was in Burford with his mother and sister and Angus was at a loose end, so Mitchell took him home for an hour and a half, where Angus entertained Mitchell and Richard Rowson with tales of India and Booker.

He said he had had to postpone Kipling to read eighty-three novels, many of them bad, which had given him a painful eye, and he saw no possibility of saving for his old age – but he put on such a show that Richard Rowson smiled seraphically throughout these complaints. Nobody believed Angus when he said he was tired, poor, old. How could he be? It was true that Cyril Connolly seemed to have died in debt, but surely Angus was selling well? Earlier this year Angus contributed to the Connolly fund, organised by Sonia Orwell to help his widow and children (he gave £50 on 18 February): it had raised some forty thousand pounds. Surely Angus was not making such a muddle of his own finances as Connolly had?

Angus also described to Mitchell and Rowson one of his more bizarre public appearances, which had taken place the week before in Sheffield at a

CHE conference. He and Tony had attended this event together, and Angus had announced his twenty-fifth wedding anniversary "but said the Gay Marxists forbade all camp jokes and complained there weren't enough gay workers, which must have been wholly misconstrued by everyone present except themselves." Angus had then gone on to mention his love for Denis Barnes: Denis and Patsy Barnes had stayed the night of 2 September at Felsham Woodside, and the old days at Oxford and a summer at Pevensey were fresh in his mind.

The CHE gathering was a proper civic event. Sheffield, the home of progressive causes, had agreed to host a conference and to give a reception in that monument to Victorian prosperity and respectability, the Cutlers' Hall. (Staid Harrogate had turned CHE down.) The Lord Mayor and Lady Mayoress were there, and so was Angus, the respectable white-haired novelist, just turned sixty-two, to affirm his support of law reform and the social and legal recognition of couples of the same sex. (This was a matter he had already with foresight raised in *Encounter* in June 1972: Angus had written a letter in response to a long piece by American academic Edward J. Mishan on "Making the World Safe for Pornography", *Encounter*, March 1972: Angus argued that there was no evidence to suggest that "to accept homosexual union as on a par, socially, with heterosexual union" would be "repugnant to the great majority of people", as Mishan had claimed.)

The reception generated a certain amount of chaos, as women delegates protested that the waitresses were not being given equal pay, but by and large all passed off well. The uniformed attendant at the City Hall was quite unperturbed and said he had seen more kissing on the football field. Angus and Tony discovered, however, that their claim of twenty-five stable years of marriage did not go down well in all quarters – they were attacked by the irascible homophobe columnist John Junor, who accused Angus and CHE of publicising paedophiles and perverts, and ironically asked in the *Sunday Express* if he should send Angus and Tony a silver spoon for their silver wedding.[10] They were also attacked from the left, by militants who accused them of being bourgeois and unliberated.

Angus McGill cheered them up – he sent them some spoons and a copy of his letter to the *Express*:

"Dear J.J.

I read your paragraph about Angus Wilson with interest and thought your suggestion a good one. I have sent a silver teaspoon to Mr Wilson and his friend with good wishes for their continued happiness." Rose Tremain and Charles Osborne and his friend Ken wrote in a similar vein, and so did several others.

*

In late September 1975, Angus and Tony went off on holiday to France,
Italy and Switzerland, staying for a while at the Cooksons' apartment in the
out-of-season ski resort of Anzères: Angus returned to lecture in Bangor
on 20 October. The misery of the Booker Dinner lay ahead. This event,
low-key by the standards of the late Eighties, could already generate a fair
amount of ill-will and envy. Angus's fellow judges were Peter Ackroyd,
Roy Fuller and Susan Hill, and between them they produced at the end of
October a very short short list, with only two books on it – Ruth Prawer
Jhabvala's *Heat and Dust*, and Thomas Keneally's *Gossip from the Forest*. This
was not popular: and the complaint was raised (for the first but not for the
last time) that these writers were not really *British*. The press was quick to
declare that the judges thought it had been a dud year: this was not very
popular either. Malcolm Bradbury remained convinced that he might
have won the prize for *The History Man* had he not been eliminated
because his colleague from UEA was in the chair: Angus was said to be
miffed because his own favourite, Rumer Godden's *The Peacock Spring*, did
not reach the short list. (Angus had not got on well with Roy Fuller, whose
views were becoming increasingly unsympathetic to him, but Peter
Ackroyd remembers Angus as a peace-maker.)*

Amidst such rumblings of discontent Angus prepared his speech, in
which he attacked the NW3 middlebrow novel, and spoke of his dislike of
"the smart icy winds round Hampstead pond", and the tedious subject-
matter of rows "looming between estranged NW parents, both working
in the media or in advertising, over the merits of the local comprehensive,
or when once more a Highgate wife had to make the momentous decision
to accept or not a threesome with the au pair girl." (Had Penelope
Mortimer remained unforgiven for her review of *The Old Men at the Zoo*?)
He went on to grumble about publishers sending in too many bad books,
critics who overpraised fleeting "masterpieces", and then himself proceeded to praise those writers who had looked beyond English provincialism – Paul Scott, Rumer Godden, and the winner, Ruth Prawer Jhabvala.

The judges had picked an Indian novel – well, an almost Indian novel.
Angus, newly returned from India, and still puzzled by the hostile response

---

* Fuller, who in 1976 briefly and uncomfortably succeeded Stuart Hampshire as Chairman
of the Literature Panel of the Arts Council, was growing curiously reactionary: he had deplored
the *Lady Chatterley* decision and disliked liberal talk about a "multi-cultural society". His
autobiographical volume about these years, *Spanner and Pen* (Sinclair-Stevenson 1991), though
it records in detail many of his public offices and quarrels, makes no mention of the Booker
episode, so presumably he thought it was better forgotten.

to *Magic*, reacted with hostility to what seemed to him the smug English world – the small world about which he had written so savagely in the early stories, with such sympathy in *Mrs Eliot* and *Late Call*. He had voted for the sun.

The evening of the award was not a success. Angus felt he had muffed his speech, partly because he had had to prepare a written version for the press, partly because the round separate tables made it difficult to speak to the whole room. He took it into his head that he was being criticised and laughed at – possibly by some of those Hampstead people who still persisted in finding their own lives of interest. Charles Osborne reported to him that Claire Tomalin, then literary editor of the *New Statesman*, had not liked his speech, and Angus stormed over to her table and shouted at her, which he was later to regret – he should have shouted at another alleged dissenter, publisher Tom Maschler, instead. It was all a disaster. He went home depressed and unhappy. The evening weighed on him for years.

There were days of anxiety and despair, aggravated by the fact that the Kipling contract did not arrive, and a Rainbird contract for a book on the history of the novel arrived with an earlier delivery date than he had expected. He was afraid that if he went to the Royal Society of Literature poetry reading he might have another outburst. He had a dream, which he reported to Tony: "somewhere at the seaside, suddenly becoming aware that valuable things of ours were being engulfed by the tide; a rush to the beach, and the rescue of the valued objects – Who's Who and Burke's Peerage. At the top of the beach a challenging voiced Audrey Brodhurst, 'Tony's Mother is better. She's a Countess, isn't she?' (Mother had been unwell with influenza.)"

Three days later, after anxieties about the shape of the book and an unsatisfactory talk about Charles Carrington's *Rudyard Kipling*, he had a coughing fit in the night and screamed that there were two men by his bed. Tony was having a rough time. At dinner in Radnor Walk a week later, on 8 December, Betjeman declared that he was afraid of dying, and talked of little but rape. (Did Tony occasionally long for younger gayer company?)

This year there was no escape from the gloom of the British winter. Christmas 1975 was spent in Suffolk, cheered by the sight of a greenfinch, and by invitations from and to Corkes and Cooksons and Gilliatts and Hampshires. On 24 January 1976 Angus and Tony drove through the snow to dine with the Reynoldses and Sonia Orwell. But mostly it was a long slog of Kipling – Colindale Newspaper Library, Malmesbury, St Osyth Priory, Guy Strutt, Somerset de Chair. Angus felt bogged down by the weight of material and of biographical detail, yet he went on acquiring more. In early February, Tony noted, he was tired and depressed by the snowy weather and the sound of sawing in the woods, and full of gloomy literary paranoia – Stephen Spender had been made President of English PEN, Malcolm Bradbury and Auberon Waugh had failed to mention him in interviews. The proofs of a reprint of *Cloche*, far from cheering him, made him think that it was a silly book, not worth a reissue, and there was silence from Paris, where he had been for three hectic days in January to promote *Magic*. So *Magic* must have failed there too. He longed for the day when he could wake up in the cottage and find he had nothing to do.

The noise of sawing in the wood got worse and worse. Angus could not work. He could not go to London as he had loaned the Regent's Park Terrace flat to Yoshi Oida – Oida was now appearing in *The Ik*, which they had seen on 27 January with Perkin Walker. Angus decamped for a few days to work at the Garden House Hotel in Cambridge, as he had done for Zola. He was beginning to feel he would never get to the end of Kipling, and here were so many other things claiming his attention – a memoir of Edmund Wilson who had died in 1972, a protest letter to British Home Stores about the forced resignation of a gay employee, an ill-attended reading at the Oxford Union, an *Observer* review, filming at the cottage and at UEA for the *Book Programme*, a week's British Council tour of Holland, an interview with Denis Lemon for *Gay News*, a drink at The Chase followed by a depressing Chinese takeaway, a meeting of the Eastern Arts Association, and lectures to write for next term. He was overtired and tense, and Tony began to wonder whether they might have not have to take an earlier holiday than planned.

The *Book Programme* was shown on Tuesday, 2 March 1976, and its shots of Angus's garden, Angus and Tony hard at work on Kipling, Angus on the campus at Earlham, elicited congratulations from old friends from as far back as Ashampstead days. Rosemary Merry, settled in Hampshire, reported that her brother Ian Calder was now living apart from his family but on friendly terms with them, and that he was drinking much less. She remembered Bletchley and Soho, Dolphin Square and Mettingham with affection, and was pleased to see Angus looking so relaxed and unpompous on the screen. But how relaxed was he? Tension is highly evident between the lines in the *Gay News* interview.[11]

Denis Lemon arrived on the afternoon of 5 March with his friend Peter Bennett, carefully following instructions about how to fit their car wheels into the deeply rutted track that led across the fields and through the avenue of trees: they taped a long interview with a grey-suited, velvet-tied Angus while they munched chocolate biscuits and sipped tea by a smoking log fire. Tony kept an anxious eye on proceedings, coming in from time to time with an armful of logs. Angus talked about his own work, about class and homosexual love, and about E.M. Forster, upon whose biography P.N. Furbank was then engaged. Angus was outspoken about Forster, whose work he found increasingly unsympathetic, whose humanism he found increasingly inadequate – although he also had doubts about his own. (Furbank, in a review of C.B. Cox's analysis of liberal humanism, *The Free Spirit*, had said of the humanist succession from George Eliot through Forster to Wilson, "Angus Wilson . . . writes under the shadow of Forster and is not able to express humanist values directly; he assumes them and teaches them how to live in the world. He is the casuist of humanism." *New Statesman*, 9 August 1963.) Angus believed that Forster could have "come out" at the end of his life, but chose not to. He claimed that Pat Trevor-Roper had said at one point to MPs "during the Wolfenden debate"

> We could always get Forster to come along and speak to you. But
> I had great doubts as to whether this was true because he would
> have got out of it in some Bloomsbury sort of way by saying
> "This is a vulgar sort of noise, and one musn't make vulgar
> noises," or something like that. But, well, he didn't speak in his
> work about it; nor did Willie Maugham.
> DENIS: Nor Coward. He was approached by The Homosexual
> Law Reform Committee for his support, but. . .
> ANGUS: I'm sure he wouldn't have done. No, they were all
> terrible, really. They were three terrible men.
> TONY GARRETT: It would have been very foolish for a highly
> successful public figure to come out alone from a whole
> generation. I think it's extremely unlikely to expect them to have
> done anything.

Angus went on to talk about Oxford days, the Sheffield conference, Baron Charlus, Gide, Fagin, and gay terminology – he still used the word queer himself, didn't quite like "gay" which sounded too "zizzy", and recorded that his brothers, when attempting to ascertain whether people were gay or not would ask them "Do you know Philip of Macedon?"

A good time was had by all, but that terrible phrase "three terrible men" – spoken of three men whom he had known and liked and respected, and who had liked him – lingered on oddly and dangerously in the newly inflammatory atmosphere of the mid-seventies. Tony, while heaping on more logs, attempted to control the flames, but Angus had become touchy. When the official interview with Lemon and Bennett was over, a bottle of sherry was produced, and Angus launched into an outburst against

Yevtushenko as collaborator – "Angus on the boil was quite a sight," remembered Lemon. Eventually Tony had to chase both the young men away.

Coming out was not easy. There must have been moments when Angus wondered whether he had been wise to abandon the policy of discretion that he had defended, in the early 1970s, to Antony Grey and Peter Conradi. It was not pleasant to receive an anonymous, impeccably typed letter correctly and very publicly addressed to the Professor of English Literature at UEA which read "Why don't you take a long rope, find a tall tree and hang yourself by the neck until you are dead – YOU DEPRAVED OLD FAGOT." And what would Tony's eighty-seven-year-old mother say if she heard Angus and Tony described as "lovers"? (Tony wrote to Lemon to say that Angus thought he was too old to be called a "lover" – surely "friends" would do?)

The battle was not yet won. Lemon believed that the British Home Stores incident reminded Angus uncomfortably of Tony's loss of his job as probation officer, and he may well have been right. Doctor Tony prescribed a holiday, but the holiday seemed to consist partly of Bentley Bridgewater's coming to stay for a few days at the end of March. Bentley too had been very depressed. They took him to Hintlesham for dinner and to Tring for lunch. It cheered him up. Then Tony and Angus went to stay a night on 30 March at Ann Fleming's, dining with the Bayleys and Stuart Hampshire: there was much Oxford talk about charm and humanism, but Ann was drinking heavily and tearful over the death of her son Caspar, who had succeeded in commiting suicide in October 1975, after a serious attempt the year before in Jamaica – he had been rescued from the sea by helicopter, but had spent much of the remainder of his short life institutionalised in England, being treated for drug addiction and depression. Caspar had been one of the lost boys. On through gloomy weather went Angus and Tony in pursuit of Kipling – to Dyrham, to Tisbury, to Clouds (designed by Philip Webb for the Percy Wyndhams) and again to Batemans. On Saturday, 4 April they went to Dymchurch, to check yet more Kipling references, then visited Denis and Patsy Barnes for lunch – always cheering – and on to Glyn and Jeanne Davies in Dover for the night.

The pressure of Kipling was intense – at the beginning of May Angus calculated that he had a quarter of the book still to write, and he had more people yet to see. It was comforting to find Amis's book described as lazy by Paul Theroux, but it made expectations of his own work even higher.[12] There was not enough money coming in – the only bright side was a low tax estimate and news of a repeat of Late Call on TV. Maybe Curtis Brown would make sure that Penguin would manage to have the novel in print with a tie-in cover this time round – and while he was on the subject, why were his short stories unavailable? He had committed himself to writing about his years at Oxford for Ann Thwaite, and was regretting it (though fortunately for posterity she urged him not to let her down, and prevailed). Proofs arrived for the text of *The Naughty Nineties* – they had to be turned round very quickly, with a dedication to Cecil Roberts squeezed in at the last moment. Whenever would he find time to write his own fiction again?

Social obligations also pressed: on 7 April he gave a party at Regents Park Terrace for some French critics who were involved with the translation and promotion of John Cowper Powys and the French magazine *Granit* which was devoted to Powys's work.[13] Viva King, Brigid Brophy, Angus McGill, David Farrer, Simon Edwards, Julian Mitchell, Denis Lemon, Bentley Bridgewater, the Reynoldses and many many more assembled to meet Diane de Margerie and Francois Xavier Jaujard. The following night, a dinner for eight, then Tring and Woburn and Bedford, and a couple of weeks later India again, in the form of an evening with the venerable Indian writer Nirad Chaudhuri at the Royal Society of Literature, which he had agreed to chair.

This occasion brought forth once more a familiar irritant, the Hampstead author Sasthi Brata, who had been pursuing Angus about bursaries and sponsors and grants since 1968, and who now said he wanted to attend the Chaudhuri evening which he gathered was to be held "by invitation only". Angus, who had ticked off Brata in their last interchange for accusing him of not having read all the Booker entries, mildly obliged, and sent two cards for Brata and his wife: his profit on it was a letter of thanks describing the speaker as a ludicrous menace[14] and retaliating with an invitation to a party in June. Then came term at UEA, where he was to take a three-hour Bloomsbury seminar (Forster, Woolf, Strachey, Roger Fry, Clive Bell) in addition to helping Bradbury with creative course work and post-graduate studies.

Viva King's autobiography appeared this spring, and having done much to encourage her to write it, he felt honour bound to review it – and did so, in *Books and Bookmen*.[15] Here he recalled the days when he had been a "nervous, voluble, painfully thin young librarian of twenty-five" and she a "formidable hostess, tough Bohemian, sharer of jokes (often bawdy) until we cried": now she revealed herself in old age, he wrote, as "an extraordinary self-knowing woman, an extrovert with exceptional powers of introspection". Willie King too was recalled – "skeleton thin, exquisite in gesture, scarlet and purple in the face, Mephistolean in the eye and dressed in shiny old blue suits." All this was all very well, thought Viva

King, but why had he gone on about her being a Becky Sharp, and why did he have to mention that one old Twenties acquaintance of his still referred to her as "Vivah Booth the dressmaker"? This was not very kind, although at least he refrained from mentioning the time when Bentley Bridgewater had made her laugh so much in the back of a taxi-cab that she had wet her knickers. ("Good old Viva no nonsense wet-your-knickers laughter" was one of the phrases Angus jotted once or twice in his notebooks.) And he did recommend the book warmly to Christina Foyle, to whom it brought back memories of early days at the Ham Bone with Nina Hamnett, and evenings with Nancy Cunard and Paul Robeson. She promised to make a special display[16] but appears to have forgotten to do so. (Angus and Tony were on visiting terms with Christina Foyle, and had several times been invited to her home at Beeleigh Abbey in Essex to see her and her husband Ronald Batty.)

Viva King had been as vivacious in her later years as in her prime, and her memoirs give a colourful account of her adventures and misadventures with her antique shop just off Sloane Square, with extravagant Arthur Jeffress and his gondoliers in Venice, with the Duke of Wellington (whom some said she hoped to marry), with the elegant ex-seaman April Ashley and with her young and untrustworthy Maori friend Mat, who was rumoured to sleep in a large basket at the foot of her bed, and who pilfered regularly from her antique shop. (April Ashley had introduced her to Mat, also a seaman, and April and Mat became violently jealous of one another.) Viva's nephew Richard Booth, lord of Hay Castle and of the second-hand book trade in Hay-on-Wye, had been warned against her by his parents in youth, and had perhaps as a consequence found her irresistible: like John Richardson, he was deeply affected at an impressionable age by her Bohemian style and entourage – not everywhere could one meet Yoko Ono and Shirley Bassey mingling with a host of antiquarians and clock experts and connoisseurs of the fine arts. Booth went on a trip to Venice with her and Cecil Gould, and Viva visited him in Hay several times, with April Ashley and her little dog Florabella: she ignored the haphazard piles of priceless and sometimes worthless books that served as mortar amidst the crumbling bricks of the castle, but took a keen interest in the onion-judging competition at the local fête.

In May 1976, a rather more secretive and reticent old lady died – Kipling's daughter, Elsie Bambridge of Wimpole Hall. There was no way of pretending that this was not good news. The way ahead was clearer now, and Angus pressed on more hopefully with the final interviews for and text of Kipling, which he was to finish in August. On 28 May he went to Penshurst where he lunched with Lady Hardinge, who had known

Kipling well. He also visited Mrs Hard, who had a film of Kipling at Bateman's which showed Kipling and his wife Carrie moving very fast in black and white. It excited Angus greatly. There was much discussion of format with his publishers – Angus was anxious that his volume should not look like a coffee-table book – and also of title. Angus favoured *From Bombay to Burwash*, and it was some time before *The Strange Ride of Rudyard Kipling* (an echo of Kipling's own *Strange Ride of Morrowbie Jukes*) was agreed.

June was a busy and blazing month. The hot summer of 1975 had been succeeded by the even hotter summer of '76 (so evocatively captured in Barbara Vine's East Anglian novel, *A Fatal Inversion*, 1987) when it seemed that it would never rain again. Angus loved it. Antonia Fraser and Julian Jebb were to film Angus and his cottage for a BBC2 programme in a series on Writers' Houses;[17] this involved various planning sessions and several days of film crew at Felsham Woodside. Antonia Fraser (who had known Angus since Reading Room days) recorded in her diary:

> June 9. Visit to Angus Wilson with Julian. Would have been wonderful and fascinating and in retrospect it was except for a) heat like the Inferno, making the train to Ipswich Danteesque without hope. b) feeling sick with exhaustion from the night before. [She and Harold Pinter had sat up all night in their London garden because of the heat.]
> The orange sun beat down on East Anglia, straight on me. When I arrived at this Beatrix Potter cottage, garden stuffed with high flowers, all the colours seemed livid, poppies, even irises, purple roses. Angus' shirt definitely cyclamen, violent, peacock *velvet* tie. Velvet! In this weather.
> He said: 'I always work *en plein soleil.*' That made me hotter than ever. But he was charming, a manic chatterer. Lunch at Carrier's Hintlesham Hall a cool treat, Italianate corridors most welcome. Julian and I had arranged this for Angus and Tony, BBC paying, to show love, but ended by finding it a great relief ourselves.

The film crew returned on 30 June, with Antonia Fraser in calmer mood: she and Julian Jebb stayed at the Mill Hotel in Sudbury.

> Two swans in the mill pond before the hotel. I joined them. Julian lurked beside the lock, in his baby blues, saying he feared the swans would attack me . . . Suffolk countryside now French with heat, poppies, corn, grasses. Julian and I decided the magic cottage was 'spooky'. On return I went to dinner [on 2 July] with

Emma [Tennant] to meet Angus resplendent in turquoise silk
Indian jacket, and Tony. Later Angus told me: 'It is a lovely place,
but perhaps its getting too isolated. Now I'm getting old, I may
have to move back to London.' We didn't know that at the time.
Maybe that's what spooked us?[18]

Angus and Tony had abandoned Antonia Fraser and Julian Jebb and the
crew in Suffolk to go to London on 30 June for two unconnected urban
events – the picketing of British Home Stores, and a celebratory dinner for
David Farrer at the Garrick.

The first of these occasions was one of the gay *causes célèbres* of the
decade: in February 1976 Tony Whitehead, a twenty-two-year-old
trainee manager at the firm, had agreed under pressure to resign after a
grilling about his appearance on a Southern Televsion documentary
programme in which he had been seen kissing his boyfriend. Outrage had
followed, in the pages of *Gay News* and with pickets at various branches,
and Angus had, as we have seen, written to BHS in protest. Gays bought
shares in the company so they could be represented at meetings, and
picketing continued throughout the country. The meeting on 30 June was
timed to coincide with the Annual General Meeting of British Home
Stores, at which the Chairman of the company, Sir Mark Turner, muffed
his lines somewhat – saying that there had been "few complaints", when
Gay News estimated a minimum of 1,500. He claimed he had been
ignorant of these figures: his excuse was that he had been in Australia.
Meanwhile, outside the headquarters in Marylebone, leading the picket,
stood Angus Wilson, FRSL, C.Litt., CBE, distinguished novelist and
CHE Vice-President, wearing a flowery shirt and carrying a large placard –
much larger than his PLR one – with its message "British Homophobe
Stores."

What did they make of that in the Garrick that evening, as Angus
sweetly sang the praises of his old editor, David Farrer, in the presence of
his old schoolmaster, John Edward Bowle? Did anybody discuss it, in this
refuge of closet gays? Or had Angus really done the unforgivable thing, and
made what Bloomsbury would have called a vulgar Bow-Wow noise?
Angus was unrepentant. He liked to claim that his BHS performance had
led to his only appearance ever, on 1 July 1976, in the Business Diary of *The
Times*.

Angus's words of thanks to Farrer on his seventieth birthday celebration,
however, had been more than formal. These two had been friends and
colleagues for many years – as Angus now revealed, they had first met way
back in 1938 or 1939 in a "very Bohemian house in Great Ormond
Street", where both had been acquainted with the slatternly caretaker,

known as Squalida Jones, and her drunken friends. "Oh Maud, she's been on the methylated!" was one of the phrases recalled from those days. Angus thanked Bowle for setting him on his course, and then he thanked Farrer for keeping him there – "such formal organisation, lack of repetition, felicity of language as my books possess I owe to David Farrer," he declared, and went on to describe his openness of mind, his willingness to embrace Angus's own experiments, his calm acceptance of Angus's queries about zoos, murders and pagan tombs. Angus offered an excellent example of Farrer's editorial tact – "She's one of the best female characters you've created, Angus, and that's why we must have only *one* specimen of her dialogue."

And he did mention the British Home Stores demonstration (muddling their name – he seemed to think they were called the Empire Stores): when he had described the scene to Farrer earlier that day, Angus said, Farrer's expression had seemed to say "I may be seventy, but do remember you are sixty-three!"

Angus, in some ways, was becoming less and less of an elder statesman: he was reverting, after his serious middle period, to the life of an *enfant terrible*. He himself was, he told the assembly at the Garrick, unlike Farrer, an "immensely impetuous character", and he had had cause, over the years, to be grateful for Farrer's amused, affectionate, occasionally irritated restraint.

★

In July 1976, Angus and Tony disappeared to Brittany for a couple of weeks' holiday, where Angus read a few unsolicited manuscripts from aspiring authors before returning to polish off Kipling. Angus struggled on, the end in sight, through an exceptionally hot dry summer punctuated by visits to Cedric Morris and Lett Haines at Benton End, to Norman Scarfe at Shingle Street, to Nicholas Brooke in Norwich. On Angus's birthday, Ian McEwan came to tea: "we sit round the table by the kitchen with him and Tony and an ex-lover who has arrived from London for the occasion. Angus is on top form – talking compulsively, first about his Kipling book which Tony is just typing up, then, when champagne appears, he indulges the wicked irony I'd almost forgotten, all breathless parenthetic qualification – 'two delightful ladies, well *quite* nice, I didn't know them *at all*, actually, I knew one . . .' "[19]

He finished his first draft, as he wrote to Peter Grose, on 21 August, and was about to take a short break – not a holiday, as he had speeches to write for conferences in Buxton and Brussels – after delivering copies to David Farrer and A.P. Watt. Then he would come back to revise.

The break was taken at The Chase at Sible Hedingham, as Tony flew off to visit his sister in Geneva. The household at the Chase remained a pleasant refuge, and Angus settled in there happily with Perkin Walker, Bob French's brother John and his wife Sheila, and their two children.

John and Sheila French have vivid memories of this interlude. They had arranged to spend the summer at The Chase while Bob French and Monty Turland were away, and were rather surprised and at first put out to find not one but two distinguished elderly bachelors in residence. They knew The Chase well and had expected to have it to themselves. They already knew Perkin Walker and had met Angus at Regents Park Terrace many times, but gin and tonic in NW1 was a different matter from five days under the same roof in the country, encumbered by their teenage boys and their Shetland sheepdog, Anteater. Martyn and Adrian would get on Angus's nerves, surely? The boys did not like the prospect of being told to keep quiet, and John and Sheila French took a portable TV to keep them out of the way.

They need not have worried. Angus had his earplugs, he explained, and anyway he and the boys struck up an immediate rapport. He would talk to Martyn for hours from his deckchair in the garden: Martyn listened, rapt, like a sketch for "The Boyhood of Raleigh". Together they would giggle as they cunningly evaded the washing-up. In the evenings there were games of Scrabble at which John French (a good linguist) excelled: Perkin and Angus, Anteater sitting on his knee, would squabble like schoolboys over every word. The generous and ample Sheila French did the cooking, and Angus and Perkin seemed to enjoy it enormously – they ate a lot of cakes between them, and on one occasion Angus helped himself to three – or was it five? – slices of date and apricot loaf. The garden, despite the drought, was looking fine, and they encouraged the petunias and roses with water siphoned off from the bath. The tomatoes ripened into a glorious excess. For Angus, this was perfect weather. John, as usual, fixed the lawnmower. He was good at that kind of thing.

And Angus talked and talked about Kipling. John French was very different from his brother Bob – Bob was pacifist, impractical, highly strung, and emotional, whereas John was in the regular army, a Lieutenant-Colonel with the Royal Engineers, and he admired Kipling's work as much as Angus did – with the exception of *Kim*, which he thought Angus overrated. John French had seen active service in Aden, Cyprus and India, and was to be recalled from the strategic reserve for the Gulf War: explosive devices were his stock-in-trade. It is easy to see why this handsome, gentle, moustached man of action appealed to Angus: he came from one of Kipling's own worlds, and spoke of it with an authority and an inner knowledge Angus had never had.

Angus not only talked: he listened. He stored away this useful source of professional information for future consultation, and when he departed, clutching a bulging bag of tomatoes, there were many expressions of mutual goodwill. It had been an unexpectedly happy week, and Angus was fortified to survive another six days alone at the cottage, with the support of the Reynoldses, Roger Gilliatt, Geoffrey Wright, Peter Hampshire and the Blackburnes. Maybe he even had the pleasure of waking up of a morning and feeling the relief of having nothing much to do.

*

The Kipling trail had been long and arduous, and it is not immediately clear why Angus had set off upon it. Dickens had seemed an obvious choice, but the Kipling connections were not so straightforward. Kipling's imperial politics and right-wing radicalism were deeply out of fashion, and Angus had never sympathised with them. On his 1975 journey to India he found that many Indians were puzzled by his quest. A few years earlier, Stephen Spender had been booed when he attempted to read from "Gunga Din", and Kipling was still more or less unmentionable in Calcutta. He was a dangerous topic: throughout his biography, Angus had to distance himself from his subject's opinions with words like "repugnant" and "repulsive", and in sentences like this: "In my own case, if I were to have to share Kipling's political standpoint to appreciate his artistry, this book could hardly have been written."[20] Why, then, write it?

The superficial answer which he often gave – and which he admitted was evasive – was territorial. He and Kipling shared Sussex and South Africa and, to a degree, a colonial childhood. But he also recognised that there was a deeper temperamental affinity which also had its roots in childhood. There was something in Kipling's relationship to his own childhood, to children, and through them to the world of animals that struck a deep psychic chord. Like Kipling, Angus set a very high value on play. Sneaking off from domestic chores with the French boys, playing Scrabble with Anteater on his knee, giggling with Perkin as they had done years ago at the Wilderness, he re-entered a harmless world which had never really existed, he became once more the spoiled child, the little Sahib.

Did Perkin Walker too escape into childhood? He apologised in a letter to Angus for having been bad-tempered during this week – although there is no evidence that he was. One wonders what Angus made of his oldest friend's inner life. In October 1976, Angus wrote a review for *Gay News* of two books, one on E.M. Forster, one on Lawrence of Arabia, in which he renewed his anti-Forster campaign – he attacks Forster for having said that Lawrence's bare, donnish, monastic room at Clouds Hill was "the real framework" of Lawrence's spirit, without mentioning the pertinent fact that it was in this room that Lawrence hired a bewildered fellow recruit, John Bruce, to beat him until the blood ran. Bruce had been reluctant to perform this task, but Lawrence had invented a persuasive fantasy in which a mythical sinister rich uncle had insisted on this punishment. To Angus, the room at Clouds Hill looked like a torture cell. Violence, sadism, masochism, and the soldierly virtues of endurance – these were all part of the Kipling story.

Kipling himself had not been a spoiled child – or not for very long. He had been separated from his parents at the age of six, sent back to England, and thrown upon the not very tender mercy of Mrs Holloway ("Aunty Rosa"), his not very loving landlady at Southsea, whose home he remembered as The House of Desolation. ("Loving" is one of the adjectives that Angus uses with a peculiar insistence, and sometimes quite obtrusively: it is particularly noticeable in the Kipling biography. It is tempting to think that he inherited it from his Christian Science childhood.) Those years at Southsea, brilliantly evoked in Kipling's story "Baa Baa Black Sheep", had been for him the equivalent of Dickens's time in the blacking factory – a wound, a creative spur, an impulse to ambition. There is no exact parallel in the life of Angus. Unlike many of the little orphans of the Raj who spent their holidays at Ashampstead, he tells us that he was indulged, petted, kept if anything too near his parents rather than cast too far away. Nor was Captain Wilson's regime as harsh as that over which the mild Captain Holloway was obliged to preside. Betty Wilson was no Aunty Rosa, branding her charges as "Liar" and speaking of hellfire.

But Angus clearly felt a kinship with Kipling. As a small child he knew insecurity and fear. Like little Rudyard, he had been inky, untidy, impractical: like Rudyard, he had been given to sudden imperious rages – Kipling's three-year-old warning to people to get out of the way because "I am an angry Rud" is a line that could well have been delivered by that truculent Bexhill baby. And like Rudyard, the unsportsmanslike Angus had eventually found release and won admiration from his peers through story-telling and creative fantasy.

The period of Kipling's youth was the period of the youth of Angus's father. They were both born in 1865, within a month of one another. Both had haunted the music halls of Villiers Street, and the Barrack Room Ballads owed a great deal to the songs Kipling had heard there, the songs that Angus himself had loved as a boy. Both knew the seedy side of

London, the City of Dreadful Night: both smoked incessantly. Willie Johnstone-Wilson liked to talk of the second sight of the Celts, to which he laid some claim: there was a similar strain in the Kipling/Macdonald ancestry, which was to emerge occasionally in Rudyard's fiction. (And in Angus's – his story of a haunting by a child, "A Little Companion", perhaps owes something to his admiration for Kipling's First World War story, "Swept and Garnished", about Frau Ebermann's visitation by dead Belgian children in her comfortable Berlin flat.) Kipling and his family had wintered in South Africa for several years at the end of the century, only six years after Maud Caney had married and come to Richmond: it was one of the ironies of Kipling's not wholly satisfactory relationship with South Africa that he never got to know Natal, where he would have found not only his "beloved Indians" but also "an Englishness and an anti-Boer sentiment that would have warmed his heart" – and keen Kipling fans amongst the Caneys and their friends.[21]

Both Angus and Kipling had known the early happiness of protected colonial life – the loving Kaffir George, the loving ayah, and the exciting snakes coiled mysteriously yet safely beneath the verandah – and both had been expelled from it into the colder world of Self-Help Britain. They knew the swords and assegais that hung proudly on the walls of the studies of parents and schoomasters. Writing about Kipling gave Angus an opportunity to explore his own colonial ancestry, as well as his responses to the lost boys and the dreadfully elegant undernourished youths who had haunted and teased him in Morocco and on his Asian tours.

> What is your name? What is your name?
> The chappering children scream.
> But "Wilson" does not satisfy:
> Impatiently they cry,
> What does it mean? What does it mean?[22]

Kim wondered, "Who is Kim?": the boys wondered, what is Wilson?: Wilson wondered, who is Wilson? In the magical Ariel-like figure of Kim, the Little Friend of All the World, Angus found some sort of reconciliation of warring sympathies in himself, and a form of redemption for all the Lost Boys. Kipling offered him this escape.*

Lecturing on Kipling in Delaware, Angus used a compelling phrase – "the traumas and delights of the nursery floor". This reverts to a period that is pre-schoolboy, pre-Stalky, pre-Ashampstead, pre-Westminster. It goes back to those nursery games with Pat and Colin, to the world of the

---

* Angus wrote about Kipling's love of children in a mysterious and very late letter to Sylvère Monod: see p.641.

dressing-up box. And from that world had grown a whole elaborate artistic fantasy. There was an element of sadism in his fantasy. Perhaps Angus was attracted by his alter ego in Kipling – by the schoolboy cruelties, the tortures, the bullying horrors he had dreaded and been spared at Westminster. To Angus, Kipling, the schoolboy with the premature moustache, was Daisy captivated by Steerforth, Daisy captivating Steerforth, and Steerforth himself, all in one.

Throughout Angus's work runs a disturbing strain of preoccupation with sadistic violence towards humans and animals. The violence is not condoned, but it is present. He recognised this strain in the works of Richardson, of Laclos, of Diderot, of John Cowper Powys: the trapped and snarling animal, the trapped and tortured human body in the cellar, fascinated him. Fragmentary notes for a lecture read "the evil of power and violence which I feel I can appreciate because they both attract me greatly. And as my parents fell through the coalholes so I see civilization as precarious, a jungle, or a zoo, in which we die if we keep without love but we also die if we do not keep . . . The Jungle. The Ice. The Ice." (The reference to his parents here would seem to be to a psychoanalytical dream in which he saw his parents walking down a London street and falling through the coal holes.) Violence and torture entered his fantasies, as they do those of many: often, as a young man, he could not resist wounding with his tongue, and even in his later fiction he admitted that he could not help giving his less intelligent characters some brilliant and occasionally inappropriate lines of repartee – he delighted too much in the sharp riposte. The phrase "s.m" recurrs frequently in the notes for his final novel, made while Kipling was still in production: "mental s.m" seems to have worried him particularly, as though he feared his own powers.

It is no accident that he picked out Kipling's periodic virulence for anxious comment: one of Kipling's sentences about ageing American womanhood – "the trained sweetness and unction in the otherwise hardish, ignorant eyes; the slightly open, slightly flaccid mouth; the immense unconscious arrogance, the immoveable certitude of mind, and the other warning signs in the poise of the broad-cheeked head" – could have come straight out of an early Angus Wilson story.[23] (We might recall here that, according to Angus's friend Murray Arbeid, Angus had a particular gift for the imitation of American matrons: and this despite the fact that, unlike Dickens and Kipling, he had no quarrel with America, and enjoyed his visits there. Indeed, he was proud of the fact that he had visited all but three of the states – Dakota, Oklahoma and Hawaii: nor can we doubt the sincerity of his expressions of enjoyment, for as we shall see he confided them to his notebook.)

Kipling influenced Angus's imagination from an early age. A curious and suggestive similarity may be noted in the plots of one of Kipling's finest late stories, "Dayspring Mishandled", and of *Anglo-Saxon Attitudes*, both of which turn on a cruel and deliberate scholarly hoax which has unforeseen and disastrous consequences: in the Kipling story, a rival in love spends years producing a Chaucer forgery which he hopes will destroy the man who insulted the woman he loved and failed to win – a parallel to Gilbert Stokesay's more casual but equally cruel planting of the pagan member in the Christian tomb. Such adult Stalkyisms, which go beyond the mere prank, were clearly once again in Angus's mind when planning the novel he began in Rome and never finished.

There was a cruel streak in both writers, but they handled their own temptations to cruelty very differently – in Angus's case, with much more seeking after self-knowledge. For men so unlike in their domestic lives they had curious temperamental affinities. Kipling had one nervous breakdown, and lived on the edge of others: he wrote with great insight about *fin-de-siècle* and war-induced nervous exhaustion and collapse, experienced within his own family through the mental suffering of his sister Trix. For him, too, the ice was very thin. Anarchy and a hereditary depression were never far away. Both Angus and Kipling were subject to unreasonable bursts of temper, which in Kipling's case made their way far too often into the works as well as the life, so that again and again Angus feels obliged to apologise for his protagonist's mawkishness, cruelty, and outbursts of unreasonable rage: the reverse side of this was a sentimental crudity to which Angus himself, a much more self-knowing artist, was less given.

The childish, simple cruelties and practical jokes of Stalky's world and of the Indian club would not, one might have thought, have appealed to Angus at all, and yet he seems to understand even these: discussing the story "A Friend's Friend", with its description of the brutal humiliation of an outsider, he says, "It is an anger we meet again throughout Kipling's work. It is a strange note of sudden intense hatred of someone as the representative of disorder or sometimes of evil mixed with an elaborate schoolboy ritual humour which when it succeeds . . . makes completely original farce, but when it fails . . . embarrasses the reader as would a sudden loss of temper on a social occasion."[24] Angus sympathises with these moments of loss of control: in life, if not in art, he was subject to them himself. And to him they represent an "almost hysteric sense of fragility and menace".

Maybe there is no need to probe further into this affinity. Maybe already there has been too much probing. Suffice it to say that Angus responded strongly to Kipling's fears of disorder in a bleak, godless, post-Darwinian world: he believed that Kipling, like himself, remained an agnostic, finding no comfort in faith. There were other bonds – an intermittent longing to get out of claustrophobic, class-ridden Britain, coupled with a deep love of the English landscape: a simultaneous attraction to and horror of the wandering, feckless, gipsy grasshopper life: a simple hatred of the English winter: a fondness despite all for some aspects of club life and ritual – all these suggest themselves. (The homosexual club, the Homintern, in some way echoes the classless Freemasonry that had so usefully extended Kipling's social range.)

For both, the refrain of "Shut, shut, shut the door, my darling" alternated with the need to jump onto an ocean liner or an aeroplane. Kipling wrote of the South Downs and the Romney marshes and Hadrian's Wall while staying in a Colonial Dutch house on Cecil Rhodes's estate at the Cape: Angus wrote of an English New Town on a hotel roof in Morocco. Writers are, as Angus suggests in his description of the composition of *Puck of Pook's Hill*, a paradoxical lot.

And it is hard to resist the notion that in his unusually sympathetic portrait of Kipling's American wife Carrie, so often blamed by outsiders for over-protecting her husband, Angus was paying a hidden tribute to Tony. He recognised that Tony's role was not always easy: perhaps Tony had succeeded even better than Carrie, who had "played with dignity, if not always with wisdom, the difficult role that is seldom perfectly played – the celebrity's helpmate."[25] Tony had, through the Kipling years, been an increasingly indispensable helpmate – chauffeur, photographer, research assistant, organiser, route planner. He had spent many hours in libraries, working on Kipling material. And as helpmate he had been asked to play roles that wives are rarely asked to play. He had waited patiently in the car at UEA, at banquets and restaurants and meetings and embassies: for hours he had sat with the chauffeurs in the pouring rain at Windsor Castle, waiting for Angus to emerge from his evening's entertainment with the Queen (June 1973), and on another occasion he had waited outside the French Embassy, listening to the badinage of the chauffeurs as they watched their colleagues try to negotiate their huge vehicles through the narrow bollards – "No, he's never going to make it, that one" – and comparing notes on which embassies entertained the chauffeurs best. "Not even a glass of water" was the verdict on the French. And so it often was – Angus drank champagne, but not even a glass of water for Tony. Tony never complained. He amused himself, with wisdom and dignity, as best he could.

★

Kipling had set Angus and Tony off along the Great Trunk Road, but he had also kept them at home. The last year of research had tied them to England, and they were still tied. In the autumn of 1976 Angus longed – and at first planned – to get back to Ceylon, and expressed his hope of getting there in many a letter. He even sounded out the possibility of writing a travel book or series of travel articles about Ceylon to support his trip. His nineteen-year-old great-nephew Mark Davies had set off on his Grand Tour the year before, in the summer of 1975, armed with many useful addresses from Uncle Angus, and had sent back encouraging reports of his reception across the continents – like Marco Polo he had departed from Venice, where had he boldly deposited his warm clothing at Peggy Guggenheim's (she did not seem *very* pleased to take it in, but never mind), and had then made his way on to Ruth Jhabvala in New Delhi, where her teenage daughters gave him a sightseeing tour in the ambassadorial car. On to the Maharajah of the Laundry Basket, who accommodated him in unusual luxury and encouraged him to play snooker and table tennis with his son Jyoti amidst the stuffed tigers: over dinner, true to form, the Maharajah produced Angus's card and said "I might just ask: please, who exactly *is* this Angus Wilson?"

Mark Davies reached Sri Lanka in December 1975, and contacted Lalith Senanayake, who held an honorary position with a Sri Lankan wildlife organisation: Lalith made him welcome, invited Mark and his travelling companion to stay at his flat in Colombo, and showed them round the city, the zoo, and the neighbouring countryside. In Goa, Mark was received by a stoned and drunken eccentric whose heavy consumption of Goanese rum alarmed his abstemious visitor: in Bombay, by Dina Mehta, whose little maid was convinced that this tall lean handsome bearded stranger was Jesus Christ. These anecdotes, relayed home from grateful great-nephew to amused uncle, had renewed Angus's thirst for the East. Clearly *Magic* had not caused lasting offence in Colombo: he hoped to get back there for the winter.

He did not make it. The Kipling research dragged on, with more visits to the Victoria and Albert Museum and the Kipling parents' home at Tisbury, interspersed with talks at Buxton (on Powys), Harrow, Haberdashers' Aske's and Stockwell College. In October (the weekend of 22–24) he went to a jolly conference at Ross Priory, an eighteenth-century mansion on the shores of Loch Lomond: this was the annual meeting of University Teachers of English in Scotland. Angus spoke on the first evening on "problems of criticism and teaching for a freelance writer" and chaired a discussion the following morning. According to Dr Hilda Spear of Dundee, and Paddy Lyons, late of UEA and now at Glasgow, it was a very convivial weekend. Angus told Lyons – Restoration scholar and Irish Gay Marxist – that his lecture equipment would consist of a "diamond tiara, a megaphone to catch the pearls of wisdom, large specs, and a false nose to make people laugh" – he did his libertarian act, to the delight of the audience. He was the comic turn. Dr Spear recalls talking about Kipling and the poets of the First World War, about whom she was to publish a volume (*Remembering, We Forget*, 1979) and attending a late-night party at the Glasgow home of Professor Alan Sandison of Strathclyde. Charles Palliser (author of the Dickensian mystery, *The Quincunx*) remembers talking about the Chicago New Aristotelians, Angus's accountant, and the disconcerting "irony that poverty meant that the bodies of Indian peasants were more beautiful because more slender than was common in the West so that what one felt was compassion mingled with desire . . . he also mentioned pornographic photographs taken in India in which whole families of thin, sad-faced people were shot engaging in every variety of incestuous sexual activity . . . I think he wasn't just trying to shock. I think he was fascinated by the complexity of his own responses to things. And I think he valued truth so highly that he felt it right and even necessary to talk about them."[26]

Angus was such a success that invitations to speak all over Scotland poured in as a result of his visit and had to be declined on Kipling grounds – years later, in 1981, a lecturer who had attended the 1976 conference still remembered it, and invited Angus to address the Scottish Homosexual Rights Group – again, he had to decline, saying he would be in the United States.[27]

He finally delivered the revised Farrer-approved text on 8 November 1976 to Viking. He was anxious to start work on a new novel, but worried, as Tony's journal notes, that the novel was finished as a "paying art form". He had to subsidise himself somehow. Lecturing in the UK was not very profitable – twenty pounds here, fifty pounds there if you were lucky, sometimes nothing at all. Lecturing abroad could be more rewarding, though on one occasion Tony got into a muddle about an offer from Austria – it looked wonderfully attractive until he realised he had misplaced the decimal point in Austrian currency. America, however, was another matter. Angus had sounded out the possibilities of teaching and lecturing in the United States in 1978 and 1979, through Ruth Emery of Anglo-American Associates, and accepted an invitation to Delaware for the autumn of 1977. This would be financially rewarding, but he worried that the teaching would interfere with his writing. Sustaining the right balance between teaching and writing was almost impossible: he was to write to John Broadbent at UEA from Delaware to enquire whether his retirement really was compulsory (it was) – his pension was, as he increasingly realised, negligible – yet part of him longed to teach less, not more.

Depression and paranoia were never far away; he worried that he had not heard from Ann Fleming, that Isaiah Berlin had cut him in the London Library. He dined with Bill Golding at the Athenaeum on 5 November: Golding was pessimistic, drinking, and wondering whether we had been right to fight the war. Angus and Tony spent the weekend with the Priestleys, where again the theme was money: why did Spender go on trying to write poetry when it didn't pay, Priestley wondered? Why didn't he try prose? Everyone was growing old: Philippe Jullian had a disastrous fire at the Moulin de Thiou at Chaumes in October which had destroyed many of his precious paintings and hangings, and as a result had become more than ever dependent on his Moroccan servant and companion, Hamoud. Angus, who did not hear the news until December, and then only through gossip, wrote in deep sympathy. "My dear, if this is true, I am so sorry, for it was a beautiful place and you had there so many fascinating objects . . ."[28]

On 17 November Angus met Jonathan Raban in the Athenaeum and over dinner confided some of his anxieties about his work: was he now too old and out of touch with the world to continue writing novels? Of course not, said Jonathan, not taking the matter very seriously, thinking it was just the mood of an unhappy moment, or a small drama cooked up to enliven the conversation. All Angus's letters of this period – turning down invitations from gay groups, literary societies, summer schools – mention that he is planning to make time to write a novel in the following year. But an undercurrent of uncertainty flows beneath these assertions. He had lost confidence. It was all very well to celebrate him, as Carol and Tim Manderson* did at a dinner for eight on 25 November, with egg mousse and devilled sauce as if by magic, fillet of pork off the map, orange dodo fool and late call for cheese, washed down by Château Hemlock 1967: Angus rose to the occasion, enjoyed himself, sparkled, charmed the Mandersons' son Dallas and shy teenage daughter Charlotte, and then no doubt went home to brood.

In early December he and Tony went off for a few days to Nice, to see Clive and Lucie, and to talk about the disposal of Colin's small estate. Clive looked a little older at last, but Lucie looked ever younger: they were as chirpy as ever. Clive had an approaching prostate operation, but by and large the boy who had been considered too tender for public-school

---

* Sales Director of Heinemann and Secker & Warburg, and a long-standing admirer of Angus's work. He was also responsible for re-launching E.F. Benson.

education was doing well, still shrewd with his money talk and his tax
avoidances, and Lucie was still careful not to overtip the waiter. Their life
was spent gadding about from Spain to the Algarve to Andorra to the
South of France. Angus credited Clive's business sense to his South African
blood and Lucie's French thrift: he himself was still all too prone to the
extravagant gesture, and it never occurred to his many younger friends that
he could not – should not – afford them. He looked, in Mary Gilliatt's
phrase, the very model of a British major novelist, and everyone thought
he could afford to behave like one.

His net income – £3,814 – for the year 1976 had been low, his expenses
high. Writing a biography was an expensive business, time-consuming,
with slow returns. Angus was worried. He was always worried. It was all
very well for Priestley to say "Try prose" – he'd been doing that for years.
Perhaps Public Lending Right, which had passed its second reading in
October and been defeated on its third in November, might make a
difference – if ever it was introduced.

Christmas 1976 was spent in Suffolk, but on Tuesday, 28 December
Angus and Tony came to London, to deliver more chunks of revised
Kipling to Secker's, and to dine with Margaret Drabble in Heath Hurst
Road. She had been to stay with them for a night at Felsham Woodside in
late November, self-invited as so many of their guests were, and had been
generously entertained at the cottage (where a mouse had invaded the
kitchen during dinner, and been noisily crunched) and at Hintlesham, the
most glamorous restaurant she had ever visited; Angus had walked her
round the woods talking wisely to her about the folly of those who tried to
live in a *ménage à trois*. He had tried it once himself, he said, and it hadn't
worked and couldn't work. She retaliated by inviting them for a meal: they
had chosen the date. It was a little close to the traumas of Christmas, as one
of the guests, the practical Dusty Wesker, pointed out; the shops had been
shut for days and people were getting tired of leftovers. But all seemed at
first to go well – the guests were Angus and Tony, Richard Rowson and
Julian Mitchell, and David Simpson, then Director of British Amnesty, of
which Angus was an active member. What an excess of handsome men,
said Dusty: was this the new-style dinner party?

If it was, it all went very wrong. Before the Weskers arrived, Julian
Mitchell, who had seen Angus on excellent form at Raleigh Trevelyan's in
October when he was still full of plans to escape to Ceylon, asked Angus
how his novel was going, and said that he had heard from Jonathan Raban
that he was anxious about it. This, says Julian, was ill-taken by Angus,
though Julian did not realise it at the time. The evening progressed with,
Julian recalls, much rival boasting about who was doing what for how

much money: I recollect little of this as I had my head in the oven for much of the time. During dinner (some form of casserole, I think) Richard Rowson spoke about Julian's forthcoming appearance on *Any Questions*, and Angus and I both said what an awful experience we had found it: Wesker said he had been on the *Brains Trust*: then Angus said he had been on the *Brain of Asia* with a pipe-smoking Alan Bullock. (This BBC radio programme was in fact called *Question Time: London Calling Asia*, on which Angus appeared seven times in 1954–5.) Julian, partly to include David Simpson, said Angus should appeal to Mrs Gandhi for the release of prisoners there, and at this point, Julian's diary relates:

> Angus suddenly stood up and announced he was leaving, I had done nothing but attack him from the moment I'd arrived. For a moment I think we all thought he was joking – but he wasn't. I went to him, apologising profusely, etc – decided I'd better leave the room, as he was now highly excited, and I seemed to be the cause: so I left, wondering who would come and fetch me back, which Maggie did, very shortly. I was shattered – he'd taken every remark I'd made and twisted it in the most paranoid way. But I had enough cool to wonder even then whether the trouble wasn't simply that he wasn't getting enough undivided attention: performer's paranoia, I mean. Anyway, I went back duly, and after dinner he came up and hugged and said he was sorry, he was an old man, very worried about his career, and why did we only ever meet at dinner parties, he was so frightened with Wesker and Maggie and me, etc. So we were reconciled; except our conversation then became more and more false and stilted . . .

Arnold Wesker also, as it happens, was keeping a diary, and he too recorded the evening, writing on 30 December:

> At dinner there was an incident. Julian, to my right, upset Angus, to my left. It flared up, suddenly. Julian was saying how good Angus was at imitating Indians and was urging him to imitate one. Angus seemed not to be in the mood – I rather got the feeling he didn't want to appear frivolous in front of me, though God knows why, *he* was the celebrity, the elder statesman, and a very delightful one too. I felt so ashamed that I'd not read any of his novels. Must amend. And Julian must have egged him to his imitations beyond endurance for he suddenly stood and said: 'Very well then I'll go.' We were all at once concerned.
>   "I'm sorry, well yes I *am* sensitive, and Julian should know this. Why does he do it? He's been doing it all evening, right from

when I came in, and just now saying 'I think Angus should be head of the world.'

I tried to assure him that was said in affection, but he was not prepared to believe it. Dusty chimed in to try to reassure him. Julian himself was quite upset and went round the table to apologise without reservation. Maggie was quite at ease and carried on serving the meal, and when Angus apologised to her she said oh it was all right, a little bit of drama was what we all needed. Something I'd never have dared say, but Angus took it very well. He became pacified finally, though remaining very frothy. Then Julian left the room. I said I hoped *he* wasn't now leaving. But it seemed not. Tony Garrett tried to explain it by saying Julian had been having flops recently with his novels and was a little sour. Maggie said he couldn't possibly mean anything serious because 'he thinks you the most wonderful person in the world, Angus.'

'Well I'm sure that's very kind of him but why then does he do it? It's not the first time.'

The evening wasn't the same afterwards. I talked to Angus about the problems I was having writing prose; then we talked about political prisoners in Russia, and about Yevtushenko. And over coffee they seemed to make friends again.

I myself also remember the outburst vividly, and how unexpected it was: Angus had jumped up from the kitchen-dining-table and stormed out into the tiny kitchenette, whither I pursued him and found him banging his head upon the refrigerator: then I pursued Julian, who had fled to the drawing-room. I remember saying to Angus that he couldn't behave like that, he was as bad as my parents who had just been with me for several days over Christmas, my mother quarrelling and squabbling with and abusing my father as was her wont until we all burst into tears. "I'm old enough to *be* your father, dear," Angus retorted angrily as I forced him back into his chair.

I was less put out by the incident at the time than I was later. I suppose I thought it was all part of inevitable Christmas misery, and of a more interesting nature than that which I endured yearly with the visit of my family: at the time, I am told, I said cheerfully to Richard Rowson (himself a born – or perhaps a made? – peace-maker) that at least the explosion had added a bit of adrenalin.

Why had it happened?

Julian Mitchell believes it was associated with Angus's unfounded feeling that we younger ones were all richer and more successful than he was, and that Julian had abandoned the novel for the theatre and television, thus in some way prostituting himself. This was a subject which had been voiced between them on other occasions, though never so emotionally and acrimoniously. Angus himself had failed in the theatre, and here was Julian talking familiarly about his television prospects (in November he had sent Angus an invitation to a BAFTA preview of a new play) and the fact that Gielgud was going to appear in *Half-Life* at the National. Julian himself was sensitive about being accused of "selling out" on the novel – and this despite the fact that he had written two volumes of (admittedly pseudonymous) gay fiction for which he could not find a publisher. His last published novel, *The Undiscovered Country*, had been a bold experimental work mixing fact and fiction: its satiric-surreal-parodistic-erotic last section, "The New Satyricon", had some prefiguring of themes and techniques in *As if By Magic*. It had been published in 1968, to critical acclaim but moderate sales, and Julian Mitchell thereafter had successfully devoted his considerable energies to stage adaptations from Ivy Compton-Burnett, screenplays, and a TV series about Lady Randolph Churchill.

A feeling that Julian had deserted the higher calling was certainly an element in Angus's outburst, but I believe there were others, of which post-Christmas fatigue was one: another was the extreme unsuitability of my small and very noisy dining area (dining-room it is not) for accommodating two voluble guests. Angus and Julian both shouted: so, I daresay, did I. Given more space and thicker carpets – indeed *any* carpets – we might not have behaved so badly. (John Alston confirms Julian Mitchell's suspicion that it was wiser not to invite Angus to dinner with other "stars" – he was happier and better company without competition from Angus McBean or Frederick Ashton.)

I dwell on this in some detail as it is the only time I myself ever witnessed Angus losing his temper. The evening had unfortunate consequences, for despite various attempts at reconciliation Julian felt the breach was never wholly healed. Angus wrote to me immediately, saying (31 December 1976):

> My dear Maggie, What a way I behaved and how my spoilt
> childhood reverberates back at me and has done all my life at the
> most unsuitable occasions and among the people I most care
> about. I liked Arnold W. just as much as I thought I should – he's
> fascinating – and Mr Amnesty (he'll forgive me for so calling him)
> is a quite exceptionally interesting and subtle person to talk to. It
> was but for my folly a wonderful evening. I have writen to Julian
> whom, of course, I love dearly. But – needing a holiday *so* much
> as I do (and being equally concerned that Tony needs one equally

desperately though he never shows a sign) things that I don't
usually regard – Julian's odd fierceness and heavy teasing when
he's in company – take on sinister shades for me – and I feel alone
and frightened. So please forgive me and thank you. Ever yours,
Angus."

To Julian Mitchell he had written even more immediately, on the day
before:

Dear Julian, I love you greatly. I am in a bit of a bad way – very
much in need of getting right away for a pure holiday – yet
there's still Kipling pictures to see to and the fucking anthology
and, altho' money at last has been settled for the next four years
(thank God) it has been a great worry. Also I have terrible lack of
confidence about my new book (but not really – only while I'm
so tired) and, in fact, I should not think about it until I've been
away and had a rest. Ceylon's cancellation was a great blow.
Given all this, my old spoilt child temperament tends to erupt (a
thing it has done all my life through sweet days and sour ones) and
I break into temper tantrums. It built up that evening because I
felt so out of it with you and Arnold W (I liked him very much
by the way) with all the theatre talk of productions here, there and
everywhere (or so it seemed it to me) and my knowing fuck all
about the theatre today. Tony rightly says – how do I think he
feels at 101 literary parties. But still I did feel isolated and then
frightened. Given this, I have to say that you who have been so
kind to me in the past as I can never forget do on social occasions
(I know not why) treat me (and perhaps some others, I don't
know) in a jolly, blustering, legpulling sort of hockey mistress way
that is so strangely unlike you that I don't know why it happens.
You say 'Hm?' interrogatively in a challenging manner and laugh
loudly on what seems a very contemptuous note. I don't think it's
my imagination – altho', of course, if I weren't in a bad state I
should know it had no relation to you at all. Love to you both and
every crossed finger for Sir John G and the archeologist which
sounds a quite splendid theme, Angus.[29]

"Alone and frightened" – "isolated and frightened" – they are strange
words from one who must surely have known that all around that table
admired him and how much some of them loved him. (David Simpson,
meeting Angus for the first time, was most impressed by his professional
grasp of human rights issues worldwide.) Julian Mitchell's teasing manner,
to which Angus refers, has never alarmed me, though I have been on its

receiving end: and it had seemed to me, on this occasion, to be part of an affectionate and intimate game. "Joshing", Renée Hampshire might have called it: when Angus joshed her, as he frequently did, she enjoyed it. But Angus, one cannot doubt, felt threatened by Mitchell's style. Jungle and ice, ice and jungle. And maybe Angus did have some reason to feel impoverished in our company: checking my own accounts for that year, I was surprised to find that I had earned £12,216 gross, compared with Angus's £11,287. I had had a good year, and so had Julian Mitchell, who earned £14,000 gross: but none of us had done as well as Wesker, whose income was £24,000. I would have assumed that Angus was earning twice as much as me. I would have been wrong.*

★

Angus needed, as he had said, to get away. January 1977 was spent in tidying up Kipling and lunching and dining with UEA friends and contacts, Rose Tremain, Jonathan Courage, Simon Edwards and Paddy Lyons: with Geoffrey Wright, Bentley Bridgewater, Michael Slater and his entourage, the Gilliatts, the Kilmartins, with designers Murray Arbeid and Freddie Fox. Angus spent a few days in Sussex on research for the new novel, and dined with his old friend George Painter, now living in Hove, on 10 January. He gave a performance at the Thumb Gallery in D'Arblay Street in London on 27 January, to launch a Penguin re-issue of the short stories with cover designs by Tony Moore: the invitations, in two tones of blue, invited guests to "Blue Suede Shoes: an Evening with Angus Wilson". Angus read from *A Bit off the Map*, brilliantly mimicking Cyril Connolly and Colin Wilson, to an audience which included Connolly's in-laws, Anthony and Tanya Hobson, and assorted young people in gumboots and evening dress. Angus went off to dinner at Langan's Brasserie, with gallery owner Francis Kyle, a Harper's lady, and a poet, and the next day he and Tony set off not for the dream island of Ceylon – that had to wait another year – but for Malaga.

They had thought to spend time in the south, but many of the old places seemed spoiled. The old-fashioned hotels had been torn down or done up, the weather was poor, the roads were bad. They stayed at first in Jerez de la Frontera, visiting Seville and Cadiz, then moved on for some days to Murcia. Alicante, Angus noted in his tiny Collins diary, was awful, and there was a very bad-tempered girl at the Phoenician excavations, but on the other hand he did take note of a very beautiful cat. It almost tempted them to stay on, but instead they drove north and settled in Madrid, where

* The pound was worth £3.19 in 1976 by comparison with 1990.

they saw their friends William and Sonia Chislett. And on Monday, 14 February 1977, Angus had a vision.

★

The vision was not religious: it was architectural. Architectural dreams had long possessed Angus. Next to literature, architecture was the art to which he responded most strongly. In a curious little chart drawn up while preparing his next novel, he listed his own ratings in two columns labelled "response" and "capacity of response" – to gardens (high in both), wildlife (high in both), buildings (high in capacity, fairly high in response), furniture (lowish, and very low), historical sense (high in both), pictures (medium and medium to low), organisation (medium) money (very low, and "very low to terror") and people (high with frequent lows). Music he did not mention at all.

His visits to Venice, to Rome, to Austria, to France, and to the churches, cathedrals and great country houses of Britain had given him much delight, and he was beginning to realise, as the wheel came full circle, how much he owed to those early, pre-conscious days in Westminster. Some of his most interesting *Observer* reviews had been on architectural themes, and Mary Gilliatt records that he had an unusually sharp eye for detail: although content himself to live in an artistic muddle, he was quick to notice the mistakes of others. Tony, too, had developed a remarkably good eye for a building: some of their happiest times together had been spent pottering around the countryside with their Pevsner in the glove compartment.

So Angus was predisposed to receive a vision. It was inspired by the Royal Palace of Aranjuez, which stands on the banks of the River Tagus about half way between Madrid and Toledo. The palace and its magnificent and extensive gardens provide a favourite weekend outing from Madrid, particularly during summer, but even in February the pink and white of the vast and imposing building glowed. It was built by the Bourbons in the eighteenth century and its slightly faded splendour – room after room of damask, marble, silk, gilt, porcelain, chinoiserie – spoke of power, possession, decay. The rococo excess enchanted. Angus had trained himself to appreciate Lasdun and Frank Lloyd Wright, but he responded even more powerfully to the elaborate, dangerous, over-reaching ambitions of the baroque and the rococo. What would it have been like, he wondered as he sat in the great formal gardens, to have such riches at one's command? What perils, what anxieties, what temptations would beset the twentieth-century owner of such a heritage?

This was the germ of *Setting the World on Fire*. It is hard to say how decisively transforming was the vision of Aranjuez, how much plotting had preceded it. Angus's notes for this novel are worryingly profuse, and it is difficult, though perhaps not impossible, to date them all (some he dates himself, but some he clearly re-annotated). He was to work on the book for more than two years, delivering his first draft in the August of 1979, and some scenes and incidents in it are clearly drawn from earlier European visits – in particular his visits to Venice and Rome when he had been appalled and intrigued by the Marcheses and Principessas who found life "so bo-aring", by his speculations about the high life as lived in the Villa Emo at Treviso. Other material accumulated during the year as he and Tony went to look at country houses in England and Scotland. But his mind also went back to the distant past – to Westminster days, to the Abbey and the cloisters and Dean's Yard, to the secret tunnel that was said to run from Ashampstead to – well, who knew where it ran, or why? – to the hidden caves quarried beneath the National Library of Wales at Aberystwyth, to the great lantern of the Reading Room beneath which he had worked for so many years, to the green Siberian marble bowl in Merton chapel, a gift of Tsar Alexander I, a bowl large enough to bathe a baby in.

And yet again he found his imagination returning to the Crittalls and the Walkers. The powerful dynasty of the Crittalls was always in his mind. There was not only Perkin Walker, ever present either in Regent's Park Terrace or at the Chase, although no longer in the best of health: there was Walker's step-aunt May, who lived nearby at Great Easton, in Essex, in a Crittall-designed house with Crittall-designed furniture: there was Perkin's scholarly cousin Elizabeth ("Biddy") Crittall, whom he had known since schooldays, and had helped in the Reading Room when she was working on the Victoria County History of Wiltshire. There was Perkin's not-very-happy sister, and her many dogs, and Perkin's nephews. Angus brooded on them all, as intensely as he had brooded on his own family. Could he imagine a family even grander than the Crittalls, with wealth so fabulous that their problems would soar into another dimension?

He thought he could. He had met the old county families in Suffolk, with their braying laughs, their double-barrelled names, their Wodehouse cries of "What? Eh, what?" He knew their rose gardens, their hunters, their paintings. He had been round Ickworth so often that he knew it as though it were his own. He had presented an honorary degree to Ketton-Cremer of Felbrigg Hall. He had watched the *nouveau riche* Robert Carrier restore Hintlesham Hall from the picturesque decay into which it had fallen. He had played a part in trying to restore the Hintlesham Festival. He had listened to Ann Fleming's accounts of her purchase of Warneford Place at Sevenhampton, near Swindon, in Wiltshire, and watched its transformation into Sevenhampton Place, complete with a garden full of urns, and, as she wrote to Angus in the spring of 1974, "too many bright yellow Daffs". (Warneford was, unfortunately, the name of the local mental hospital, and Sevenhampton Place sounded much better.) He had visited the eccentric gay left-wing Lord Faringdon of Buscot Park, who had insisted to visiting Russians that they should not tip the staff – "*pas de pourboires, s'il vous plaît, nous aussi nous sommes socialistes.*" He had never been to Renishaw, but he had heard many stories of the Sitwells. He had spent a night at Chatsworth and visited Harold Acton at La Pietra. His new admirer, Max Egremont, lived at Petworth House in Sussex, and Angus and Tony were to visit him there on a couple of occasions. Kipling had brought him into contact with Sussex gentry and grand houses in Wiltshire, and Ann Thwaite and Frances Hodgson Burnett between them had given him the entrée to Penshurst and an introduction to Lord de L'Isle. His old pre-war friend, architect Ian McCallum, had created the American Museum with its fine gardens at Claverton Manor, overlooking the Avon valley just outside Bath; McCallum, the Museum's first director, had worked on the project from 1959 onwards and Angus and Tony had visited several times, admiring the growing arboretum, the colonial herb garden, and the replica of George Washington's garden at Mount Vernon on the Potomac.

Could he "do" the English aristocracy, with its strange mixture of barbarian indifference to culture, its cultured obsession with its own history, its intermittent patronage of the arts, its occasional talented artistic sport? He thought he could. Ever eager to extend his fictional territory, he had already travelled a long way from South Kensington. There were high risks involved – he had said, in Japan in 1969, that he had "tried to cut out the more provincial aspects of my writing, but there's a limit to what I can do, because I have a particular kind of provincial mind and if I deserted all my provincialism then I would cease to exist."[30] But the risk might be worth it. He was fascinated by the fate of this caste which had clung on so tenaciously through rising income tax, death duties, drug scandals and the mockery of *Private Eye*.

The research promised to be entertaining. Angus and Tony returned from Spain on 18 February 1977, and one of their first social engagements was to attend the Memorial Service at St Margaret's, Westminster, for Cecil Roberts, who had died in late December, leaving Angus a crimson mandarin dressing-gown. Roberts and his chatter of the titled rich of Europe had gone forever, along with most of his best-selling novels and his hundreds of patriotic poems, broadcasts and speeches, but he had handsomely endowed the Manuscript Room of the new Public Library in his birthplace, Nottingham, and presented thirty years worth of diaries and correspondence to Nottingham University. A few pilgrims continued to visit his former home, Pilgrim Cottage at Henley-on-Thames – his account of his life there had run through twenty-four editions, but he himself had recognised that Immortality was Dead, along with the Collected Edition – he and his once-famous colleagues, H.V. Morton and Richard Church, had long been "wringing their hands in rage and anguish to see their life-work on the bonfire,"[31] and now he had at last joined his life-work.

Angus and Tony said their farewells to the game old boy, who had suffered both success and neglect with panache, lunched after the service with John Betjeman and Philip Dossé (of *Books and Bookmen*) and dined that evening with Peter Conradi, whose tales of his grandmother Florence Josephi-Conradi at once made their way into the notebooks. She was, says Peter, "an American, patrician, Edwardian; hence both, in AW's language, smart, & also vulgar in her interest in smartness. Her elder sister married a Sulzberger (owners of N.Y. Times) and her great-niece (I was at their odd wedding in Paris with my grandmother) married Adrian Berry (Telegraph) whose mother I think features in Waugh diaries. In the 1920s she briefly ran a shop with hand-painted (hers) lampshades. 'Beauchamp Place no doubt' said AW, who loved 'mapping' his friends and was struck that it was Hanover Square . . . her greatest coup was designing lampshades for Sandringham, and thereafter she had an imaginative, partly real relationship with Queen Mary . . . I recounted to AW what she had said when I asked her about homosexuals – 'What they *do* is *quite disgusting*; but they do have *perfect manners* luckily. . .' "[32]

A couple of weeks later Angus and Tony dined with Jack Plumb, whose fascination with the aristocracy and Princess Margaret was itself an object of fascination for Angus. They lunched with Bentley Bridgewater and Janet Shand-Kydd, whose royal connections were also interesting. A week or two later they dined with Harold Pinter and Lady Antonia Fraser – now there was a social combination to exercise the imagination . . . Angus's mind was turning over very fast.

Then on 15 April Angus and Tony set off up north to see some gardens and some architecture. It was largely but not exclusively a Vanbrugh tour. They visited Castle Howard in North Yorkshire, spent a couple of nights in Scotland with Steven Runciman in his Johnstone border tower, then moved on to stay with Mary and Gerry Cookson in County Durham. The Cooksons had left Suffolk and moved north to reclaim the family estate at Consett from the coalfields: Angus, on arrival, professed himself so shocked by the raw bleak post-industrial landscape that he refused to get out of the car. How *could* you have left Suffolk and your beautiful garden at The Chantry, he cried to Mary, who protested that she needed time to work a horticultural transformation.

Angus missed Mary Cookson in Suffolk: she had been one of his favourites, he told her, a beauty and daughter of a beauty, a gracious hostess, a great gardener, a talented painter, a generous friend, a woman of culture, a mother-in-law of a Cavendish – why, she even had a brother who was a distinguished poet *and* a friend of Bentley Bridgewater! (Mary Cookson's brother was Richard Murphy, who was even then taking part in the Writers' Workshop in Iowa.) Mary could talk to Angus about his favourite island, Ceylon, for she had been born there, the daughter of a diplomat. Suffolk had need of her, how *could* she have deserted him and all her friends?

The Cooksons were delighted to see Angus, who greatly amused them, and they helped to direct him towards the architectural sights of the neighbourhood – Lanercost Priory, Wallington Hall, Clapheaton Hall, the coastal town of Alnwick, the gardens at Howick Hall, the little port of Craster, the ruins of Dunstanburgh Castle. On 20 April 1977 Angus and Tony went to Vanbrugh's curious fortified masterpiece, Seaton Delaval Hall, to which they were given special pre-arranged out-of-season access by Lord Hastings's sub-agent: they looked at the Vanbrugh Town Hall in Morpeth, then drove down to Newcastle (good food at the Imperial Hotel) and on to Bishop Auckland, Castle Barnard and a night at Holker Hall at Cark-in-Cartmel, the home of Mary Cookson's daughter Grania and her husband Hugh Cavendish.* The next day they went to Cartmel Priory and Kilwick hall, and then back home for the beginning of term at UEA and the proofs of Kipling.

*

Angus, as usual, taught (this year mostly Dickens and Dostoevsky) through the summer term. Despite the fact that teaching interrupted his fiction, he was already beginning to worry about the drop in his income when he reached retirement age the following year, and had written to Terry Kilmartin in April enquiring about the possibility of a more regular relationship with the *Observer* as reviewer.

There were other summer distractions apart from teaching – a lecture and a dinner in Brasenose for John Edward Bowle, followed by a meeting at Corpus with the well-connected Singhalese postgraduate student Rajiva Wijesinha to plan the next dream visit to Ceylon: a meeting with Prime Minister Callaghan on 12 May about Public Lending Right, and an

---

* Now Baron Cavendish of Furness.

ill-attended talk for the Shirley Society in Cambridge. (Callaghan considers the introduction of cats' eyes and Public Lending Right to be among the high points of his political career.) Ian McEwan came to tea at the cottage on 28 May 1977, to be briefed for his imminent trip to the Iowa Writers' Workshop – Ian was impressed by the off-campus range of Angus and Tony's friends there, who included not only the pheasant-shooting Tina Bourjaily but also a whole unfamiliar world of firemen and owners of poodle parlours. Angus and Tony both seemed on top form at this meeting: plans for the novel, said Angus, were going well.

Angus continued to pursue the architectural theme. In May 1977 he and Tony went to Blenheim, in June to Belton Park and Grimsthorpe Castle in Lincolnshire, and in July to Woburn, Chicheley House, and Burghley House. On 28 June Angus spoke at the RIBA on Sir Denys Lasdun, who was receiving the Royal Gold Medal: Angus had already presented Lasdun with an Honorary Degree in 1974, when he had warmly praised the Royal College of Physicians and the nearly completed National Theatre, and had rejoiced in the fact that Lasdun was designing a country house in Berkshire – this was good news, he had said, for "those of us who regret that the English rich turn only to period houses for their country life". He now updated his assessment with a paean of praise for the National Theatre in action ("such a promenade, such a display place, such a theatre of the crowd") and with affectionate words about UEA and its thriving student city in the valley of the Yare. Yet his own mind was working backwards. He concluded his oration with a comparison of Lasdun with Vanbrugh, who forces us "to face the transcendent", and mentioned that in his schoolboy days he had dreamed of recreating a Covent Garden piazza, a Bartholomew Fair. He was now well advanced in the process of the creation of his own imaginary Vanbrugh palace.

Angus peppered friends and acquaintances with queries about houses, art collections, art collectors, and, in particular, Vanbrugh. The conception of his novel was changing as he digested the information that came in. Novelist and magazine-maker Emma Tennant gave a large garden party in May at which she engineered a conversation between Angus and Bevis Hillier, whom Angus had first met with the Gilliatts: at this point, Hillier recalls, the novel was to be "about a young man who inherits a stately home – then either he opens an antiques market in it or is exploited by people who do." Hillier provided details about Vanbrugh's Mince Pie House in Blackheath (demolished in 1902) and introduced Angus to Peyton Skipwith of the Fine Art Society.

Robert Carrier and many others talked to him about dealers and galleries. In an early form, the novel seems to have turned on a wicked/

corrupted aristocratic art dealer, a ruthless Iago figure – *grand danger de libel*, Angus warned himself repeatedly, but that would be part of the zest of the book. The theme of the deliberate, sadistic destruction of innocence, probably of a mental rather than a physical nature, now haunted him. It was in part a further stage of the Kipling journey, which had led him into darker places than Kipling himself would have been prepared to recognise. But there would be physical sado-masochism too – some Proustian deviation, perhaps, or some T.E. Lawrence expiation? Violence and anarchy would undermine the grand fabric of his construction: his mind turned to the curious and successful career of Gerard Reve, now the proud owner of a fortress near Dieulefit in the South of France. (Reve had become so respectable through his excesses that he had even been invited to sit on a committee to advise the Dutch Queen about the possibility of her abdication.)

Bullying seemed once more to preoccupy Angus as it had done in earlier years, when he wrote on Evil: in April he wrote a curious, confusing little article for a slot called "Private Line" for the *Observer* in which he seemed to suggest that the 1970s had seen an increase in the romanticising of "bullies, intriguers, and ruthless cold hearts", and cited Inspector Barlow of *Z-Cars*, the anti-heroes of Simon Gray's plays, and Johnny Speight's creation, the racist monster Alf Garnett, as characters who "touch again and again on this exciting nerve", perhaps without their authors' direct knowledge or responsibility. "Little Hitler," he complained, was no longer a name of contempt, but one of admiration. Our values were changing. The submissions to the Eastern Arts Anthology alarmed him by their high proportion of brutal "horror comic" sick jokes, *à la* Polanski or Hitchcock. He noted an excessive pleasure in attacking the frail, the old, the sick.[33]

This was not comfortable material, and he wished to refuse comfort. Maybe he sensed, as several of his friends thought and one or two very unwisely suggested, that this would be his last book. And if it were to be so, it must not be a compromise. Banish optimism, banish false cheer. If the end be darkness and destruction, then let the darkness come. Jolly Angus lunched at Langan's, dined out with the Wollheims and the Snows, sparkled at Ann Fleming's and as Guest of Honour at PEN, was one of the judges of a Silver Jubilee Beauty Competition for Miss Bradfield St George and displayed himself in butterfly-brilliant robes as he received an Honorary Degree at Leicester. (The Public Orator, Dickens scholar Philip Collins, was famous for his witty orations; Angus was invited to reply on behalf of the Graduands.) He went to see *Jumpers* and took Kazu Serikawa to *Julius Caesar*, he encountered Nathalie Sarraute at the French Embassy, he went to a party at Buckingham Palace and celebrated an extravagantly early candle-lit Christmas of oysters and guinea-fowl in mid-August at Hintlesham Hall in the company of Robert Carrier, Angus McBean, Murray Arbeid, Frederick Fox, and Sir Frederick Ashton (they were all photographed for the *House Beautiful* Christmas issue) – but all the time his mind was pursuing its own preoccupations: he even wrote in his pocket diary on 1 July 1977, the last day of term, as though to admonish himself and strengthen his own resolve "Novel notes – nothing else on this holiday." (Early Christmas seems to have been a feature of Suffolk life: Angus's neighbour from Yorkshire, Mrs Thomas, who lived in the cottage over the field, surprised him one year by inviting him and Mr Tony to Christmas dinner in October. Angus protested that it was a little early, to which she replied, "Yes, but Hubby and I wanted to get it over with." Angus said he would consult Tony, when he got back from visiting his mother, to which she retorted, "Oh, he's got a mother then?")

The notes grew and grew – notes on terrorism, the Red Brigades, Lully, Vanbrugh, the baroque, adultery in the armed forces, the price of Dior suits, Westminster schoolwear in the 1950s. Angus drew family trees and chronologies and corresponded with his old schoolmaster Laurie Tanner – now nearly blind – at Westminster. He asked a neighbouring Norfolk squire, John Alston, about arable farming. By the time he and Tony set off for Newark, Delaware, on 6 September 1977 he had accumulated a mass of possibilities. "On the eve of leaving Felsham Woodside," he noted, in a little blue notebook covered with stars, outlining yet more plot – then broke off: "No, no. All this a huge novel before the novel starts."

The outward journey via Brussels, New York and Philadelphia was unusually unpleasant, bedevilled by delays caused by "fuel conservation policy", and their anxious hosts lost track of them for a whole day: but eventually, after a night in a Holiday Inn, they arrived at the spacious campus, modelled on Thomas Jefferson's University of Virginia in Charlottesville. It had a fine carillon which played God Save the Queen specially for them – a pleasanter welcome than they had first received in Iowa City. They had left the cottage in Suffolk to the care of Michael Slater and his friends John Grigg and Q, and the London flat to a succession of visitors – mostly Davieses, but also at one point the Chisletts from Madrid and Kazu Serikawa from Japan. (Tony had written to the Chisletts apologising for dust, and recommending the Trattoria Lucca round the corner and the nice family who ran it.) Throughout the autumn, both Mrs Revens and Michael Slater sent reports on the cottage and on one another's good behaviour: the principal subjects of discussion were the cats, Ada and Victoria, the latter of whom was not quite so good. Ada

quickly became friendly and agreed to sit upon a Dickensian knee, but the
farouche Victoria would hardly speak to anybody for the first weeks, and
seemed to spend her time murdering and crunching up blue tits, rabbits
and squirrels, or fighting with Ada.

It took Angus and Tony some time to master the noise insulation of the
brick Colonial-style house they had taken in South College Avenue in
Newark, but eventually they conquered it – though they continued to be
disturbed by traffic to the steelworks and rock groups in a nearby fraternity
house. Angus hoped to get on with the novel in Delaware, but found that
teaching, socialising and lecturing took up much of his time. The
University specialised in chemical engineering (the whole region is
dominated by the Dupont Corporation) but the English faculty was large,
friendly and well paid (as, indeed, was Angus – $20,000 for the semester –)
and the students seemed bright. Shakespeare scholar Professor Jay Halio,
one of Angus's greatest advocates in the States, was his contact at Delaware,
and he and his first wife June entertained Angus and Tony generously – as
did many others.

Angus got on well with the formidable Dean, Helen Gouldner, and he
also very much liked a quiet, charming young academic called Hans-Peter
Breuer, a Victorian expert whose interest in Samuel Butler endeared him
to Angus: Angus persistently addressed him as "Dear Boy". ("Dear Boy"
was Angus's favourite term of endearment: Glen Cavaliero rejoiced in the
fact that Angus continued thus to address him when he was well into his
fifties.) Breuer and his High School teacher wife Angela were modestly
surprised by how much Angus and Tony seemed to enjoy their evenings
with them and their children. They talked a lot about Bexhill, of all places:
Angela's father, a Czech Jewish refugee doctor, lived there, and one of
Hans-Peter's curious ambitions was to retire there one day. Breuer was
musical, and anxious to persuade Angus that Newark had a fine orchestra –
he played in it himself. But to this overture Angus did not seem overly
receptive. To Hans-Peter Breuer fell the duty of introducing Angus's
formal lecture on Kipling, a task which, according to Tony, he
accomplished with more grace and knowledge than many who had
assumed this role, and Breuer himself never forgot Angus's final,
reverberating epitaph on the art of biography – that in the last analysis, the
human personality is not open to invasion.

Newark itself was as uneventful though not as quiet as Bexhill. Not
much went on there apart from the busy social life of the campus, which
encouraged Angus to eat and drink more than he wished and gave him
some bad attacks of hiatus hernia – "eating and drinking even moderately
when exhausted is bad for me," he wrote to Tom Rosenthal at Secker &

Warburg.[34] One of the town's livelier characters, the South-African born playwright Drury Pifer, desribes Newark as "an unhappy little village, a sort of Siamese twin with the University and a Chrysler factory joined by a common traffic jam. The place was designed for dog carts and must now accomodate enormous truck-trailers hauling dozens of new automobiles . . . Engineers and chemists inhabit the boring suburbs where the only sound is that of the television set, the lawn mower, and the odd teenager going insane. Artists may be found in woodsy nooks like Landeberg, Arden, or New Castle . . ."[35] It did, however, rejoice in one historic restaurant, the Deer Park, where Edgar Allen Poe had once got so fabulously drunk that he missed the literary event he had come to Newark to attend. Angus and Tony got to know it well.

Everyone was well disposed to the new Distinguished Visiting Professor. The President of the University, E.A. Trabant, who met Angus at a football game, discovered that Angus liked to write out of doors, and offered him the use of his own neighbouring garden, so when opportunity offered Angus would gather up his notebooks, make his way through a gate in the picket fence, and settle himself upon the President's lawn amongst the cardinals and mocking-birds. It was much pleasanter there than in the dark and windowless basement of the Memorial Hall, where he shared an office with Jay Halio. The surrounding hillside country was attractive, despite encroaching golf courses and "developments", and Angus and Tony liked to go to the pretty – some thought over-pretty – small town of New Castle on Delaware Bay: William Penn was said to have landed here, and the ancient town retained some streets near the water paved with ancient, buckled brick. A summer's walk along the Strand by the river offered glimpses of snug domestic interiors with "a display of well polished old furniture, oil portraits and every sort of bourgeois art object from pewter bowls to paintings of mallard ducks."[36]

In New Castle, Angus would sit out of doors on a specially purchased $3.99 folding chair on the great expanse of lawn sloping down to the river in the battery park: here he would work, punctuating his day with lunches or dinners of excellent fresh fish, caught that very morning, and that very morning ruined by the American method of instant cooking in order to reheat. Other longer excursions were taken to the Victorian resort of Cape May on the coast of New Jersey, to Lewes (which presented him with its keys) and to Dover, the old capital of Delaware: Angus also discovered, to his delight, a small town called Seaford. This was the Sussex of the States. At the Bombay Hook Reserve, through Halio binoculars, he and Tony admired large flocks of Canada geese, ducks, avocets, and egrets – the noise of flying and honking was astonishing.

All reports confirm that Angus was extremely popular with faculty and students, and that he seemed to be happy there. Barbara Gates* recalls that he loved not only the quaintness of New Castle, but also the garish lights of the supermarket fringe of Newark: he had treated her to his aria upon the beauties of Los Angeles. Anthony Storey, Yorkshire novelist, psychologist, and neighbour from Bury St Edmunds, who succeeded Angus as Professor in Residence, recalls that Angus was remembered with great affection. Yet filling his creative writing class had not been easy. Students were more anxious to learn technical writing and journalism than to learn how to write fiction, and had to be encouraged to sit at the feet of the famous guru from England, of whom many of them had never heard. Drury Pifer joined the class, partly to swell numbers, and records that Angus's manner was "friendly, affectionate and forgiving . . . he made up in angelic sweetness of manner for all we lacked in genius."

Pifer also sensed that while in Delaware Angus was living in at least three separate worlds – that of the gay community in town, that of the university itself "where he placidly attended his classes and engaged in a desultory way with teaching or showed up at the occasional faculty party to engage in tepid conversation," and that of *Setting the World on Fire*. Angus was interested in, but not deeply engaged with, the social composition and problems of the community – there were rednecks and KKK in the notorious Cecil County, Maryland, just south of the University, and the blacks had tried to burn down the neighbouring town of Wilmington on the day that Martin Luther King died. But this kind of arson, which gripped and fascinated those who lived with it, was not on Angus's agenda.

*

Angus and Tony were in the States until 21 December, thus missing the publication of Kipling, which appeared in the UK on 7 November 1977. It was dedicated by Angus to Patrick Woodcock, "on whom I rely so much."

Angus had asked not to be sent bad reviews, and those that reached him were reassuring. Snow, Powell, Anthony Burgess, Michael Ratcliffe and John Carey all came out strongly in his favour: Snow particularly pleased Angus by praising Tony's photographs. Some (including George Painter, Craig Raine in the *New Statesman* and John Shearman of the Kipling Society in private correspondence) questioned Angus's views on what Angus considered the needless obscurity of "Mrs Bathurst"; others took issue over his intepretation of the bleak "Mary Postgate"; Benny Green in

* Barbara Gates, nineteenth-century scholar and author of various works on Victorian literary depression and suicide.

the *Spectator* felt that Angus tried too hard to defend his subject against Edmund Wilson's Freudian interpretations; but most agreed that his appreciation of the Indian stories and Indian society was first-class, and that his sympathy with his subject was remarkable.

Anthony Powell noted that Wilson, a cat-lover, could even speak with moderation of the sixteen-year-old Rudyard Kipling, accompanied by Gilbert Murray, throwing stones at a cat in Kensington Gardens. Charles Carrington, who more than twenty years earlier had published the standard Kipling life,[37] was also very friendly in his piece in the *New Review*, though Angus felt he could have been a little more generous about the fruits of Angus's original research – for example, his examination of the social background and failing fortunes of the Holloway family, or his discovery, though Terence Rattigan, of a connection between Rattigan's illiterate Irish great-grandfather, a private in the Indian army, and the inspiration for young Kimball O'Hara. But, by and large, Angus and his publishers were satisfied with the warmth of the reception, summarised by Tony Gould in *New Society*, who wrote "I don't know which to admire most in Angus Wilson's book: his critical acumen, his biographical insight, or his refusal to play down the awfulness of Kipling's politics."[38] Angus wrote happily to Jeanne Davies that the reviews had been superb, indeed "almost ecstatic".

The book sold moderately well, and reprinted in February 1978. Over the next few months, scores of Kipling letters poured in, some from correspondents thanking Angus for thanking them in the acknowledgements, some expressing a delighted recognition of his evocation of Pellitti's coffee-house in Simla, some taking him to task on minor points of detail or interpretation. (Shavian scholar Stanley Weintraub was pleased to point out that Kipling and Shaw met at Hardy's funeral, not at Barrie's.) Paul Theroux wrote requesting help with research on Kipling's in-laws, the Balestiers: a man who had met Angus while working in a bank at Berkeley wrote with warm admiration. The Viking edition, published in March 1978, eliminated some "dangling modifiers" that had been hanging around in the English text – the phrase caused Angus lasting amusement. But most curious of all was a letter from his old friend from Ashampstead, Tom Wood, now living in retirement in New York – did Angus remember, he asked, seeing Kipling taking tea in Brown's Hotel some time in the 1920s? (As Angus never seems to have mentioned this, the answer would appear to be no.)

Amidst the good reviews and flattering letters, less happy news filtered through to Iowa from England – the suicide in early November of Keith Vaughan (his executor was Patrick Woodcock), and the even more distressing news of the suicide of Philippe Jullian. Jullian had never entirely recovered from the shock of the disastrous fire which had destroyed his Moulin at Chaumes in October 1976. He moved back to Paris, but the five flights of stairs to his fifth-floor apartment in the rue de Miromesnil exhausted him, and in the summer of 1977 he found rooms in a palatial building in the rue Saint-Florentin, near the Place de la Concorde. His faithful servant Hamoud reluctantly postponed a visit to his wife in Marrakesh in order to help with the removal, and on 23 September 1977 Hamoud was stabbed to death by a fellow Moroccan in Drancy. The motive was not discovered. Jullian was plunged once more into despair: Hamoud had beeen everything to him, he had been as a son to him, he had never loved anyone as he loved Hamoud . . . he was growing old, ill, he had no more books to write, he was guilty of Hamoud's death by keeping him in Paris. On 28 September 1977, alerted by anxious friends, police broke into his apartment and discovered his body hanging from a hook behind the front door. His ashes were scattered at Père Lachaise on 12 October.[39] All his French friends were appalled: André Bay, Angus's publisher at Stock, wrote in distress saying that Philippe's death was too awful to describe.

This was a terrible ending for the dandy hero of Angus's youth. Jullian had skated elegantly on the thinnest of ice, and he had gone under. Angus contemplated the blackest of dénouements.

In Delaware, Angus managed to write some 10,000 words of the new book. He was determined to spend as little time as possible in England when he got home in December. England was full of worries and dilemmas. Earlier that year, in July 1977, had come the depressing result of the Mary Whitehouse-instigated *Gay News* trial, which convicted the magazine's publisher and its editor Denis Lemon on the antique charge of blasphemous libel for publishing a poem by James Kirkup. In April, Angus had after much heart-searching decided he could not appear as a witness at the trial, on the grounds that the resulting publicity might put at risk his American lecture plans for the next two years – he had always been foolish over money, he wrote to Denis Lemon, and had failed to put aside for his own age and Tony's. His visiting professorships would, he hoped, bail him out. "It would be very wrong of me to risk that now, and very unfair to Tony."[40] (Bernard Levin and Margaret Drabble had appeared at the Old Bailey for the defence in the trial, but evidence as to literary merit was considered inadmissible: they could speak only for the character and reputation of the magazine, not on the quality of the poem or reputation of the poet.)

But the matter had not rested there, nor ever would: his old friend and colleague Tony Dyson was pursuing him to support a new Charter of Homosexual Rights, and although Angus admired his initiative he simply could not get his mind round the problem. He wanted time to write his novel. He hoped the new anti-homosexual feeling was no more than a Whitehouse fringe. But he could not disregard the subject altogether – several times he anxiously asked his agent, Peter Grose, whether the comparatively modest sales of his much-admired fiction might reflect an anti-homosexual prejudice.

The only thing to do was to press on with the novel, in which he was willing to court disaster. As he had told Ken Tynan a few years earlier, in fiction he would not compromise. Whatever the effect upon sales, he would continue to take risks.

26

THE COLD LAIRS

Angus and Tony flew back from Delaware to England on 21 December 1977, after an end-of-term flurry of farewell parties, essay-marking, and writing of graduate reports. There was no stopover in Lisbon this year, for they planned to fly off almost at once for their long-delayed break in Ceylon – or Sri Lanka, as it was now more widely known. But before their departure, they spent Christmas at Felsham Woodside entertaining Jaidev from Simla.

Jaidev had been at UEA for the autumn term on a British Council grant, working on Angus Wilson while Angus Wilson himself was far away in America. He had written his PhD thesis on Angus's work for the University of Meerut, and was now engaged in further studies which were to result in various essays on Wilson's work.[1] Lorna Sage and Jon Cook had done their best to help in Angus's absence, and now Angus, who liked Jaidev very much, did his best to remedy this chronological mismatch by an intensive burst of hospitality, introducing Jaidev to the English festive season by taking him to several parties at the Corkes. Jaidev expressed himself overwhelmed by this undescribable kindness, and later confessed that at the cottage he had been in terror of using the bathtub or the loo because of the terrifying noise of the cistern – a farcical fear that he felt the creator of Hamo would appreciate. Jaidev had a quick understanding of Angus's tensions and terrors and fears of falling – both physical and metaphorical – about which Angus talked to him at length.

Angus then lunched in London with Rebecca West and on 9 January 1978 flew happily away. He assured Tom Rosenthal and David Farrer that he was really going to get on with the novel seriously this time – though he was also planning to keep a journal with the hope of publishing a travel book. Angus and Tony had been dreaming of Ceylon for years now, and at last they were off.

Their aim was to travel for some of the time, but to settle for much of their seven weeks in a beach villa, at Uswetakeiyawa, some ten miles north of Colombo, where Angus could write in peace. Tony's mother wrote to them there "Now you are on your own and quiet you will both be better":[2] and Tony sent many cards back, describing their travels to Jaffna (where Angus scribbled away in the Palm Court Hotel) and Kandy and Anuradhapura. He reported that Angus was getting on well with his novel, had mislaid his travellers' cheques, had had his hair cut (by Tony) and looked, as a result, very peculiar.

Angus and Tony explored the Wilpattu Jungle Reserve on the west of the island – this was real jungle, an unspoiled Mowgli paradise with bears, wild boar, leopard and buffalo, crocodile and deer – and Angus, with interpolations from Tony, recorded their travels in his Sri Lanka Journal.[3] This contrasts oddly with his earlier light-hearted Indian travel pieces. He still responded as strongly to the landscape and the extraordinary wildlife, but there is a curious uncertainty in his observations about people which tends to confirm the fears of some of his younger friends – that he had, over the past year or two, somehow lost his nerve. Particularly striking is an episode in a hotel in Jaffna when a little girl started screaming over breakfast at the sight of Angus and had to be forcibly removed. "Later she appeared on the hotel roof where I was writing. From the scattered toys it was clearly a playroom of hers. Violent screams again and her nurse rushed out to remove her. She was obviously horrified at the sight of the ogre again, and in the panic of retreat her little shoes fell off and lay pathetically overturned on the floor. All this did not help my writing confidence: I love small children and they usually love me . . . Later, the girl's father came to apologise: it seems that my white hair made the girl think of Father Christmas, and as Christmas was over, it was unseasonable and frightening of FC to appear again.

"It made me feel older, and fell in with my spoken and unspoken emphasis on being old (serves me right), because apart from financial worry and tummy pains I do not feel old at all."[4] Almost as sad is a question he puts to himself after watching a small staff disagreement between an English manager and a young Singhalese receptionist in a Tourist Hotel: "Is this Singhalese umbrage? Or is it just youth? Here is a novelist's dilemma: did I once know more surely or did I presume more easily?"[5]

To write his novel he had to dispel or ignore these doubts. The scenery helped – he could sit on his balcony at Uswetakaiyawa amidst geckoes and scuttling land crabs, looking over the pool and the garden to the sea, interrupted occasionally by a scarlet woodpecker. And he and Tony were well attended by Robert, who cooked and shopped for them and sweetly fed the land crabs upon rice: Angus was at first puzzled by the way Robert kept referring to "Our Lord", for surely Robert was a Buddhist? Did he mean the Lord Buddha? " 'I cured Our Lord of diarrhoea by giving him burnt toast; and then I cured his cold by making him inhale the fumes of coriander seed.' It was then clear that he was referring to a previous tenant, Lord Maugham."[*6]

News of Angus's presence got around, and one of the admirers who walked along the beach for a look at the famous author by his pool was the Canadian Singhalese-born poet and novelist Michael Ondaatje, who was back in Sri Lanka on the first of his reconnaissance trips to research his own colourful family history.[7] Ondaatje wrote a poem about the village where Angus had taken up residence – "Uswetakeiyawa" – which means the Village of Thorn Fences. It describes "the grey silver of the Dutch canal/ where bright coloured boats lap like masks in the night", the mongrel tailless rice hounds, the women and lean men bathing half naked in the water, the smell of curry and toddy, the sound of the ocean, the mystery of a night drive from Colombo.[8]

This was an exotic oriental backcloth for a novel which deals with a very British form of the exotic. Angus sat on his balcony, struggling with his explorations of the baroque and the classical, of chaos and order, of creativity and destruction. The theme of his last short story, "The Eyes of the Peacock", kept returning to him – a big room, a child, a grandmother. He made himself see the old person through the child's eye – at once frightening and fascinating. In his Kipling book, he had written with a particular emotion of "The King's Ankus", in his view the best of all the Mowgli tales, and had noted that Kipling's descriptions of the very old white cobra that lived deep in the Cold Lairs, guarding forgotten treasures, suggested a sense "of something repulsive and frightening that, if we are honest, we must admit to find in some very old people."[9] He was himself powerfully to evoke this sense in his portrait of ninety-year-old great-grandfather Mosson, head of the Mosson dynasty, and keeper of the Mosson hoard.

There were cobras at Cubile Mare. " A beach walk. 'You want to see cobra, sir?' No thanks. Then surrounded by twenty-eight small children and one puppy, all chappering at once. A slightly older girl with a broom, giggling as she swings it violently over her head. She reduces all the other children to rolling-about fits of laughter with her imitation of my voice."[10]

---

[*] Lord Maugham, better known as Robin Maugham (1916–1981), novelist, playwright and travel writer, and nephew of Somerset Maugham: his novel, *The Servant* (1948), was filmed by Joseph Losey with a screenplay by Harold Pinter.

★

It was by and large a good time, but when they left Ceylon, on 27 February 1978, the novel was still far from complete – indeed, Angus was to scrap much of what he wrote there, as he felt that he was trying to include too many generations of history for one narrative. The shape of the book kept changing as new ideas kept crowding in. There was to be a Vanbrugh house in the heart of Westminster, with a vast Vanbrugh Hall and a green malachite bowl; there were to be two brothers, one representing common sense and the classical, the other the risk-taking baroque; and there was to be a final Dostoevskian, Powysian dénouement of arson and anarchy. This point he seems to have reached. But there were many unanswered questions, and his own sympathies were by no means clear. He seems at first to have intended the younger classical brother, Tom, nicknamed "Pratt", to have been a prig and a bore, anxious to turn his older brother's inheritance into a dead, historical, commercially-run National Trust property – he was called Pratt after the architect Sir Roger Pratt, who in real life had been commissioned by the King as one of the three supervisors of the rebuilding of the City after the Great Fire, and in Angus's story had been the first classical designer of the fictitious Tothill House. (Pratt appealed to Angus partly because most of his works, including Clarendon House, had not survived.)

The artistic, ambitious, theatrical, histrionic brother, Piers, took his nickname "Van" from Vanbrugh, who had designed the magnificent baroque Great Hall at Tothill, scene of much of the novel's action: he too in earlier drafts appears as largely unsympathetic. He was originally conceived as a ruthless destroyer and a sadist, as well as an over-reacher. Art could destroy as well as create, as Dickens discovered. Van was to unite some of the best blessings of existence – he was handsome, tall, blond, bisexual, aristocratic, fabulously wealthy, *and* a winner of the coveted Christ Church history scholarship. Surely he, like Phaeton, must ride for a terrible fall? And if he did, would we the spectators applaud, or condemn?

These were questions that went to the heart of Angus's explorations of his own nature. He had accused Kipling of a final artistic failure through his lack of introspection. If he himself should fail, it would not be for the same reason.

★

Meanwhile, England reclaimed him for his last term's teaching at UEA, which was this year to appoint him Professor Emeritus, and to offer him an Honorary Degree. His last series of lectures was entitled "Thin Ice and the

English Novel", in which he spoke on Jane Austen, Dickens, Kipling, Woolf, John Cowper Powys and Henry Green, and dwelt on the dangers of taking too many risks.

He and Tony had missed the worst of a harsh winter, and Michael Slater begged without much response to be sent a bill for the heaps of logs that he and Q had consumed at Felsham Woodside. (Q had secretly been writing a novel there: he had to walk miles, as Colin Wilson had done years earlier, to buy the smallest item, and discovered in the pub that Angus was known locally as "The Telly Man".) Tony's mother in Tankerton was not at all well, and had been made very miserable by the bad weather – she had spent some months the year before in South Africa with Philip and Nancy Garrett, and the contrast was bleak. Bentley Bridgewater, Honoria Wormald informed them, had had an accident: but Val Graham-Young had got a fine new black cat called Thomas. There was a lot of catching up to do. In their absence in Sri Lanka requests for lectures and invitations to parties, dinners, lectures and feasts had accumulated, and Angus rushed from one old friend to another, missing Denis and Patsy Barnes's Ruby Wedding but remembering to send them a congratulatory telegram. On 4 March he wrote to Andrew Hodges, who was planning a biography of Alan Turing:

> I do remember Turing, but I am afraid I can tell you nothing of importance – I hardly knew him, not at all at Bletchley.
>
> I am writing a new novel so I am cutting myself off; I can't say when I shall surface though I must do in September to go to teach in America. I really don't want to think about anything but my novel, and especially not about Bletchley!
>
> I am sorry to be unhelpful but I have just come back from blissful peace working in Sri Lanka to a mailbag full of letters, requests for this and demands for that.*

It was impossible to cut himself off. Despite his good resolutions, engagement followed engagement. There was no time to read Glen Cavaliero's novel, and not much time to look at his own. He had decided to return the advance on the projected Rainbird book on fiction, but accepted a commission to write an introduction to *Kim* for Macmillan and agreed to edit a Portable Dickens for Viking. Americans arrived in droves, as they did every summer: in April he charmed the students of a London Study Group for Colegate University, and alarmed Frederick Busch, the

---

* Angus wrote to Hodges again on 20 April 1983 "Thank you. I have really enjoyed Enigma. The narrative moves superbly on both social England and US and on personal emotions. I was totally absorbed."

organiser, by throwing "a smashing fit of coughing" at The Lamb in Lamb's Conduit Street: he had choked on a bone.[11] Hans-Peter and Angela Breuer came to stay at the cottage, and Angus dined with George Ford in the Garden House Hotel in Cambridge. (They talked about Vanbrugh, and had an argument about whether there was a house by him in Somersby, next to the Tennyson house: "I was right as it happened," noted Ford, on what was to be their last meeting.) The new Sainsbury Centre, itself an ambitious architectural venture, opened with fanfares at UEA in April, and Angus's Farewell Party was held there in June. Angus went to a dinner in the Zoo hosted by Lord Zuckerman where he met the Queen Mother in jade green and diamonds. He and Tony dined with the Reynoldses and Sonia Orwell, with Martyn Goff, with Rose Tremain, with Peter Conradi and his friend Jim O'Neill. (Angus had told Conradi he would be happier if he found someone to live with; he had, Conradi said, been right.) At Felsham Woodside the nightingales sang: Ian McEwan heard them when he spent three nights there in late May, and fell asleep to their music after a long, late, sad talk with Angus, in which Angus had expressed his fear that the young were no longer interested in what he had to say, that he himself no longer understood his readership.

Angus had been in a mood of gloomy pessimism, sitting by the Victorian screen with his back to the garden, talking while Ian drank wine and listened to American jazz on the old gramophone. Tony was away visiting his mother, who had had an operation earlier in the month – Tony had left meals for them, and Mrs Revens came in to see how they were surviving. During the daytime, Angus went upstairs to write, but Ian was restless: he walked the woods amidst the wild garlic, brooding on *The Comfort of Strangers* and wondering whether Angus was not perhaps striving over-anxiously to stay in touch. Could the contemporary world be rendered in fiction at all, McEwan asked himself?

By this stage McEwan had published two volumes of short stories – an unconventional début which bore some similarity to Angus's own, and indeed his stories were often compared to Angus's early work. It did not seem to occur to Angus, as he complained about the prevailing nastiness of the submissions to the Eastern Arts Anthology, that his own most dazzling protégé, although so gentle and pleasant in person, was hardly distinguished, as a writer, by niceness. (On this or some other occasion Angus talked to McEwan about his time at Bletchley Park, perhaps sowing a seed for McEwan's television play about Bletchley, *The Imitation Game*, ("Play for Today", directed by Richard Eyre 1979, transmitted April 1980). This play irritated some of Angus's old Wrens: McEwan, although of pro-feminist intentions, had misunderstood the role of women at Bletchley:

any intelligent young woman with good German would at once have been put on a course and promoted, not victimised, or so they claimed.)

*

At the end of June, after seeing Jonathan Miller's *Orfeo* at Snape and lunching with Paul Bailey at the Zoo, Angus and Tony flew off for a short holiday to France and the Pyrenees – to Bayonne, St Sever, Pau, Biarritz, Sauveterre, Lourdes, Bordeaux. (At Lourdes Angus got in a highly emotional state and wanted to try to help to cure the sick.) Despite the proximity of Snape, opera was not close to Angus's heart: had he been wise to invent a plot which involved so much knowledge of baroque music, he wondered, as he enjoyed the "lovely cross country journeys" he commended to his diary. The Pyrenees, however, proved a little vertiginous. Both he and Tony wished that Clive and Lucie, whom they visited in Pau, did not have such a passion for mountains. They returned on Thursday, 6 July and on Sunday, 9 July 1978 Margaret Garrett died at 2.30 in the morning in Whitstable and Tankerton Hospital. Tony's sister, Genifer, was with her. Tony's last postcard to his mother from Bayonne had said "Thinking of you all the time. You seemed a bit better when I left on Monday morning." This was the last of the dozens of cards which he had sent her over the years from round the world: she kept them all. Angus noted in his pocket diary "Margaret died," and wrote a long letter of sympathy to the family.

Tony disappeared to Kent for the week for the funeral, leaving Angus to cope with a speech at the Kipling Society (with which, inevitably, Angus had become deeply entangled: just as he had become President of the Dickens Fellowship through writing about Dickens, he was now fated in good time to become President of the Kipling Society).* He was comforted by Bentley Bridgewater, by lunch with Bob French at the Zoo, by dinner in Hampstead with Tony Dyson and his friend Cliff Tucker. On 14 July Angus noted in his diary in a prematurely wavering hand "self Zoo alone luncheon".

Without Tony, he was no longer quite steady. Over a *tête-à-tête* at the Trattoria Lucca in Camden Town with P.N. Furbank on 6 May, the day of Mrs Garrett's operation, he had talked at length about himself, his Oxford days, and the BM. He had talked of Tony's mother, acknowledging her as a model for Sylvia in *Late Call* – throughout his letters of this period he referred to Mrs Garrett's illness as "a family illness". He had also spoken of

---

* He was Vice-President of the Dickens Fellowship (1972–3), President (1974–5): President of the Kipling Society (1981–8): and President of the John Cowper Powys Society (1970–80).

page
115

"Its all this pride he pleads for in that very chapter," Elinor swept on, disregarding authority's intervention. "It destroys all his intuitive love. As if Dostoevsky hadn't created Myshkin around half a century before."

"Birkin fails, y'know," Ned was on the defensive.

"Oh ! if its failure that is the sign of sanctity," *The awful Elinor person said, waving her well structured head on its long preRaphaelite neck,* Dostoevsky's divine idiot wins everytime - a rare Chinese porcelain smashed to fragments, Aglaya married lovelessly to a Pole ! - think of what that meant for Dostoevsky! - a prostitute murdered in her own blood with a fly buzzing round her head, and Myshkin himself at the end, a babbling idiot. Oh yes, if failure was the answer, Myshkin has it over Birkin every time. Failure's no good, Ned, its just as concrete and material and choking as success. Myshkin's divine idiocy has something more than that, a surrender, a comic dissolution of the self that at least looks on towards non-being." *The awful sweetness, of Elinor's high class American accent brought Alexandra near to screaming pitch.* Alexandra looked desperately towards Ned for a refutation, she hoped a fierce, overwhelming refutation, but, at any rate a refutation. He looked quizzically at Elinor for a moment, "If she's got a paperweight, take it away from her, somebody," he said, burying his head *in his arms,* ~~once more.~~ He appeared to go to sleep.

"Oh, no !" Elinor cried, "not British humour !"

Alexandra kept her eye on Elinor's plump arm, and, *fell to* stubbing her cigarette out in ~~the~~ tin, she felt it burn deep into that too smooth flesh. *(one of the many boot polish tin lids on the Seminar Table*

Alexandra felt as though in throwing at him and killing him. or, more likely, dissolving into the hopeless crying that today so near anyway nowadays. To boast of Birkin's failure to make a real relationship with Gerald, to excuse Lawrence. because of it, when the whole of their tippling, the whole of them deceit 3E3, Rodrigo herself - Ned was glad was that Birkin need not have failed that humour ... that the old bad lines of man/woman could be dissolved into man/woman may ... Other combinations of love you could think of. And Ned was denying it just for this angel protection a catastro ...

41 Angus Wilson writing in the garden at Felsham Woodside

42 Angus Wilson with
Terry Kilmartin,
Felsham Woodside,
July 1972

43 Angus Wilson
with Rose Tremain
in Orford, on the
Suffolk coast

44 Angus Wilson embarking on the Writers' Tour
in March 1969 with (left to right) Nell Dunn, J. O. Jones,
Margaret Drabble, Charles Osborne and Christopher Logue

45 Angus Wilson lecturing at the Dickens Festival, London 1974

47 Angus Wilson with giraffes in Sydney Zoo, 1966

48 Angus Wilson writing on a Cairo houseboat, amongst laundry, 1966

49 Angus Wilson on a beach in Trinidad, 1968

50 Angus Wilson being
presented to the
Queen at the Royal
Society for Literature
(left to right Ruth Pitter,
Rebecca West, R. A. Butler)
(*Camera Press*)

51 Angus Wilson campaigning
in protest outside
the head office of
British Home Stores,
30 June 1976

52 Angus Wilson with a former student (Jonathan Courage) at the apartment in Les Glaniques, St Rémy, 1988

53 View of St Rémy from the window of Angus Wilson's apartment

54 Sir Angus Wilson
(photograph by Sally Greene)

his affair with the dazzlingly beautiful Ian Calder: when Ian deserted him, he told Furbank, he would have been "nearly broken by it if he had not found Tony."[12]

Tony cancelled his carefully laid plans to take his mother on holiday to the Lake District and he and Angus both began to prepare (dentist, eye checks, visits to Patrick Woodcock) for their next trip abroad. Angus did a little work on his new Portable Dickens project, and on 16 August 1978 entertained Michael Slater, John Grigg, and the Japanese Dickens scholar Professor Matsumura at Felsham Woodside.* On Angus's sixty-fifth birthday, Angus and Tony dined with Maggie Bishop, recently retired in her pretty cottage at Boxford: she baked a large angel food cake, which delighted him – "No one ever made me a birthday cake before!" Yet he managed to quarrel on this same occasion with her other guests, the Reynoldses: he teased them for being turncoats about socialism, and they got quite annoyed with him.

On 30 August Angus and Tony flew off to Chicago, for another ten-week stint in Iowa City; this time Angus was to wear the title of Ida Beam Visiting Professor.

They were to stay once more at the Kerns' in Ridge Road. They liked the house. Angus had worked well here in 1971. He hoped he would be able to finish the novel here.

*

An unusually extended passage in Angus's notebooks for *Setting the World on Fire* describes his feeling of delight at being back at work, and shows the precariousness of that delight – a contrast which was to be the very theme of the novel itself. "My first day of work at Ridge Road seemed so wonderful – especially after what must be deep tension from at least end of Sri Lanka (and February) and above all, after Thursday's outburst. [Outburst unexplained] But in bed with 90 degrees heat and cars and T tells me this morning a pop concert nearby, there was a tension (I had gone to bed too late) – then endless fussing about what I could have been writing here last time – and the dates after NLM (which appeared at Berkeley time) and before C.D. (pubd 1970) and surely not written away from home and the reference books – tho the last chapter was written on the roof at Tripoli so perhaps the first chapters *were* written in the garden here. Anyhow I decided nothing was written here and that seemed to undercut all my delight and assurance about the day's work and the future writing here so

* Professor Masaie Matsumura of Konan University translated *The World of Charles Dickens* (published by Eihosha, 1979) and met Angus several times through this project: he kindly sent me a tape of the lecture "What Sort of Man a Novelist Is?" which Angus gave in Kyoto in 1969.

that I unpicked everything in the sleeplessness – and the heat – and the 3 minute interval car swishes and was left with bladder tension and a blank. But this morning detailing to Tony I have reconstructed . . ."* Then follow pages and pages of plotting and replotting, of invocations of Firbank and Peter Conradi and Rex Whistler and Edith Sitwell and John Osborne and Nick Furbank and Chris Arnold and Julian Mitchell and Jean Corke and Maggie D. (He notes at one point that he must avoid common sense and optimism of Jean Corke and Maggie D., must make himself go for the bitter hopeless ending – then goes back to annotate his own note with "This not fair, perhaps, to either of them?")

The notebooks for this novel are like a dialogue with all the people, living and dead, he had ever known throughout his life. The action was to be deliberately confined to a square mile or two of Westminster – and most of it would take place within one building – but into this small, classical space would converge many familiar ghosts. His father's talk of dogfights in Paris, mistresses in St John's Wood, and visits to the wounded in the Field Hospital in the Great War would emerge in Great-Grandfather Mosson: his mother's Christian Science would be faced, mocked, but in a measure accepted in Great-Grandfather's American daughter-in-law Lady Mosson: the cadging dandy aesthetes Colin and Pat would emerge again (though in heterosexual Edwardian *chasseur-de-femme* guise) as Useless Uncle Eustace. Even the Rua da Lapa where the brothers had lived for so long got into the novel: Eustace, approving of Salazar's grip of law and order, takes himself off there to avoid the increasing turbulence and anarchy of Britain. (Angus's pondering on Christian Science and what it had meant to him and his mother emerges in a wonderful note to himself about Mrs Revens, who had asked him, à propos of broken dustbins, for "the name of that stuff – what's it called – that stuff that mends everything." Angus had murmured, *sotto voce*, "You mean love.")

Angus himself would be split between the two brothers – the sharp-tongued artistic theatre director, Piers, and the chaos-fearing gourmet lawyer, Tom, whose sensitivity expresses itself in spells of acute vertigo. As the scheme of the novel developed, both brothers became more attractive – Tom's priggishness and fears more deeply understood, and Piers's cruelties less malicious, less deliberately wicked. Angus was intent on investigating, possibly for the last time, his own desperate need to be loved (which, he notes, had been spotted by George Steiner on first meeting at the Powys conference in Cambridge) and his own power to harm, which so often threatened to alienate that love. What was the source of this contradiction in him, and was it a necessary conflict in every artist?

---

* He had been working on *As if By Magic* at Ridge Road. Interesting that he forgot it.

He still had not finished the research for the book, research which had begun with the vision at Aranjuez and the travels to Castle Howard and Blenheim. The key text within his text was Lully's opera, *Phaeton*, with a libretto by Quinault. Angus discovered that one of his neighbours in Ridge Road was the poet, Donald Justice, who happened also to be an excellent pianist.* So Justice obligingly played the score, and Angus listened.

Lully, like Phaeton himself, had been ambitious: he had prospered as composer at the court of Louis XIV, the Sun King, had married well, made a fortune, and produced three daughters and three composer sons (one of them godson of the king himself). But he had also been a practising homosexual. Did that make his art buggers' art, Angus, through Uncle Eustace, asked himself? *Was* there such a thing as buggers' art? Why were even heterosexual men of the theatre like John Osborne so fascinated by camp? He remembered the dreadful fate of Pasolini, who had died so violently in 1975. (One evening over dinner at the Trattoria Lucca in Camden Town, he and Paddy Lyons had once talked about gay and camp art: they agreed that they both disliked Derek Jarman's *Sebastiane*, and Lyons had recommended to Angus the gentle, interminably flowing fully-dressed Jamesian almost-lesbian movie, Jacques Rivette's *Julie et Céline vont en bâteau*. It is not know whether Angus ever took up this recommendation.)

Phaeton was the main text, but there were many more subtexts. The plot of Phaeton is prefigured in Piers's first schoolboy production of *Richard the Second*, and in references to Ibsen's *Master Builder*. Vanbrugh himself enters as playwright as well as architect, with quotations from *The Provok'd Wife* – Sir John Brute in drag as the Queen of the Welshmen. Dostoevksy's scenes of disorder lie behind the dénouement, as they had behind the orgy at Vardon Hall in *Hemlock*. Readings of Proust inform the death of Sir Hubert Mosson, who dies by falling downstairs in dubious circumstances in a brothel in Arnos Grove. The Angry Young Men – Colin Wilson, John Osborne, Edward Bond, perhaps the Storey brothers – appear *en masse* (not very convincingly) in the anarchist playwright Ralph Tucker. Virginia Woolf's *Between the Acts* was a powerful shaping force, and one that Angus had to warn himself against – he had at one point thought of writing the novel as a sequence of historical scenes tracing the history of Tothill House and the Mossons, and his use of Ralph's historical pageant-drama has clear echoes of Woolf's own pageant novel. (Angus had expressed his admiration of *Between the Acts*, as we have seen, in his letter to

---

* Donald Justice: awarded the Pulitzer Prize for his *Selected Poems*, 1979, and author of several books of poetry and a libretto.

Leonard Woolf, written in April 1962.) An odd echo of his very early reading of Wyss's *The Swiss Family Robinson* seems to appear in his treatment of the gourmet greed – a dominant motif throughout the book – of Tom and his uncle Eustace: was this perhaps some reference back to the clever greedy little son, Ernest Robinson, who is reprimanded by his father for thinking too much of culinary delicacies such as turtle-egg omelette and shipwrecked Westphalian ham? Angus must surely have identified with this member of the Robinson family.

Perhaps the novel has too many sources, too many references. Auberon Waugh had blamed *As if By Magic* for being too professorial, too literary: this novel was just as bad – or just as good. Malcolm Bradbury believes that Angus may have come to think that his connection with UEA and the teaching of literature, creative and academic, was in some way harmful to his own creativity: what had begun as liberation and experiment had ended in a kind of over-loading. Angus was certainly aware of this danger. Yet he could not help himself. Not only did he continue to refer to other works of art throughout the novel: he also invented ones that did not yet exist. Why not call the family Rose, and the book *The Wars of the Roses*? After all, the boys' mother was to be a famous shrub-rose grower. It was an idea. And what a good subject for a play George III would make, thinks Piers – the old king, tormented like Great-Grandfather by his protectors, powerful yet powerless – he could see it all, and would have been able to see it on stage a decade or so later when Alan Bennett independently hit on the same idea. And does not the feast that Tom prepares to be served at Tothill after the performance of *Phaeton* oddly foreshadow the film of *Babette's Feast*? Its Oeufs Mollets La Vallière, Sole Colbert, and Ortolans en petit chariot d'Olympe; its Pommes de terre à la Dauphine, Sorbet Soleil and Coupe Phénix must have delighted Angus's foodie spirit as he invented them: but the word foodie, of course, had not been invented in 1978.

*

While he was working away on the novel in Iowa – which had by now acquired its title, *Setting the World on Fire* – he was also teaching, lecturing, being interviewed and meeting friends old and new. There were picnics at the Bourjailys, dinners with the Engles, cocktails with a Professor Furia, and luncheons with novelist and academic Fred Busch, who was in charge of the Writing Program in Jack Leggett's sabbatical absence. (Busch recalled Angus "wrapped in coats, and blankets, outside in front of the home he and Tony were renting. He was doing research – on Lully? – and was totally happy to be at work. He struck me as one of those splendidly eccentric Englishmen Abroad – almost too cold to work, but *out there in it,* braving the world and not quite aware he was braving it." Busch also recalled that Angus and Tony threw a party for spouses – mostly wives – of Angus's graduate students – "they felt it important that Tony cook for, and they both serve, the women who worked as waitresses and secretaries while their husbands attended school."[13]) English friends turned up – David Hughes from London and Provence was teaching in Iowa City that semester, and vividly recalls a river trip along the Mississippi from Dubuque in mid-October – "a crazy day of non-stop ebullience". In late October Paul Bailey blew in for a much-needed weekend break from the wilderness of North Dakota, where he was teaching. He had to change flights three times and got stuck in a snowstorm at Sioux Falls. Angus and Tony threw a drinks party for him on 28 October, and introduced him to some not very entertaining townsfolk and students: Paul Bailey had to sing for his supper (which he ate, with Angus, Tony and creative writing student Charles Clayton, at the Carrousel). In November Peter Conradi appeared and was taken out to the charming soft green Amanas: Conradi thought he noticed, for the first time, a real depression in Angus.

Back home, in late October, Pamela Warburg had died: when the news came, Angus had already written a tribute to be delivered at Fred Warburg's forthcoming eightieth birthday celebration, in which he spoke of Fred and Pamela's support during the "disastrous first night" of *The Mulberry Bush*, and harked back to his disastrous Booker speech – "I have expressed . . . my dislike for English Literature that is confined to SW or NW – my remarks were not well received and I shall not repeat them. In those days my range itself was very English, and if I have achieved a wider sense, I think it a great deal due to Fred . . . I knew that he thought of literature in world terms and not in London publishers' gossip." There is something a little gloomy in these memories, as though Angus were dwelling more on defeats and discomfitures than on triumphs.

Angus was worried about money. He had negotiated various lecture deals in the United States extending over the next two years, incidentally getting himself into a muddle about an invitation to Santa Cruz, which he had to turn down in favour of the more lucrative Ann Arbor. Pay continued to be a priority: he had been wryly amused when Graham Watson, the new chairman of Curtis Brown, had written to *The Times* (10 September 1977) assuring its readers that authors like "C.P. Snow, Patrick White and Angus Wilson appear to be able earn a decent living by their pen", when in fact Angus increasingly had to subsidise his writing by visiting professorships. This autumn he was supplementing the Iowa money by giving lectures at the Universities of Minnesota and Wisconsin, and at Grinnell College in the plains of Iowa, where a typhoon all too appropriately blew through the Four Winds Motel. At Winsconsin, on 3 November, he was interviewed (and very well interviewed) by Betsy Draine for *Contemporary Literature*[14] to whom he spoke with animation of his own family's histrionics, and of family life as play-acting and ballet – one of the key set-pieces of the new novel, "The Family Lunch", was to be a spectacular family row over a Mosson luncheon which schoolboy Piers tries to orchestrate both for his own advantage and for the aesthetic pleasure of control. Betsy Draine questioned him about nihilism and his vision of Armageddon in *The Old Men at the Zoo*, and what he now thought of what he wrote then, and he replied "I think three things: I think how marvellous ordered life is. It allows me to do the things I want. Then I think, Oh, if only I could get away from this ordered life to the wild. And then I think, Oh, God help us – the best thing is if we'd all blow up. 'A good old, rare old Armageddon!' So, I'm dealing with the appeal of the apocalypse very much in my present novel . . ." He went on to say that as he grew older "I'm more turned off from people than I used to be. I like people, but I get very quickly bored with groups of people, whereas I am passionately drawn towards watching bird life and going to look at buildings and so on. Now what is the meaning of this?" (Angus was a great one for the rhetorical question: the habit is catching.)

Well, what did it mean? Was a preference for birds and buildings a prelude to a more complete withdrawal? It is clear that Angus was still struggling to comprehend both himself and the world he inhabited, and still had faith that he could use the novel as a means of exploration. But there is also a dark note of despair, of possible defeat. As he repeatedly reminded himself, this time there would be no happy ending, no stoic compromise. He had in the past tried too hard to stay in the ordered world of faculty parties and committee meetings and honourable citizenship. He would have to risk all.

Perhaps it was already too late. Drury Pifer, who had talked with him at Delaware while he was working on the novel the year before, had speculated that there might be "a doubly and triply hidden Angus who saw through the nest of hypocrisy to the dark sexual center of the world where awful things were going on in the name of love, an Angus who, had he expressed himself, would have created a body of work that might have changed the nature of literature. But this great hermaphrodite never quite got loose and instead we were given the middle age of Mrs Elliot [*sic*], and certain attitudes. In short, it seemed to me, when Angus spoke about his family and their escape to South Africa, that he was touching on a great theme that was never grappled with in his work. Perhaps the great loss was his decision (one must consider the time he lived) to make himself respectable when, had he followed in his father's footsteps, he might have written a truly disreputable literature that made the gay experience accessible to the imagination – the way Tolstoy made Karenina our access to adultery. Hearing him speak of his family, and realizing how hard he tried to tell the truth, to throw open the door to what others might consider shameful but which he wanted to treat as a subject for art, I felt that he veered away from the dark side of his true fascination whenever he sat down to write. If his father was disreputable, well, he would make up for it. Too bad, I say.''[15]

This is speculation, but one must feel that Angus would have understood every word of it.

★

Angus and Tony left Iowa on 19 November 1978, and came home to a hard frost and the news of the death of Viva King and a cold London Christmas. They cheered themselves up with a festive outing to see Anthony Quayle in Toby Robertson's production of *King Lear* at the Old Vic on 23 December, and had a drink with Peter and Polly Jenkins in Clapham on Christmas Day. (Polly remembers he was on good form, and thinks he had spent the day working.) Then it was back to Bury, and back to work on the novel. Angus embarked on 1979 with a bad cold. But it was worse in Iowa – letters filtered through from the violent Siberian blizzards and snowdrifts of the Midwest telling Angus and Tony how lucky they were to have escaped. Refugees appeared upon their doorstep – one "crazy boy" made his way all the way from Iowa City and had to be put up in a hotel in Bury. They also made welcome the black South African writer and journalist Miriam Tlali, from Soweto and Iowa, whom Angus and Tony had got to know well that autumn, and liked very much.

They went to some trouble to entertain her – finding her accommodation in the Royal Commonwealth Society and contacts in the publishing world and PEN, showing her round London, taking her to lunch at the Zoo, and throwing a large party for her at Regent's Park Terrace on 26 January, to which they summoned writers, critics and old friends. She was delighted with their hospitality, and sparkled in response – everyone took to her and wrote to tell Angus so. Other South African writers, including J.M. Coetzee and poet Stephen Gray, had made their way to Iowa, but Miriam Tlali was the first woman from Soweto to find an international voice. Her first novel, *Muriel in Metroland*, was published by Longman later this year: it was a notable first.

Angus, meanwhile, was working on his last. He had been writing hard through the last weeks of December, putting the telephone under a tea-cosy and leaving Tony to field all demands by saying he was away. To Tony, too, was left the task of sorting out the problems arising from a transfer of his backlist from Penguin to Panther Books at Granada, who demanded quotes from the distant past to adorn their new jackets. Tony had been keeping cuttings for years, with the help of a press cutting agency and on one occasion of Val Graham Young – (*Cuttings Muddled by Val GY*, read, reproachfully, the labels on some of the Scrap Books) – so in theory everything was pasted in and labelled, but it was odd how some things went missing when one most needed them – where, for example, was that glowing review of *Hemlock* by Evelyn Waugh? Surely it must be somewhere in the filing system? (It wasn't.)

In January 1979, both Tony and Angus attended the haunted Perkin Walker's Northcliffe Lectures on witches (later published as *Unclean Spirits*) – in late December Perkin, like Donald Justice before him, had played Lully's *Phaeton* to Angus on the piano, explaining the score as he went, while Tony made a recording. Angus was now coming up for what he hoped was the last stretch of the book. In February, after a Kipling lecture in Sussex and a night at The Old Ship in Brighton, he and Tony flew to Pisa, to spend a couple of weeks in Florence. There Angus worked on the final chapters, breaking off for little architectural and artistic forays to churches and galleries, and a visit to Harold Acton. (One of the principal characters of the novel in progress was a stylish and very wealthy Italian from Turin who tries and fails to marry into the Mosson family: she then turns terrorist and attempts to use the Mossons to blow up the Ministry of Defence. At this point in the novel's evolution she was called Marina Guzzi, Angus seemingly unaware of the inevitable association of this name with Motoguzzi motor-bikes and Gucci shoes: he was to rename her, with advice from Muriel Spark and Harold Acton and Alberto Arbasino, as Marina Luzzi.)

Harold Acton was still living in antique marble grandeur in his vast mansion, La Pietra, at Fiesole, and there he received Angus and Tony for lunch: they overheard him say loudly to Anglo-Florentine biographer Joan Haslip "That's Angus Wilson, he once wrote a novel called *Anglo-Saxon Attitudes* which had quite a success, but he's not done anything much since."* Equally disconcerting was a dinner with Ian Greenlees of the British Council; he and his friend Robin Chanter sat at either end of a very long thin table, staring fixedly at Angus and Tony from a great distance. (Paul Bailey was given similarly uncomfortable treatment:

---

* Joan Haslip (1912–1994), author of biographies of *Lucrezia Borgia* (1954), *Catherine the Great* (1976), *Madame du Barry* (1991) and many others.

disconcerting people by staring at them and bickering between themselves was their Machiavellian stock-in-trade.)

Angus was able to find these episodes quite entertaining, for his mind was on other things – the novel was coming to its explosive climax, as his anarchist-terrorists mined their way beneath the very foundations of Westminster. He had written earlier when plotting this finale "All move to some great scandalous London festival in which the arson takes place. Dost. But watch lest soc. asp. of Fest smothers the psychol. interplay of characters – I do want in this book to go deeper and more lovingly (but watch that, too, for you must write books you can write best rather than books to win approval or show every side of yourself before you die").

How oddly that word *lovingly* strikes there. And how calmly, how bleakly strikes that phrase, "before you die".

★

So he himself suspected this book might be his last. He was not yet old, but death seemed to be all about him. His witty diffident BM colleague Noel Sharp had died in Stowmarket at the end of December, and Angus wrote a warm letter of sympathy to his widow Rosemarie. (Sharp was the nephew of the poet William Sharp, who wrote under the female pseudonym of Fiona McLeod: Noel Sharp's domestic entanglements were thought to have suggested some of the background of *The Old Men at the Zoo*.) Letters of condolence and Memorial Services were to become all too frequent over the next year.

After his fortnight in Florence, Angus flew back to Paris for a couple of days on 26 February 1979 to lecture for Sylvère Monod at the Sorbonne, and was greeted by Sonia Orwell at a British Council reception: she was not looking too good, though George Melly, whom she brought with her as her guest, proved the life and soul of the party. Sonia Orwell had gone to live in Paris, thinking it would be pleasanter and cheaper to manage there on her dwindling and badly managed finances, but it had all proved a disastrous mistake: she wrote to her friends in England complaining about being in exile. She should never have gone, and now she could not afford to come back. Money and health failed, she was smoking too much, the French were unfriendly, and she lived in a hole. It was an awful warning – and not the only one. Had not Cecil Roberts written to Angus from the Grand Hotel in Rome in 1972, complaining of a duodenal ulcer, gout and neglect, and crying out like Cassandra "If ever you thought of living abroad, don't! In this long illness I feel the want of a home, apart from the enormous expense of doctors and hospitals etc, and ever-rising hotel bills, and nothing to show for it."

On the other hand, there was Stephen Spender, younger than ever as he commuted between the Mas St Jerome in Provence and his pretty, tilting Wedgwood-blue house in St John's Wood. Surrounded by a loving family, Spender celebrated his seventieth birthday with a glittering party at the Royal College of Art on 28 February. Angus and Tony went, as did the Glenconners, the Wollheims, the Snowdons, the Longfords, Isaiah Berlin, and Ann Fleming escorted by Pat Trevor-Roper: Philippe de Rothschild provided the Mouton-Cadet, and four students from the Royal College of Music played a fanfare. It was all very jolly. If life was like this at seventy, it was worth staying on for.

★

On Sunday, 11 March 1979, both Angus and Tony noted in their diaries "Novel finished." At what time of day this completion took place is not clear: Angus had spent the Friday being interviewed by Christopher Bigsby of UEA and visiting Peter and Eve Hampshire at Stowmarket, on the Saturday he had lunched with Jorn Langberg and his friend Ivar, and on Sunday he had lunched with the Corkes. But at some time over the weekend an ending had been achieved. It was to be another few months, however, and another trip to the States later, before he handed the finished work over to David Farrer.

They set off to Atlanta on 25 March 1979, after sorting out a visa muddle, visiting dentists and accountants, making a will, attending a PLR victory party with Michael Foot, taking tea with Fred Warburg, dining with Terry Kilmartin at the Escargot, lunching with Rajiva Wijesinha at the Zoo, and saying a temporary farewell to many of their Suffolk friends. Their contact in Atlanta was Professor Jack Biles, who, with his wife Edith, looked after them well. Angus and Tony stayed in a house on North Garden Lane, Loring Heights, set in woodland – Tony recalls that the dogwood, both pink and white, was ravishingly pretty in the spring sunshine, and a compensation for missing the spring flowers at Felsham. The cottage had been lent this time to one of Monty Turland's partners at Casson-Conder, Michael Cain: his wife Patricia sent Angus and Tony photographs of their own hellebores and hollyhocks and poppies, and of Victoria eating a squirrel. *Harpers & Queen* were producing an illustrated article on Angus's garden that was to appear in July: from Georgia, Angus wrote to Ann Barr with a brief description of his Suffolk demesne, with its "hellebores, daffodils of every kind, anemone blanda, forget-me-nots, fox gloves, aquilegia, parrot and bizarre tulips, tree paeonies, rugosa and other shrub roses, lupins, oriental poppies . . ."

Several of these flowers made their way into *Setting the World on Fire*, including the parrot tulips, and the Cuisse de Nymphe, or Great Maiden's Blush, which Hilary Spurling had so admired on her visit in the summer of 1973: as in *The Middle Age of Mrs Eliot*, Angus had amused himself by creating two characters – Ma and Uncle Eustace – with a serious and scholarly interest in gardening. He had much pleasure in contrasting their rigorous middle-class plantsman scholarship with Lady Mosson's Constance Spry arragements and her vulgar spiritual passion for blue. (Gardening snobberies continued to enchant Angus and annoy his friends: one of his stories was of the short, spare, military Colonel Barcock who came to the cottage to advise on a windbreak, and suggested laurentinus. Angus said, "Oh dear no, how terribly suburban," to which the Colonel replied, "Oh, really? I'm afraid I don't know the suburbs.")

Angus and Tony were in Atlanta through April and May, a visit unmarked by much incident, although there was a bad moment when Angus managed to mislay his passport, Identity Card, Barclaycard, Zoo Card and 140 dollars when he took his jacket off in a hot gay bar one evening. Luckily it was still there when Tony went to reclaim it the next day. (Poor Kazu Serikawa, who had arranged a rendezvous with them while in the States, was not so lucky – he lost his luggage and all his notes on English dialect in Los Angeles and never found them again.)

Otherwise it was the usual round of lectures, interviews, dinners and teaching, enlivened by glimpses of bluebirds, pelicans, terns, tortoises, porpoises, terrapins, a black rat snake, and Stephen and Natasha Spender, with whom they made a more successful rendezvous for a night in the Ramada Inn at Chattanooga on 12 April – Spender was teaching at Vanderbilt University, Nashville, where he was feeling (though only temporarily) "ill-housed and neglected". (The next day Angus and Tony drove through the Chattamoochee National Forest.) In May Angus and Tony visited Savannah and Charleston, and Angus gave guest lectures at various places, including the University of Missouri at St Louis, where he saw the Mississippi in flood. Angus was teaching a mixed diet of Kipling, George Eliot, Samuel Butler and Richardson, planning articles on *Kim* and *Clarissa*, and wondering how much work there was still to do on the novel.

They flew back on 31 May 1979, an exceptionally easy flight for once with Delta Airlines, and Angus advised himself in his diary in somewhat Lewis Carroll style to "Rest until rested" before tackling his introduction to *Kim*, his travel notes on Ceylon, and the novel revisions. He was also beginning to think about writing his autobiography: in June Peter and Sally Carter and their mother Val Carter from Natal visited him in Felsham Woodside, and Angus made a point of asking Val if she would look out for any photographs of the Caney grandparents.

Through June and July he worked, with Tony fending off callers: one of Angus's few exceptions was for the Chelmer Arts Festival, at which he had agreed to appear on 4 July, without fee. July also brought Honorary Degrees from both UEA and Liverpool, and after receiving them Angus was driven off by Tony to spend some days in vertiginous Andorra with Clive and Lucie, who had rented a house there – Tony had made all the arrangements for this visit, but Lucie, as she admitted in her replies, after all these years *still* did not know his surname. While they were away they missed a chance of catching up with old friends – John Wain was giving a reading of his work at the Nomad Puppet Theatre, in Kingly Street just off Oxford Circus, where Pat Calder had for three years been running a small studio: Ian Calder wrote asking Angus and Anthony if they would like to come. (The "Anthony" seemed strange after all these decades of being addressed as "Tony".) Ian and Rosemary Merry would be there, Calder said. Ian Calder's letter confirms what Rosemary Merry had written to Angus – that Ian, although separated from Pat, was still on good terms with his family. Angus, after the traumatic meeting in Tokyo in 1969, was perhaps not anxious to see Ian Calder again, however much he had reformed. (Both the Calder parents were now dead: the Rev. Mr Calder had been swept out to sea in 1964 while playing with his grandchildren on the beach at Thorpeness, and Molly Calder died in a car accident in 1974.)

Angus returned from Andorra to collect the professionally typed copies of *Setting the World on Fire* and on 14 August delivered one set to David Farrer, who had just returned from a holiday with Melvyn Bragg in Cumbria. Angus and Tony waited anxiously for Farrer's response. It came promptly, only a week later, in a form that cannot have been wholly reassuring. Despite the usual phrases about its being "a very remarkable novel" Farrer expressed doubts about the slow opening, the "welter" of characters, the repetition of theatrical set-pieces, and the over-long descriptions delaying the exciting climax. He worried that calling the Mosson boys by two different names – Piers/Van and Tom/Pratt – might confuse the reader. Angus, encouraged by Tony, stuck to the dual names: the nicknames struck them both as entirely characteristic and evocative of a certain aspect of English society. (Bump Walker, Perkin Walker, Uncle Pink, Gollie Gillespie, Puff Wormald, Tooker Hammond . . .) But Angus made some adjustments to the dénouement, which in the finished version appeared to several readers not so much long-drawn-out but as somewhat perfunctory and unprepared.

Farrer was a little out of his depth – indeed, John Blackwell at Secker & Warburg, who had written a report on the novel and discussed it in detail with Farrer, notes that they were "*all* out of our depth (or, it being August,

David and I were). Bluntly, it was pretty evident we had a problem . . . this was not going to be the commercial success Angus was expecting and needing. Now, how does one set about conveying that news, fast, to an author – any author? Out of our depth? The water was way over our heads."

"The dialogue scintillates," Farrer wrote, "but it also sometimes drags, and I have a feeling that your enthusiasm and your pen occasionally run away with you a bit, and mitigate against the general scintillation." This comment was not wholly helpful, though his suggestions for chapter headings were. Nor was Angus quite happy about the fact that Peter Grose had just moved from being his agent at Curtis Brown to become his publisher at Secker & Warburg: he sensed, in conversation over lunch on 5 September, that Grose did not really like the book, and took a dim view of the future of the book trade. Would *anyone* understand the novel, would anyone buy it? Tom Rosenthal's response was slow to arrive (he had been on holiday, then in Vienna on business): when it arrived in early October it made up in ardour for what it lacked in promptness, but then Tom was a dear and *always* enthusiastic, and his enthusiasm was so warm that one doubted that it might spring more from friendship than from discrimination . . . however, he was quite right about the need to promote Uncle Jim from the rank of Major to Lieutenant-Colonel, and about the title of Sir Hubert Mosson. He was probably also right to suggest that now at last was the time for a *Collected Short Stories*. They could appear along with the new novel and with Peter Faulkner's critical study, *Angus Wilson: Mimic and Moralist*.

1980 would be Angus Wilson year.

★

August was punctuated not only by first handing over, then rethinking the novel, and by planning a 1980 South Bank Show with Melvyn Bragg: there was also the usual relay of visitors. Kazu Serikawa arrived, as did Dina Mehta and her daughter Huzan from Bombay. She had just won a BBC-sponsored competition with her play *Brides are not for Burning*, and arrived in England for a two-week visit. Angus invited her for a sunny day out in Cambridge on his 66th birthday, and they explored the town, lunched, and took tea by the river by a weeping willow, where they talked of William Golding. Bentley Bridgewater came to stay, as usual. Angus and Tony did the rounds of the Suffolk neighbours, and on 4 September they dined at Long Melford with Professor and Mrs Greenhut from Ann Arbor, with whom they were to do a house exchange. Mrs Greenhut had arrived with vast quantities of luggage and ate her trout very slowly, but she was a great cat-lover and assured them that Ada and Victoria would be in safe hands. (She discovered that they liked Cheddar cheese.)

Angus and Tony arrived in Ann Arbor on 6 September 1979, and were met by James Gindin. This was Angus's second visit to the University – he had given a lecture there in October 1971, but on that occasion Tony had kept himself very much in the background, arriving to collect Angus by car the next day and whisking him away quickly away to the northern lakes. This time Tony would not be able to be so discreet. They found that the Greenhut house in Ferdon Road with its scrupulously neat garden was fine and the resident cat affectionate, although fat and lacking half its tail. But Angus was tense – "tired, muddled, anxious and lacking in self-confidence," Tony noted in his diary. "Difficult sort out whether genuine tiredness owing genuine hard work, or neurosis, or just too old to cope with so much. Tiresome waiting for Viking novel comments following enthusiastic telegram. Paranoia about Observer again – 'They don't want me, they make no offer for future.' Fussing again about 81.82 finances One short recurrence of diverticulated colon. Hse good and plenty opportunity sit in garden. Super fall weather. Cat okay, but really I wouldn't have cats – so much fuss about food – abs. hell when you stagger down in the morning."

Angus fretted that he had not been invited to give a public lecture, and the staff seemed remote after the friendliness at Delaware and Iowa City. Tony suspected that this was part of the "prestigious university syndrome" that they had encountered before at Johns Hopkins, Harvard, Princeton, Oxford and Cambridge – Jack Plumb always seemed so much better at managing this kind of thing. Despite the many feasts to which Angus was invited at Oxford, he continued to feel somewhat slighted by his old university, and never recovered from the shock of coming down one morning while visiting Merton to find the breakfast he was about to eat whipped away from him with a reproachful "That's *Professor Coghill's* breakfast, Sir." And how Madeline House (now dead, poor thing) had gone out of her way to point out to Tony that Angus was not a *real* professor! No, the academic life had its drawbacks, and Ann Arbor embodied some of them. There were too many students, and some of them, he wrote to Tom Rosenthal, were stoned and schizoid.

Life on these US tours presented Tony with particular difficulties. While Angus was being lionised or grumbling because he was not being lionised, Tony had to amuse himself as best he could, while making sure that Angus did not boil over. His position was anomalous. He usually managed to get himself onto good terms with his neighbours, exchanging domestic small talk and consulting friendly faculty wives about how to work the washing-machine – he startled one in Iowa with his quaint

British wartime enquiry about how long he should boil Angus's handkerchiefs. Many he charmed, and one or two innocents fell hopelessly in love with him. He was amused in Wisconsin on one occasion to find himself observed from a café window by a group of young women students, whispering, laughing and pointing: they beckoned him over and told him they had been awarding points to passers-by for their appearance, and he had won the High Street Beauty Contest with Ten out of Ten. But there was a sad undercurrent to all this, and to Tony's unfailing good manners. Some sensed a remoteness and distance in him. He remained unknown.

He was kept busy on one level, with the secretarial work which Angus increasingly neglected. Angus was becoming "infuriatingly nonchalant" about checking his typescripts and "unbelievably woolgathering over his papers"; Tony found himself having to make decisions that should really have been taken by Angus himself. Tony grew depressed, had bad dreams, and wondered if he was, like his father, drinking too much.

> 7 Oct. Relaxing in evenings can be a strain. Same as Suffolk. A. reading all day, would like not and yet can't think of anything else to do. Conversation can all too easily lead to irritable discord over finance. Usually by late evening I am content to read. However couldn't manage Heart of Midlothian – too bitty in the first chapters. Found life of Yukio Mishima . . ." [The life of Mishima took him back to musings about Mishima's visit in the spring of 1965 to Felsham Woodside. See p.348 above.]

> 8 Oct. Rain cold. A. "I am an embittered old curmudgeon."

There were brighter moments. Fortunately it was an unusually warm autumn, and Angus could spend time in the garden. They met the poet Geoffrey Hill at drinks with the Gindins: Angus liked him and was comforted to find that he too seemed embittered – "Superb reviews, he says, UK, USA, no sales." There was a successful trip out to Olivet where Angus lectured at the Michigan College English Association, and visits to the Kellogg Bird Sanctuary and the rural lake coast of Northern Michigan. They discovered the Cleveland Art Museum – a Midwest Florence with "fantastically rich picture collections" from motor money, they wrote to Jeanne and Glyn Davies. And they loved their visit to Palmer House, a Frank Lloyd Wright building in Ann Arbor inhabited by a retired professor who was into music, yoga and mystery novels – Tony made extensive and appreciative notes on the architecture, and a celebratory haiku:

> To be frank, poor mouse,
> There is no hole in the plan
> Of a Frank Lloyd house.

James Gindin, like Jay Halio, was a long-term admirer of Angus's work and had written about it from 1958 onwards; Angus was to reciprocate with a friendly review of Gindin's *The English Climate*,[16] in which he wrote of Gindin's relationship with various English worlds – the "Coketown beast" tamed by the Welfare State, and the genteel *rentier* south and south-west of Galsworthy. Gindin, who had first visited Angus and Tony in Felsham Woodside in 1964/5, was a handsome worldly Anglophile ex-Air-Force ex-*New Yorker* journalist who had nearly settled in England with his wife Joan in the 1950s: Joan had been working in television, he with educational programmes for the American Armed Forces. But they had returned to the US and academe, and were pleased to have enticed Angus back to Ann Arbor: it gave them an opportunity to talk nostalgically about England, about Dolphin Square and Anthony Blunt and socialism in the 1930s and Gorley Putt and Arthur Mizener and the death of liberalism. They also talked about Rebecca West, whom Gindin had met and interviewed at length, and the Yugoslav days of the Johnstone-Wilson brothers. Angus seemed to understand the amateurism and lack of careerism of Gindin's immediate post-war generation, which was glad, simply, to have survived. Angus appreciated the situation of women like Joan – "educated, capable, but for years willing to scrap jobs they were good at for children, husband's leaves in Europe, whatever, never having thought the institutional or hierarchically professional role mattered, thinking themselves amateur, though just as good at what they do as the institutionally professional."[17] On many evenings in America, Angus listened with sympathy and courtesy to these women: he received confidences that could not be spoken within the resident community. He was an unpaid amateur therapist, a confessor, a confidant.

He was also an amateur teacher: when confronted with the need to teach the work of a contemporary American, he suggested Kurt Vonnegut, but was told by Gindin that Vonnegut was ten years out of date, why not try Bellow instead? (On Drabble's visit to Ann Arbor, Vonnegut drew a rapturous crowd of about 2,000 students: but by this time he had become a travelling peepshow.) Keeping up was hard work, even on a part-time basis. Students loved it when Angus arrived with great bundles of notes and cried out "Lord Lummy!" in his eccentric English way as the papers drifted to the floor, but Tony began to think it perhaps was too much of a strain. And Angus sometimes said some very odd things. There was one evening at dinner when a sad poet asked Tony where he was born.

"I told him about Finchley. A. interrupted rather like Plumb, 'Yes, yes, following 1914 war big development of council houses and bungalows.' "

It was time to get away before the next outburst. The autumn wore on, and Angus spent Thanksgiving Day in bed. After a painful dinner on 18 December 1979 at the Michigan Society of Fellows, where Angus had to give an amusing speech and Tony found himself stuck betwen two mathemeticians, they flew away, on the 20th, to Portugal.

Oh, the relief of the beautiful palace of Seteais and its lemon groves and wonderful blue European views! Seven sighs of gratitude they heaved, as they settled in for a couple of weeks of pure escape and irresponsibility. Back in Bradfield St George the Corkes could not think what had happened to their old friends. But Angus and Tony were far away from the delights and rigours of an English Christmas. They sat in the gardens at Seteais, as Margaret Yourcenar and Agatha Christie had done before them. The porter at Seteais still remembers Angus with his notebook on his knee. They strolled down the hill to Sintra, past the fantastic architecture of extravagantly rocky follies, and wandered in the lush but ordered walks and gardens in the little town below: they visited the Botanical Gardens of Lisbon in the sun, warmed themselves gently in the Estufa Fria with its perilously lurching statuary and its swarming fish, lunched in Cascais and drove out for the day to Mafra: they lunched and dined with John Cobb and Dickie Wyatt and David Ponsonby and Luis Ribiero and Michael Woolley, and met Nicholas Shakespeare with the delightful Susan Lowndes Marques in her charming house perched on the hillside at Monte Estoril.* No work was done, apart from a brief interview with a Portuguese newspaper, in which Angus could play the easy role of Distinguished Writer on Vacation. The relaxation was wonderful, and they had earned it. Next year was intended to be the Annus Mirabilis, the Angus Wilson year, but whatever else 1980 promised, it held two more long tiring teaching stints in America. After Atlanta and Ann Arbor would come Minneapolis and Delaware. Now was the time to recoup and relax and breathe deeply. Back home waited the mail bag.

---

* Susan Lowndes Marques (1907–1993), niece of Hilaire Belloc and daughter of Marie Belloc Lowndes, was married to the proprietor of the *Anglo-Portuguese News*, who died in 1976: she entertained many literary visitors to Portugal, including Waugh, Huxley and Greene, and with Ann Bridge wrote a guide to Portugal (1949). She was widely known and loved for her charitable works in the English community.

27

ANNUS MIRABILIS

The next two years were to be a puzzling and paradoxical prelude to a puzzling and problematic decade. With one hand Fortune heaped honours upon Angus: with the other she began to pluck them away. One of the items that arrived in the mailbags of 1980 was a letter at the end of April from 10 Downing Street asking Angus if he would accept a knighthood. He would, and he did.

He admitted to a childish delight in this honour, but that delight was somewhat marred by the veiled or direct criticisms of some of his friends, who thought that he should not have accepted it, and particularly not from Mrs Thatcher, who annoyed him so much in every possible way. How surprising that Mrs Thatcher should admire his books! and that he should appear in the same Honours List as Mary Whitehouse! some teasing friends wrote. Ina Chaplin, who was not teasing, and who remained as radical as ever after her years on the left with Holborn Council and the GLC, wrote to say that she was shocked that Angus had accepted, and how much, incidentally, she had disliked *The Old Men at the Zoo*. Would Angus please now write her a book she *could* enjoy? Angus knew how the Honours system worked – indeed he had advised on it himself – but nevertheless such comments could irritate.

Mrs Thatcher, leader of the Conservative Party from 1975, had come to power when the Tories won the election in May 1979, and had immediately irritated Angus and Tony by setting herself up as St Francis of Assisi and declaring that where there was discord, she would bring harmony, and where there was despair, she would bring hope. But she had been getting on their nerves for quite a long time before that. As early as November 1970 Angus had mentioned her in an attack on the new conservatism of Kingsley Amis: he had ended his review of Amis's *What became of Jane Austen?*[1] with a sigh of regret for the lost radical Amis, and the conclusion that maybe he was drifting towards God – but "Meanwhile he seems, for want of a better craft, to have boarded the ship of conservative realism, where his tenor voice is no doubt most welcome to the Skipper, and is sailing towards the old decencies (bad teeth and less education for the mass of people) made new, guided by the twin beacons of Mrs Thatcher's ear-rings."

Mrs Thatcher was increasingly becoming a bogey figure to them both, mentioned with a mock horror that was to become all too real as her real power grew. They talked about her a great deal. A letter from myself to both of them, written on 26 November 1976, concludes "Just got back from my driving lesson. My instructor is a very uncaring person who thinks all tramps, squatters and foreigners should be put in a big pit and covered in petrol. He wanted Franco rather than Thatcher. Oh Dear" – a note which sounds like part of a continuing conversation with them about her. Many other friends noted their pronounced dislike of her, which time did nothing to diminish. As the full scale of her monetarist policies became clear during the 1980s, Angus increasingly feared the destruction of the remains of his liberal humanism. Would all that he valued be dismantled? He feared so. And he feared a new wave of philistinism which would demolish all he had worked for in the arts. As the decade wore on, he was to feel increasingly out of step.

The honour which was offered to him was not a political honour, and he was under no illusion that Mrs Thatcher personally admired his work. (He had better hopes of the Queen and the Queen Mother, or so he pretended: "*La reine me lit, j'en suis sur*," he was to tell the French culture programme, *Apostrophes*, in March 1981: a remark quoted approvingly by Anthony Burgess in the second volume of his memoirs.)[2] Few politicians in recent years have been noted for their affection for serious literature, but the new Tory administration perhaps excelled itself in its ignorance. When William Golding won the Nobel Prize in 1983, Downing Street rang around to enquire from the arts world who he was. "Author of *Lord of the Flies, Pincher Martin, The Spire*," the reply began, to be interrupted by "No, no, that's not what we meant, what we meant was, is he *divorced* or anything, or can we send him a congratulatory telegram?"

Had it *regretted* its honour to Angus? Had nobody told them that he was a campaigning homosexual? Certainly the government had not been aware that it was not a good idea to try to introduce Mrs Gandhi to Salman Rushdie, or to try to persuade Angela Carter to become Chairperson of the Literature panel when she was known to be only months from death. And I myself remember sitting next to a Minister for the Arts at a dinner in the Savoy and mentioning, for lack of anything better to say, that Arnold

Bennett had loved the Savoy and had an omelette there named after him. "Oh, and is Arnold Bennett here tonight?" came the quick reponse. (The Minister later asked me whether the London Library was part of the British Library when, floundering yet more deeply, I mentioned that I had seen Enoch Powell there that morning. This was the Minister for Arts and Libraries.) Another Minister, addressing the Royal Society of Literature, congratulated its fellows upon the success of literature as demonstrated by "increased productivity" – if more titles were being published every year, then surely literature must be doing *very* well? (This ex-Minister was shortly to become involved with some kind of commercial lottery.)

No, it was not a very literary administration, and no doubt handed out some of its honours to the right people purely by mistake. But most of Angus's friends were to rejoice with him. When the news of his knighthood broke in July 1980, he was inundated with letters from all quarters – from the beaches of Bexhill, from Old Boys at Ashampstead and Westminster, from Caneys in South Africa, and from John Edward Bowle priding himself on his other pupil knights, Bill Deakin and Frank Byers. Fans and friends wrote and telegrammed from the world over. Anne O'Donovan said how pleased his old father would have been (and how shocked Willie had been with her in the old days for living at Epsom and never studying the form). Neville Blackburne recalled the year he and Charles and Geoffrey Wright had converged on Lyme Regis to meet Angus and Bentley Bridgewater on holiday – Angus had then been worrying about the risk of leaving the BM and his pension, but how wonderfully now, at the height of his profession, he must feel that the gamble had paid off! Old Ashampsteadian Michael Pitt predicted that a suite of rooms at Merton would surely follow. Peter Jenkins wrote saying Sir Angus would be the very model of a shooting and fishing baronet of the lowlands, and Cecil Gould was pleased to find some evidence that officialdom was maturing in its attitudes to homosexuality.* Bentley Bridgewater, who had just returned from driving over the Rockies with Raymond Tyner, sat down to pen his jet-lagged congratulations at midnight. Neighbours in Regent's Park Terrace told him he had added glitter to the terrace, and George Sacks pulled himself together to write in "from Timon's cave". Even Colin Wilson sent congratulations from his distant anchorage at Gorran Haven. It was all very heart-warming, and as publishers and Christina Foyle noted with delight, the news had come at just the right time for the maximum publicity for the new novel, scheduled

---

* Cecil Gould, art historian, keeper and Director of the National Gallery 1973–8, an old friend from BM days.

to appear in July. Surely a knighthood would sell more copies! And how the Americans would love it! Now he could put up his lecture fees.

This was all very well, but the lectures still had to be given, and the book still had to be published and meet the cold breath of the younger critics. Angus had worried about publication through the spring of 1980, while far away in Minneapolis. The year had begun with a flurry of home engagements – talks at Westminster School (28 January) and at Lancing (6 February), where he spoke of his father; an address to the Ladies' Club at the Athenaeum; a talk on Kipling at PEN (30 January); a visit to Felsham Woodside from Miriam Tlali – and a quick trip to see Clive and Lucie in Nice. Then, at the end of March, he had departed to Minneapolis, to teach and lecture and to write an introduction to the *Collected Stories of Elizabeth Bowen.*[3]

He sent his friends back home many jolly postcards of the Badlands, and although his public lectures were somewhat unsupported he as usual made a lasting impression on some of his students. Karen Wadman, who described herself as "the oldest graduate student at Minnesota", attended his course on the Child in Literature, and remembers his brilliant reading of Kipling's "Baa Baa Black Sheep": he talked to the class about his own childhood – about the unvetted and untrained servants of the Edwardian era, about the nanny who had been caught hovering over his crib with a pair of scissors in her hand.

Karen Wadman was working on Henry James, and Angus talked to her about James's short story, "The Pupil", a curiously powerful and melodramatic little tale about the relationship of a neglected child, Morgan Moreen, with his tutor, Pemberton. The cosmopolitan Moreens bear a striking relationship to the feckless Johnstone-Wilsons, with their charm, their style, their cadging, their ruthlessness. "Mr Moreen had a white moustache, a confiding manner and, in his buttonhole, the ribbon of a foreign order – bestowed, as Pemberton eventually learned, for services. For what services he never clearly ascertained: this was a point – one of a large number – that Mr Moreen's manner never confided. What it emphatically did confide was that he was a man of the world." Pemberton is baffled by the family, which lived on macaroni and coffee, overflowed with music and song, and "talked of 'good places' as if they had been strolling players. They had at Nice a villa, a carriage, a piano and a banjo, and they went to official parties." Pemberton takes a great liking to his intelligent, unwanted, cynical, sickly little pupil, and promises him "great larks", but as the Moreens never pay him any wages he eventually finds himself having to threaten to abandon his little friend. The family's fortunes sink lower and lower and after much Jamesian psychological manoeuvring Pemberton finds himself offering to take on Morgan as his own responsibility: whereupon the child instantly dies, of a mixture of joy, humiliation, and a weak heart.

With this fable, Karen Wadman observed, Angus identified strongly. He still saw himself, in his late sixties, as the vulnerable child.

As a professor, Angus made himself accessible: he would come in to his seminars early to chat, would take students out to lunch with Tony two-by-two, seeming to prefer very dark very American road-houses to more pretentious restaurants. Some of the students, engaged in serious literary theory and deconstruction, found his style a little old-fashioned: others found it a relief. He responded, glowing, to admiration, and when Karen Wadman invited him to her home for Mother's Day, with motley guests including her own mother and Madonna Egan (nun, graduate student, and Dickens scholar) he was the life and soul. She noted that Tony kept a close eye on Angus: Angus's very friendliness, she speculated, could leave him vulnerable.

The term in Minneapolis was punctuated by excursions – one to Iowa City to see old friends and to give a reading, one to see Frank Lloyd Wright's Johnson Wax Factory in Racine, and one on 25 May 1980 to New York where Angus was made an honorary member at the annual ceremony of the American Academy of Arts and Sciences. Robertson Davies, the first Canadian to be made a member of the Academy, was invited to give the acceptance speech: he thought Angus was a bit miffed not to have been asked himself, or so he told Drabble when he met her in Toronto in April 1992. Angus Wilson and Robertson Davies had much in common; both were born in 1913, both had had an Oxford education and a youthful love of the theatre, both had written generous many-peopled novels which combined scholarship with satiric wit, and both were excellent performers. (As we have seen, Robertson Davies had written to congratulate Wilson on his book on Dickens.) There to watch this performance was a distinguished gathering which included old friends Eudora Welty, Hortense Calisher, Dwight Macdonald and Nadine Gordimer.

On 3 June 1980 Angus and Tony flew home, via Milwaukee and Chicago, to face the music and set the world on fire. Great things were being planned. Ann Fleming, to whom the book was dedicated, was determined to give a party for Angus: so was Christina Foyle, and the publishers were anxious for Angus to meet and charm the booksellers. Melvyn Bragg had already started to put together a South Bank Show. Publication, once a quiet affair, was becoming in the Thatcherite Eighties an exhausting and vulgar round of interviews and appearances and book signings. Writers had to learn to sell their own books, and woe betide them if they were crippled, ugly, frail, shy, or had speech defects. There was no escape from the glare – and it has to be said that Angus himself, at the Arts Council, had done much to make the writer more accessible to the public, to give the writer a human face. But this had been done in the name of education and communication rather than commerce. The tone was different now: the word "hype" was on everybody's lips.

Angus, with his knighthood impending, was considered by those who did not know him well a natural self-publicist and salesman, but his publishers and agents, who knew him better, had learned to be cautious, knowing his horror of bad reviews and his dislike of meeting false-faced grinning critics. And he himself was apprehensive. The wounds inflicted by the reviews of *As if By Magic* had not healed, as he revealed in a pre-publication interview with Ronald Hayman when he said they had "upset and destroyed" him. And now he had to put on a good face for the cameras.[4]

There was no way of telling how the book would be received. Angus knew he had taken risks with it and had no idea how readers and reviewers would react. His old and dear friend Jean Corke, whose "optimism" he had determined to banish from his novel, bravely read the proofs upon her death-bed: she died of cancer on 9 July aged fifty-three. She said she had enjoyed the book, but would she ever have said otherwise? Nor would his publishers ever breathe a word of warning. So one just had to wait, with Peter Grose's gloomy predictions rankling somewhere at the back of the mind. And amidst the hype, he made time to to write to Martin Corke:

Saturday 13 July
My dear Martin,
    In all this last week of hectic and often idiot publicity that I have gone through, amid endless changing faces and meaningless names, one thought has been constant with me – that I have lost in Jean one of the best and the most rewarding friends of a very people-filled life. Anger with myself that I have not spent more time with her has alternated with gratitude to her for giving me so much of herself and wonder that someone could, in the years I have known her, absorb so much of life so eagerly (almost greedily), profit by what she learned and found so much rewarding, and also (this is the extraordinary thing) give out so much at the same time. Surely it is very rare for someone to be at once an eager learner and a wise teacher as she was. Anger that someone so rare should be cut off so young is one's first reaction; but then when I think of how she responded so continuously and

so fully I must give thanks for the wonderful years of absorption and reception that one saw in her every look and speech during this last dozen years or so. She was someone very rare who did what she wanted without being wayward or self consciously rebellious. But, of course, on occasion she defied with profit. And of course, equally, she could not have done so satisfactorily without your love and support, Martin. I have thought, through all this weeks's screams, champagne and journalism both laudatory and snide, of all of you, – each individually so very interesting and have only been able to hope that you will reward all I got from Jean (and, I know, her affection for me) by seeing that we go on seeing each other as and when you wish – and Martin, of course that Tony and I enjoy your friendship and affection which was essentially interwoven (and will continue to be) with all that we got from Jean. Love to you all from Angus.

The knighthood was announced to the press on 14 June. The *Daily Express* was not pleased: William Hickey (7 July 1980) declared "Our latest nancy knight, author Sir Angus Wilson, has dedicated his new novel . . . to Anne Fleming, widow of the red-blooded James Bond writer. Heaven only knows what 007's creator would have thought of it all . . ." and John Junor in the *Sunday Express* tried to crack a joke about whether Tony Garrett would now have to be addressed as Lady Wilson. (As we have seen, it was in fact Ian Fleming's admiration for Angus Wilson that had brought Angus and the Flemings together in the first place. Ironically, both Hickey in his article and Angus in his dedication addressed her as Anne: she herself almost always signed herself Ann. As with the Blackburnes, Angus had been a little careless in spelling out his compliment, but Ann Fleming, whose own spelling was not perfect, did not seem to mind; she had written to him on 27 May to tell him it was "a marvellous and absorbing novel", and thenceforward proudly referred to it as "*my* book".)

Angus was undeterred by William Hickey's predictable hostility to his knighthood: one of the very first official letters he wrote under his new title was to the Greek Embassy protesting about the prosecution of a Greek gay magazine, *Amfi*: he recived in reply a report on the state of the law with regard to homosexuals in Greece. Apart from the homophobic press, the public and the profession were delighted.

The book was published on 7 July. The reviews, when they came, were a mixed bunch. There were plaudits for its virtuosity and its elegance, but there were also attacks. Critics tended to love or hate it. Auberon Waugh in the *Evening Standard*, predictably, hated it and found it "virtually unreadable", the *Daily Mail* found it "arid", and Paul Ableman in the

Spectator complained that there was far too much architecture. (The complaint was echoed, silently, by Julian Mitchell, whose professional opinion was that the many pages Angus had devoted to establishing the extraordinary fiction of Tothill House could have been achieved on film by one camera shot.) For the defence spoke up Drabble (though I note I was dissatisfied with the dénouement), Anthony Burgess (very warmly), David Holloway, Michael Ratcliffe, Thomas Hinde and Bernard Bergonzi. Angela Carter credited him with a desire, particularly admirable in a Grand Old Man of English Letters, to detonate the traditional English novel. Nicholas Shrimpton, in *Quarto*, was exercised by the ending, and the dangerous late balancing-act between order and chaos, between Tom and Piers: he was astonished to find "so much moral energy released so late" and was left (as I think was I) with "a strange sense of important things only just said." Several sat on the fence. David Lodge praised its "high seriousness", but found the identification of art with hereditary wealth and privilege uncomfortable, and Christopher Ricks in a long and generally appreciative piece in the *London Review of Books* came down on the side of declaring the book an ambitious but honourable failure: Angus's daring attempt to embody the charade-quality of society had about it a certain stageyness which he could not overcome: ". . . what this new novel gathers to itself, what it makes so much of, to the point at which questions not just of genre but of medium become too much for it, is the especially taxing mode of masque."[5]

Graham Lord in the *Sunday Express* was less measured: "TV viewers watching the flat, soporific Melvyn Bragg interviewing Sir Angus Wilson may have wondered how such a twittering old woman got a rare literary knighthood, or why he is such a literary guru . . ."[6] and he condemned the novel as a book about "a pair of pompous snobbish conceited schoolboys."

Some writers try to avoid their reviews: others cannot resist reading them. Angus veered towards the latter position. It is clearly one's duty as an author to try to make oneself read reviews of books based on fact – in order to correct mistakes rather than to score off those who erroneously detect them, though the latter instinct after years of goading can occasionally prove irresistible.* With fiction the question is different.

---

* I have swallowed much humble pie over my edition of the *Oxford Companion to English Literature* – indeed, I recollect with horror that Angus himself gently pointed out to me that in my first edition I had his birthplace as South Africa rather than Bexhill-on-Sea. "You know, dear girl," he said obliquely over supper one evening in Camden Town, "it is very strange how some people believe I was born in South Africa. I was really born in Bexhill." He then embarked on a tactful small speech about Bexhill which, had I then known I would one day be writing this book, I would have written on the tablecloth or engraved upon my heart. (I did rush home and alter his birthplace for the first reprint.)

Angus himself acknowledged the distinction in an interesting letter about his not wholly unfavourable review of Ruby Redinger's life of George Eliot. He had concluded by remarking that it was jarring to find that someone who had worked on George Eliot for fifteen years should "feel able to alter her normal English usage of 'obliged' in her letters to the alien American 'obligated'."[7] This comment had drawn a letter of impassioned objection from a friend of the author's, protesting that Redinger would never have done such a thing, that it would have been abhorrent to her as a scholar to have done so, and that Redinger had quoted from Gordon Haight's edition of Eliot's letters: she, the friend, was writing to complain, as Redinger herself preferred not to see any reviews of her book and had not read this one. Angus (who was in the right on this occasion) replied pointing out the page numbers to instance his objections, and continued "I am sorry that Professor Redinger prefers not to see the reviews of her book. I can understand that a fiction writer might not wish to read reviews, but I find it odd in an academic."[8]

Angus could not help reading his own reviews, though Tony tried at times to protect him. He had to know the worst. At the end of his pocket diary for 1980 Angus lists the reviews for *Setting the World on Fire*.

Bad	E. Standard
	E. News
	Sunday T
	S. Express
	Spectator
Poor	Vogue
	Harpers
	Eastern D.P.
	TLS
	London Review
Good	S. Telegraph
	Yorkshire P
	Birmingham P.
Very good	Times
	Financial Times
	Guardian
	Telegraph
	Listener
	Quarto
	Now
	Economist
	Western Mail.

Angus put a good face on the reviews good, bad and indifferent, writing to André Bay at Stock (who liked the book very much) that the reception had been magnificent: indeed, this is the line he took with all his correspondents, in marked contrast to his open admission of pain over the reception of *Magic*. At Ann Fleming's dinner party at Brooke's on 9 July, surrounded by friends, he sparkled: he sat next to and charmed Caroline Egremont, wife of his admirer Max Egremont. There were dinners and celebrations and no murmurs of libel – not even any dangerous identifications, though one or two in private thought they spotted the original of Marina Luzzi. (She, like Mrs Curry, was found implausible by some and all too recognisable by others: and although she stood for so much that Angus abhorred, he admitted to a small identifcation with her anarchic spirit. She, like him, felt that in the midst of society she was desperately lonely – "You know 'ow lonely I have been.") Despite Auberon Waugh the novel stayed on the best-seller lists, so perhaps all the junketing had been worth while.

★

Tony had managed to slip away for a few days to Holland in June, but Angus stuck it out through the summer of 1980 in London and Bury. On 11 July he attended the annual Election Dinner at Westminster, to be fêted as the man of the moment and to hear himself mentioned in verses –

> This literary lion eschews the platitudes,
> The easy exploitation of the tragic.
> His comic theme is Anglo-Saxon Attitudes
> A world is conjured up As If By Magic.

He had been living much in the past of late, reliving his schooldays, walking round the square mile of Westminster and Victoria which he had known so well, describing through Piers's eyes a taxi ride past "the Army and Navy Stores, the neo-Byzantine wonder of the Roman Catholic Cathedral, the Victoria Palace with its habitual Crazy Gang signs", a trip which had been followed by a precociously sophisticated Sole Dieppoise with Marina Luzzi in Overton's narrow dining-room. Much had changed – the school now admitted girls, and that ink-spotted uniform was a thing of the past – but Overton's was still exactly the same, and as Angus looked around the great hall and ate his smoked trout and chicken supreme and raspberry pavlova he saw how much here was unchanging. How fortunate he had been in his schooling. How lucky that he had not, so early, fallen through the ice into the dark water that had claimed so many of his brothers.

The boys still sang. On his programme Angus scribbled a note on the "shrill high treble" of one of the singers. He had got Westminster right – the odd misquoted epitaph from the cloisters, perhaps, as various friends were eager to point out. But he had done it. The boy with the hair now sat at High Table, a Knight Bachelor.

Life was not all nostalgia. He saw and previewed for television the new theatrical wonder of the RSC's *Nicholas Nickleby*, he lunched at the pleasant little fish and oyster restaurant at Orford on his birthday, he met Paul Binding and Peter Conradi and Norman Scarfe and Clive Sinclair. Sinclair was a product of UEA, but he had not known Angus personally there – he had seen him lecturing, small and portly with glasses that kept slipping off his nose, but he met him now, in the summer of 1980, at a party at Felsham. Angus did his Indian Maharajah, and Sinclair, who had just read the new novel, found it hard to break in with words of appreciation: but then sent him his second collection of stories, *Hearts of Gold*. Angus promptly responded by postcard:

> 11 August, 1980
> I found *Hearts of Gold* quite wonderful, especially the title
> story . . . And all this despite my immense distaste for football,
> cunts, and national movements of any kind. So it had to be a very
> good book . . . and it was. Angus.

Angus remained in buoyant and outgoing mood, jotting down ideas for short stories on bits of paper, menus, invitations. He dined with Paddy Lyons at the Trattoria Lucca in Camden Town, and was on skittish form, urging Lyons to try the chicken *alla principessa* ("the campest thing on the menu") and suddenly demanding of him in all seriousness "And would *you* adopt a child?" (Lyons came to think that perhaps *As if By Magic* was not so much about sex as about wanting to have a child, and about the fear of the destructive powers of love: Angus often remarked that Dickens had almost destroyed his own children through excessive and possessive love.*) Angus caught up with his correspondence with friends and ex-students, writing a kindly letter to me on 4 August about my novel *The Middle Ground*, and mentioning *en passant* that "ever since I was sixty, I should say, I have somehow found it hard to remember middle age, although childhood and adolescence have poured into my mind." The Hobsons

---

* He expressed this view in a TV interview with John Pitman, *The Other Half*, 1983, when both he and Tony said they loved children but feared they would have been bad parents.

arrived from Wiltshire to take a holiday on the Suffolk coast at Aldeburgh, in a cottage quaintly called Correggio: Angus and Tony went over for a lunch of plaice and then walked upon the beach, with Angus in the highest of spirits, chatting of Harold Acton and Ian Greenlees in Florence and their euphemism for going to an old people's home – "Time *he* went to Monte Carlo," they would say of a failing friend, or occasionally of themselves. To Angus this summer, Monte Carlo seemed far off. As they walked along, Angus spotted a woman lying on the beach wrapped in a tartan rug like an Egyptian mummy and said he longed to go over to her and say "I'm sure *your* mother wasn't an actress" – he had always wanted to begin a novel thus. He was not even cast down by Hobson's criticisms of details in the novel – surely Angus had got some of his military nuances wrong, and one of the boys was taking far too many A-Levels even for a genius? Hobson believed that Angus identified himself with Van the artist, and that Tony was Pratt the practical man (with whom Hobson himself also identified), but Angus insisted that he himself was both Van and Pratt.

A teasing reminder of an old pot-boiler arrived, in the form of a letter reminding him of the thin ice of writing about the British class structure: his correspondent informed him (without a murmur of complaint) that the caption to one of the photographs in *The Naughty Nineties* was wrong: the gentleman pictured skating on thick ice in St James's Park on page 55 was not "a Gentleman's gentleman" at all, but her husband's grandfather, Sir Edward Pollock. He wrote at once to apologise, and informed the publishers.

Angus and Tony lunched with Perkin Walker's Aunt May, the Chisletts came for the night, and they dined with the Reynoldses and Stephen Jones, now curator of Gainsborough House, soon to be curator of Leighton House. The tone of Angus's letters at this time is quite jolly – a word he himself uses several times. He had survived the ordeal by fire. And on 28 August 1980 he and Tony heard and saw a corncrake in the field.

The new novel had divided his friends as well as the critics. Some admired it greatly: Fred McDowell at Iowa thought it was "incandescent". Anne-Marie Meyer wrote warmly, and so did Paddy Lyons. Lord Hastings was grateful to receive a complimentary copy, and glad that Angus's visit to Seaton Delaval in April 1977 had born fruit. Some it took by surprise: Angus had sent a copy to Lieutenant-Colonel John French, who had advised him about Uncle Jim's regimental career and changing army etiquette – would Jim have been able to divorce and remarry a brother officer's widow without resigning from the regiment, Angus had wanted to know, and John French had done his best to explain. A gift copy arrived in a Jiffy Bag at Christchurch in Dorset, where the Frenches were then stationed, but Sheila, an alert army wife, had been taught to be suspicious of unexpected packages and she very sensibly classified it as a possible bomb, likely to set the house if not the world on fire. She placed it safely in the middle of the lawn at the bottom of the garden. As John French said in his letter of thanks, such a reception was a sad reflection on the state of the world. And Angus's novel had not been over-fanciful. That spring had seen the SAS attack on the Iranian Embassy in Knightsbridge, and in August a bomb blast at Bologna station which might have been planned by the Luzzi herself killed eighty-four people.

Some had reservations about the book, although they did not necessarily express them to Angus. Anthony Symondson, who thought *Magic* much under-rated, did not like the new novel at all, and considered Angus's apprehensions about writing about the upper classes justified: in the only one of his diaries to survive his becoming a Jesuit in 1989, he recorded (21 August 1980) that Bentley did not like the book either, and neither, from hospital, did Honoria Wormald. She disliked the characters, especially Van. She thought Angus's non-fiction – Zola and Dickens – better than his fiction, and complained that he would not recognise what he could do well. "It is a bad book in which he makes upper class people speak and behave as if they were in a hotel lounge. Bentley is dining with Angus twice next week – once alone and then with a party from their Bletchley days. 'I don't want to be have dinner with those people, but Angus involved me.' " Symondson and his friend the journalist Gavin Stamp were also harsh on Angus's architectural allusions – did he not know that the term "mansards" could not apply to baroque architecture? (Symondson had a specialist interest in architecture – fostering the cult of Comper was one of his enthusiasms.)

On 3 September 1980, after their dinners with Bentley Bridgewater, Angus and Tony flew off to Delaware once more for another term's teaching, leaving Felsham Woodside to the care of Ian McEwan and Penny Allen – Mrs Revens liked Penny very much and wrote to tell Angus so. (Ian was to describe the wood and the cottage and the stuffed birds in *The Child in Time*, Cape, 1987.) In Newark they were greeted by old friends, in the form of Jay and June Halio, the Breuers, the Pifers, the Bohners, and many others who remembered them well. It was another term of interviews, honking geese, creative writing students, departmental picnics, faculty parties and visits to the pre-Raphaelites in Wilmington: on 19 October Angus lectured with panache on "Prudence and Courage in Jane Austen", coming down firmly against the small world of Emma and Mr Woodhouse and on the side of the courage of Anne Elliot in *Persuasion*, who opted for a life of alarms and trial by water. *Setting the World on Fire* was published by Viking on 30 October, and various telephone interviews marked the occasion.

It was at this period that Jay Halio noticed how anxious Tony was to keep bad reviews from Angus's attention. Halio had wanted to show to Angus Ann Tyler's review in the *New Republic* which, although full of qualifications, Halio had found very interesting, but Tony thought it would be ill-advised. And it was bad news, of a non-news sort, that the novel had not reached the Booker shortlist back home – the prize was won this year by William Golding's *Rites of Passage*. It was just as well that they had not been around to endure the gossip.

Angus, in fact, took the news of Golding's success very well: he had long admired his work, and had been cheered to receive a very friendly card from him from a Golding family holiday in Brittany in August, congratulating him on his K ("it shines like a candle in all the dark wastes of unworthy awards!") and telling him that Ann was reading his *Kipling* with the greatest enjoyment – it eclipsed the weather and the yelling of babies. A copy of Golding's own new novel, the one they had discussed at the Athenaeum, would soon be on its way. This was disarming, and Angus was quick to congratulate Golding on his Booker success. Although he described himself as an embittered old curmudgeon, Angus was not an envious man. Paranoid at times, but not envious.

On 18 December Angus and Tony flew off to Martinique for a holiday. They had much enjoyed their earlier visit, but found it sadly altered. Mass tourism had discovered it, and jumbo jets from France, the USA and Canada arrived by the minute. They escaped to a small seaside resort called Robert, on the far side of the island, but even here the crowds arrived: suddenly President Giscard turned up out of the blue and started to address them from a balcony. They flew home, on 3 January 1981, and retreated to Suffolk and their muddy neglected garden.

*

What, then, of 1980? A good year, or a bad? The Angus Wilson industry flourished. Averil Gardiner from Newfoundland had approached him for approval to write a Twayne biography, Professor Kerry McSweeney of the Queen's University, Kingston, Canada wanted to edit a collection of his critical writings, and J.H. Stape from Vancouver had investigated the possibility of a detailed bibliography of his works. Sussex wished to give him an Honorary Degree, and his fellow knight and RPT neighbour Sir Victor Pritchett had included a piece on his work in the volume of essays, *The Tale Bearers* (1980). Peter Faulkner's full-length study had received respectful attention. And Angus had been invited to be the star speaker at the Shakespeare Birthday Celebrations in Stratford-upon-Avon.

But despite all this acclaim, there were fears lurking just below the surface. He was even suspicious of his ostensible admirer, Kerry McSweeney, who had not much liked *As if By Magic* – the last thing Angus wanted was a critical reappraisal by McSweeney which described his new novel as a further failure of creative power. One could not avoid the fact that a dominant theme of *Setting the World on Fire* was a fear of falling. Emma Tennant pointed this out as she sent him a copy of her own book on the same theme, *Alice Fell.*[9] Fear of falling, fear of being sent to Monte Carlo, fear of running out of funds, fear of not being able to write. The wealth of the Mosson brothers attracted some critical hostility: few reviewers noted that they very nearly lost it, and that their childhood, like Angus's, was overshadowed by a threat of being disinherited and left to fend for themselves. In the event, Piers inherits only by default, through his uncle's fall – a squalid fall down a flight of suburban stairs in a brothel.

Angus might have reached the top of his profession in the eyes of the world, but he knew that it had not brought financial security; serious novels were simply not selling as they had once done. He had a bee in his bonnet about airport bookshops, of which he saw so many – ten years ago you could find serious novelists like Dickens and Iris Murdoch there, but now you found only "big, promoted blockbusters" and books boosted by TV adaptations.[10] He gloomily foresaw the commercial triumph of hype.

From the top, where could one go but downhill? Angus no longer felt quite happy as he descended the great staircase of the familiar Athenaeum. He held on to the rail, and took little steps. And getting up all those stairs to the top floor at Regent's Park Terrace was not as easy as it used to be.

*

The New Year found Angus hard at work writing about two of the authors who had most influenced him. He was working on a 10,000-word introduction to a Viking Portable Dickens, and on a long piece on Proust for the *Observer* to coincide with the publication of Terry Kilmartin's new translation.[11] Proust, appropriately enough, took him back into the past – to his first adolescent readings, to the summer vacation from Oxford when he made his way through the volumes in French, to his wartime reading when he was "in the depths of the most complete despair that I have ever ever known". Proust took him back to Philippe Jullian, whose illustrated edition he had reviewed thirty years earlier in the *Observer.*[12] and to George Painter, whose two-volume biography he had also reviewed. (The second volume was dedicated to Angus.) Painter now wrote to Angus from Hove about Proust and Dickens, confirming that there was, alas, no positive confirmation of Proust's familiarity with Dickens's works, but agreeing that any sensitive reader must feel his presence in *A la recherche*.

Angus was also called upon to write a brief note on the death of Sonia Orwell – another exercise in time regained, as he recalled her voice with its "idiosyncratic combination of pitch and inflection" when she rang him at the Museum out of the blue all those years ago to tell him so improbably that Connolly wanted two of his stories for *Horizon*.

He turned down invitation after invitation, but managed at last to fit in the Queen at Buckingham Palace on 10 February 1981 for his somewhat delayed Investiture. Tony proudly drove him to the palace in their new little blue Citroën 2CV, purchased in January 1981 for £2692.58; they were accompanied by Ann Rosenthal, who delighted in the Palace's sniffer labradors. The next day Angus re-enacted the day's events with "a wild twinkle" over lunch at the Zoo to an appreciative Denis Lemon, who wanted to hear every detail of the dubbing. Angus also talked at great length to Denis about his fears for Tony's future, and his own new fear of losing his way in the middle of lectures. He was financially dependent on his United States engagements: what would happen to him and Tony if the time came when he could no longer perform? What would happen if the United States authorities turned nasty about his visa? This had been a long-standing worry: the restrictions on visas for homosexuals and members or one-time members of the Communist party or other Un-American undesirables remained shrouded in uncertainty and it was hard to find out what the rules were. In the case of eminent persons (such as Sir Peter Pears in 1980) restrictions could be declared "non-meaningful", particularly when the Freedom of Information Act was invoked, but one could not rely on an arbitrary benevolence.[13] Things could go wrong for homosexuals at any time – and, with the advent of AIDS, were shortly to do so. Angus was prescient in these matters.

With most of his friends, however, he seemed as confident as ever. That very same evening he had dinner with Perkin and Luigi Meneghello, and to Meneghello he seemed on good form – not a hint of mental impairment, not a whisper of poverty. Angus invited June Halio to lunch in the Zoo on the 25th, and that evening he and Tony came to dinner with me and Nell Dunn, and again he seemed very chirpy – he gave me a long list of contacts in Poland, which I was to visit in March 1981 on a British Council lecture tour. On the 27th he dined in Norwich with the Bacons and the Sainsburys, a combination of names which he found irresistibly funny: on 14 March he presided over a large family reunion of Erskines and spent the night with Jeanne and Glyn Davies before setting off with Tony for France by Hovercraft. (Cousin Vivienne Erskine, the daughter of Bessie Frank and Val Caney, was now living in Kent with her husband Thomas Erskine.)

In France, again, Angus sparkled. *Setting the World on Fire* was being published by Stock – ominously, his only foreign publishers to come through with an immediate offer. He embarked on a busy week of interviews and discussions. Paris loved Angus. It loved his flowing white hair, his apple-green tie and his red socks. He was a character, a real English eccentric. Novelist and journalist Pierre Combescot accused him of having read so much Dickens that he had turned into a cross between Mr Pickwick and a baby caught with his finger in a jar of jam. And Angus confided to the *Magazine Litteraire* that he was "*un vieux snob esthétique*": he also said how much he disliked Walt Disney's *Fantasia* and how much he had admired de Montherlant. He read at the elegant British Council building on the rue de Constantine, in English accompanied by a French translation, from "Que mangent les Hippopotames?" and "La Ciguë et après".

At the end of the week Angus and Tony set off from the Hôtel Racine for the South to see Clive and Lucie in Cannes. Angus flew back on his own to Paris to appear on 27 March on Bernard Pivot's famous French culture programme, "*Apostrophes*", in company with William Styron and Italo Calvino: they discussed the post-Auschwitz novel and the Tower of Babel, then Angus briskly flew back again to Cannes. Clive and Lucie had embroiled Angus and Tony in April in an extremely elaborate correspondence about a dog from a kennels in Taunton: as Captain Clive's hand was by now almost totally illegible and his instructions obscure Tony had had to step in to sort out the muddle. But Angus and Tony seemed to bear the captain no ill will: in the last few years Angus had become closer to his only surviving brother.

After Cannes, Angus and Tony travelled on, through Aiguilles, Saint Marcelin, Aix-les-Bains, Geneva, and finally home on 12 April via Arras, Troyes and St Omer, where they met a lady who had actually read *As if By Magic*. Angus happily noted down the lovely but stormy weather, the delightful museums, the cathedrals, and the drunken waiters of Ham.

★

Angus had meant to have an easy summer and take on no new engagements; already he was regretting having said he would speak at Stratford. (When he got there, he spoke largely about Dickens and *Nicholas Nickleby*, and hardly mentioned the Bard at all, some complained.) Since his knighthood yet more requests had poured in, and he dealt with as many as he could, sometimes for no fee at all – he would not dream of accepting money for reading an unpublished novel by his old friend Wilson Knight, who had taken over as President of the Powys Society, and although he agreed to appear at Great Cornard Upper School in Sudbury he said that as a Patron of the Eastern Arts Association he could not be paid. He wrote an introduction to stories by a Singhalese friend, Suvilamee Karunaratna, and gave away a lot of money to other writers when he presented the Society of Authors Awards on 3 June. This was no way to get rich. Various trips to America were already organised – Pittsburgh in the autumn, St Louis in 1982 – but it would be cheering to have some kind of windfall himself. Royalties were not looking good.

There was a murmur of interest from television, on which so many impecunious writers pin vain hopes. Since the successful dramatisation of *Late Call* in 1975, there had been no major offer, although there was a continuing ripple of interest in the possibility of adapting *Anglo-Saxon Attitudes*: Julian Mitchell's friend, the New Zealand producer Andrew Brown, was passionately keen on this project and had bought a year's option on it for two hundred pounds in 1974. This idea had gone underground, but now there was talk of the BBC making *The Old Men at the Zoo*. Maybe it would work out this time. But anxieties nagged and snagged – so many of these projects collapsed.

Angus and Tony dined with the Priestleys on 24 April, just before the Shakespeare celebration, but found that Jacquetta was worried about Jack – he was on the whole well, but suffering from a vagueness and memory loss that she knew could only get worse. John Pattisson had died on 10 May and Fred Warburg on 24 May, and Tony's sister Genifer was seriously ill in Vevey. Angus refused to speak at a proposed Memorial Service for Fred Warburg – he felt he had said all he had to say in his message from Iowa in 1978 for Warburg's eightieth birthday celebration.

At the end of June he wrote a letter to Neville Blackburne which sums up his apprehensive mood at this time.

24.6.81

My dear Neville,

I should have written to you before to thank you for your letter which moved me greatly. You and Charles have made life much easier for me by making me feel that I am not only seen as witty, bitchy, tiring and spoilt. The adaptation to old age, much decreased income etc is not made easier by a lot of awarding of honours, praising on television etc etc (much though I ought to be grateful for these.) However, not too many more 'events' – David Farrer's 75th birthday, visit of my US publisher and

Perkin's retirement party this week, P.E.N. next; and after that only I.L.E.A. and the Sussex degree before we go. Last week I was amazed at what I did get thro' tho' it gave me drowsiness and an itching rash – but broadly speaking I feel much less tense, tho a bit scared of what I'm going to do when Tony goes as he must to see his sister for ten days but we have plans. Money, at any rate, has been worked out, altho' investigation proved that about £7,000 of large sums forecast by agents and publisher was a 'computer mistake'. At least now I only cry when the wireless or the TV are on. Diana Cooper's memoirs have largely saved my life – they're so good and her life seems to have been lived with exactly the same emotions that mine has – I bless her.

As for Tony (who has given me *all* that's most precious in my life) he is 52 next month. But we're doing all we can and must just hope.

Geoffrey and Michael were sweet recently. Also Eve and poor dying Peter (months only I should think.)

     Love to you

     Angus

P.S. If you can tell me of any poems concerned with places in, scenery of or life Norfolk Suffolk or Cambridgeshire (not Cambridge itself) – it would help with a small money-earning project I'm committed to.[14]

And so it all came to pass. On 28 June a photographer came from the *Tatler* and photographed Angus and Tony together, smiling, relaxed and contented, as they took tea in the sunny cottage by the red Chinese wallpaper and the Victorian scrap screen: Victoria sat on Angus's knee as he chatted on happily about his new knighthood and his fondness for offal and the flamingoes of North Carolina as though he had not a care in the world. This was a very different scene from the *Tatler* photograph of the solitary Angus with gin bottle which they believed had caused so much trouble all those years ago: when the 1981 picture finally appeared a year later Rosamond Lehmann wrote to tell Angus how delighted she had been to see him and Tony "both looking so bonny". But on 4 July 1981 Peter Hampshire died, and ten days later Ann Fleming: Angus and Tony went to Ann's funeral service at St James's, Sevenhampton, and spent the night with Michael Howard at Eastbury.

On 20 July Angus spoke at the Sussex Congregation dinner, and met Alan Tuckett, once his student, and once married to another of his students, Penny Allen McEwan: he saw Joan but not George Painter, who was not well and unable to come from Hove. On 25 July Angus took himself off by train to stay with the Cooksons at Whittonstall near Consett, while Tony went off to see his sister: Tony felt he was leaving Angus in good hands, he wrote to Clive and Lucie, for the Cooksons would make him very comfortable, and "I believe that he may meet one or two members of the aristocracy – so important in the summer I always think." And so he did – the Cooksons took him to dinners and drinks, to castles and cathedrals – "a very pretty woman", he noted at one point in his diary. (Who was she, one wonders?) He always told Mary Cookson, herself a very pretty woman, that she and Mary Gilliatt and Annie Fleming were his three favourite ladies – Annie was gone now, Mary Gilliatt was off to New York, and Mary Cookson in the wild north. His friends were scattering.

Angus returned from Whittonstall on 1 August to a meeting at Regent's Park Terrace with Troy Kennedy Martin over the script of *The Old Men at the Zoo*: Tony remembers that he seemed oddly detached from the whole process, as though he hadn't really grasped what was happening. A Suffolk summer of old friends and mild sightseeing followed, then, after a sticky evening at the Travellers with Bentley Bridgewater arguing about opera with a visitor from Minnesota, they flew off on 28 August for Pittsburgh. Felsham Woodside was to be left to the care of Professor Tobias and his wife, who were to have a sad time of it, presiding over the demise of Victoria. There were to be many visits to the vet, and many anxious dispatches from Mrs Revens; Victoria died, Tony gravely noted, on the night of 19 October. Her hunting days were over.

But Pittsburgh was a success, says Tony. Angus bore the title of Mellon Professor, the weather was good, they liked the Tobiases' house, and they found the historic industrial city interesting. Built on the confluence of two great rivers, its dark Satanic mills now shone in the smokeless air, and the night views over the city lights were dazzling: steel money had gone into culture and learning, indeed into a great Cathedral of Learning, in front of which Angus was photographed for the local *Pitt News*. Angus sent an enthusiastic postcard to the Painters: "Pittsburgh is a fascinating mixture of the tail end of 1880s industry, magnificent modern building, wonderful wooded mountains in the redgold of the Fall." And there were many pleasant outings to what Angus described as the "wonderful countryside" of Maryland and West Viriginia – splendid waterfalls, notes Angus, in a hand that is becoming noticeably more spidery, and a wonderful day sitting out in the sun by the water at Ohiopyle. He liked to make fun of the vision of himself white-haired upon his folding chair, telling interviewers that children and wandering hikers mistook him for George Washington or Einstein.

In October he went to Toronto to appear at the Harbourfront

International Authors' Festival (fee one thousand Canadian dollars): this went well, and the sun shone brightly upon him, though he was to be roundly ticked off by organiser Greg Gatenby for his enthusiasm for the dolphins and manatees emprisoned in Pittsburgh Zoo. Another guest at the Festival was D.M. Thomas, who heard while he was there that the Booker judges, chaired by Malcolm Bradbury, had narrowly decided to give the prize to Salman Rushdie's *Midnight's Children* and not to its rival, *The White Hotel*.

In November Perkin Walker came over to Pittsburgh from Cornell to see them for a few days, and expressed a warm admiration of the station hotel restaurant. Angus was now thinking quite seriously of writing his autobiography, as he told several interviewers: did he, one wonders, mention this project to the reticent Perkin Walker, who would have been obliged to play in it, perhaps unwillingly, at least some part?

In December the weather changed and snow began to fall. Angus and Tony were glad to fly off to a holiday in Portugal on the 17th, where Bentley Bridgewater was due to join them for Christmas. They stayed once more in style at Seteais at Sintra, and strolled amongst the box hedges and topiary: they took their usual tours round the countryside, visiting churches and *quintas*. Susan Lowndes Marques invited them once more to Monte Estoril, with Bentley, and they met there her sister Lady Iddlesleigh, who had once so improbably been engaged to Stephen Tennant. Life in Portugal was very pleasant in its way, and expatriates like Mrs Marques's amiable friend Norman Field could enjoy a mild climate, low taxes, and an agreeable social life. Was it not pleasanter here than in dark, cold, muddy Suffolk? Food was cheap, even luxury hotels were relatively cheap, the architecture was a superbly fantastic riot of Gothic and baroque, canaries sang in all the windows, and very little news came through of Mrs Thatcher: perhaps the brothers had done wisely to settle themselves in the Rua da Lapa, with its splendid views. Angus and Tony wandered round the romantic little Ruritanian domain of Sintra, and visited the famous English gardens at Montserrate, and gently thawed.

But the mud called them, and back they flew to England, to the Corkes and the Queen Mother and Terry Kilmartin and the London Library and Eve Hampshire and Gaia Mostyn-Owen and engagements cancelled through bad weather. Plumb was much on the scene, inviting Angus to Christ's to give a reading, to lunch, to dine with the Prince and Princess Michael of Kent. There were speeches in schools, and lunches with Bentley Bridgewater in Woolpit, and a supper with Wendy Rintoul. (Wendy Rintoul was working on her dictionary of the originals of fictional characters, eventually published in 1993:[15] although she must have suspected the originals of several of the Old Men at the Museum, she restricted herself to identifying Willie King as Matthew Price. She also more questionably identified Arthur Calvert in *Late Call* as Angus's father – an identification made by several readers. But although Willie Johnstone-Wilson was, like Calvert, a storyteller and a romancer, he came from a very different social background – Calvert had risen from the ranks and been gassed for his country during a hard-fought First World War, whereas Willie, as we have seen, had never been nearer to battle than a visit to see his wounded son in a field hospital.) On a bitter February day Angus turned out with Antonia and Harold Pinter, V.S. Pritchett, Stephen Spender and Francis King to demonstrate outside the Polish Embassy with a petition for the release of writers imprisoned in Poland. On 3 March Angus spoke at the King's school, Ely, and caught the attention of a curly-headed schoolboy called James Winch who was studying *Anglo-Saxon Attitudes* for A-levels: Angus, with characteristic impulsive generosity, invited James to ring up one day and invite himself to tea. Everything was going along quite calmly, apart from a problem with the lower eyelid (Angus) and a touch of lumbago (Tony): even the TV adaptation (to be directed by ex-UEA student Jonathan Powell) seemed on course. But suddenly a storm blew up out of nowhere over nothing.

The Book Marketing Council, in January 1982, had released to the trade a list of twenty "Best of British" writers which it planned to promote in the second half of February. Angus's name was not on it. When he discovered his omission (through an article in the local paper) he was deeply upset and annoyed. Why had he not been selected? The panel, chaired by Frank Delaney, had included Martyn Goff, who had always professed to admire his work so much: why had he not voted for his old friend? Goff made things worse if anything by saying that he had stood up for Angus and had been over-ruled. Peter Grose and Tom Rosenthal at Secker tried to reassure him that the whole thing would be a damp squib. Angus rang me in a state of distress rather than annoyance to complain that he wasn't on the list, and to ask me what I knew about it. I was almost as ill-informed as he was – like him, I had heard through indirect channels, and the first I knew of the scheme came from a news-cutting sent to me by a friend in New Mexico. I told Angus that the whole thing seemed to be just a commercial lottery, not to be taken seriously at all. Doris Lessing and Philip Larkin weren't on the list either, so what on earth was it all about? At the time of this conversation, I was not aware that Desmond Clarke of the BMC had told the *Sunday Times* that I had been approached early and had agreed to be on the list – an event of which I have no recollection whatsoever – but it may well be that Angus had seen this announcement.

Maybe Clarke had indeed approached my publishers, but certainly nobody had asked me, as I wrote to Angus when I had had time to think about it. Moreover I soon discovered that my principal publishers, Weidenfeld & Nicolson, had refused to sponsor me, so I was supported instead by Thames & Hudson, with whom I had recently published a book on landscape called *A Writer's Britain*, with photographs by Jerzy Lewinski. (An additional irony of this whole affair is that Angus himself had been approached before me by Thames & Hudson to write this very book, and had declined because he was too busy – a fact which he courteously never mentioned to me, although he gave my book a friendly review.)

So low was my interest in the BMC project that I (along with half the other authors) had not turned up for the group publicity photograph, as I was staying in Suffolk with my parents who were unwell. I remember my own feeling of indignation as I realised that this nonsense might endanger my friendship with Angus: I also remember my amazement that Angus should be so hurt. He said what struck me as a very strange thing during that phone call. He said he was going to see his brother and sister-in-law in France, and was afraid they would make fun of him. There you go, they would say, you think you're so famous, such an important author, and you're not even amongst the top twenty.* (Anthony Burgess responded to this initiative by compiling his own list of the best 99 post-war novels, on which Angus featured twice.)

I was taken aback by his vulnerability. I believed, like Tom Rosenthal, that such pinpricks from people so inferior in judgement to himself should not touch him. But they did. Angus's premonitions had been right. The new market economy brought with it into the literary world a new wave of malice, competition and distortion. It pitted writer against writer. Those of us who wanted to stay sane would have to keep very calm, I remember thinking then. And Angus was not very good at keeping calm. He had got things out of all proportion.

He did go off to Cannes to see Clive and Lucie: he and Tony flew off to Nice on 23 March 1982 after dining at Wendy Rintoul's the night before with Natasha Spender and Igor and Annabel Anrep. Angus took with him to France a copy of Massingham's *The Harp and the Oak*: A.N. Wilson had approached him in October 1981 to contribute a piece on a "Forgotten Masterpiece" for the *Spectator*,[16] thanking him the while for presenting him with the Somerset Maugham prize for *The Healing Art* at

---

* They were: Beryl Bainbridge, John Betjeman, Malcolm Bradbury, Anthony Burgess, Margaret Drabble, Lawrence Durrell, John Fowles, Leon Garfield, William Golding, Graham Greene, Ted Hughes, John le Carré, Laurie Lee, Rosamond Lehmann, Iris Murdoch, V.S. Naipaul, V.S. Pritchett, Rosemary Sutcliffe, Laurens van der Post and Rebecca West.

the Society of Authors Awards, and indirectly apologising for being an "annoying near namesake." It was just as well that Angus did not appreciate quite how annoying this coincidence of names might eventually become.

Angus and Tony stayed in Nice for a week, then came home, saw a few people – including, on 31 March, the Pinters whom they invited to dinner at the Athenaeum to meet Ian McEwan and his friend Polly. (Ian and Harold Pinter got on well: Pinter was to write the screenplay for McEwan's 1981 novel, *The Comfort of Strangers*.) Angus gave a few interviews, wrote a lot of letters saying No, read Wilson Knight's novel, and sent a fine recipe for pigs' trotters to Connie Brothers in Iowa. (Angus was serious about offal and trotters and Bath chaps, which he used to buy from Paxton and Whitfield in Jermyn Street, so conveniently near the London Library.) But beneath the surface, Angus was frequently on the verge of serious depression: Thatcher's England seemed no more congenial to him, and in some ways it grew more menacing – all around him were stories of cuts in educational spending and the arts, and friends were being forced into early retirement. A sympathetic letter from Gerard Reve, dated Good Friday (9 April) and clearly written in response to some *cri de coeur* from Angus, attempted to offer comfort – Reve had by now become a devout Catholic, and wrote with feeling about his own problems with drink and boys and the ephemeral nature of passion, all now he hoped in the past, and tried to reassure Angus about the permanent triumphs of Angus's own life as a writer. How fortunate, too, Angus had been with Tony, wrote Reve. In a world of danger, risk, and destructive psychopaths, not everybody could know such happiness.

At the end of April 1982 Angus and Tony whizzed off again to France on the Hovercraft, after spending a night with Jeanne and Glyn Davies in Dover. They were off once more to the Cooksons' apartment at Anzères amidst the Alpes Valaisannes, high above St Moritz, taking in a visit to Tony's sister Genifer on the same trip: they sent me a postcard of an appallingly vertiginous dangling ski-lift saying "Here we are, but luckily we're grounded in a small house lent to us at Anzères. Strange mixture of summer – very hot sun – spring – wild crocuses – and winter, evening snowfalls. See you at Ipswich, I believe!! Angus, Tony." The sun shone brilliantly upon the snow, but at Evian Angus noted in his diary "Wonderful day but deep depression." On the way home he sent a postcard of the Musée Martin Gray (at the Château de Gray, in the Haute-Saone) to Elizabeth Jane Howard telling her how much he had been enjoying reading her novel *en route*, and complimenting her on the sympathy, good sense and truth to life of her treatment of "the gay world"

– this novel was *Getting it Right*, and its hero was a non-gay hairdresser, Gavin Lamb, who could well, Angus speculated, have taken his girlfriend Jenny on one of his educational trips to the Musée.[17] On the way home they also admired the superb stonework of the cathedral at Noyon and Angus made several spidery architectural jottings about it. He sent me a postcard of the cathedral: the sins of the BMC had been forgiven, and we were to meet in public on 7 June for the launch of the Ipswich and Suffolk National Book League, with Frank Muir and my parents. (Angus wrote to say that he had found my mother very lively – not everyone's view of her, but like his own creation Meg Eliot he did bring out the best in people. The Ipswich and Suffolk National Book League still flourishes, thanks in part to the strong support of publisher and author James and Jean MacGibbon, who live overlooking the estuary at Manningtree.)

Angus and Tony tried once more to spend a quiet summer without too many public engagements. At the suggestion of Michael Slater Angus spoke at a Summer School on Kipling on 10 August (he was now President of the Kipling Society): he also met his bibliographer-to-be from Toronto and Vancouver, John Stape, and had one or two television meetings over the forthcoming *Zoo* series. But most of his engagements were social. Juliet Corke married a Frenchman and Angus spoke at the wedding in fluent French, recalling the little tabby kitten she had once given him, *"un beau petit chat rayé"*, which he had promptly and unprophetically given an Italian name – Giuseppe. Muriel Spark came to visit her old friend Guy Strutt, whose family had known the Kipling family well and who had offered (too late) to introduce Angus to Mrs Bambridge at Wimpole Hall: they all lunched together. Geoffrey Wright celebrated his seventieth birthday, and many old friends and acquaintances converged upon the Guildhall in Bury, including Bentley Bridgewater, Steven Runciman, Bunny Roger and Hermione Hammond in her old Fortuny dress. Geoffrey could look back with satisfaction on a varied musical career – and, like Angus, he could look back on a life which had mingled success with stress. After his sparkling début with the Gate and Cochran Revues he had moved on to study composition at the Guildhall, to write a symphony and chamber works, to conduct *The Threepenny Opera* and Osborne's *The Entertainer* at the Royal Court, and to compose ballet music and song cycles while working for some years with the Architects' Department of the LCC and the GLC. After his retirement to Suffolk he had continued to compose, working on several productions in association with the Theatre Royal at Bury, and this very year the Friends of the Theatre revived his *Lydia Languish*, written many years earlier with a libretto by his old friend Sandy Wilson.

Time was passing, although Geoffrey himself looked remarkably fit and young for his age. In our seventies, we begin to hear the music of the *danse macabre* striking up – the music of the rattle dance which Geoffrey had already composed, abortively, for the projected and abandoned television musical of "Totentanz" in the summer of 1963. In our eighties and nineties we hear it in earnest, and Patrick Woodcock had already noted amongst his distinguished ageing patients the rattling and jingling of the dancing skeletons, all concealments, all pretences stripped away. Bunny Roger declared in mock-horror, of a photograph taken at Geoffrey Wright's party of Angus and Frith Banbury and himself in a white suit suggestive of Monte Carlo in the 1920s, "We look like the three witches in Macbeth!" Almost time to go to Monte Carlo for good for some of them, perhaps . . .

The young cheered one up. Angus and Tony lunched with their sparkling fast-talking American friend ("our newest and best friend") Benjy Cohen, and entertained the Chisletts, who had recently adopted two delightful little Mexican boys – the Chisletts were singularly soft of heart, and wherever they went they collected people and creatures, accumulating not only a human family but also a menagerie of homeless and sometimes tailless dogs, cats and birds. Angus and Tony went with the Blackburnes for an injection of undergraduate youth by the Cambridge Footlights: but Angus, feeling giddy, wished he had not sat in the Circle.

In June Angus sent a telegram to *Gay News* congratulating it on its tenth birthday. In July he got a letter from Lucie from the Hotel Faro in the Algarve, hoping he had recovered from his "virus": "We heard from friends in England that they had a mysterious virus that gave them pneumonia – loss of weight and sickness? They blame the invasion of England by coloured people etc . . ." Doubtless he dismissed this as a typical piece of Anquetin/Johnstone-Wilson xenophobia.

On 3 August Angus and Tony spent a "fascinating" day in Harwich, and on the 11th, Angus's sixty-ninth birthday, they lunched in London with their St Louis exchanges, the Schwarzbachs, and discussed their respective cats and their diets – an Ada for a Plantagenet. They left for St Louis on 26 August 1982, and settled into what was now a familiar routine – a night in a Ramada or Holiday Inn followed by a few days getting to know their new home and its resident cat, and meeting students and faculty. Then would come teaching and lectures and excursions into the countryside, and the correction of the proofs of the Viking Portable Dickens. By now, over the years, they had collected many American ex-students to add to those from UEA who kept in regular touch about their careers, marriages and divorces – some prospering as writers, others finding quite different professions. Charles Clayton from Iowa, Dan Saferstein from Ann Arbor, Bruce and

Linda Belzowski, Kelly Cherry from Pittsburgh, David Kaplan from Iowa, all wrote regularly, and others wrote when in need of a reference or professional advice or even an address to visit in Europe: Angus never declined. (His kindness was legendary: rumour had it that at UEA his marks were conspicuously higher than those of his colleagues, but upon examination it was revealed that students tended to produce better work for Angus because he was so encouraging. And the more he encouraged, the more he was pursued.)

The American excursions, however, always offered enjoyment as well as work. Here they looked forward to the Art Gallery and the Zoo, and a visit in October to pay their respects to the birthplace of Anita Loos's Lorelei of Little Rock, Arkansas. Angus took to singing "My muddy old buddy the Wabash" wherever he went, perhaps a little too persistently for Tony's comfort. He ate walnut ice cream on the shore of the Mississippi, went on a boat trip on the *Huckleberry Finn*, picnicked at a Benedictine monastery, and enjoyed "the incredibly lovely view in changing lights" of New Harmony, Indiana, where a highschool boy in a huge bow tie acting as waiter in the elegant modern inn announced to them that their Prince had had a baby. (The news was not wholly new, as the baby had been born in June – Angus claimed to be chuffed that he was called William in honour of the Johnstone-Wilsons.) They loved New Harmony, and wandered happily in its maze: Truth was said to stand in its middle, but they found her not. Angus had a revealing fondness for places which combined aesthetic and social endeavour: New Harmony, with its Owenite aspirations, attracted him as Mogador-Essaouira had once done, though he sent a postcard to the Painters saying that Philip Johnson's "Roofless Church" was a very peculiar piece of work and reminded him of "what I was brought up to call a Kaffir Kraal!"

Angus's enthusiasm for the varied American landscape had not waned with the years, and his love of Americans persisted – he disliked the obsession with sports, but the genuine "snob-free air" of the country continued to delight him.

"I am a gipsy," he told an interviewer the following year: he said he planned to write two volumes of autobiography, one about his earlier years, and the other about his wanderings in America – it would be called "Cottages, Cars and Cats".[18]

Another interesting piece of news from England reached them: Angus was told over a dinner by lawyer Joseph Cohn ("a phenomenal Anglophile" who wore handmade English shoes and inhabited a turn-of-the-century mansion in St Louis) that Margaret Drabble and Michael Holroyd had married. Cohn, who had discovered that he would be meeting Angus, had panicked that he would have nothing to say to this eminent guest whose work he much admired, and had rung his friend, musician Steve Brown – another Wilson fan – to consult about topics of conversation: Brown, who happened to be one of Drabble's only regular correspondents, had just received a card with news of the marriage, and suggested this might be a useful bit of gossip. So Cohn duly raised the matter, and was delighted by Wilson's astonishment – "I do believe," wrote Brown, "that giving Angus Wilson this surprise was one of the happiest moments in Joe's life. According to Millie, Joe's wife, they went on to have quite a good discussion of Angus Wilson's books, as of course Wilson was pleased to meet someone who had probably read everything he'd ever written . . ."

Angus and Tony went back and dashed off a congratulatory telegram to the Holroyds: Cohn's news was shortly confirmed in November by a letter from Natasha Spender, thanking Angus for a donation for one of their good causes, saying "you sound irrepressibly cheerful in St Louis", and adding that Drabble was married and was also very cheerful although worried about her father's illness. (The Holroyds had married quietly, indeed more or less secretly, in September 1982, and the news had leaked out slowly.)

But despite the fun and the outings, there was an ever-present current of anxiety, which rumbled around them like the frequent storms of the Midwest and ocasionally broke out in violence: on 2 December a tree crashed with a tremendous bang in Stanford Avenue, and blew open the French windows at the Schwarzbachs's home. Angus did not seem to notice. He sat in the dining-room quite unmoved. It was his lack of response that upset Tony.

While they were away, Angus Wilson productions continued at home – *East Anglia in Prose and Verse*, an anthology edited and introduced by Angus, dedicated to Mr and Mrs Revens, and with "research by Tony Garrett" appeared, published by Secker & Warburg, to pleasant reviews and a warm handwritten letter of appreciation from the Queen Mother. (When they came home in December there was a party at the Angel Hotel in Bury to celebrate its publication: Tony made a little speech in which he said all the research had been done in the University of Pittsburgh. The East Anglians did not find this amusing.) Angus was elected President of the Royal Society of Literature, and offered an Honorary Degree from the Nouvelle Sorbonne. Angus and Tony had stopped subscribing to a press-cutting agency and were now dependent on reviews forwarded from Secker & Warburg, and Tony was finding it difficult from such a distance to keep a close eye on Angus's promotion. He wrote dozens of letters from

St Louis to Curtis Brown in London and New York, and to Secker and Granada, and did his best to see that the new Granada Panther paperbacks were properly distributed, to make sure that Wimpole Hall and the National Trust displayed Angus's Kipling book prominently, to effect a tie-in with a reprint of *The World of Charles Dickens* and the spectacular commercial success of the RSC's *Nicholas Nickleby*. He feared that the chance of a TV tie-in with *The Old Men at the Zoo* would be botched, as it had been so disastrously by Penguin for *Late Call*, and wrote anxious letters trying to check that everything was being done to sell Angus's work at home and abroad. For Angus and Tony were off abroad again – to India, for the British Council, in the New Year. The gipsy life continued.

Angus admonished himself to rest before he took off again on his travels. "Sleep," he wrote longingly on several pages of his diary after their return to England on 11 December 1982. And maybe he did sleep, in the intervals between seeing Alan Gray and Bentley Bridgewater, Patrick Woodcock and Maggie Bishop, Martin Corke and the Reynoldses, Geoffrey Wright and Michael Colborne-Brown, the Blackburnes and Jack Plumb. Old friends all – though on 29 December a new friend, Pittsburgh-born Joseph Kissane of Columbia University, came for an extended interview. Kissane was to prove one of Angus's most discriminating and appreciative allies in the academic world.

28

ZOO PARTY

1983 was Angus's seventieth year, and it brought with it all that should accompany old age – as honour, love, obedience, troops of friends. But it also brought a few tempests.

In early January, Angus flew off alone to Paris for a couple of nights, to be presented with an Honorary Degree at the Nouvelle Sorbonne alongside William Golding. Sylvère Monod, to whom Angus had dedicated his Portable Dickens, presented Angus for his degree, and threw a party in his fifth-floor apartment for his white-maned pride of British lions: the Monods had recently had a lift installed and Angus did not have to negotiate the steep flights of stairs. He talked brilliantly in a French that – like Dickens's own – was quick but not perfect, making sure he spoke to everybody. There was no sign of any mental or physical deterioration, but nevertheless it was a taxing programme for a man no longer young, and a day later he and Tony flew off together to Bombay for a British Council lecture tour, luckily interspersed with some breaks for rest.

They were away for six weeks, and covered the country – from Bombay to Poona, Bangalore, Hyderabad, Madras, Trivandrum, Bhubaneshwar, Calcutta, Delhi and Lucknow. These trips were exhausting, with flights leaving at four in the morning, long waits in airports, and hundreds of new faces a day. In Bombay he met the wry and enigmatic poet Nissim Ezekiel, in Poona he met the famous old champion of the untouchables, Mulk Raj Anand, and in Delhi he saw Anita Desai – but he also met hordes of eager young students and academics, all anxious to tug at the guru's sleeve. Indians, as he had discovered on previous visits, were not all quiet contemplatives: many of them were even more busy and bustling and inquisitive than Americans. Nevertheless, some of them had a kind of second sight. Jaidev, on whose academic career he had kept an anxious and protective eye, had written in his New Year's greetings that he had "foolish and irrational fears" about Angus's health. Would it stand up to this gruelling schedule?

There were bad moments, like the one when Tony tried to pack Angus off on his own from Calcutta to lecture in Delhi and Lucknow: Angus made his way back through the barrier, with the help of a kindly Indian gentleman, in a panic because he'd lost his ticket. "It's in your copy of *Nostromo*," said Tony. And indeed it was. But Tony feared they might not be so lucky every time.

Amidst the rush and the social whirl they found oases of peace – sitting in palm groves, visiting ruins and palaces and temples, and calling in at the lavatory of Mamallapuram Township (price 10 paise per person for using lavatory once, as recorded on the carefully cherished receipt dated 22 January 1983). And wherever Angus lectured – on Dickens, on Brontë, on Woolf, on himself – he left behind him a trail of astonished delight, which Michael Holroyd and I picked up when we travelled in his footsteps the following year – ah, Sir Angus, how he loved the birds! Here he stopped, here on this very corridor in the University of Bhubeneshwar, and cried out, look at that butterfly! Sir Angus was so witty, so clever, so tireless, such fun! He noticed so much, he was so kind to everyone! (Raleigh Trevelyan and Raul Balin, travelling even more immediately in his wake, found the beggar girl attached to the hotel in Bangalore giving an excellent imitation of the temptingly imitable Sir Angus.)

But he was also tired. Dina Mehta, meeting him again in Bombay, thought he looked "rather weary", and on his return he wrote to her that he had returned

> . . . utterly exhausted by my tour, although I am more in love
> with India than ever and not in Miss Jefferson's way,* for I was
> as much horrified as I was delighted this time – the lively, elegant
> boys and girls/even women and men) who delight me so to watch
> are in part, I fear, so elegant because they are so ill fed (I would
> not face this on my first two visits-but even now I would argue
> that a workloaded middleclass Thatcherite life is the end of all
> liveliness all richness and diversity of living and I fear that we shall
> turn in the West into Benthamite high producing, technological
> workday people who after work simply watch and eat and never
> come alive. My only surviving brother (87 – 17 years older than
> me) has been seriously ill. He is incredibly tough and is now,
> nursed by his tough French wife (81) well on the road to

* Maybelle Jefferson, a character in Mehta's story "The New Broom" from her collection, *The Other Woman*.

recovery. But the shuttling between here and Cannes where they live has been very consuming.

I have also started on some short stories. Perhaps inspired by you. I found yours superb and within an apparrently small circle of life enormously rich and varied. Moving – and (see Miss Jefferson) often very funny. Thank you. And I hope we meet again. Tony sends his best regards,

　　Yours
　　Angus Wilson.

This is a sombre though spirited letter, and Angus's underlying mood remained tense and sombre. A trip to see Clive and Lucie in Cannes in February was cancelled because of Clive's illness. David Farrer died in harness at the end of the month – an old friend whose loyalty to Angus and his work had never been in question. Angus's troops seemed to be thinning out. And in March, another storm broke, similar in tone to the Book Marketing Council débâcle and the Julian Mitchell row.

This time the focus of Angus's paranoia was Terry Kilmartin, who in an unguarded moment over lunch on 2 February the year before had seemed to say that he had not admired *Setting the World on Fire*, and thought Angus's writing days were over – at least, he had implied, he assumed that Angus would produce no more novels. Kilmartin had also, or so Angus remembered, reproached Angus for accepting a knighthood. These were the last things that Angus wished to hear: as he told Dina Mehta, he was trying to goad himself on to write some long short stories, which, in view of his off-repeated dismissal of his own interest in the form, might in itself suggest a fear of waning powers. (Tony, aware of Angus's reluctance to tackle a full-length novel, had encouraged the idea of writing short stories.)

Angus's professional relationship with Terry Kilmartin had had its difficulties – with Angus alternately hurt that he was offered so little reviewing, and insisting that he was too busy to take on any more for months. For many years now books had pursued him to Suffolk and round the globe, and copy had been turned in not always very tidily but with a high degree of reliability. But Angus suspected that Terry Kilmartin and Miriam Gross were no longer so interested in what he had to say, and was depressed that the *Observer* had not been able to offer him the assurance of a written contract for regular reviews. In the autumn of 1982 he had sent in his last two pieces for the paper, from Stanford Avenue, St Louis: the first, which appeared on 3 October 1982, was a friendly review of Peter Quennell's *Customs and Characters*, a collection of "slender anecdotes" about Edwardian and between-the-wars figures like Diana Cooper and Greta Garbo, and the second, which appeared on 31 October 1982, was a review of Angela Carter's *Nothing Sacred*. Angus was well aware that Carter (who had taught for a while at UEA) was a writer whose name carried much weight with the younger generation, and he wrote in praise of her bravery in "keeping alive of the erotic, the physical, even the sado-masochistic in all her complicated explorations of the social shape of our times", but he also chided her for allowing the strength of her feminist and social convictions to prevent her from "empathising with a great part of her characters."

This, apart from his choice of three Christmas books – Elizabeth Jane Howard's *Getting It Right*, Eudora Welty's *Losing Battles*, and Carter's *Nothing Sacred* – was the last he wrote for Terry Kilmartin. He had informed Kilmartin, in a letter from St Louis dated 20 October 1982 that he could review no more until the spring, as he was busy with exams and lectures, and would then be off to India for the British Council ("with a bit of holiday thrown in"). Kilmartin had accepted this, perhaps too readily. The *Observer* at this time was well supplied with a team of distinguished reviewers which included Paul Bailey, Anthony Burgess, D.J. Enright, Philip Larkin and Lorna Sage – and on 10 October 1982 reviews had appeared by both Kingsley and Martin Amis. There was no shortage of quality criticism, and Angus may have felt insecure in the face of it, even though, as he said, he sometimes felt he would like to give up journalism altogether.

Angus and the Kilmartins had, until this period, always got on well together in personal terms. Angus and Tony had taken a kindly interest in their son Christopher when he was at school at Nowton Court, and the Kilmartins had been to stay for many a weekend in Suffolk – indeed, as Kilmartin was quick to point out in self-defence, he and Joanna had been to Felsham Woodside for the night in early March 1982, five weeks after the alleged insults.

Angus's mounting tensions belatedly erupted into a flurry of letters, apparently prompted by a chance meeting at a W.H. Smith Prize Luncheon on 16 March 1983 at the Fishmongers' Hall: the prize had gone to his namesake A.N. Wilson for *Wise Virgin* and Angus had been placed at table next to his old acquaintance Norman St John Stevas. (Did they, one wonders, mention Mrs Thatcher?) At some point at this event he and Kilmartin met, and words were exchanged. Angus wrote two letters two days later, one official and one personal: in the first he said he would write no more for the *Observer*, and in the second he claimed that Kilmartin's remarks had been "central to the recurring bouts of depression and frustration that I have suffered in this last year." He brought up Kilmartin's "expressed distaste" for *Setting the World on Fire* and his misinterpretation of Burgess's favourable *Observer* review of it, and also recalled his critical remarks about Angus's review of a travel book by Paul Fussell:[1] more generally, he alleged that "most strangely" Kilmartin had complained of his support for the homosexual cause and his liking of the company of women. "I don't too much enjoy pub life if that is what mens company means to you," wrote Angus – and "as to my enjoyment of womens friendship, if what you don't like is my overt support for womens causes, I plead guilty."

In response, Kilmartin pleaded innocent: he said he was very shaken by Angus's unexpected attack, and that his remarks had been totally misunderstood and misremembered. Tom Rosenthal joined the fray, loyally taking Angus's side, and emotionally defending him against both Kilmartin and Jonathan Raban, whose name now seemed to have become attached to the squabble as someone who had lost faith in Angus's fiction – a reference back, perhaps, to the Julian Mitchell episode. Raban and Kilmartin were unforgivable, Rosenthal declared. Rosenthal himself recalled having had a terrible dinner at the Athenaeum with Angus after the publication of *Setting the World on Fire*, during which Angus had told him that Kilmartin had told him he ought to give up writing fiction.

A storm in a teacup, but quite an ominous little storm. These outbursts were frightening. Angus had not arrived at the complacent or well-armoured serenity that sometimes accompanies old age – he was as morbidly sensitive as ever, indeed was perhaps becoming more and more vulnerable. Jonathan Raban believed that he had taken fright – " *Setting the World on Fire* seems to me to have fright written on its every page – fright at not moving in the right circles, not being in the centre of things. I can't help feeling that from *No Laughing Matter* onwards (which is a book I revere, but the rot does seem to start there), Angus began to confuse post-modernist aesthetics with a social world from which he felt he was being increasingly excluded. He wanted to be in the swim – the same swim as fancy p.– mods as Barth and Hawkes and Butor and Co. This is, I know, very crudely put . . . but when Angus asked me if he was too old to write more novels, I now wonder if what he meant was too old to write post-modernist novels of the kind that would seize the attention of 'the young'.

"I have a hunch that his time at UEA . . . may have led him into an agonising misreading of the value of his own work. 'The young' were into movies, not novels, (a point I remember him making many times), and if they were into novels, they weren't his kind of novel. (He detested Fowles's *The Magus* – and I can see now exactly why; it was a great success with 'the young', and it was a piece of tricksy, seminarish fiction-of-fiction writing of the kind that made Angus feel prematurely old.) I think he saw his own wonderful style of very heightened social realism as having gone the same way as the teddy boys, Knightsbridge hostesses and old men at the zoo who had lived inside it . . ."[2]

Was there a pattern to these outbursts? Peter Conradi, a sharp and affectionate Angus-watcher, had tried to follow the thread, and had noticed that Angus had a remarkable capacity for loyalty even to people he did not much like – indeed he was loyal even to the rejected friends of his friends, and would enquire with a curiously long-lasting solicitude about a not particularly attractive or interesting couple to whom Conradi had once introduced him at his cottage in Wales – but once Angus fell out with somebody, the rift tended to be serious. Sonia Orwell, Terry Kilmartin, John Bowen, Anthony Blond, Julian Mitchell . . . all had offended, and not all had been forgiven.

Many people had managed to quarrel with the theatrical and unpredictable publisher, Anthony Blond, whose most faithful author Simon Raven liked to refer to Blond's publishing company as "Blond's Folly". Angus had known Blond on and off over many years – Ann Dent from Bletchley Park, when married to her first husband Anthony Rubenstein, had invited Angus Wilson, the rising literary star, and publisher Blond to dinner together, and had been worried by strange undercurrents of tension between them – was Angus, she wondered, anti-Semitic?* Their relationship was never comfortable. John Bowen, who had been a good friend, denies that there was anything that could be described as a quarrel, though he admits that he and Angus had somewhat drifted apart, as Bowen himself became more successful and less of a listener – "and by the late sixties a listener was what one was required to be." Bowen recalls the conversation about the East India Company at Tom Rosenthal's party for *As If By Magic*: clearly it registered with both of them. But he and his friend, novelist David Cook, were not struck off the guest list, and there was no real ill-feeling on Angus's side.[3]

The subject of politics could spark trouble. This spring, Angus, prompted somewhat by Barley Alison (like him hitherto a long-term Labour Party supporter), joined the SDP, a move which did not go down too well with lefties like Simon Edwards (who continues to describe himself as an unreconstructed Stakhanovite) – but Simon, lastingly devoted to Angus, managed not to quarrel over the issue. The very

---

* Ann Dent (now Ann Langford Dent) had taken up her interrupted training as an artist after the war, and after this dinner (some time in the Fifties or Sixties, she thinks) she painted a large blue-eyed bow-tied Angus. He was an impatient sitter ("when he switched off he switched off") but she noted that success had made him much better-looking and pleasanter of manner than he had ever been at Bletchley.

thought of Mrs Thatcher continued to enrage both Angus and Tony – though they continued to spend pleasant evenings with conservative squire John Alston and his friend Milo O'Sullivan of Besthorpe Hall in Norfolk, disagreeing about politics in a way that never grew sharper than teasing.

But there is no doubt that journalistic opinion was continuing to thicken against the liberalism Angus represented: in the 1980s writers who were or had been left-wing were portrayed in the press as naïve, fellow-travelling, deluded, or hypocritical. Some of these charges were grossly unfair. History was being rewritten, often with little regard to the facts. In 1981 the OUP had published a symptomatic volume by Paul Hollander entitled *Political Pilgrims: Travels of Western Intellectuals to the Soviet Union, China, and Cuba 1928–1978* in which writers and artists like Bernard Shaw, Sartre, de Beauvoir, Mary McCarthy, Simone Signoret and Susan Sontag were castigated at times somewhat indiscriminately for their gullibility abroad and their susceptibility to the hospitality of socialist or communist régimes. It was all too easy to slip, by association, the names of writers like Angus into a list of the deceived and seduced: Hollander writes "Simone Signoret and Yves Montand, the French actress and actor, were entertained by Krushchev and virtually the entire Politbureau. Simone de Beauvoir, Sartre, Angus Wilson, Magnus Enzensberger, and other European writers were flown 'aboard a special plane' to Krushchev's 'country place in Georgia . . . a vast wood, planted with the rarest and most beautiful trees in the whole Union. Krushchev greeted us pleasantly . . . he took us to see the swimming pool he had made by the shore; it was immense, and all round it had a glass wall that could be made to disappear by pressing a button – he did so several times, with great satisfaction.'

"Often the purpose and result of such attentions were either to send some specific political message through selected individuals . . . or else to make a lasting, favorable impression on individuals who were considered important or potential opinion-makers capable of influencing public opinion in their own countries."[4]

This seemed fair enough, as far as it went, but the writers who were alleged to have been hoodwinked were quoted very selectively and given no right of reply: no mention here of those icy vigils on pavements outside embassies on behalf of imprisoned Polish or Hungarian writers, no mention of those telegrams sent, those lists of signatures collected by PEN and Amnesty International. One would not guess from Hollander's extract from de Beauvoir's account of the Krushchev meeting in 1963 that far from being seduced, she had, as we have seen, been highly critical of the whole exercise. And it is comic to find Hollander citing in a list of excessive eulogies of hosts by guests, in a chapter entitled "The Techniques of Hospitality", a stoic Mary McCarthy in wartime North Vietnam, patiently putting up with these luxurious attentions: ". . . each time I went to the outlying toilet, the young woman interpreter went with me as far as the door, bearing my helmet, some sheets of tan toilet paper . . . and at night, the trusty flashlight." A far cry, one might have thought, from a Chinese banquet.

But the left and liberalism were now out of fashion, like an old tune. Journalist Paul Johnson had now travelled so far from the base of his *New Statesman* days that he was eager to accuse anyone who did not travel with him of travelling with the enemy. Those who were not for Mrs Thatcher were against her, and mysteriously even those who had spoken up loud and clear against the Soviet Union and its treatment of dissident intellectuals were now portrayed as its apologists. Trying to set the record straight was exhausting.

It was an uneasy climate, and one in which temptations to paranoia were felt by many less naturally susceptible than Angus. It was easy to misread signals. A case in point was provided by an *Observer* Profile of Angus, published on 7 August to celebrate his seventieth birthday. It was intended as a tribute, but he did not receive it in that spirit. It is not a soft piece, though it hailed him from the start as "an authority against authority" and praised his works highly: but it did not hesitate to examine (not to condemn) the direction of his recent fiction. ". . . ironically, as Angus Wilson the elder statesman of letters became more established, Angus Wilson the novelist was becoming less so. The same imaginative restlessness and generous identification with the future that one can trace in all these activities [i.e. Arts Council, teaching the young etc.] made *No Laughing Matter* (1967) a difficult novel for his readers to take. It was allusive and dense with self-consciousness . . . His knighthood, in 1980, coincided with the publication of the least read of his novels, *Setting the World on Fire*, rather as if, a friend sadly said, the honour was a recompense for neglect. The earlier novels, too, seemed to be slipping mysteriously out of reach. The reasons are doubtless ultimately to do with the pervasive revulsion against the political doings of that Other Wilson, which discredit, it sometimes seems, any liberal' values that happened to be canvassed at the time. A desert of scepticism divides us from the fertile ambiguities of *Anglo-Saxon Attitudes*.

"Comparison with Malcolm Bradbury's *The History Man* would provide a measure of that gulf. Bradbury was recently described in the the *Sunday Times* as the new unoffocial novelist laureate, partly, seemingly, on the grounds that his novel's eloquent disillusionment with libertarian

cultural aspirations had helped Margaret Thatcher win the 1979 election
... be that as it may, it's indisputable that Wilson's virtues are, currently,
intensely unfashionable. Like Sir William Empson, another White Knight,
he pursues complexity, ambivalence, diversity, as moral aims and matters
of conscience."

And there was more among the same lines. This was not perhaps the
ideal seventieth birthday present – who would not prefer to be told that he
is the greatest writer of the post-war world, and beyond the vagaries of
fashion? – but it is by no means as offensive as Angus suspected: the target is
Thatcher's new Britain (and possibly even the trend-conscious Bradbury
himself) not the adventurous Angus Wilson. Being in fashion in
Thatcher's Britain, as the *Observer* suggests, was hardly an accolade. But it
was hard for Angus and Tony to read this calmly, and they naturally
preferred the warmer and less questioning tribute in *The Times* – written,
ironically but not very surprisingly, by Malcolm Bradbury himself. One
cannot help feeling that the right balance was struck by the shrewd but
good-hearted Maggie Bishop, who wrote to Angus on 14 August,
thanking him for sending her a copy of the Bradbury piece, but continuing
"I still insist – as a fairly detached reader – that there is considerable
affection in the Observer feature." (There was – it was written by Lorna
Sage.)

The unestablished Angus continued to raise eyebrows. His seventieth
birthday was a major event, and major festivities were planned: there was
to be a great party at the Zoo followed by a dinner at the Garrick in July,
and a mass release of Granada paperbacks, as well as approaching fanfares
for the September showing of the Troy Kennedy Martin-Stuart Burge-
Joanathan Powell TV adaptation of *The Old Men at the Zoo*. All this might
have seemed quite enough to be going on with, but Angus and Tony were
to add a surprise ingredient to the festive mix.

In April Angus had received a letter from Patricia Holland, a researcher
at the BBC, asking him if he would be willing to consider appearing in a
series of programmes about partners and their "long-term relationships",
with John Pitman as reporter – the producer would be Edward Mirzoeff,
who had recently made a documentary about Westminster School. Angus
wrote back on 18 April inviting her to tea at Regent's Park Terrace –
"Tony Garrett will be there (I am assuming you mean him when you talk
about partnership)." And so it very rapidly went on from there. The BBC
discovered that in Angus and Tony it had not one but two natural
performers, and it planned its film sequences to display them both – filming
at the cottage of daily life and social life, filming at the Zoo, filming of Mrs
Revens, even filming of the retiring Perkin Walker. Jonathan Gili, friend

and colleague of Jonathan Powell, who had first met Angus twenty years earlier on that summer visit with Paul Binding, would direct. It would be something quite exceptional, an intimate portrait of two men in a stable, happy marriage, talking about their lives together. Tony would be seen as cook, secretary, chauffeur and friend, chopping parsley, shopping in the supermarket, typing Angus's appallingly untidy manuscripts, sparkling over a lunch table.

Angus and Tony seem to have had no qualms about accepting this challenge, nor indeed to sense that it was a challenge. They had "come out" long ago and their support for the liberation movement had not wavered – although the advent of AIDS had suggested to them as to others the possibility of a new wave of homophobia, illustrated by contradictory newspaper cuttings about American state law and visa regulations which they now began to collect. ("Court prohibits Ban on Homosexual Aliens" read one headline from the *New York Times*, 8 September 1983.) But by and large gay liberation seemed to be making real progress: Angus had given a favourable review to the *Penguin Book of Homosexual Verse*,[5] of which the very title would have been unthinkable only a few years earlier, and as we have seen had read with fascination the proofs of Andrew Hodge's scholarly and ground-breaking biography of Alan Turing. Of course there was still the *Sunday Express* to contend with, and in April he and Tony had written a letter of support to the beleaguered gay activist Peter Tatchell after he lost the Bermondsey by-election to the Liberal Simon Hughes. Peter Tatchell had faced a particularly unfortunate combination of circumstances: Bob Mellish, former Labour Chief Whip and the long-standing member for Bermondsey, had resigned from Parliament, and when Peter Tatchell was selected to fight his seat Mellish campaigned against him with the slogan "Which Queen will you vote for?", whipping up anti-homosexual feelings in the neighbourhood and ensuring that this safe rock-solid Labour seat was lost.[6] But this, Angus hoped, was not representative of the feelings in the country at large. His own constituency was more enlightened, more tolerant.

Angus had not of late sensed much hostility, despite the odd mad anonymous letter: his personal charm and integrity in public office had made him acceptable even to those who had admitted that they did not as a rule like homosexuals. Martyn Goff records that there had been some anxiety in the book trade when Angus was about to be appointed Chairman of the National Book League – was it really a good idea to have two known homosexuals as Chairman and Director? – but Angus had made himself both useful and popular. Victor Bonham-Carter of the

Society of Authors, who confessed to an "in-built distrust" of homosexuals, said that he excepted Angus: "I always found him friendly and
generous, never bitchy in my hearing about anyone though he may well
have been at other times . . . he was helpful in the worst period of the PLR
campaign."[7] Joanna Richardson, biographer and member of the Royal
Society of Literature committee, had resisted in committee his election as
President of the RSL in 1982, but she was out-voted, and Mrs Schute, the
Society's secretary, was impressed by his diligence at the RSL.

So no great risk seemed to be associated with making a programme
about his life with Tony. It seemed a jolly idea – a victory celebration over
sorrows past. During June and July the BBC pursued them with
interviews, and they both talked freely about themselves and their
relationship. There were one or two tiny shadows – Mrs Revens was
certainly willing and eager to appear in her role as faithful apple-cheeked
housekeeper and cat protector, and assured them (on the fifth anxious
enquiry) that she quite understood what the programme would reveal, but
some of their Suffolk friends seemed a little reluctant to appear as
ornaments at a televised lunch or dinner. One or two of them – who had
been more than happy to invite Angus and Tony to their homes, to accept
their hospitality, to laugh their heads off at Angus's jokes – were shy of the
camera, and indeed said they found the whole thing really a bit
unneccesary. Gay Lib had gone too far. It was undignified. Why flaunt
oneself? The attitudes of discreet gay Bloomsbury mingled with those of
the smart or stuffy heterosexual county in a mild disapproval of such
exhibitionism.

But some rejoiced. One-time protégé of Jack Plumb, historian Neil
McKendrick and his wife Melveena were very happy to be invited to appear
in the inner circle at Felsham Woodside, and so were Benjy Cohen and
Janet Shand-Kydd, who got in a bit of a muddle with the technology –
when the sound man, hoping to pick up some witty conversation,
interposed a microphone wrapped in an old sock between her and her
neighbour, she assumed it was something to eat, and declined it politely
with a "No, thank you very much." Emma Tennant would have loved to
be there, and was disappointed when she had to cancel because she fell ill.

The interviews gave both Angus and Tony a chance to talk with some
seriousness about their relationship – though both were highly conscious
of the effect they were making. Tony proved a polished performer: he had
travelled a long way from Finchley and the YMCA. They both revealed
and concealed their lives with an adept smoothness, like any mutually
supportive long-married couple. Yes, they said, they occasionally irritated
one another – Angus's untidiness, Tony's repetitive jokes and puns. Yes,

Angus had used Tony for Eric in *Hemlock*, a little for Tom in *Setting the World on Fire* (that famous *béarnaise*), perhaps even a little, unconsciously, for Hamo's Sam Weller in *Magic*, the comic Cockney Erroll. Angus worried about having swallowed up Tony's life: Tony described his anger over the probation-officer episode, his feeling that he should perhaps have spoken up at the time. No, they said, they had not been without sexual adventures on the side, but they had long given up the easy promiscuity of their early years in favour of a settled life together: Tony said that when he did have "flings" he always told Angus about them, and never saw them as a threat to his life with Angus – "it was talked about or known between the two of us, and I think that was the important thing . . . it would never have occurred to me to try to keep [secret] something so intimate, I mean important as that, or potentially important . . ." Angus did not regard these diversions as serious either: both made clear, when interviewed together or separately, that they expected to stay together, though Angus ended on a characteristically wry note – yes, he sometimes worried that Tony would walk off the edge of a cliff by mistake, but he knew that was not what interviewer John Pitman meant about worry about their future :

> ANGUS: . . . you say do I get worried would he go off with
> someone else, no, it never enters my head. Of course in a book
> that would be the very moment when you expect it to happen,
> but I don't think it will.
> PITMAN: It would only happen in a book?
> ANGUS: Ah it won't happen to us, I don't think, I really don't
> think.

They both spoke with confidence, ably playing their role as stable, teasing, tolerant partners, presenting a united front to the world. They would not desert one another. But when questioned about the future, a shadow of uneasiness crept into their answers. They had not been sensible with money, they knew. They could not really see very far ahead. Tony was willing to push Angus's wheel-chair, but would Angus be able to push Tony's? (Laughter.) They refused to look ahead. They could not envisage anything beyond a life of work and travel.

The sequence at the Zoo had a different, crazier tone to it than the cottage sequences. This party was indeed, as many were to point out, one of the wildest, most Wilsonian events imaginable, uniting the fantastic, the delightful and the macabre to the most astonishing degree. It was not quite a rare old Armageddon, but it had a touch of the end of the world about it. The weather and the beasts did their best and their worst. In the morning, as Angus and Tony strolled through the zoo discussing their party outfits –

a peacock shirt and turquoise trousers, perhaps? – the sun seemed well inclined, but by the time guests began to arrive in the evening the heavens had opened. There was a deluge. The animals roared and trumpeted and hooted and catcalled as the thunder crashed. They cried out to Angus, who for many years had heard them calling to him as he lay tucked up aloft in his bed in nearby Regent's Park Terrace. Where was the ark? They would surely drown.

Champagne and canapés circulated, umbrellas dripped, guests chattered and mopped and mowed. And what guests! Here was a terrifying, a stupendous gathering from all the seven decades of Wilson history. Here were great-nephews and nieces, here were old boys from Westminster, here were colleagues from UEA and Holland and India and the Arts Council, here were poets and novelists and biographers and publishers, here were beauties and grotesques, here were rose-growers and Kipling scholars and Dickensians and contributors to the *SM Times*. Here were sons who would not speak to their fathers, here were (or were not) husbands who failed the feast for fear of meeting their ex-wives. Anne-Marie Meyer and Lady Antonia Fraser Pinter found themselves wearing identical dresses of Jean Muir spots. Karl Miller mislaid his umbrella. Peter Jenkins met John Petch and Geoffrey Wright from his Suffolk youth – he hadn't seen them for years. Some sneaked off through the rain to gaze at the poor sodden tigers in their cages. Some stayed to cheer. Lady Bonham-Carter, Peter Price, Ludo Pieters, Christopher and Helen Morris, the Painters, Hermione Hammond, Denis and Patsy Barnes, Ian McCallum, Bentley Bridgewater, Raymond Tyner, Steven Runciman, Patrick Woodcock – there they all were, milling and thronging.

The camera dwelt on Charlotte Bonham-Carter with a particular delight. She was of the essence of Wilson. She was a redoubtable first-nighter, opera-lover and party-goer, and had been much admired by Philippe Jullian – Angus recorded that Jullian, having searched in vain for her eccentric achievements in *Who's Who*, threw the volume to the floor with a cry of disgust – "Oh, what an 'orrible book!" Charlotte was now old, long widowed, and had long been hooped with arthritis, but nothing prevented her from attending social and artistic occasions, and she was sometimes to be seen at several a night, occasionally popping in, it was alleged, for the interval at the Royal Opera House: tiny, fragile, with head cocked enquiringly upon one side like an inquisitive bird, she never listened for long. At one party she asked of a friend, "How's your husband?" "I'm afraid he died a couple of months ago," came the subdued reply. "Fascinating, fascinating!" cried Charlotte, and moved spryly on. And here, at the Zoo, she was in her element.

She was quite oblivious to the presence of the cameras: others were more self-conscious. Conradi's friend Jim O'Neill was convinced that he had been mistaken for his fellow Canadian, Angus's editor and admirer Kerry McSweeney, and was being pursued by the jib-boom and the camera for good takes of intellectual conversation: the uncut version of his interchange with Stephen Jones ran:

O'NEILL: Oh God, this is supposed to be a literary party. What the hell are we to talk about, they're recording all of this crap?
JONES: Talk about literature, ask me about Dickens.
O'NEILL: Have you read *Nicholas Nickleby*?
JONES: No.

(Only the last two lines survived: Jones received several copies of *Nicholas Nickleby* for Christmas that year.)

The family was there in force. Jeanne and Glynn Davies, who had just celebrated their Ruby Wedding with Angus in attendance, were there, and so were some of the Scotts. The South African branch, including Angus's godson Chrispen (son of Penelope Holt), sent many greetings. Despite his gipsy life, Angus had done his best to keep in touch with his relatives, and had made welcome any South Africans who arrived in England.* Of his great-nephews and nieces, he was perhaps closest in temperament to nephew Mark Davies, who continued to share Angus's globe-trotting instincts and his concern about global politics, but Angus had also gone out of his way to talk to Sybil's daughter Georgina at her grandmother Betty Wilson's funeral, and shortly afterwards had taken her out to lunch at Wheeler's in London. He thought he would have liked to have children of his own, he had told John Pitman in an interview for the *Couples* programme: certainly he proved a more benevolent uncle than many elderly bachelors, and his sense of family duty and connection was surprisingly strong. Nevertheless, it was a bit of a worry to have everyone from his past life all jumbled up together like this . . .

Some guests didn't make it to the party. Bunny Roger got the date wrong and arrived a day late with pounds of melting chocolates. Charles Carrington wrote saying he was too old – his wife was in hospital "and I ought to be". John Bowle from Oxford and Harold Acton from Fiesole ("in my seventy ninth year") also declined on grounds of age. Angus was showered with messages both for this event and for his "real" birthday in August – very queenlike to have two birthdays, some commented – he was

---

* A South African relative lay in the family mausoleum at Kingston – old BW's great-grandson, Frederick Caney Slingsby Mann, son of Angus's cousin Betty Caney by her first husband, was interred there in 1975. He was Penelope Holt's brother.

inundated with greetings telegrams, with pretty floral cards, with elegant British Museum cards, with tasteful Old Masters and tasteless naked boys, with kitsch and camp and coy. One of the most beautiful messages was a card of dried flowers from Genifer Garrett and her friend Vreni from their home by Lac Léman in Switzerland.

It was all very exciting, and, as Angus said in his speech, "macabre". After the big bash, a mere thirty or so retired to the Garrick for dinner where Antonia Fraser spoke most affectionately of Angus and his work, and Tom Rosenthal presented him, on behalf of his various publishers and his agents – Secker, Granada, Viking, Stock and Curtis Brown – with a handsome set of the Nonesuch Dickens. It had all gone off very well, despite the storm. It had been utterly exhausting, but never mind, off they staggered the next evening to Claridges to help Steven Runciman celebrate his eightieth, then on to Soho to dine with Geoffrey Wright and Michael Colborne-Brown. Angus was still a chicken in comparison to some of his guests. (Geoffrey Wright and Bentley Bridgewater had been so excited the night before that they had gone home in one another's coats.)

*

The summer was divided between Suffolk and London, and broken up by days of filming for the BBC programme. Tony escaped from being a couple for a while and spent a few days alone in London while Angus tried to work and went to stay for a couple of nights with Benjy Cohen at Shingle Street. (Angus and Tony, as they had told the BBC cameras, had to get away from one another from time to time in order to remain a happy couple.) Benjy Cohen had bought the house on the strand with its magical horizontal view of the eastern sea from another Suffolk friend, Norman Scarfe, and there he lived with his race-horse training friend Charles Jerdein: he remembers that he and Angus talked about Willie Johnstone-Wilson's "weakness for the gee-gees" and the odd way in which Plumb, Stephen Spender and Michael Howard always seemed to fall on their feet in the poshest of the American universities, while Angus and Tony wandered the Midwest. (Benjy Cohen had still not quite recovered from the shock of reading the entire works of Emma Tennant in order to be able to converse intelligently with her over the televised luncheon, only to find that she had been unable to come.)

Tony returned to the fold, and other visitors descended, including Anne Thomas from New Vernon, New Jersey, soon to join forces with John Stape as official bibliographer. She arrived upon a bicycle. (Tony had helpfully sent her a booklet on *Where to Stay in East Anglia* and she was cycling around the Bed and Breakfast circuit.) The clever off-beat good-looking schoolboy James Winch, whom Angus had met at the King's School, Ely, invited himself to tea with his Suffolk neighbour Caroline Dibert: they both lived in a village near Sudbury. Later Winch invited Angus and Tony back to Sudbury and entertained them with his own songs on the guitar and his standard student special of steamed spaghetti, steamed vegetables, and mackerel fried in garlic with tomatoes. They had seemed to enjoy it very much, he said. Rothschilds at Rushbrooke and Reynoldses at the Manse also provided entertainment, and in London Angus dined at the Zoo with Drury Pifer and his wife Ellen – a doubly appropriate location, for this year Pifer had a play on at the Young Vic entitled *A Day at the Zoo*.

Angus celebrated his second, real birthday on 11 August 1983 at the Old Rectory, Great Whelnetham, with his old friend Martin Corke, who was almost exactly ten years younger than he was: it was a beautiful summer evening, and Martin Corke in his short-sleeved striped blue cotton shirt glowed benignly on the sunny lawn. Tony, ever correct, was wearing a jacket and tie. The Corkes, though correct in some ways, and familiar with the ways of the old county régime, were also unconventional – and ever tolerant. Martin and Jean Corke, and now Martin and his second wife Frances, had provided an oasis of hospitality, comfort and culture in what Angus sometimes described as a philistine county: they were rare friends, in fair and foul weather. They drank Angus's health in Taittinger 1973, and dined on *salade de fromage de chèvre au noix* and *pintade au vinaigrette framboise*, accompanied by Château Cos D'Estournel 1962: a Château Coutet 1937 was served with the Black Forest Gâteau.

On 30 August a collection of Angus's critical writings, *Diversity and Depth in Fiction*, edited by Kerry McSweeney, was published: it was dedicated by Angus to Ian Watt who had introduced him to life as a professor of English Literature. It contained pieces stretching back over his literary career – from his early hostile broadcast on Woolf to his revised view of her published in 1978,[8] from the "Evil" lectures to his tributes to J.C. Powys and Proust. It was on the whole respectfully reviewed: John Bayley (with whom Angus, when they met, loved to talk about "the novel") wrote about it in the *Times Literary Supplement*, interestingly questioning Angus's views of "evil": "Wilson himself has portrayed some notably bad characters, like Mrs Curry . . . yet I wonder whether his rather too overt authorial hint that she 'embodies evil' is really any more effective than the similar suggestion about Kurtz and evil which Conrad gets into *Heart of Darkness*. As he remarks, 'our transcendent sense of evil is being destroyed all the time by our psychological knowledge.' We no longer think of it as something that comes from outside to destroy us." Bayley goes on to consider Wilson's views of the "evil" figures in James – the valet in *The Turn of the Screw*, Osmond and Mme Merle in *The Portrait of a Lady*, Kate Croy and Merton Densher in *The Wings of the Dove* – "James had invoked both the transcendental and the all too sordidly right and wrong, and has got caught between the two."[9]

This analysis prompts a new glance at Angus's continuing and not always very clearly expressed obsession with the difference between "evil" and "right and wrong", which he had confronted again in fictional terms in *Setting the World on Fire*: in this novel, interestingly, he introduced for the first time a full-scale treatment of the Christian Science he had made such fun of so often, and which he felt had helped to kill his mother – "poor darling," as he told John Pitman. The Christian Scientist, Lady Mosson, is pitted against the forces of random terrorism, and is inevitably found deeply wanting – but she is also found deeply wanting on a simpler, psychological level, as a mother who had kept her only surviving son in a state of dependent sexual arrest. There is some muddle here, if Angus is indeed trying to portray "evil" in his terrorists – might they not too have had mothers who were Christian Scientists? – and increasingly one suspects that what he really disliked about Christian Science was not so much its denial of evil as its denial of sexuality and complexity. His invocations of "evil" as a positive force which we neglect at our peril hint at some major denial in himself – a fear not so much that evil exists, but a fear that there is *nothingness* instead of the goodness and sweetness that Mrs Eddy had believed in so powerfully. *Boum boum*, as Forster said, as Mrs Moore heard, in the one novel of Forster's that Angus continued to admire.

This utterly hollow sound was perhaps more frightening to Angus than any Mrs Curry, any Marina Luzzi, any corrupting valet, any Mary Postgate, any hijacker or crazy fundamentalist or gunman. It was not human evil that terrified, it was the absence of any possibility of human good, inevitable when one rejected – as one had to, as Angus did, as poor Hubert Mosson did – when one rejected all that early cloying unreal sweetness. Sweetness was denial, and must itself be denied. For a humanist who denied the possibility of transcendence, this left nothing, and nothing was surely a worse fear, as Bayley hints, than any vague metaphysical *fin-de-siècle* nastiness invoked by Conrad, Ford Madox Ford or Henry James.

On 29 January 1984, Angus wrote – or rather Tony typed, possibly from dictation or notes? – a long letter in response to questions from a Dutch academic, Christiaan van Minnen, in which he tried once more to unravel his ideas on evil:

You may indeed say I am concerned with evil. Why am I so

fascinated by it? I think two facts of my youth may be relevant: one that I was brought up by my Mother in the religion of Christian Science, where evil existence if [for is] denied, as is that of sickness or death. The unbearable sweetness of all this became repulsive to me soon after my Mother's death when I was coming sixteen years old. Indeed I have probably over simply attributed much of my naivete and I have a lot of it to this Christian Science upbringing. This also is probably naive. I think it is also the case that though I never became a Catholic, two of my older brothers – some fourteen years older than me – attempted to convert me and used my innocence about evil in their attempts. It remains for me very important because otherwise a rational humanist my consciousness of something going beyond right and wrong especially in the modern world is constant with me. It is something that I am glad to share with William Golding.

Some of my 'evil people' do come over as grotesques but that is in part because they are not seen from the inside, and in part because they are culpably (or may be not) perpetual children. This is certainly true of Inge . . .[10]

"Or may be not." There is surely a deep conflict here, a conflict which exercised him until the end of his life.

A very different review from John Bayley's appeared the following spring in the *Atlantic Monthly*, May 1984. Here Martin Amis wrote with some affection about Wilson's "delightfully personal, impressively ama- teurish, and thrillingly unsystematic" approach to criticism – not for him the world of hermeneutics and syntagmatics, *lexia* and *irreali*, and political, sexual and ethnic dialectical imperatives. No, as a practising novelist rather than an academic he boldly, confidently and routinely committed the Biographical Fallacy, the Intentional Fallacy, and the Affective Fallacy. Amis enjoys this, but wonders whether Wilson's own great tradition is not a little fossilised, and the consensus which he assumes already lost: he also (probably more annoyingly to Angus) complains about the constant distraction of the "mandarin brio" of his prose.

Martin Amis had understandably become something of a bogey figure to Angus, like Bradbury before him – the young, alarming and brilliant representative of an incomprehensible new order which could chat idly about post-modernist aesthetics if only in order to dismiss them. Amis himself says he was not aware of being cast in this role: he had been conscious that his review of *Magic* had not pleased either Angus or John Gross, but had thought his own real liking for Angus's early works would temper indignation: he had also greatly admired *No Laughing Matter*, which had seemed "a formation of everything he had done". Amis's own feeling was that the energy of undisclosed homosexuality trapped in the earlier novels had been released, in *Magic*, too rapidly, too playfully, and too uncertainly, and he drew a comparison with E.M. Forster's *Maurice*, which also suffered from an uncertainty of tone. He said he and Angus had met and talked several times after the *Magic* review, and Angus had never brought the subject up. They had also corresponded, quite amiably, when Martin Amis had been working as an editor at the *New Statesman*: Martin had asked Angus to contribute on more than one occasion, and Angus had declined with characteristic civility. But beneath the civil surface, he had continued to prick and bleed. (Martin Amis, in an interview in the *New Standard*, 7 August 1981, had volunteered that he liked Led Zeppelin, Bob Dylan, Bellow, Nabokov and Borges, and "Among English authors I like, apart from my father, Anthony Burgess and the early Angus Wilson.")

*

In September 1983 Angus and Tony were off once more to to Delaware, on what was to be their last visit: their exchange, Professor Jack Robinson, arrived on 1 September and they departed a week later. Unlike Professor Schwarzbach, who was to write with nostalgic rapture about life in the cottage, and about Ada, Mrs Revens, and the medieval wood, Professor Robinson proved to be not wholly enchanted by English country life: taps leaked, radiators were not adequate, and the Johnstone-Wilson 2CV was a "lousy ten cent" job, not at all what you would expect of a knight. But in Apple Road in Delaware Angus and Tony were comfortable enough, surrounded by old friends: they took themselves off once more to Bombay Hook, where Angus sneezed and a thousand snow geese took off in alarm. Some of their old friends were back in England: Angus wrote to Frith Banbury in September saying that at his zoo party he had "intended to introduce hundreds of people to hundreds of other people, and some people to the animals, but none of this was achieved. There were two people whom I particularly wished you to meet: Drury and Ellen Pifer. Drury is an American playwright . . . at present working with the Young Vic who are doing one of his plays. When in the US they live in Wilmington and Ellen is one of the professors at the University of Delaware, and has written a first rate book on Nabokov. They are a lively and amusing couple . . . we shall miss them on campus here." (Dated Ith [*sic*] September, 1983.) Banbury and the Pifers did indeed meet, and had much lively and amusing gossip about their old friend Angus.

The Pifers were in England, but Perkin Walker was in America, and he came to visit from the Folger Library. Joe Kissane was in frequent touch about the issue of *Twentieth Century Literature* which he was now editing to celebrate Angus's birthday: Kissane had diligently obtained contributions from many friends old and new, including Perkin Walker, Hortense Calisher, Patrick White, Lorna Sage, Clive Sinclair, Rose Tremain, Peter Conradi, Jaidev, F.S. Schwarzbach and Vance Bourjaily: he also assembled some fine photographs, including one of Angus as a little boy in Durban being pulled along in a little cart by a huge Zulu in fantastic fancy dress and feathers.

The issue (Volume 29, Number 2, Summer 1983, published by Hofstra University Press) was launched on 11 November with a party on Long Island, but, as Tony wrote to Mike Shaw, now Angus's agent at Curtis Brown, only Mick Jagger, Elizabeth Taylor and the Queen seemed to sell books these days. They dined on Thanksgiving Day (temperature 62 degrees, followed by sleet) with June and Jay Halio, and Angus pursued a hectic social life as well as a heavy teaching programme until flying to Lisbon on 18 December.

They had missed *The Old Men at the Zoo*, which had been shown in September, with a cast of fine old men which included Robert Morley, Marius Goring, Andrew Cruickshank and Maurice Denham: it was well received, but Tony had once more been agitated about whether or not Granada were promoting the paperback properly, and disappointingly, there had as yet been no American sale. Tom Rosenthal confirmed that the Granada sales had indeed been disappointing – the series had been too "sophisticated" for the common reader, and not long enough to build up the *Brideshead* response. I enjoyed the series and apparently talked about it and the book at what must have been tedious length to Emma Tennant at a party at the Pinters: I also wrote to Angus and Tony and received a postcard (of Schaefer's Canal-House, Chesapeake City) thanking me – "No other friends have said a word but the producer wrote that he was happy with the reception."

Once more Angus and Tony stayed at Seteais above Sintra on their Portuguese stopover: once more they visited Mafra, Belem, Palmela, Setubal, the Estufa Fria and Mrs Lowndes Marques. On Christmas Day 1983 Angus recorded that he had the pleasure of sitting in the sun in a formal garden: after Christmas lunch at the Pena Palace they walked back to Sintra.

They had intended to fly from Lisbon to Cannes to see Clive and Lucie, but a collision on the runway at Madrid airport (93 dead) had put Tony off the idea of flying, and they drove instead, across a mysteriously beautiful and wintry Spain – through Badajoz, Merida, Oropesa, Madrid and

Zaragossa. It was freezing cold: the dreaded year of 1984 came in with bitter chill.

1983 on balance had not been a bad year. There had been many high points – a visit to the Egremonts at Petworth in April, the party at the Zoo, the Presidency of the Royal Society of Literature, the invitation to make *Couples*. (Angus at the end of his pocket diary sums up the year thus: "*Tides* – Clive well, a non-abrasive phone call, TV programme request for me & T., R.Lit. Soc., K.S., Paris, Lewes – Brighton, Petworth etc. – events *always* overtake each other. If not you wouldn't notice them.") But there had also been deaths – they had lost not only David Farrer, but also Angus's French translator, Anne-Marie Las Vergnas, who had died of cancer in April, and Wim Schumacher, who had suddenly and quite unexpectedly dropped dead in a shower while on holiday with Michael Goodall in November. Mrs Revens was still going strong, but her husband Albert was very ill, as was Genifer Garrett in Switzerland. And Mrs Thatcher had won a landslide victory in June, prompting Tony to dash off a protest letter to a bishop on the BBC's "Thought for the Day" who had sounded far too pleased about it. Tony was getting into the habit of writing protest letters. There was much to protest about. Angus, speaking to a French interviewer for the "magazine freudien" *L'Ane*, No. 13, Nov.–Dec. 1983, had commented once more on Mrs Thatcher's faith in the work ethic and neo-technology, and her appeal to Victorian values which Dickens would not have appreciated: he also deplored her lack of interest in the arts, endorsing the widespread suspicion that she liked only opera because it kept visiting heads of state quiet for a few hours. (This issue also contains interviews with Frank Kermode, Richard Cobb, Malcolm Bradbury, Ernst Gombrich, J.B. Trapp, Karl Miller, John Sturrock and D.P. Walker – an unusual selection of British intellectuals.)

On the credit side, *The Old Men at the Zoo* and *Diversity and Depth* had been well received, and *Firebird 2* had printed his Sri Lankan Journal – but where was the new work? Angus's pocket diary for this year has tiny jottings which look like ideas for stories – for example "Lucia Lomax, former star of some kind, gets madder as she's driven to command attention in the local city. (Me in Bury)" and "Cuckoo – let one of her two mockers at the party speak of repoussé – you must be used to *that*, dear." These speak for themselves. So, too, does an undateable scrap written on the back of a cheap white paper table napkin :

Story (me?)
The really feeling, amusing, lively man (woman?) entertaining and making two lots of people (with an interval) feel that they're really wanted and helped – but wittily with feeling anecdote. But as we

[illeg.] how he (she?) identifies with the shaped, inhuman, natural (or artifical world) and how drearily the human world presses.

And yet again, in another note to himself – "In the flat alone – in the cottage alone – in love with terror and death?" It was not, he said to himself, that he did not enjoy gossiping with Benjy Cohen about his father and Jack Plumb, or supping with Geoffrey Wright and his friend Michael, for he did. But there was also something in him that now pulled him towards the inhuman, towards nothingness, towards the abyss. Human beings he found "inadequate and flat". Was this new mood a product of old age? And could he write about it?

Angus told John Pitman in July that he had already given up reviewing, and that perhaps in a couple of years time "what I'll give up will be teaching and then I'll go on writing until I fall, whatever fall means." A fear of falling possessed him – Tony would leave him by falling off a cliff, he and his works would fall into oblivion. "Whatever fall means," falling was on its way.

29

FEAR OF FALLING

In 1984 Angus hoped to start work on his autobiography. He had agreed to speak at Writers' Day for PEN on March 24, and would use the opportunity not merely to rehash his old favourite of "Angus Wilson on Angus Wilson" (although that was still his title) but also to try to delve more deeply into his own childhood. Many impulses had been pushing him this way – over the past few years he had given extensive autobiographical interviews to Jay Halio and Joe Kissane, and there had been requests to write his biography, including a not-very-serious one over dinner from me, which he had roundly rejected. "You've better things to do with your time, dear girl," had been his line, but Tony had murmured that really he wanted to keep the horrors of their lives a deep secret. But the *Couples* programme (now renamed *The Other Half*) had been an exercise in limited disclosure, and on 27 February 1984 he was to give an even more revealing talk in Cambridge on "The Bad Old Days" to the Alternative Homosexual Group. ("A very good occasion," he told his diary: his audience agreed.) Those long short stories did not really seem to be getting anywhere very fast, so perhaps now was the right time to address the past in a new way. (He had promised Tony Dyson he would write at least three volumes.)

Despite his acute vulnerability to criticism Angus could also produce a contradictory and curiously dogged persistence, a gift for shrugging off even his own paranoia when he had to. He continued to have need of this gift. As usual, both compliments and brickbats reached him from the outside world – two of his novels were included in Burgess's list of the best 99 published in the *New York Times Book Review*, 5 February 1984, none in a BMC and PA promotion for the "Best Novels of Our Time" on 22 February. (Tony indignantly refused on his behalf an invitation to the luncheon.) 22 February also brought, more happily, the first fruits of the long campaign for Public Lending Right: Angus's share of the kitty was £696.81. *The Other Half,* shown on the Leap Date of 29 February, brought both praise and blame, though the praise greatly outweighed the blame: ironically, Angus had to watch it with his friends in Regents Park Terrace without Tony, as Tony was in Switzerland for his sister's funeral.* The broadsheets and the tabloids were united in admiration. Nancy Banks-Smith in the *Guardian* (1 March 1984) particularly admired the perform-ance of Mrs Revens, "A sturdy figure in saxe-blue", and Angus's meditation on what he would wear for the zoo party . . . " 'a gold and, oh, lovely kingfisher blue shirt. With a rather pleasant pair of light blue trousers.' ('I think you should have trousers,' said Tony, with a lifetime's timing . . .')" Valerie Grove, Julian Barnes, Lucy Hughes-Hallett, Herbert Kretzmer, Maureen Paton in the *Daily Express,* and many others spoke warmly of Angus and Tony's courage, dignity and wit, and of the unsensational nature of the reportage: the columnist Tailgunner Parkinson in *New Society* was to take the opportunity (on a second showing) to lament at length Tony's loss to the probation service, and Tony's one-time supervisor at the LSE, Kit Russell, wrote to say how pleased she had been to see him and Angus looking so well.† Even the provincial press approved. Richard Ingrams in the *Spectator,* while unintentionally betraying only the most superficial acquaintance with Angus's work, was one of the rare dissenting voices: he considered Wilson a "preposterously self-satisfied old boy" and came up with the puzzling view that the final sequence at the Zoo "brought home better than anything the essential absurdity of his existence."[1] Now what could he have meant by that?

The BBC received various telephone calls of protest and some of thanks, and quite a few mildly obscene letters protesting against the programme's "muck" and "filth" and "perversion": the *Radio Times* printed one of the more carefully worded protests, which in turn elicited a flood of letters in support of Angus and Tony. And personal letters of appreciation poured in to them both from friends of yesteryear and yesterday and tomorrow: one woman wrote to Angus reminding him that he used to dine in her restaurant in the Old Brompton Road some sixty years ago, and asking after Pat and Colin. Michael Howard wrote from Oxford saying that they both looked so handsome and so clever that he was sick with envy but proud to know them both, and please would Angus

---

* Genifer Garrett had worked for many years for a Greek shipping company, in Genoa, then as secretary to the owner in Switzerland: she shared a house by Lac Léman with a German-Swiss friend.

† Mrs Kit Russell, *née* Stewart, married to cellist Sheridan Russell, was Tony's Field Work Tutor at the London School of Economics: she was also a friend of Denis and Patsy Barnes.

come soon to talk to the boys of Oriel? The Blackburnes, Perkin Walker, Glyn and Jeanne Davies, Alan Gray, Pat Trevor-Roper, Pam Schute from the RSL, Frank Thistlethwaite, Stuart Hampshire, Angus McGill, Anne-Marie Meyer, Bob French and Monty Turland, and many many more both known and unknown, gay, straight, closeted and out, wrote in, several praising Tony as the "star of the show"; Tony Dyson said how much his eighty-four-year-old mother had enjoyed the whole pro-gramme. Tony Garrett also received the first of a batch of interesting intellectual fan mail from a dramatic young woman in Cambridge, Nemone Thornes, who implored him to come to her party at Newnham College on 20 June. (He did: she proved to be very glamorous and a keen fan of John Cowper Powys.)

Angus battled on through the spring with various public engagements – he seemed always to be writing "four minute speeches", one visitor complained, though some of them were in fact much longer. He became a Vice-President of the Gay Humanists, he answered literary questionnaires from France and Holland, and spoke at a Writers' Guild Day on George Orwell at the Barbican in January. One of his fellow panellists was Angela Carter, whose long grey hair fell over her face as she talked: Angus regarded her with interest and respect, both as an icon of the "young" and as someone who, like him, had been fascinated by the ambiguities of Japan (indeed, she had known Ian Calder there, though Angus may not have known this). The other panellist was Salman Rushdie, whose work Angus much admired – he had invited him to dinner at the Athenaeum and had talked to him very much in a fatherly "handing-on-the-baton" tone, Rushdie remembers.

In March Angus went with Tony to Paris, gave a reading for the British Council, saw his publishers, and dined with Christine Jordis. His speech to PEN at the Purcell Room in the Queen Elizabeth Hall on 24 March 1984, chaired by Antonia Fraser, was a *tour de force*, and brilliantly delivered (it is preserved in the National Sound Archive)[2]. It shows not the slightest sign of waning powers of concentration or delivery: at his usual speed he rushed through his Regency-Victorian family, his story-telling days at Westmin-ster, the economic gloom of his youth (which he compared to the current economic climate*), the BM Catalogue, the bombing at the BM, his own "nervous upset", his career as a novelist, his admiration for Rushdie's combination of reality and fantasy, his intermittent sense of frightening loneliness, his faith in the form of the novel. (Towards the end he admitted

---

* In his 1981 piece on Proust Angus had referred to the 1930s as a "time of domestic depression and military threat" similar to the climate of Britain in 1981: now, two years after the Falklands, the comparison seemed even more apt to him.

"I have lost a lot of my readers with my later novels.") It was a performance showing considerable self-knowledge. Stephen Spender wrote to him from Provence congratulating him warmly, and crying out in indignation against George Steiner and his whole approach to literature – Steiner had insulted Larkin and seemed to expect us all to curtsey at the very name of Borges. (Steiner, who had spoken after Angus, had delivered the Dawson Scott Memorial Lecture on "The Home Ground Under Siege".)

Angus addressed the Kipling Society at a luncheon in May, and spoke on *Clarissa* at the RSL. He attended a party on 19 June at Leighton House to celebrate Drabble's putting to bed of the fifth edition of *The Oxford Companion to English Literature*: Angus was one of many celebrated guest-entries to be seen wandering through the peacock-tiled halls and the sultry garden. Iris Murdoch, the Pinters, Julian Mitchell, Salman Rushdie (too young to be an entry, but a valued adviser on Magic Realism, Indian literature and other matters), and many other friends old and new were gathered together, and Angus, in peacock tie to match the décor, was very much a Guest of Honour. (His friend Stephen Jones was now curator at Leighton House, and had been responsible for the booking: Drabble had caused some confusion with the caterers by insisting on two kinds of white wine – a dry Chablis, and a sweeter Gewürztraminer specially for Angus, who could not tolerate very dry wines.) On 5 July he lunched with the *Sunday Telegraph* at Simpsons, presented the C.Litt. to William Golding at the RSL, and spoke *in absentia* on Graham Greene and Samuel Beckett, both of whom had somewhat surprisingly accepted. Again, he brought up the topic of evil, and how delighted he had been as a young reader to encounter it in *Brighton Rock*.

But he was not well. He had been taken ill on 11 April, and spent over a week in bed. At first he said it was flu, then he said it was a virus, but whatever it was it lingered on for many weeks and he was obliged to cancel several engagements. Kind friends were upset by his appearance, and wrote him well-intentioned letters about his diet: he might loathe salad and vegetables, but he ought to *try* to eat more of them. He and Tony took a holiday in France and Holland in May, and spent a night with Patsy and Denis Barnes in their charmingly irregular historical house, The Old Ship, in Kent on the way back, but Angus did not really seem to recover properly. He was not on his usual top form at the RSL, as he had been at PEN in March. He could usually pull himself together to sparkle "like a chandelier" (Josephine Pullein-Thompson's phrase) but the effort was now visible, and sometimes he could not make it.

On 3 July 1984, Drury and Ellen Pifer visited Angus and Tony for lunch at Felsham Woodside, and Pifer found the whole visit very disturbing –

"we felt we were intruding on some private catastrophe." Tony picked them up at Stowmarket and drove them to the cottage and seemed in a state of "barely suppressed violent irritation" – no doubt aggravated by the fact that his little car had not only been impeded by bales of hay dumped dangerously upon the road but had also broken down beneath the weight of his guests. (Pifer, extremely tall and craggy, who had survived a rigorous but adventurous outdoor childhood in South Africa to become a helicopter pilot before he took up writing, was not the kind of man to be crammed easily into a 2CV.)

Pifer found that Angus was confused, tended to totter and trip over things, and seemed bewildered as Tony tried to preserve the formalities and serve the meal with his usual precision. Pifer felt Tony was "berating" Angus in reproach for his illness: Angus himself hardly spoke, except to mention that a rock star had bought a big house nearby and came and went by helicopter – "his books were out of print, and that rock singer sailing over his house in a private chopper was a sign of the time. The way Angus spoke of the rock star, with amused bemusement, was characteristic of him, for he preferred to be amused by all the silly nonsense than to grizzle away on the dark side. But the dark side was pressing very hard on that day in Bury St Edmunds . . ."[3] (The rock star was Bill Wyman, guitarist with the Rolling Stones.)

Tony was becoming anxious. He thought that Angus's health problems seemed evident to all but their local GP and Patrick Woodcock, both of whom considered Angus would be well enough to embark on a teaching stint in Tucson, Arizona. Angus's teeth were not good – he had made a comic feature of his dental problems in the *Couples* programme, and Tony had warned me to provide soft foods only when he came to dinner with us on 13 June after the RSL: new dentures were on the way but not yet installed. (We had scallop soup and a little salmon trout, as I recall: the soup went down well and Angus politely cried for more.) Angus gave a reading in Cambridge on 13 July to assorted international academics for the British Council Cambridge Seminar, and I remember seeing him cross the court at Trinity, walking anxiously with little steps as though the great formal empty space alarmed him.

Perhaps the Pifers had not seen him at his best. The week in which they saw him was a tiring week in a busy month, with a lunch in Bury with Christopher and Pamela Bigsby and Malcolm Bradbury on 9 July to meet Arthur Miller and his wife, and a crisis meeting about funding of the NBL with Arnold Goodman on the 12th: the gloom of Arts Council cuts was spreading and Angus had already struggled unsuccessfully to persuade Marghanita Laski that the budget for literature should be trebled, not reduced. She didn't agree at all. She couldn't really see the point of funding literature – which was unfortunate, as she was Chair of the Literature Panel. Angus wrote miserably to a colleague who had resigned from the Eastern Arts Association that these were dark days for public support for the arts, with literature the most shamefully treated of all – a revolution was taking place, and as with all revolutions very bad things would follow in its wake. To leave all to private patronage seemed to him a doomed policy.

Maybe, after all, Arizona would be just what he needed. He could get away from all this. He had always loved the sun.

★

Angus and Tony flew off to Boston on 21 August 1984, and on to Tucson two days later: the Fall semester began earlier than they had at first expected, and Angus was disappointed that the dates prevented him from attending a seminar in Vermont organised by Saul Bellow. He was still in principle game for new enterprises, and reluctant to turn them down.

They found themselves well placed in a fine apartment in Tucson, but one wonders how Angus regarded his heavy teaching duties and the strain of meeting and getting to know so many new people. The money was good – a gross fee of $25,000 – but the work was demanding. He taught classes on Charlotte Brontë, James, Dickens, and gave interviews and readings, but his notes in his diary about these activities become almost indecipherable. He and Tony ate in Joe's Oyster Bar, made a trip to the Sonora Desert Museum, and visited Salt Lake City, but cancelled the Grand Canyon (as too vertiginous): they also cancelled by telegram a lecture in Boulder, Colorado, as Tony felt that Angus would not be up to the extra travel and stress in a full teaching week.

There was a pleasant interlude in the form of a vacation with Joe Kissane, some of which was spent visiting the Frank Lloyd Wright architects' training centre at Taliesin West. Angus and Tony got on very well with Kissane, who had done such a good job the year before with the *Twentieth Century Literature* edition on Angus's life and work: Joe Kissane had written his dissertation at Columbia on Samuel Richardson and Jane Austen, which made an added bond of literary sympathy.(And he had been born in Pittsburgh, about which they also talked a good deal: his mother still lived there.) Angus had felt able to talk very freely to Kissane in their taped interviews of December 1982 and again in March 1984.

Now, in early November, Tony and Angus drove to Phoenix in a temperature of 80 degrees, where they met Joe and a friend of his, David Delong, who was doing research there and had arranged for a private tour:

Kissane thought that Angus looked well and lightly tanned from the Arizona sunshine, but he did not seem to have quite his usual energy.

"David Delong met us at a restaurant in Phoenix the night before . . . to give us our instructions for the tour. Tony remembered that in his previous meeting with David [at the Hofstra party], pleased to be speaking with an architect, he offered some criticism of Frank Lloyd Wright's Fallingwater . . . only to discover that David is a member of the board that supervises the operation of Fallingwater. David was amused and he and Tony found each other quite compatible.

"The drive to Taliesin West is through Phoenix to Scottsdale, past housing developments, and stretches of desert. Indira Berndtsen greeted us when we arrived and guided us through. She and Angus took to each other at once. He explained that he was having trouble walking – moving slowly and stopping frequently – because he had lumbago. She, too, had a back problem and they chatted their way through Mrs Wright's living room, the theater, and architect's work rooms. They compared notes on gardens here and abroad . . . Angus was as absorbed by the plantings as Tony was by the architecture at Taliesin which he said he liked better than Fallingwater. Angus was particularly delighted with a citrus orchard, unusual because a mountain rises sharply behind it. It was while chatting about the plants that Angus suddenly toppled over. I don't remember that there was any preparation, no slow sinking to the ground. He just suddenly went down.

"He was up again fairly quickly. At the time, it seemed that the fall must have been related to lumbago but in the light of what happened later I think Tony is right that this difficulty in maintaining his balance could have been an early sign of the difficulties he had the next year in Iowa . . ."[4]

Angus was stumbling, and back home things were falling apart. The roof was in a bad way at Regent's Park Terrace and needed expensive repairs. In the same week in late September Mark Barty-King left Granada and Tom Rosenthal left Secker & Warburg: all their seeming allies were deserting them. Mark Barty-King had gone to Corgi Books, and to let them know about this he kindly sent a press release in which he boasted that authors he had published in the past included "Robert Ludlum, Barbara Taylor Bradford, Erica Jong, Jacqueline Briskin and Eric Van Lustbader." Maybe they would be better off without Mark Barty-King? But then again, maybe not. The tide was flowing the wrong way for them: Angus's letter about VAT to the Society of Authors (October 1984) ended thus: "VAT on books will mean less books, less employment in the book trade, and more expensive books. Best sellers will continue to cruise luxuriously round the world, but the rest will be told to sink or swim while the Government sells off the lifebelts to the private sector." (He was offered a token fee of ten pounds for this, which he waived.)

Tony tried to keep things ticking over, responding by telegram from Tucson to various invitations – "duties in the desert" was the formula he found to excuse their absence to PEN, President Mitterand, Rose Tremain, Christina Foyle and the retiring Lord Franks. Invitations were pleasant, but honour brought with it obligations, and they were frequently obliged to pay up not only for a share of their own communal roof, but for the roofs of others – for a Christ's College building fund, for retirement gifts and memorial lectures. They tried to shed unncessary subscriptions, Angus on several occasions declining to be a patron of a new good cause on the grounds that he could not afford it, but unlike Sir Walter Elliot and his daughter Elizabeth in *Persuasion* they found it difficult not to be charitable: they were an easy target for appeals that touched them in any way personally. (At an even more dire moment in their lives, they were to contribute £100 to a fund in memory of A.J. Ayer.) Nor were they very good at extorting money from their debtors. Knights were supposed to give many services for free. The BBC reluctantly agreed to pay a small disturbance fee for Angus's recorded obituary on his old friend Jack Priestley, who had died in August, just short of his ninetieth birthday: one can't help feeling that Priestley would have driven a better bargain.

The view from the desert of life in England was not overwhelmingly alluring: in October the IRA had blasted the Tory Party conference hotel in Brighton, and the miners' strike continued to tear the nation apart and fill its television screens with images of civil war. Nevertheless in November Tony was alarmed to receive a letter from Nemone Thornes which reported that a friend of a friend had read somewhere that he and Angus were planning to leave England and live abroad. How on earth had this got about? It was not the first such rumour to reach them, Tony replied, and it was true that they had talked of moving to "various places like Dover, Dignes, Aigues-Mortes, Norwich, London, Weymouth, Amsterdam, Reading – but mainly to annoy the local Suffolk folk.

"We have made no plans, so much would be involved, not least finding the cash to make a move . . . but there is some substance in the rumour: Angus loves the sun, and as we get older the garden will become a problem without help. And Thatcher England does not help us keep calm . . . Nor does Reagan America, for that matter . . ."[5]

On 14 December 1984 they set off, via Houston, for France – to Paris, Montpellier, Aigues Mortes, and then to Cannes, to see Clive and Lucie. They were beginning to prospect around their old haunts for somewhere to live, and visited Patrick Woodcock who seemed to have settled pleasantly into encroaching semi-retirement near Uzès – he had left the National Health Service for private practice in 1967, to Honoria Wormald's disgust, and was now spending much of his time in France. But the weather in Cannes that year would hardly encourage anyone to become an exile – it was bitterly cold and covered in ice, and the palm trees had died of frostbite. Angus had another fall, on the steps at the Hotel el Puerto where they were staying – but, said Tony, it was so dreadfully slippery that *anyone* might have fallen. On the credit side, the expatriate life had done wonders for Clive, who would be ninety the following year, but was still skipping around like a forty-two-year-old. He and Lucie were ready with advice about buying property in France – whatever you do, they urged, *don't sign anything*. Both had a horror of documents, and had been shedding them through the years.

Angus and Tony flew back on 15 January 1985 over a snow-covered France to yet more snow in Suffolk. Tony had been noting the weather and temperatures almost daily. The Midi had not come very well out of this meteorological testing, but then Suffolk didn't come well out of it either – the winds were bitter, the road to Bury was cut off in February by thick snow, Angus's eyes ached, and he retired to bed with a heavy cold. Everything seemed so difficult. Michael Slater had kept Ada and the cottage warm for them over a mild and sunny Christmas, but now the cold and damp set in for weeks. They crawled out for visits to the dentist and doctor and chiropodist, and made a few sallies with their old faithfuls to the cheerful new fish restaurant, Mortimer's, in Bury. But one fish restaurant does not save a winter, and the winter was very bad.

The spring was to be even worse.

THE LAST OF ENGLAND

They had decided that they would leave England. They had had enough. Suddenly everything began to happen very rapidly. In January 1985, Angus was still telling correspondents that he saw ahead some "lovely free time" to write, and he and Tony were planning to take Perkin Walker, who had been stoically undergoing debilitating treatment for cancer, on a convalescent tour to Lincoln and York. But on 10 March Perkin Walker suffered a massive haemorrhage and died. His last note to them, dated 25 February, had arranged to meet them for dinner in Camden Town at the Bistroquet to discuss their trip – but, ominously, he had asked Tony if he could drive him there, as he was not well enough to walk. (Perkin had up to this point insisted on taking the bus from Camden Town to University College Hospital in Gower Street for his chemotherapy sessions for cancer of the oropharynx. He died in the hospital.)

This was a terrible blow. He was Angus's oldest friend, and he was also their London landlord. They would be friendless and homeless. It was a disaster. They had been thinking for a year or two of looking for a more convenient *pied-à-terre* in London (preferably without any stairs), and had made one or two enquiries, but they had not seriously addressed the problem. They would have to move fast. Perkin, they knew, had left the house to his nephews: all his tenants, who had been living there on such favourable and on the whole friendly terms, would have to think again. The little community would be broken up forever. Angus and Tony sent flowers to the funeral on the 19th, with the messages "With all my love to a great and generous friend for nearly sixty years, Angus" and "With all my love for a true and constant friend, Tony."

As if to compound the tragedy, a day after the news of Perkin Walker's death came news of the death of Ian Calder. The old order was passing away so fast that they could hardly take it in. They had not seen or heard much of Ian Calder of late, but Angus had never forgotten his first great love: he had heard from Pat Calder in April 1974 about his impersonation of Henry VIII for American tourists in the "1520 A.D." Olde Elizabethan restaurant in St Martin's Lane, he knew Ian had suffered from gout and angina, and he had heard of his cancer of the throat and his subsequent silence. Angus had heard from both Pat Calder and Rosemary Merry of his efforts to live at peace with himself at last. Now Ian Calder too was gone. (Curiously, in May he was to receive from Pat a letter to him from Ian Calder from beyond the grave – Ian had written it after the John Wain poetry evening at the little theatre in 1979, and had forgotten to post it. She had found it while sorting out his papers. It was friendly, cheerful, even hopeful, and Pat in her covering note said that she believed that at the end Ian had found release from the hell into which the conflicts of his own nature so often plunged him.)*

The two Renaissance scholars – Perkin Walker the silent who had published several distinguished volumes, and Ian Calder the voluble who had published nothing – they had both gone, both dead of cancer of the throat.

Angus's own health now took a turn for the worse, as it had the spring before. In late March 1985 he had an attack of what was diagnosed as labyrinthitis: he woke up at four in the morning and found he had completely lost his sense of balance. He was referred to Dr R.S. Kocen at the National Hospital, Queen Square for examination and a brainscan. He told Dr Kocen his medical history – years ago he had smoked 70 cigarettes a day, he still drank alcohol regularly, and he suspected that his father might have suffered from "luetic disease" (i.e. syphilis). He said he found himself slower, his handwriting slightly impaired, and that he suffered from memory lapses – also that he had on several occasions (including the one in Tucson, Arizona) fallen backwards for no evident reason. Dr Kocen tested for Parkinson's but the tests were not positive, though he suspected there might be some "early Parkinsonism" – Kocen's diagnosis, on the basis of the brain scan, was that Angus was probably suffering from cerebro-vascular disease (insufficient blood supply to the brain) and normal pressure hydrocephalus (i.e. unexplained pressure not caused by an obstruction). A shunt operation to relieve pressure on the brain by draining fluid from the somewhat enlarged ventricles to the heart was a possibility, but Dr Kocen did not think Angus's condition severe enough to warrant surgery – Angus's mind was still clear and alert, and he was functioning in most respects normally. Kocen told Angus that the situation should be kept under review.

* Pat Calder still runs a small puppet theatre in Tooting.

Angus and Tony wrote about all these disasters to Clive and Lucie, who themselves had been in the wars: in February they had been burgled, Lucie had had a bad fall and several stitches in her head and forehead, and they had been in trouble with their passports and "documentation" – trouble from which Tony had to rescue them. They wrote to thank him most gratefully.

Where to turn, and what to do next? On one level life had to continue as normally as possible, but it was clear some action would have to be taken. Angus had got it firmly into his head that he would sell the cottage and go to France – Tony was attracted by the idea of Paris, but Angus longed for the sun. (Angus told the local vicar, Jim Hobbs, whom he encountered on the sugar-beet clamp at Gorse corner, that it was the climate that was driving him away from Suffolk – it had been an exceptionally wet spring.) They no longer even considered the possibility of trying to buy somewhere in London: property prices were ludicrously high.

Their state of disorientation was not apparent to all comers. On 24 April 1985 Angus spoke wittily and well as he presented prizes for a charity for expatriates called Focus, along with writer Bel Mooney and publisher Peter Mayer, and on 30 April Angus, along with many past dignitaries of the National Book League, appeared at a celebratory dinner at the Garrick for Lord Goodman, attended by the Duke of Edinburgh, where Angus appeared to be on perfectly good form. (I was there as a past chairman – not one of my happier roles.) On Wednesday, 1 May he attended the annual luncheon of the Kipling Society, where he sat at the high table with Professor Ranjan Goonetilleke from Sri Lanka: Goonetilleke found him very good company, the kind of person "who endeared himself to one instinctively and instantly" – though he did also note that Angus apologised for his lack of sense of balance, laughing it off by saying that though he might look drunk, he wasn't.[1] That very afternoon he went to see Kocen, and professed himself reassured by the results. But with close friends, he revealed his anxieties. On 29 April, Angus had dined at the Bistroquet with Tanya and Anthony Hobson, who had been acutely aware of how much he had aged since his Zoo party. He came down the stairs at Regent's Park Terrace very slowly and walked with tiny steps to the restaurant: over dinner he talked about financial troubles, about the neglect of the Suffolk garden, about Perkin Walker's death, about troubles with the woman in Regent's Park Terrace who shared their bathroom and left her knickers hanging everywhere. Angus spoke of their plan to go to France; Hobson reminded him of the fate of Sonia Orwell, who had moved to Paris to save money and translate, but had found the French very hostile and had ended up old and ill in a poor basement flat off the Luxembourg.

Was Angus listening? It seems not. In mid-May 1985 he and Tony set off to house-hunt in St Rémy. Stephen and Natasha Spender had offered to lend them their house near St Rémy as a base for exploration, and they had gladly accepted. The Mas St Jerome near Mausanne les Alpilles had received and bewitched many literary visitors over the years – it was a large-ish farmhouse, restored by the Spenders from a pile of rubble, with pale green-blue shutters and reddish biscuit-coloured tiles and a large garden and a fish in a pond and roses and olive groves and a most wonderful view of the dry sunny rocky Provençal landscape. (Iris Murdoch had been inspired by it for her novel *Nuns and Soldiers*,[2] dedicated to Stephen and Natasha Spender: she wrote lyrically of the little blue butterflies, the rosemary and lavender, the cicadas, the light-charged oleanders, the rocks and the moths.) The only worry for Angus was the staircase, which was open and had no stair rail – Tony wondered how Stephen Spender himself had managed. Spender was getting on in years, although he never showed it, and he had had terrible trouble with his knees a few years ago. (Stephen had been rather peeved that Angus had not gone to visit him in the Royal Free Hospital in Hampstead.)

The weather was as seductively warm and lovely in Provence as it was tiresomely wet in England. Angus and Tony drove around, visiting estate agents, looking at properties, seeing a friend or two, and driving over to see Clive and Lucie for lunch on the day of Perkin Walker's Memorial Service. Angus made an appointment with the local doctor, and was delighted to find he was one of the most handsome young men in France – Dr Arnaud was a doctor out of a television series, dark, handsome, articulate, well-read. Their delight was mutual. Dr Arnaud loved Angus, and longed for him to settle in the neighbourhood, or so he told the Spenders.

Natasha Spender had thought they were using this visit simply to explore the neighbourhood and experiment with the idea of settling there: she was astonished when she heard that they had made an offer on an apartment in the heart of St Rémy. Was not this a little impulsive? Were they really wise to rush in like this? And was it true that the flat was on the *fiifth* floor?

Over the next years friends were to discuss their decision *ad nauseam*, on the whole coming with some hindsight to the conclusion that the whole idea had been madness. But it did not seem like that at the time. Angus and Tony were anxious to leave Suffolk. The Mrs Tiggywinkle cottage had served its turn. Angus had arrived there by accident, and now it was time –

more than time – to depart. They felt they had already been there too long. Suffolk society was at times irksome. They were not willing to settle into a life of retired and cosy obscurity, in an atmosphere of semi-failure and diminished status. And the garden was becoming more of a burden than a pleasure. It reproached them. In March 1980 Angus had written to Norman Scarfe saying that his Minneapolis visit would be his last spring visit "for the garden needs us in spring (you see my Xtian Science upbringing has not been wholly wasted as far as prose goes)."[3] (Angus's last completed work of fiction, "Cuckoo", was to explore for the last time, and most perceptively, the gardening metaphor that had run through his work from the early stories onwards – gardens were not always pleasant places, and the uses to which we put them are not always benign.)

Angus and Tony came back to England, now, on 3 June, to try to sell Felsham Woodside, and to pick up for a while the threads of daily life. Angus had shelved the idea of writing his autobiography: he did not seem to be writing anything, though he was planning an introduction to a collection of travel pieces. He publicly announced his decision to leave England in a Profile by Craig Brown in the *Spectator*, published on 15 June: his sadness at this decision, Brown said, was evident. "A linguist and a lover of café society, Wilson is bound to survive his self-imposed exile. But what of Britain without him?"

(Craig Brown had met Angus at dinner in College Street in Bury St Edmunds with bookseller Stephen Du Sautoy and his wife Alison: the Du Sautoys served Angus gazpacho, which he seemed to enjoy, and were upset when later in the evening he dramatically announced "If I eat cucumber I *die*!" They watched him anxiously – but, as Stephen Du Sautoy noted, he survived.)

Craig Brown had got his interview, solicited by a letter of 14 April mentioning previous meetings with the Du Sautoys and Janet Shand-Kydd, but nearly all requests for Angus's attention were politely turned away by Tony with the phrase "he is not very well at present." Nevertheless, Angus officiated at the RSL on 12 June 1985 and came to dinner with us in Hampstead afterwards: he had certainly aged, and spoke in a slightly rambling manner, but we saw nothing in him that would make the idea of his moving to France seem madness. On the contrary, it seemed an enviable notion and he spoke of it with pleasure. He and Tony were still entertaining in Suffolk – on Sunday 16 June they gave a party for David Plante, Charles Jerdein, Benjy Cohen and Janet Shand-Kydd (described by Tony to another proposed guest as "A Canadian author, a horse-trainer turned art dealer, a high-born American, and the former wife of the Princess of Wales's mother's present husband").[4] They saw Rajiva

Wijensinha from Sri Lanka in Camden Town, and Rose Tremain and her second husband Johnny Dudley at the oysterage in Orford. Tony went off to Amsterdam for a few days in early July, and while he was away Sybil and Dick Scott came to spend a night at Felsham Woodside, and potential buyers came to look at the cottage. The Scotts were delighted by the garden which Angus was so soon to leave – they had never seen it before.

Pleas from the outside world still reached them: on 18 June they wrote and sent cheques in support of the Defence Fund for the Gay's the Word Bookshop in Marchmont Street, which was being prosecuted for selling obscene material, and were warmly thanked by Andrew Hodges. (The shop, set up in 1979, had been raided by Customs and Excise in April 1984.) Angus's statement of support read:

> It took until 1967 to get the anti-homosexual laws changed. It took that long to get some justice. I was a member of the Homosexual Law Reform Committee which campaigned. We assumed that this first step to equality would soon be followed by others.
>
> It is incredible that in 1985 we should be witnessing further persecution: in this case the stock seizure and impending prosecution of that fine homosexual bookshop, GAY'S THE WORD.
>
> As a writer I have had to protest sadly often against the persecution of writers in many parts of the world. It is utterly disgraceful in this civilized country that we should have to protest against censorship of reading material.
>
> It is shameful that prosecutions can still be brought by individuals or officials under long-outdated laws.
>
> It is intolerable that officials should have such wide-ranging powers of indiscriminate seizure of books.
>
> It is even more intolerable that those powers should be exercised.
>
> Sir Angus Wilson

(After protests by PEN and other bodies the case was withdrawn.)

Angus was still trying hard to respond to requests – in July he cancelled a tentatively arranged appearance with Chris Bigsby at the British Council seminar in July, but managed to conduct a seminar in a Summer School for Michael Slater in August. He was up and down – fine one moment, confused the next.

Throughout this period, Tony tried to cope politely with the annual spring and summer influx of North Americans. They wrote from Iowa, from Ann Arbor, from Delaware, from St Louis, from Georgia, from Pittsburgh, and now, of course, from Tucson: they sent photos of their babies and their cats and their wives and their gay groups, they sent short stories and dissertations, and round-robin letters about their family activities.

Joe Kissane came over from New York for April and was entertained and taken to Kew – but then Joe, as Tony later wrote to him, was a perfect gentleman whose mother should be proud of him. Kissane was always tactful: he understood their difficulties. During this visit, Kissane talked to and taped conversations with several of Angus's friends, including Bentley Bridgewater, Pat Trevor-Roper, Martyn Goff and Wendy Rintoul: he was thinking of writing some kind of biographical sketch – but not, he reassured Tony, a Holroyd job.[5]

Not all were as perceptive. Yet over the years Angus and now Tony had responded to visitors with an almost indiscriminate politeness, offering hospitality at home and in restaurants, tours of Cambridge or Ely or Ickworth or London, sending guide books when they could not act as guide in person. Even now they kept it up, and if their hearts sank at the sight of letters beginning "Seeing the two of you is high on my list of must-dos" they never betrayed it. Angus's imitations of Americans may have been unkind: his courtesy to them was impeccable. As late as September 1985 he was thanking Professor Joseph Prescott of Michigan for sending him a copy of his book of *Aphorisms and Other Observations*: Angus sent a card in his own wavering hand – "The aphorisms are splendid and set me to think about life's meaning without pomposity."

At the end of July, Tony flew off to France to sign the first documents for the purchase of the St Rémy apartment. Various friends had offered guarantees of loans to tide them over in case they did not manage to sell Felsham Woodside as soon as they hoped, but it was all rather nerve-wracking. The die was cast. The cottage sold for £74,173.66 to Keith and Penny Turner (Penny Corke, daughter of Martin and Jean) who also agreed to take on Ada. (At the time of writing, Ada is still alive and well, and has moved in to the Old Rectory with Martin Corke and his second wife Frances.*) Tony was able to write to their guarantors – Lord Goodman, Peter Grose for Secker & Warburg, the Corkes, and John Alston and Milo O'Sullivan, formally releasing them from their obligation and thanking them for their generosity. The estimate for removal was £4090.00. The telephone in Regent's Park Terrace was cut off. This was the end of England.

On 30 August 1985, BBC "Newsnight" showed an interview with

---

* Martin Corke died in January, 1994.

Angus (filmed the day before) in which he announced that he was leaving Thatcher's Britain. He had had enough. He felt unappreciated. He had always loved France and the sun, and the French had a higher regard for writers than the English. He would go where he was wanted.

Several of his friends, catching sight of this by accident, were shocked. What on earth had come over him? Michael Pitt, the Ashampstead schoolboy for whom Angus had bought his first Pimm's so many years ago in The Star in Alfriston, thought Angus looked as though he had turned into one of his own characters.* One or two wrote accusing him of making empty gestures, of having thrown in the towel. Others felt there was something slightly grotesque about the sight of this portly red-faced well-fed white-haired knight walking down the front steps of the Athenaeum while complaining that he was impoverished and unloved. Did he not look the very model of the establishment he now intended to desert? Others muttered that he had fallen into Mrs Thatcher's trap – she it was who had politicised everything, and Angus had allowed himself to be driven into a corner. These were difficult times.

"Territory, status, And love, sing all the birds, are what matter," W.H. Auden had written.[6] Angus and Tony were uprooting themselves from their territory, but they embarked on their new adventures with high hopes. They would listen to the birds of Provence.

★

To Tony was left the upheaval of packing and removal. He put Angus in a hotel for three nights in Long Melford while he struggled with thirty years' accumulation of papers and books. Luckily Angus was curiously indifferent to furniture and objects (though the stuffed birds made their way to St Rémy) but he would fuss about the books. Some were left in Martin Corke's garage, but many, many packing cases were filled and loaded. Into the bottom of one of them, pushed down beneath some cushions, went the notebooks in which Angus had recently been working. They did not turn up for some years. Paintings were donated to suitable institutions, and some of their more valuable books (including the Nonesuch Dickens) were sold. The apartment in St Rémy was not large.

They now began the long round of their farewells. Numbers of people claim to have dined with them on their last night in England, and certainly there were many last suppers. There were many East Anglian lunches in the Old Fire House and the Old Bakery, and there was a meal at Simpsons

---

* Michael Pitt, now a historian at the University of Reading, had been a schoolboy at Ashampstead from 1938, had attended Lewes Grammar School while still lodging with Betty Wilson, and then had lodged for a while in Violet Bridgewater's basement in Clareville Grove.

with a convalescent Arnold Goodman. (The Bradburys thought that Angus, over an excellent meal in Ely, was excited, perky, and full of hope, but Elizabeth noted that he was walking very badly, and she drove away full of worry.) Everyone wanted to say goodbye – Harold and Antonia, Maggie and Michael, Geoffrey and Michael, Bill and Gwen, Monty and Bob, Alan and Lionel, Pat Trevor-Roper . . . To some, it did not seem as great a break as it in the event proved to be – Angus and Tony would surely be back, over the years, for meetings, for more evenings with their friends. For those who saw them only a few times a year, it was not really the end, it would not make such a difference. Angus was still perfectly on the ball – it must have been at this last meal in the Bistroquet that he ticked me off so obliquely for telling the world he was born in South Africa.

On 15 October 1985, Angus revisited Dr Kocen, who found the clinical picture unchanged. Angus had had no more falls, although he was still a little unsteady on his feet, especially on uneven pavements. There seemed no reason to suspect that his condition would deteriorate rapidly, and there was no need for an operation. (His skin condition remained somewhat puzzling.) On 22 October Angus and Tony went to lunch with Sybil Scott in Seaford, where she had come home to settle after many wanderings abroad. She and Dick Scott now lived not far from Ashampstead, still a school but now renamed as Newlands Manor School: the spacious grounds had been eaten away by developers, but the creeper-covered house itself still looked very handsome, and its old myths – of the underground tunnel, the famous Great Dane, the eccentric Johnstone-Wilsons – still lingered. Angus and Tony then went on to stay for a couple of nights with the Egremonts at Petworth – their second visit since Max Egremont had written his fan letter out of the blue about *Magic*. The first visit had been before a "brilliant" Kipling lecture at Sussex University on 26 April 1983, Lord Egremont recalls: Charles Carrington had been in the audience, and Angus had been on top form.

Egremont always found Angus very entertaining, and charming with his children – he particularly enjoyed the manner in which Angus addressed an elderly female relative of his who was taking a very long time over telling a story – "Get it out dear, get it out!" Angus had cried impatiently.

(Egremont also liked and respected Tony, and was touched by Angus's insistence on the equality and openness of their relationship: yet again Angus had made sure that Tony did not get the "Come in after dinner" treatment. In his letter of invitation (17 June 1985) Egremont had said "I have been meaning anyway to write to say how much we both enjoyed the programme about your lives together. You were most impressive and so supremely natural which I could never be on television. We were delighted to see it got such excellent well-deserved reviews.")

Angus and Tony then moved on to Michael Howard and Mark James in Eastbury: Angus gave a talk in Oxford to the Rhodes Society at Oriel on 25 October. In Oriel, the old trouper gave a charismatic performance, and the kids loved him, Howard remembers – but Mark James (himself much younger) was shocked to see how doddery Angus had become. Angus could hardly walk unsupported, and looked vacant for long periods of time – had he had a heart attack, James wondered, and wonders still. Were they really well enough for the move? Geoffrey Wright and Michael Colborne-Brown remember a moment of horror at their last supper at Shrub Cottage near Bury – Tony looked white with exhaustion from weeks of packing and worry, but Angus seemed not quite to have taken the whole situation in: at one point he said "Of course if we don't like it in France we shall just come back again –" at which the weary Tony looked whiter than ever.

The psychic Jaidev had written to Angus in July, "Please don't fall." Dr Kocen, in a report written after Angus's second visit to him on 15 October 1985, had been more technical. "On examination he shuffled a little and was unsteady. Cranial nerves were normal, there was a suggestion of slight cogwheel rigidity, perhaps a little more on the left than the right in the upper limbs, tendon reflexes were symmetrical with ankle jerks absent, plantars flexant. The computerised Brain Scan shows generalised ventricular enlargement. The sulci were not as prominent as the somewhat enlarged ventricles. The appearances were suggestive of communicating hydrocephalus. I reviewed the clinical picture on the 15th October 1985. There has been no significant change (since May 1, 85) in the patient's symptoms and I am writing this report purely to have him take it with him as he is likely to travel and stay abroad for significant periods of time in the forthcoming future." Tests for AIDS and syphilis, Kocen reports, proved negative.

Armed with this report at last they set off, as so often in happier times, via a night with Jeanne and Glyn Davies in Dover, then onto the ferry, and on a long, slow journey through France to their new life.

They also took with them the last note from Mrs Revens, whose husband Albert had died the year before. It said,

> I have gone to save saying goodbye. Thanks for everything, all the best.
>
>   E. Revens.
>   You don't want me weeping on your hands.

★

The apartment overlooking the square in St Rémy was on the sixth floor, even higher than rumour had reported, but it had a lift with its special key which took you right up to the top floor and inside your own home: Les Glaniques, as the conversion was called, was the highest building in town, once an old chardonniers' workshop, dating from 1907, and the modern penthouse commanded a spectacular view of the Place de la République, the domed church of St Martin, the tiled rooftops, and beyond them, in a great circular sweep, Avignon, Mont Ventoux, the Luberon, Tarascon, Beaucaire, and the strangely carved bony white peaks of Les Baux and the Alpilles.

While settling themselves in Angus and Tony stayed for a few nights at the modest and deeply French Cheval Blanc in the corner of the square. It was ruled by a mini-skirted Madame, some large dogs and a gentleman in a beret: other family members could be seen and heard noisily enjoying themselves in its dining room just off the first-floor landing. While Angus and Tony were there they enjoyed visits from Natasha Spender and from Terry and Joanna Kilmartin, who, somewhat ironically, were to be amongst their closest English neighbours. A telephone was installed in the flat in Les Glaniques, and Angus and Tony moved in, to receive their first calls from Clive Johnstone-Wilson and Bentley Bridgewater. They had not yet been forgotten. They had not yet sent out change-of-address cards, as they were due to go to Iowa for a last teaching stint in January 1986, and they had decided to wait until they returned to St Rémy in May to announce their official change of residence.

It was a short winter in St Rémy, and they hardly had time to settle into the life Stephen Spender said he imagined for them – of bières and berets in the Café des Arts – before they were back again, on 16 December, to make a programme in London with poet and biographer Ian Hamilton for *Bookmark*. Hamilton had given Spender what he considered a "HOR-RIBLE" review for his recently published Journals – perhaps Angus was unwise to accept an interview with such a cut-throat. As Angus and Tony waited for their flight in Marseilles airport, they met a pleasant young aspiring novelist, Teddy St Aubyn, who said he was a friend of Janet Shand-Kydd's son Adam. They exchanged addresses. He seemed very polite, and so, when it came to it, was Ian Hamilton. (Edward St Aubyn was not polite about the wealthy expatriate world of the British and Americans in Provence in his first novel, *Never Mind*, published in 1992 by Heinemann: set back in the sixties, it offers a devastatingly macabre and tragi-comic child's-eye view of drugs, drinking, incest, child abuse, sado-masochism, and other forms of high living – a vision that the younger Angus would probably have saluted.)

Ian Hamilton's programme – a profile of Angus and his work – is curiously affecting. One sees it now with hindsight but with hindsight the fragility revealed by the camera is striking. Sir Angus walks with a stick: he peers anxiously down from a gallery in the Reading Room: he hesitates, a little lost, as he gazes at a shop window. He looks cautious and wary and puzzled. The world had become baffling to him – and this he revealed in what he said. He spoke freely about Mrs Thatcher and her values, offering the remarkably detached view that "neurotic people seek embodiment of what they fear" – and for him, she had been it. He had summoned her up. An hysteric himself, he considered Mrs Thatcher an hysteric. It took one to know one, as Hermione Hammond had said. Angus had cared about England, about English literature, English painting, English scenery – and these things were no longer valued. All that anyone cared about now was monetary success.

He tried to relate this to his own family's financial fecklessness and gradual decline. They had, he said, considered themselves civilised though poor – but they knew that all the same that they were "lovely people". It is not clear whether Angus endorses this view of the Johnstone-Wilsons or not. All he knows is that there had been "a total change of climate which I found very difficult to take."

He is on surer ground when talking about Bletchley Park, the Museum, Dolphin Square, but really comes to life when describing Charlie, the Cockney butcher-boy who had tried to blackmail him. "He was fun," says Angus defiantly, grinning wickedly. "He was my idea of what a young man should be to be attractive" – but he was "not at all nice." The blackmail was "the nasty side of a rather wonderful thing" – and Angus admitted he had got frightened and forked out quite a lot.

When questioned about his work, he was cautious – his books did not sell, they were middle-class, they were of the past, he admitted: adding sweetly, "I am seventy-three, you know." (In fact, he was only seventy-two.) He could not work in England now because of the politics – they weighed on him, they destroyed the freedom of the imagination. That was why he had gone to France. He had gone to make a new start.

In notes that he made in preparation for this interview, Angus dwelt much on his youthful homosexual adventures, as though he was determined to be fully open at the last. There would be no more concealments. "Lavatories graffiti from 12 (Liverpool St – first trip abroad to Holland) very powerful in teens – one or two v impressive and interesting – have outlived all the great porn I've read. Never cottaging but once with messenger boy from Travel Bureau – cottaging not for me but for many the central feature of their lives – relief from home – size of cocks – class breakdown – DANGER. John Gielgud following the Montagu case seemed to us to portend prosecution. (Perkin comments on Paddington Stn) Pickups – Gloucester Road – Butchers or fishmongers shop – The relief of Corsica or Marseilles where it was all a regular thing, – But 15/16 La Ciotat – affront – scorn of the parting pickup." And again, in a separate aside, "From Nancy Boy to Gay via Pansy and Queer." In these notes, he also refers to the Villiers St episode at the Faulkner Hotel. (Villiers St had also appeared, in *No Laughing Matter*, as the site of the theatrical agencies from which Marcus Matthews – and in real life, presumably, Colin and Pat – had tried to find work as film extras.)

Only the butcher-boy got into the Hamilton interview, an interview which contrasts interestingly with a much jollier and more informal conversation with travel writer and journalist Duncan Fallowell, who called in on his travels to see Angus in snowy St Rémy: the piece appeared originally in *Time Out*.[7] Here, Angus had clearly been on his most relaxed and scatty form – munching meringues, covering himself with sugar, chattering on about his father, Zulu George, the OUDS, Lawrence Durrell, Iowa, and anything else that came or was put into his head. Fallowell suggested to him that it was odd for someone who had vertigo to choose to live in a penthouse: would he be able to sit on the balcony with his back to the railings to work in the summer?

"No, I couldn't. I'd think all the time that a mountain was going to come and strangle me. Perhaps I could write indoors, against the windows, with the windows shut. But I don't know if I can get sunburnt with the windows shut, and I like to be sunburnt."

"I'm afraid you can't get sunburnt that way."

"Oh . . . then perhaps I could sit on the balcony with something over my head. You see, I'm not afraid of falling down. I'm afraid of falling up. That's why I find New York so difficult because I think I'm going to be sucked upwards."*

An Alice-through-the-Looking-Glass response worthy of the Old Master, who was obviously enjoying both his guest and the meringues.

*

Angus and Tony flew to Chicago, via Paris, on 14 January 1986, on their last American journey. In Chicago they saw Jordan and Anita Miller of Academy Chicago (distributors of the Granada fiction paperbacks and *The*

---

* The White Knight in *Through the Looking Glass*: "Now the reason hair falls off is because it hangs *down* – things never fall *upwards*, you know."

World of Charles Dickens), and then drove on to Iowa City where it was soon apparent to Jack Leggett, the McDowells, the Kerns, Sandy and Susan Boyd, Connie Brothers, Donald Justice, Tina Bourjaily and other old friends and acquaintances that Angus was not the Angus they remembered. He seemed confused, did not always recognise people, had tinges of paranoia – America suddenly seemed to him to be full of Japanese, or so Justice remembered his saying. All of them recall incidents when he seemed to lose his way. Like his father Willie in 1938, Angus would set off to a familiar place and forget where he was going. The spring was to be littered with a trail of cancellations and broken engagements and hospital appointments. At least one of his students, David Kaplan, felt protective about him – "I think many other students – with the intolerance of youth – were less tolerant, perhaps because they didn't understand just how sick he was."[8] James McPherson, black short-story writer and fellow teacher at the Workshop, remembers with pleasure Angus reading from his fiction on 6 March at the English-Philosophy Building – and recalls also conversations with Angus about the sad new monetarism and philistinism on both sides of the Atlantic. Angus was a gentleman, said McPherson: the first knight he had ever met, and an honor to the honor.*

This semester, Angus taught for the last time his course on Children in Literature and paid his final tribute to Virginia Woolf, who in *The Waves*, through the stream of consciousness, had brought to perfection "one of the major revolutions" of fiction –a revolution in thinking for one who had declared in California in 1960 that "interior monologue writing is a disaster . . . the most heavy, ugly & cumbersome form that has been invented."[9] Her death, the news of which had come to him forty-five years ago in March 1941 as he sat on a train delayed in the bitter cold for three hours by a time-bomb, still affected him – indeed, in some ways it affected him more. It had been the end of an era – "Her suicide in the shallow river of the Sussex Ouse in the Winter of 1941 ended, perhaps, a cultural era, she was the last of the cultured elite, the end of an experiment in English intellectual aristocracy, but no English speaking novelist of significance can write again as though her four great novels had never been written." In the margin of this comment he had scribbled "My own walks there with the desperate sadness of adolescence." He linked his fate with hers. Another era was coming to an end. The world that he had known was disintegrating, and so was he.

Angus's health was very worrying – swollen ankles, shortness of breath, skin problems – and Tony's was not good: he was suffering acutely from

---

* James Alan McPherson, author of *Hue and Cry* (1969) and *Elbow Room* (1977). He won the Pulitzer Prize in 1978.

stress and came out in a rash. Tony was not the calm operator he had once been: at times he seemed quite testy. He read *Barnaby Rudge* to calm himself down but it did not quite do the trick. He was worried about all the problems waiting in France – taxation, pensions, health insurance, social security. Should they become French *résidents*, as Gerard Reve, now the owner of four homes round Europe, had advised? Their income had dropped sharply in the preceding year, and it was hard to know where further funds would come from – Angus was clearly not up to any further teaching engagements, royalties were down, some of his books were out of print, and the only new book in the pipeline, a collection of travel articles called *Reflections in a Writer's Eye* (dedicated to Jaidev) received scant attention in the press, and some of that hostile. Secker published in it January, but cautiously, with a small print run: Tony was deeply upset by Alan Ross's review in the *Guardian*[10] which accused Angus of publishing left-overs – and indeed it was a fact that only two short pieces, on Arizona and Martinique, were previously unpublished. "Sir Angus is an old dear, as observant as a gekko, often extremely funny and disarmingly frank. Alas, the human qualities that make him as a story-teller and a companion so immensely agreeable are present in these various anecdotes only in the smallest doses . . . Perhaps now that he is back in his beloved France, he might consider writing stories again." This advice from a one-time friend could hardly have seemed more unwelcome or irrelevant.

(Alan Ross and Angus had had many friendly contacts over the years, most of them, as we have seen, connected with the *London Magazine* or India or both – Ross had been born in Calcutta, and in his review failed to praise Angus's reflections on India, accusing him of "garrulousness – what old India hands call 'Cochin-leg' ". Ross, like Angus but even more gravely, was subject to fits of deep depression. In 1962, when Ross was going through a crisis, Angus wrote to John Lehmann – "As I suffered a similar experience, my sympathies are very real."[11])

Tony, in his depression, was briefly cheered by a request from the British Council in India to use his Kipling photographs in an exhibition, but had to write back saying the negatives were buried in the muddle of unpacked boxes at St Rémy. Pat Trevor-Roper wrote reassuringly to say that it sounded as though there was nothing wrong with either of them that a soft summer in Provence would not cure, but meanwhile they had to endure a winter in Iowa. It was some consolation to hear that the weather in England was appalling. In Bury, John Petch had died very suddenly, and poor Betty Blackburne was very ill. Life would have been no better back at the cottage.

They had rooms, this time, in Iowa House, the university Guest House, but it was in the Holiday Inn that Angus collapsed and from which he had to be taken by ambulance to hospital. The night before, on 12 April, he had woken at five in the morning and fallen out of bed while trying to find his spectacles: he claimed to have lain there for two hours, unable to get up, before somebody from Iowa House Reception rescued him. The next day, which was a Sunday, he felt well enough to go out for an evening meal, but before setting off for the Inn he called to Tony from the lavatory, where he had wet his trousers: he was clinging to the cistern, unable to straighten up. Tony helped him to change, and off they went to dinner, Angus proceeding with enormous difficulty. The Inn was in the centre of town, only a few minutes walk from the university buildings, and Angus and Tony often ate and entertained guests there: they had once thrown a large party there for everybody they knew in town. This evening, Angus had a brandy and ginger ale and ate a light meal of salad and fish, but he did not really seem to know where he was and was almost completely silent. "Glazed and gaga," said Tony later. At the end of the meal, at about 7.30 p.m., Tony helped Angus to the Gents, but again, he was almost unable to walk or stand. Once more in the corridor he seemed unable to move in any direction, and held on to the telephone booth for support. Tony then sat him on a chair in the corridor while he summoned an ambulance. He thought Angus might have had a stroke, and so did the paramedics – one male, one female – who within minutes put him on a stretcher and whisked him to hospital.

He was kept in the Department of Internal Medicine at the University for just over a week, and the diagnoses were "1) early demential syndrome, probable normal pressure hydrocephalus with Parkinsonian features; 2) hypertension times 15 years; 3) psoriasis; and 4) probable history of vertebral-basilar transient ischemic attacks." The report later noted that his "gait was remarkable for small narrow based shuffling steps and he was noted to turn en bloc."

Whatever all this meant, it did not bode well. Was it possible to struggle on in Iowa? Angus was put on a salt-free diet and medication, and told to lose weight. Luckily it was near the end of their long stay, and the friendly little town rallied round loyally. Angus himself rallied: astonishingly, he returned to give his classes at the Writers' Workshop and also managed to give a talk on 5 May 1986 at the Gay People's Union, where he was on his best and most brilliant form. Disclosure, in these late years, compelled him. Connie Brothers deeply regretted that the speech had not been taped for the archives. Then, on 8 May, Angus and Tony set off for St Rémy, via Chicago, Paris, and Marseilles. It was a long journey and Angus was no longer as happy or co-operative a passenger as he had been: he needed wheelchairs at the airports.

★

The soft summer of Provence awaited them. Now they could settle in to their new life, and get to know the shops, the cafés, the restaurants, their neighbours. Tony had to dash back to England in June to hire an estate car to clear their remaining possessions from Regent's Park Terrace, but for Angus nothing urgent waited. He could relax. He wrote, in a quavering hand, to the Chisletts in Madrid on 19 May, "yes, Spain will be one of the first targets for next year – but maybe you will like to visit old friends in Provence! 'Old' is it. This water on the brain is nasty to deal with but I think I'm winning through. How odd it was to be in the USA for the first time . . . and find it a bit distasteful. Europe is not there anymore, we know European people. It was all Chinese, Japanese, Taiwanese, Hispanic American. American people are busy changing themselves to fit this new life. They were awfully kind to us as always and Iowa looked lovely as too did Chicago, *but* (and it is a niggling but) the Japanese are welcome because they are business people. The yuppees welcome them all flying back . . . God is back in US mouths now. I was feeling a bit senile for all that."

Angus felt European. He was at home in the South of France, and he had always particularly loved this landscape. He had loved it from early years, from his intoxicating and sexually liberating schoolboy visits to the Anquetins at La Ciotat, through his pursuit of Zola on those exciting, occasionally stormy excursions with Bentley Bridgewater, Pat Trevor-Roper, Chris Arnold and Tony Garrett – and in his book on Zola he had written of Zola's own love of "the bright colours and sweet scents . . . the white, rocky hills, the vineyards, the twisted fig-trees and the lush overgrown estates." (Chapter One, "Early Life.") By a curious not-quite-coincidence Angus's French school text of Daudet's *Lettres de mon moulin* survives: it is a Harrap Modern Language Series Text, published in 1927, and it bears witness to Angus's early love of Provence – the English introduction describes the Camargue, la Crau, the Alpilles, the village of Paradou, Arles, Nîmes, Tarascon, Avignon: young Johnstone-Wilson had adorned the fly leaves with various inkblots and, happily, in pencil, had noted "Se griser = be in an ecstasy" "s'enivrer = wallow in or be in an ecstasy". He had known ecstasy here: maybe he would know it again.

The countryside round St Rémy was famed for its recuperative powers: there was a temple to Valetudo, the God of Health, in the semi-excavated and herb-scented Roman site of Glanum just up the hill to the south of the town – Glan was the name of an ancient divinity with healing powers who dwelt in a cave, and whose shrine dated back to the fifth or sixth century BC. The ruins of three fluted columns mark the temple, and water still rises from the source to fill a pool restored by Agrippa in 20BC. Across the olive grove from the Antiquities stood the church and hospital of St-Paul-de-Mausole, where Vincent Van Gogh had accepted treatment and painted orchards and quarries and irises and pine trees. Van Gogh had written many a letter to his brother Theo about the cypresses, the poppies, the "little mountains, grey and blue" and "The very, very green cornfields and pines": and he had painted here the yellow reaper, Death. (On the change-of-address card he sent to George and Joan Painter, Tony wrote, "Van Gogh was cared for in the town, but he needed care, so far we do not, just – Love Tony.")

Tony loved the flower-filled Romanesque cloisters at St-Paul: he and Angus were to spend many hours sitting there, reading or dreaming. Tony was musing on the nature of purgatory and trying to read Heidegger: the "practising atheism" which he had professed in conversation with John Pitman for the *Couples* programme was under siege. Religion interested him more and more. Many a virgin on many a hillside watched over them: Notre Dame du Bon Remède would come to their help, and so, perhaps, would les Saintes Maries de le Mer.

This was a painter's landscape of light where every view recalled a masterpiece. Augustus John, who had stayed here with Dorelia in the late 1930s, just before the outbreak of war, had described it as "an endless sequence of exquisite landscapes", and had regretted to his neighbour Marie Mauron that he could not himself do it justice: "*ces Alpilles attendent encore leur peintre – mais ce n'est pas moi. Regardez! Ces jeux de gris, de bleu, de rose, ces touffes de plantes aromatiques, en boules, taches, traits sur le roc de toutes couleurs insaisissables, me désespèrent.*"[12] Old friends from England envied their retreat to paradise. Iris Murdoch, who remembered St Rémy with a particular affection, wrote to wish them well in their new home. Viola Hall, now eighty-six, an old friend from British Museum days and Viva King's salon, recalled a happy fortnight in St Rémy many years ago – enchanting dancing in the streets, with girls and boys dressed in mauve. Now her travelling days and the "*temps de cérises*" were over, but there were still pleasures left – "the sunshine, brother, and the wind on the heath,"[13] she quoted.

The small town itself was a delight. It was just the right size. It preserved some of its old medieval walls, and a walk round its tree-planted circular boulevards could be accomplished in half-an-hour. (Van Gogh had painted the plane trees and the road-menders of the Boulevard Mirabeau in December 1889.) It had a bookshop, many restaurants, excellent

markets and food shops, and just the right amount of historical interest – it
was no museum or mausoleum (though there was an Hôtel de Sade, and a
Fontaine Nostradamus in honour of one of its most famous sons). It was a
fruit and market-gardening centre, and had a busy commercial and cultural
life. Provençal poetry as well as impressionist painting informed the
atmosphere – Frédéric Mistral of nearby Maillane was well remembered.
(Local historian and writer Marie Mauron, widow of Charles Mauron,[*]
died this year; her funeral on 3 November was a low-key affair, Tony
noted in his diary, as he watched from the balcony.)

Mistral's poetry recorded a way of life that still survived, and Tony
learned to track its lyrical landmarks:

> *Dins lou Camin dis Abeie*
> *Au clar pais de la Tarasco*
> *A Mont-Majour, au Trau di Masco,*
> *L'ai acampado, a passa tems,*
> *E messo en rimo aquest printems . . .*
>
> *Dans le Chemin des troupeaux transhumants,*
> *Au clair pays de la Tarasque,*
> *A Montmajour, au Trou des Masques,*
> *Je l'ai recueillie autrefois*
> *Et je l'ai rimée ce printemps*
>
> (Nerto-Nerte)

On 19 May this year came the Grande Fête de la Transhumance, when
the streets were filled with shepherds moving their sheep along the ancient
way from Arles to their summer pastures in the Alpilles: one had a
wonderful view of the migration from the top of Les Glaniques. Less
agreeable were the regular festivals when crazy young men chased crazy
young bulls round and round the town and crashed ritually and bloodily
into shopkeepers' plate-glass windows, and once into the ground floor of
Les Glaniques itself – this was also bull-fighting terrain, and Tony disliked
this even more than he had disliked the Suffolk hunt.

In the good weather there were many little cafés where one could sit on
the street and watch the world go by – and all within a few minutes' walk
from their front door. No more was Angus isolated in the dark cottage
when Tony went out: he could sit up in his eyrie and watch the life of the
square below, or gaze at the clouds and the mountains, or wait at a
pavement café while Tony did the errands. The lady in the bakery, the lady

---

[*] Charles Mauron (1899–1976), pioneer of psychoanalytic literary criticism, wrote on
Baudelaire, Mallarmé and Van Gogh. Marie Mauron (b.1896) wrote novels and books on local
lore and history.

in the laundry, the lady in the cheese shop, the lady in Vêtements Peyrache, soon got to know Monsieur Tony, whose French was improving rapidly from a regular reading of *Le Monde*. (But he found the meetings of the Glaniques co-operative association quite tricky to follow, and wished Angus were up to writing protest letters about lift doors and dustbins and fire precautions – all these responsibilities now fell on him.)

Angus and Tony ate out a good deal, both in St Rémy itself – at the Bistro des Alpilles, and at the little Vietnamese restaurant, Le Mandarin – and took short excursions into the neighbouring countryside to Mausanne and Maillane, and to Les Doctrinaires and the Café Nautic on the quay in Beaucaire. It was pleasant to drink a *kir* or a *vin blanc* at the Café du Progrès, eat at the little family restaurant of L'Oustalet in Maillane just across the road from the Museon Mistral, and to visit the Mistral mausoleum in the cemetery, modelled on Queen Jeanne's pavilion at Les Baux. They avoided the citadel of the rocky promontory of Les Baux itself – too many tourists, and far too precipitous.

They made valuable friends both amongst the expatriates and the local community. Their circle widened to include Margaret Reinhold, a handsome, colourful and dynamic South-African-born psychotherapist with a wholly sympathetic weakness for stray cats: her friend and frequent house guest, neurologist and ceramic artist William Gooddy, who pleased her by taking excellent photographs of those cats: Pamela Rachet (painter, and half-sister of Neal Ascherson) and her French husband Antoine: Robert Ferec, interior decorator: Ann Cox Chambers, American millionaire, diplomat and hostess, who occasionally gave grand musical soirées when she happened to be in residence: and Canadian writer John Ralston Saul and his Hong-Kong-born wife Adrienne Clarkson, publisher and television presenter. This exotic, bilingual and high-powered couple had a house nearby perched on the ancient rocky hillside of Les Eygalières and they spent their time commuting dashingly across the Atlantic, sometimes breezing in for a long weekend.

A little further afield were the painter Barbara Robinson (whose husband Walter had now died), Quentin Crewe and Patrick Woodcock: Wendy Rintoul had a house which she visited in the summer, and Hampstead bookseller Ian Norrie and Christine Brooke-Rose were both looking for properties in the neighbourhood. In summer many visitors passed through – Ludo Pieters from Rhoon, who was so charmed he thought of buying a house there himself, and Anthony Hobson, who wrote that driving north away from Provence felt a little like dying.[14] Bentley Bridgewater and Richard Brain of the *Times Literary Supplement* and their young friend and minder Ian Munday (dubbed by Angus

"Squirrel Nutkin") arrived for several days on a spree, Nicholas Brooke and his second wife Julia popped in, and Simon Edwards turned up with yet another wife or girlfriend. Michael Slater came with an entourage, and Kazu Serikawa came all the way from Yokohama. Patsy and Denis Barnes, Sybil and Dick Scott and Ian McEwan all sought them out. So did Dick Ashby from Ashampstead, who had written to Angus a long letter about the old days when he used to read *Kim* by torchlight under the bedclothes in Landseer dormitory – *Kim* had given him a lasting love of India and he still enjoyed an annual regimental dinner singing Kipling's "Screw-Guns" to the tune of the Eton Boating Song.

In the autumn the martins gathered like bees on the dome of the church, and the summer visitors thinned out and began to fly away home. In late October Tony nipped back to London to visit the dentist, installing Angus in comfort in the Hôtel Le Castelet during his absence: Angus rang Michael Slater anxiously from the hotel to find out where Tony was and whether he was on his way home.

Was Angus trying to write at this time? Possibly. He wrote to Nicholas Brooke's first wife Pamela at some point in October saying that he was upset that he had lost his notebooks for his new work – a novel, as she understood it. These were the exercise books lost in the box beneath the cushions: Tony says he remembers Angus mentioning them a few times, but then he seemed to forget all about them. Was their loss still weighing on him?

The weather stayed fair and in November they went to see Clive and Lucie in Cannes. They had hoped for a mild winter, but the weather became increasingly cold, and the roof leaked: snow threatened, then fell, as it had done the year before on Duncan Fallowell. "A hellish winter here," wrote Tony miserably to Perry Knowlton at Curtis Brown, New York, and he told Simon Edwards that St Rémy was beginning to pall. He noted van Gogh's letter to his sister, written nearly a century earlier in November 1889: "Do not imagine that it is less cold here than in Holland. The winter has only just started, and we shall have it until the end of March. Only less rain than in Holland, an unbearably harassing wind which is very cold and dry and clear but severe spells of cold weather . . ."

Dr Arnaud, who had received the medical reports from Iowa, believed that Angus's condition could be stabilised with the right mix of medication. Angus's walking was still poor, and he suffered from indigestion and nausea, but his psoriasis had improved slightly. There did not seem to be any point in consulting a neuro-specialist in Avignon, though various enquiries were made – Arnaud knew that the possibility of a "shunting operation" had been mentioned by Dr Kocen, but Arnaud did not think this advisable. Tony tried to keep Angus walking, as Arnaud recommended, and on some days he seemed fine, on others sleepy or tottering: they managed an expedition in early December to Valence and Lyon without mishap. A week later they went to Avignon, and visited the Petit Palais, but Angus seemed worried by the cobbles and the downward slope.

Mentally, his state was equally uncertain. He wrote a page or two on Dickens for a programme in which he still hoped to take part, and sent tributes for Anthony Burgess's seventieth birthday and Terry Kilmartin's retirement from the *Observer*: he wrote in detail to Julia Brooke about some short stories she had been writing, and answered many queries from Chen Ruilan in Beijing University who was translating *Late Call* into Chinese. But he was often confused: he had delusions at night that his father or some other older man was in the apartment, and would sometimes start up with a pile of books or papers saying that he had to go and give a lecture or attend a meeting. Tony would have to calm him and settle him back in bed.

In the New Year of 1987 Angus and Tony carried on as best they could, visiting Lucie and Clive in Cannes in early February, and spending a few nights at the Hôtel de Noailles in Montpellier at the end of the month. Tony kept a bulletin of Angus's progress for Dr Arnaud: he reported no problems en route to Montpellier or at the Art Gallery the next morning, but on the half-hour walk back to the hotel after a two-hour rest in a café Angus was "tottering forward, and at one point staring wide eyed ahead with teeth bared." Then on 1 March, back at St Rémy, there were no problems.

On 14 March Angus and Tony dined with the Hobsons at the Hôtel de L'Europe in Avignon. This was the second time the Hobsons had seen them in France: they had lunched together in August 1986 at the Mas des Madames, near Barbentane, and Angus, in a grey suit and orange knitted tie, had seemed vague, and had thought he lived at St Denis, not St Rémy: this time, when he appeared at the hotel, he held himself very upright and still. With his ivory-knobbed cane, wrinkled walnut-dark face, and clouds of white hair, he looked like an Indian idol, and it was of India and of Kipling that he talked.

Angus and Tony might have continued like this for years, with good days and bad days, or so thought Dr Arnaud: but three weeks later, on 10 April 1987, Angus fell heavily, tripping over the small step from the balcony into his bedroom. He broke the neck of his femur. Tony found him lying on the floor, and got him into bed; it was not until the morning, when Angus was still in great pain, that Tony realised the extent of his injury. Angus had had several falls before in the apartment, but this was by far the most serious, and in Dr Arnaud's view it greatly precipitated his final deterioration. Angus was taken to the Polyclinique St Jeanne D'Arc fifteen miles away at Arles, where the break was mended with a metal plate.

There, eleven days later, on 22 April, Peter Conradi and Jim O'Neill went to visit Angus. Peter found him "a little distrait, ODD fellow in his chair, blanket over his tummy and legs.

"Hello, David, as I kissed him, then reverted to 'Peter'. He was bubbly and confused . . . What a nice shirt (to Jim): do you always wear it? later, – Do you always come around and visit just like this as you are, or do you sometimes move around with a small flock of *dogs*, Scottish terriers perhaps. (This was prescient: we acquired a dog ten days or so later.) On greeting, Angus looked quizzically, and used his standard opener 'You look like someone famous, I can't think who, one has only to look at you, and one realises that something about you, that you're *alright*.' On his confusion he said, 'I don't know WHO I am or WHAT I am or WHY I am.' "

They continued to talk, in an inconsequential and surreal way, of living abroad, of Alphonse Daudet and his Moulin at Fontvieille near Arles, of Angus's wicked family, of Simon Edwards, of how much nicer publishers' wives were than publishers, of the snobbish dullness of French society. Peter thought that Angus's false teeth (which he would occasionally now take out at table and lay upon his plate) gave him "a mad look, half (I unkindly thought) Old King Cole, half Sugar-Plum Fairy: enjoying a laugh at his own expense, and at the expense of frailty and sadness, a bit the air of a pantomime dame . . ."

(Old King Cole, Sugar-Plum Fairy, Mr Toad, Widow Twankey, Margaret Rutherford, guru, swami, Miss Marples – with age Angus grew ever more androgynous in appearance, though even his earliest appear-ances – Leila at Ashampstead, Emmy with the Merton Floats – had been gipsy-like. There is a story that Charles Monteith, switching on television, once mistook Angus for an old gipsy woman – his long flowing hair, his beads, his Moroccan cheesecloth shirts, gave him the aspect of a fortune teller. Perhaps he *was* a fortune teller: the sibyl of his own unwritten Roman novel, *Improbable Nonsense* – and it was no coincidence that he had referred to himself in his 1973 letter to Connolly as a "disgruntled clairvoyant lady".)

Tony was pleased to see Peter Conradi and Jim O'Neill: they were the first non-medical visitors he had allowed near Angus. Tony asked their opinion: they diplomatically said they had found Angus more cheerful than he had been for years, despite his accident – maybe the shock had pulled him out of his depression? "Maybe we should arrange a shock or accident for him like this every week," said Tony mordantly. "Or maybe not."

Tony joined Conradi and O'Neill in Ménerbes for dinner and they talked about their French friends and neighbours – how incurious Patrick Woodcock seemed about Angus's health, how snobby and dotty were others. One of the things that Angus had said to Peter in the Clinic was that he had not realised until recently how Tony "didn't like France *or anything to do with the 1900's!!* An extraordinary collocation." Maybe they would go back to England after all. (Conradi found it interesting to talk to Tony without Angus's incessant interruptions: getting to know Tony better was the one benefit of Angus's illness.)

★

Tony did not dislike France, but he was understandably finding life there difficult. At bad moments it felt as though they had left claustrophobic, spiteful, cosy Suffolk for its replica in claustrophobic, spiteful, cosy St Rémy. It was becoming clear that Angus would never work again, and yet more engagements had to be politely cancelled – a carefully planned trip to Madrid in late April to take part in a conference and see his Spanish publishers for the launch of *The Old Men at the Zoo* was now impossible, and Tony failed to get the conference organisers to pay, although he sent them a draft of Angus's proposed speech. (The Chisletts did their best to sort these matters out, and were disappointed and distressed not to be able to welcome Angus in Spain.) The RSL in June and a possible lecture in Durham were also cancelled. There was no hope now that Angus could ever accept Jaidev's invitation to visit Simla. Even the mildest and least taxing engagement was beyond him. It would be difficult enough to get him back on his feet.

And beyond the immediate medical emergencies long-term financial problems loomed. It had been enormously difficult to sort out the claim on Angus's Health Insurance in Iowa, there were income-tax complications on the horizon, and, horror of horrors, they were just about to wake up to the fact that because of the peculiarities of French inheritance law, Angus would not be able to leave his half share in the jointly-owned apartment, his only capital, to Tony, for Tony was neither his spouse nor his next-of-kin.

Nobody had warned them about this, although many later said they had known about it all along: the only person who had given any kind of an oblique warning was Genifer Garrett, who had written to Tony a few months before her death a letter (dated 12 December 1983) mentioning the oddities of Swiss inheritance law. But it had not seemed relevant then.

Now Tony began to hear nightmare stories of other dispossessed gay couples, and of couples where preventive action had been taken by the older adopting the younger. (Douglas Cooper apparently, had adopted his friend for this reason.) But maybe it was already too late for all that. Angus's 1972 letter to *Encounter* about homosexual marriage and the legal rights of gay couples did not look so impractically avant-garde in this alarming new context.

The first task, however, was to get Angus back onto his feet, if possible. After three and a half weeks in Arles, he was taken to a Re-education Centre in Nîmes to learn how to walk again with a frame. The prospect of a bleak new regime dawned, of wheelchairs, nurses, physiotherapy, tests, examinations, incontinence protection pads, and yet more drugs. Apart from the anxiety, it was all very expensive – the journeys to and from Arles and Nîmes added greatly to normal living costs. Luckily Angus had become an EEC pensioner with an official number in the French social-security system just a week before his fall, so hospital expenses were minimal – Tony did worry that in Nîmes he ought to have a private room, as he snored so loudly and talked so much in his sleep, but the nice young man recovering from a motor accident in the next bed assured Tony that he had earplugs and did not mind. Much of the time Angus was a "sweet and good" patient, but there were worrying bursts of aggression, and a good deal of confusion – Margaret Reinhold, one of his most faithful visitors, says that he seemed convinced that the hospital overlooked the docks. When she tried to correct him, he was quite firm about it. She was wrong, he was right.

Margaret Reinhold thought that he had little insight into his own condition – he did not understand what was happening to him, and resented the fact that his power was slipping away. Tony was taking over, making decisions, signing cheques, and Angus did not like it. Although most of the time Angus was patient with his own illness (a view confirmed by Dr Arnaud and the nurses, Claudine and Nanette, who were to care for him at the apartment) he could also be infuriatingly naughty and play the *enfant terrible*. Everyone forgave him, for everyone knew he was ill. He liked to talk to Margaret Reinhold about his South African childhood: she had been brought up in Durban on the Berea, and they exchanged gossip about life in Natal. He told her about the little girl he had loved in Durban – his mother had not approved because she was his landlady's daughter, and he had never loved another girl since. Rough sailors from Marseilles were what he really fancied, he told Margaret – harking back, perhaps, to those teenage visits to La Ciotat. (Others said he said he fancied rickshaw boys, or golden ephebes, or sophisticated older men – he certainly knew how to confuse those who liked to dwell knowingly on *les secrets de boudoir*. Tony commented on Angus's revelation about sailors, "Well, that really *proves* he was dementing . . .")

Margaret Reinhold was a qualified doctor and Tony turned to her for advice on Angus's medication. She expressed doubts about a regular prescription for a drug called Sinemet which could have side effects of "paranoia, hallucinations and depression", and suggested Angus could be taken off it for a trial period at the Clinique while under medical supervision.

Yet, despite his confusion, Angus could be in his own way quite clear at times, and he wrote three cards from Nîmes in his own hand to the Chislett boys, Tomás and Benjamin, who had sent him get-well drawings: one card showed a view of the hills near St Rémy, one was a reproduction which said "Vincent Van Gogh who painted this lived a large part of his life in a chain of hills on to which my flat here looks all the time and with very little interference." The third, in response to a drawing of a goat from four-year-old Ben, said, "I think your goat was better than this one. A very nice nurse from Marrakesh insisted that the goat was the key to my recovery. I have registered my view that the goats that take orders from me are very well – but those who know outside of goat life are less reliable. Uncle Angus."

Tony's own health was continuing to be of concern to himself and his friends. He was tense, he had developed a maddening tinnitus, his teeth were in a bad way, and he had neurotic fears of choking at the dentist. The journeys to and from Nîmes were tiring, and Angus was not always pleased to see him – sometimes he asked Tony why he had bothered to come, though on other occasions he was friendly and lucid, and would apologise for fits of temper – "I am sorry about it, but I must burst out." On some days he hardly made much sense, but on 21 May 1987 he was "able to read and appraise his short stories which could possibly be included in the Collected Volume; but by supper time (6 pm) bland indifference, childishness, confusion.

'What shall I be doing tomorrow?'

'Physiotherapy.'

'What is that?' "

Angus was making very little progress in learning to walk again. Others around him in the Clinique were doing much better. And to crown the terrible spring, in May Clive died.

31

THE HOWLING MISTRAL NIGHT

Clive Johnstone-Wilson, born in Richmond on 2 September 1894, and considered too delicate to go to school, died on 22 May 1987. The circumstances of his death were bizarre and macabre. Clive's little brother Angus was lying in bed at the Clinique in Nîmes when he took it into his head to ring Clive at his apartment in the rue Jean-Baptiste Dumas in Cannes. Lucie answered. Tony Garrett's medical notes record:

> At 4pm phone call to his brother Clive. Lucie [Clive's wife] answered. A. did not seem to realise who she was – but then grasped and spoke rather at random with her, then passed phone to ACG.* Her voice very faint, but she seemed to be fairly lucidly saying Clive on floor, blood had come from his mouth; she had covered him, but could not lift; against calling Porter or Monsieur Raymond (a friend) and when I asked if she had called their Doctor, she said she had at lunchtime but he was not there. And anyway Clive would not go to hospital and she, Lucie, would not open the door to any other doctor. She agreed that I should call Docteur Maison-Neuve again for her. Which I did. He not there, but receptionist said, of course she would send another Doctor, and I urged this as emergency. Told A. He seemed not to grasp any of it.
> ACG left for St Rémy, phoned again Lucie to find out if anyone had come, and was answered by Police who announced that Clive was dead and that Lucie had been taken to Cannes General Hospital.
> 23.5.87 A. wet in night.

---

* In notes and diaries Tony Garrett usually refers to himself as ACG – for Anthony Charles Garrett.

Very lucid with visiting niece and her husband [Jeanne and Glyn Davies], but they noticed some confusion pm. Told him about Clive, he really showed no emotion. I asked nurses to keep an eye on him that night. I said I thought I should go as soon as possible to see Lucie, but I had to go for a blood test and dentist, and he said "why don't I go to Lucie?"
24.5.87 During whole day – another visit from niece and her husband – very much on top form – memory good, witty, and only one confused remark – "Why don't I come to dinner with you all?" He was able to talk with affection and understanding about Clive and Lucie.

Clive had died intestate, and to Tony was left the business of arranging a funeral, trying to sort out Lucie's affairs, arranging for a priest and a mass to be said. Lucie was too frail to attend the service at Abadie on 26 June, and Tony was the only mourner. Lucie could not look after herself any longer (however had they managed for so long?) and Tony arranged for her to be taken from the hospital in Cannes into the Pension Mariquita at Magagnosc near Grasse. There was thought to be some money in Andorra, but nobody knew how to get hold of it. Lucie was confused, and did not seem to understand that Clive was dead. When Tony first visited her in Nîmes, she had said to him, "Tell me, Tony, is Clive dead?" and Tony had murmured sympathetically "Yes, Lucie": her satisfied response was, "Oh well, that's good to know – he was *such* a liar." It was another fine old Johnstone-Wilson muddle. Patiently Tony set about trying to sort it out, corresponding with Lucie's "Tutelle des Incapables Majeurs", Claude Sellame, about Lucie's finances, her family connections ("*aucune*") and trying to establish whether Lucie was eligible for an army widow's pension from Britain.

Captain Clive, with "his freckles, his screeching voice, his dyed red hair and very white face", with clothes that some of Angus's friends said looked like a bookie's, was gone at last, and Angus was the last of the line. Amongst Clive's effects was a gold watch, a gift from Alan Rook, inscribed with the date 1963. Alan Rook himself was still alive: he was to die three years later, in 1990, and left his estate and vineyard at Stragglethorpe Hall, Lincolnshire, to the family of his brother Michael Rook, a pilot who had been killed in a flying accident just after the war (after surviving The Battle of Britain, Russia and North Africa). The nephew, also Michael Rook, records that he benefited from this generosity because Alan's friend and companion, retired actor Denis Woodford, died first.[1] Had Alan and Clive been in touch at all in later years, since Clive and Lucie left England? There is no record.

Tony, meanwhile, was facing a bleak future. He was writing around for support – he approached Iowan friends Sandy and Susan Boyd, now in Chicago, to find out if there was any fund in the United States that might be asked for help – not as a charity but as an award for "services to literature", and they in turn wrote to Hortense Calisher at the American Academy of Arts and Sciences. In England, Tony thought of the Royal Literary Fund and a Civil List Pension – the RLF was to help, but the Civil List, despite strongly-worded letters of support from many eminent authors, did not. I note that I myself wrote a letter to the Secretary of Appointments at 10 Downing Street urging his case, but have no record of any reply. (Angus himself had once sat on the RLF committee, and had to resign in December 1966 because he was too busy to attend meetings. The RLF has a history of such ironies.) Various friends sent private donations when they heard of Tony's plight (and the Society of Authors said Angus could have an honorary membership without paying his subscription) but Angus's lack of progress at Nîmes made survival in the eagle's nest at St Rémy seem much more doubtful: although it was so central, there was the problem of the lift door, which sometimes stuck, and the flat was too small to take a wheelchair easily. Angus and Tony would be cooped up. (Tony resisted a wheelchair, some said stubbornly.) Friends at home began to enquire into the cost of nursing homes. The answers were frightening.

Angus's future income was totally unpredictable – there might be a windfall at any moment, but it seemed unlikely that things would improve dramatically. Great question-marks hung over French income tax, and over the taxability of the sale of a second batch of manuscripts to Iowa. Well might Angus quote to Tony – as he often did – some of the last words of Arnold Bennett to his common-law wife, Dorothy Cheston Bennett – "Everything is going wrong, my girl." (Bennett's obsession with money had long worried Angus – and even Bennett had muddled his finances, partly through excess generosity.)

Although sales had dropped in England, Angus continued to receive a steady flow of enquiries from academics and admirers and autograph-hunters around the world. Thesis-writers from India and Germany and Holland still pursued him, and it was Tony who had to type out and on occasions to compose replies. How much this interest would add up to in terms of hard cash one could not tell: was Angus doomed now, like his hero John Cowper Powys, to be a forgotten genius, one of the great unread? Did Angus recall the time he had spent approaching the wealthy for a fund for Powys? (Henry Miller had sent a very dusty answer.)

Public Lending Right for this year brought in £812.81 – so somebody was still reading Angus Wilson. A photograph of Angus, taken by Ian

Munday in the St Rémy apartment appeared in the September 1987 issue of the *Tatler*, in a short article and photo-collage on expatriates and holiday visitors in the South of France: it proclaimed "Sir Angus Wilson has chosen to live in a modern flat in St Rémy where friends gather to admire the view from his picture windows." Other celebrities listed included Jackie Onassis in Bagnols-sur-Cèze, Mai Zetterling and Daphne Fielding in Uzès, Peter Mayle at Ménerbes, the Spenders and Conrans at Mausanne-les-Alpilles, and Lawrence Durrell at Sommières: at least the South of France was more chic than Powys's last resort of Blaenau Ffestiniog. Angus is seen wearing the red dressing-gown inherited from Cecil Roberts: in the original photograph Hiram Winterbotham, Tony Garrett, and Richard Brain had also appeared, but they had been neatly excised by the *Tatler*.

In January 1987 Susan Keable, a mature graduate student who had met Angus in 1977 when she was planning a dissertation on his works, had written a long letter to him about his critical reputation and why he was currently underrated: she concluded "But – and there's no way of putting this tactfully, so you will not I hope be hurt – I am absolutely certain that, on your death (sorry, I said I couldn't put it tactfully) EVERYONE will start saying what a shame it was that your books weren't readily available, *all* the posh Sundays and literary magazines will carry lengthy and adulatory reviews . . . and so on, and so on." (14 January 1987) Angus wrote back on 26 January:

Dear Sue,

What a lovely letter to receive! . . . You are surprisingly prophetical because you speak with taste and certainty of my forthcoming death. Alas I fear this may be nearer to prophesy than I would have thought a year ago. What worries me of course is the opposite to your fears – not that people will regret the lack of interest in my work when I die, but that they will simply not notice that I have died. It would be a shame I think where there is so much work which, however faulty, is original and deep-seeing . . .

I hope that the bibliography of my work which has just been completed by Drs John Stape and Anne Thomas – and will I think be published in the States by GK Hall this year – will provide a basis for more worthwhile work on my books – do refer to it and see what you think. I am sure that whatever work you do will be of the greatest interest. I shall be coming to the UK in June and will I am sure have a day to spend in Cambridge. Can we meet then?

But he did not come to Cambridge – his broken femur intervened – and they did not meet again. He did not reach the Royal Society of Literature that year – Steven Runciman, who received a C.Litt. that autumn, wrote from Elshieshields to say that he had hoped to have had a chance of seeing Angus – "Some day I hope that you will be able to come again to this land of your ancestors. But in the meantime you are probably better off in Provence than in the bleakness of Britain. I have not been to St Rémy since 1912 – but I loved it then." (5 November 1987.) Ronald Blythe, reporting to Angus on the RSL ceremony, said that "Poor Rosamond Lehmann was too ill to receive hers and sent a niece.* But Stephen Runciman (85?) trotted up like a lad." (9 November 1987.)

*

As the year wore on, Tony wrote more and more letters – to Martin and Frances Corke, to Mike Shaw at Curtis Brown, and to publisher Graham C.Greene (a friend of Martin Corke, a director of the Greene King Brewery, and nephew of Graham Greene). They are long and often desperate letters. The Clinique insisted on sending Angus back to St Rémy on 8 August, but it had admitted defeat in its attempts to get him to walk again. He could manage only one or two "dragged steps", and for those he needed firm support from Tony. A physiotherapist in St Rémy, M. Casals, was engaged to visit Angus to try to get him moving, with some small success, but it was not easy. Angus was stuck in the flat until November, when he was able to take his first outing in the car – he seemed to enjoy it, but on future excursions was not always co-operative: he would turn himself into a "sack of potatoes" and Tony had physically to lift and lug him about. Sometimes Angus would sit in the car and refuse to get out. Sometimes Tony, in a mixture of anger and despair, would leave him there for an hour or more until he agreed to be moved. (On one of these occasions, in April 1989, by bizarre coincidence, Gerard Reve arrived on an unannounced visit from Montelimar, and witnessed the whole drama, as Angus sat angrily in the little 2CV and would not budge: Reve helped to get Angus up to the apartment, where he fell asleep – thereafter Angus made no mention of Reve's visit and seemed not to have taken it in at all.)

There were visitors, and some of them more congenial than Reve, who annoyed Tony by his insistence on his own financial success, and by ticking Angus and Tony off for selling Felsham Woodside too hastily. Others were more tactful. Rose Tremain – who was to be one of the most willing organisers of the rescue operation – arrived in August, and so did

---

* Mrs Schute from the RSL wrote that the award had been collected by a charming granddaughter.

Jonathan Gili, his wife Phillida, and their three children. (Fourteen-year-old Daisy kissed Tony on parting and told him he was wonderful, which was good for morale.) Yoshi Oida, touring with Brook's *Mahabharata*, popped in: Bob French and Monty Turland came for a week. On 24 August John Stape, co-editor of the forthcoming bibliography, called, and Tony noted that he "stayed from 11 am to 3.30 pm. AW talked coherently with him all the time. Bed 8pm. During day, he seemed to be walking more easily . . . said he was looking forward to M. Casals' next visit."*

The autumn brought Kazu Serikawa, the Barneses, the Sauls, and Mike Shaw. These visits were "life-saving", Tony wrote to Mike Shaw; despite the unfailing kindness of their French friends Tony was isolated, shut up in the flat evening after evening with no one to talk to, and a great deal of wiping up to do in the bathroom. (Tony took to tape-recording poetry to fill in the time – the poets and history of the First World War increasingly compelled his attention.) Either Nurse Claudine or Nurse Nanette came in every day for forty minutes or so, and they found Angus on the whole very amusing, but there was still a lot of nursing left to Tony. One of the notes left by Claudine for Tony reads:

"*Monsieur Garret,*

Sir Angus est têtu, moi aussi! Je lui ai fait son shampooing, ce fût long et 'douloureux'! Lorsque vous verrez le Docteur Arnaud veuillez svp lui demander de renouveller le traitement pour le psoriasis. Merci beaucoup, Amicalement."

Tony was seriously beginning to think they would be better off in England, but Dr Arnaud advised against a move before the winter, and Margaret Reinhold also firmly believed they should stay where they were. Everything was unpredictable – neither their finances nor Angus's condition could, despite the best efforts of many well-wishers, including Arnold Goodman himself, be intelligently assessed. (Goodman expressed himself astonished by the French inheritance laws, which must have been some comfort to Tony.)

In England, Mrs Thatcher was still in full voice, and on 16 October 1987, the great hurricane blew. Letters from back home were full of it. The old mulberry tree at Ashampstead was uprooted, though there was a hope it might be saved, and a pine and a yew crashed onto the roof of St Peter's Church, Blatchington, Seaford, where Angus had given away his niece Sybil Wilson as bride to Richard Scott on 4 September 1948. Maybe it was better to stay put.

---

* The Bibliography by John H. Stape and Anne N. Thomas was published by Mansell in 1988 with a lucid foreword by Angus himself, saying that he found their "fine, detailed listing brings alive, it seems to me, the very meaning of the life of a man of letters, however unmodish that expression may be."

★

Angus and Tony were to stay in St Rémy for another two years. It was a period of profound uncertainty. It was not without its better moments – *The Collected Stories* were published by Secker in the New Year of 1988 and were very well reviewed. On 15 January 1988 Tony wrote to the Corkes that Angus had been "affectionate, lucid, alert, intelligent" all day – "Were it not for his walking which does not seem to improve, I would have said he was as he might have been any evening five years ago. It is a very confusing illness." And he concludes "It is true that Angus benefits – as a writer – from the French Tax Benefit of a 25% reduction in his taxes (where else would this happen, one asks?)"

At the end of January, Tony and Angus set off to visit Lucie in her Maison de Retraite at Grasse, Tony noting that Angus's walking was very poor, and that he was very self-conscious about it with strangers. But the visit was a success, and Tony found Lucie in much better health than the summer before – hopping about with great agility, looking twenty years younger, her hair short and smartly cut and un-hennaed. Angus managed nights in hotels (with drawsheets) and meals in restaurants without too many disasters. Back in England the surprisingly practical Barley Alison had recruited an old childhood friend of hers who lived in Cannes to keep an eye on Lucie when she first moved into the home, but Lucie had resisted visits both from Barley's friend Mrs Montagu and from Lady Buchanan Jardine of the British Association of the Alpes Maritimes on the grounds that her room-mate might be jealous – but now Lucie seemed much better. (Barley Alison had written many chatty and supportive letters to Angus and Tony, in which a surface Barley-esque breathless dottiness always concealed a fund of good will and common sense: her letter of 7 November 1987 enquiring of Tony if Angus was up to signing bookplates for Secker for his *Collected Stories* is a masterpiece of tact.)

On the first of February, Angus wrote (or Tony wrote for him) a letter of resignation to the Royal Society of Literature: he resigned as President of the Kipling Society at the end of March, and a year later, in October 1989, was to cancel his membership of the Imperial Society of Knights Bachelor – the subscription was fifty pounds a year. Tony, increasingly, was becoming Angus's voice, and it is hard to tell how much of the late correspondence Angus dictated himself, and how much Tony was obliged to improvise. On 3 March 1988 Tony accepted on Angus's behalf the task of writing an "Encounter" in a series of biographical sketches in *The Yale Review*. Angus said he would like to write a piece about Perkin Walker, but in the event Tony had to compose most of the piece himself – he gave an account of Perkin Walker's family, his cyclamen socks, his hospitality, his "atrocious" taste in hybrid tea roses, and his habit of taking his books "to some dreary local public house" where he would study Hebrew amidst "the deafening noise of rock music and video-games . . . I am not aware," wrote Tony, "that his long study of religion ever tempted him from his firmly held, slightly sad, pessimistic humanism." (Tony himself was tempted: he was moving slowly away from humanism and the atheism he had once professed towards religious faith.)

This sketch was an unacknowledged substitution for Angus; in rather more light-hearted vein, Tony had stepped in to write a contribution published in the *Car Owner*, September 1987, in which he had described his many years of chauffeuring Sir Angus – "who would have written this article himself, but is in hospital with a broken leg which was *not* caused by my driving."

Tony also continued his flurry of correspondence about legal matters – the adoption route seemed unlikely, but there was a possibility of a *"vente en viager"* which would enable Angus to sell Tony his share in the apartment by some method which would avoid the penal French inheritance tax of 60% – Tony would buy Angus out by monthly instalments, or something like that. It was very confusing, and Tony admitted that he did not have a head for this kind of problem, though the useful French lawyer introduced to him by John Ralston Saul did his best to explain.

Spring brought visitors, but not necessarily good weather – Michael Howard, staying for Easter in a gîte belonging to a nephew at St Rémy, said it was bitterly cold and horrible, but he and Mark James thought Angus and Tony were comfortably ensconced – more comfortably than they were in their gîte, clearly – and that Angus was "genially dementing". They had several pleasant meals together, and were amused by the arrival of Bentley Bridgewater and his curious assortment of lively young friends – Silenus with his rout, they noted. (Bentley was now suffering from Parkinson's, but the quality of his life – and for once the phrase is wholly appropriate – had been immensely improved by the arrival of Ian Munday, who tidied up "the old codger", as he called him, and sorted out the chaos in which he nested – he bullied him, teased him, amused him, and drove him about. He had even, as Tony wrote to Geoffrey Wright, introduced into his Bloomsbury flat "a TELEVISION, something Bentley had resisted since it was invented.") Michael Howard recalls a dinner in a farmhouse somewhere in the neighbourhood with Angus and Bentley both sitting in high-backed chairs like two old icons, staring at one another across empty space, with nothing much to say, after all these decades of intimacy. Were

the Spenders there? Howard and James cannot be sure. But they do recall
wondering why Angus and Tony had allowed themselves to get into such
a muddle with the inheritance tax – they had surely heard of the
tremendous row about the Somerset Maugham estate, over which the
daughter had sued. (They had, though they had perhaps not seen its
relevance: by bizarre coincidence, an article in the *Daily Telegraph*
announcing that "Sir Angus yields to lure of South of France", in which
Angus had described his desire to live in the sun and his inability to cope
with his Suffolk garden, had been accompanied on the same page by the
news of the death of "Maugham's 'patient and loyal' secretary". Their old
acquaintance Alan Searle, aged 80, had died in Monte Carlo on 25 August
1985, and the report noted that he had "featured prominently in a series of
legal actions in the 1960s, when Mr Maugham attempted to adopt him as
his son and heir. The French legal tussle was fought with a bitterness that
dismayed Maugham's circle, beginning with his daughter, Elizabeth, Lady
John Hope . . ." who had successfully applied to have the adoption
annulled, and had received a massive settlement. Searle had eventually
been left with "the contents of the Villa Mauresque, plus £50,000, and the
author's manuscripts and the copyright on Maugham's work for 30 years."
The copyright on Searle's death had passed to the Royal Literary Fund.)

Things were ordered better and less litigiously in Yale. In North
America, by this time, it was not uncommon for gay couples to be offered
the same contractual terms for accommodation, pensions etc. as a married
couple – what came to be known as "spousal benefits" – the only problem
would be with medical insurance, where the spectre of AIDS arose.

The Chisletts came to St Rémy, and Graham C. Greene, and Tim
Neighbour, and Simon Edwards, and Jonathan Courage, and a German
academic friend of Peter Conradi's who was writing on Angus's work.
Ronald Crichton, an old British Council friend from Oxford days, tried to
make it from Eastbourne, where (on Bentley Bridgewater's advice) he had
retired, but he didn't manage it – he too was suffering from the long after-
effects of a bad fall, and was full of sympathy for Angus and Tony's plight.
Bridget and Michael Erskine, son and daughter-in-law of Vivienne Caney
Erskine, enjoyed a pleasant lunch at Glanum: both were doctors, she
specialising in geriatric medicine, and she comforted Tony by speaking
highly of geriatric care in France. Geoffrey Wright and Michael
Colborne-Brown visited and took some jolly photographs, and Jacquetta
Priestley called in with her friend Diana Collins: she was saddened by the
sight of Angus staring blank and melancholy at his immense view, but says
that Tony entertained them well. Barbara Gates from Iowa remembers
sitting with Angus as he gazed at the bell-tower of the church and

imagined young men climbing it, "and thinking he could go to Nîmes with a friend and myself and Tony, when in fact he could no longer really go anywhere. And Tony, in a Van Gogh hat, looking as tired and sad as anyone I have ever seen, asking me what I thought of Angus . . ."[2]

And so it continued: Angus at times quite alert and taking an interest in visitors, at other times blank or rambling – often he did not recognise the apartment, insisted it had other floors, that it was in a university, that he could hear voices, that his parents were about to arrive by train, that he was being called for a play reading . . . sometimes he was aggressive, sometimes he apologised for being difficult. (On one occasion in February 1988 he had burst out at Tony "You have battened on me all the time I have known you": he apologised the next day.) In May Tony managed to get him to Grasse to see Lucie again, and Angus and Lucie had a reasonable conversation – but on the way back to St Rémy Angus objected when Tony emptied the urine from his *pistolet* – "I shall need that at the customs" – and thought he was on his way to Cape Town. But then, a day later, he managed to write a long letter to his niece.

Negotiations about a possible return to England continued, compli-cated by the fact that Angus could still take in some of his correspondence – sometimes two letters were necessary, one for Tony's eyes' only and one that Angus could see. Tony at times felt strongly that he wanted to come home – to be near old friends, near the British Library. He worried that he was drinking too much in France, but did not want to come home to be buried away in the country – and wherever he was, what would he live on? Angus was no longer paying him any salary, and was incapable of making any decisions – he told Tony one evening that he had no idea that they had purchased the apartment on a permament basis – "My idea was that we could have somewhere to go for a month or two . . ." Against leaving was the fact that the health care in France was very good but, he had written to Martin Corke, "I am worried that if I fall ill there will be no one else to help him . . . anxiety over present and future finances makes me an anxious and temperamental nurse."[3]

In July the flat in St Rémy was valued at 670,000 francs. Novelist and civil servant P.D. James, alerted to Angus's condition by her friend Francis King, generously offered the free use of her house in Oxford, but this had to be declined as Angus would have been unable to manage the stairs. (No offer of a suite at Merton arrived.) Various friends offered temporary accomodation, and investigated yet more nursing homes. Tony's resentment at what he considered Patrick Woodcock's bad or inadequate advice broke out in a letter addressed to their old friend, written on 15 February 1989: Tony claimed that Woodcock should have warned them, on medical evidence, against the move to France. He admitted that his own mind – distressed by his sister's death and Perkin Walker's death – had not been clear, but he had not realised that Angus's mind was only working at half capacity. Now he found himself in poor health, tormented by dreams, and temperamentally unstable – "It is a dismal point to have reached in a successful relationship of forty years. When occasionally love does shine through a break in the clouds over Angus's mind, my response is impaired, blunted. I am often too tense, too unforgiving, too ready to blame . . . The future is blank, unthinkable . . . I am not attempting to shuffle off my responsibilities. But I believe that much of the desperation of the last three years could have been avoided if we had remained in the UK."

Patrick Woodcock was shocked and distressed by this reproachful and accusing letter. He had been shocked by the spectacle of Angus's deterioration, and what seemed the deterioration of his relationship with Tony – at times it seemed as though they had come to hate one another. Angus had bullied and dominated Tony, and he was still doing so – he was deliberately naughty, he peed on the floor and sat in the car on purpose. Tony had his own revenge. Others made similar observations. Tony manhandled Angus as though he were some wretched obese doll. Tony let Angus's hair grow long and wild until he looked like the White Queen in *Through the Looking Glass*, and one afternoon a friend's hairdresser boyfriend from Marseilles cut it *en plein air* in Margaret Reinhold's garden and much improved him – it should have been cut long before.

Julian Mitchell and Richard Rowson, calling in on Angus and Tony in August 1989, were distressed by what they found:

August 3rd . . . went to lunch with Angus and Tony . . . Angus almost immobile, and his mind – well, who knows? He looks just the same, which is very disconcerting, and smiles, and makes conversation, and often makes sense, but then it goes. "You're just in time for the sextet" he said when we arrived, but I don't think there was music on. The rooms were lined with books, a lifetime's reading, unopened now . . . Tony talked the whole time, like someone who has had no one to talk to for months. He half-carried Angus through to the small dining room. There was a portrait of A by Barbara Robinson whom I once met at Ivy's; she has just done another one of him. A told me with assurance that their flat had three floors: Tony looked astonished – they have one – . . . A kept forgetting words: got in a complete jumble when he got in pain from sitting. We were talking about Wootton Underwood: 'I blame Gielgud and all those people for the pain in my bum.' Tony moved him, but he was getting tired. He ate and drank well, though . . .

(Next day? Tony had meanwhile heard from Martin Corke about the place near Bury and had decided to take Angus back to England. I was worrying about the finance.)

It isn't just A, who has something in the way of annuity and royalties . . . but Tony, who has no money of his own. What is *he* to live on, how is *he* to cope. It's ghastly. Still, in England he will be, I hope, less lonely. Out there must have been hell on earth. Still, it's a four-day journey, and A is incontinent and wakes in the night with psoriasis and scatters his skin around the room and – Oh, God.

Hell on earth? Not quite, perhaps. But at this moment it must have seemed that this is what the French experiment had been.

★

The French adventure ended badly, but not all of it had been a disaster. If Angus's health had not failed as seriously and as mysteriously as in fact it did, he and Tony might well have enjoyed a long and reasonably happy retirement in St Rémy. They were by no means as isolated as they appeared to Julian and Richard on this fraught occasion: they had many friends in the neighbourhood, and not a week passed without several social engagements, with Margaret Reinhold, with the Rachets, with the Kilmartins and the Spenders and their frequent house-sitters the Elstobs. (The Elstobs entertained Angus to a meal of tripe, having been assured that he liked it: he demonstrated his appreciation by eating three platesful.) At some times of year they were almost overwhelmed with visitors from England and America. St Rémy itself was a negotiable little town, and it offered pleasant excursions. Angus enjoyed them though he was not always quite sure where he was. (One day, when Tony took him to the Abbaye St Michel de Frigolet, on a pilgrimage to visit Notre Dame du Bon Remède who had saved the monks of Montmajour from malaria, Angus whispered from his wheel chair to some nuns *"Est-ce-que c'est permis pour les anglais d'entrer ici?"*)

Not that it was always sunny – the weather could as be appalling as in England, and everybody complained when the Mistral blew or when snow fell – everyone except Pamela Rachet, who declared that she hated hot weather. Her idea of a holiday was an annual trip to rainy Scotland – and snowy Iceland would be pleasant, she thought. (She still lives happily in Provence.) The Mistral was a well-known hazard, and many hours were spent discussing its odd behaviour and complaining about it. Virginia

Woolf and Vanessa Bell had encountered it when they visited St Rémy from Cassis in April 1928: Virginia had loved Van Gogh's asylum and the cloisters of St-Paul and said she hoped she'd be shut up here "next time she went cracked" – "The whole country round here is most beautiful, only in the teeth of the mistral, which was so strong the day we drove back that it really almost stopped the car at times."[4] Tony noted the Mistral blowing in July 1986 for days, and again in mid-August: it blew in January 1987 and a great deal in March 1988 and no doubt on many other occasions he did not trouble to record – in short, it could blow at any time of year. It got on his nerves, even though he also disliked the very hot weather. (But on 30 May 1988, he noted a healing rainbow over St-Paul.)

Tony's feelings about France were inevitably coloured by financial anxiety and anxiety about his own future and Angus's health. Certainly he did not dislike it, as Angus had declared in his outburst to Conradi in the Clinique. He liked St Rémy, and valued his friends there. Had he and Angus been *rentier* millionaires, like Hiram Winterbotham at Apt, or in receipt of a large, secure, occupational pension like other retired neighbours, they would never have regretted their decision. And then again, if Angus had not fallen, if he had remained mentally confused but mobile, then the sheer physical strain on Tony would have been much less. Conversely, if Angus's mind had not failed, then he would have gone on writing, and other problems would not have arisen. (On 1 January 1988, he declared to Tony at four o'clock in the afternoon "Shortly, I shall go to a remote farm and write, and you will find work in St Rémy . . .") If Angus had been able to go on writing, his finances would have not have been so steadily and severely depleted. If he had been able to publish stories or a volume of autobiography, the back-list of his fiction would have been given a new lease of life. It had been a bad sequence that could not have been fully foreseen.

Tony bought Angus two large lined exercise books, one yellow, one blue, while they were in St Rémy and encouraged him to start to write his memoirs. The yellow one, entitled "The Flying Spur, Vol I", contains nothing but five lines of indecipherable handwriting and a few wavering scratches. The first few pages of this book have been torn out and inserted in the blue one, entitled "The Flying Spur Vol II", which contains fifteen pages of notes and, on the back leaf, a legible page of accounts of "Francs in my possession at hotel." Some of the notes make a kind of sense – one reads "? Seirkawa [sic] and a French girl? Japanese Guide? Travail tales ? Witness my sudden heart beats" – another "Try to relate", and yet another "Röslein auf den Heiden – the deep firm voice of the *contralto* – *Janet Baker*." Then there are several attempts at autobiographical notes –

"Mother Father 1883 Hynd Wood – Tillett – Phil – Anquetin – Maud's maiden name" – other scraps which look like notes for a short story – and what seem to be two pages of sustained effort:

"First Wednesday in February [deleted] March

Midnight. Howling mistral night. My attention incessantly drawn to the either a) events of my own life and that of surrounding people and every – being powerful is the frightening picture they provide of what is happening [illeg] or/everything a death of what might have been" – and so on, for another page and a half.

The memoir was never written, although Angus had days of complete lucidity, when he could have worked. He could talk intelligently about Flaubert and Zola, work with his bibliographer, and he could still give interviews – on 5 December 1987, according to Tony's notes, he was interviewed by a journalist from Paris: "AW spoke in French all the time, was tired at end, but seemed to cope well." On 10 November 1988 he wrote in his own illegible hand a letter to Sylvère Monod about Kipling which Monod took to be an accusation that Kipling took too much interest in boys: it seems to offer a comparison between Dickens's treatment of childhood and Kipling's, and mentions Kipling's desire "desperately to make love to children without offending anyone – I don't think he was able to do it but necessarily got closer than any other writer . . ." The letter (confused yet clearly trying to express a complex thought-process) concludes "I shall stay in Provence for a while until my mood of self-distrust gets better. Then I shall go to England and I hope to France and somewhere along this lonely line do let us meet. Yours Angus. (Angus Wilson.)"

There were still flashes of great perception in the midst of the howling mistral night. The old Angus was still there. Arnaud said that after the fall, "he was not the same man . . . It was a very great pity for me to meet him so late in his life. He liked to talk to me about his travels. For two years he was not so bad, but the last year he went downhill . . ."

32

THE VOYAGE HOME

"Je considère cela comme un naufrage ce voyage ci on ne peut pas alors comme il vaut et comme il vaudrait non plus."

"I think of it as a shipwreck, this journey. Well, we cannot do what we like, nor what we ought to do, either."

Vincent Van Gogh, on leaving St Rémy for the North, May 1890.[1]

After agonising indecisions, in the summer of 1989 Tony gave up the struggle to stay on in the apartment in St Rémy, and arranged to install Angus in a nursing home in Suffolk. Accommodation had been arranged by the unfailingly helpful and patient Martin Corke (who happened, providentially, to be chairman of the local health authority). Angus greeted news of the move with "total blandness and unconcern", though he had seemed at times to approve the idea of moving to a residential home: an added misery for Tony was his feeling that perhaps Angus was "longing for a time AWAY from me. That I shall be homeless doesn't seem to worry him."[2] He wrote again to Martin Corke on 2 August, "It is all hell, and I am wracked by doubts ... the dispersal of our home, my impending homelessness, the return under ignominious circumstances to somewhere we had left with high hopes, somewhere which still for me (despite of course all dear friends) reverberates with the informer's voice."

Tony and Angus set off, by car, on 7 September 1989. It was a ghastly journey. Was Tony punishing himself and Angus by insisting on driving, rather than flying? Each hotel presented the obstacle of drawsheets and incontinence pads, and Angus's skin flew off in all directions. They took four days over the journey, spending the first night at Lyon, then on to nights in Auxerre, Arras, and Calais. On 11 September they caught the Hoverspeed to Dover, where they were met on disembarkation by Glyn and Jeanne Davies: Jeanne had cooked Angus a batch of her delicious

Welsh cakes. Angus did not seem to know Jeanne, although he had revived so much in her company on her last visit to France: he sat in the car, opened the parcel of cakes, and started to eat them at once. That night Tony installed him in Pinford End, and handed over all his medical documents to Dr Adams.

The nursing home cost two hundred and ninety pounds a week – £1160.00 a month. Tony had calculated Angus's income for 1988 thus:

Pension from UEA	£325.00
Barclays Bank deposit	£137.57
Legal and General/Norwich/Eagle Star	£4437.07
State Retirement Pension	£2695.93
Public Lending Right	£573.61
Royal Literary Fund Grant May 85	£5000.00
Literary earnings (including £2700 option on novel [*Anglo-Saxon Attitudes*] and £2700.00 advance for short story collection.)	£7334.44

Tony himself had minimal savings, and was dependent on Angus's income: he was as yet ineligible for any pension, though he was eventually to apply for (and be granted) an Attendance Allowance. It was going to be a close-run thing, and without the help of the Royal Literary Fund would have been impossible.

One wonders if Angus ever remembered Ian Watt's view that any pension from UEA would be derisory.

★

Angus was settled into Pinford End House, which was hidden away in the little criss-cross maze of country lanes just beyond Bury St Edmunds. Many a visitor who did not know the area was to get lost on the way. It was on the Nowton Court side of Bury: great changes had taken place at the Court since Betty Blackburne's recent death. A large and cheerful Memorial Service for her, with 400 guests, had been held in April 1988, when her good heart and her idiosyncracies, particularly her erratic driving, were affectionately celebrated: she had been a familiar figure, rushing to do her shopping hunched over the wheel of an enormous Rover, and when cautioned one day for speeding, she had excused herself to the police officer by saying her eyes were so bad she couldn't see the bloody dials. Now Charles and Neville Blackburne were retired to the Small House in the grounds, and the Court had been sold – it was being expensively landscaped and redeveloped as a finishing-school for young

Japanese ladies. As once the chopper hovered over Felsham Woodside, so now the Japanese strolled along the English prep-school lawns and took lessons in English etiquette from Douglas Blyth's second wife Lucy. Even Suffolk was changing. Lord Stradbroke, who had boasted to Angus that his grandfather had been appointed Lord Lieutenant of the County 129 years earlier, had passed away in 1983: he had been succeeded (after the rapid death of an intermediary) by an Australian farmer who gave his address as The Old Booralong Road in New South Wales.[3]

Tony, who visited Angus daily, stayed with friends. Many were anxious to help – Jacquetta Priestley offered the use of her London attic at Albany, and wrote to Tony with much sympathy, glad that Angus was comfortably settled with nursing care, but "all the same, what a dire thing the end of a true life can be".[4] In Suffolk, Tony went first to the Corkes, then moved on to the home of Jorn Langberg at Hillwatering, Langham, near Bury.

Langberg had not been in touch with Angus and Tony since their disappearance in 1985, and had not been forewarned about their removal either – he had been a little hurt when they simply vanished, and had assumed that they had gone off, like his friend Robert Carrier, as tax exiles. He did not blame them, as Felsham Woodside was gloomy and inconvenient in the winter. Only a few postcards had arrived to track their progress, and now suddenly here was Tony on his doorstep, in a terrible state, tired and shabby.

Jorn Langberg, whose own companion Ivar had died young in the autumn of 1988, did his best to help. True to the dictates of his profession, he tried to smarten Tony up and reintroduce him to the world of fashion, but Tony would not have it – he preferred his own "understated" English look. The 1960s had suited Angus and Tony, Langberg remembered. They had been at their best in the happy days of early Sixties suits, flared trousers, large lapels, kipper ties in mauve or fuchsia – they had never quite grown out of it, despite Langberg's hot tips from Dior over the years. Those had been happy days, the party days at Hintlesham Hall.

Tony stayed at Hillwatering for some months (Langberg flew off to the better weather and better parties of South Africa for much of the winter) and then moved on in February to Bob French and Monty Turland at The Chase at Sible Hedingham. A routine developed with almost daily visits to Pinford End, when Tony would read aloud – mostly from history books – to Angus, or talk with him and other residents. Tony made himself useful there – Uncle Tony was always ready to chat to a nurse or an elderly inmate or to help to push a wheelchair. Angus continued much the same – sometimes lucid, sometimes thinking he was in France or South Africa. Visitors made very different reports of him. Jean McGibbon, who had known Helen Pattisson in her youth, came over from Manningtree to see Angus and found he remembered Helen well: his short-term memory was poor but he could recall the past and when Jean left he said "No one ever talks about Helen – you don't know what this has meant to me." (According to Jean, Angus was with Helen a night or two before her death from cancer and a brain tumour on 3 January 1956 – Angus was probably the last person to see her alive, apart from her family, and it was rumoured that she, like her husband, had committed suicide, unable to bear her illness.)[5]

Graham C. Greene visited regularly, when he went to meetings of the Greene King Brewery. Benjy Cohen called in, and John Alston, and Bob French and Monty Turland, and Geoffrey Wright, and Pat Trevor-Roper, and Mike Moorcock, and Simon Edwards, and of course Bentley Bridgewater. Simon Edwards went three times – on two of these visits he and Angus talked in a rambling way of Pope, Dryden and South Africa, but on the last occasion Edwards took his baby, which he decided was a mistake – Edwards had wanted to introduce his late-born offspring to his surrogate father, but Angus, all hunched and shrivelled in a vivid purple V-necked sweater, appeared deeply puzzled by the unexpected apparition of little Jack. Natasha Spender came with Maggie Drabble, though they arrived rather late having been lost in a fog: they found Angus polite, smiling, chatty but confused, and oddly mesmerised by a photograph in the *Sunday Times* (5 November 1989) of a severe bespectacled Elisabeth Lutyens looking a hundred years old. She clearly worried him – he took no interest in the article above her picture, which was a reappraisal of his own novel, *No Laughing Matter*.[6] He also talked of South Africa and thought he might still be able to take part in a – what was the word? a group? – he tried hard for it, nearly got it, and then Tony produced it for him – a Symposium.

By strange coincidence, Drabble called again on another visit almost exactly a year later, on 22 November, the day of Mrs Thatcher's resignation: Drabble had not heard the news, as she had been listening to Timothy West reading Trollope on cassette instead of attending to her car radio, but as Tony walked across the carpark of the pub of their rendezvous to greet her she could tell that something dramatic had happened, for his face was illumined with a curious delight: "She's gone!" he said, almost with disbelief, "She's gone!" Angus had outlived the Thatcher era, which he and Tony believed had caused so much harm: in vain had Bentley teased them that they had "gone over the top" about Mrs T., for Tony continues to maintain that her "revolutionary government" had done enormous damage to the country.

Others who called in included Jay Halio from Delaware, accompanied by Tony Storey from Bury St Edmunds: Halio was shocked "not so much by Angus's condition – this, I think, was one of his better days – but his drastically reduced circumstances. A bon vivant and world traveler, he was now reduced to a small room with a bed and bureau and few other pieces of furniture, and on the door of his room was the nameplate, 'Sir Angus Wilson.'[7] Storey, who went on several other occasions, said that Angus "was quite flirtatious – tried to make contact, but couldn't." He, and other callers, noted brother Pat's photograph on the shelf by the bed.

Maggie Bishop from Boxford proved an extremely reliable visitor. She popped over frequently, and was always greeted warmly – "You're looking very well, dear, *much* better than you looked in London." – "You're a very good-looking woman, dear!" – but she was not sure if he really knew who she was. (She had never known him in London.) But what did it matter? He was pleased to see her. She would offer to fill in for Tony when he had to be away. (One of her stories was that Geoffrey Wright, sitting with Angus in front of the television in his little room, remarked of the Orthodox Communion Service which they seemed to be watching "I didn't realise they dipped the bread in the wine." "Oh yes," said Angus happily, "and there are prawns in it too.")

Angus's behaviour was sometimes unexpected. Penny Corke went to see him once a month or so, and on one occasion he wanted to go to the loo – would Penny take him, he didn't want the nurse. She wheeled him in and sat him down. "Don't go, dear," he said, and she sat there with him watching his poor scratchy peeling legs, while he told her that it was easier to pretend he was mad – "it's very distressing, it's easier to be in another world." And one day he said to Tony, "You know, sometimes I think I'm losing all touch with reality."

There were others to keep an eye while Tony was away sorting out affairs in France or in London. In St Rémy, the Rachets were advising on the sale of the apartment at Les Glaniques: it was not a good time to sell in France, and it was not a good time to buy in England. Since the sale of Felsham Woodside the British property market had been through one of its periodic bursts of mad inflation and Tony would find it very hard to find anywhere to buy within his budget, even when he managed to sell.

The apartment at Les Glaniques had been bought for 700,000 francs in July 1985: it was sold in May 1990 for 830,000 francs. The removals from France cost £3,500, Tony owed a personal loan of £4000, and was faced with storage charges for furniture unless he found somewhere to buy soon.

★

On the financial front, many friends made efforts to help. It was difficult to appeal too openly for funds, as the RLF (which expected discretion over its pension) might feel obliged to withdraw its support if too much came in from elsewhere. At UEA, a celebration dinner had been organised by Jon Cook with a not-so-secret agenda of fund-raising: the event took place on 9 June 1989, and there were speeches in praise of Angus by Ian McEwan, Lorna Sage, Malcolm Bradbury. Tony, then still in France, sent a message of thanks. Jon Cook was one of Angus's many loyal friends at UEA. Cook had gone to UEA in 1971, influenced partly by the fact that Angus and Bradbury were both on the faculty: he had studied with Ian McEwan, attended Angus's Dickens lectures, and had talked to Angus about Freud and fiction. Cook himself was appointed to the faculty in 1973, where he had greatly valued Angus's "free-spirited, migratory, subversive" influence: although he had not seen him since 1978, he had heard news of him through Ian McEwan and Rose Tremain, and it was while on a walking holiday in France with Ian McEwan in September 1988 that he heard at the Kilmartins of the difficulties at St Rémy. He had returned to consult Pat Hollis, then Dean of the School of English and American Studies, and Malcolm Freegard, recently retired director of the University's Audio-Visual Centre (another old friend of Angus's) and together they planned this event: over four months they managed to raise £10,000.

Rose Tremain was equally devoted to the cause. On 19 May 1990, she published an article in the *Independent Magazine* in which she described her great debt to Angus and her affection for him: it ended "Angus is now 76 and gravely ill. He will write no more books . . . His novels no longer sell widely and Tony struggles to find the money to pay the nursing-home bills. Has the world forgotten what a great writer Angus Wilson was and what a distinguished and heroic life he led? It seems as if it has. Try as I may, I can find no comedy in this."

The article produced a wave of sympathetic response and cheques from well-wishers, including £1,000 out of the blue from a total stranger, Victoria Wood, who had long admired Angus's work. Michael Moorcock, an old friend with whom Angus had many times discussed the trials of a writer's life, generously and impulsively sent £500. The *Evening Standard* picked the story up, and so did several other papers. The tone on the whole was friendly, though there was evidence of some *Schadenfreude* – some enjoyed nothing better than to see a good man down and out, and began wilfully to exaggerate the extent of Angus's poverty and critical neglect. (There were one or two who muttered that Angus and Tony had always been extravagant – all those winters abroad, all those expensive hotels . . .) Auberon Waugh's attempt at an apology for his cruel reviews was not well received. Eva Tucker (who had memories of attending the first night of *The Mulberry Bush*) wrote to the *Independent* the next week to say that the best help for Angus Wilson and his reputation would be the re-publication of his works, and soon this was in hand: Peter Carson at Penguin agreed to bring out new paperback editions of all the fiction and of *The Wild Garden*. I meanwhile signed a contract to write this biography for Secker & Warburg, BBC *Bookmark* was planning a TV Profile with Nigel Williams as presenter, and a television adaptation of *Anglo-Saxon Attitudes* was on the way. (Tony Lacey of Penguin Paperbacks was later to record accurately that "the idea of re-issuing Wilson came up two years ago at a lunch with Margaret Drabble, who is working on his biography, and Peter Carson editor-in-chief of the Group. We all discovered we were Angus Wilson fans and realised you couldn't get his books.")[8]

Angus sat in Pinford End, taking little of this in. It was hard to know where his mind was. One close observer was the thin and bearded Derek Longmire (a Catholic, and godfather to poet and translator Oliver Bernard): Longmire was then living in Diss and working as a handyman at Pinford End. Longmire would stop and chat for a few minutes every now and then, and Angus seemed so articulate that it took Longmire some time to realise that much of what Angus said was gibberish. There were flashes of wit and clarity – Angus took in the demolition of the Berlin Wall, spoke of Virginia Woolf, and wanted to take Longmire out for a meal. In Longmire's view the caring staff at the home had no idea of "what kind of person they had on their hands" – they would persistently switch Angus's radio onto Radio Two, and Longmire would switch it back to Radio Three. (In Tony's view, the staff understood Angus's musical tastes better than Longmire: unlike Longmire, Angus had no fondness for Messaien.) At mealtimes, Longmire would often sit with Tony and with David Chandler, the owner of the home, and Angus liked to sit with them and try to join in the conversation – it disturbed Longmire when a nurse would come and almost forcibly wheel a reluctant Angus away, saying in a loud cheerful voice "Come on, now, Angus, it's time to go" as he clung to the tablecloth.

One day, Derek Longmire found Angus watching *Batman*. He asked him if he was enjoying it. No, said Angus, he found it terrifying. Longmire was not sure if Angus could switch his set off unaided. There sat Angus, transfixed, watching the appalling vertiginous skyscapes of Gotham. He had never liked skyscrapers, he had never enjoyed New York. He was afraid of falling upward. Batman swooped and soared.

In February 1991, Tony was called back to France once more for the death of Lucie. This was a sad and lonely affair. Tony wrote to her Tutelle:

Angleterre, le 14 fevrier 1991
Chère Mlle Sellame,

   Le Mardi, j'étais à Grasse pour les obsèques de Madame Lucie
Johnstone. Comme avec son mari, j'étais le seul de dire 'aurevoir'. Elle
reste parmi les oliviers et des mimosas des petits collines.
   Priez-vous d'avoir la gentilesse de m'informer des circonstances du décès
de Madame Johnstone. Priez-vous aussi de me fournir avec un certificat du
Cimetière à Grasse, avec les details d'emplacement. J'ai oublié de
demander ce document ce jour la. C'était un jour de tristesse.
   Avec mes sentiments les plus amicales,
   A.C. Garrett

Mlle Sellame wrote back to say that she had been "*souffrante*" and
therefore had been unable to attend the "*obsegues*" (sic) and could he let her
know about Lucie's family. Tony wrote back on 8 March to say that as far
as he knew Lucie had "*aucune de famille*".

*

Angus himself now began to deteriorate. Tony was somewhat distracted
by the BBC, which was beginning to film for its *Bookmark* programme,
and by Anglia TV, which was also planning a documentary about Angus.
But there was no avoiding the signs of decline. On Sunday, 26 May 1991,
Tony noted in his diary "A. very low. 'How do you feel?' 'Pathetic.'" The
last time Maggie Bishop saw him, at Tony's request, he had been put to
bed and hardly looked up when she came to him. She held his hand for ten
minutes, then left. (Tony, says Derek Longmire, would sit holding Angus's
hand for hours.) On 27 May Angus was in bed all day, made comfortable,
but "very low". He had had a stroke. Tony, who had alerted his friends to
the possibility of Angus's imminent death, was called at about six in the
evening on 30 May by a nurse who said she thought he ought to come: he
sat in Angus's room all night, listening to his stertorous breathing. Angus
seemed deeply unconscious, and there was little change, so in the early
morning Tony slipped back to the flat to collect a toothbrush, and while he
was away, at ten minutes to seven in the morning, Angus died. Derek
Longmire went in to work that morning at 8 a.m., and found there was
need of him – the lock on Angus's door had broken, and nobody could get
back in to the room. Longmire adjusted the handle and made his way in
and there was Angus dead looking exactly the same as Angus alive, with a
slight smile on his face. Longmire conversed with him while he fixed the
lock, rescuing the springs from the barrel which had jumped all over the
bed. "Never mind, don't worry, I'll fix it, Angus," he said.
   It had been a long watch, as Tony said to me on the telephone that night.

(I rang quite by chance from Porlock on the night of 31 May, and the note with news of Angus's deterioration waited for me in London.)

The next morning, the news was announced to the nation on the radio. The letters began to pour in, the obituaries to appear. Tony marked the day in his diary with the sign of the cross.

*

The announcement read: "Wilson, May 31st, at Pinford End Nursing Home, Suffolk, peacefully after a long illness, Sir Angus Frank Johnstone, Kt., C.B.E., C.Litt., F.R.S.L., author and Professor Emeritus of the University of East Anglia, beloved friend of Tony, treasured uncle of Jane and Glyn, Sybil and Dick, and dear great-uncle of Nic, Penny, Mark, Georgina, Sally, Angus. Private cremation. No flowers please, but donations if desired to the Royal Literary Fund, Temple Chambers, Temple Avenue, London EC4 0DT."

The funeral took place very quietly, at Risby Crematorium, on Thursday 6 June 1991. There was no music, nothing but a prayer-book service. The clergyman who officiated was a friend of Michael Colborne-Brown: Michael attended the service with Maggie Bishop at Tony's request. James McGibbon went with Ronald Blythe, but they were uneasy, feeling perhaps they should not have been there. Tony arrived alone in the 2CV and sat at the front with Martin Corke. Members of the staff and Dr Adams from Pinford End also attended.

After the service they all stood about in the desolate carpark with its tiny newly planted trees, lost in the flat prairie country of Suffolk. Tony looked very grey.

Derek Longmire and his wife Judith took Angus's clothes to Oxfam, at Tony's request.

33

AMONG THE TREES IN THE DARK WOOD

Susan Keable had rightly predicted that the media coverage of Angus's death would be extensive, and some of it penitent in tone. Malcolm Bradbury, who was frequently solicited by the media for instant obituaries, was on the radio the morning after Angus's death, and there were long tributes in *The Times*, the *Daily Telegraph* (David Holloway and anon), the *Independent on Sunday* (Lorna Sage), the *Independent* (Francis King), the *Guardian* (Ronald Blythe and Rose Tremain), the *Financial Times* (Anthony Curtis), the *Observer* (Paul Bailey), the *New Statesman* (Paul Binding), and many others. Several foreign papers, including *Le Monde* and the *Frankfurter Allgemeine Zeitung*, covered the news of his death, and the *New York Times* in its farewell somewhat bizarrely claimed that he had written more than fifty books. Peter Burton in *Gay News* annoyed Norman Scarfe by dragging up Angus's old antagonism to E.M. Forster, and Francis King revived the old story of Angus's running naked round the lake at Bletchley Park: David Holloway saw Angus as the last of the old men of letters: others saw him as a wicked social critic or a benign friend, a champion of gays or a friend of women. (Clive Sinclair, writing for Joe Kissane for Angus's seventieth birthday, had hailed him as "the thinking person's Evel Knievel": numbers of women had entrusted their marital or maternal secrets and worries to Angus and saw in his loss the loss of a unique confidant.)[1] Michael Slater achieved a remarkable double by writing tributes both in *Capital Gay* and *The Dickensian*. (The first managed to squeeze in a nostalgic mention of happy days with Ada and Victoria at Felsham Woodside.) Glen Cavaliero in the *Powys Society Newsletter* (July 1991) remembered Angus's spirited appearance at the first Powys conference at Churchill College in 1972, "talking non-stop and sheltering from the disheartening rain beneath a gigantic multi-coloured striped umbrella." Many of the obituaries paid tribute to the devoted care which Tony Garrett had taken of Sir Angus in his last years.

More private letters also came in, including an aria from Penny McEwan in France on Angus's great teaching days, and a haiku from Kazu Serikawa:

> In a masterless garden
> A solitary white rose
> In bloom in the rain.

Kazu Serikawa was not the only one to grieve for Tony. All Tony's friends were "worried about Tony". Tony had been through a long period of great strain, and his financial future was still very uncertain. In the winter of 1991 he had managed to buy a small two-bedroomed flat in a new development overlooking allotments in Bury St Edmunds, where he settled in modest comfort. Many worldly goods had been shed in the last migration: the parakeet had gone to nest in Provence with a delighted M. Peyrache, and the little stray kitten which had adopted Uncle Tony at Les Glaniques had gone to join Margaret Reinhold's collection of strays.* The Victorian scrap screen found its home with the newly appointed Professor of Victorian Literature, Michael Slater, in Bloomsbury: the olive-green rocking chair in which Angus had written *Hemlock* made its way to the Suffolk home of Graham and Daphne Reynolds. Grandmother Tillie's massive portrait moved up to North Yorkshire with Great-Niece Georgina. A little Gothic wickerwork chair found a home with Peter Conradi and Jim O'Neill. Papers were dug out of Martin Corke's garage and brought to the biographer in Hampstead. In the flat in Bury Tony kept Barbara Robinson's early portrait of Angus, some pictures of St Rémy, a falling Phaeton given by Anthony Symondson, some views of Rome from Cecil Roberts.

When Angus died Tony quixotically returned the last part of Angus's pension to the Royal Literary Fund. Some at the RLF were interested in testing the idea of giving Tony a grant as though he were "a widow or dependent child" but Tony rejected this, saying it was unnecessary. ("Think I shall be OK," was his own laconic reflection pencilled on this offer.) Tony had a natural extravagance, some thought – Martin Corke complained that he would insist on buying his potatoes from Marks & Spencer instead of from the greengrocer. And the generous habits he had learned with Angus died hard. He found it very hard to go anywhere as a

---

* Margaret Reinhold's *Watchers By the Pool: The Cats of the Mas des Chats*, with photographs by William Gooddy (Souvenir Press 1993), gives a good picture of life round St Rémy.

•

guest without a gift of wine or chocolates or a painting purchased from an exhibition by a friend.

He was not extravagant on his own behalf. He lived monastically. His secular friends worried that Tony was becoming religious. He talked a good deal about St John of the Cross and Hildegard of Bingen, and liked to disappear to visit the nuns and brood with some suspicion on T.S. Eliot at nearby Hengrave Hall. (Though Tony was not too devout to recount with pleasure the story of what the Mother Superior of Hengrave Hall had said to Angus, when he went to visit Siegfried Sassoon when he was at Hengrave in retreat: how amazing it was, she said, that people with all kinds of diseases and sores used the same pool at Lourdes, often losing their plasters in the water, and yet no one became ill thereby – that, she said, for her, was the true Miracle of Lourdes. Both Angus and Tony relished this tale.)

In his new flat, Tony, who had whiled away evenings in St Rémy by recording Rupert Brooke, Wilfred Owen, and Shakespeare sonnets, now made a recording of Francis Thompson's "The Hound of Heaven":

> I fled Him, down the nights and down the days;
> I fled Him, down the arches of the years;
> I fled Him, down the labyrinthine ways
> Of my own mind . . .

He struggled with the difficult stanza form, and mastered it with much skill. What would Angus, Vice-President of the Gay Humanists, have made of this?

(On 15 May 1994, Tony Garrett, some of whose earliest letters to Angus had recorded that he was wrestling with the problem of sin, was confirmed in the cathedral church of St James in Bury St Edmunds.)

*

On 23 July 1991 Tony went off to France to get away from it all, but he had a fall in the street in Paris (of which he remembered nothing) and woke up in hospital on Thursday 25 July with a badly sprained wrist. He returned to write a letter of mild protest to Richard Rogers about the vertiginous lifts at the Pompidou Centre (and for once he received a very civil reply) and to appear with his arm in a sling at Bentley Bridgewater's grand eightieth birthday party on 9 September in the Conservatory at the Barbican. Bridgewater sat amidst the ferns, receiving his guests grandly, like a Roman Emperor. Tony looked pale and romantic, as though he had survived a duel.

Tony's teeth were still giving him trouble, and so was his tinnitus: he also feared he was suffering from gallstones. So many years of being saintly Uncle Tony had taken their toll. Bentley Bridgewater, meanwhile, was whizzed off to France, Parkinsons and all, on a surprise birthday holiday treat paid for by his friends – a surprise which at that age might have killed a lesser man.

Tony was kept busy, organising the Memorial Service, sorting and packing Angus's archives, and being interviewed for the BBC and the Anglia Saffron production made by David Spenser. The Memorial Service took place at St James's Church, Piccadilly, where Angus's grandparents Thomas Johnstone-Wilson and Matilda Barns had been married in 1864. Tony himself read Sir John Soane's "Epitaph on his Wife", and Ian McKellen (now much involved with gay rights and the campaigning organisation, Stonewall) read Shakespeare's Sonnet 116 and W.H.Auden's "The Novelist":

> For, to achieve his lightest wish, he must
> Become the whole of boredom, subject to
> Vulgar complaints like love, among the Just
>
> Be just, among the Filthy, filthy too,
> And in his own weak person, if he can,
> Dully put up with all the wrongs of man.[2]

Drabble gave the address. The service was packed with friends from all periods of Angus's life – from distant Westminster and BM days, right up to young James Winch from Suffolk, who had been on the Heriot trail to Morocco and was lucky to get back alive after a serious motor accident. The youngest member of the congregation was Simon Edward's baby son: amongst the older were numbered Steven Runciman, Arnold Goodman and Sir Victor Pritchett. Sir Joshua Rowley, Lord Lieutenant of Suffolk, attended and UEA turned out in force. (Clive Sinclair was awarded a knighthood by The Times reporter.) Maureen Duffy, who came both as a Gay Liberal Humanist and as a good personal friend, was delayed at the entrance by her unwillingness to be classed as Miss or Mrs. Her novel, Londoners,[3] had given a vivid and immediately recognisable portrait of Angus as Hector, lunching with Duffy's narrator in the Zoo, "his skin scorched by the years and his travels, the eyes the blue of a seafarer too under the white lion's mane, bleached by sun and time. Our soft pigskin becomes reptilian as we age: turtle, tortoise, frog, lizard. Hector is a smiling, leathery washerwoman . . . Hector hasn't grown old or tired or bilious. He believes still. I am lifted by his sprightliness." And so, remembering him in his prime, were many.

★

The two television programmes inevitably had something of an elegiac tone to them, filmed as they were in the days immediately before and after Angus's death. *Bookmark*, made by Nadia Haggar with Nigel Williams as presenter, was shown on BBC2 on 3 October 1991: it was entitled "Skating on Thin Ice", and it included tributes from Bentley Bridgewater, Rose Tremain, Ian McEwan, Paul Bailey, Jeanne and Glyn Davies, and Jonathan Powell, and some fine clips of Angus at his mischievous best. Some thought it played too much on the "Forgotten Novelist" aspect of Angus's last years: a writer who has truly been forgotten does not fill a large Memorial Service, nor do all his titles make their way back into print *en masse*. Too much was made of the confusion between A.N. Wilson and Angus Wilson – the one in print, the other neglected. (Secker & Warburg, who had published both, were very indignant about this.) And some would have liked to have seen a little more of the Old Angus, and a little less of Nigel Williams. But by and large the programme was well received, though there were those who preferred the more lyrical approach of the Saffron production, "In a Suffolk Garden", which dramatised seashore extracts from "Necessity's Child" and included interviews with Paul Binding, Francis King and Michael Slater, as well as some very pretty shots of the masterless garden in full bloom at Felsham Woodside.

Anglo-Saxon Attitudes was altogether a more robust and entertaining experience. Andrew Brown had at last achieved his long-held ambition of producing this work, for which he won a BAFTA award. It was skilfully dramatised by Andrew Davies, who negotiated the novel's complex time-scheme with professional expertise, and it contained several excellent performances, including those by Douglas Hodge and Richard Johnson as Gerald Middleton young and old, by Dorothy Tutin as Gerald's ex-mistress Dolly, and by Paul Firth as the gay waiter, Vin Salad. Pat Keen, who had appeared decades earlier in *The Mulberry Bush* at the Oxford Playhouse, played the blackmailing Alice Cressett, and Elizabeth Spriggs was splendid as Gerald's wife Inge: in the Christmas party scene in which Inge terrorises the local village children she managed to look remarkably like an illustration, from Margaret Murray's *The God of the Witches*, of Queen Lucia of Sweden with a round of wax tapers on her head. The series was widely admired, won a large following, and kept the Penguin reprint in the best-seller lists for weeks. (Andrew Brown did not long outlive this triumph: he was to die, in Sydney, on 17 May 1994, at the age of fifty-five.)

Other celebratory memorials included an evening of readings organised by Jon Cook at UEA, a memorial evening at PEN (with reminiscences from Michael Slater, Francis King, Rose Tremain, Tony and others) and launches of the Penguin reprint, including one at Waterstone's in Earls Court, at which Tim Waterstone spoke of his great respect for Angus's work. Waterstone, born in Glasgow in 1939, and brought up in the vague liberalism of the 1950s, remembered the shocking impact of the short stories and his first reading of *The Middle Age of Mrs Eliot* when he went up to Cambridge in 1959. Paul Bailey on this same occasion also spoke very warmly of Angus and his work – he recalled his generosity to younger writers, his dislike of fashionable minimalism, his love of the loose and open-ended novel.

*

After Angus's death, the lost notebooks from 1985 turned up in their hiding-place, where they had been stuffed away during one of the removals. Tony discovered some late autobiographical notes, and the manuscript of two stories, one finished, one unfinished. Tony eventually forced himself to type them up: it cannot have been an easy or welcome task.

In his last years, Angus, as he had written to Dina Mehta, had had various ideas for long short stories: the finished story, called "Cuckoo", seems to have been brewing since 1983. There were other ideas which never came to anything – one, entitled "Left, Right, Centre" was to be based on the Russian professor Valentina Ivasheva, whom Angus had met in Moscow, and then again twice when she visited England: Angus and Tony had given her lunch in Norwich, at the old Royal Hotel, where by chance they also met the novelist Desmond Stewart,* one-time admirer of Mosley, and nicknamed "Florence of Arabia" by David Carritt for his passion for the Arab World.[4] Ivasheva and Stewart, the Left and the Right, had met previously in Cairo, and they got on famously in Norwich, united by their powerful anti-Semitism. Ivasheva was an impressive woman – stocky, abrupt, aggressive, importunate, Anglophile, and distinctly paranoid – though, as Angus speculated, she was paranoid with some reason, for wherever she went on her licensed trips to England, chasing up novelists to interview, the tireless KGB went too.

The theme of Soviet anti-Semitism and the Stewart character's "anti-black, pro-Mussulman" position was one which Angus could have handled well – Clive and Lucie, like Colin, had remained xenophobic to a marked degree in their long years of exile, and there was something in Angus that was imaginatively tempted by these dangerously incorrect

---

* Desmond Stewart (1924–81) was the author of several works of fiction and non-fiction set in Egypt, the Middle East and Scotland: his mother was a Stirling of Muiravonside.

characters. Indeed, his fascination with the incorrect was so strong that he himself was occasionally taken to task for xenophobia. A Dutch academic, Menno Spiering, had written a paper on "Evil Europeans" in *The Old Men at the Zoo*[5] in which he concluded that the novel, "written in 1961, the year the Macmillan administration first applied for membership of the EEC," comes down on the side of a "Little England", back-to-the-country-cottage policy, and that its portraits of pro-Europeans (Englander, of German-Swiss descent, and the uni-European neo-Fascist Blanchard-White) are deliberately hostile and anti-European. According to Spiering, the fact that the novel's narrator, Simon Carter, is rescued from war and famine ₁y a countrywoman living in a wattle-and-clay cottage with a garden ₁ ll of early roses and oriental poppies indicates that Wilson as novelist h₁ d voted against internationalism and for the essential goodness of English country life – an interesting reading, but one which is somewhat at odds not only with Angus's own known political affiliations (he always voted and spoke up for the EEC) but also with all he had written over the years about the town-country opposition in English fiction. His country-woman is of the hard-boiled variety – far from living the good life, she longs for "proper tinned stuff from Norwich", while her son repeats with laughter and satisfaction "I reckon old Norwich has about copped it."

Arnold Simmel, as we have seen, reacted with mild indignation to the character of the ungrateful German-Jewish refugee, Kurt Landeck, in *The Mulberry Bush*: when *Anglo-Saxon Attitudes* was shown on television, Claire Tomalin recoiled in alarm on behalf of her French ancestry from the cruel portrait of Marie-Hélène Middleton, while writer and critic Monica Lauritzen protested from Gothenberg that Inge was a most unrepresentative Scandinavian. A more sympathetic reading of Angus's treatment of foreigners came from Pauline Paucker, who in a discussion of the image of the Jew in British fiction wrote with approval of the portrait of refugee Frau Liebermann – "one of those bores who have charm" – in *No Laughing Matter*, and of the meeting at Kingsway Hall when a German-Jewish writer appears at first to actor Rupert Matthews as "a disagreeable self-opinionated monster" but who speaks so well of the plight of European writers "who must speak in a half-tongue, not our own" that Rupert is overwhelmed and ashamed.[6]

★

Several other ideas for short stories came to nothing. One, called "Golly", was to have been based on Madge "Golly" Gillespie – an oppressed spinster, put down by her smarter, more beautiful sister. A more substantial but unfinished text called "My Little Folly" (to which Angus had referred when being interviewed by John Pitman for "The Other Half") deals with the reminiscences of the elderly survivor of an Edwardian artistic set called "Le Cercle", who possesses what he boasts of as "a little folly" in Oxfordshire – the folly turns out to be a squalid mess, and the plot was to have involved some grim practical joke about a dying cat and the mysterious death of one of Le Cercle's stars, Lady Alma. (Back to Kipling and Stalky, again, and to a name – Lady Alma – remembered from one of the rare girls at Ashampstead. George Painter says that Angus once told him he had stamped on a dying cat in a gutter to put it out of its misery. And there had been another story, about Forrest Fulton cutting off the head of a tortoise. And there were those moths Angus had burned in the flame at Watchet. The cruel deaths of the helpless haunted Angus to the end.)

"Cuckoo", fortunately, is finished. It is a stream-of-consciousness piece, giving the memories of a heavy late-middle-aged woman, a one-time specialist in French literature, sitting in a canvas chair in a herbaceous-bordered vast-lawned Edwardian garden. Joan looks back to Mummy, to her own days as a Wren, to her wild Bohemian hard-drinking sister Liz, now old and paralysed, to Liz's wartime parties, Liz's fatherless daughter, and Liz's marriage of convenience to a closet queen. She looks back to her own marriage to art historian Derek Rodmell. As she sits in the garden and recalls the past, the cuckoo's song changes from Mummy saying "That's true, that's true," to Liz saying "Fuck you, fuck you." The present is represented by her great-niece Harriet, a student at UEA: Harriet's grandmother Liz lies paralysed upstairs in bed.

This is the last of Angus's gardening stories, and it is worthy of its predecessors. All the flower snobberies which had diverted Angus over the years and annoyed some of his friends find here their final resting-place: more significantly, so does a peculiar, almost distressing Van Gogh-like intensity of response to nature.[7] Joan, admiring her green lawn and her slugless flower beds, turns her back "on the jungle-like mass of trees and bushes that swallowed and devoured each other's shapes, great waves twisting and boiling down to the sands" and from time to time, in her reverie, she seeks escape from the past – but is it escape? – in "the dark red, almost black parrot tulips glistening and glittering in the light breeze", in "the yellow and gold of the trolius, whose heads moved gently like great buttercups", in the deep burning fiery-red euphorbias. "Intensity, fierceness and delicious relaxation could and did coexist in the visual world. All her muscles relaxed, all her senses surrendered, she knew it." The flowers are her refuge, as they had been for Bump Walker, for Molly Calder, for Ella Sands in *Hemlock*, for Miranda Searle in "Fresh Air Fiend": they are also her one remaining intensity. (Intriguingly, not unexpectedly, a quote from Frances Cornford's poem – "O why do you walk through the fields in gloves, Missing so much and so much? O fat white woman whom nobody loves . . ." – surfaces in these very late notes: an echo, perhaps, of a memory of Molly Calder marching over the fields from Chris Arnold's cottage to Angus's while he was in the middle of writing *Anglo-Saxon Attitudes*.)

As Angus had withdrawn from people into the study of birds and architecture, so too Liz attempts to withdraw into tulips and lilac as she faces dreadful wartime memories of the billeting officer and the evacuees; of her own volunteering to join the Wrens; of Liz's contempt ("Oh you silly little cunt!"); of her boyfriend Colin from Bletchley blown to pieces by a bomb at Earls Court on his day off from Bletchley Park. And then she had gone to Bletchley without him – "she found herself – brilliant linguist – sent to Canaan-Bletchley – the Promised Land. Without Colin, a Promised Land was one hundred years in the wilderness. Clearly now she must leave the comforting calm order of the flower beds and meet the fierce battle among the trees in the dark wood . . ."

The garden is invaded by the distant roar of motor cycles from the village six miles away (as the chopper had invaded the peace of Felsham Woodside) and the noise of the cuckoo begins to drive Joan crazy: when great-niece Harriet returns from a job interview, Joan tells her to "go and get Derek's gun from the library" and shoot the bird. It would make a good fry-up.

"You're cuckoo yourself," Harriet answered. "Isn't that the word they used for mad people when you were a kid?"

"Cuckoo" – this was the Thirties slang that Hermione Hammond and Angus had both used to describe and dismiss their mental illnesses. And baby Angus had several times felt himself to be a cuckoo in the nest, supplanting his brothers, supplanting his landlady's own son in Simpson, pushing little Carol Wardale in St Andrews into the box-room. A cuckoo in Cloud Cuckoo Land. Years ago John Cowper Powys had written to invite him to visit him in his Nephelococcygia in Ffestiniog, and Angus had found his own imaginary city of birds amidst the clouds at St Rémy.

This last story, "Cuckoo", ends as Joan tries to pull herself together, to face the present. She makes her way back to the house, away from her threatened garden, but she stumbles on the brick terrace, as Angus was to stumble on his St Rémy balcony. She feels a give in her knee socket, and her final reflection is "The show won't go on for long."

For Angus, the show had dragged on for another six years, but there is no escaping the sense that he knew the end was coming. He was no self-deceiver. This last story bears a curious if indirect resemblance to Virginia

Woolf's last novel, *Between the Acts*, which is a contemplation at once of the continuity of English history, the menace of war, and the approach of death. Even Joan's married name, Joan Rodmell, is a Woolf echo. Woolf and Wilson had travelled a journey of breadown and recovery and breakdown which had some heroic similarities. Neither had settled for optimism. Both had gone on until they could go no further. Neither knew how to relax in the canvas chair and empty the mind. Neither knew how to give in.

Angus Wilson was a writer who wished to know himself as well as others. His last years, between the writing of "Cuckoo" and his death at Pinford End, were full of confusion and forgetfulness and moodiness — some of it, perhaps, as Margaret Reinhold speculated, drug-induced. (Was the illness itself in part a result of those many years of nightly barbiturates, Tony wondered?) Yet many of those who observed or visited him during this period bear witness to a sense that Angus himself was still there, still alert, still questioning. Physiotherapist M. Casals said that in the apartment at St Rémy Angus would point to the sky and say with wonder "Are they clouds? Are they birds? Do you see them?" (Delusions of clouds of birds, Angus had noted forty years earlier, had haunted Zola when he was on the verge of breakdown.) M. Casals could not see the birds, but he believed that Angus could – "*pas de la confusion*", he insisted. Like old Mrs Swithin in *Between the Acts*, Angus could see the birds and beyond the birds.

On Angus's death someone wrote to comfort Tony by saying that the Angus that he knew had died long ago. Yet in a strange sense this was not true. Angus's personality was so powerful and his own testing of it so tireless that even at the end he was still the Angus Tony had known. As Peter Conradi and Ian McEwan, his old students, both noted, neither old age nor dementia had been able to destroy him. He sat, and smiled, and was himself, even in the dark wood.

APPENDIX I

Letter to David Farrer, Secker & Warburg

Felsham Woodside, Bradfield St. George,
Bury St. Edmunds, Suffolk.
Telephone: Rattlesden 200.

Tuesday 7th March 1967

My dear David,

Your comments and suggestions were as always most helpful, and I have incorporated most of them. Where I have felt that you did not wholly comprehend the fault has been no doubt either through the difficult circumstances in which you read the book or in a certain failure of communication on my part.

All one's books are 'the most important'. But this novel has a certain breadth of scope, a certain new note of compassionate ribaldry and a fresh approach to novel writing which, if it succeeds, should command me serious and delighted attention. I am sure that some shaping can go a long way to curing its present faults: a lot of this I have just done – cutting Gladys, removing, as you suggested Quentin's article etc etc. But for the better purpose of any shaping or abbreviation we may still need to do, I here offer an outline of the book's theme to assist your second reading. Please do however remember that I have been very anxious to avoid the book becoming simply a thematic shape in any passages except the comic dramatic interludes of the family plays. For the rest I have wanted the individual lives of the six children to be a struggle sometimes successful, sometimes not, against their background but always flowing, changing and filled with life. For this reason, if we shape more we must avoid changing the novel from the story of living people into a comic ironic pattern book.

The children, as you know, and as the Game shows, stand each opposite to an adult member except for Quentin who has lived in privilege apart from them, and all the time threatens to be the lonely embittered self-appointed judge. Gladys is always on the edge of Regan's self-destructive clowning, and ends as a good sort clown. Rupert is always in danger of the sort of vain self-approving comic philosophising of Billy Pop and at the end succumbs to it. Margaret is threatened by Mouse's self-destructive irony and is still fighting her lonely battle at the end. Sukey is the heir to her grandmother's garrulous sentimental indulgent comic reminiscence; she sacrifices her husband and her children to this in a lunatic pact with God and ends on the surface a respectable woman with a nearly dotty secret life. (This is the only point where I fear you had seriously misunderstood – I believe it was my fault for cutting out an absolutely necessary Sukey episode and leaving in unimportant ones; I have amended this.) Marcus, always threatened by the Countess' powers of malice and seeking like her a warm family around him to vent it upon, does eventually, partly by realising his active instead of his passive sexual nature, come through to some sort of crazy victory surrounded by his Moroccan 'family' and running his much needed factory. Quentin, the Judge, with his equally lonely but scared need to feed himself on women plays a brave and courageous political role until overcome by lonely self pity he sacrifices himself to the success of cheap television nihilism. So much for them all in stark outlines. But I have tried in the book to give this the clothing of real life so that even when shaped it will be real life rather than played out morality. The scene in the Laughing Mirrors Hall provides a direct clue.

As to the middle section, from 1925 to 1937, where, interspersed with the light pastiches of Shaw, English version Tchekov and ending with Rattigan and Beckett, the six children "Grow up", this is based upon an ironic treatment of the themes – marriage, self-reliance, responsibility, companionship, sense of the past, and love of beauty (Regan's 'don't mix up with the muck'), which were offered to them as the marks of adult life by their absurd elders. Once again these themes, though twisting in and out in various ironic ways, are always kept subordinate to the life of the characters.

Of course, in another sense the whole story is a paradigm of the history of the British middle class during this period. For this reason in part, and in part because the final defeats and victories of the characters only emerge at the end, I regard the post war episodes (particularly the events of 1956, Suez, Hungary and Look Back in Anger) as absolutely essential to the book. It is by no means pure chance that in these last sections the scene shifts considerably from England, is dominated by ex-Colonials, television, and the new uncomprehending generation who are taking over from our six protagonists – as you say an anti-climax for the middle class.

I think that I have pointed a great deal of this up in the changes I have made. How much more cutting we must make must depend on the amount of words the typist eventually discovers, but as you will see from the account of the novel any cuts we must make will have to be delicately excised in view of the interweaving complexity of the themes.

　　　Yours ever,
　　　Angus

Angus Wilson's Outline of *No Laughing Matter*

NO LAUGHING MATTER is the story of six people called Matthews (three brothers and three sisters) who come from a 'hopeless', shabby genteel, not very respectable, 'Bohemian' middle class family. Considering their 'ghastly' upbringing they all succeed admirably in life, thanks to their toughness and humour, their seriousness and their competitive individualistic energy. Yet through these very same qualities some of them are tripped up very badly at times during their lives – but then the increasing demands of the world outside (the world of Hitler's camps and Stalin's camps, of Guernica and Adowa) put a heavy strain on all sturdy, humourous English middle class privacy and individualism during the inter-war years. Each Matthews chose a different path – writing, acting, business, journalism, art patronage, bringing up a family – and pursued it with a different humour – irony, clowning, wit, invective, whimsicality, sly fun – yet none quite escaped from the battery of world events in those 'political decades', and some never recovered from it. In crises they often herd together to seek refuge, as they did in their childhood, in play-acting, mocking their elders in "The Game" – a tradition derived from their two hard-boiled, failed parents whose own lives are one long second-hand play – watered down versions of the wit of Maugham, of the paradoxes of Shaw, or the nostalgias of Chekhov, the plays which delighted their class and generation on the London stage. But the Matthews, parents and children alike, have high survival powers. Where did this toughness come from? Some credit must be given to the oldest generation whose financial patronage hangs over the early childhood books of the novel like a Santa Claus who refuses to come down the chimney.

GRANNY MATTHEWS, widow of a wealthy Victorian business man, for whom solid dividends, servants, lap dogs, sables, saddle of mutton, Stilton cheese, and a chauffeur driven car are a necessary part of a cosy, tranquil, family life. For whom Lloyd George meant the monstrous deprivation of a footman who had been expert in brushing the gentlemen's top hats. A big, heavy meal in the company of her beloved son Will and her beloved grandson Quentin and she is content so long as no one upsets her beloved Pom.

On the other side of the family stands GREAT AUNT MOUSE (Miss Rickards) with a background of more cultured professional people – service officers, doctors, dons – but with no less dividends. A pioneer traveller in Africa and Asia, and, through the 'Circle', in psychic realms, her dry irony reduces all around her to the desert sand she loves so well. But neither Granny Matthews' ample egotism nor Mouse's thin spinsterish hardness can prevent Mr and Mrs Matthews (Will and Clara, Billy Pop and the Countess) from squeezing the last golden sovereign or unwilling cheque out of them.

BILLY POP (the father of the family) wrote in his youth a story that got into "The Savoy", he knew some of the great men of the nineties – and remembered having met many more of them as the years went by. But it is long now since he had a story even in "The Pall Mall Magazine". A writer with a trickle of sporting and historical novels behind him, he has settled down on his private income and wits to cultivate his Muse, search for the mot juste and ponder over his memoirs in as much comfort as he can get for himself. He is an intensely 'philosophical' man, never troubling himself with the distresses of other people, preferring to greet his childrens' unhappiness with a blithe whimsicality, unless he is too greatly incommoded when he can bite. He is only moderately faithful to his wife in a marriage chiefly remarkable for survival, but then his infidelities in the pre-1939 world would hardly show because – shocking to say (and how much she loved people to say it)

THE COUNTESS (his wife) was a very Fast Woman. The countess lives in a world of dreams of elegance and luxury and adoring men, though, in actual fact, her life grows more squalid with age. For ever pursuing the joy of life, she can forgive no one else – and especially her children – for sharing in it; nor can she and her husband ever forgive seriousness so that it comes natural to them to see their children as prigs. As her own beauty and youth leave her she uses her sharp and witty tongue to punish others (especially her children) for their youth and talents. Yet in a moment if she wishes can turn her malice into great fun. A consciously 'dance mad' mother she is never so happy as when netting her own blue trout at the Piccadilly Restaurant. This tough, age-hating couple are killed at last by a German bomb, yet ironically not dancing to Al Bowlly at the Café de Paris but (ugh, dowdy thought) in a private hotel during the Baedeker raid on Exeter Cathedral – a death that changes Rattigan suddenly into the *theatre of the absurd*.

But not only egotism and energy keep the Matthews parents going their own sweet way – England's pre-1939 class system proves a great aid in the person of REGAN (Henrietta Stoker) the faithful old cockney cook. She prepares superb food (she wouldn't be there if she didn't). She drinks (but you can't have everything in return for a damp basement and irregular wages). Above all, she is the Countess' delight with her quaint cockney clowning When the cat is killed by a Taxi Regan calls it a 'dispensation', years later when a taxi knocks her over, her sister says the same.

And so to our six characters in search of fulfilment.

QUENTIN, the eldest, becomes at last the famous television star, Q.J. Matthews, cynical, witty prophet of woe of the post '45 world, who delights television audiences by his dandyish disgust for the Common Man. But he has travelled a long hard path before he takes this dubious turning. Young wounded subaltern of the 1914 trenches, young don who leaves Oxford to help the coal strike, expelled from Hitler's Germany and from Stalin's Russia, his implacable hostility to the Communists in the Spanish Civil War and to France earns him the hatred of all proper-thinking people of Right and Left, and a beating up from Irish Catholic unemployed. His lonely tough fight against social injustice is made tolerable for him by his popping in and out of bed with every easy-make girl he meets; or is it?

GLADYS – Podge – her ample figure makes her from the start the warmhearted clown of the family; she is also the independent girl, the woman with a business head. She is rewarded by lifelong, happy devotion to an engaging crook and a long severe prison sentence as a consolation prize. It is perhaps only in later comfortable widowhood among the English taxation exiles in Portugal that she loses her courageous individualism, though never her generous optimism.

RUPERT – the handsome, tall blond dreams from the nursery of the stage. Standing in the broken down, grubby bathroom of his family home, he longs for a play in which, scarlet dressing gowned, he will engage in battle not only of words but with elegant scent bottles and tortoiseshell hairbrushes flying across the room in a witty play set in Cannes or Paris. What better aim for the '20s theatre of "Our Betters" and "The Vortex"? Thanks to his flirtatious practice with his mother he becomes the stage partner of a famous ageing star; then on to more serious triumphs in Chekhov and Shakespeare in the thirties. But he takes his wife off the stage and makes her a lady, only to find that bills for his sons at Eton and his daughter's coming out make a transfer to the film studios an economic necessity. How he meets the Jimmie Porter trend in Suez year is one of the comeuppances that that horrible year brings to all six of them.

MARGARET, the 'highbrow' of the family, ironic, beloved of her Great Aunt Mouse, is, with her stories based on her family life, the first to win worldly success. But her most valuable literary weapon, her irony, is also to some extent her worst enemy in life as she finds on her first visit abroad to the South of France in a comic but touching first sexual experience. Throughout the novel her life and her work are interwoven through two marriages, political engagement, devotion to the Arab rudely shattered for a time in Cairo in 1956, but above everything else the fight to create fiction that can reflect both wit and compassion.

SUKEY, her twin sister is solely concerned to get away from the bohemian squalor of her family, to become a conventional wife and mother, to live in the country. She does not make the grand county marriage she dreams of, but as a prep-school master's wife she gives her life to her three sons, especially the youngest. All is so neat and peaceful in the world she creates, but her illusions are shattered by outside events that practical homemaking cannot control; and she loses everything in an irony of war. The strange consolation she finds, parodies in a way the search of her eldest brother, Quentin.

MARCUS the youngest, hated by his mother for coming so late, naturally plays the feminine role in the family games. Taken early from school, given no pocket money, he ostensibly makes do by odd jobs as a film extra in "Ben Hur" or a model, but in fact earns a more dubious wage in Piccadilly. Taken up by a rich young Jewish aesthete, Jack Pohlen, he becomes a famous host of the 'twenties and foremost, knowledgeable collector of Klee and Kandinsky. But he, too, veers between the hard chic of his mother's teaching and the warmth of his own feelings. It is his warmth that involves him with Ted, the unemployed boy from Bermondsey and his respectable, friendly working-class family. It is also his warmth (and his deep devotion to Jack) that involves him by chance in the demonstrations against the Fascist march through South London. But his arrest in Tooley Street earns him a fine of £10 and more importantly the loss of the respectable pickup Ted and his family, like Marcus' mother, the Countess, they find such public behaviour 'common'. But all the things that happen to Marcus are paradoxical, including a shift in his sex life that leaves him at the end of the novel patriarch-matriarch to a Moroccan family in Mogador and owner-manager of a Robert Owen type scent factory among the sand dunes.

APPENDIX 3

Letter to David Farrer, Secker & Warburg

(Undated)
(July 1972)

My dear David,

You may imagine how pleased I was to get your letter of praise for AS IF BY MAGIC.

You are right it is an ambitious book, though not technically anything like such a headache as NO LAUGHING MATTER. It is essential that we see that these ambitions are as far as possible carried through to the reader more successfully on first impact that OMAZ (altho' that has gained ground with readers continuously – but we don't want to wait, we want a direct impact). I think MAGIC has two advantages over OMAZ. People are no longer surprised that my work should mix realism with fantasy; the action is not laid in the future so simple people cannot think it is meant to be some sort of Science Fiction.

But what I am sure needs doing and you can help me here to the greatest extent is a signposting, a constant (but not too obtrusive) insistence on the theme, so that the reader is always aware of the track he is on.

My theme is as always *humanistic*. Life today is junglelike (hence the setting side by side of the boy who is too old for the pederasts in his cruel jungle setting with the Little Mam too old to command men's attention in the new concrete jungle of London), it is complex, it is inhuman in its materialism. But the magic we lack is a concern for involvement with others, a concern for human beings however hopeless/and indeed for animal life however hopeless like the Sirenae (dugongs etc.). To this extent the title should read sarcastically or indignantly AS *IF* BY MAGIC – as if the complex, delicate problems of human beings can be solved by any old magic formulae, whether Hamo's attempted disinterested scientific 'Magic' (parodied by Zoe's belief that everything can be 'cured'), or by the younger generation's natural but panic flights into 'old' magic, irrationalism, drugs, 'intuitive' wisdoms. Both hopelessly ignore social and human concerns. Where they lead Hamo we see in his farcical adventures in Asia (farcical-cruel) and where they lead Alexandra, Ned, Rodrigo we see in the killing of the goat in

Morocco. Where they lead both together we see finally in the irruption in Goa, which could be a terrible disaster but ends in pathetic farce.

Almost everybody in the book (except perhaps the Dissawardenes with their old-fashioned honour) seeks a short cut answer to a long term (eternal?) complex human problem. The 'magics' they offer are many and fashionable: G.N.P., rat race (Perry, Martin, Leslie, etc.), sexual perfection (Hamo), sexual magic (Alexandra's tripling), the wisdom of old age (Alexandra's search for it with her elders who are all as lost as she is, and the Japanese traditional concern for the wisdom of old age which leads poor Hamo into his gerontophilic hornets' nest); the new fashion of the wisdom of youth (the Vicar, even Sir James in appointing Rodrigo, the Uncles' tastes that lead Hamo into the most terrible parody of his own sexual heartlessness and failure – the pederastic jungle orgy); opting-in (the Colombo world of the Jayasekeres – keeping up with the Joneses); opting-out (the Commune, Thelma); Elinor's search for Nirvana; Rodrigo's dandyism; Alexandra's constant search for literary hero types which leads her to see Hamo's muddle as divine idiocy; to Cronnall, Sir James's attempt to hitch 'magic' to his mammon wagon. All are deceptions, substitutes for the hard job of using reason and industry and intuition and compassion to solve even a little bit of the muddle with humaneness and awe for the natural world and the complexity of human beings. There is no formula to success (no magic); but also there is no escape from trying to solve it, from injecting the magic of feeling into life, the only so-called escape is into the sort of materialist death that swallows up Perry (the most self deceiving of all) and Erroll and Leslie in Corfu. At the end Alexandra sees this insufficiency of magic formulae – there is no 'Abracadabra', no ignoring the future as the old prefer to do, no ignoring the past as the young try to do, no putting all our hopes on to future generations. Only doing what she can, as competently as she can, as unselfdeceivingly as she can, as unsentimentally as she can (and yet, as she is well aware, nothing is perfect – she is in danger of being a power wielder, a hard, unmated, rich mother), but she must do what she can.

The two pilgrimages run thro' different seas. Hamo's absurd adventures become yet ever more terrible as he sees what he has been doing – and then he acts too quickly, is a 'divine idiot' but dies absurdly and by the wrong hands for his folly. Alexandra begins with selfish youngness, yet always seeking to be honest, having the courage to have her baby, finding thro' this a temporary resting place in motherhood which brings her in touch with human warmth and intuitive living, but is ultimately too narrow. She is bounced out of it by the impact of events – the hypocrisy of the Commune over the goat, the swami, the riots, Hamo's legacy, Aveling; at last settling, rightly I think, for what she *can* do in a field where she *feels* deeply – and fairly aware of the limits of life. A Shavian sort of heroine, as she sees for herself; courageous; imperious a bit, intensely feminine.

I'm terribly pleased that Hamo worked for you – I was afraid he was too wooden and selfish to command sympathy. Alexandra to me is my triumph because it's no easy thing for a sixty year old to get inside a twenty-two year old girl – but I believe she is real and what many girls are like today – I set her beside

Meg Eliot and Sylvia Calvert in my portraits of women. But the young must judge.

A word about the orchestration of the book – Mime (the battery hens) leads through to a monstrous breeding of abnormal plants -so that the scene is set both in A's world and H's for the mixture of science and magic – then to Hamo's inner life and A's lostness (shown here (1) Hamo in the setting of his desert flat, (2) Alexandra against the obliquity and neglect of her parents). We are taken through this scene first thro' Alexandra's eyes (her desire to cut all off but herself, her scary thrill (the 3 in bed), her terrors (the faces) and her view of Hamo) – then we see thro' Hamo (his desire to shut all off but himself, his thrills and his memories of the failure with Leslie which are his "faces", his view of Ally and her young men). If we can cut this conversation down, do let's do so – I cut it many, many times, but it *is* necessary to give the younger generation's, Ned's, contempt even hatred for science, and to introduce Sir James in relation to the young – one of these tiresome preparations for later developments. As to "Lord of the Rings", I think it's important that they should half-jokingly follow it because of its magic properties – but perhaps we can reduce it and indeed "Women in Love" too. Then the disastrous tripling and Hamo's disastrously farcical beginning to his journey.

Now, Book 2 – First Alexandra in search of wisdom at her conventional seat of wisdom the University (disastrous), then her flight North (the mysterious North, Ned, Brian are always values just beyond the grasp of the materialist South East and are a kind of false magic), then her repair to her elders, shocking Martin's sense of property by her naive revelations of shoplifting – then to Japan, land of sense of property and traditional belief in the wisdom of old age. I wish I could cut down Senator Tarbett a bit. I *have* done so, but he is a bore and as such has to go on rather. He is Hamo's first inkling that it may not be possible to separate his scientific work from politics – but he puts it on one side. Then the gerontophile brothel ("They're either too young or too old" covers this and the jungle orgy). Now from Japan, pretended worshipper of age, to the old Needhams and then to the Little Mam in the concrete jungle and so to the boy too old for the pederasts' taste thrown out into the pool. I *must* keep this scene. First, I think it's one of my best pieces of comic horror writing with its parody of the European agrobusiness exploitation of Asia (so vital to Hamo's realisation of what has happened to Magic-rice) disguised in sexual terms, and also its parody of Sade – the double revelation to Hamo that his view of the distasteful (small boys) is no less equalled by the uncles' distaste for his tastes, *and* that their ruthless exploitation is only an exaggeration of his own (from this comes the haunting by the uncles = Alexandra's faces) – then the first moment of real tenderness with the boy thrown out by the uncles and by the hybrid 'Magic'. From here we go to the 'commune' in Morocco exploiting the local community, and to the community of Colombo's smart set exploited by Hamo's sexual desires.

After that plot takes over from orchestration. I think rightly, otherwise the book would be too schematic.

I write all this as a help, I hope, to you to help me to signpost the book. Cuts may be required and, if I can, I will make them, but more important, I think, is direction and emphasis.

Parentheses. You're quite right. It's a vile Jamesian habit I've got into. Tony has cut many of them, but any you can get rid of, please do.

Travelogue. I don't want to cut out any episodes – tho' I did for a while hesitate about Japan but I think it's necessary. However, if we can remove "local colour" etc. without removing life, please let us do so.

I hope this is some help to you, as I know you will be to me, David. It *is* an ambitious book but it could be, not perfection that doesn't happen, but a very telling novel. Perhaps exceptional in a mature novelist really dealing with the young of today.

I look forward to our working on it. As always, I suspect, when we get the right clue, the amount of work will be small but it must be the right work.

    Love,
      Angus

ANGUS WILSON LTD & A.F. JOHNSTONE WILSON COMBINED
SUMMARY OF RESULTS
1959–1985

Year	Income	Expense	Net Income	Dir. Rem. & Sec. Sal	Travel	Enter-tainment	Motor Expenses
1954	1,449	529	920		188	108	
1955	1,441	492	949		128	132	
1956	3,542	925	2,617		261	190	140
1957	5,130	1,076	4,054		381	187	96
1958	3,466	1,264	2,202		246	262	168
1959	5,671	2,527	3,144	780	328	408	281
1960	3,737	2,555	1,182	681	644	429	161
1961	5,507	4,053	1,454	2,297	639	293	151
1962	6,154	3,859	2,295	2,104	522	281	287
1963	5,595	4,233	1,362	1,958	753	339	168
1964	5,117	3,978	1,139	1,464	922	361	183
1965	6,938	3,825	3,113	1,498	774	448	132
1966	6,624	4,394	2,230	1,623	786	649	205
1967	9,163	4,312	4,851	1,768	1,085	357	200
1968	12,088	2,923	9,165	1,380	60	228	219
1969	5,962	4,072	1,890	910	1,712	20	344
1970	11,058	5,447	5,611	2,119	1,489	97	226
1971	11,071	5,024	6,047	1,668	1,663	179	248
1972	7,500	4,403	3,097	1,567	1,002	125	345
1973	13,699	6,112	7,587	3,624	454	165	398
1974	14,264	9,188	5,076	4,880	2,466	48	386
1975	9,909	7,412	2,497	3,131	1,986	36	501
1976	11,287	7,473	3,814	3,500	710	309	568
1977	18,981	13,599	5,382	6,786	1,475	181	499
1978	14,445	12,130	2,315	3,883	2,718	561	439
1979	17,237	16,257	980	7,673	2,350	153	382
1980	25,210	17,436	7,774	8,524	1,691	49	681
1981	20,303	14,475	5,828	7,355	243	138	496
1982	20,930	17,167	3,763	9,013	239	155	1,016
1983	32,419	22,227	10,192	12,959	3,183	724	1,008
1984	23,435	16,836	6,599	11,083	784	230	592
1985	7,721	11,375	(3,654)	7,394	375	891	560

| | 347,053 | 231,578 | 115,475 | | | | |

ANGUS WILSON LTD
SUMMARY OF LIMITED COMPANY BALANCE SHEETS

Year	Bank	Current Assets	Liabilities	Directors Cur. A/C	Net Assets	Capital	Profit & Loss A/C
1954	0	0	0	0	0	0	0
1955	0	0	0	0	0	0	0
1956	0	0	0	0	0	0	0
1957	0	0	0	0	0	0	0
1958	0	0	0	0	0	0	0
1959	1,565		(672)	(60)	833	100	733
1960	683	27	(231)	262	741	100	641
1961	2,211		(1,886)	436	761	100	661
1962	1,563		(1,612)	907	858	100	758
1963	885		(1,340)	1,381	926	100	826
1964	469		(932)	390	(73)	100	(173)
1965	312	387	(932)	262	29	100	(71)
1966	891		(942)	231	180	100	80
1967	600		(1,314)	209	(505)	100	(605)
1968	563	31	(142)	(720)	(268)	100	(368)
1969	147		(50)	(386)	(289)	100	(389)
1970	814		(326)	(418)	70	100	(30)
1971	1,429		(655)	(580)	194	100	94
1972	1,228		(115)	(893)	220	100	120
1973	1,960		(1,268)	(301)	391	100	291
1974	298	12	(280)	(10)	20	100	(80)
1975	1,197		(949)		248	100	148
1976	417		(259)	(59)	99	100	(1)
1977	4,874		(1,366)	(3,195)	313	100	213
1978	2,717		(2,450)	(1,684)	(1,417)	100	(1,517)
1979	3,396		(1,562)	(2,133)	(299)	100	(399)
1980	1,671		(2,435)	(23)	(787)	100	(887)
1981	6,453		(3,033)	(3,276)	144	100	44
1982	1,954	4,393	(2,600)	(3,414)	333	100	233
1983	15,796	890	(6,793)	(2,598)	7,295	100	7,195
1984	6,771	6,198	(2,559)	(839)	9,571	100	9,471
1985	2,386	3,385	(1,846)	(30)	3,895	100	3,795

BIBLIOGRAPHY

The Wrong Set and Other Stories
    Secker & Warburg 1949
    William Morrow, New York 1950
    Penguin Books 1959

Such Darling Dodos and Other Stories
    Secker & Warburg 1950
    William Morrow, New York 1951
    Penguin Books 1960

Emile Zola: An Introductory Study of his Novels
    Secker & Warburg 1952
    William Morrow, New York 1952
    Revised edition Secker & Warburg 1964

Hemlock and After
    Secker & Warburg 1952
    Viking Press, New York 1952
    Penguin Books 1956

For whom the Cloche Tolls: A Scrapbook of the Twenties
    Illustrated by Philippe Jullian
    Methuen 1953
    Secker & Warburg 1973
    Penguin Books 1976

The Mulberry Bush: A Play in Three Acts
    Secker & Warburg 1956

Anglo-Saxon Attitudes
  Secker & Warburg 1956
  Viking Press, New York 1956
  Penguin Books 1958

The Middle Age of Mrs Eliot
  Secker & Warburg 1958
  Viking Press, New York 1959
  Penguin Books 1959

The Old Men at the Zoo
  Secker & Warburg 1961
  Viking Press, New York 1961
  Penguin Books, 1964

The Wild Garden or Speaking of Writing
  Secker & Warburg 1963
  University of California Press 1963
  Penguin Books 1992

Late Call
  Secker & Warburg 1964
  Viking Press, New York 1965
  Penguin Books 1968

No Laughing Matter
  Secker & Warburg 1967
  Viking Press, New York 1967
  Penguin Books 1969

The World of Charles Dickens
  Secker & Warburg 1970
  Viking Press, New York 1970
  Penguin Books, 1972

As If by Magic
  Secker & Warburg 1973
  Viking Press, New York 1973
  Penguin Books 1976

The Naughty Nineties
  Eyre Methuen 1976

The Strange Ride of Rudyard Kipling: His Life and Works
   Secker & Warburg 1977
   Granada Publishing – Panther Books 1977
   Viking Press, New York 1978
   Penguin Books 1979

Setting The World On Fire
   Secker & Warburg 1980
   Viking Press, New York 1980
   Granada Publishing – Panther Books 1981

Diversity and Depth in Fiction: Selected Critical Writings of Angus Wilson,
edited by Kerry McSweeney
   Secker & Warburg 1983
   Viking Press, New York 1984

Reflections In A Writer's Eye: travel pieces by Angus Wilson
   Secker & Warburg 1986
   Viking Press, New York 1986
   Paladin Books 1988

Angus Wilson: A Bibliography 1947–1987
   by J.H. Snape and Anne N. Thomas,
   Mansell Publishing Limited, London and New York 1988

Unless otherwise stated, all unpublished Angus Wilson material is in the Special Collection of the University of Iowa. The Secker & Warburg Archive is held in the University of Reading.

SOURCES

Below are listed, with dates and places where recorded, all the interviews on which the biography is based, with thanks to all who gave their time. The word "interview" has been stretched to cover taped interviews, interviews recorded in note form, telephone conversations and informal conversations.

Anrep, Annabel – Highgate 28.11.91.
Arnaud, Dr – St Rémy Easter 1993.
Arnold, Christopher – London 4.7.91, 6.2.92 and various other
    conversations.
Bailey, Paul – London 24.11.92.
Banbury, Frith – London 27.6.92.
Barnard, Eileen – Blackheath 3.12.90.
Barnes, Denis and Patsy – Wittersham 20.5.91.
Bayley, Professor John – Oxford 23.11.93 and letter.
Berlin, Isaiah – London 17.2.93.
Beyts, Major A.J.A. and Mrs Joan Beyts – London 19.12.92.
Binding, Paul – London 25.1.94.
Bishop, Maggie – Boxford 15.12.92.
Blackburne, Charles and Neville – Nowton Court 26.2.92.
Booth, Richard – London 31.1.92.
Bourjaily, Tina – Iowa 20.6.93.
Bowden, Russell – London late 93/4.
Bradbury, Malcolm – London 18.11.93.
Bragg, Melvyn – London 5.2.93.
Breuer, Hans-Peter – London 17.10.92.
Brewis, Rachel – Winchester 10.4.91.
Bridgewater, Bentley – London 16.10.90, 1.11.90, 21.5.91. and many other
    conversations.

Brodhurst, Audrey – London 30.1.91 and again in March 92.

Brome, Vincent – London 26.3.93.

Brooke, Nathalie – London 6.1.93.

Brooke, Nicholas and Julia – Corsham 27.5.92.

Brooke-Rose, Christine – London/Bletchley 19.10.91 plus several letters.

Brothers, Connie – Iowa June 93.

Brown, Justin – Telephone Australia 20.6.92.

Brown, Merle – Telephone Durban 2.7.92.

Calder, Pat – Tooting 11.11.91.

Calisher, Hortense – London 28.4.94.

Campbell-Johnson, Alan and Fay – London 20.4.91.

Caney, Dr Edmund – Durban December 1990.

Caraman, Father Philip – Telephone 11.8.93.

Carter, Peter – London 14.5.92 plus letters.

Casals, M. – St Rémy Easter 1993.

Cavaliero, Glen – Cambridge 17.9.91.

Chambers, Ivan – Telephone 5.4.92.

Chilver, Sally (*née* Graves) – Oxford 23.3.93.

Chislett, William and Sonia – Madrid 24.1.92 and various letters etc.

Cobb, Richard – Oxford 5.7.91.

Cobley, Roger and Brian – Westward Ho! 13.8.91.

Cohen, Benjamin – Shingle Street 14.12.92.

Cohn, Mildred – London 27.7.92.

Colborne-Brown, Michael (with Geoffrey Wright).

Conradi, Professor Peter—London 22.9.92 and many letters.

Cookson, Mary – London 25.11.92.

Corke, Martin – Suffolk 25.6.91 and many conversations, letters, etc.

Coulson, George (and Thomas Hutton) – Diss 25.2.92.

Courage, Jonathan – London 14.7.92.

Crichton, Ronald – Eastbourne 24.5.92.

Crittall, Elizabeth – Kelvedon 15.5.91.

Culmer, Philip and John – Woodbridge (with John Culmer) 27.10.91 and
  letters.

David, Gwenda – London 3.4.93.

Davies, Jeanne and Glyn – First meeting Dover 20.2.91 and several others.

Dawbarn, Carol and Bob – Sedbergh 30.11.92.

Deakin, Sir William – London 18.2.92.

Dent, Ann Langford – London 30.11.94.

Dick, Kay – Brighton 26.3.92.

Dizikes, John and Ann – Cambridge 12.7.91.

Duffy, Maureen – London 5.2.92.

Duncan, Ben – Cambridge 22.10.92.

Du Sautoy, Stephen and Alison – Bury St Edmunds 17.9.92.

Edwards, Simon – London 2.11.92.

Egremont, Max – London 28.5.92.

Engle, Hualing Nieh – Iowa June 1993.

Erskine, Vivienne and Thomas – Aylesford 6.12.90.

Farrell, Kathleen – Brighton 26.3.93.

Fincham, Paul – Woodbridge 14.2.92.

Ford, George and Pat – London 28.7.92 and many letters.

French, Robert and Turland, Montagu – Sible Hedingham 15.2.92.

French, John and Sheila – Barton Stacey 21.12.92.

Furbank, P.N. – London 28.11.91.

Gandy, Professor Robin – Cambridge 15.1.92.

Gates, Professor Barbara – London 7.3.93.

Gilliatt, Mary – London 29.7.92.

Gindin, Professor James – London 8.9.93.

Glenville, Peter – London 30.10.90.

Goff, Martyn – London 1.10.92.

Gombrich, Sir Ernst and Ilse – London 27.3.92.

Goodman, Lord Arnold – London 19.2.92.

Gorer, Richard – Heathfield 1.2.93 plus correspondence.

Gowrie, Lord – Telephone 15.4.94.

Graham Young, Valentia – Letheringham 17.1.92.

Gray, Alan – London 17.5.91.

Grey, Antony – London 17.12.91.

Grose, Peter – London 26.1.93.

Halio, Professor Jay – London 9.8.93, letter 1.11.92.

Hammond, Hermione – London 1.4.93.

Hampshire, Stuart – Oxford 15.1.92.

Harris, Philip – London 23.3.92.

Hillier, Bevis – London 27.11.91.

Hobson, A.R.A. – Fordingbridge 24.9.92 and letters.

Hodges, Andrew – London 17.5.92.

Hoff, Harry – Dolphin Square, London 23.3.92.

Howard, Professor Sir Michael – Eastbury 23.7.92.

Humm, Maggie – London 14.7.92.

Humm, Peter – London 14.7.92.

Ineichen, Pamela – Telephone Lisbon June 1992.

Ironside, Virginia – London 20.1.93.

Jack, Gavin – Durban 31.12.90.

James, Mark – Eastbury 23.7.92.

Jenkins, Dr David (with Miss Beatrice Davies) – Interview and tour
    Aberystwyth 27.8.93.

Jenkins, Janet – Bury St Edmunds, London 9.1.93.

Joll, Professor James – London 13.3.92.

Justice, Donald – Iowa June 93.

Kermode, Frank – London 5.5.92.

Kern, Alex and Jean – Iowa June 93.

Kissane, Joseph – London 1991 and other meetings.

Kocen, Dr R.S. – London 22.2.94.

Langberg, Jorn – London 27.11.92.

Lassalle, Judith – London 17.2.92.

Lemon, Denis – Exeter 19.9.92.

LePan, Douglas – Toronto 20.4.92.

Longmire, Derek and Judith – Kendal 1.12.92.

Lukas, Andrew and Elizabeth – Stroquhan 1.12.92.

Lyons, Paddy – Telephone 6.10.93.

Marques, Susan Lowndes – Monte Estoril, Portugal 1.6.92.

McDowell, Fred – Iowa June 93.

McEwan, Ian – Oxford 22.2.93.

McGibbon, James and Jean – Manningtree 15.9.91 and documents.

McGill, Angus (with Conradi) – London 22.9.92.

McKendrick, Neil and Malveena—Cambridge 21.7.92.

Meneghello, Professor Luigi and Katya – London 24.3.92.

Merry, Rosemary and Ian – Hartley Wintney 9.4.91 plus many letters etc.

Meyer, Anne-Marie – London 24.3.92.

Mitchel, Stuart – Welwyn 7.7.92.

Monod, Sylvère – London 18.1.92.

Moorcock, Michael – London 13.12.91.

Morris, Christopher and Helen – Cambridge 26.6.91.

Morris, Norman – Manchester 20.11.91, 19.3.92.

Murdoch, Iris – Oxford 23.11.93.

Nachtsheim, Hubert and Ursula – St Rémy Easter 93.

Naipaul, V.S. – Telephone 31.3.92.

Neighbour, O.W. – London 28.2.91.

Norrie, Ian – London 7.12.92.

Oida, Yoshi – Telephone 1992.

Oliver, Professor Roland – Newbury 27,8.91.

Osborne, Charles – London 16.11.93.

Osborne, John and Helen – Craven Arms 21.11.92.

Painter, George and Joan – Hove 16.12.90, 26.6.91.

Panting, Anthony – Langport 18.3.92.

Parnis, Sandy – London 3.2.92.

Peterkiewicz, Jerzy – London 3.3.92.

Pitt, Dr Michael – Shillingford 4.7.91.

Plumb, Sir John – Cambridge 13.2.92.

Powell, Albert Baden – Simpson 14.1.93.

Priestley, Mrs J.B. – Chipping Camden 3.5.91.

Prosser, David – London 19.2.92.
Ratcliffe, Michael – London 93.
Reekie, Miss M.P. (now Mrs Howard) – Porlock Weir 3.8.92.
Reinhold, Margaret – St Rémy Easter 93.
Revens, Mrs – Gedding, Bury St Edmunds 25.6.91.
Reynolds, Graham and Daphne – Bradfield St George 27.9.92.
Richardson, John – London 24.5.92.
Rickwood, Jean (née Napper) – Market Harborough 10.7.91.
Ridley, John – Letters 28.2.91.
Rintoul, Wendy (née Charles) – London 13.5.91.
Robert, Judge Hywel ap (Hywel Jones) – London 21.9.91.
Robin, David de Montpied – Telephone 16.7.91.
Robinson, Barbara – Telephone 23.7.92 plus later meeting in London.
Roger, Neil – London 9.9.92.
Rook, Agnes – Hadleigh 25.9.92.
Rook, Robin – London 30.9.92.
Rose, Pamela (née Gibson) – London 12.3.92.
Rosenthal, Tom – London 16.9.92.
Rothschild, Lady Tess – Cambridge 21.7.92.
Rubens, Robert – London 29.10.92.
Runciman, Sir Steven – Elshieshields 11.5.92.
Sage, Lorna – London 12.3.92.
Sage, Vic – Norwich 17.11.92.
Scarfe, Norman – Woodbridge 14.2.92.
Schofield, Michael – London 14.9.92.
Schweitzer, Pamela – 14.7.92.
Scott, Sybil and Richard – Seaford 17.2.91.
Screech, Professor Michael – Oxford 8.11.92.
Serikawa, Kazu – Porlock Weir 14.8.91 and letters.
Settle, Mary Lee – Long Melford 26.9.92.
Shannon, Richard – London 2.12.92.
Slater, Professor Michael – London 30.9.91.
Smith, Vivian and Sybil – London 1.7.92.
Spender, Sir Stephen and Natasha – London 31.1.91 and many
    conversations.
Storey, Anthony – Bury St Edmunds 11.11.93.
Tanner, Michael – Cambridge 26.2.92.
Thistlethwaite, Professor Frank – Cambridge 22.10.92.
Toeg, Victor and Laetitia – London 27.7.92.
Trevor-Roper, Patrick – London 16.5.91.
Tuckett, Georgina – Great Ayton 11.11.92.
Turland, Montagu – Sible Hedingham 15.2.92.
Turner, Penny Corke – London 4.10.91.

Underwood, B.F. – Interview and tour Seaford 14.1.93.
Wadman, Karen – London 27.7.92.
Wadsworth, Barbara – London 18.5.92.
Wain, John – Oxford 27.10.91.
Waley, Pamela and Daniel – Lewes 11.1.92.
Watt, Ruth and Ian – London 1.10.92.
Wilson, Colin – Gorran Haven 23.8.92 plus letters.
Winch, James – London 8.2.93.
Wollheim, Ann – London 11.2.92.
Wollheim, Richard – London 8.7.92.
Wood, Laurence and Rona – London 13.4.91.
Woodcock, Dr Patrick – London 10.3.93.
Woodward, Professor and Mrs L.J. – St Andrews 10.5.92.
Wright, Geoffrey – Bury St Edmunds 25.6.91.
Wyndham, Elizabeth – Chalfont St Giles 4.7.91.
Wyndham, Francis – London 12.2.92.

NOTES

All quotations from Angus Wilson's work, and the page references, are from the Penguin Books editions.

CHAPTER ONE (pp.1–11)
1. Reverend Robert M Brown, Chapter 11 in *The County of Dumfries*, ed. George Houston (Collins, Glasgow, 1962).
2. *The Wild Garden* p.73.
3. J.A. Froude, *Thomas Carlyle: A History of the First Forty Years of his Life 1795–1835*, Vol. 2 p.358 (Longmans, 1882).
4. W.A. Wilson, *Tynron*, printed in Dumfries (1957).
5. *Scottish Diaries and Memoirs 1550–1746*, ed. J.G. Fyfe pp.76–7 (Stirling 1927).
6. Lord Lindsay, *The Lives of the Lindsays*, Vol 2 Ch XVIII p. 315 (Wigan, 1840).
7. Letter from Thomas Carlyle, dated 16 November 1840. *The Collected Letters of Thomas and Jane Welsh Carlyle*, Vol. 12, ed. C.R. Sanders and K.J. Fielding (Duke University Press 1985) p.326.
8. Basil Handford, *Lancing College: History and Memoirs* (Phillimore, 1986).
9. *The Wild Garden* p.69.

CHAPTER TWO (pp.12–22)
1. *Market Rasen Mail*, 14 September 1878: the paper still survives.
2. AW to Hon. Lionel Caney, 6 February 1957: Angus did not believe the story himself.
3. Ian Morrison, *Durban: A Pictorial History* (Cape Town, 1987).
4. Val Caney's diary and other Caney papers are preserved in the Killie Campbell Africana Library in Durban.

CHAPTER THREE (pp.23–38)
1. *Bexhill Chronicle*, 15 August 1914.
2. *Setting the World on Fire*, Ch. 7, "The Family Lunch" p. 200.

3. Fr. Rolfe, *Hadrian the Seventh* (Chatto & Windus 1904).
4. "Homage to Firbank", *Observer*, 1 April 1973.
5. Philip Hoare, *Serious Pleasures: The Life of Stephen Tennant* (Hamish Hamilton 1990) Ch.7 p.87.
6. Lord Eden to MD, 10 January 1994. Sir Timothy (d.1963) was the elder brother of Sir Anthony Eden.
7. *Five Dogs and Two More* (Longman 1928).
8. *The Tribulations of being a Baronet* (Macmillan 1933).
9. *The Wild Garden* p.140.
10. Memory of Mrs Mary Reid of Dunscore. Taped November 1993.
11. "Bexhill and After", *Spectator* 200, 9 May 1958 pp.583–4, reprinted in *John Bull's Schooldays*, ed. Brian Inglis (Hutchinson 1961).
12. "Anglo-African Attitudes", *Trifler*, Westminster School, July 1960, pp.9–10.
13. Guy McDonald to MD, 18 January 1991.
14. *The Wrong Set* (1949).
15. *The Strange Ride of Rudyard Kipling* p.4.
16. Ibid. p.21.
17. AW to her daughter Penelope Holt, 4 July 1976.

CHAPTER FOUR (pp.39–47)
1. Jeremy Lewis, "Seaford's Treasure Trove", *Spectator*, 13 April 1985.
2. "Bexhill and After", *Spectator*, 9 May 1958 pp.583–4.
3. "Rex Imperator", *Arena*, no. 2, September 1949: *Such Darling Dodos*.

CHAPTER FIVE (pp.48–64)
1. "Bexhill and After", *Spectator*, 9 May 1958 pp.583–4.
2. Bernard Adams to MD, 3 February 1991.
3. B. Urquhart, *A Life in Peace and War* (Weidenfeld & Nicolson 1987).
4. Christopher Isherwood, *People One Ought to Know*, Illustrations by Sylvain Mangeot (Macmillan 1982).
5. Brian Urquhart, ibid.
6. Bevis Hillier, *Young Betjeman*, Ch 7 (Murray 1988).
7. "Bexhill and After", loc.cit.
8. Debating School Minutes, Westminster.
9. AW to Michael Barrie, 13 May 1976.
10. *Times Literary Supplement*, 30 December 1929.
11. J. Ridley to MD, 28 February 1991.
12. D.P. Walker's tribute appeared in *Twentieth Century Literature*, 29 (Hempstead, NY, Summer 1983).

CHAPTER SIX (pp.65–75)
1. Peter Copley to MD, 7 May 1991.
2. "My Oxford", *Encounter*, 48 April 1977 and *My Oxford*, ed. Ann Thwaite (London, Robson, 1977) pp.91–109.

3. Ibid.
4. Ibid.
5. Ibid.
6. Ibid.
7. Richard Lamb to MD, 12 May 1992. Richard Lamb is the author of several books on the Second World War, including *Montgomery in Europe 1943–45* (1983), *The Drift to War 1922–1939* (1989), *The War in Italy 1943–45* (1933).
8. *Sunday Express*, 2 August 1953.

CHAPTER SEVEN (pp.76–88)
1. Notebook labelled "Seven Ages of Man: Autobiographical piece for the Observer", on "Reputation".
2. K. Betterton to MD, 6 August 1991.
3. John Halperin, *C.P. Snow: An Oral Biography* (Harvester Press 1983) p.143.
4. *The Library of the British Museum*, ed. P.R. Harris (The British Library, London, 1991) Ch. 7, "Some Memories" by Alec Hyatt King p.252.
5. Peter Fryer, *Private Case – Public Scandal*. AW review in *Observer*, 16 October 1966, "Eros Denied in the British Museum".
6. Hyatt King, op.cit. p.246.
7. John de Villiers, *My Memories* (Grant Richards 1931) p.59.
8. *The Wrong Set and Other Stories* (1949).
9. *The Wild Garden* p.103.
10. Valentine Cunningham, *British Writers of the Thirties* (OUP 1988) Ch. 6 p. 201.
11. Sybille Bedford, *Aldous Huxley*, 2 vols (Chatto/Collins 1973, 1974) Vol. I p.327.
12. Arnold Simmel to MD, 23 November 1991.

CHAPTER EIGHT (pp.89–115)
1. Talk at PEN Writer's Day, 24 March 1984, National Sound Archive, British Library.
2. John Forsdyke, *The British Museum Quarterly* Volume XV 1941–50 (London 1950).
3. Angus Calder, *The People's War* (Jonathan Cape 1969) p.214.
4. *Adam*, ed. Miron Grindea (1966).
5. *The Road to Sinodun* (Rupert Hart-Davis 1951) pp.26–7.
6. See Angus Wilson's Introduction to *The Aerodrome* (Bodley Head, 1966).
7. S. Gorley Putt, *Wings of a Man's Life*, "H.M.S. Bletchley Park" (Claridge Press 1990).
8. John Croft to MD, 7 May 1991.
9. For an account of work on naval hand signals and the Reservehand-verfahren (RHV) cipher see "Navy Ultra's Poor Relations" by Christopher Morris, Ch. 24 in *Codebreakers*, ed. F.H. Hinsley and Alan Stripp (OUP 1993).

10. Alan Pryce-Jones, *The Bonus of Laughter* (Hamish Hamilton 1987) p.129.
11. S. Gorley Putt, op. cit.
12. C. Morris in *Codebreakers*, p.242.
13. John Halperin, *C.P. Snow: An Oral Biography* (Harvester Press) 1983 p.217.
14. *Seven Ages of Man*: Notebook, op.cit.
15. *The Wild Garden* pp.19–20.
16. Jean Medawar, *A Very Decided Preference*, "War Years in Oxford" (OUP 1990) pp.58–9.

CHAPTER NINE (pp.116–127)
1. Basil Creighton (1885–1989) was a poet, novelist, translator and collector: Angus reviewed favourably his Meredithian pastiche novel, *The Leaden Cupid*, in the *Listener*, 4 May 1950.
2. Viva King, *The Weeping and the Laughter* (MacDonald and Jane's 1976) pp.37–40.
3. Ibid, p.117.
4. "Ivy Gripped the Steps": *Horizon*, September 1945. For AW's comment, see his Introduction to *The Collected Stories* (Cape 1980) p.11.
5. Jean MacGibbon, *I Meant to Marry Him* (Gollancz 1984) p.112.
6. "Totentanz", *Such Darling Dodos and Other Stories*.

CHAPTER TEN (pp.128–155)
1. *Seven Ages of Man*: Notebook, op. cit.
2. See "The Library's Losses from Bombardment", by A.F. Johnstone-Wilson, *The British Museum Quarterly*, Volume XV (London 1952) pp.9–11.
3. *Spectator*, 6 May 1960: "New Woman", review of *Nancy Astor* by Maurice Collis (Faber).
4. Routledge 1943.
5. Lindsay Drummond 1948.
6. *The Wild Garden* p.23.
7. Jeanne Davies to MD n.d. [1991].
8. The notebooks are now in the Iowa collection.
9. *The Wild Garden*, p.21.
10. BBC European Division, January 1957, with Charles Roetter, *et passim*. It should also be noted that Angus himself, when looking through the Iowa notebooks, was surprised to see evidence that he had been trying to write before this episode.
11. *The Wild Garden*, p.21.
12. The British Museum: "Some Impressions of one who works there." Iowa Draft, Box 8, Notebook 5.
13. "Lower Depths of Literature", a review of Gissing's *New Grub Street*, *Observer*, 21 May 1967.
14. "The British Museum Reading Room", July 1939: *Collected Poems* (Faber) p.161.

15. Tony Garrett, recording: Hall-Carpenter Archives.
16. See Francis King, *Yesterday Came Suddenly* (Constable 1933) pp.102–5.
17. *Under the Dome*, May 1949.
18. *Tatler*, 6 April 1949.
19. *New Statesman*, 3 December 1949.
20. London: Secker & Warburg, 24 March 1949; New York: William Morrow, 15 March 1950.
21. *The Wild Garden* p.53.

CHAPTER ELEVEN (pp.156–174)
 1. *The Daily Telegraph Book of Bon Viveur in London* (H.A. & W. Pitkin Ltd London 1953) p.161.
 2. Ghislain de Diesbach, *Un esthète aux enfers* (Plon, Paris 1993) p.215.
 3. *The Weeping and the Laughter*, p.129.
 4. Cecil Beaton, "Bright Old Things", *Observer*, 28 June 1953.
 5. Edmund Wilson, *The Fifties*, ed. Leon Edel (Macmillan 1986) p.207.
 6. Ghislain de Diesbach, op. cit. p.220.
 7. *Les Morot-Chandonneur, ou une grande famille, décrite de Stendhal à Marcel Aymé, peinte d'Ingres à Picasso* (Plon 1955).
 8. Letter to Lady Pamela Berry, 22 February 1952. *The Letters of Nancy Mitford*, ed. Charlotte Mosley (Hodder & Stoughton 1993).
 9. Letter to Lady Pamela Berry, 22 May 1952, ibid.
10. *Spectator*, 28 July 1950.
11. *Listener*, 3 August 1950.
12. *Tribune*, 11 August 1950.
13. *The Wild Garden* p.50.
14. Rosemary Merry, *A Crack in a Wall* (Envoi Poets Publications, Newport 1993) p.36.
15. *The Wild Garden*, p.29.

CHAPTER TWELVE (pp.175–189)
 1. "A Book in my Life", *Spectator*, 26 June 1982.
 2. Averil Gardiner, *Angus Wilson* (Twayne 1985).
 3. Evelyn Waugh, "A Clean Sweep", *Month* (Nov.8 1952) pp.238–40.
 4. Stevie Smith, "Succès de Scandale", *World Review*, October 1952.
 5. Donald Gordon to AW, 21 July 1952.
 6. Stephen Spender to AW, 29 July 1952.
 7. Angus Wilson to J.B. Priestley, 19 August 1952, letter in Harry Ransom Humanities Research Center, University of Texas at Austin.
 8. Edith Sitwell to AW, 29 July 1952.
 9. E.M. Forster to AW, 18 July 1952. Letter in Iowa Special Collections.
10. AW to E.M. Forster. MS in King's College, Cambridge.
11. *Hemlock and After*, "Camp Fire Cameos", Ch. 5.
12. 4 October 1952. Letter in Gorer Collection, University of Sussex.

13. John Richardson, "New Short Stories", *New Statesman*, 12 August 1950.
14. Angus Wilson, "Through the Country", *New Statesman*, 13 June 1953.
15. Peter Hennessy, *Never Again* (Cape 1992) p.427; Michael Frayn, "Festival", Ch.15, *Age of Austerity 1945–1951*, by various authors, ed. M. Sissons and P. French (Hodder & Stoughton 1963).

CHAPTER THIRTEEN (pp.190–208)

1. Harry Guest to MD, 14 December 1993.
2. "The Always Changing Impact of Virginia Woolf", *Studies in the Literary Imagination*, 11 (Fall 1978). The letter from Woolf which AW mentions here does not survive, though there are two letters in *The Letters of Leonard Woolf*, ed. Frederick Spotts (Weidenfeld & Nicolson 1989), dated 8 March 1962 and 22 April 1962 in which Woolf responds to an article by AW "Against New Orthodoxies" in *Books and Bookmen* March 1962, p.149. See below, Chapter Seventeen.
3. AW to P.H. Newby, 4 May 1951, BBC Archives, Caversham.
4. Letter from W. Plomer, dated 28 August 1950, held in the National Library of New Zealand (incorporating the Alexander Turnbull Library) in Wellington: quoted in *William Plomer, a Biography* by Peter F. Alexander (OUP 1990) p.259.
5. Edith Sitwell to AW, 2 July 1953.
6. 28 July 1953, *My Sisters and Myself: The Diaries of J.R. Ackerley*, ed. Francis King (Hutchinson 1982) p.203.
7. *Brick*, no. 42/43 Winter/Spring 1992.
8. *Diaries*, ed. Graham Payn and Sheridan Morley (Little Brown 1982).
9. Edmund Wilson, *The Fifties* (Macmillan 1986) p.105, p.113.
10. See Trevor-Roper's Preface to Yorke-Long's posthumously published volume, *Music at Court: Four Eighteenth-Century Studies* (Weidenfeld 1954).
11. Francis King, *Yesterday Came Suddenly* (Constable 1993) p.128.
12. Ewing Lectures (California 1960).
13. *Anglo-Saxon Attitudes* p.172.
14. Somerset Maugham to AW, 7 June no year.
15. Peter Glenville, letter n.d..

CHAPTER FOURTEEN (pp.209–225)

1. *Almost a Gentleman* (Faber 1991) p.18.
2. Binkie Beaumont to AW, 18 April 1956.
3. BBC Third Programme Tribute to George Devine, 5 November 1966.
4. Norman St John Stevas to MD, 9 April 1994.
5. 19 August 1955: Lord Chamberlain's Papers in British Library.
6. Nancy Spain, "Oh, No . . . Angus Wilson's Gone Serious", *Daily Express*, 12 May 1956.
7. See Sidney Campion, *The World of Colin Wilson* (Frederick Muller 1962) pp.137–8.
8. See Brigid Brophy's biography of Ronald Firbank, *Prancing Novelist* (Macmillan 1973).

9. Peter Wildeblood, *Against the Law* (Weidenfeld 1955). It includes the above quotation from the *Sydney Morning Herald*.
10. James Kirkup to MD, 17 June 1992.
11. James Kirkup, *I, of all People* (Weidenfeld 1955) p.181.
12. *The Decline of Hell* (Routledge & Kegan Paul 1964) and *Unclean Spirits* (Scolar Press 1981).
13. *Tirade*, December/November 1983.
14. Gerald Reve, *Brieven Aan Wimie 1959–63* (Veen, uitgevers Utrecht 1980) p.85.

CHAPTER FIFTEEN (pp.226–251)

1. It was published in the *Texas Quarterly*, Autumn 1961.
2. "Night and Day in Tokyo", *Lilliput*, July 1958.
3. Moravia to AW, 27 October 1957.
4. Donald Keene to MD, February 1992.
5. Tokunaga to MD, 1 March 1991.
6. "Some Japanese Observations", *Encounter*, December 1957; *Lilliput*, op.cit.
7. Donald Richie to MD, 17 April 1994.
8. 14 October 1957, Secker & Warburg; 24 October 1957, Viking, New York.
9. *Manchester Guardian*, 27 February 1953.
10. *Isis*, 4 June 1958.
11. *Hemlock* notebook, Box 4, Iowa.
12. *Il Mondo*, 9 June 1959, and in Arbasino's collected essays, *Parigi o cara* (Feltrinelli 1960).
13. Richard Gorer to MD, 10 May 1993; 1 July 1993.
14. AW letter to Hemmings, dated 1954: Hemmings asked permission to sell in Society of Authors sale 4 December 1981.

CHAPTER SIXTEEN (pp.252–283)

1. *Belfast Telegraph*, 17 February 1959.
2. "Nabokov's Basement", *Spectator*, 20 March 1959.
3. *Which of Us Two* (Viking 1990) p.166. Letter to MD, 21 September 1992. Second quote p.226.
4. J.B. Priestley to AW, 30 November 1956.
5. Michael Rook to MD, 17 April 1994.
6. A. Jussawalla to MD, 17 July 1992. Philip Romans had taught in India, in Baroda, between the wars.
7. Sewell Stokes, *Court Circular* (Michael Joseph 1950).
8. "A Book in my Life", *Spectator*, 26 June 1982.
9. Letter in McFarlin Library, University of Tulsa.
10. Sally Toynbee to MD, 10 November 1992.
11. George Ford, diary entry.

12. *The Wild Garden*, p.50.
13. *An Edmund Wilson Celebration*, ed. John Wain (Phaidon 1978) p.33.
14. Edmund Wilson, *The Sixties*, ed. Lewis M. Dabney (Farrar Straus & Giroux 1993) p.50.
15. *New Republic*, 15 November 1980, "South African Witness": a review of Alan Paton's *Towards the Mountain*.
16. "No Future for Our Young" draft in Iowa.
17. Randolph Vigne to MD, 20 December 1992.
18. *Cronaca di Agrigento*, 10 March 1961.
19. Reprinted in *Reflections in a Writer's Eye*.
20. Edmund Wilson to AW, 7 November 1961.
21. "Beyond the Fringe", *Times Literary Supplement*, 29 September 1961.
22. E. Waugh to AW, 19 September 1961.

CHAPTER SEVENTEEN (pp.284–307)
1. Rebecca West, *Black Lamb and Grey Falcon*, Vol 2 p.556; Vol 1 p.143, p.162 (Macmillan 1941).
2. Tape made by Princess Abida and her son for MD.
3. Letter to AW, 14 July 1983.
4. *The Invasion* was broadcast by "ABC Armchair Theatre", 31 March 1963.
5. *All Authors are Equal*, (Hutchinson 1973) p.281.
6. The lectures were broadcast on the BBC Third Programme in December/January 1962/3, and printed in four instalments in the *Listener* (27 December 1962–17 January 1963). A version was published in *Diversity and Depth in Fiction*, 1983.
7. It finally appeared in *Reflections in a Writer's Eye*, 1986.
8. Colin Wilson to A.W., 29 July 1960, 2 October 1962.
9. *Sunday Times*, "The Seven Deadly Sins", 10 December 1961. *Encounter*, "Fourteen Points", 18 no 1, January 1960.
10. *Recollections of the Powys Brothers*, ed. Belinda Humfrey (Peter Owen 1980), pp.262–4.
11. Subsequently in *Moderna Sprak* 1961, *Books and Bookmen* March 1962, and finally as "Letter from London" in *Diversity and Depth in Fiction*, 1983.
12. Letter 8 March 1962, *Letters of Leonard Woolf*, ed Frederick Spotts, (Weidenfeld & Nicolson 1989) p.520.
13. Leonard Woolf Papers, University of Sussex.
14. "A Man from the Midlands", *Times Literary Supplement* 12 July 1974.

CHAPTER EIGHTEEN (pp.308–327)
1. "Mary, Quite Contrary", a review of *On the Contrary*, *Encounter* no. 18, 6 June 1962.
2. Neal Ascherson, *Observer*, 26 August 1962.
3. "Brief uit Edinburgh", from *Op weg naar het einder*, Amsterdam, G.A. von Oorschot 1963: "Journey towards the End"; this publication was to prove a watershed in Reve's career.

4. *The Letters of J.R. Ackerley*, ed. Neville Braybrooke (Duckworth 1975) p.220.
5. AW to Anthony Thwaite, 2 October 1962.
6. *The Times*, 31 March 1963.
7. Jay Halio to MD, 1 November 1992.
8. "The World of J.C. Powys", *Observer*, 23 June 1963.
9. James Kirkup, *Me All Over* (Peter Owen 1993) p.17.
10. "The Soviet Style", *Observer*, 12 July 1955.
11. Simone de Beauvoir, *Tout compte fait* (1972), translated as *All Said and Done* by Patrick O'Brian (Weidenfeld 1974) p.313.
12. Angus Wilson, "On a Black Sea Holiday with Mr K", *Daily Express*, 16 August 1963; "Black Sea Notebook", *Observer*, August 1963: both reprinted in *Reflections in a Writer's Eye*.
13. Iowa MS draft for *Express* article, see above.
14. *The Sixties*, ed. Lewis M. Dabney (Farrar Straus & Giroux 1993) p.258.
15. *Daily Express*, 30 September 1963.
16. *Writers at Work: The Paris Review Interviews, Second Series*, introduced by van Wyck Brooks (Secker & Warburg, London 1963).
17. *Times Literary Supplement*, 21 November 1963.
18. *Times Literary Supplement*, 28 November 1963.
19. Cyril Connolly, "Glimpses of a Charmed Circle", *Sunday Times*, 10 November 1963.
20. Stephen Spender to AW, 12 November 1963.
21. D.P. Walker to AW, 24 October 1963.

CHAPTER NINETEEN (pp.328–344)
1. Letter in Harry Ransom Humanities Research Center, Austin, Texas.
2. John Osborne to AW, 9 June 1964.
3. V.S. Naipaul to MD, 6 April 1992.
4. *Late Call*, p.69.
5. "Long-distance perspective", *Observer*, 10 September 1961.
6. *Queen*, 2 December 1964. "Mellow Wasp in New Town" by Elizabeth Smart.
7. AW letter, 16 October 1963.
8. Originally published in the *New Statesman* as "The Old, Old Message", 23 December 1950.
9. Fred Warburg to AW, 30 December 1964.

CHAPTER TWENTY (pp.345–361)
1. "Broken Promise: The English Novel 1912–22", broadcast 22 March 1951, reprinted in the *Listener*, 12 April 1951.
2. Fred Warburg to AW, 6 February 1964.
3. Fred Warburg to AW, 27 April 1966.
4. "Waiting for the Real Sade", *Observer*, 13 December 1964.
5. John Croft to MD, 7 May 1991.

6. Paul Bowles, *Without Stopping* (Peter Owen 1972) p.338.
7. Harry Ransom Humanities Center, Austin, Texas.
8. Tony Garrett, letter to MD n.d.
9. *Mainichi*, 10 April 1965: translated by Kazu Serikawa.
10. "The Incestuous Muse", shown on 5 September 1964.
11. This was MD.
12. "Cold War Fiction", *Observer*, 30 August 1964.
13. "It seems", *Decanter* 1, Summer 1965.
14. *Bulletin*, 23 March 1966.
15. *Reflections in a Writer's Eye* pp.7–8.

CHAPTER TWENTY-ONE (pp.362–381)
1. *Listener*, 17 October 1968.
2. To Monica Jones, 13 November 1962. *Selected Letters*, ed. Anthony Thwaite (Faber 1992) p.346.
3. See Charles Greville, "Sacked when the Arts Council discovered what IT is all about", *Daily Mail*, 15 February 1967.
4. AW to Edna O'Brien, who had been organising a statement for the *Daily Express* from "non-Jewish writers, artists, directors, musicians and university professors" on behalf of Israel's "normal and unthreatened continuity". (Angus had assumed it was intended for *The Times*.)
5. 5 April 1967, to Jeremy Murray-Brown at George Allen & Unwin.
6. Letter to MD, 9 November 1992.
7. Letter in Orwell Papers, University of Sussex.
8. *Stephen Spender Journals 1939–1983*, ed. John Goldsmith (Faber 1985) p.257.
9. Melvin Lasky to AW, 6 July 1967.
10. Iowa Notebook.
11. AW to Julian Mitchell, 4 November 1967.
12. "The Unhidden Persuaders, No. 3" by Jeremy Hadfield, *Smith's Trade News*, 30 September 1967.
13. Fred Warburg to AW, 27 October 1967.
14. Julian Mitchell to AW, 20 October 1967.
15. *Listener*, 10 October 1968.
16. AW to Frank Thistlethwaite, 5 August 1968.

CHAPTER TWENTY-TWO (pp.382–409)
1. Edmund Wilson to AW, 21 July 1950. Possibly *Dickens and the Divided Conscience*, in *The Month* 189 No 3, May 1950.
2. *The World of Charles Dickens*, Chapter 2 pp.63, 64.
3. D.P. Walker to AW, 18 May 1970.
4. *Dickens the Novelist*, by F.R. and Q.D. Leavis, reviewed in "In the Great Tradition", *Observer*, 18 October 1970.
5. Michael Slater to AW, 20 June 1971.
6. Interview in *Sunday Times*, 31 August 1969.
7. AW to Kenneth Tynan, 22 September 1969.

8. Kenneth Tynan to AW, 3 October 1969.
9. "Courage of Conviction", a review of Angela Carter's *Nothing Sacred*, *Observer*, 31 October 1982.
10. By Reiji Nagakawa (Shueisha Co. 1967).
11. Yukio Mishima to AW, 26 July 1969.
12. James Kirkup, "Gay Boys", reprinted in *The Penguin Book of Homosexual Verse*, ed. S. Coote (1983).
13. *Reflections in a Writer's Eye*, p.8.
14. Harry Guest to MD, 14 December 1993, and H. Guest, *Traveller's Literary Companion to Japan*, (In Print 1994) p.330.
15. AW to Tony Garrett, n.d.
16. *An Autobiography*: Vol 2, *Growing 1904–11*, Ch. 2 (Hogarth Press 1961).
17. Interview with Tim Devlin, "Angus Wilson and the Art of the Unexpected", *The Times*, 30 May 1973.
18. Russell Bowden to MD, 2 February 1994.
19. J.B. Priestley, *Instead of the Tree* (Heinemann 1977) p.7.
20. Antony Grey to AW, 4 August 1970.
21. *Observer*, 16 January 1977: AW review of *Frederick Rolfe, Baron Corvo* by Miriam J. Benkovitz, "The Quest for Rolfe".
22. "Angus Wilson's Traditionalism", by Valerie Shaw, *Critical Quarterly*, Spring 1970. Reprinted in *Critical Essays on Angus Wilson*, ed. Jay L. Halio, Boston (Hall 1985).
23. Gordon Carroll to Michael Holroyd, 20 June 1969.
24. Gordon Carroll to Michael Holroyd, 12 November 1973.

CHAPTER TWENTY-THREE (pp.411–446)
1. Charles Dickens, *The Mystery of Edwin Drood*, ed. Arthur J. Cox (Penguin Books 1974): Introduction by Angus Wilson.
2. *Emile Zola*, Ch 3, "Les Rougon-Macquart: The Form of Expression".
3. *Public Lending Right*, ed. Richard Findlater (André Deutsch 1971).
4. See Malcolm Bradbury to AW, 2 April 1971: University of East Anglia file, Letters.
5. Harry Ransom Humanities Research Center, Austin, Texas.
6. David Farrer to AW, 12 September 1971.
7. Roy McGregor Hastie to MD, 18 June 1991, 2 July 1991.
8. AW to Tom Rosenthal, 8 November 1971.
9. *The Daily Iowan*, 3 December 1971. Interview Mary Zielinski.
10. T. Roethke, *Collected Poems* (Faber 1968) p.267.
11. Published in *Iowa Review*, Fall 1972 pp.77–195.
12. Robert Lambert to MD, 5 December 1992.
13. Gavin Jack to AW, 17 July 1972.
14. "Homage to Firbank", *Observer*, 1 April 1973.
15. David Farrer to AW, 3 April 1973.
16. AW to David Farrer, 7 April 1973.
17. Jonathan Raban to MD, 27 September 1993.

18. John Betjeman to MD at TV Centre in the 1960s during a "Take it or Leave It" programme.
19. "Busting Out all Over", *Observer*, 27 May 1973.
20. "Kith of Death", *New Statesman*, 1 June 1973.
21. "The Professor and a Cast of Thousands", *Evening Standard*, 29 May 1973.
22. "The Wayward Wilson", *Spectator*, 2 June 1973.
23. AW to John Plumb, 8 June 1973.
24. P.N. Furbank to AW, 11 December 1972.
25. Anthony Symondson to MD, 30 July 1993.
26. Max Egremont, 18 October 1973.

CHAPTER TWENTY-FOUR (pp.447–469)
1. Hilary and John Spurling to MD, 17 November 1993.
2. AW to Miriam Gross, 4 February 1981.
3. Claude Simon won the Nobel in 1985. Angus Wilson's oration was reprinted in *Diversity and Depth in Fiction*, ed. Kerry McSweeney (Secker & Warburg 1983).
4. *A House in the Country: The Second Home from Cottages to Castles*, with photographs by Brian Morris (Hutchinson 1973).
5. *Sheffield Morning Telegraph*, 13 December 1973.
6. Leo Caney to AW, 5 February 1974.
7. "The banned biography", *Observer*, 8 October 1978, AW review of *Rudyard Kipling* by Lord Birkenhead.
8. AW to Tom Rosenthal, 28 January 1974.
9. Muriel Spark Papers, Special Collections, National Library of Scotland in Edinburgh.
10. John Cobb to AW, 27 July 1974.
11. Notes for Kipling lecture.
12. Tony Garrett's Journal.
13. Julian Mitchell, Diary, unpublished. Peter Jenkins wrote to Tony on 21 December 1989: "Angus was immensely kind to me – as were you – when I was a precocious and pretentious young man. Indeed my very first published piece – in the New Statesman – was the result of his intervention with John Freeman."
14. *The Strange Ride of Rudyard Kipling*, p.178.
15. *Sunday Sun*, Baltimore, 10 November 1974. Interview with Patricia K. Grant.
16. Letter in McFarlin Library, University of Tulsa.
17. 9 September 1952. Evelyn Waugh Papers, British Library.
18. *Writers' Favourite Recipes*, ed. Gillian Vincent (Corgi 1978) p.159.

CHAPTER TWENTY-FIVE (pp.470–517)
1. "Love in a Cold Climate", *Observer*, 2 February 1975. The letters were edited by Neville Braybrooke (Duckworth 1975).
2. *Literary Review*, No.28, November 1980.

3. Published 13 December 1975, *Sunday Times* Colour Supplement, and in the *Collected Stories* (Secker & Warburg 1987).
4. D. Nichols to AW, 31 March 1975.
5. *Return to Kipling's India*: 20 June 1976: reprinted as "New and Old on the Grand Trunk Road" in *Reflections in a Writer's Eye*.
6. *Debonair*, Bombay, October 1976.
7. Article by Dina Mehta in *Times of India*, 9 February 1992: and Dina Mehta to MD 25 February 1992.
8. *Private Eye*, 2 May 1975.
9. AW to Alan Ross, 17 August 1975. Letter in Brotherton Library, University of Leeds.
10. *Sunday Express*, 31 August 1975.
11. *Gay News* No. 92, April 1976.
12. Paul Theroux to AW, 1 January 1976.
13. *Granit* 1–2, 1973, 480 pages.
14. S. Brata to AW, 5 May 1976.
15. "Beneath the Surface", *Books and Bookmen*, June 1976.
16. Christina Foyle to AW, 1 May 1976.
17. "Angus Wilson Lives Here" was shown on BBC2 on 3 January 1977.
18. Antonia Fraser, unpublished diary, and letter to MD, 28 March 1994.
19. Ian McEwan diary, unpublished.
20. *The Strange Ride of Rudyard Kipling* p.218.
21. Ibid. p.228.
22. *Reflections in a Writer's Eye* p.157.
23. Rudyard Kipling "The Prophet and the Country", *Hearst's International Magazine*, October 1924; *Debits and Credits* (Macmillan 1926).
24. *The Strange Ride of Rudyard Kipling* p.70.
25. Ibid. p.278.
26. Charles Palliser to MD, 18 April 1994.
27. David Jago to AW, 4 June 1981.
28. AW to Philippe Jullian, 15 December 1976.
29. The anthology was *Writers of East Anglia*, edited and with an introduction by Angus Wilson (Secker & Warburg 1977).
30. Transcript of answer to unrecorded question following his lecture on "Is the Novel a Doomed Art Form?" at Sophia University, Japan, 29 September 1969.
31. Cecil Roberts to AW, 30 January 1972.
32. Peter Conradi, letters to MD, 13 July 1993, 21 September 1994, 24 September 1994.
33. "The Modern Bully", *Observer*, 13 March 1977.
34. AW to Tom Rosenthal, 3 December 1977.
35. Drury Pifer to MD, 15 November 1993.
36. Ibid.
37. Charles Carrington, *Rudyard Kipling: His Life and Work* (Macmillan 1955).
38. Tony Gould, "World of Action", *New Society*, 10 November 1977.

39. See Ghislain de Diesbach: *Philippe Jullian, Un esthète aux enfers* (Plon 1993).
40. AW to Denis Lemon, 25 April 1977.

CHAPTER TWENTY-SIX (pp.518–541)
1. Notably "The Function of *The Idiot Motifs* in *As If by Magic*", *Twentieth-Century Literature*, Hempstead NY, Summer 1983.
2. Margaret Garrett to Tony Garrett and AW, 23 January 1978.
3. Published in *Firebird 2* (Penguin 1983), and reprinted in *Reflections in a Writer's Eye*.
4. Ibid. p.169.
5. Ibid. pp.161–2.
6. Ibid. p.161.
7. Published as *Running in the Family* (McClelland & Stewart, Toronto, 1982).
8. Michael Ondaatje, *Rat Jelly & Other Poems 1963–78* (Marion Boyars 1980, London, Boston)
9. *The Strange Ride of Rudyard Kipling*, p.127.
10. *Reflections*, p.161.
11. Fred Busch to MD, 10 March 1993. Angus enjoyed Busch's novel, *The Mutual Friend*, and volunteered a blurb for it for Harper & Row.
12. P.N. Furbank, diary notes.
13. Fred Busch to MD, op.cit.
14. *Contemporary Literature*, Madison, Winter 1980.
15. Drury Pifer to MD, 15 November 1993.
16. "A Biographer in Search of Himself": *Michigan Quarterly*, Summer 1980. Review of Gindin's *The English Climate*.
17. James Gindin to MD, 26 May 1992.

CHAPTER TWENTY-SEVEN (pp.542–570)
1. "Right about Turn", *Observer*, 22 November 1970.
2. Anthony Burgess, *You've Had Your Time* (Heinemann 1990) p.368.
3. *The Collected Stories of Elizabeth Bowen* (Cape 1980).
4. Ronald Hayman interview, *Books and Bookmen*, July 1980.
5. "A House and its Heads", *London Review of Books*, 7 August 1980.
6. "The South Bank Show", 29 June 1980, interview with readings.
7. "Mary Ann into George", review of *The Emergent Self*, *Observer*, 7 March 1976.
8. AW letter dated 25 April 1976.
9. Emma Tennant, *Alice Fell* (Cape 1980).
10. *Sunday Telegraph*, 29 June 1980.
11. "A La Recherche de Marcel Proust", *Observer*, 1 March 1981.
12. "Marcel Proust", *Observer*, 10 September 1950.
13. Mary Lago to MD, 9 February 1994.
14. This was *East Anglia in Verse and Prose*, ed. Angus Wilson, research by Tony Garrett (Secker & Warburg 1982, Penguin 1984).

15. M.C. Rintoul, *Dictionary of Real People and Places in Fiction* (Routledge 1993).
16. "A Book in my Life", *Spectator*, 26 June 1982.
17. Elizabeth Jane Howard, *Getting It Right* (Hamish Hamilton 1982).
18. *East Anglian Daily Times*, 29 August 1983.

CHAPTER TWENTY-EIGHT (pp.571–592)
 1. "When the going was good", *Observer*, 22 March 1981, a review of *Abroad* by Paul Fussell.
 2. Jonathan Raban to MD, 27 September 1993.
 3. John Bowen to MD, 9 September 1994.
 4. "The Techniques of Hospitality: A Summary", Ch. 8 p.361.
 5. *The Penguin Book of Homosexual Verse*, edited by Stephen Coote (1983).
 6. For an account of this incident, see Chris Smith, "The Politics of Pride", in *Stonewall 25*, edited by Emma Healey and Angela Mason (Virago 1994).
 7. Victor Bonham-Carter to MD, 3 June 1991.
 8. "The Always Changing Impact of Virginia Woolf", *Studies in the Literary Imagination*, Fall 1978.
 9. *Times Literary Supplement*, 16 September 1983.
10. C.L. van Minnen, "Enkele vragen aan Angus Wilson", *Wildgroei*, March–April 1984.

CHAPTER TWENTY-NINE (pp.593–601)
1. *Spectator*, 10 March 1984.
2. "Angus Wilson on Angus Wilson": PEN Writers' Day, 24 March 1984. The British Library, National Sound Archive.
3. Drury Pifer to MD, 15 November 1993.
4. Joe Kissane to MD, 31 December 1991.
5. Tony Garrett to Nemone Thornes, 16 November 1984.

CHAPTER THIRTY (pp.602–627)
 1. Rajan Goonetilleke to MD, 13 October 1994.
 2. Iris Murdoch, *Nuns and Soldiers* (Chatto & Windus 1980).
 3. AW to Norman Scarfe, 9 March 1980.
 4. Tony Garrett, 5 June 1985.
 5. Joseph Kissane kindly made these tapes available to me.
 6. W.H. Auden, "Thanksgiving for a Habitat", *Collected Poems*, ed. E. Mendelson (Random House 1976) p.519.
 7. *Time Out*, 16–22 January 1986: *To Noto, or Sicily in a Ford* (Bloomsbury 1991) pp.46–7.
 8. David Kaplan to MD, 18 May1992.
 9. Notes for Ewing Lectures.
10. "A Touch of the Sun" *Guardian*, 30 January 1986.
11. Postcard 16 June 1962 etc.
12. Michael Holroyd, *Augustus John* (Heinemann 1975) Vol. 2 p.146.

13. Viola Hall to AW, 29 August 1986.
14. Anthony Hobson to AW, 10 September 1986.

CHAPTER THIRTY-ONE (pp.628–641)
1. Michael Rook to MD, 30 June 1992.
2. Barbara Gates to MD, 31 October 1992.
3. Tony Garrett to Martin Corke, 21 February 1988.
4. Letter from Vanessa to Quentin Bell, 17 April 1928: *Selected Letters*, ed. Regina Marler (Bloomsbury 1993) p.332.

CHAPTER THIRTY-TWO (pp.642–650)
1. Letter from Vincent van Gogh to his brother Theo, 2 May 1890, *Complete Letters* (Thames & Hudson 1958) Vol. III p. 264.
2. Tony Garrett to Martin Corke, 19 July 1989.
3. Lord Stradbroke to AW, 13 February 1973.
4. Jacquetta Priestley to Tony Garrett, 4 October 1989.
5. From notes written for MD by Jean McGibbon, April 1993.
6. An edited extract of "Angus Wilson and the Family Romance" by Margaret Drabble, first published in Vol 5 of the *European Gay Review*, 1989.
7. Jay L. Halio to MD, 1 November 1992.
8. Anthea Hall obituary, *Sunday Telegraph*, 2 June 1991.

CHAPTER THIRTY-THREE (pp.651–660)
1. *Twentieth-Century Literature*, op cit, p.133.
2. W.H Auden, "The Novelist", *Collected Shorter Poems 1933–38* p.124.
3. Maureen Duffy, *Londoners*, (Methuen 1983), pp.120, 123.
4. See Francis King, *Yesterday Came Suddenly* (Constable) p.86.
5. Published in *Englishness: Foreigners and Images of National Identity in Postwar Literature* (Rodopi, Amsterdam, 1993): also in Yearbook of European Studies: *Annuaire D'Etudes Européennes I. Britain in Europe.*
6. *Second Chance: Two Centuries of German-speaking Jews in the United Kingdom*: co-ordinating editor Werner E. Mosse (Tubingen). Pauline Paucker, "The Image of the German Jew in English Fiction" (Leo Baeck Institute 1991) pp.315–333.
7. For a discussion of Wilson's horticultural accuracy, see "Gardens in Fiction: Angus Wilson", by Peter Parker, *Hortus*, Vol 6 no. 3 Autumn 1992.

INDEX